*A*dventure Guide to

Switzerland

Kimberly Rinker

HUNTER

HUNTER PUBLISHING, INC,
130 Campus Drive, Edison, NJ 08818
☎ 732-225-1900; 800-255-0343; fax 732-417-1744
www.hunterpublishing.com

Ulysses Travel Publications
4176 Saint-Denis, Montréal, Québec
Canada H2W 2M5
☎ 514-843-9882, ext. 2232; fax 514-843-9448

Windsor Books
The Boundary, Wheatley Road, Garsington
Oxford, OX44 9EJ England
☎ 01865-361122; fax 01865-361133

ISBN 1-58843-369-2
© 2004 Hunter Publishing, Inc.

This and other Hunter travel guides are also available as e-books through Amazon.com, NetLibrary.com and other digital partners. For more information, e-mail us at comments@hunterpublishing.com.

Cover photo: *Aletschwald forest near the Aletsch Glacier, Canton Valais*
Back cover: *Chillon Castle, on the shores of Lake Geneva*
All photos © ST/swiss-image.ch & picswiss.ch.

Maps by Lissa Dailey, © 2004 Hunter Publishing, Inc.

1 2 3 4

Contents

CENTRAL SWITZERLAND

Maps

Introduction

Mention Switzerland and people typically think of the Alps, Heidi, cheese, yodeling, chocolate and St. Bernards. Yet, this relatively small country – 15,941 square miles (414,466 square km) of land and inland water – offers much more than you might expect. Nestled in the heart of Europe, the Swiss Confederation (the country's official title) is home to over seven million people who speak four national languages, including their indigenous tongue, **Romansh**. The Latin name for Switzerland is "Confederatio Helvetica," from which the abbreviation "CH" comes. You'll notice the "CH" on many buildings, products, cars and on postal codes throughout Switzerland.

For the first-time traveler, Switzerland is a dream come true. The country – which celebrated its 700th anniversary in 1991 – is clean, the local people and those in the tourism industry are helpful and courteous, and the public transport systems are unmatched anywhere in the world. Local roads and highways (autobahns) are extremely easy for the neophyte visitor to navigate. The experienced explorer can return time and again to this small, mountainous country and always find a new peak to ascend, another pass to hike, an isolated lake to swim or fish in, and another small village to investigate.

In addition to the striking beauty of its Alpine scenery, Switzerland is Europe's center for international banking and manufacture of quality goods. And and is home to a variety of unique customs and traditions. Nearly 70% of the population speaks German, 19% speaks French and about 9% speaks Italian. The ancient, traditional Swiss language of Romansh is spoken by a very few.

Landlocked by Germany on the north, Austria and Liechtenstein on the east, Italy on the south and France on the West, Switzerland contains several glorious mountains that rise above 14,000 feet (4,300 m). The three major regions of the country are divided by a series of mountainous belts that run northeast to southwest. This trio of regions – the **Jura**, the **Swiss Plateau**, and the **Alps** – all follow this directional pattern, and are altered only in certain spots by the rivers that run between mountains. While the largest area of the country is in the Rhine Basin, a small area in the south is drained by the Ticino, and in the southwest by the Rhône.

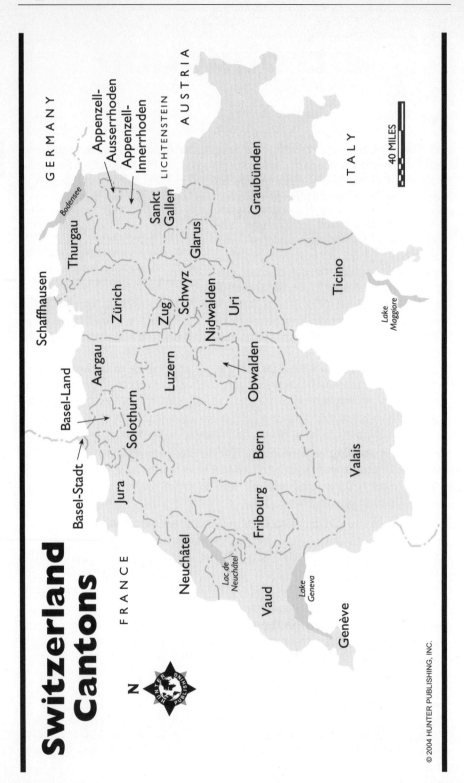

Switzerland
Cantons

Neutrality is another Swiss tradition, and one that is carried out through the country's 26 **cantons**, each of which contains a local governmental unit. As one of the most advanced industrialized nations in the world, Switzerland also has the distinction of being one of the oldest democracies. The federal government, with its headquarters in the capital of Bern, has a somewhat restricted jurisdiction and limited powers. A Federal Council heads the executive branch of the government, and a president and vice-president are chosen from among the Council's seven members. Both federal and cantonal court systems exist, and a Council of States is made up of 46 members – one or two members from each of the cantons. Election methods and office terms are decided by each canton individually.

Switzerland offers the traveler a wide array of climates and settings. One morning you might be on top of the Klein (small) Matterhorn, observing Alpine peaks in a snug down ski jacket in the mountainous canton of Valais. The next afternoon you could be sipping a glass of wine under a palm tree on the banks of Lake Lugano in your swimsuit. The following night would find you strolling across the Chapel Bridge in the Old Town of Lucerne, wearing a T-shirt and jeans, while the picturesque Alps loom up in the background.

From the high-speed trains that can whisk you from Bern to Paris in only four hours to Zermatt's famous Gornergrat Railway, no trip would be complete without at least one ride on the indefatigable Swiss Federal Rail system. A relaxing journey on one of Switzerland's many waterways gives a different perspective on the beautiful scenery, which seems never-ending.

So sit back, relax, and enjoy a trip that's sure to bring you lots of chocolate, cheese, stunning scenery and fresh, crisp mountain air – complemented by Swiss cuisine, efficiency, and a rich history.

■ What This Book Will Tell You

For over 20 years I have been living in and visiting Switzerland on a yearly basis. My job in this Alpine country has been as a writer, farm hand, and tour guide. Needless to say, I've gotten to experience Switzerland as the Swiss do, and have been able to visit the little out-of-the-way places few tourists ever visit. This book will help guide you to those places, as well as to the traditional hot spots.

If you want to experience the Alps at their finest, then the traditional towns of Zermatt, Davos, Interlaken and St. Moritz are for you. Besides spectacular mountain scenery and snow sports opportunities, these areas offer superb accommodations, fine eateries and a lively nightlife.

However, for those who want to shuffle along the path less traveled, we'll also take a walk to less-frequented areas such as Saas-Fee, Leukerbad, Vevey, Zofingen, and Langenthal. In these quaint places, you'll see more of the real Swiss – how they live, work, make a living, and how they celebrate.

Switzerland keeps evolving, and yet in some ways, it never changes. Yodeling, Emmentaler cheese, milking and watchmaking are still part of the culture after hundreds of years, enriched by all the modern conveniences, which are never far away.

■ How This Book is Organized

After this introduction – which gives you a broad overview of Swiss life and culture – we'll tell you how to get the most out of your visit. You'll learn about the seven regions of Switzerland, and the cantons (areas akin to our state counties) within those regions, as well as their major attractions and cities.

Within each canton profile we'll highlight the history of the region and then give some basic information – accommodations, restaurants, best sights, and don't-miss spots. Of course, some cantons, such as Zug or Appenzell-Innerrhoden will have less to see and do than the cantons of Bern, Valais, or Graubünden. We'll also provide you with extras, such as where to find the best Swiss porcelain or finest Swiss lace, for example. You'll get information on the best times of the year to visit certain areas, and insights into traditional festivals, such as Bern's Onion Festival and Basel's Faschnacht, as well as the annual national Schwingfest.

As many Swiss would say, "Viel spass und viel Glück!" – Have fun and much luck!

The Seven Regions of Switzerland

For the purposes of this book, we have divided Switzerland into seven distinct regions in order to help you with your travels throughout this beautiful and unique country. Swiss geography was originally formed through the development of glaciers. Switzerland became a stunning mixture of valleys, gently rolling hills, ominous mountains, and streams, rivers and land-locked lakes – all the result of glaciers. Over time, and as more areas became part of the Swiss Confederation, the development of the cantons evolved. Starting with the original three cantons of Switzerland (Schwyz, Glarus, and Uri), another 23 eventually joined them, each with its own unique history, culture and traditions.

This guide begins by examining the northern region of Switzerland, and then moves to the southeast, before covering the middle of the country. We then make our way up to the northwestern and southwestern sides of Switzerland, before journeying farther south to the most mountainous portion of the country.

© 2004 HUNTER PUBLISHING, INC.

Introduction

Switzerland

Principal Cities, Mountain Ranges & Lakes

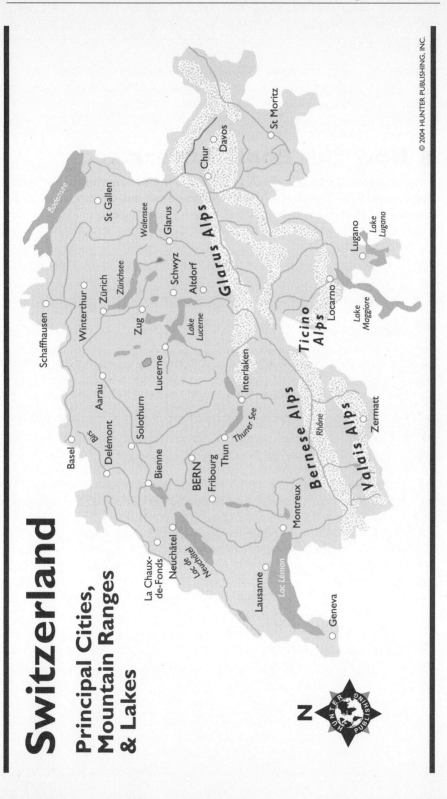

N

■ History

 Geography played a vital role in the history of the development of Switzerland. The brutal terrain provided a barrier of unity for the Swiss, and gave them independence from outside neighbors. Switzerland was once part of the mighty Roman Empire during the first century BC. A Celtic tribe known as the Helvetii was conquered by the Romans and continued to live under their protection, until the Germans invaded the area in the fifth century. The country eventually became part of the Holy Roman Empire again in the 11th century after a series of battles.

In 1291 the three cantons of Uri, Schwyz, and Unterwalden banded together and formed the **Swiss Confederation** – celebrating their independence from all other factions on August 1st of that year, which is still celebrated as the national independence day throughout Switzerland.

During the centuries that followed, more cantons were added to the young country. Lucerne joined in 1332, Zürich in 1351, Glarus and Zug in 1352 and Bern in 1353 as territorial expansion accelerated. However, at times small wars would break out between the cantons, as each one struggled for military control and power. Cantons Fribourg and Solothurn were admitted to Switzerland in 1481, Basel and Schaffhausen in 1501, and Appenzell in 1513.

As additional cantons were added, Switzerland's economy flourished. Silk goods, linens, wool and cottons experienced the greatest growth and, by the 18th century, Geneva had gained a reputation for clock production. Zürich became the center for literature and new ideas. Napoleon had a short stint of supervision over Switzerland in the late 1790s, which gave France the ability to recruit 14-15,000 men for his national army. After his demise, Switzerland was forced to develop a new constitution, which was christened the **Pact of 1815**, giving Swiss citizens freedom of religion, of movement, and freedom from occupation. The cantons of Valais, Neuchâtel and Geneva were officially established at this time as well.

Since the mid-1800s, Switzerland's history has remained fairly quiet, and the Swiss have remained unyielding in their commitment to neutrality, even as the European Union evolved and developed all around them. During both world wars, Switzerland was faced with hostile neighbors, and was able to maintain neutrality and become a center for international organizations, such as the Red Cross.

Modern Switzerland has not been unscathed by 20th-century wars, however. In the mid-1990s the Swiss government was accused of selling weapons to the Nazis, and many people who had family members perish in the Holocaust filed lawsuits against Swiss banks, accusing them of illegally keeping money and other assets deposited by victims both before and during World War II. In 1998 several Swiss banks agreed to a $1.25 billion settlement, but the government did not opt to participate in the settlement. To this day, the Swiss remain adamantly opposed to joining the European Union.

WILLIAM TELL

"Switzerland has had but one hero, William Tell, and he is a myth," wrote English author and humorist Max Beerbohm. Legend never really says if Tell was a man or a myth, but you can find a statue of him in nearly every town, village and city in Switzerland. The Swiss see Tell as a symbol of independence and the love of liberty, which has characterized this tiny country for centuries.

Made universally popular by 18th-century playwright Friedrich Schiller, the story of William Tell came to be considered fact. According to Schiller, Tell refused to bow to a hat owned by Gessler – the governor of Uri, Schwyz and Unterwalden – when that hat was placed in the market square of the town of Altdorf. Tell was taken to Gessler, where he was told to shoot an apple off of his (Tell's) son's head. Tell proceeded to split the apple with his first two arrows, and as he did this, he explained to Gessler that he would shoot Gessler himself if he tried to harm Tell's son. Tell was put into irons for his brash speech, but soon escaped to kill Gessler, and was later one of the leaders responsible for Switzerland's independence.

The Land

■ Geography

Though Switzerland appears to be all mountains, the geography offers a wide variety of features. For instance, the **Jura Mountains** – which form part of the French/Swiss border – provide a setting of lush pastures and green meadows. Lying between the Jura and the Alps is the **Central Plateau**, where nearly two-thirds of the Swiss make their homes. Herein lie the majority of family farms and major cities as well. As one passes to the south and southeast, the **Alps** rise up as rocky crags, snowy peaks, glaciers and gorges. Peaking at 15,203 feet (4,635 m) is the highest point, **Dufourspitze**, in the Monte Rose group near the Italian border. There are 50 peaks that tower higher than 12,000 feet – among them, the famous Matterhorn, the Eiger, and the Jungfrau. Still farther south, the Alps plummet into **Ticino**, home to palm trees, warm Mediterranean breezes, and heavy Italian influences.

■ The Alps

There are many distinct regions of the Swiss Alps. These relatively compact (by North American standards) mountain ranges cover 60% of the country, and are home to glaciers that comprise about 772 square miles of land (2,000 square km). Switzerland is also home to the most extensive glacier range in Europe, the **Aletsch Glacier**, which covers 65 square miles (169 square km). **Mount Rosa**, at 15,203 ft (4,634 m) is Switzerland's highest peak.

The Alps actually are formed of two parallel mountain ranges: the **Bernese Oberland** in the west-central part of Switzerland move north into the Glarus Alps, while the southwestern **Pennine Alps** continue on into the **Lepontine Alps** and the **Rheatian Alps**. The Bernese Alps (Bernese Oberland) rise to 14,022 feet (4,300 m) at the **Finsteraarhorn**, and to 13,642 (4,146 m) at the **Junfgrau**, the highest peaks in that region. This area can be crossed at only two places in the 110-mile range: either the difficult and steep **Grimsel Pass**, or the much easier valley of the **Reuss** – itself a narrow and deep crossing.

The towering Pennine Alps are separated from the Bernese Alps by the valleys of the upper **Rhône and Rhine rivers**, whose waters discharge in opposite directions. These two valleys are linked by passes at their heads, and contain most of the Alps' population. The southern range can be crossed by a number of passes, none of which are easy, and many of which are closed in the wintertime or made extremely dangerous due to massive amounts of snow and ice. The **Simplon**, the **St. Gotthard** and the **St. Bernard passes** are used the most.

The Alps got their name from the Celtic word for height – alp, itself derived from the Latin albus, meaning white. Both words help to describe these snow-topped mountains that have been a home for the Swiss people for centuries, as well as a route for explorers, traders, and armies throughout history.

Today, many people who live in the Alps are either farmers or involved in some aspect of tourism. Flocks of sheep and herds of cows are taken into high pastures during the short summer months to get fat on the rich grass that grows there, and then are brought back down for the winter. The climate tends to be a bit gentler on the southern slopes, and many of the lower mountains are covered with grapevines, while corn is grown in the valleys. Citrus fruits, such as oranges and lemons, can be found near the Italian border as well.

Land used for agricultural purposes reaches to 4,921 feet (1,500 m), and up to this height is dominated by dense forests. You will see Norway Spruce (a mountain species found on north-facing slopes), Larch (a conifer

Introduction

– found mostly in cantons Valais and Graubünden – that sheds its needles in the wintertime), and other lesser spruces, as well as fir and pine trees. Above 7,220 feet (2,200 m), the forests cease and are suddenly replaced by Alpine mountain pastures (alpe), which are home to a wide array of flowers and hardy berries. At 9,842 feet (3,000 m) only moss and lichen can be found among the rock faces and in crevices.

Due to the shortage of good farmland and unpredictable climate conditions, living in the Alps has never been ideal. Additionally, there is always the threat of the occasional avalanche, which can bury entire villages and shut off access roads for long periods of time. Years ago the people who inhabited the Alps did so to avoid wars, which were commonplace in Europe.

Avalanches

 Avalanches often occur when the first snows follow unseasonably cold temperatures. A season with steady snowfalls is preferable to a season where heavy snowfalls are mixed with weeks of rain, snow-drought and severe temperature changes. They can also occur after a very heavy snowfall which is accompanied by wind, especially on a sunny afternoon during which some of the snow begins to thaw.

The Swiss are much more accustomed to avalanches than are visitors, and tend to be more careful than tourists. In fact, the **Weissfluhjoch** (Swiss Avalanche Institute) predicts that an average winter will claim the lives of over 100 skiers and mountaineers, compared to 10-15 avalanche fatalities in the US.

There are two main types of avalanches – the **slab** and the **loose snow**. Loose snow avalanches can be wet snow or dry powder, whereas slabs are formed by snow that is blown by wind onto slopes, breaking into blocks if the slope avalanches.

Danger spots include gullies, routes that traverse beneath a cornice, and slopes with uncut grass beneath them. Conversely, safe areas include ridges, undulating ground, if it is not too steep, and heavily forested areas.

It is imperative to check local avalanche forecasts regularly. People are most often caught in avalanches because they disregard local warnings. Avoid skiing "off-piste" (off the marked ski run), and adhere to all local rules. That means staying on marked runs and avoid skiing through avalanche fences that have been set up to protect people from avalanches. While spontaneous natural avalanches do occur, the majority of them are caused by skiers who have little knowledge of the risk.

■ Rivers, Lakes & Streams

Switzerland has often been called Europe's "mother of rivers," as the melted waters from snow and glaciers drain down into two of the continent's greatest rivers – the **Rhine** and the **Rhône**. The **Ticino River** joins the **Po** in Italy, while the **Inn** combines with the **Danube** on the Austrian-German border. Waterfalls abound through Switzerland, and can provide spectacular photo opportunities. Nearly all of these waterfalls and rivers eventually make their way to the European shores, hundreds of miles south.

Over 1,500 lakes and ponds abound throughout Switzerland, and nearly every major city was founded near a major waterway. Zürich, Geneva, Lucerne, Neuchâtel, and Lugano are all examples. There are countless numbers of streams and small rivers throughout the country, some quietly gliding down mountains, while others pass over rugged gorges, creating wild foam as they strike boulders and rocks below.

Water is one of Switzerland's few natural resources and, as such, is used as a primary source of energy. At high Alpine levels, dams hold back glacial waters, which are used to drive power station turbines. While this hydraulic power produces over 50% of Switzerland's energy, a good deal of water is also need for agriculture. The area north of the Alps typically generates an adequate amount of rainfall on an annual basis, but southern Switzerland often tends to be arid. In the canton of Valais, for instance, irrigation ducts known as *Suonen* in German, or *bisses* in French, are cut from tree trunks or carved into the cliffs. These carry water from Alpine regions to thirsty fields many miles away.

■ The Climate

Switzerland's climate is greatly influenced by the Alps, although in some parts of the country these giants offer protection from the often-fierce elements. Though temperatures tend to vary with the altitude, one can expect warm summers and cold winters. The summers are shorter and winters longer in the Alps, with the first snows falling near the end of September. Peaks at 9,000 feet

(2,740 m) and higher usually stay snow-topped all year and rain falls throughout the country during all four seasons. Rainfall can be heavy in the summer months, especially in the valleys. In the winter, a dismal fog can hang over the valleys while, thousands of feet above, skiers bask in the warm rays of sunlight.

The *Föhn* is a unique wind typically occurring in the cold season, and one that unbalances the Alpine weather patterns. It usually begins in the upper Aare and Reuss valleys and is caused by a drop in the barometric pressure along the slopes of the Alps. In the Italian region of the country, the *Föhn* causes thunderstorms and heavy rainfall, while in other areas forest fires can break out and avalanches occur. For all its disastrous affects, the *Föhn* also reaps certain rewards for Switzerland – enhancing vegetation and flora growing times and shortening the lifespan of snow on many Alpine grazing pastures. That allows farmers to put their animals out to pasture earlier in the year than they normally would.

■ Flora & Fauna

While Switzerland has nearly every kind of flower that can be found anywhere else in the world, it is renowned for its famed **edelweiss.** The unofficial national flower (*Leontopodium alpinum*) is strictly protected throughout the entire country, and grows on dry meadows and rocky areas in strong sunlight up to 10,168 feet (3,100 m) above sea level. It is characterized by its beautiful, delicate, tiny white flowers with six to seven thin petals, growing two to four inches tall.

Other flowers considered primarily Alpine plants typically only grow from June through August. The beautiful **Alpine columbine**, which grows in rocks and bushes, has wide dark blue and purple petals, growing eight to 12 inches high. The **martagon lily** can be found in damp wooded areas and moist meadows and can grow to be quite tall (12-44 inches). This lilly has pink-purple petals with a red-orange middle.

The **Alpine aster** can be found among rocks and on dry hillsides from 5,000 feet (1,524 m) and above, and it has bright purple petals with a middle golden crown. This large, flat flower has a short stem, and is easily spotted because of its rich tone. The **blue gentian** is also found above 5,000 feet and is comprised of compact pod-like flowers in various colors, growing to 24 inches tall. **Bear's ears**, found above 3,200 feet (975 m) among fallen rocks and in crevices, produce large, flowering leaves with tiny daffodil-like flowers, which develop earlier than most Alpine plants, usually in April.

Other rarities include **fire lilies** and **lesser gentian**, which manage to survive and thrive on mountain plateaus. Another typical flower is the **Alpine androsace**, which has small blossoms and short stalks, blooming in various colors from purple to white. It grows in tiny, fragile bushes, each with up to 3,000 blooms, and in some rare cases can be found at 13,000 feet (4,000 m) above sea level.

The Swiss take pride in their gardens, and countless flower boxes can be found – filled to the hilt with geraniums – throughout the spring, summer and fall. There are numerous flower parks that you can explore.

Flower Journeys – Must-See Gardens & Parks

Alpine Gardens, started in the 1930s, is home to over 500 types of flowers on the Schynige Platte, high above Interlaken in the Bernese Oberland. Though these flowers bloom only between June and the end of September, it is well worth the trip (aboard a 19th-century rack-and-pinion railroad that takes 50 minutes) to ascend from Wilderswil via this antiquated mountain train. Just opposite the gardens you'll get a spectacular view of the Jungfrau, Eiger and Mönch as an added treat. For information, contact Wilderswil Tourismus at ☎ 033-822-8455 or at www.wilderswil.ch.

The **Botanical Park of Gambarogno** is on a hill between Piazzogna and Vairano, on the Gambarogno side of Lake Maggiore in the canton of Ticino. The garden is tended by Otto Eisenhut, who has thousands of colorful flowers spread out over 20,000 square yeards (17,000 square m) – including 950 species of camellias and 350 species of magnolias. In addition, Eisenhut has peonies, azaleas, rhododendrons, pines, junipers, ivies and firs. To find the Botanical Park, you have to drive from Vira up to Piazzogna. Once there, it is best to pick up the Madadin-Gerra or the Magadino-Indemini bus line. The bus stops at the Restaurant Gambarogno and the park is only a two-minute walk away. For information, contact the Gambarogno Turismo at ☎ 091-795-1866 or online at www.gambarognoturismo.ch.

Alpine Garden Thomasia in Le Pont de Nant has been in existence since 1891 and showcases over 3,000 plants and Alpine mountain flowers natural to the area. This valley between the Grand and Petit Muveran mountains in the Lake Geneva region provides a wide array of vegetation, including blueberries and gooseberries, and was proclaimed a nature reserve in 1969. The Garden is open from May until October, daily, from 11 am. You can go from Lausanne via Bex to Le Pont de Nant. ☎ 024-495-3232, www.villars.ch.

San Grato Botanical Park is in the village of Carona, on the Arbostora Hill, above Lake Lugano, and is a 30-minute drive from Lugano. Starting at the summit of Monte San Salvatore, a perfect walk follows the Sentiero dei Fiori (Flowers Path) which takes a visitor through Carona and up to the gardens. The flora includes rhododendrons, azaleas and camelias in a wide range of colors. Contact Lugano Turismo at ☎ 091-923-3232 or check their website at www.lugano-tourism.ch.

The Adelboden Flower Trail, open from May to October, provides one of the best walks anywhere in Switzerland. Along with gorgeous scenery and beautiful Alpine flora, along the trail you'll find detailed information on all the flowers, as well as a drawing of each one to help you identify them. The walk takes about 45 minutes and is well worth it. Contact Adelboden-Tourismus at ☎ 033-673-8080 or e-mail them at info@ adelboden.ch for information.

The **Conservatoire et Jardin Botaniques**, in Geneva, contains 70 acres (28 hectares) of plants, trees, flowers, rock gardens, streams and waterfalls, with greenhouses sheltering tropical plants from five continents. From Geneva's main bus terminal, you can take Bus 4-44-18 to get there. Operating hours are from 8 am to 7:30 pm, April-September, and 9:30 am to 5 pm from October-February. ☎ 022-418-5100, wwwcjb.unige.ch.

Wild Animals

A typical variety of animals can be found here: squirrels, snakes, moles, and other ground rodents, as well as a wide range of birds and bats.

Bearded vultures were once completely extinct in Switzerland, due to hunting caused by the belief that they would kill sheep, goats and even small children. These birds cannot chew bones to break them, so they drop their prey from high in the air to the rocks below, then swoop down to swallow their meal. They were successfully reintroduced into Switzerland in 1991.

The **golden eagle** is Switzerland's largest bird of prey, and is easy to distinguish from the bearded vulture by the form of its tail. The golden eagle's tail is shaped like a rectangle, while the bearded vulture's tail is arrow-shaped.

The **marmot** remains the favorite meal choice for both the golden eagle and the bearded vulture. These small mammals have dens throughout the country, feeding on the sweet grasses during the summer and retreating to their dens to hibernate during the winter months.

Elk, **chamois** and **deer** are also found throughout Switzerland, and all have adapted to the steep and rocky mountain areas, and thick forests, where they like to hide and forage for food. Because they lack natural predators, these animals are hunted at various times throughout the year.

Domesticated Animals

Milk, meat, eggs and other animal products account for more than two-thirds of agriculture production in Switzerland. Several varieties of cattle, pigs, goats, sheep, horses, chicken and rabbits are all productive livestock. In addition, turkeys, ducks, geese, mules, llamas, ostriches, bees, and even bison are slowly gaining popularity.

Simmental and **brown Swiss** are the most popular breeds of **cows** in Switzerland, with about 1.7 million of them on the farms. The number of dairy cows has dropped significantly in Switzerland since the mid-1970s, due to fewer farmers in the business, and heightened production methods.

 Though pork is a meat of choice for most Swiss people, a limit of 1,000 **pigs** per farm applies throughout the country. About 1.4 million pigs live on Swiss farms – mainly family farms – and producing feed for pigs is the second most important activity of Swiss agriculture.

 Goat raising has plummeted in the last century in Switzerland. Once home to 420,000 goats, the entire country now supports just under 60,000 animals, with 9,000 registered goat keepers. Only seven breeds are recognized and supported by the government. The most common – the **Saanen goat** – accounts for one-fourth of the total Swiss goat population. The chamois-colored mountain goat is second and the Toggenburger goat third. Six out of 10 goats live in the cantons of Bern, Ticino and Graubünden, and 80% of all goats reside with their handlers in mountainous areas.

Nearly half a million **sheep** feed on the lush green pastures of the Swiss countryside. These hardy animals are able to graze where cattle cannot venture – on high meadows and steep slopes – and are seen as a great help for cultivation of the landscape.

 Horses – once used primarily for agricultural labor – are now either used for sport or as meat for human consumption. Heavy draft horse types are now being cross-bred with thoroughbreds in order to produce a leaner, more athletic animal. Swiss horses are known to excel in national and international dressage, jumping, and three-day event competitions. Also, consumption of horsemeat by the Swiss continues to rise. In the past, most of the horse meat was imported, but since the early 1990s farmers in the Jura region have stepped up their horse production in order to meet the demand for meat.

 Over 6.3 million **chickens** are cultivated in Switzerland annually, one-third of which are laying hens, and two-thirds for human consumption. Half of the chickens and eggs produced each year are consumed domestically, as the average Swiss resident will consume 90 eggs and 25 pounds of poultry annually.

Unlike the US and other countries, industrialized animal production is not possible in Switzerland, due to limits on the number of animals each farm may keep, and animal and water protection laws. Also, livestock buildings are subject to approval by local authorities. As a result, about one-third of Swiss farmers opt to specialize in crop farming, vegetables and flowers, or fruit and wine production.

Switzerland is home to seven official breeds of **dogs**, and the breeding of these canines is overseen by the Schweizerische Kynologische Gesellschaft (SKG), which is the equivalent of the American Kennel Club.

Swiss mountain dogs (Sennenhunde), of which there are four varieties – Bernese mountain dog, appenzeller, entlebucher, and great Swiss mountain dog – were once used to pull carts and as general all-purpose farm dogs. They date back to the time of Julius Caesar and can now be found on farms and in homes as house pets. During the mid-1800s their popularity waned and the breed almost disappeared. However, their spark was rekindled by crossing the remaining purebreds with smooth-coated St. Bernards during the early 1900s. These dogs are very friendly and typically have a white chest, white feet and a white tail tip, a black coat, and bronze touches on their cheeks, above their eyes and on all four legs. They are usually around 29 inches tall and weigh between 110 and 140 pounds.

St. Bernards evolved from rescue dogs to become farm dogs and household pets. Usually between 125-175 pounds and some 28 inches tall, they are second in popularity to the Bernese mountain dogs.

During the 11th century a hospice was founded by monks in the St. Bernard Pass (8,100 feet/2,470 m) as a refuge for explorers and travelers, and the dogs were kept to help stranded and injured people, who fell victim to snowstorms.

In 1884, the Swiss St. Bernard Club was founded in Basel. In 1887, the St. Bernard was officially recognized as a Swiss breed, and since then has been known as the national dog of Switzerland.

Gentle Giants: When the St. Bernard Pass was used by Napoleon and his 250,000 troops as they crossed the Alps in May 1800, not one soldier lost his life in the chilling and treacherous mountains. According to legend, the dogs and their handlers that guided the troops and travelers were so well organized that, between 1790 and 1810, not a soul perished on the pass. The St. Bernards' broad chests were said to have helped clear paths for travelers as early as the mid-1700s. These gentle giants were also known to have an uncanny ability to navigate through heavy snowstorms and fog, as well as an excellent sense of direction. During the early years the dogs were accompanied by local monks. Over the last two centuries that these dogs have patrolled the St. Bernard Pass, more than 2,000 travelers have been rescued.

Barry, the most famous of all St. Bernards, lived in the local monastery from 1800 to 1812, and alone helped to save

40 people from certain death. In 1813 the aging Barry was brought to Bern by one of the monks, and he passed away there two years later. His body was put on exhibit in the National History Museum in the Swiss capital, where it can be admired today.

Swiss hounds (Schweizer laufhunde) are medium-sized game hunting dogs used for hunting with a rifle, and are excellent on rough terrain. Typically they have long muzzles and lean ears with a "racy" look to them indicating speed and agility. They are generally used to hunt deer, hare and fox. The four varieties include the Bernese, the Jura or Bruno, the Lucerne and the Schwyz hound. They are typical of hunting dogs found in the US such as bluetick hounds and springer spaniels.

The **smaller Swiss hound** is a cousin of the variety described above. In the early part of the 20th century, a system of hunting in preserves was introduced in a few of the cantons. Since the medium-sized Swiss hounds were too fast for enclosed preserves, it was thought that a smaller, shorter dog would be more appropriate. Through cross-breeding and stock selection, the **Niederlaufhund** – short-legged scent hound – was born. Most have short, stocky legs, and attractive coats similar to the Swiss hounds.

Government

 Switzerland is a republic, made up of 23 full cantons and three half-cantons – Appenzell, Basel, Unterwalden – for a total of 26. While the structure of government varies slightly from canton to canton, there are basic similarities. Each canton has an administrative council and a type of legislative assembly, though election methods can differ widely. Referendum techniques and popular incentive are used by most cantons, while a few others utilize the ancient custom of Landesgemeinde – an annual open-air assembly of all citizens that are at least 18 years old. This Landesgemeinde has power of legislation and must approve all laws and regulations drafted by the body of people within the canton.

Each canton is entrusted with powers in all matters that are not federal in nature, which means each canton has control over health, education and sanitation, for example. However, cantons must also conform to standards set by the federal legislative body in the capital of Bern. Cantons are also required to adhere to federal standards in regard to military training. Police and the court system are handled on a cantonal basis, with the exception of the Federal Court, Switzerland's highest tribunal.

■ Political Parties

There are four major political parties in Switzerland and several minor parties. The Christian-Democratic People's Party defends the interests of Roman Catholics and cantonal rights. The Radical Democrats represent the liberal center, while the Social Democrats are moderates who tend to favor greater federal action in social reform. Founded in 1971, the Swiss People's Party has less support than the other three major parties, and tends toward more liberal views. Other smaller parties exist as well, such as the Green, Liberal, Independent, and Communist parties.

■ The Court System

The Swiss court system is headed by the Federal Court in Lausanne. This court does not have the power of judicial review of federal legislation, but instead functions as a court of appeal for the cantonal court systems, which are responsible for trying cases at the lowest levels. The Federal Court also serves for trials concerning treason and for disputes between cantons, or between the confederation and a canton.

■ The Military

The military in Switzerland is geared solely to defense. The Swiss have a system in place to destroy every tunnel, bridge and pass leading into or out of Switzerland in the event of a national emergency. All men between the ages of 20 and 42 must serve in the military. Those who cannot serve for various reasons are subject to a special tax.

Military training is divided into three periods, with duties becoming less demanding with age. At age 20, men undergo 15 weeks of basic training. Between the ages of 21 and 32, reservists participate in 10 three-week refresher courses. Those aged 33-42 undergo 39 days of training annually for the militia. This modern plan was initiated in 1995 in response to international threats of terrorism. Soldiers usually keep their uniforms, weapons and ammunition in their homes.

Often, when they are not serving their military time, men will participate in a unique exercise called **Waffenlaufen**. Dressed in their military uniform and carrying a backpack and rifle, they'll embark on an 18- to 24-mile course at a fairly swift pace.

Cantons are able to promote soldiers to the rank of captain, but only the federal government can promote a man higher in rank – up to colonel during peacetime. During times of emergency the Federal Assembly will elect a single man to the rank of general, which has occurred only five times since 1848.

The Economy

Switzerland has long been known as one of the most prosperous countries in the world. Since the Middle Ages, commerce has been at the heart of the Swiss economy and due to the country's neutral status, it also became an ideal place for banking and a safe haven for foreign investments.

Besides banking and commerce, **tourism** is a major industry, with the visitors sometimes outnumbering the locals. These foreigners help to support hotels, restaurants, bars, and all forms of transportation. Internationally known resorts such as St. Moritz, Gstaad, Interlaken and Zermatt help to promote tourism with their year-round accessibility. The excellent railway system and highways, bridges, cable cars, funiculars and ski lifts make mountainous areas accessible that were not so a hundred years ago. Also, you can easily access Switzerland from Italy, France, Austria, and Germany on the passenger ships that ply lakes Geneva, Lugano and Constance.

About 75% of Switzerland is used for various types of **agriculture** or **forestry** and, of this, only about 10% is used for crops, such as potatoes and grains. Vineyards encompass another small percentage, while about 40% of the land is used for grazing. Dairy farming is the most productive branch of agriculture, supporting the production of milk, cheese, butter, and chocolate. However, only about 4% of the Swiss labor force is involved in some type of agriculture.

Switzerland is home to some 35,000 acres of vineyards, with the top wine-producing regions being Valais, Vaud, Geneva and Ticino – all located, not surprisingly in the southern areas of the country. The white and red wines from Valais are especially popular and can match fine wines found anywhere else in the world.

Engineering, **textiles** and **chemical production** are the leading manufacturing industries, utilizing about 20% of the Swiss labor force. Switzerland has nearly no mineral fuels, and thus has to import about 80% of its energy needs. This affected the growth of many manufacturing plants, who had to wait for the country to develop its hydroelectric power. Engineering facilities are near Zürich and Basel primarily, while textile producers – second only to engineering plants – are found mostly in northeastern Switzerland. Most chemical plants are in Basel, and they concentrate on the production of pharmaceuticals and dyes rather than on traditional chemicals or fertilizers.

Switzerland was a founding member of the European Free Trade Association in 1960, but chose to stay out of the European Economic Community (EEC or Common Market) – later called the European Union (EU). The United States and Japan are Switzerland's chief non-European trading partners. Swiss foreign trade consists of the exportation of engineering, chemical and textile products, while the top imports are agricultural products, machinery, transportation and construction equipment.

CURRENCY

The Swiss currency is "Schweizerfranken" – Swiss Francs or Franken. CHF or SFr are often used to represent Swiss francs when written, such as 15SFr. One Swiss franc equals 100 "rappen." When exchanging money it is best to go to a bank or currency exchange – hotel rates can be obscenely high. Exchange rates at the time of publication were 1SFr=US$0.73 or £0.46.

The People

■ Languages

"Unity through diversity" is the motto of the Swiss people, and loyalty to a specific canton, hometown or village tends to be strong. Diversity is accentuated by the four languages – German, French, Italian and Romansh, each of which has many regional dialects. Also, the German spoken by many Swiss is not "Hochdeutsch" or high German – the German taught in schools – but Swiss German or "Schweizerdeutsch." Swiss German can sound completely different from canton to canton, and usually reflects the people and their society, changing as you travel from north to south or from east to west.

At the borders where Switzerland meets with other nations, languages usually change gradually, and most people living in border towns grow up bilingual as a result. In all schools children are required to learn a second spoken language and usually a third written language. Where the German-speaking part of the country merges into the French-speaking area, this is known as "Röstigraben" – literally, "hashed potato dish." This signifies a separation not only of languages, but of cultures and ideals as well. The French and Italian speakers often feel intimidated by the overwhelming number of German speakers, especially on political issues. In general, the French and Italian speakers tend to be a bit more liberal, while the German speakers are more conservative.

Switzerland is predominantly German (74%), while 20% are French and just 4% are of Italian descent. Romansh and other nationalities account for the remaining 2%. In terms of religion, 48% are Roman Catholic and 44% Protestant.

■ Education

The cantons are responsible for education of children, most of whom attend public schools from ages five, six or seven until age 16. Private schools are very expensive, and many Swiss believe that a child only attends a private school if he can't make it in a public school. The cantons vary on education levels and rules, which can prove difficult for parents who move to a new canton in the middle of a school year. For instance some cantons start to teach foreign languages in the fourth grade, while others start in the seventh.

Public schools begin with Kindergarten, followed by Volksschule (elementary school), then Gymnasium (secondary school), and finally Universitäten (universities). After elementary school, children may choose to go to a middle school or they can begin an apprenticeship in a variety of trades – everything from cooking and banking, to farming and horsemanship. After finishing their apprenticeship it is then possible to continue an academic career at a secondary school or at a "Fachhochschule" (FH) – technical college. There are eight universities in Switzerland – six are run by cantons and two run by the federal government.

THE NICETIES

When speaking with the Swiss, always use the correct forms of address, such as Dr., Frau (Mrs.), Herr (Mr.), followed by the family name, until you are invited to use a first name. When greeting or saying goodbye, shake hands with the adults and then the children. It is traditional to greet the Swiss in most any setting with "grusse" (pronounced *grear-sa*), which means "greetings." While nearly all of the Swiss speak some English, most appreciate foreigners who attempt to speak their language.

If you are invited to a Swiss home for dinner, drinks or conversation, do accept and be sure to bring along some type of small gift such as chocolates, wine, a plant or a bouquet of flowers. Above all, be on time, and try not to overstay your welcome. If wine is served, wait until the host has made a toast before taking a drink, at which point all the guests will say "Prost" (pronounced *"Prosht"*).

Swiss Festivals

Many of the Swiss festivals are based on ancient folklore. For instance, the Appenzell farmer dons his golden cow earring and a bright red and yellow traditional Sunday suit in April on the day of Alpine procession – **Alpaufzug**. This is the time when an Appenzeller farmer leads his cows up to their mountain pastures for the summer. His loud greeting made with the Alpine horn is meant to express his thanks to God for a beautiful life. This is one of the many deeply rooted Swiss customs.

Chästeilet is another tradition – celebrated when the summer's cheese is distributed, accompanied by flag swinging, and more Alpine horn music. When grapes are harvested, the Swiss living in the southwest and in Canton Ticino often celebrate the following year's wine with the boisterous celebration known as **Fêtes de Vendanges**. In Basel and Lucerne particularly, **Fasnacht**, or Fools Night, is celebrated with loud music, drums, drinking and scary costumes designed to allow "fools" to drive out the evil spirits of the area – beginning at 4 am.

Each year, a large weeklong festival known as **Schwingfest** is held – the city varies from year to year – celebrating the Swiss love for wrestling. This is not the WWF type, but wrestling in the ancient Roman style made popular during the time of Caesar. It is a particularly strong tradition in the town of Gonten, in the canton of Appenzell Innerrhoden.

There are also celebrations and festivals much subtler than Fasnacht or Schwingfest. One of the most interesting is the **Onion Festival**, held each November in Bern, near the Parliament Buildings.

Food

Everyday traditions revolving around foods are widespread. Take **raclette**, for instance. This dish is made up of a three-month-old loaf of Bagnes cheese, which is cut in half and placed over an open fire to melt slowly. When melted, it is scraped onto a plate, spiced with pepper and added to pickled onions and sour gherkins, along with small, boiled potatoes. This popular Swiss dish hails from Canton Valais.

Another traditional Swiss dish is **fondue**, a mixture of Gruyère and Emmentaler cheeses, garlic, wine and kirsch (cherry brandy). Fondue is typically prepared in an earthenware pot over a tiny stove in the middle of the dinner table. Guests are given a long fork, on which they place small chunks of bread. They then dip the bread into the fondue, and try their best not to lose the bread in the cheese mixture. If a guest loses his bread in the fondue pot, he or she must then forfeit either a bottle of wine, or a kiss to the host/hostess and other members of the opposing gender seated at the table. Fondue is really a specialty of the western cantons of Switzerland, but has become a national and worldwide favorite. There are several varieties, but the best-known is the Neuchâtel fondue, which includes wine, Emmental (Gruyère) cheese, garlic, paprika, pepper and corn flour. You'll also find other fondues such as the fondue Waadtländer, where the only addition to the aforementioned recipe is butter. Fondue Genfer (Geneva) adds egg yolks, nutmeg and cream to the mixture for added flavor.

Birchermüsli is a popular dish that originally came from Zürich – now it is a national favorite, consisting of fruits, porridge, milk, grains and nuts.

Eieröhrli are giant, wavy, pancake-sized egg cakes that come from a very old Zürich recipe and are usually displayed in bakery windows during carnivals. They are made with eggs, flour, lard, butter, salt and sugar.

Emmentaler schnitzel is a dish of veal cutlets that have been rolled in flour, egg and breadcrumbs, then fried in hot butter and Gruyère cheese.

Kartoffelpfluten are hot potato dumplings.

Spätzli and **knöpfli** are varieties of small dumplings found throughout the German-speaking areas of Switzerland. Spätzli means "little sparrows," while knöpfli means "little buttons," but these are basically the same mixtures of flour, eggs, salt, butter, breadcrumbs, onions and grated cheese.

Züpfe are the braided golden-brown breads that are made especially for Sunday dinners in the canton of Bern. They are thick at one end and taper down at the other, with a thick, crisp crust and tender, light bread inside the loaf.

Other Swiss favorites include **rösti** – crunchy fried potato cakes – and **bündnerfleisch**, thin slices of meat dried in the open air. These are often dipped into fondue-like pots containing various types of sauces.

The Adventures

■ Winter Sports

 Switzerland is home to a wide variety of winter sports, and is known for having some of the best ski areas anywhere in the world. The winter season typically runs from December to April, although above 8,202 feet (2,500 m) it lasts from November to May because of the excellent snow coverage most years.

The Swiss Ski Federation is located at Haus des Skisports, Worbstrasse 52, Postfach 478, CH-3074 Muri bei Bern. ☎ 31-950-6111. They can provide information and maps on ski resorts and difficulty levels of slopes. Beginning skiers should contact the **Swiss Ski School Federation**, at Oberalpstrasse, CH-6490 Andermatt. ☎ 41-887-1240, ☎/fax 41-887-1369.

InterSport (www.intersport.ch/rent), **Rent-A-Sport** (www.rentasport.ch) and **SwissRent** (www.swissrent.ch) offer rental equipment. You'll find 90 shops in 65 different locations throughout Switzerland, and you can reserve your equipment via the Internet prior to your trip and it will be waiting for you when you arrive.

Cross-country skiing (known as *Langlauf* in German) is very popular in Switzerland. Some of the best cross-country trekking regions are in the canton of Graubünden, which has 94 miles (150 km) of pistes near St. Moritz. At Laax-Flims near Chur and Davos, there are 47 miles (75 km) of trails and many in the Gstaad region as well.

Ski touring is a combination of cross-country and downhill skiing. Great itineraries abound between Chamonix, Zermatt and Engadine. This sport is for those who are experienced and in good shape, and it's usually undertaken with an experienced guide.

Skijoring is an exhilarating sport where you are towed on skis behind a galloping horse. You must be in excellent physical condition to attempt this. Skijoring races on snow are held in St. Moritz on a regular basis.

 Zorbing is the latest craze is, for those people who just can't get enough excitement in their lives. For this sport, you are strapped inside a giant plastic ball – arms and legs spread out – and then hurled down the side of a mountain.

Snowshoeing is another sport for the physically fit, allowing you to explore off the beaten path. Most excursions are taken with an experienced guide.

Dogsledding abounds throughout most of the ski resorts in Switzerland. You can get information on local runs at the various tourist offices.

Other snow sports include **snowboarding** and **mono-skiing** (parabolic skiing), which is much like snowboarding (you use a single, wide ski and your feet are side-by-side). This sport is most popular in the areas of Les Diablerests, Saas-Fee and Laax. World Cup events are held in these three areas every year. **Snow biking** or **snow-bobbing** are also popular (basically cycling on snow). Ice sports include **ice hockey**, **curling**, and **luge**.

■ Summer Sports

 Cycling, hiking, swimming and skating are all popular in Switzerland. In the last five years Switzerland has initiated a number of **in-line skating** routes of 124 miles (200 km) each.

The most popular are those from Geneva to Brig, from Zürich to Yverdon-les-Bains, and from Bad Ragaz to Schaffhausen.

You can rent **bikes** at nearly every major train station, and cycling shops are abundant throughout Switzerland. You can arrange for a bike prior to your trip at www.rent-a-bike.ch. Prices vary, but they average around 25Sfr daily, and all types of bikes are available, from simple models to 21-gear mountain bikes.

Hiking is the number one recreational activity here. Trails are well-marked and are color-coded to indicate levels of difficulty. For instance, bright gold signifies that a trail has suitable paths for all levels of hikers. Bergweg (mountain way) path signs are white-red-white and are for experienced mountain walkers. The highest Alpine paths are coded blue-white-blue, and should never be attempted without the proper equipment and experienced mountain guide.

Hikers will want to check out **Eurotrek**, at Freischützgasse 3, CH-8021 Zürich. They provide maps and excursion information for hiking (known in German as *Wanderweg*). ☎ 01-295-5555, fax 01-295-5640, www.eurotrek.ch.

If you want to **golf** in Switzerland, take along your handicap card and lots of cash – this is one of the most expensive pastimes in Switzerland, and is generally a sport of the wealthy.

There are some 90 **riding stables** throughout Switzerland, with the majority in Canton Jura.

You can **bungee-jump** at a number of spots throughout Switzerland, but some of the best places are found at Engleberg in Titlis for 150Sfr, at Brunnen in the Urmiberg Valley, and at the Gorge of the Inn in Scoul.

To experience Switzerland in a **hot-air balloon** is extraordinary. Located 43 miles (70 km) west of Zürich and 50 km east of Bern, in the town of Wolfwil, **Funks Ballonfahrten** offers flights from one to six hours, ranging in price from 280Sfr for a one-hour excursion to 1,950Sfr for a six-hour journey. A variety of trips are possible. ☎ 62-926-2277, or ☎/fax 62-926-1611 for information. Located at Vordere Gasse 27, Wolfwil 4628.

Hot springs are natural hot baths for which Switzerland is famous. The best are found in Leukerbad, Yverdon-les-Bains and Caunausee in Films.

Shooting is a very popular sport among men, and there are some 3,600 shooting clubs throughout Switzerland.

Travel on a Budget

■ Camping & RVing

Switzerland is home to over 450 camping sites. Only a handful are open in the winter months, and about a third have accommodations for handicapped travelers. Contact the **SC (Schweizer Camping) Office** for their *Campingführer* (guidebook) at CP176, CH-1217, Meyrin. ☎ 22-785-1333, www.camping.ch.

■ Farm Stays

Those wishing to trek through Switzerland on a budget will find that the Swiss offer clean accommodations, even when sleeping in a barn! The latest trend for students and frugal travelers is called ***Schlaf im Stroh***, literally "Sleeping in Straw." Farms throughout Switzerland allow travelers to sleep in their barns on a deep bed of straw. The cost is around 18Sfr and includes breakfast. A sleeping bag is required. Check out their website at www.agri.ch/stroh, or contact the founder of this group, Christian Stahli-Fehr, at Bois du Fey, CH-1430 Orges. ☎ 24-445-1631.

Along the same lines, you can stay with Swiss families in their farm houses. **Swiss Holiday Farms** can give you a list of welcoming farms. Contact Schweizer Reisekass (Reka), at Neuengasse 15, CH-3001 Bern. ☎ 31-329-6633, ☎/fax 31-329-6601, www.reka.ch.

■ Swiss Mountain Huts

For those who are hiking, biking or just wandering, a stay in one of the many Swiss mountain huts is a game experience. Many of these huts are owned by the **Swiss Alpine Club** (SAC) and others are privately owned. The paths and trails leading to them are generally well-marked and not very demanding, but don't forget your hiking boots, a compass, and maps. These huts offer basic accommodations amid the Alps, so be ready to bunk down hard and enjoy the beautiful scenery. Rates are 43-65Sfr per night, but if you join the SAC, you'll get a discount. A reservation is strongly suggested. There is no age limit, but lights out are at 10 pm each night, with no exceptions. Most of the huts offer a simple range of dishes, and vegetarian meals must be ordered in advance. Most offer mattresses with woolen blankets, but visitors are strongly advised to bring their own sleeping bag, along with toilet paper and a torch lamp. The Association of Swiss Hut Warders has a great website at www.bergtourismus.ch/e/huetten.cfm, and you should give it a look before you go. Schweizer Hütten, Pius Fähndrich, Neudorfstrasse 2,

CH-6312 Steinhausen. SAC (Schweizer Alpen Club), Monbijoustrasse 61, Postfach 23, CH-3000 Bern. ☎ 31-370-1818, fax 31-370-1890.

■ Bed & Breakfasts

These abound throughout Switzerland. Contact Rolf Suter, Bernstrasse 6, CH-3067 Boll. ☎/fax 31-839-7484, www.homestay.ch.

■ Hostels

For more traditional economy travel, you can hook up with the **Swiss Youth Hostels** for a $25 annual fee. Schaffhausenstrasse 14, CH-8042, Zürich. ☎ 01-360-1414, fax 01-360-1460, www.youthhostel.ch. Members of the **Swiss Backpackers** pay no fee. Contact them at Postfach 530, CH-8027, Zürich. ☎ 01-201-7072, www.backpacker.ch.

■ Postal Bus Excursions

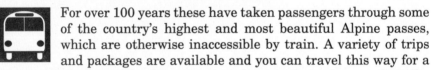

For over 100 years these have taken passengers through some of the country's highest and most beautiful Alpine passes, which are otherwise inaccessible by train. A variety of trips and packages are available and you can travel this way for a day or a week. One of the finest is a four-day trip that takes you from the Alps in Switzerland's oldest city – Chur – to the palm trees of sunny Lugano, passing through St. Moritz and Italy along the way.

Swiss postal bus on the Klausen Pass, between Glarus and Uri

For older folks and for people who don't wish to drive themselves, these trips can be a real treat. Postal buses combine trips throughout Switzerland with overnight stays at Best Western hotels. The drivers are very friendly and usually able to converse in English as well as other languages. Below are just some of the most popular trips, where you'll see a lot of sights for your dollar. Reservations are mandatory, and you must have your passport to cross any borders. Also, timetables and fares are subject to change at any time, and routes can be altered due to weather conditions. You can combine these routes, or travel on only part of these excursions.

For most single journeys, fares start at 62Sfr for adults, and 31Sfr for kids ages six to 16. Children up to six ride free with their parents. For reservations and information, contact **Die Schweizerische Post** (Swiss Post) at Post Auto Tourismus, Aareckstrasse 6, Postfach 449, CH-3800 Interlaken. ☎ 33-828-8838, fax 33-828-8839, www.postbus.ch. You can also contact **Switzerland Destination Management** at Toedistrasse 51, Postfach CH-8027 Zürich. ☎ 800-100-200-30, fax 800-100-200-31, www.sdm.ch.

The Historic Route Express

Flüelen-Altdorf-Klausenpass-Linthal

This excursion begins on Lake Lucerne, where you'll board the historic paddle steamer *Uri* for a trip into central Switzerland. You'll get grand views of Pilatus, Rigi and the Fronalpstock. When you reach Flüelen., a Postbus will be waiting for you. You will first visit the William Tell monument in Canton Uri, and wind your way past tiny villages before climbing the northern slope of the Schächental and eventually the Hotel-Restaurant Klausenpass. You can stay overnight here if you like as this is the highest point on the Klausen Pass road at 6,392 feet above sea level. When you depart from this stop, you wind your way toward the village of Linthal via the Urnerboden plateau, which offers impressive views of the Clariden massif. Contact the Swiss Post, CH-6454 Flüelen. ☎ 41-870-2136, fax 41-870-9474.

The Julier Route Express

Chur-Lenzerheide-Julierpass-St.Moritz

This journey begins at the city of Chur in Canton Graubünden and is a highly scenic route. You'll board the post bus in Chur's old town, traveling through Malix, Parpan and Valbella. From here the valley opens into the Lenzerheide plateau, where you'll find sporting activities and adventures year-round. You'll then travel through the village of Lenz and on to Savognin, a ski resort village, before reaching Bivio, the final village on the road to the Julier Pass. This pass divides the northern section of Graubünden with the Engadine and the Italian-speaking valleys of Bregaglia and Poschiavo. You travel southward to Silvaplana and soon arrive at the sophisticated outpost of St. Moritz. Contact Swiss Post, CH-7003 Chur. ☎ 81-256-3166, fax 81-252-6279.

Napoleon Route Express

Domodossola-Simponpass-Brig-Saas-Fee

Domodossola – in Italy – is the starting point for this postal bus tour. To get there, take the Centovalli Railway from Locarno – a stunning 34.1-mile ride over 348 curves, 83 bridges and through 31 tunnels. From Domodossola you'll travel to Gabi (Simplon) to visit a hotel where Napoleon stayed in 1806. You'll then travel to Simplon Dorf, an Italian-style village and on to Simplon Kulm, the summit of the Simplon Pass at 6,756 feet (2,060 m). From here you'll continue onward to the sunny plateau villages of Belalp, Riederalp and Bettmeralp, before you reach Brig. From Brig you'll travel on to the "Pearl of the Alps" which is Saas-Fee. For information and reservations, contact the Swiss Post, Bahnhofstrasse 1, Postfach 650, CH-3900 Brig. ☎ 27-922-0055, fax 27-922-0056 (Monday-Friday from 8:15 am-noon, 2-5:30 pm).

Romantic Route Express

Andermatt-Gletsch-Meiringen-Gr.Scheidegg-Grindelwald

The first leg of the journey begins in Andermatt and takes you over the Furka Pass to Gletsch, allowing for fantastic views of the Rhône Glacier. From here you'll ride around a series of hairpin turns to the summit of the Grimsel Pass before coming to Meiringen. You'll continue onward to the Bernese Oberland, eventually reaching the village of Grindelwald. Swiss Post, Aareckstrasse 6, CH-3800 Interlaken. ☎ 33-828-8828, fax 33-828-8829.

Ticino Route Express

Oberwald-Nufenenpass-Airolo-Gotthardpass-Andermatt

This trip starts out in Oberwald, a typical Valais village, and brings you to the Nufenen Pass and the western edge of the canton. From the Nufenen Pass you'll descend to Bedretto, a small village that has been devastated by avalanches time and time again, before reaching Airolo. The journey then takes you through the Gotthard Pass and on to Andermatt. La Posta Svizzera (Swiss Post), Agenzia Leventina, CH-6780 Airolo. ☎ 91-869-1353, fax 91-869-1170 or Swiss Post, Poststelle, CH-6490 Andermatt. ☎ 41-887-1188, fax 41-887-1736.

The Palm Express

St. Moritz-Lugano

Beginning in St. Moritz, the postal bus will take you along the lakes of the Upper Engadine before crossing the Maloja Pass. From here you'll descend into the Bregaglia Valley and on to Castasegna, where you'll cross into Italy. You'll travel on to Lake Como, where you'll see many lakeside resort villages. Eventually, the bus will climb again, reaching the village of Gandria as you cross back into Switzerland and then to your final destination of Lugano. The Palm Express also stops at these spots on Lake Como: Sorico, Gera Lario, Domaso, Gravedona and Dongo. Contact the Swiss Post in St. Moritz, CH-7500 St. Moritz. ☎ 81-837-6764, fax 81-837-6760 or the La Posta Svizzera, Via Serafino Balestra, CH-6900 Lugano. ☎ 91-807-8520, fax 91-923-6939.

Four Passes of the Central Alps

The Oberalp, Gotthard, Nufenen, and Furka Passes

This journey is one of the most impressive excursions found anywhere in Switzerland. You'll travel via Flims to the Oberalp Pass and then on to the St. Gotthard Pass. From here you'll drive through the Val Bedretto before climbing to the Nufenen Pass and eventually to the Furka Pass. Returning, you travel through Andermatt and across the Oberalp back into Graubünden. On Tuesdays in July, August and September. Contact Swiss Post, CH-7003 Chur. ☎ 81-256-3166, fax 81-252-6279.

Three-Pass Tour of the Bernese Oberland

The Susten, Furka and Grimsel Passes

The trip begins by ascending the Susten Pass for superb views of the Stein Glacier before stopping in Andermatt for lunch. Afterwards, you'll travel to the Furka Pass for its views of the Rhône Glacier and the village of Gletsch. It's then on to the third and final pass – Grimsel Pass – before returning alongside the waters of Lake Brienz to your starting point. This trip is available every Tuesday and Thursday from Interlaken. Swiss Post, Aareckstrasse 6, CH-3800 Interlaken. ☎ 33-828-8828, fax 33-828-8829.

Soglio to Chiavenna

This route starts at Chur and takes you through the Lenzerheide Plateau, the Julier Pass and the Upper Engadine, before journeying over the Maloja Pass and then down to the Bregaglia Valley and the village of Soglio. The return trip brings you back via the Italian town of Chiavenna and along the Splügen Pass road to Andeer, Thusis and Chur. On Tuesdays only in July, August, September and October. Contact Swiss Post, CH-7003 Chur. ☎ 81-256-3166, fax 81-252-6279.

The Bernina Pass to the Livigno Dam

This journey takes you from Chur across the Lenzerheide Plateau to the narrow Albula Pass and into the Upper Engadine before continuing to Pontresina and the Bernina Pass. You'll travel into Italy, along the Livigno dam and then back into Switzerland – passing through the Munt la Schera tunnel, the Ofen Pass road and finally to Zernez. Returning, you'll take the Fluela Pass to Davos, then Wiesen, and eventually Chur. On Thursdays only in July, August, September and October. Contact Swiss Post, CH-7003 Chur. ☎ 81-256-3166, fax 81-252-6279.

■ Tips for a More Enjoyable Trip

Supermarkets

 Coop, **Denner** and **Migros** are all large supermarket chains with stores throughout Switzerland. Many of these grocery stores – besides providing fresh, canned and prepared foods for hikers, backpackers and budget travelers – also offer self-service restaurants. Generally, the food is quite tasty. The salads and vegetables are always fresh. But frugal travelers beware – you pay based on the weight of your plate. It's worth it, though, and the settings are usually clean, bright and efficient. Also, especially in the Denner stores, you can find exquisite Swiss chocolate at much lower prices than in conventional tourist haunts.

Business Hours

 Most offices and banks close for lunch in Switzerland, typically between noon and 2 pm. All business are closed Sunday, and some on Monday as well. Banks are usually open from 8:30 am to 4:30 pm during the week.

Retail shops & outlets are usually open every day but Sunday, and most typically have a day or half-day during the week when they are closed as well. Some close during regular business lunch hours, but the train station shops usually stay open later, some until 9 pm.

Mail

 Rates for mail are either first-class airmail or second-class surface mail. Letters mailed to the US typically cost 1.80Sfr or more first class and 1.40Sfr second class.

Gas Stations

 Nearly all have automated pumps that are open 24/7. They will accept major credit cards and Swiss currency. In the larger cities those with food shops are open from 6:30 am-9 pm.

Customs

 Upon arrival in Switzerland from North America or a non-European nation, you may bring 400 cigarettes, 100 cigars, or 500 grams of tobacco. You can also bring up to two liters of alcohol (up to 15 proof) or one liter over 15 proof. If you are coming into Switzerland from another European country, you can bring 200 cigarettes, 50 cigars or 250 grams of tobacco.

Electricity

To use North American devices you'll need to bring a converter and adapter, as Switzerland's electrical current is 220 volts and 50 AC cycles. You can find these converters and adapters at most electronics stores.

Embassies & Passports

Citizens of the US, Canada, Great Britain, Australia and New Zealand need only a valid passport to enter and stay in Switzerland for 90 days or less.

The **US Embassy** is in Bern at the Jubilamstrasse 93, CH-3001 Bern. ☎ 31-357-7011.

The **Canadian Embassy** is also in Bern at Kirchenfeldstrasse 88, CH-3005 Bern. ☎ 31-357-3200.

The **United Kingdom Embassy** is on Thunstrasse 50, CH-3015 Bern. ☎ 31-359-7700.

The **Australian Consulate** is in Geneva at Chemin de Fins 2, Cast Postale 172, CH-1211 Geneva. ☎ 22-799-9100.

Emergency Services

Anglo-Phone is an English-language hotline that provides information to travelers. Calls cost 2.20Sfr per minute and lines are available from 9 am-7 pm, Monday-Friday, and from 9 am-1 pm on Saturday. For all medical emergencies and ambulance service, call 144.

Swiss Holidays

January 1, Good Friday, Easter Sunday and the following Monday, May 1-Labor Day, Ascension, Pentecost, August 1 (Swiss Independence Day), December 24, 25 and 26.

■ Swiss Associations & Clubs

Swiss Automotive Club
Wasserwerkgasse 39
CH-3011 Bern
☎ 31328-3111, fax 31-311-0310

Swiss Camping Association
Verband Schweizer Campings
Seestrasse 119
CH-3800 Interlaken
☎ 36-23-3523

Swiss Hiking Federation
Im Hirshalm 49
CH-4125 Riehen
☎ 61-606-9340, fax 61-606-9345

Association of Swiss Hut Warders
Schweizer Hütten
Neudorfstrasse 2
CH-6312 Steinhausen

SAC (Schweizer Alpen Club)
Monbijoustrasse 61
Postfach
CH-3023 Bern
☎ 031-370-1818, fax 031-370-1890, info@sac-cas.ch

Swiss Spa Association
☎ 41-726-5216, fax 41-726-5217

Swiss Ski School Federation
CH-7526 Graubünden
☎ 81-854-0777, fax 81-854-0053

Touring Club of Switzerland
9 Rue Pierro-Fatio
CH-1213 Geneva
☎ 22-737-1212

Swiss Youth Hostel Association
(Open to all age travelers)
Mutchellenstrasse 116
Postfach CH-8038 Zürich
☎ 1-482-4561, fax 1-482-4578

The Swiss Adviser
(Travel Services)
Postfach 103
CH-1000 Lausanne 19
Fax 2-184-4114

The Swiss National Tourist Office
Gare de Bern
Case Postale 2700
CH-3011 Bern
☎ 31-22-7676

Red Cross International
Ave de la Gare 10
CH-1003 Lausanne
☎ 21-329-0029

Services for Disabled Travelers
Mobility International Switzerland
Postfach 129, Feldeggstrasse 77
CH-8032 Zürich
☎ 01-383-0497

Swiss Invalid Association
Froburgstrasse 4
CH-4600 Olten
☎ 62-207-8888, fax 62-8889

■ Important Swiss Phone Numbers

Police 117
Fire 118
Ambulance 144
Swiss Rail Info 41-067-1050
Weather 162
Road Conditions 163
Crisis Line 143
Time 161

■ Swiss Internet Sites

www.sbb.ch . . . . Rail schedule
www.schweizferien.ch . . . . Basic info
www.ethz.ch/swiss/Switzerland . . . . Basic info
www.switzerland.isyours.com . . . . Basic info
www.switzerland.com . . . . Basic info
www.tele.ch . . . . Swiss television info
www.swissinfo.org/eng . . . . Basic info
www.burgen.ch/ . . . . Mountain info
www.backpacker.ch/ . . . . Backpacker hostels
www.bnb.ch/ . . . . Bed & breakfasts
www.avis.ch. . . . . Avis Rent A Car
www.crossair.ch. . . . . Crossair (Switzerland's domestic airline)
www.europcar.ch. . . . . Europcar Rent A Car
www.hertz.ch. . . . . Hertz Rent A Car
www.swissair.com. . . . . Swissair
www.snowsports.ch . . . . Swiss ski & snowboard schools

www.swisshiking.ch/ . . . . Swiss hiking
www.swissgolfnetwork.ch./ . . . . Swiss Golf Association
www.barguide.ch/ . . . . Bar guide
www.events.ch./ . . . . General info
www.cinemachine.ch/ . . . . Cinema info
www.kino.ch . . . . Cinema info
www.swissart.ch/. . . . . .Swiss art network

■ Swiss Foods

Berner Platte (Bernesdish) – a mixture of bacon, sausages, ham, boiled beef, pickled cabbage (sauerkraut), potatoes and green beans
Bündnerfleisch – dried meat from the Grisons region (raw beef smoked and served in thin slices)

Fondue – in the form of cheese or meat fondues, usually contains a center pot of melted cheese or hot juice into which meat or bread is dipped

Geschnetzeltes kalbsfleisch – minced veal or calf's liver with cream

Gnagi – knuckle of pork (a popular snack, traditionally eaten at 4 pm in Bern)

Kalbsbratwurst – veal sausage

Lake Geneva perch – reported to be the finest fish in Switzerland

Leberspiessli – calf's liver cooked on a spit with bacon

Leckerli of Basel – spiced bread with honey and almonds

Rösti – national dish of diced, boiled and fried potatoes with onions and bacon bits

Schaffhauserzungen – baked biscuits with fresh cream

Schnitzel – fillet of veal or pork chop

Wurst – sausage

Zug kirsch cake – a tasty honey-based cake from Zug

■ Swiss Hotel Terms

Café – tea room

Garni – hotel without a restaurant

Gasthaus – an inn, possibly without a restaurant

Grotto – rustic bar with light snacks and drinks

Kurhaus – spa

Pension – a small, inexpensive inn

Wirtschaft – local inn or pub

21 Places You Must See

Here are the top 20 places you should visit in Switzerland. See the pages indicated for full details. Enjoy!

AUTHOR'S
PICK

Nowhere is Switzerland more epitomized than in the wonderful, auto-less Alpine village of **Zermatt**, home to some of the world's most spectacular mountains, including the mighty Matterhorn. The Gornergrat-Bahn takes you up to a plateau at 10,171 feet (3,100 m) near the Matterhorn, where you will have fine views of the peak. Here you can enjoy a fine meal or even stay overnight. This railway leaves from near the Zermatt train station. Also, it is well worth your time to take the Klein Matterhorn cable car up to the top station at 12,533 feet (5,265 m). The views are spectacular. This cable car is at the opposite end of the village from the Zermatt train station, and is usually loaded with skiers. This is one of the most unusual and most romantic cities on the planet (can you tell I like this place?). Don't miss it! Located in Canton Valais. See page 451.

A day spent in **Lucerne** (Luzern in German) is one of the best you'll have on your trip. Besides the spectacular scenery of mountains like Pilatus, you can stroll through the Old Town, across the famous Chapel Bridge, and then take a relaxing afternoon sailing on one of the many ships that depart regularly from the Vierwaldstättersee dock. Luzern offers some of the best shopping anywhere in Switzerland. Located in Canton Lucerne. See page 187.

The Alpine Grand Canyon in the Alpenarena of Flims-Laax-Falera features the Rhine Gorge and its bizarre rock formations, which can be experienced on foot, or by car or train. However, one of the best ways to see this natural wonder is via a river raft. Tours of this area on rafts take place from May through October, with the help of professional guides. The rapids are mild and suitable for almost anyone. This is a great trip. See page 124.

Chillon Castle near Montreux on Lake Geneva is an ancient fortress at the foothills of the Valais Alps. This is absolutely the most impressive castle in Switzerland, and can be reached by a two-mile walking path from Montreux. It is one of the best-preserved medieval castles found anywhere. Located in Canton Vaud. See page 393.

The Schilthorn, atop Piz Gloria, enables you to marvel at the breathtaking 360-degree panorama of over 200 mountain peaks dominated by the Eiger, Mönch and the Jungfrau. You can either sit inside the world-famous revolving restaurant or stand outside on the observation deck, where portions of the James Bond film *On Her Majesty's Secret Service* were filmed. A great place on sunny days, horrible during a snowstorm – and be prepared… some days they won't let you back down if a storm is too violent down below. Located in Canton Bern. See pages 356-57.

Mürren is a friendly and car-free summer and winter holiday resort situated on a sun-drenched mountain terrace, and provides hikers with one of the best bases for exploring the Alps along well-marked trails. Expect to spend at least six hours if you decided to venture down the main hiking trail here. Also, you'll want to spend a day riding the 23,000 feet of aerial cables that connect Mürren with the top of Piz Gloria at 6,900 feet (2,100 m). This ride takes you through a series of stops and is Switzerland's longest cable car ride. See pages 356-57.

St. Moritz is the winter resort playground of the rich and famous. Known for its unending miles and miles of ski pistes, snowboarding runs and spectacular upper-crust shopping, St. Moritz is also a hiker's paradise during the summer months. It is also home to the "White Turf," featuring the best of Switzerland's equine athletes racing on snow. Thoroughbred racing, harness racing, polo and racing on skis are very popular during the winter months, and are sights not to be missed. You can join in the fun as well by taking one of the many horse-drawn sleighs that serve as "taxis" in St. Moritz. Located in Canton Graubünden. See page 148.

Zürich's Bahnhoffstrasse is one of the finest shopping areas anywhere in Europe. During Christmastime, the streets are lined with tiny lights, while people window-shop to their hearts' delight. Vendors line the streets offering toasted almonds and hot cider, and the lure of fresh-baked goods and Christmas cookies are everywhere. See pages 41-54.

Harder Kulm is Interlaken's mountain and offers great views of the famous holiday resort between the lakes of Thun and Brienz and the entire Jungfrau region. This area is especially good if you're traveling with children, who will undoubtedly love the Wildlife Park at the valley station, and the trip to the top by funicular. Located in Canton Bern. See page 349.

Engelberg is in central Switzerland, and is a great destination for families and for sports enthusiasts. The area boasts a top ski school and Switzerland's biggest paragliding school, as well as other snow sports. There are over 50 miles (80 km) of ski and snowboard trails, and 9,900-foot (3,018 m) Mt. Titlis provides a wide array of downhill runs. There are also 25 miles (40 km) of cross-country ski trails and 20 miles (32 km) of winter hiking trails available to wanderers of all levels. Also, the Engelberger Monastery give tours of its interiors, and of its dairy, where visitors can indulge in fondue, for starters. See page 263.

Bern, the capital of Switzerland, is in the canton of the same name, and is a versatile city that has combined the wonderful cobblestone streets of the past with all the modern conveniences any traveler could want. The historic clock tower, once the western entrance to the city, is always a treat for the first-time visitor, as is the Bear Pit – housing Bern's bears – the long-time symbol of this glorious city, which has remained unchanged for centuries. See page 309.

ove: The Aescher Restaurant near Wildkirchli, on the face of the Ebenalp (see page 109)

Below: Castle of Salenegg in Maienfeld, Graubünden

The Faelensee mountain lake at 4,800 feet in the Alpstein Mountains (see page 109)

Brienz, on the shores of Lake Brienz, overlooks the picturesque Giessbach Falls and surrounding Alpine peaks. This town is famous for woodcarving and most of the carved wood you'll find in Switzerland hails from this region. The Brienz Rothorn Bahn gives you a breathtaking panoramic view of the Bernese Alps on a wonderful old steam locomotive. The three-hour ascent peaks at the summit of Rothorn 7,700 feet (2,350 m). Located in Canton Bern. See page 353.

Gruyères is a beautiful medieval village overlooking a crest of a small mountain just south of Bern and north of Lake Geneva. You can follow the cobblestones through the quaint village up to the unique castle which looms like a king over the small fortress-like area. This is also the location for the famous cheese of the same name – and a visit to the small factory/museum at the base of the mountain is imperative. Here you can sample the rich cheese, quiche and fondue, of course. Located in Canton Fribourg. See page 427.

To get to the highest train station in Europe, you need to ride a series of trains and trams to the **Jungfraujoch**, which sits just 300 feet (92 m) below the summit of the Jungfrau. The train journey makes a complete circular trip from Interlocken East train station. You'll pass through the villages of Lauterbrunnen and Wengen, riding up to the Kleine Scheidegg, the last stop before the Jungfraujoch. The last part of the journey takes nearly an hour as the train just creeps along – at one point going through a four-mile (6.5-km) tunnel. Up here one finds an ice palace carved into the glacier, dog-sled rides, shops and restaurants. Located in Canton Bern. See page 349.

Saas-Fee is at the end of the Saas Valley, on the west side. At the fork in the road if you went east, you'd be heading to Zermatt. Saas-Fee is in the middle of 12 mountains, sitting atop a terrace high above the valley. The village is closed to traffic, and all cars must be parked at the edge of town in a parking garage. This is *the* town for hikers. It is where the Swiss go, when they want to hike or ski. Located in Canton Valais. See page 460.

Lugano, with its heavy Italian influences, is another must-see part of your journey, along with Zermatt and Lucerne. The streets of the Old Town are closed to cars, making this a great walking city. You can also take one of the many steamers for a couple of hours or for an all-day journey on beautiful and relaxing Lake Lugano. This is a great romantic spot for couples. Located in Canton Ticino. See page 468.

Geneva, though modernized, still retains the charm of old Switzerland, particularly in the Old Town, where strolling along the maze of cobblestone walkways seems idyllic. A 12th-century cathedral – St. Peter's Church – dominates this area of Geneva and, if you climb to the top of the north tower of the church, you'll get a great view of the city and her Alps. Also, Geneva is a good spot if you're looking for fun day-trips. There are a handful of tiny artisan-splashed villages on the French side of Lake

Geneva, which are worth exploring for an afternoon. Yvoire (pronounced EVE-wa) is one such spot that should not be missed. See page 371.

Appenzell is very popular with the tourists, and for good reason – in no other Swiss town does folklore ring out so strongly. The buildings in this small village are painted with bright landscapes, flowers, people, animals and designs of all sizes and shapes. In addition, the town is known for its great cheeses and exquisite embroidery. Located in Canton Appenzeller Innerholden. See page 106.

The Glacier Express is more of a must-do, rather than a must-see, although expect to see quite a lot on this 7½-hour journey through some of the most treacherous mountain passes Switzerland has to offer. This train crosses 170 miles (274 km), passing from southeast Switzerland to the eastern part of the country – beginning in Zermatt and ending in St. Moritz – crossing some 291 bridges and moving through 91 tunnels. The trains are very modern and come complete with dining cars and large windows to view the spectacular scenery. See page 150.

The Engadine Region is enclosed by beautiful mountain ranges and highlighted by the winter-sports resort of St. Moritz. In lower Engadine is where you'll find heavily forested valleys and the Swiss National Park – a 55-mile wildlife sanctuary that is a haven for hikers and wanderers. Located in Canton Graubünden. See page 115.

Zürich, view of the river Limmat and the Old Town,
with Lake Zürich in the background

Zürich & Northeastern Switzerland

Northeastern Switzerland encompasses the cantons of Zürich, Schaffhausen, Thurgau, St. Gallen and the two Appenzeller (Ausserrhoden and Innerrhoden) half-cantons. It is a region known both for its sophistication (in Zürich) and for its ultra-traditional side (Appenzell). Since many visitors arrive in Zürich, at the main airport or train station, this can often be a good starting

point from which to see the region, either via car or *bahn* (German for train). Excluding the cities of Zürich and Appenzell, this region is often overlooked by foreign tourists. For instance, Canton Thurgau lacks the industrial development that plagues a good part of Canton Zürich. Here you'll find fruit groves, meadows and pastures that are great for relaxing walks or long hikes. The houses are half-timbered and many feature red beams that enrich the glow of stone walls. Canton Schaffhausen, which sits to the north of Zürich, often seems more a part of Germany than of Switzerland. With its picturesque villages along the Rhine River, Schaffhausen is home to one of Europe's finest natural wonders – the spectacular Rhine Falls. It is also the home of some lovely vineyards. Farther east lies the canton of St. Gallen, with the half-cantons of the Appenzells firmly entrenched within it. These cantons offer more of the refreshing Swiss countryside – gently rolling hills, the clanging of cow bells from afar, and small farms dotted throughout the land. Here, you'll find the men and women sporting traditional Appenzeller costumes of red vests, black pants and ornate embroidery work. Along the far eastern and northeastern edges of the area is Lake Constance or the Bodensee as it is known in German. With its gentle mountain slopes and crystal blue waters, relaxing shipboard excursions and walks are popular here.

For a pleasant five- to seven-day trip through this region, we recommend using the city of Zürich as your base. If you're driving or traveling by train, you're only a short distance from most destinations here. After several days exploring Zürich, you can travel north (on Highway 1) and spend an afternoon in the artsy city of Winterthur, before heading north (along Highway 4) to Schaffhausen, where we suggest an overnight stay.

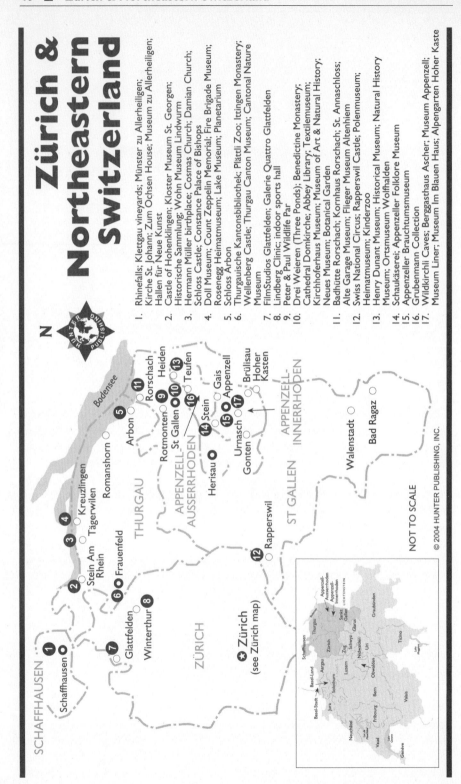

Zürich & Northeastern Switzerland

1. Rhinefalls; Kletgau vineyards; Münster zu Allerheiligen; Kirche St. Johann; Zum Ochsen House; Museum zu Allerheiligen; Hallen für Neue Kunst
2. Castle of Hohenklingen; Kloster Museum St. Georgen; Historische Sammlung; Wohn Museum Lindwurm
3. Hermann Müller birthplace; Cosmas Church; Damian Church; Schloss Castle; Constance Palace of Bishops
4. Doll Museum; Count Zeppelin Memorial; Fire Brigade Museum; Rosenegg Heimatmuseum; Lake Museum; Planetarium
5. Schloss Arbon
6. Thurgauische Kantonsbibliothek; Plättli Zoo; Ittingen Monastery; Wellenberg Castle; Thurgau Canton Museum; Cantonal Nature Museum
7. FilmStudios Glattfelden; Galerie Quattro Glattfelden
8. Lindberg Clinic; indoor sports hall
9. Peter & Paul Wildlife Par
10. Drei Weieren (Three Ponds); Benedictine Monastery; Cathedral Domkirche; Abbey Library; Textilemuseum; Kirchhoferhaus Museum; Museum of Art & Natural History; Neues Museum; Botanical Garden
11. Badhütte Rorschach; Kornhaus Rorschach; St. Annaschloss; Alte Garage Museum; Flieger Museum Altenhiem
12. Swiss National Circus; Rapperswil Castle; Polenmuseum; Heimatmuseum; Kinderzoo
13. Henry Dunant Museum; Historical Museum; Natural History Museum; Ortsmuseum Wolfhalden
14. Schaukäserei; Appenzeller Folklore Museum
15. Appenzeller Brauchtumsmuseum
16. Grubenmann Collection
17. Wildkirchli Caves; Berggasthaus Ascher; Museum Appenzell; Museum Liner; Museum Im Blauen Haus; Alpengarten Hoher Kaste

N

SCHAFFHAUSEN ❶
Schaffhausen ○

Glattfelden

Winterthur ❽

❼

Stein Am Rhein
❷
❸
Tägerwilen
❹ Kreuzlingen

Frauenfeld ❻ ○

Romanshorn ○

Bodensee

Arbon ○ ❺

THURGAU

Rotmonten ○ ❾
St Gallen ❿ ○
APPENZELL
AUSSERRHODEN

Herisau ●

Rorschach
❶❶
Heiden
Teufen ○ ❶❸
❶❻ ○
Stein ❶❹ ○

Brülisau
Hoher
Kasten
Gais
Appenzell
❶❺ ○ ❶❼
Urnäsch ○
Gonten ○

APPENZELL-
INNERRHODEN

Rapperswil
❶❷ ○

ST GALLEN

Walenstadt ○

Bad Ragaz ○

★ Zürich
(see Zürich map)

ZÜRICH

NOT TO SCALE

© 2004 HUNTER PUBLISHING, INC.

You can then travel via secondary road or rail to Kreuzlingen, along the shores of Lake Constance for half a day, continuing onward to the lakeside village of Arbon. Better yet, take one of the many ship excursions available from Kreuzlingen. You can cross the lake and spend the rest of your day in Germany or simply sail on the lake, enjoying the tranquil waters and lovely scenery. From Kreuzlingen or Arbon you can head south to St. Gallen for another overnight stay and spend a day exploring this city and its surrounding villages. From here, it's a short hop to Appenzeller land and Mt. Santis, where we suggest another overnight stay. Then travel west along Road 8 to Jona, a village on Lake Zürich. From there, you can take a ship back to Zürich.

Canton Zürich (ZH)

■ At a Glance

 Located in the far north of Switzerland, Canton Zürich has been a member of the Swiss Federation since 1351 and is home to 1.3 million people. With German as the primary language, this canton is dominated by the capital, "Stadt Zürich," which is also the largest town in Switzerland, with approximately 348,100 residents.

The **arms** of Canton Zürich are probably derived from the banner of the city, which was divided diagonally into silver and blue. The oldest use of the divided shield as the coat of arms of the city or canton dates from 1389, when it appears as a small shield in the seal of the Court of Zürich.

Stadt Zürich

Zürich is Switzerland's most populous city and is famous as the intellectual and cultural capital of the nation. In 1916, the Dada movement emerged from Cabaret Voltaire, at nearly the same time when Lenin and Trotsky were running around in the city.

Set 1,200 feet (400 m) above sea level, Zürich straddles the Limmat River at the south end of the city, which is home to 1,030 fountains. The old town contains most of the major sights, including 16th- and 17th-century houses, guildhalls, courtyards and innumerable winding alleyways.

■ Information Sources

Tourist Offices

 The **Zürich Tourist Office** is in the Hauptbahnhof on Bahnhofstrasse 15, CH-8023 Zürich, and is open November-March, Monday-Friday from 8:30 am-7:30 pm, Saturday and Sunday from 8:30 am-6:30 pm; April-October, Monday-Friday from 8:30 am-9:30 pm, Saturday and Sunday from 8:30 am-8:30 pm. There is also an office in the airport, in Terminal B, open daily from 10 am-7 pm. Hauptbahnhof on Bahnhofstrasse 15, CH-8023 Zürich. ☎ 1-215-4000, www.zurichtourism.ch.

The **Zürich Tourism Convention Bureau** offers all types of services for business travelers. Open Monday through Friday from 8:30 am-6:30 pm, the office is Bahnhofbrucke 1, CH-8023 Zürich. ☎ 1-215-4030, fax 1-215-4099, congress@zurichtourism.ch.

Post Offices

The main post office, the Sihlpost, is open Monday-Friday, 7:30 am-8 pm, Saturday, 8 am-8 pm, and Sunday, 11 am-10:30 pm, at Kasenmenstrasses 95/99 CH-8023 Zürich. ☎ 1-296-2111. There is also a post office in the Hauptbahnhof open Monday-Friday from 7:30 am-6:30 pm and on Saturdays from 7:30-11 am.

Codes

The **postal codes** for Zürich are CH-8023 to 8023 and the area code is 1.

Disabled Travelers

The *Wheelchair Guide for the City of Zürich* is an accessibility guide to Zürich's attractions, theaters and restaurants. You can find it in the Tourist Office at the Hauptbahnhof and in bookstores throughout the city.

Health Care

Most doctors in Switzerland speak English, and English is understood at these emergency numbers:

- Ambulance, ☎ 144
- First Aid, ☎ 47-4700
- Poisonings, ☎ 251-5151

A number of hospitals offer 24-hour emergency care, and both doctors and dentists can be reached at the **Zürich Universitätsspital**, Schmelzbergstrasse 8, 100, CH-8008 Zürich. ☎ 1-269-6969.

For eyeglass troubles, contact **Götte Optics**, Bahnhofstrasse 100, CH-8023 Zürich. ☎ 1-211-3780.

There is also a 24-hour drugstore service at **Bellevue Apotheke**, Theatrestrasse 4, ☎ 1-252-5600.

Internet Access

Most hotels provide some type of Internet access or will assist you with an occasional e-mail addressed to the hotel. You can also check out the **Internet Café**, at Uraniastrasse 3, in the

Zürich

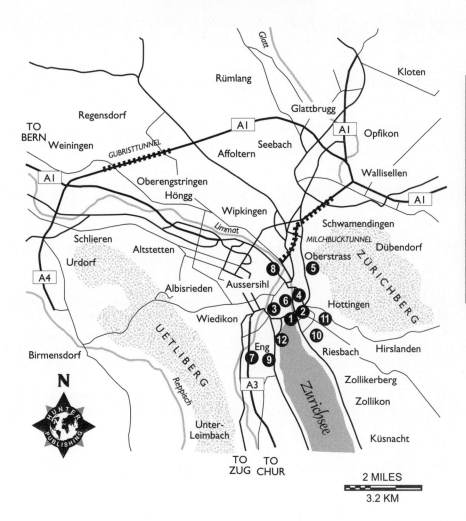

1. Fraumunster church
2. Grossmunster church;
   The Bellerive Museum
3. St. Peterskirch
4. Rathau; Stussihofstatt Fountain;
   Johann Jacob Museum
5. Zoologisches Museum;
   Zürich Zoo
6. Zurich Toy Museum
7. Rietberg Museum
8. Schweizerisches Landessmuseum
   (Swiss Land Museum)
9. Belvoir Park
10. Chinagarten
11. Old Botanical Garden
12. Quayside Park

Urania Parkhaus. This café is open most days from 9 am until midnight. ☎1-210-3311. A few banks have Internet terminals in their lobbies as well.

Money Exchange

Banks abound in Zürich. ATMs are abundant as well, and most accept major bankcards and credit cards. They dispense Swiss francs at the going rate of exchange. Most hotels will also exchange money, but at much higher rates. Train stations outside of the city will usually exchange money as well. The **Union Bank of Switzerland** at Shop Ville, ☎ 1-234-1111, or the **Swiss Bank Corporation**, at Bahnhofstrasse 70, ☎ 1-224-2142, are both open Monday-Friday from 8 am-6:30 pm and on Saturdays from 9 am-4 pm.

There is also a currency exchange office at Minervastrasse 117 at the Hauptbahnhoff (near Track 16) that is open daily from 6:30 am-10:45 pm, ☎ 1-383-6560. There is also an automated machine just outside the office for use during and after office hours. An American Express office is at Bahnhofstrasse 20, ☎ 1-211-8370, open Monday through Friday, from 8:30-6 pm, and on Saturday from 9 am-1 pm.

Newspapers, Magazines & Radio

Die Neue Züricher Zeitung (NZZ), *Der Tages-Anzeiger* and *Der Blick* are the daily Zürich papers. *Der Züricher Wocheplan* is a weekly paper that details local happenings. International papers such as *The International Herald Tribune, USA Today,* and *The Daily Telegraph,* are available at most kiosks and in bus and train stations. English-language Sunday papers are available at the Hauptbahnhof and at the airport. The local radio station is Radio 24.

Telephones

Most public phone booths accept major credit cards and pre-paid calling cards. For local operator assistance, dial 111; for international operator assistance, dial 1159. The Zürich Hauptbahnhof offers phone, telex, and fax services from 7 am-7 pm, Monday-Friday and on Saturday and Sunday from 9 am-9 pm.

Translators & Interpreters

Dolmetscher und Ubersetzung Vereiningung provides translation services in all European languages. Located at the Lindenbachstrasse, CH-8008 Zürich, the office is open Monday through Friday from 8 am-noon, and from 1-5 pm. ☎1-360-3030, fax 1-360-3033.

■ Getting Around

The best way to see Zürich is on foot or by tram. Public transportation is excellent in Zürich and provides convenient and frequent stops to every niche of the city. Fares can be expensive, but deals are always available. Check out fares at three places: the airport train station (Kloten Bahnhof), the main railway station (Hauptbahnhof), and the tourist information office inside the Hauptbahnhof. ☎ 1-215-4000.

Tours

The Zürich Tourist Office in the Hauptbahnhof can arrange private tours based on your preferences. Prices begin at about 250Sfr for half a day and can go up to 340Sfr for a full day. ☎ 1-215-4088. These are great for folks traveling with elderly parents, or for those who want to get a full historical education on Zürich; otherwise, this option is a bit pricey for the economical traveler.

You can sign up for more traditional city tours at the **Zürich Excursions** desk in the Tourist Office. Walking tours, bus tours and tours that combine boat rides with cable cars are included here. Prices for these are more reasonable at 20-40Sfr per person. Zürich Excursions can also arrange for side-trips to other Swiss cities and towns. ☎ 1-215-4000.

Taxis

Taxi stands are throughout the city, and are available 24 hours a day. They're found at major hotels, restaurants, bars and by the train stations, but cannot be hailed from the street. These are terribly expensive; the rates are calculated by a meter at 3.2Sfr for each kilometer traveled, with a base fare of 8Sfr.

Rail

The rail system is superb, and trains are marked and referred to by their initials, which var according to the local language of the region – in Zürich's case, SBB (Schweizerische Bundesbahnen). Intercity (IC) trains provide express service between Zürich and other main cities of Switzerland, while Eurotrains (EC) run between Zürich and over 200 European cities. For all train reservations, schedules and information, go to Zürich's main train station or call ☎ 1-030-0300.

Buses & Trams

Zürich's VBZ Zuri-Lines (local city trams and buses) work in tandem with the greater Zürich transport system (ZVV). These intricate networks operate daily from 5:30 am until midnight. ☎ 1-212-3737. It is advised to purchase your tickets before boarding the trains from either the ticket counter or through various vending machines at most stops. If caught without a ticket, you'll pay a fine of 60Sfr. A single ticket – costing 3.60Sfr – is good for one hour, and is valid for both buses and trams. Tickets are available as Kurzstrecken (short trip) for 2.10Sfr if you are only traveling one or two stops; as Tageskarte (day passes); and as Mehrfahrtenkarte (multi-ride). For information, ☎ 1-821-3850.

Funiculars

 There are three funiculars in Zürich. One goes to Dolder, where there are sports facilities, hiking paths and a luxury hotel with a panoramic view of the region. Another, the Forch narrow-gauge railway, departs from Stadelhofen railroad station (the S-18 line), which you would use if you plan to hike and wander outside the city limits. The UBS Poly (near the Rutli Hotel) is an ancient railway that takes you to the Polyterrasse for a marvelous view of the city – in just three minutes. These trams typically cost between 6-10Sfr, depending on your destination, and are operated on a daily basis.

Driving

 If you prefer to drive around Zürich, you'll have no problems, unless you like to speed. Speed limits are strictly enforced, and fines are very high. Parking in downtown Zürich can be difficult on the street, but parking garages abound – just look for

View over the River Limmat of Zürich and the old quarter

the bright blue parking signs. Rates are anywhere from 6-10Sfr per hour in public garages. You can rent a car at the airport or at locations within the city limits.

> *If you want to get a true taste of what living in Zürich is like, the Zürich Tourist Office (☎1-215-4000) will arrange for you to meet a family or person(s) close to your own age and occupation.*

■ Adventures

On Foot

Zürich abounds with "**Vitaparcours**" – woodland hiking, jogging and exercise routes. Any hotel can direct you to the nearest trail, and the **Sportamt der Stadt** in Zürich, at Station Letzigrund, Herdenstrasse 47, will provide you with maps. Their phone is ☎ 1-496-9393. The nearest trail to the city is in the Fluntern district on the Allmend. To get there, take Tram 5 from Bellevueplatz, or Tram 6 from the Bahnhofplatz.

TOURS

If you want to take a guided tour through Zürich itself, the city offers a very good two-hour tour through Old Town. Tours are operated from May through October, Monday through Friday at 2:30 pm in English and German, and on Saturday and Sunday at 10 am in English and German, and at 2:30 pm in English and Spanish. From November to February, these tours are offered only on Wednesday and Saturday at 10 am in English and German only. Tours begin in the main hall of Zürich's main train station (Hauptbahnhof). Prices are 18Sfr for adults and 9Sfr for children ages six to 16, and free to youngsters under age six. ☎1-215-4000 for information.

For those who enjoy **running** and **jogging**, the **Dolder Grand Hotel** offers a running path that winds through nearby forests for both guests and non-guests alike. At the north end of the city is the **Allmend Fluntern**, a large public park complete with numerous jogging paths and trails very near the Zoo. To get there, take Tram 6. The **Allmend Sportplatz**, near the city center, offers a conditioned track. To get there, take Tram 13 and get off at the last stop.

Uetliberg and **Zürichberg** are the closest hills just outside of the city and are excellent sites for hiking and mountain biking, and numerous other mountain areas abound nearby for winter sports. If you like to picnic, then take the Uetlibergbahn from the Selnau station in Zürich to Uetliberg. Cost is about 15Sfr for a round-trip ticket and this popular ride takes about a half-hour each way. Uetliberg is situated on a 2,800-foot (840 m) hill near the Sihl River, with abundant scenic views. From the drop-off station, you can hike another 15 minutes to the summit, where you'll find a restaurant, café and small observation tower. The view from the top of the tower on a clear day is spectacular. ☎ 1-206-4511 for train information and schedules.

On Water

 Visitors will find that Zürich is a dream for outdoor sports and recreation. Besides mountains, there are several beaches along the shores of Lake Zürich. These – the **Strandbad Mythenquai** and the **Strandbad Tiefenbrunnen** – are generally open from May through August. Besides sunbathing, you can also rent boats to take on the lake from the numerous vendors lined up along Limmatquai, Stadthausquai and Seequai. Prices vary and are negotiable. A public pool is at Sihlstrasse 71, and includes a sauna as well as outside pools.

You can also take a **boat trip** from Zürich and visit some local lakeside villages. One such tiny town deserving of a day-trip is **Rapperswil**, which is across the lake from Zürich. Boats leave from the main port at Burkliplatz and General Guisan Quai. Rapperswil is a quaint little village with cobblestone streets and a small castle. You can eat in one of the tiny family-owned restaurants there and walk along the tree-lined path that edges Lake Zürich.

There is also a boat ride that gives the visitor insight into the city's history, architecture and bridges, cruising along the Limmat River. Boats depart from in front of the Landesmuseum, near the main train station. Contact the Zürichsee Schiffahrtgesellsschaft (ZSG), Mythenquai 333, CH-8038 Zürich. ☎ 1-48-713-33.

On Wheels

 In Switzerland cyclists are subject to the same rules that apply to cars, but many roads throughout the country and in Zürich have special bicycle lanes, and in many places the bike lanes have their own traffic lights. Signs for cyclists are in red with black figures, and in Zürich many of the bike routes are away from areas of heavy traffic. Bikes for tourists can be rented for one day at no charge, though there is a refundable deposit of 20Sfr (and you must leave your passport as well). Reservations are recommended and should be made no later than by 6 pm of the previous day. To rent a bike, go to Zürich's main train station, Platform 18.

On Snow

 The small range of mountains just outside of Zürich, which includes Uetliberg, provides skiers with a limited amount of options. For those who enjoy **cross-country skiing**, the **Albis Pass** has a 7½-mile (12-km) trail that stretches to Uetliberg. There is another trail that belongs to the Albis cross-country ski school. For **downhill skiing**, the nearest location is at **Hoch-Ybrig**, an hour from Zürich. To get to Hoch-Ybrig, take the train to Einsiedeln and transfer to the bus for Weglosen; that brings you to a cablecar, which then lifts you to Hoch-Ybrig. There are five ski lifts and two chairlifts at Hoch-Ybrig and rental equipment is available. ☎ 55-414-6060 for information.

Ballooning

 To experience Switzerland in a hot air balloon is extraordinary. Located just 42 miles (68 km) west of Zürich and 31 miles (50 km) east of Bern, in the town of Wolfwil, **Funks Ballonfahrten** offers flights from one to six hours, ranging in price from 280Sfr for a one-hour excursion to 1,950 Sfr for a six-hour journey. A variety of trips are possible. ☎ 62-926-2277, or fax 62-926-1611 for information. Vordere Gasse 27, CH-4628 Wolfwil.

Golf

 If you enjoy golf, there are several courses close to Zürich, but take along your handicap card and lots of cash – this is one of the most expensive pastimes in Switzerland, and generally reserved for the elite. Check out the **Dolder Golf Club** at Kurhausstrasse 66, ☎ 1-261-5045, or the **Golf and Country Club Zürich**, slightly southeast of Zurich in the suburb of Zumikon, ☎ 1-918-0051.

■ Sightseeing

 Although Zürich is highly industrialized, the skies remain clear since the factories are powered by electricity. Zürich is situated between the wooded slopes of the Uetliberg and the Zürichberg, and the southern portion of the city is divided by the River Limmat. It's here, where the Limmat meets Lake Zürich, that visitors can take a sailboat excursion on the lake. This city is ideal for exploring in an unhurried fashion and the Old Town is a great place to people-watch and window shop.

Churches

Besides the fountains, churches are Zürich's main landmarks. Most significant and impressive are the Fraumünster, Grossmünster, and St. Peterskirche – each with its own contrasting styles.

The **Fraumünster** was built in the 13th century to replace a convent for noblewomen, which had been there since 853. It has been greatly modernized since then. Among other things, the artist Marc Chagall designed the stained-glass windows in 1970. Admission is free and guided tours are available. The church is at Fraumunsterplatz, ☎ 1-211-4100, and is open Monday-Saturday from 9 am-12:30 pm and 2-6 pm; Sunday after mass until 4 pm in the winter and until 6 pm in the summer. Fraumunsterplatz, CH-8001 Zürich. ☎ 1-211-4100, fax 1-221-2078.

The **Grossmünster** was built between 1100 and 1250 on the site of a ninth-century church, and is dedicated to the patron saints of Zürich. Artist Augusto Giacometti designed its stained-glass windows. It's found at Zwingliplatz and Münsterplatz, ☎ 1-252-5949. The church is free but to climb the towers costs 3SFr. The climb is well worth the 3Sfr and provides excellent views of the city. Open Monday-Saturday from 10 am-4 pm and after Sunday services until 4 pm.

St. Peterskirch is one of the oldest in Europe and has the largest clock face of any church in Europe. Built in the 13th century, the church was altered and the clock added in 1705. The clock is 28.6 feet in diameter and the minute hand alone is 12 feet long. St. Peterhofstrasse, ☎ 1-211-2588. Open Monday-Friday 8 am-6 pm, Saturday from 8 am-4 pm; Sunday service is from 10-11 am. Concerts are held occasionally on Saturdays. Admission is free.

Landmarks & Historic Sites

The **Rathaus** is Zürich's Renaissance town hall that dates back to the 1600s. The richly ornamented building is still the seat of city and cantonal parliaments. There are no tours of the interior, so you'll have to be content with the outside view. Limmatquai (at Rathausbrucke).

Stussihofstatt Fountain dates back to 1574, and has been restored many times, but still retains its charm, and is typical of the more than 1,000 fountains found in this city. On Niederdorfstrasse in Old Town.

Museums

The Bellerive showcases displays of modern art, including those by William Morris, Emile Galle, Diego Giacometti and Sonia Delaunay, to name a few. A rich commercial art collection is on permanent display. Guided tours every Thursday at 5:30 pm. Closed Mondays. Open Tuesday-Thursday from 10 am to 8 pm; Friday from 10 am-5 pm; and Saturday from 11 am-5 pm. Located on Hoeschgasse. ☎ 1-383-4376. Adults 6SFr.

Johann Jacobs began a coffee, tea, cocoa, chocolate and biscuit business in 1895 in Bremen, Germany, and the name Jacobs soon became synonymous with coffee throughout most of Europe. This museum was founded in his honor in 1984 by his great-grandson.The **Johann Jacobs Mu-**

seum has displays on the cultural history of coffee, along with porcelain, silver and graphic arts. Guided tours are offered on the second and fourth Friday of every month at 5 pm; Friday and Saturday 2-5 pm; Sunday 10 am-5 pm. Free. Seefeldstrasse 17, (at the corner of Feldeggstrasse). ☎ 388-6151.

Kunsthaus Zürich is a museum of fine arts displaying paintings, sculptures and graphic arts, mostly from the 19th and 20th centuries, many by Swiss artists. Highlights are the Dada collection, works by Munch, Giacometti, Chagall and Mondrian. Since 1976 it also housed the Swiss Foundation for Photography (SSP) and exhibitions by the world's leading photographers are held on a regular basis. Tuesday-Thursday 10 am-9 pm, Friday-Sunday, 10 am-5 pm. 10Sfr for adults. Audio guides available in English, French and German for 6 Sfr. Heimplatz 1. ☎ 1-253-8484; www.kunsthaus.ch/e/ssp/stiftung.html.

The **Rietberg Museum** is housed in Villa Wesendonck, a beautiful mansion in Rieter Park with a view of the lake. The permanent collection features non-European art, including famous works from India, China, Africa and Japan. Museum hours, Tuesday-Sunday, 10 am-5 pm. Villa hours, Tuesday-Saturday, 1-5 pm, Sunday, 10 am-5 pm. 3 Sfr-12 Sfr. Gablerstrasse 15 (take Tram 7). ☎ 1-202-4528, www.rietberg.ch. The Rietberg is actually made up of a pair of villas set in a tranquil park just southwest of Zürich city center. **Villa Wesendonck** – which was built in 1857 by German industrialist Otto Wesendonck – is on the right and was modeled after Villa Albani in Rose. **Villa Rieter** – the smaller of the two museums – is on the left. Villa Wesendonck houses the main collection of non-European artwork and was home to composer Richard Wager in 1857. Villa Rieter houses several ever-changing collections of Asian, Indiana, Chinese and Japanese art on two floors. The grounds and buildings themselves are stunning and a stroll around the area is well worth it.

Schweizerisches Landesmuseum – The Swiss National Museum – is housed in a 19th-century castle, and details the history of Switzerland from prehistoric and Roman times through the Confederation. One particularly interesting exhibit is a display of arms and armor with Swiss-made weapons from medieval times, including impressive crossbows and swords. Another exhibit features book-inscription from the Middle Ages. Tuesday-Sunday, 10:30 am-5 pm (Thursday to 7:30 pm). Free admission, though special exhibitions run 8-10 Sfr. Museumstrasse 2 (behind the Hauptbahnhof). ☎ 1-218-6565.

The **Zoologisches Museum** is part of the University of Zürich and has displays relating to all aspects of the animal kingdom. Popular attractions include hands-on exhibits with sophisticated microscopes and various forms of insect life. The exhibits of a giant crab and a giraffe are also well done. Tuesday-Friday, 9 am-5 pm, Saturday and Sunday, 10 am-4 pm. Free. Karl Schmidstrasse 4. ☎ 1-634-3838.

Zürich & the Northeast

The Zürich Toy Museum provides an impressive display of toys from centuries past. This museum (Zurcher Spielzeugmuseum) appeals to kids of all ages, as it houses over 1,200 antique toys from all over Europe. Monday-Friday, 2-5 pm, Saturday, 1-4 pm. Free. Fortunagasse 15 (at the corner of Rennweg). ☎ 1-211-9305.

Parks & Gardens

Belvoir Park is the city's largest park, and it offers spectacular floral displays and pleasant walks. Take Tram 7 to Billoweg or walk from Bellevueplatz along the west side of the lake.

Chinagarten is one of the most significant Chinese gardens outside China. Beautiful plush gardens are highlighted by Chinese pavilions of various shapes and sizes and white zigzag bridges, complemented by a wonderful tea house, where visitors can sample over 30 different types of teas. All the materials used to construct the buildings – including wood, stones and bricks – were imported from China. March-October daily, 11 am-7 pm. 4 Sfr. On the west bank of the lake, just past the Bellerive Museum. ☎ 1-435-2111.

The **Old Botanical Garden**, belonging to Zürich University, contains more than a million and a half plants. Take a pleasant walk either through the gardens or in the wooded area nearby. Monday-Friday, 9:30 am-6 pm. Free. Zollikerstrasse 107 (take Tram 2 or 4 to Hoschgasse). ☎ 1-634-8461.

Quayside Park runs alongside the promenade, ending at the rhododendron garden at Zürichhorn, home to a sculpture by Swiss artist Jean Tinguely. It's a great place for walking. In summer, you can swim in designated areas. A small marina, a restaurant and numerous kiosks are in the park. Take any of the trams passing through Bellevueplatz (Nos. 2, 4, 6, 8, 11 or 15).

The **Zürich Zoo** is superb, featuring more than 350 species from around the world, and including an aquarium and open-air aviary, along with special enclosures for red pandas, snow leopards, clouded leopards, tigers and Indian lions. March-October daily, 8 am-6 pm, November-February daily, 8 am-5 pm. Zürichbergstrasse 221 (on the Dolder Hill – take Tram 5 from Bellevueplatz or Tram 6 from the Hauptbahnhof). ☎ 1-254-2500. Admission is 16SF for adults, 8SF for children, 5SF for students, and children under five are admitted free.

■ Where to Stay

Hotel Baur au Lac – this family-owned hotel (since 1844) is discreet and exclusive, with a reputation as one of the world's leading luxury hotels. It is next to the Schanzengraben Canal – just three minutes from the Bahnhofstrasse – in a private lakeside park. The hotel is also home to **La Terrasse**, a French restaurant popular for its Sunday brunch. There are 107 rooms and 18 suites. Expensive ($$$$), but worth it. Everyone should stay here at least once! Talstrasse 1, CH-8022 Zürich. ☎ 1-220-5020, or toll free in the US at ☎ 1-800-223-6800, fax 01-220-5044.

HOTEL PRICE CHART	
$	30-75Sfr ($20-$49)
$$	76-205Sfr ($50-$109)
$$$	206-299Sfr ($110-$200)
$$$$	300Sfr+ ($200+)

Another unique hotel in Zürich is the **Storchen Zum Hotel**, the only one that is on the Limmat River. This beautiful building looks more like someone's private mansion than a hotel, and is great for romantics and writers, with 73 rooms. One of the oldest hotels in Europe – having been built in 1357 – it provides great views of the river. Also pricey ($$$-$$$), but also worth it, at least once. Weinplatz 2, CH-8001 Zürich. ☎ 01-227-2727, or toll-free in the US at ☎ 1-800-457-4000, fax 1-312-4468.

X-Tra Limmathaus Hotel Limmat is a good, average-priced hotel ($$) with all the basics – clean rooms, close to the train station, and only 25 minutes from the airport. It is well known to many famous artists and musicians, who like to hang out here. Though it doesn't offer parking, it is close to two public parking garages on the Limmatstrasse 118, CH-8005 Zürich. ☎ 1-448-1595, fax 1-448-1596.

If you like to party, than the **Zic Zac Rock Hotel** is for you. Just seven minutes from the main train station in the heart of Zürich's party district, this hotel offers 32 budget rooms ($) for the frugal traveler. Each room is dedicated to a rock star or group, and American cuisine is served in the hotel's **Rock Garden** restaurant. Marktgasse 7, CH-8001 Zürich, ☎ 1-261-2181, fax 1-261-2175.

The **Zürich Youth Hostel** is just 100 yards (90 m) west of the Wollishofer railway station and five miles (eight km) from the Zürich airport. The hostel has 292 beds, with rooms of all sizes and prices, starting at 32.50Sfr per person. $. Mutschellenstrasse 114, CH-8038 Zürich. ☎ 1-482-3544, fax 1-4820-1727; www.youthhostel.ch/zuerich.

■ Where to Eat

For a fancy try at traditional Swiss and international dishes, check out the **Kronenhalle** – one of the best restaurants in Switzerland. Over the years, it's been frequented by a who's who list of the rich and famous. Placido Domingo, Joan Miro, Igor Stravinsky, and Pablo Piccaso are just a few of the celebrities who have dined here. The Kronenhalle is a five-story building with two elegant dining areas, adorned with original art works by Chagall, Matisse, Picasso, Miro, and Klee. Reservations are required for lunch and dinner. ($$$$). Ramistrasse 4 at Bellevueplatz, Zürich, ☎ 1-251-6669.

Originally built as a mill 300 years ago, the **Blaue Ente** (The Blue Goose) was converted into a modern restaurant in 1985 and is one of the most popular in the city. Located on the eastern shore of Lake Zürich, this restaurant features duck in every form and is very popular with artists, musicians and theater buffs. Open daily for breakfast, lunch and dinner. ($$$). Seefeldstrasse 223, CH- Zurich. ☎ 1-388-6840.

DINING PRICE CHART	
Prices based on a typical entrée, per person, and do not include beverage.	
$	15-25Sfr ($10-$16)
$$	26-45Sfr ($17-$29)
$$$	46-70Sfr ($30-$47)
$$$$	71Sfr+ ($47+)

The Reithall (Riding Hall) is a must for any horse enthusiast. Originally a horse stable that housed military horses, it still contains hay racks and feed bins along its stone walls. Swiss and traditional fare at mid-range ($$-$$$) prices. Gessnerallee 8, Zürich. ☎ 1-212-0766.

Crazy Cow Leoneck is a fun place for lunch or dinner at medium prices ($$). The specialty is the "Crazy Picnic," with grilled pork sausage, cheese and Swiss cider served on a patch of grass. Leonhardstrasse 1. Zürich, ☎ 1-261-4055.

Raclette Stube is a cozy and charming little restaurant, perfect for sampling fondue and raclette. Open Tuesday through Sunday for lunch and dinner, reservations required. ($$). MasterCard only is accepted. Zahringerstrasse 16, Zürich. ☎ 1-251-4130.

Zeughauskeller is a popular hangout in a former arsenal built in 1487, which is known for its rowdy atmosphere and good food at average ($$) prices. Traditional dishes such as sauerkraut, Wiener schnitzel, and potato salad are served, along with a great variety of beers. The Swiss favorite – Hurlimann Beer – is dispensed from 1,000-liter barrels, and the owners (Kurt and Willy) are usually around to talk with guests. Reservations are recommended. Bahnhofstrasse 28a, at the corner of In Gassen, Zürich. ☎ 1-211-2690.

Café Schober is a nice little tearoom that offers a break from walking through the Old Town. It serves homemade Swiss chocolates and desserts, and a light lunch menu is also offered. Open Monday-Friday, 8 am to 6:30 pm, Saturday, 8 am-4:30 pm, and Sunday from 10 am-5:30 pm. ($-$$). Napfgasse 4, with the entrance on a dead-end street nearly hidden by greenery. ☎ 1-251-8060.

Movenpicks are a chain of restaurants suiting travelers on a budget or with children. The food is surprisingly good, the menus lengthy, and the prices good ($-$$). They have some of the best ice cream in Switzerland. You'll find them throughout the city. One central Zürich location is at Beethovenstrasse 32. ☎ 1-288-5464.

Winterthur

This is the second-largest city in Canton Zürich and the sixth largest in all of Switzerland, with 92,000 inhabitants. Located to the north and east of Zürich, Winterthur has a reputation as a city of culture, due to its fine art collections and various museums, of which there are 16 – including Oskar Reinhart's museum, a photography museum and others featuring artists from the 15th century to the present. There are also a variety of different musical groups and theaters. Winterthur received city status in 1264, though it dates back to Roman times. Eighty years ago various surrounding communities became a part of Winterthur, expanding its boundaries even farther. About one-third of the city is modernized; the rest is farmland or forests. The Zurcher Hochschul Winterthur (Zürich High School Winterthur) and the International School are both well-established institutions. A day-trip to Winterthur from Zürich (except on Mondays, when the 15 museums are closed) is an excellent way to see a wide array of artwork easily and quickly. A one-day museum pass costs 20Sfr.

THE LINDBERG CLINIC

All Swiss hospitals provide excellent and modern health care services. Winterthur is home to the Lindberg Clinic, an independent facility providing hospital, surgical and clinic options for patients. Should you become sick or injured while traveling in Switzerland, this would be one of the top hospitals you could choose. It is easily accessed from all routes and is only 15 minutes by train from the Zürich airport. Schickstrasse 11, CH-8400 Winterthur, ☎ 52-266-1111, fax 52-266-1166.

If you're up for some indoor fun in wintertime, then check out Winterthur's **Tempo Drom Block Sportanlage**, an indoor fun hall featuring a 1,082-foot (330-meter) kart track, a sand-filled volleyball field, roller skating, skateboarding, and climbing walls. Lagerplatz 17 in Winterthur. ☎ 52-204-0700. It's open Monday through Saturday from 2 pm to midnight and on Sundays from 10 to 10.

■ Getting Around

 As with many Swiss cities, the Old Town or *Altstadt* is the place to be, and is best explored on foot. There are many shops and street cafés where you can browse and linger, savoring freshly steaming baked goods, and the aroma of strong Swiss coffee.

■ Where to Stay

Hotel Loge is a five-minute walk from the rail station in Old Town and provides quiet and comfortable lodgings. It features a tall, beautiful doorway in an old five-story stone building. ($$). Breakfast included. To get there by bus, take Bus No.1, toward Oberwinterthur

HOTEL PRICE CHART	
$	30-75Sfr ($20-$49)
$$	76-205Sfr ($50-$109)
$$$	206-299Sfr ($110-$200)
$$$$	300Sfr+ ($200+)

and get off at Stadhaus. Oberer Graben 6, CH-8400 Winterthur. ☎ 52-268-1200, fax 52-268-1233, www.hotelloge.ch.

Zentrum Töss is a large Swiss-style hotel that has clean rooms at reasonable prices ($$). A 20-minute walk from the train station, or take bus No. 1, toward Töss, and get off at Zentrum Töss. Zucherstrasse 106, CH-8406 Winterthur. ☎ 52-202-5321, fax 52-202-8549.

Glattfelden

For those who enjoy checking out artwork by local artists and those from neighboring countries, the **Galerie Quattro Glattfelden** is worth a visit. Operated by owner Arlette Quattropani, the gallery has been in operation since 1985, and spotlights works by hopeful artists – both Swiss and foreigners. Glattfelden is a tiny Swiss village, only 15 minutes by train from Zürich and about 10 minutes from Winterthur. The gallery is in the village center across from the post office at Juchstrasse 9. Hours are Monday-Friday from 10-8, and on the weekends from 10-5. ☎ 1-867-05-62, galerie@quattropani.ch.

Glattfelden is also the home of Switzerland's largest film studios, **FilmStudios Glattfelden**, with over 34 sets for television production. Open Monday-Friday from 6:30 pm, Saturday from 2:30 and Sunday from 10:30 am. Spinnereistrasse 9, CH-8192 Glattfelden. ☎ 1-886-6675, fax 1-886-6661.

Canton Schaffhausen (SH)

■ At a Glance

Schaffhausen is the northernmost canton in Switzerland, encompassing just 115 square miles (299 square km), with 33,275 German-speaking citizens who are predominately Protestant. The south side of this canton backs up against Canton Zürich along the Rhine river, while the rest shares the outer border of Switzerland with Germany. Schaffhausen joined Switzerland in 1501, and retains a great deal of its medieval charm even today. Over the years Schaffhausen has become known as a center of high trade and industry, brought about by 19th-century hydroelectric expansion within the city. However, 45% of this canton is still used for agricultural purposes, despite the high level of industry here, which remains fairly concentrated. This canton also has one of the highest rates of foreigners living within its borders, as a large number of asylum seekers – primarily Sri Lankan immigrants – have migrated here.

Schaffhausen is also the only canton in Switzerland to have experienced bombing during the Second World War. On April 1, 1944 nearly 100 citizens of the town of Schaffhausen were accidentally killed by Allied bombers who mistook the area as a German target. Less than one year later, on February 22, 1945, 16 people in Schaffhausen and nine in Stein-am-Rein were also killed in a similar bombing expedition. Some historians have theorized that the bombings were not mistakes, and were in response to Schaffhausen munitions factories supplying arms to the nearby Nazis. This theory, however, has yet to be proven, and records are still sealed regarding these events.

The **coat of arms** for Schaffhausen is represented by a black ram dancing on two legs against a golden background. This crest is believed to have been developed as early as 1396, but wasn't declared official until 1512.

Schaffhausen

Schaffhausen is the capital of the canton of the same name, and is a busy modern town outside of its medieval city center. For years it has acted as a bridge between Switzerland and Germany, exporting and importing products. Goethe was a frequent visitor to Schaffhausen in the late 1700s, and he reportedly remarked that the inhabitants must be "very curious folk," due to the great number of peep-holes that can be found throughout the city. As a result, Schaffhausen was nicknamed Erkerstadt or the "City of Dormer Windows." The city is 32 miles north of Zurich and just 17 miles north of Winterthur.

■ Information Sources

Tourist Office

This is directly underneath the city's big clock tower, on Fronwagplatz 4, just one block east of the train station. Here, you'll find excellent walking maps of the Old City, along with other information. Open Monday-Friday, 9 am-5 pm, Saturday, 10 am-4 pm, Sunday from 10 am-1 pm – July through September. From October through June it is open Monday-Friday, 9 am-5 pm, Saturday, 10 am-noon. ☎ 52-625-5141, fax 52-625-5143, www.sh.ch.

Train Station

This is at the northwestern corner of the Altstadt. Here you can find a currency exchange (Monday-Saturday, 7 am-7 pm, Sunday, 9 am-7 pm). You can also rent bikes, store luggage or rent lockers here.

Post Office

The Schaffhausen post office is directly across from the train station, at Bahnhofstrasse 34. Open Monday-Friday, 7:30 am-6:30 pm, Saturday, 8 am-12:30 pm. CH-8200, Schaffhausen 1. ☎ 52-632-6222, fax 52-624-0295.

Codes

The **postal codes** for Schaffhausen are CH-8200 to 8202, and the **area code** is 52.

■ Getting Around

One of the most fascinating ways to experience Schaffhausen is by boat. You can take trips up or down the Rhine from May through September, leaving from Freier Platz, at the southeast edge of the Schaffhausen Altstadt. This is also a great area for extended hikes along the river or through the nearby hills. The Schaffhausen Tourist Office can provide you with free maps of hiking and biking trails, and boat excursion information.

■ Adventures

On Foot

 No visit to Schaffhausen would be complete without a hike to the **Rhinefalls**. As Europe's largest and most powerful waterfall, it falls from a height of 70 feet (21 m) and reaches its highest flow during the month of July. The scenery around the falls is spectacular, with green forests and mist that arises from the grassy river banks below. To get there, walk 1.8 miles (2.9 km) from Schaffhausen to **Neuhausen** city center, where signs will guide you to the falls, just a quick five-minute walk away. There are walking trails all around the falls, but in the summertime, this area is overrun with tourists and souvenir vendors, so late fall or early spring are great alternatives.

You can also take a boat ride (in June, July and August from 10 am-6 pm, and in May and September from 11 am-5 pm) to the rock in the middle of the stream near the falls. You can climb up the rock to gain an even more impressive view of the Rhinefalls. Contact **Verkehrsverein** at Industriestrasse 39, CH-8212 Neuhausen am Rheinfall. ☎ 52-672-7455. Be sure to take in the nearby **Schloss Laufen**, which sits on a cliff directly above the falls on the south side. There are also **paragliding** and **passenger flight tours** over the Rhinefalls available from local vendors. If you're into **river rafting**, then contact **Rhein Travel**, Schlauchbootfahrten, CH-8455 Rudlingen. ☎ 01-867-0638.

An Excursion to the Vineyards of Klettgau

Only a few minutes away by car lies the famous wine-growing region of Klettgau. Its green rolling hills make this area ideal for bike tours and hiking. What about a carriage ride through the heart-warming vineyards, followed by a wine-tasting party?

On Water

 For a lovely boat trip, board one of the many ferries in Schaffhausen for a trip to **Stein am Rhein**. Contact the Schweizerische Schifartsgesellschaft Untersee und Rhein from April through October. CH-8202 Schaffhausen. ☎ 52-625-4282. If you are a bit more of a daredevil, than catch up with **Rhyfall-Mändli**, a local operator of speedboat rides that take you right up to the Rhinefalls. These are very popular and reservations are highly recommended. Open June to August from 10 am-6 pm, and in May and September from 11 am-5 pm. Cost is 65Sfr. ☎ 52-672-4811.

On Wheels

There are also numerous bike paths in Schaffhausen that will bring you to the Rhinefalls and beyond to such villages as Rheinau (home to a Baroque monastery) or to Rüdlingen, where you can sample some of the locally grown wines.

■ Sightseeing

Walking through Schaffhausen's Altstadt – which is at the foot of the **Munot** battlements – you'll find historical architecture dating back to the Middle Ages. The Munot fortress itself dates from 1564 (it was built after writer Albrecht Dürer published a book in 1527 in Nürnberg describing such a place) and has a covered footbridge across a moat, a tower, a spiral ramp inside (one of only three in Europe) and a circular viewing platform. Admission is free to the Munot, which is open daily from May to September, 9 am-8 pm, and from October to April, 10 am-5 pm.

Fronwagplatz is the city center's long square, and here sit two distinguished medieval fountains – the **Metzgerbrunnen** and the **Mohrenbrunnen**. The former was built in 1524 and the statue that sits atop it is of a Swiss mercenary, while the latter was built 11 years later in 1535 and features a Moorish king. Also worth notice is the **Fronwagturm**, a lumbering tower that was once home to huge market scales. Now you'll find a clock and astronomical device built by Joachim Habrecht in 1564 with 10 different available readings. Nearby, at Fronwagplatz 3 is the **Herrenstube**, a Schaffhausen society house and a popular drinking establishment of local noblemen that was originally built in the 14th century and restored in 1984. Throughout this area you'll find medieval and Baroque facades on houses and buildings. Be sure to take a stroll down the **Vordergasse**, where you'll find Renaissance frescoes, dormer and bay windows, woodcarvings and local shops. Also, don't miss Schaffhausen's **Zum Ritter**, acclaimed as home to one of the best preserved Renaissance frescos north of the Alps, on the Vordergasse. This 1570 fresco depicts the virtues of Swiss knights (*Ritter* in German).

Churches

Münster zu Allerheiligen, or Cathedral of All Saints, is one of the highlights of the Altstadt, dating back to 1049 (the original building was later replaced with the current structure in 1103). The Romanesque church tower and the adjoining Gothic cloister (the largest in Switzerland) are open Tuesday-Sunday from 10 am-noon, 2-5 pm. Outside of the cathedral wall is the circular path around the **Junkernfriedhof** (nobleman's cemetery). In the courtyard is the 1486 **Schiller Bell**. Legend has it that this gigantic ringer inspired German poet Friedrich Schiller to write his *Song of the Clock*. However, Schiller never was in or even near Schaffhausen, leaving one to ponder why his name was connected to the bell in the first place.

Kirche St. Johann is a five-naved Gothic church at the east end of the Vodergasse. Built in the 11th century, the structure has been expanded six times. Open April to September, Monday-Saturday from 9 am-6 pm, and from October to March, 10 am-5 pm, Monday-Saturday.

Landmarks & Historic Sites

The Zum Ochsen House (at Vorstadt 17) features a striking Renaissance fresco along with a five-paneled dormer window. Formerly a Gothic inn, the building was remodeled in 1608. The panels pay tribute to the five senses and show a woman holding a cake, a flower, a glove, a mirror and a medieval stringed instrument. Walk north from the Zum Ochsen House, past the **Zum Grossen Kafig House** (at Vorstadt 43) to the **Schwabentor** – the northern gate of the city. This tower was built in 1370, and during renovations in 1933 a plaque was added that shows a boy holding a pig under his arm while trying to avoid traffic, and the inscription: "Lappi tue d'Augen uf," which means "Silly people keep your eyes open." This was in reference to the traffic that had become heavy during those years as Schaffhausen grew into a more industrialized city.

Museums

The **Museum zu Allerheiligen** is in the same complex as the **Münster zu Allerheiligen** and, while a great museum historically, is a bit hard to follow, offering little in the way of information. There is a lot of religious art, military history, and the like, but finding out who did what, why and where becomes the problem. This is worth a visit on a rainy day – though it is a frustrating experience overall unless you're very patient, like dark, damp places and can speak German. Open May to October, Tuesday-Friday from 10 am-noon, 2-5 pm, Saturday-Sunday from 10 am-5 pm and from November to April, Tuesday-Sunday from 10 am-noon, 2-5 pm. Admission is free, www.allerheilgen.ch.

Hallen für Neue Kunst (Contemporary Art Museum) presents works from 1960s artists to the present. Open May to October from 2-5 pm and on Sundays from 11 am-5 pm. Cost is 14Sfr. Baumgartenstrasse 23, CH-8200 Schaffhausen. ☎ 52-625-2515, www.modern-art.ch.

■ Where to Stay

Rheinhotel Fischerzunft is an ultra-modern hotel with unique charm and an excellent restaurant known throughout Europe. Located on the river, this one-time fishermen's guild house features 10 distinct rooms. Open year-round, the restaurant is closed Tuesdays. ($$$-$$$$). Rheinquai 8, CH-8200 Schaffhausen. ☎ 52-632-0505, fax 52-632-0513.

Park Villa is a historic mansion found at the edge of Schaffhausen's old town, featuring chandeliers, Persian rugs, and other stunning décor. ($$$-$$$$). Parkstrasse 18, CH-8200 Schaffhausen. ☎ 52-625-2737, fax 52-624-1253.

HOTEL PRICE CHART	
$	30-75Sfr ($20-$49)
$$	76-205Sfr ($50-$109)
$$$	206-299Sfr ($110-$200)
$$$$	300Sfr+ ($200+)

Kronenhof is ideal for the business traveler, as well as the tourist. ($$-$$$). Features a fine restaurant and bar. Kirchhofplatz 7, CH-8200 Schaffhausen. ☎ 52-625-6631, fax 52-624-4589.

Hotel Bahnhof is a clean, comfortable and striking inn near the train station for the ultimate in convenience. Contains a stylish restaurant and cozy bar. Breakfast included. ($$). Parking available. Bahnhofstrasse 46, CH-8200 Schaffhausen. ☎ 52-624-1924, fax 52-624-7479.

Hotel Promenade is a gorgeous building on the west side of the town, just outside of the Altstadt, and just north of the Rhine. Run by the Sonderegger family, this hotel offers all amenities, including a cozy restaurant featuring Swiss and international dishes with generous helpings. ($$). Fäsenstaubstrasse 43, CH-8200 Schaffhausen. ☎ 52-630-7777, fax 52-630-7778.

Gasthaus Löwen is an old comfortable inn with nicely renovated rooms located 1½ miles (2.4 km) north of Schafhausen center in Herblingen. ($$). Im Hösli 2, CH-8207 Herblingen. ☎ 52-643-2208.

Youth Hostel Belair is just half a mile west from the train station, and is open from March until the end of November. The hostel is a former manor house which dates back to the 16h century, and is quite impressive. You can rent bikes here too in this 87-bed facility. ($). Randenstrasse 65, CH-8200 Schaffhausen. ☎ 52-625-8800, fax 52-625-5954, www.youthhostel.ch/schaffhausen.

Hostel Schloss Laufen am Rheinfall, is an old castle sitting atop the Rhine Falls just 1½ miles (2.4 km) west of Schaffhausen center. It's open to anyone, but is used primarily by backpackers. It is easily reached by trail or train (the second stop from Schaffhausen). Reservations are recommended. Breakfast, lunch and dinner are available in the castle's Bannerstube at very reasonable prices ($-$$). Open mid-March to mid-November. ($). ☎ 52-659-6152, fax 52-659-6039.

Camping

 Camping Rheinwisen is on the south bank of the Rhine at Langwiesen, 1.2 miles (1.9 km) southeast of the center of Schaffhausen. Open May-September. ($). ☎ 52-659-3300.

■ Where to Eat

Gasthaus Adler features regional and seasonal specialties. The cozy, wood-paneled dining room has seating for 70 people, while the beautiful outdoor garden terrace has room for 120 guests. Excellent fare and a large wine list at reasonable prices ($$-$$$). Open Tuesday-Saturday from 8:30 am-11:30 pm, Sunday from 9 am-10 pm. Closed Monday. Vorstadt 69, CH-8200 Schaffhausen. ☎ 52-625-5515, 52-625-5819.

DINING PRICE CHART	
Prices based on a typical entrée, per person, and do not include beverage.	
$	15-25Sfr ($10-$16)
$$	26-45Sfr ($17-$29)
$$$	46-70Sfr ($30-$47)
$$$$	71Sfr+ ($47+)

Restaurant Gerberstube is a former 17th-century guildhall that is run by the Guidi family, and considered to be the finest Italian restaurant in the region. Reservations are required for lunch and dinner. ($$-$$$). Open Tuesday through Saturday from 11 am-3 pm, and from 6-10:30 pm. Bachstrasse 8, CH-8200 Schaffhausen. ☎ 52-625-2155.

Mexican Restaurant Tequila serves up hot and cold dishes in traditional Mexican style, and offers take out dishes, and a buffet in a fun and lively atmosphere. Run by the Keller family, it also features live music. Open Tuesday-Sunday from 5-11 pm, closed Monday. ($-$$). Fischerhauserstrasse 57, CH-8200 Schaffhausen. ☎/fax 52-625-7020.

Confiserie Reber is a great little shop where you can pick up all kinds of tastey goods – fresh-baked breads, cakes, tortes and the like. Lis and Laurent Perriraz are the owners of this shop, which has been a baking business since 1896. ($). Open daily 8 am- 6 pm. Vordergasse 21, CH-8202 Schaffhausen. ☎ 52-625-4171, fax 52-625-4195.

Stein am Rhein

This is a simple country town 12 miles (19 km) east and slightly south of Schaffhausen, sitting on the north bank of the Rhine river, at the western basin of the Untersee. This old village features half-timbered houses with ornate facades with detailed designs. The first bridge built over the Rhine by the Romans is here. You can catch buses into the German town of Singen from here, where you can pick up rail connections to most European cities.

■ Information Sources

Tourist Office

 The Stein am Rhein Tourist Office is at Oberstadtstrasse 10, and is open Monday-Friday, from 9-11 am, 2-5:30 pm. CH-8260 Stein am Rhein. ☎ 52-741-2835. For information regarding adventure tours within the area, contact Tourismus Stein am Rhein, Chlingeweg 1, CH-8260 Stein am Rhein. ☎/fax 52-741-2044, www.ostschweiz-i.ch.

Train Station/Post Office

 The train station is on the south bank of the Rhine at Bahnhofstrasse. It offers **bike rental** (Monday-Saturday, 6:30 am-7:30 pm, Sunday 7:15 am-7:30 pm) and a **currency exchange**. It is also home to the Stein am Rhein **post office** (open Monday-Friday, 7:30-11 am, 3-6 pm, Saturday 8-10:30 am).

Codes

The **area code** for Stein am Rhein is 52, and the **postal code** is CH-8260.

Internet Access

 This can be found at **Kiosk Charregass**, near the Tourist Office. You'll also get good, cheap pizzas and snacks here too. Open Tuesday-Sunday from 10 am-11 pm. 12Sfr per hour. Oberstadtstrasse 16.

■ Adventures

On Foot

 Consider taking one of the footpaths up to the **Castle of Hohenklingen**, which is a fairly steep path among vineyards and woods. Located two miles (3.2 km) north of the city. The tourist office can provide you with maps and directions. The view from the top provides you with a fine look at Stein am Rhein and the Alps beyond.

On Water

 Countless boats make their way to Stein am Rhein on a daily basis, and full-day and half-day excursions are available.

■ Landmarks & Historic Sights

The town hall (**Rathaus**) is hard to miss in the city center (**Rathausplatz**), a large square that is home to a number of half-timbered houses and buildings. The Rathaus was built in 1540 along the Hauptstrasse (Main Street). Two miles (3.2 km) north of the town sits the **Castle of Hohenklingen**, while the **St. George Kloster** is one of the best-preserved Benedictine churches around. Originally built in the 11th century, it is now the home of the **Kloster-Museum St. Georgen**, displaying fine art and local historical artifacts. The interior is filled with stunning murals by 16th-century artists. Admission is 3Sfr. Open March to October, Tuesday-Sunday from 10 am-noon, 1-5 pm. ☎ 52-741-2142.

■ Museums

Historische Sammlung (Historical Museum) can be found inside the Rathaus on the second floor and is available by appointment only for a viewing fee of 3Sfr. If you're into medieval armor and weapons, as well as stained glass and porcelain, you'll like this exhibit. ☎ 52-741-2142.

Wohn Museum Lindwurm is found in a 19th-century structure that was once a meeting place for local officials. This museum gives insight into how inhabitants of Stein am Rhein once lived through exhibits and artifacts. The farm exhibition often features live animals as well to complement their displays. This museum also presents an open-air play known as *No e Wili* (*Still Another Time*) every 10 years (the next presentation is in 2005). Open March to October, Wednesday-Monday from 10 am-5 pm. Admission is 5Sfr. ☎ 52-741-2512.

■ Where to Stay

Hotel Rheinfels sits directly on the banks of the Rhine river in a perfect medieval setting (it was built in 1448). Inside, you'll find suits of armor and tons of antiques, paintings and stately wallpaper and carpeting. Most of the bedrooms overlook the water, but be

HOTEL PRICE CHART	
$	30-75Sfr ($20-$49)
$$	76-205Sfr ($50-$109)
$$$	206-299Sfr ($110-$200)
$$$$	300Sfr+ ($200+)

sure to request this type of room when making your reservation. Run by Edi Schwegler-Wick, who cooks in this popular restaurant. ($$-$$$). Open mid-March to mid-December. Breakfast included. The restaurant is open daily except for Wednesdays. CH-8260 Stein am Rhein. ☎ 52-741-2144, fax 52-741-2522.

Hotel Chlosterhof is just east of the Rathausplatz on the Rhine and was once a show factory. The 69 rooms are of various shapes and sizes, and offer all modern amenities. Many of the rooms look upon the Rhine, and **Le Bâteau**, the in-house restaurant, serves up gourmet meals, while **Le Jardin** is a popular in-house café with the locals. ($$$-$$$$). Oehningerstrasee 201, CH-8260 Stein am Rhein. ☎ 52-742-4242, fax 52-741-1337.

Hotel Adler is known for its outstanding façade, with Rhenish legends depicted in traditional medieval style, while inside the 25 rooms are comfy and stylish. Built in 1461, but an addition was added in 1957 that doesn't have the character of the original building. ($$-$$$). Rathausplatz, CH-8260 Stein am Rhein. ☎ 52-742-6161, fax 52-741-4440.

The **Youth Hostel** offers 121 beds from March through mid-November. ($). Hemishoferstrasse 87, CH-8260 Stein am Rhein. ☎ 52-741-1255, fax 52-741-5140, www.youthhostel.ch/stein.

Camping

This is popular in and around Stein am Rhein. On the eastern side of the village you'll find **Grenzstein**, ☎ 52-741-5144, fax 52-741-4552; and **Hüttenberg**, ☎ 52-741-2337. Both are open year-round. **Wagenhausen**, open from April to October, is on the western side. ☎ 52-741-4271, fax 52-741-4157.

■ Where to Eat

Sonne is considered to be the best restaurant in town, next to the **Rheinfels Restaurant**. Featuring Swiss and French fare, the Sonne is housed in a 15th-century building that is a perfect blend with the fine cuisine you'll find prepared by owner/chef Philippe Combe. Wild game, locally caught fish and river crabs are the specialties, along with a generous wine list. Reservations re-

DINING PRICE CHART	
Prices based on a typical entrée, per person, and do not include beverage.	
$	15-25Sfr ($10-$16)
$$	26-45Sfr ($17-$29)
$$$	46-70Sfr ($30-$47)
$$$$	71Sfr+ ($47+)

quired. ($$-$$$$). Rathausplatz 127, CH-8260 Stein am Rhein. ☎ 52-741-2128.

Spaghetteria serves up inexpensive pasta dishes and is home to the world's longest piece of spaghetti. ($-$$). Open mid-March through October, Sunday-Thursday from 9 am-11 pm, Friday and Saturday from 9 am-midnight. Schifflände 8, CH-8260 Stein am Rhein. ☎ 52-741-2236.

Le Papillon is a perfect cozy stop for a late night drink, in the Hotel Chlosterhof. With views of the river and with a wood-panelled interior, this is a great spot for romantics. Open nightly from 6 pm to whenever. Oehningerstrasse 201. CH-8260 Stein am Rhein. ☎ 52-742-4242.

Canton Thurgau (TG)

■ At a Glance

 Thurgau is 391 square miles (1,013 square km) of mostly roll-ing countryside and flatlands that stretch along the shores of the seemingly never-ending Lake Constance. The canton sits in the northeastern corner of Switzerland on the south side of Lake Constance (The Bodensee) and is bordered on the west by Canton Zürich and on the south side by the canton of St. Gallen. Lake Constance is the second largest lake in Switzerland after Lake Geneva, stretching 162 miles (261 km) along the border of Switzerland, Germany and Austria. It is nine miles (14 km) across at its widest point, and in the summer is a popular spot for swimming, fishing, boating, sailing and windsurfing.

Thurgau first became part of the Swiss Confederation in 1803, and can trace its history back to the Roman times (Roman settlements have been found in the Thurgau region of Arbon). With a population of 209,362 German-speaking, mainly Protestant citizens, Thurgau is often referred to as "Mostindien" or "Cider India" by the locals, in reference to the great number of apple orchards that abound in the area. Locals often say that there are more apples than people in Thurgau – hence Cider India as a reference to India's high population. Here you can take long hikes through the flowering orchards of Upper Thurgau in the far eastern edges of the canton. You'll see many half-timbered houses with red beams and white panels set magnificently on huge stone bases.

There are eight regions within Thurgau: **Diessenhofen** sits at the far northwestern edge of the canton, while **Steckborn**, **Kruezlingen**, and **Arbon** lie against the shores of Lake Constance. **Frauenfeld** – home to the canton capital city of Frauenfeld – sits at the far west, while **Weinfelden** is smack in the middle and **Bischofszell** is at the far eastern edge, just below Arbon. **Münchwilen** is the southernmost section of the canton. Throughout the canton you'll find an overabundance of monasteries, fruit plantations, wineries, forests and meadows worth exploring on foot.

The **coat of arms** of Canton Thurgau is defined first by a diagonal line that runs from left to right, with the right background in white and the left background in a deep emerald green. Two prancing golden lions sit within each section of the shield, representing the counts of Kyburg.

Frauenfeld

T his is the capital of Canton Thurgau – a small village west of Kreuzlingen that sits on the banks of the Murg River. Frauenfeld is also home to most of Thurgau's cantonal museums.

■ Information Sources

Tourist Office

The Tourist Office of Canton Thurgau can help you with maps, hotels and excursions. Thurgau Tourismus, Gemeindehaus, CH-8580 Amriswil. ☎ 71-411-8181, fax 71-411-8182.

Post Office

Frauenfeld post office is open Monday-Friday, 7:30 am-6 pm, Saturday, 8-11:30 am. Rheinstrasse 1, CH-8500, Frauenfeld. ☎ 52-728-9540, fax 52-728-9545.

Codes

The **area code** is 52 and the **postal code** is CH-8500 for Frauenfeld.

■ Getting Around

You might want to opt for the **Thurgau Day Pass**. At just 27.50Sfr, this covers all types of travel within the canton (rail, bus, boat) for one day. Available at the Tourist Office.

■ Adventures

On Wheels

You might want to take a drive east on Highway 7 to the town of Lipperswil if you have children, where you'll find the amusement park known as **Conny Land**. There is a good children's zoo here and lots of attractions for the little ones. Open daily from 9 am-6 pm.

Sports

One of Switzerland's 11 racetracks is found in Frauenfeld, and includes a 1,500-meter turf course and a 1,500-meter steeplechase course. Both tracks are slightly less than one mile. The Swiss Derby is held here annually in June. The track is also home to a pleasant restaurant and bar area. Rennenverein Frauenfeld.

Bahnhofstrasse 61, CH-8500 Frauenfeld. ☎ 52-728-9225, fax 52-728-9226.

■ Landmarks & Historic Sites

 Thurgauische Kantonsbibliothek is the main library for the canton of Frauenfeld, and is just five minutes from the main train station. Promenadenstrasse 12, CH- 8501 Frauenfeld. ☎ 52-724-1888, fax 52-724-1899.

The **Plättli Zoo Frauenfeld** is in the southernmost part of the Frauenfeld, and is open daily year-round – in summer from 9 am-7 pm, and in the winter from 9 am-5 pm. Admission is 10Sfr for adults and 5Sfr for kids from ages four-15. The zoo features tigers, lions, leopards, camels, owls, monkeys and lamas, and includes a petting zoo for children, and a small kids play area that has bumper cars. There is also a decent restaurant on the grounds, offering seasonal specialties such as grilled dishes, salads, vegetarian fare, rösti, cheese fondue and wild pig. Open Monday-Friday, from 8:30 am-midnight, and on Saturday and Sunday from 9:30 am-11 pm. ($-$$). You'll find the zoo and restaurant at Hertenstrasse 41, CH-8500 Frauenfeld. ☎ 52-721-1648. The restaurant phone is ☎ 41-52-720-8191, fax 52-721-8845.

Just about a mile northwest of Frauenfeld in the little town of Warth, across the Thur River, is the **Ittingen Monastery**, which was founded in 1152. It was destroyed by a fire in 1524, but the church was rebuilt in 1549-53 and then refurbished during the 1700s. The renovation from that era has left behind a beautiful example of the Baroque style of architecture.

Wellenberg Castle is just east of Frauenfeld on Road 14 in the small village of Weinfelden, where you'll find a 13th-century castle, which is the seat of the cantonal parliament for six months out of the year (the other six months the cantonal parliament is held in the capital of Frauenfeld).

■ Museums

The **Thurgau Canton Museum** is housed in an 18th-century castle in the upper part of the city, while the **Cantonal Nature Museum** is in the old village center, near the library. Both museums are OK, but if your time is limited, go to the Wellenberg Castle instead.

■ Where to Stay

 The Feldbach Hotel is one of the finest hotels in the area, a few kilometers north of Frauenfeld in the seaside town of **Steckborn**. From Frauenfeld, travel east on Road 14 for about two miles (3.2 km), and then follow the signs north to Steckborn, a quick 15-minute trip. Here you'll see the Feldbach Hotel on the Untersee shoreline. It's a beautiful, restored 13th-century convent with an ornate Baroque tower that you see as you enter. The hotel offers free bike rentals for guests and it caters to disabled travelers as well. Worth the trip. CH-8266 Steckborn. ☎ 52-762-2121, fax 52-762-2191.

HOTEL PRICE CHART	
$	30-75Sfr ($20-$49)
$$	76-205Sfr ($50-$109)
$$$	206-299Sfr ($110-$200)
$$$$	300Sfr+ ($200+)

The **Youth Hostel Rüegerholz** has 38 beds and is open from January 1-16, from February 16-October 31, and from December 1-31. ($). Festhüttenstrasse 22, CH-8500 Frauenfeld. ☎/fax 52-721-3680, www.youthhostel.ch/frauenfeld.

■ Where to Eat

Roter Ochsen (The Red Ox) serves up excellent Swiss food in a clean, white-walled dining room. This is worth a visit. ($$). Open daily. Zurcherstrasse 224, CH-8500 Frauenfeld. ☎ 52-721-1257.

Kreuzlingen

This is a unique town in that it connects with a similar city (Constance) set neatly on the border of Switzerland and Germany. The town of Constance was, in fact, part of Switzerland until 1805. Kreuzlingen is best-known for its **St. Ulrich Kloster Church**, which is home to a Holy Cross that was brought to this area in the 10th century, and is housed in the Church Tower. The current structure was built in the 17th century and the Baroque interior was completed in the 18th century. After several fires throughout the ages, the building was renovated in 1967. This church chapel has ornate woodwork and figurines representing biblical characters and scenes from the 18th century.

■ Information Sources

Tourist Offices

The Tourist Office is in the TCS travel office at Hauptstrasse 39, CH-8280 Kreuzlingen. Hours are Monday-Friday, 8:30-noon, 1:45-6 pm, Saturday, 8:30 am-noon. ☎ 71-672-3840, fax 71-672-1736. For information regarding **Lake Constance** and the region, contact **Tourismusverband Ostschweiz** (The Tourist Association of Eastern Switzerland) at Postfach, CH-9001 St. Gallen. ☎ 71-227-3777.

Post Office

Located on Nationalstrasse 3, the Kreuzlingen post office is open from Monday to Friday, 7:30 am-6 pm, and on Saturday from 8 am-noon. ☎ 71-677-9911, fax 71-677-9915.

Codes

The **area code** for Kreuzlingen is 71 and the **postal code** is CH-8280.

■ Getting Around

This canton is a cyclist's paradise, with lovely bike paths throughout the region. There are also countless hiking paths. The Tourist Office can provide you with maps and routes for both types of exercise.

■ Adventures

On Water

There are countless swimming pools and free public beaches in Kreuzlingen, as well as the **Sailing School of Kreuzlingen**, ☎ 71-688-8020. You should also check out the beaches here, which are some of the few with sand in the country. Sunbathing is done on the grassy areas just west of the shoreline. Public beach information is at ☎ 71-688-1858.

■ Landmarks & Historic Sites

Just west of Kreuzlingen on Road 13 lies the town of **Tägerwilen**, which will be a point of interest for wine enthusiasts. This is the birthplace of Hermann Müller (1850-1927), who produced the Müller-Thurgau grape, which is a cross between Riesling and Sylvaner. In **Tägerwilen** you'll also find the churches of **Cosmas** and **Damian**, and looming boldly above the village is the **Schloss Castle**, built in 1661. Near the castle is the **Constance Palace of Bishops**, which was rebuilt in 1876 and 1894 after its destruction in 1499.

■ Museums

The **Puppenmuseum Jeannine**, or Doll Museum, is in the Tenant's house of **Schloss Girsberg** and contains 500+ rare dolls from throughout history. Attached to the Doll Museum is the **Graf-Zeppelin Erinnerungszimmer** (Count Zeppelin Memorial), which pays homage to the count who lived here from 1890 to 1900 while working on his air balloons/dirigibles at Girsberg. Open March 1-January 6 on Wednesday and Sunday, from 2-5 pm, or by appointment.

The Feuerwehrmuseum (Fire Brigade Museum) gives a curious introduction to the history of fire-fighting in the area, but you must make an appointment to visit it. Löwenstrasse 7, CH-8280 Kreuzlingen. ☎ 71-677-6370.

Rosenegg Heimatmuseum features furniture, weapons and important papers from Kreuzlingen's history. Open May to October on the first Sunday of the month, from 2-4 pm. Barenstrasse 6, CH-8280 Kreuzlingen.

The Lake Museum is on the north end of the town in **Seeburg Park** (a refuge for fallow deer and fowl). This museum tells the story of Lake Constance, complete with shipping models and fishing history. Open November-March on Sunday from 2-5 pm, and in April-October on Wednesday, Saturday and Sunday, 2-5 pm.

The Planetarium was built in June 2002. Open daily from 9 am-5 pm. Admission is 12 Sfr for adults, 10Sfr for youngsters. ☎ 71-677-3800, fax 71-677-3801.

■ Where to Stay

Hotel Krone is a 300-year-old inn that offers a quiet romantic spot in a beautiful tiny village just outside of the northern edges of Kreuzlingen. ($$-$$$). Seestrasse, CH-8274 Gottlieben. ☎ 71-666-8060, fax 71-666-8069.

HOTEL PRICE CHART	
$	30-75Sfr ($20-$49)
$$	76-205Sfr ($50-$109)
$$$	206-299Sfr ($110-$200)
$$$$	300Sfr+ ($200+)

Schlössli Bottighofen is a castle that was built in 1640. It sits on the shores of Lake Constance. Simple-looking on the outside, it is anything but that on the inside – being meticulously and tastefully decorated. Open year-round, with two in-house dining areas. ($$-$$$). CH-8598 Bottighofen. ☎ 71-688-1275, fax 71-688-1540.

Hotel Schiff is slightly farther north of Kreuzlingen on Road 13 and is a relatively new hotel that appears to be more Italian than Swiss. The stucco design contrasts nicely with the blue waters of the Untersee. This hotel is handicapped-accessible and has two dining rooms that serve up excellent locally caught fish and provide a good list of local wines. ($$-$$$). Closed February. CH-8268 Mannenbach am Untersee. ☎ 71-663-4141, fax 71-663-4150.

Zum Blauen Haus is a restaurant and piano bar in the historic Gebuden area of Kreuzlingen. ($-$$). Hauptstrasse 138, CH-8280 Kreuzlingen. ☎ 71-688-2498, fax 71-699-1406.

Bahnhof Post Hotel offers clean, comfortable rooms across from the train station. ($-$$). Nationalstrasse 2, CH-8280 Kreuzlingen. ☎ 71-672-7972, fax 71-672-4982.

The Plaza Hotel offers comfortable, modern facilities. ($-$$). Lowenstrasse 23, CH-8280 Kreuzlingen. ☎ 71-672-6868, fax 71-672-8233.

The **Youth Hostel Villa Hörnliberg** is in the park behind the train station and offers 96 beds. Open March 1-November 31. ($). Breakfast is usually included. Promenadenstrasse 7, CH-8280 Kreuzlingen. ☎ 71-688-2663, fax 71-688-4761, www.youthhostel.ch/kreuzlingen.

Camping

Fischerhause is the local campground, just one mile from the tourist office, near the lake, and with many activities and services for families. ($). Open April-October. ☎ 71-688-4903, fax 71-688-1776..

■ Where to Eat

Park Kafi is one of the best spots we could find here, serving pasta, vegetarian dishes and great salads at reasonable prices. ($-$$). Open daily until midnight year-round. Hauptstrasse 82, CH-8280 Kreuzlingen.

Romanshorn

This is about 12 miles (19 km) south of Kruezlingen on the shore of Lake Constance. Ferry services abound here to most ports on the lake, and especially popular is the service between Romanshorn and Friedrichshafen. Here you'll find sailing and waterskiing schools, swimming pools, tennis courts, a park and a small zoo.

■ Information Sources

Tourist Office

The Tourist Office at Romanshorn is within the train station and is open daily in the summer, and from Monday-Saturday in the winter. ☎ 71-463-3232, fax 71-461-1980.

Ferry Services

Contact the Schweizerische Bodensee Schiffahrtsgeseelschaft at ☎ 71-446-7888. The ferries run hourly from 8:30 am-7:30 pm, May to October.

Post Office

 The post office is open Monday-Friday from 7:30 am-6 pm, Saturday from 8 am-noon. Bahnhofstrasse 2, CH-8590 Romanshorn. ☎ 71-466-7666, fax 71-466-7660.

Codes

The **area code** here is 71 and the **postal code** is CH-8590.

■ Adventures

On Foot

 This area offers many walking paths for visitors, and the Tourist Office will provide you with maps of hikes for all levels of hikers.

On Water

 Information on Romanshorn's **public grass beach** can be found by phoning ☎ 71-463-1147. You'll also want to take a trip to **Mainau Island**, which is about four miles (6.4 km) north of Kreuzlingen on the lake. This island is a weird paradox, with palm trees and tropical plants, while the Alps loom boldly in the background. The island contains a botanical garden worth exploring. It is on the grounds of a residence where a Teutonic Knight once lived. Contact the Schweizerische Bodensee Schiffahrtsgeseelschaft at ☎ 71-446-7888 for departure times.

■ Where to Stay & Eat

Most of the good restaurants in this village are affiliated with the hotels.

HOTEL PRICE CHART	
$	30-75Sfr ($20-$49)
$$	76-205Sfr ($50-$109)
$$$	206-299Sfr ($110-$200)
$$$$	300Sfr+ ($200+)

Park Hotel Inseli is probably the best hotel in the area, sitting on the lake and surrounded by a grove of trees. The in-house restaurant offers French cuisine, and there is a café as well with a sun terrace for summertime dining. ($$$). Inelistrasse 6, CH-8590 Romanshorn. ☎ 71-463-5353.

Hotel Garni is near the train station and has clean, comfortable rooms. ($$). Bahnhofstrasse 56, CH-8590 Romanshorn. ☎ 71-461-1080, fax 71-461-1069.

Hotel Bodan is just across from the train station on the Bahnhofstrasse and features an inexpensive in-house restaurant that serves hearty meals at cheap prices. ($-$$). CH-8590 Romanshorn. ☎ 71-463-1502, fax 71-463-1501.

The Youth Hostel is only a short walk from the train station, at Gottfried-Keller Strasse 6 and is open from March-October. ($). There are 114 beds. CH-8590, Romanshorn. ☎ 71-463-1717, fax 71-461-1990.

Camping

Strandbad Amriswil is the closest camp grounds, in nearby Uttwil, just west of Romanshorn. ☎ 71-463-4773.

Arbon

Arbon is a quiet little village filled the distinct half-timbered houses that dot this region. It's worth a half-day of exploring – wandering through the old village and stopping for a local coffee or tea and biscuits. It was known as Arbor Felix during Roman times and is one of the best spots along the lake.

■ Information Sources

Tourist Office

The Arbon Tourist Office is with the local travel agency at Bahnhofstrasse 40, a few steps away from the train station. Open Monday-Friday from 8 am-noon, 2-5:30 pm, Saturday, 9 am-noon. ☎ 71-447-8515, fax 71-447-8510.

Post Office

The Arbon post office is open Monday-Friday from 7:30 am-noon, 1:30-6 pm, Saturday from 8 am-noon. Friedenstrasse 7, CH-9320, Arbon. ☎ 71-446-3471, fax 71-446-7945.

■ Adventures

On Foot

For a good hike, walk east to the old fishing hamlet of **Horn**, which is an ideal base for further walks. The village itself has no real outstanding sights, but you might want to spend a night at the **Hotel Bad Horn**, a large blue and white inn ($$$-$$$$) built in 1827 that is home to two outstanding restaurants – the **Captain's Grill** and the **Glottasteube**. ($$-$$$). Seestrasse 36. CH-9326 Horn. ☎ 71-841-5511, fax 71-841-6089.

On Water

For information on Arbon's "tough on the feet" rocky, stone beaches, call ☎ 71-446-1333.

■ Landmarks & Historic Sites

Schloss Arbon is a 14th-century castle that overlooks the town from a small hilltop. The inside contains a technical school and a small museum featuring Roman artifacts and former industries within the region. Open May-September, from 2-5 pm, otherwise open Sunday from 2-5 pm. Closed December 1-March 1. Admission is 2Sfr for adults, 1Sfr for kids. Hauptstrasse. CH-9320 Arbon. ☎ 71-446-6010.

■ Where to Stay

Hotel-Restaurant Park provides clean and comfortable lodgings. ($$). Parkstrasse 7, CH-9320, Arbon. ☎ 71-466-1119, fax 71-466-2226.

HOTEL PRICE CHART	
$	30-75Sfr ($20-$49)
$$	76-205Sfr ($50-$109)
$$$	206-299Sfr ($110-$200)
$$$$	300Sfr+ ($200+)

Hotel Metropole is across from the train station with clean rooms that all face the lake. Comfortable with modern anemities. ($$). Bahnhofstrasse 49, CH-9302 Arbon. ☎ 71-447-8282, fax 71-447-8280.

Hotel Rotes Kreuz was built in 1760 and is modest and clean. ($$). Hafenstrasse 3, CH-9320 Arbon. ☎ 71-446-1914, fax 71-446-2485.

Gasthof Frohsinn is a unique spot for beer and bowling fans. With an in-house brewery and an in-house bowling alley (Kegelbannen), this simple inn with modest rooms is open year-round, and is a good spot for those who like to try something really different. ($-$$). Romananshornstrasse 15, CH-9320 Arbon. ☎ 71-447-8484, fax 71-446-4142.

Hotel-Restaurant Krone offers simple clean rooms and simple good meals at reasonable rates. ($-$$). Bahnhofstrasse 20, CH-9320, Arbon. ☎ 71-446-1087.

Garni Sonnehof is the local pension, which can be found at Rebenstrasse 18, in a quiet neighborhood. Rooms are clean, simple and charming. ($-$$). CH-9320 Arbon. ☎/fax 71-466-1510.

Camping

This can be found at **Strandbadcamping Buchhorn**. ☎ 71-466-6545.

■ **Where to Eat**

Gasthof Frohsinn has two splendid dinning rooms that serve vegetarian and stir-fry dishes. Closed Sunday and Monday. ($-$$). Romananshornstrasse 15, CH-9320 Arbon. ☎ 71-447-8484, fax 71-446-4142.

DINING PRICE CHART	
Prices based on a typical entrée, per person, and do not include beverage.	
$	15-25Sfr ($10-$16)
$$	26-45Sfr ($17-$29)
$$$	46-70Sfr ($30-$47)
$$$$	71Sfr+ ($47+)

Restaurant Metropole is housed in the hotel of the same name, serving Swiss fare and locally caught fish in hearty portions. Dishes are neatly prepared. Located across from the train station. ($$). Bahnhofstrasse 49, CH-9302 Arbon. ☎ 71-447-8282, fax 71-447-8280.

Northeastern Switzerland

The cable car connects Wangs in the St. Gallen Rhine Valley and the ski area of Pizol, with the peaks of Gonzen and Alvier in the background

Canton St. Gallen (SG)

■ At a Glance

The canton of St. Gallen is comprised of 1,256 square miles (3,265 square km) with 48% of the land being used for agriculture. This eastern canton, which surrounds the two half-cantons of Appenzeller, contains 90 municipalities. Slightly over 20% of the 444,000 citizens are foreigners in St. Gallen, which is probably due to the fact that textile factories here employ a large number of workers, who are always in demand. St. Gallen is the sixth largest canton in Switzerland in terms of area and the fifth largest in population – mostly made up of German-speaking Roman Catholics.

The **coat of arms** is represented by a symbol for the union of the regions that formed this canton in 1803.

Stadt Sankt Gallen

This is the capital city of the canton and is home to just over 75,000 citizens. It is approximately nine miles (14.4 km) southwest of Lake Constance and contains one of the largest shopping areas in Eastern Switzerland – being home to many textile and embroidery factories. As the largest city in Eastern Switzerland, it is known historically as the "Finger of God" – referring to the Irish Monk Gallus, who in 612 wandered through a valley and fell onto a thorn-bush. Gallus took this as a sign that had placed his finger at the spot where he should erect the village of St. Gallen. Legend has it that he then befriended a wild bear who helped him to build a monastery. The city sits between the Appenzeller Alps and the Rosenberg foothills, exactly 53 miles (85 km) east of Zürich, and is a great town to explore on foot. The town center is a shopper's paradise, with countless boutiques, cafés, restaurants and shops. The old part of the city was first established in 1454 and contains a remarkable Abbey Library.

■ Information Sources

Tourist Office/Train Station

St. Gallen's Tourist Office is at Bahnhofplatz 1A, near the **train station.** If you're a hiker, be sure to ask for copies of the *St. Gallische Wanderweg* map of walking paths. Open Monday-Friday, from 9 am-noon, 1-6 pm, Saturday from 9 am-noon. CH-9001, St. Gallen. ☎ 71-227-3737, fax 71-227-3767.

Post Office

The St. Gallen post office is at Bahnhofplatz 5 and is open Monday, Tuesday, Wednesday, Friday from 7:30 am-6:30 pm, Thursay from 7:30 am-8 pm, and Saturday from 7:30-4 pm. ☎ 71-499-7304, fax 71-499-7320.

Codes

The **phone code** is 71, and the **postal code** is CH-9000.

Internet Access

This can be found at **The Media Lounge**. Open 9 am-9 pm Monday-Friday, and on Saturday from 10 am-5 pm. Cost is 1Sfr for five minutes. Located at the Katerinengasse 10, CH-9000 St. Gallen.

■ Getting Around

The best way to see the city of St. Gallen is on foot. The Altstadt has a wide array of oriel windows, fancy murals, wood-carved balconies and half-timbered houses. Walk down the Gallusplatz, Spisergasse, Kugelgasse and Schmiedgasse to view some of the fanciest buildings in the old village. A lively market takes places each week at the Marktplatz on Wednesday and Sunday.

The terrain here is mostly flat and allows walks through forests, meadows and over low hills. There is also a self-service funicular – the **Mühleggbahn** – that takes you to a lovely spot on a hillside, allowing great views of the area. Wooden stairs at the top lead you to a small park. It's at the far end of the Altstadt (Old Town) near the Abbey. Open daily from 6 am-11:30 pm. Cost is 1.7Sfr. ☎ 71-243-9595.

■ Adventures

On Foot

The St. Gallen Tourist Office offers both private and public walking tours of the city. Individual walking tours are arranged privately, while the public city walks have set schedules. From June 2-October 19, the public walks take place Monday, Wednesday, and Friday beginning at 2 pm and on Saturday at 11 am. These walks take you through the old city, to the Textile Museum, the Cathedral and the Stift Abbey Library. Cost per person is 15Sfr. During Christmastime, the Tourist Office features a Christmas walk for one hour, beginning at their office and ending up at the St. Katherine Cloister, where you'll be treated to a steaming glass of spicy Swiss cider.

For some great walking paths and fun for the kids, check out the **Peter & Paul Wildlife Park** in Rotmonten, a quick ride from St. Gallen. Here you'll find numerous trails that make for a relaxing walk while viewing various types of wildlife, including marmots, lynx, wild pigs, wild cats, Alpine ibex, and herds of red and fallow deer. The park is open year-round and has a good restaurant on the grounds. To get there, take Bus No. 5 from the St. Gallen train station to Rotmonten, then follow the signs on foot (about 15 minutes) to the park. Park, ☎ 71-244-5113; park restaurant, ☎ 71-245-5625.

On Water

 The **Drei Weieren** (Three Ponds) near St. Gallen are a great spot for relaxing, sunning, swimming and walking. The trio of small ponds includes the Mannerweier, a free swimming pond, the Chrüweier, a family pond, and the Fraurenbad, or ladies' pond. To get there take Bus. No. 2 from the St.Gallen train station to the Muhlegg funicular for St. Georgen. There are several restaurants and kiosks near the ponds as well.

Golf

 The **Säntis Park Golfplatz** is a family-friendly sports park that includes an 18-hole golf course (cost is 60-70Sfr per person), sauna, massage, playgrounds, bowling and miniature golf. Open daily from 9 am-11 pm. To get there from St. Gallen, walk or drive 2½ miles (four km) east on Highway 1, exit at Gosau. Golfpark Waldkirch, CH-9000 St. Gallen. ☎ 71-434-6767.

■ Landmarks & Historic Sites

 The **Benedictine Monastery of St. Gallen** is now home to the canton's government offices, the cathedral and Abbey Library, in the center of town. The **Cathedral Domkirche** is a double-towered church that was build in 1756 and is an excellent example of Swiss Baroque architecture. Open daily from 9 am-6 pm, Sunday 12:15-5:30 pm. Admission is free. Klosterhof. ☎ 71-227-3488, fax 71-227-3381.

The **Abbey Library** (Stiftsbibliotheck) was built in 1763 and contains over 130,000 books and papers from the eighth century to the present. The building has beautiful woodworking throughout and Rococo architecture, stucco art and painted ceilings. Open May-October, Monday-Saturday from 9 am-noon, 2-5 pm, Sunday from 10:30 am-noon. In June and August it is also open on Sunday from 2-4 pm. Adults, 7Sfr, students and seniors, 5Sfr, kids under 15 get in for free. Located in the Klosterhof (Abbey Yard). CH-9000 St. Gallen. ☎ 71-227-3416.

■ Museums

St. Gallen is famous for its textiles, so don't miss the **Textilemuseum** if you're into embroidery and lace. It contains examples form the 14th century to the present. Open Monday-Saturday from 10 am-noon, 2-5 pm. Vadianstrasse 2, CH-9000. ☎ 71-222-1744. If you stroll along the **Museumstrasse**, you'll find the **Kirchhoferhaus Museum**, which includes prehistoric relics and silver collections, as well as the **Museum of Art** and **Natural History**, where you'll find Impressionist art and precious stone collections. The **Neues Museum** spotlights prehistoric collections and domestic ware throughout the centuries. Actually, though, it is easy to get burned out on museums in St. Gallen – they are all good, but not spectacular unless you are really into a particular area of interest. I would recommend the Textilemuseum above the others, simply because it is the most unusual.

■ Parks & Gardens

 St. Gallen has a lovely **Botanical Garden** on the northeastern outskirts of the city, featuring over 7,000 species of plants from all around the world. It is open daily from 8 am-6 pm, while the greenhouse is open from 9:30 am-noon, and from 2-5 pm.

■ Shopping

 If you're into embroidery work, fine linens, handkerchiefs and the like, then you'll love this town. Many of the shops in town carry high-quality work. **Rocco Textil** features custom-made embroidery and linens exclusively from St. Gallen. Spisergasse 41. ☎ 71-222-2407. Since 1883 the **Sturzenegger Broderie** has delighted locals and visitors alike and is one of St. Gallen's better-known embroidery houses, with the factory just a block down the street. Marktgasse 21. ☎ 71-222-4576. **Saphir**, at Bleichestrasse 9, sells high-quality fabric by the yard or roll, as well as embroidered handkerchiefs, lace and table linens from St. Gallen. ☎ 71-223-6263. **Graphica Antiqua** sells paintings of Swiss landscapes from all regions of the country at all price ranges. Marktgasse 26, CH-9000 St. Gallen. ☎ 71-223-5016. **Hiking gear** can be found at **Transa**, on St. Leonhardstrasse 20. ☎ 71-222-3666. Or check out **Ochsner Sport** in the suburb of Winkeln, Im West Center. ☎ 71-310-0988. If you've got a sweet tooth, stop in at **Maestrani Schweizer Schokoladen** on St. Georgenstrasse 105, CH-9000 St. Gallen. ☎ 71-228-3824. They have some of the finest chocolate found anywhere.

■ Where to Stay

 Einstein Hotel was built in the 1850s and was previously an embroidery factory that was renovated into a hotel in 1983. The marble lobby is impressive and so are the prices here ($$$$+). Located in the historical district, it also includes a fine restaurant and piano bar with all modern amenities. Berneggstrasse 2, CH-9001 St. Gallen. ☎ 71-227-5555, fax 71-227-5577, www.einstein.ch.

HOTEL PRICE CHART	
$	30-75Sfr ($20-$49)
$$	76-205Sfr ($50-$109)
$$$	206-299Sfr ($110-$200)
$$$$	300Sfr+ ($200+)

Hotel Walhalla is in the shopping district across from the train station and is just a few minutes walk from the Old Town. Swiss and Mediterranean cuisine are served in the fine in-house restaurant. Breakfast is included. ($$$-$$$$). Bahnhofplatz, CH-9001 St. Gallen. ☎ 71-222-2922, fax 71-222-2966. In the US/Canada, the toll free number is ☎ 1-800-528-1234, www.hotelwalhalla.ch.

Hotel Ekkehard is in the center of town and offers clean and comfortable accommodations with a good in-house restaurant that serves Austrian dishes. Closed mid-July to early August. Breakfast included in rates. ($$$). Rorshacherstrasse 50, CH-9000 St. Gallen. ☎ 71-222-4714, fax 71-222-4774.

Hotel Dom is near the Cathedral and this simple inn is charming, quiet and very reasonable, in typical Swiss style – clean and comfy. ($$). Werbergasse 22, CH-9000 St. Gallen. ☎ 71-223-2044, fax 71-223-3821.

The St. Gallen Youth Hostel has 88 beds and many amenities, including nearby hiking trails, tennis and swimming opportunities. Open from early February to December 1. ($-$$). Jüchstrasse 25, CH-9000 St. Gallen. ☎ 71-245-4777, fax 71-245-4983, www.youthhostel.ch/st.gallen.

Jona-Rapperswil Busskirch is south of the city of St. Gallen and is a youth hostel with 74 beds near the bike trails. Open from late January to late October. ($). Hessenhofweg 10, CH-8645 Jona. ☎ 55-210-9927, fax 55-210-9928, www.youthhostel.ch/jona.

■ Where to Eat

 The **Weinstube Zum Bäumli** is one of the oldest restaurants around – having been in business in St. Gallen since the 1600s. The food is local and cheap, but the wine list is one of the best in this area of Switzerland. Closed Monday and Sunday. ($-$$). Schmiedgasse 18, CH-9001 St. Gallen. ☎ 71-222-1174.

Restaurant Neubad is in a 300-year-old building in the historic district that includes two restaurants – a bistro on the first floor and an expensive dining room on the second floor. Menus are seasonal, wild game is the specialty, and the salads are always spectacular – some of the best around. ($$-$$$). Reservations are recommended. Open Monday-Friday from 10 am-2 pm, 6-10:30 pm. Closed in July for two weeks. Bankgasse 6, CH-9001 St.Gallen. ☎ 71-222-8683.

DINING PRICE CHART	
Prices based on a typical entrée, per person, and do not include beverage.	
$	15-25Sfr ($10-$16)
$$	26-45Sfr ($17-$29)
$$$	46-70Sfr ($30-$47)
$$$$	71Sfr+ ($47+)

Restaurant Einstein is in the hotel of the same name and offers great views of the area on the fifth floor. Hearty portions in a sublime and relaxed atmosphere. ($$-$$$). Open daily from noon-2 pm, 6-10 pm. Berneggstrasse 2, CH-9000 St. Gallen. ☎ 71-227-5555.

Concerto is housed in the Tonhalle concert hall, with a glass terrace that serves a wide array of international dishes at varying prices. ($-$$$). Open daily. Museumstrasse 25. CH-9001 St. Gallen. ☎ 71-242-0777.

Am Gallusplatz serves up French and Swiss cuisine in a dining room that was built in 1606. With five- or seven-course "Surprise" menus that always include wine and champagne, the menu changes weekly. Reservations are recommended. ($$-$$$$). Open Tuesday-Friday and Sunday from 11:30 am-2:30 pm, 6 pm-midnight. Saturday from 6 pm-midnight. Closed from the end of July to mid-August. Gallusstrasse 24, CH-9000 St. Gallen. ☎ 71-223-3330.

Rorschach

This is St.Gallen's main port city, set along the southern shores of Lake Constance (Bodensee). With 10,800 citizens, this lakeside city sits at the foot of the Rorschacher Berg (3,154 feet/961 m), and is a popular site for piano and metal working industries. Since 947, when Rorschach was awarded the "marktrecht" (literally the market right or permission to become a trading and marketing center), it has grown into one of the most important trading centers on the southern side of the Bodensee. Here you'll find the impressive **Kornhaus**, built in 1746. The main harbor of Rorschach contains a local museum that features a collection of prehistoric items from the area, while the **Seepark** with its impressive fountains is a good spot for a romantic evening stroll. The main road of the town that runs parallel to Lake Constance is dotted with beautifully decorated houses, some dating back to the 18th century. High above the city sits the former **Mariaberg Monastery**, which has been an educational training facility since the Middle Ages.

Albula Route viaduct , Rhaetian Railway in Canton Graubünden (see pages 29, 156)

*St. Moritz seen from Suvretta over Lake Champfer,
with Piz de la Margna in background (see page 148)*

Ibexes on the Pilatus in Central Switzerland (*see pages 190, 259*)

Above: Postal bus in Soglio, with Sciora Mountains in the background (see pages 29, 1

Below: View of Lake Lucerne from Mount Rigi, with the Bürgenstock Peninsula and Pilatus Mountain behind (see page 190)

■ Information Sources

Tourist Office

The Rorschach Tourist Office is at Hauptstrasse 63, Postfach, CH-9401 Rorschach. ☎ 71-841-7034, fax 71-841-7036. Open from the end of March to the end of October, Monday from 2-5:30 pm, Tuesday-Friday, from 9:30 am-noon, 2-5:30 pm; November to mid-March from 2-5:30 pm daily; mid-June to the end of September on Saturdays from 9:30-noon.

Train Station

The nearby train station rents bikes for 26Sfr per day.

■ Adventures

On Foot

Hikes are numerous throughout the area. Here are a few easy ones, suitable for almost anybody. All are well-marked, and all are round-trip walks.

Hike One: From Rorschach grab one of the many boats along the docks to Rheineck. Here you'll follow the signs along the well-marked path to the Alten Rhein. This lovely, easy path will give you a relaxing walk through a beautiful setting for about an hour. The ship will return you to Rorschach, and these usually leave every hour on the hour.

Hike Two: Grab one of the many postal buses from Rorschach to Goldach and walk to Untereggen, Büel, Alteburg, Egg, Eschlen, Iltenried, Schloss Sulzberg, Goldach, and then return to Rorschach via postal bus.

Hike Three: For a bit longer excursion (2½ hours), take the rack-railway Zahnradbahn (RHB) from Rorschach to Wienacht and once here follow the trail from Unterbilchen, the Rossbüchel, Koblen, Hasenhus, St. Annaschloss and back to Rorschach.

> *The abbreviation RHB stands for the Rorschach-Heiden-Bergbahn (Rorschach-Heiden-Mountain train), a rack-railway mountain train that runs between the villages of Rorschach and Heiden in the canton of St. Gallen. For the Bergbahn Rheineck-Walzenhausen, designating mountain train service between the villages of Rheineck and Walzenhausen, the abbreviation is RhW.*

Hike Four: Known as the Drei Schlosser Hike (the Three Castles), this 2½-hour excursion has you leaving Rorschach via the main train station toward Strandbad. From here, follow the signs to Schloss Wiggen,

Linkonsberg, Schloss Wartensee, Vogelberg, Hof, St. Annschloss, Loch, and back to Rorschach.

Hike Five: For a lovely three-hour walk, take the rack-railway Zahnradbahn (RHB) to Heiden, then walk to Frauenrüti, through Grub, Rossbüchel, Fünfländerblick, Fonberg, Hüttenmoos, Chürzweb and back to Rorschach.

On Water

 Most of the sporting activities in Rorschach revolve around the water. The tiny public beach is very popular; call ☎ 71-841-1684 for times and information. If it's sailing your interested in, then check out the **Segelschule Rorschach Stadler Ag** at Hauptstrasse 93, CH-9401 Rorschach. ☎ 71-844-8989, fax 71-844-8988. The **Delfino Segelschule** at ☎ 71-845-4020, fax 71-845-4022, three miles (4.8 km) east in the city of **Staad** at Hauptstrasse 8, is also a sailing school.

At the Tourist Office you'll also find information (maps) on **in-line skating** and **roller blading** treks throughout the area. **Paragliding**, or "Gleitschirm" as it is known in German, features tandem flights from the local Flugschule (or flying school). Contact the Tourist Office for information or go to www.swipt.ch. You can rent pedal boats at various spots along the shoreline. These **"pedalos"** are available from May 1-August 11, 10 am-9 pm, and from August 12-April 30, 1:30-6 pm. The Tourist Office can also help you arrange combination trips with **bicycling** and ships, or go to www.tourenguide.ch.

Strandbad Rorschach has a sandy beach and funpark with a water slide and swimming pool, as well as miniature golf and beach volleyball. Open in May from 9 am-8 pm, June through August from 8 am-9 pm, and September from 9 am-8 am daily. Jugendherberge am See. CH-9400 Rorschach. ☎ 71-844-9710, fax 71-844-9716. Reservations for miniature golf (open daily from 10 am-closing) at ☎ 71-844-9716.

It is also fun to discover the Rorschach area via ship. At the **Schifffahrtsbetriebe**, you'll find three ships that offer different cruises and amenities. The **Rhyspitz** caters to large groups and features a pleasant ambiance, buffets and banquets. The **Rhynegg** is a double-decked boat with upper and lower viewing areas, and a good on-board kitchen. The **Alte Rhy** is a cozy smaller version of the aforementioned two. Schiffahrtsbetriebe Rorschach, Kornhause Postfach, CH-9401 Rorschach. ☎ 71-846-6060, fax 71-846-6061.

You can also take a nostalgic trip with either a **Rosa** (red) or a **Schwartz** (black) **Dampflokomotive** (steam locomotive). This mountain train (Bergbahn) comes in two colors and gives you a round-trip tour of the area, along with a postal bus and ship excursion. First you'll take the rack railway RHB to Heiden, then you'll travel 23 miles (37 km) by postal bus (or you can walk for 2½ hours via the Witzwanderweg) to Walzenhausen. From there, you'll pick up the RhW to Rheineck, and from here travel by ship back to the port of Rorschach. Postfach 247, CH-9410 Heiden. ☎ 71-891-1852, fax 71-891-1459, www.ar-bergbahnen.ch.

■ Landmarks & Historic Sites

The **Badhütte Rorschach** first opened in 1924, and is comprised of three ramshackle huts that sit over the water on the shores of Lake Constance. Designed by the Swiss architect Koepplin, they are open May 15-June 16 from 9 am-7 pm; June 17-August 15 from 8 am-8 pm; and August 16-September 20 from 8 am-7 pm.

The **Kornhaus Rorschach** was built in 1746. A former grain house, it is now a museum that is home to historical documents from the region. Open by appointment only. Contact the Tourist Office for reservations. ☎ 71-841-7034.

St. Annaschloss belonged to the Edeln of Rorschach – a worker for the St. Gallen Abbey – in the 12th and 13th centuries. It is now the private home of a Swiss painter – set at 1,864 feet (568 m) elevation. He creates landscape portraits of the surrounding area from here.

■ Museums

Alte Garage Museum is a must for any car or motorcycle enthusiast, as it features historic and classic vehicles. Open April, May, June, September and October on Wednesday and Saturday from 1:30-5:30 pm and Sunday from 10 am-5:30 pm. Open July and August daily from 10 am-6 pm. Cost is 7Sfr for adults and, for kids over seven, 4Sfr. ☎ 71-841-6611.

Flieger Museum Altenheim features historic airplanes in this flying and flight museum. Open Saturday from 1:30-5:30 pm. Cost is 8Sfr for adults, kids 4Sfr, and kids under seven free. ☎ 71-737-8104.

■ Where to Stay

Parkhotel Waldau is a former private boys school that has since been renovated into one of Rorschach's finest inns. This hotel has many amenities for sports enthusiasts, including tennis courts, two swimming pools, a fitness center, sauna, etc., as well as one of the

HOTEL PRICE CHART	
$	30-75Sfr ($20-$49)
$$	76-205Sfr ($50-$109)
$$$	206-299Sfr ($110-$200)
$$$$	300Sfr+ ($200+)

best restaurants in town. ($$-$$$). Seebleichestrasse 42, CH-9400 Rorschach. ☎ 71-855-0180, fax 71-855-1002.

Hotel Mozart is one of the best in the village, between the lake and the center of town. There are half a dozen rooms with views of the lake in this granite building, and its **Café Mozart** is well-known for its great variety of teas and pastries. ($-$$). Breakfast is included in the rates. Hafenzentrum, CH-9400 Rorschach. ☎ 71-841-0632, fax 71-841-9938.

Rorschach See has 60 beds and is near all of the biking trails. Open early January to late October. ($). Churnerstrasse 4, CH-9400 Rorschach. ☎ 71-844-9712, fax 71-844-9713, www.youthhostel.ch/rorschach.see

Rorschach Berg has 20 beds and is open from early January to the end of October. Near the mountain lift. ($). Im Ebnet, CH-9404 Rorschacherberg. ☎ 71-841-5411, www.youthhostel/rorschach.

■ Where to Eat

Ristorante-Pizzeria Mama Mia has some of the finest pizza in the area and includes a nice garden terrace. ($-$$$). Mariabergstrasse 7, CH-9400 Rorschach. ☎ 71-841-1278, fax71-841-1389.

Restaurant Rosengarten offers up what most people want in Rorschach – good fish – and that's the specialty here. The terrace overlooking the lake has seating for 50 people. ($-$$$). Thurgauerstrasse 22, CH-9400 Rorschach. ☎ 71-841-1582, fax 71-841-1590.

DINING PRICE CHART	
Prices based on a typical entrée, per person, and do not include beverage.	
$	15-25Sfr ($10-$16)
$$	26-45Sfr ($17-$29)
$$$	46-70Sfr ($30-$47)
$$$$	71Sfr+ ($47+)

Schloss Wartegg features creative cooking with vegetarian dishes. CH-9404 Rorschacherberg. ☎ 71-858-6262, fax 71-858-6260.

Bad Ragaz

The home of Johanna Spyri's **Heidi** is in this tiny village, also known as "Heidiland," in the far southeastern edge of Canton St. Gallen. You can get there via Highway 13 from the north, where it is only a few miles south of Met, or from the south, via Chur (in Canton Graubünden), which is only a 15-minute train ride away. One of the main attractions here is the extensive range of wellness activities, including hot baths, such as the **Tamina Therme** spa, hiking, skiing and wandering through the car-free Bahnhofplatz. At Tamina, you can purchase a two-hour pass allowing you to sample spas, pools, and lounges at your leisure. Open daily from 7:30 am-9 pm. ☎ 81-303-2741, fax 81-303-2733, www.resortragaz.ch.

Or you can take a cable car from Bad Ragaz to **Paradiel** at a cost of 33Sfr (for adults, 21Sf for kids), and from there you hike 90 minutes to **Heidi's house**. Here you learn about the Heidi story and have lunch on the Schwarzbüel Alp. Open March-November, 10 am-5 pm. ☎ 81-330-1912.

Or contact Ferienregion Heidiland, Postfach 90, CH-7320 Sargans. ☎ 81-720-0820, fax 81-720-0828, www.heidiland.com.

■ Information Sources

Tourist Office

The Bad Ragaz Tourist Office at Maienfelderstrasse 5 (☎ 81-302-1061, fax 81-302-6290) can help you plan a number of small excursions but, if you head up to the Tamina Spa, make sure to take plenty of money with you because this place isn't cheap! Great facilities overall, however, www.badragaz-tourismus.ch.

Trains

Bad Ragaz and the Pizol region are served by regular trains, as well as by a mountain railway, and a narrow-gauge train. Information on both is available at ☎ 81-720-4820.

■ Adventures

On Foot

Besides the spas and thermal baths, there are plenty of hikes – 37.2 miles (60 km) of trails – and 25 miles (40 km) of easy walking paths, suitable for handicapped and wheelchair-bound persons.

On Wheels

You'll find 86 miles (138 km) of mountain bike trails and 31 miles (50 km) of marked roller blading and skating paths.

On Snow

In the winter this area is a sports enthusiast's paradise, with 14 superior ski runs totaling 25 miles (40 km) on **Pizol**, winter hikes, sledding, tobogganing and cross-country skiing. A one-day adult pass costs only 45Sfr, and a kid's pass is just 30Sfr. For local information on snow sports, ☎ 81-302-1190. The Pizol area includes four gondolas, three chairlifts and six ski lifts. For Alpine ski and tobogganing information, ☎ 81-720-4825.

■ Where to Stay

 Termalbader & Grand Hotels Bad Ragaz is the only health and spa resort in Switzerland with an 18-hole golf course. Comes complete with thermal baths, which have been in use since 1242, saunas, massages, two luxury hotels and five restaurants. ($$$$-$$$$+).

HOTEL PRICE CHART	
$	30-75Sfr ($20-$49)
$$	76-205Sfr ($50-$109)
$$$	206-299Sfr ($110-$200)
$$$$	300Sfr+ ($200+)

Both hotels offer packages, but none are cheap. For example, a three-night stay with various amenities, including facial treatments, parafin hand baths, massages, etc., starts at 1,020Sfr or $680. A similar six-night package starts at 2,490Sfr or $1,660. This resort spares no expense, and includes an 8,200-square-foot (738 square m) fitness oasis. Be prepared to pay dearly, though you won't be disappointed by the treatment you receive here. It is all first-class. CH-7310, Bad Ragaz. ☎ 81-303-3030, fax 81-303-3033.

If you want to bunk down in Bad Ragaz for reasonable rates, then check out **Hotel Bergadler** at Bahnhoffstrass 29. ($-$$). A comfortable home-style setting with great breakfasts. Closed February. ☎ 81-302-1813, fax 81-302-4445.

Another unique place to rest your weary bones is at the **Mountain Lodge Gaffia**, in the Pizol Region. This unique hotel is made of large boulders and blends in well with the surroundings. It is ideal for families, large groups or the lone hiker and offers a great vantage point for those wishing to hike into the Weisstannen Valley, the Heidalp, the Calfeisen Valley or the Pizol. Comfortable and rustic accommodations at reasonable prices. ($$-$$$). Maienfelderstrasse 5, CH-7310 Bad Ragaz. ☎ 81-302-1061, www.gaffia.ch.

The Toggenburg Valley

This is seven miles (11 km) south of Mt. Santis on Highway 16, and is north of the Churfirsten range on the Thur River. This idyllic setting is seldom visited by foreigners and offers a quiet respite from the hustle and bustle of such resorts as St. Moritz or Davos. Here, you'll find three ski resorts – **Wildhaus, Unterwasser, Alt-St. Johann** – that have joined together to form a snow sport area popular with the local inhabitants. The area contains three mountains – **Gamserrugg** (at 6,809 feet/2,075 m), **Chäserrug** (at 7,419 feet/2,262 m), and **Wildhaus** (at 3,280 feet/1,000 m) – all of which can be reached by railways, cable cars and lifts. Wildhaus entertains 31 miles (50 km) of downhill ski runs, 27 miles (43 km) of cross-country ski runs and 17 miles (27 km) of ski-hiking trails. Similarly, Unterwasser has 31 miles (50 km) of downhill runs, 28 miles (45 km) of cross-country trails and 17 miles (27 km) of ski-hiking paths. A one-day ski pass for all three sites is just 45Sfr; a five-day pass is 178Sfr, and a seven-day pass is 222Sfr. Each resort offers a ski school. ☎ 71-999-9911 for information and lessons.

Walenstadt & the Churfirsten

Walenstadt is at the foot of the Churfirsten mountain range, where the Seez river meets the Walensee. The town is well known for its eighth-century church and town hall, which are worth a half-day visit. However, the real reason to visit this lakeside village is for the hikes and relaxing walks, and for the frequent ferries that cruise the lake, stopping at various villages along its edges. The Churfirsten Alpine range lies just north of the Walensee, and is a great area for a variety of hikes. Most of these are best attempted in the spring or summer, when the southern slopes of the Churfirsten are free of snow. The **Walenstadt Tourist Office** can provide you with maps of the area, and assist you with other travel needs. Bahhofstrasse 19. ☎/fax 81-735-2222.

■ An Adventure on Foot

 For an easy five-hour hike that offers great views of the slopes between the Walensee and the Churfirsten, grab one of the postal buses that run many times daily from the Walenstadt train station up to **Knoblisbühl Höhenklinik**. Once here, you'll follow the winding road uphill through a forest that eventually comes to an open area littered with small farmhouses. Continue on and you'll soon come to the **Bergrestaurant Schrina** at Hochrugg. Open only in July and August, this hotel/restaurant offers clean, plain rooms at very cheap rates ($). Call ahead if you plan on staying overnight. ☎ 81-735-1630. You can continue on past **Paxmal** westward, where there's a peace monument that was created by artist Karl Bickel; it took him 25 years to complete. Half a mile later, the path splits, and you'll want to go to the right, over the grassy hilltop of the Rutz. From here, the path veers more to the right again (back east), at times steeply. Continue eastward, eventually reaching the Schrina ridge. Here, you'll find the Obersäss stone house and barn, and there are spectacular views of the Walensee and the Churfirsten along the way. After over an hour, you'll come to the **Tschingla Restaurant**, past the **Palis** ridge at 5,382 feet. This restaurant is open from June to late September and offers similar rates to the **Bergrestaurant Schrina** ($). Continuing past the restaurant, the trail winds a bit, passing a few solo farmhouses and steadily declining until you reach **Brunnen** after another hour. The trail descends through small meadows, tiny vineyards, and lightly wooded areas. It is easy to follow, however, being marked with small yellow diamonds. This will lead you back to Walenstadt. You'll want to bring a small backpack, with water, soda, munchies or a lunch. This hike can be made in less time if you are a serious hiker, however.

Untertoggenburg

This is a region of St. Gallen between the easternmost town of **Wil** and the capital St. Gallen on Highway 1. Here you'll find Alemannic farmhouses and 18th-century manufacturers' buildings dating from when this area was a hub of the textile industry. The village of **Flawil** is just south of Highway 1 on the Glatt River and, with 9,000 inhabitants, is best-known for its weaving and spinning industries. A quick stop at the nearby village of **Burgau** is worth a visit, as this town dates back to the 17th century, with its houses reflectiing that era. Farther south you'll find the village of **Degersheim**, which is home to **Retonio's Magic Casino** – a unique spot with a store selling magicians' tools of the trade, including magic wands, top hats, card trick, etc., as well as automated pipe organs. The town of **Lichtensteig** can be found by traveling south on Highway 16 from Wil. With 2,200 citizens this village features half-timbered houses and the **Toggenburg Heimatmuseum**. This museum displays local art, crafts and musical instruments. While here, you can also check out **Fredy's Mechanical Music Museum**, in the **Haus Zur Frohburg**.

Rapperswil

This town is found on the north shore of Lake Zürich, on a tiny peninsula that is still part of Canton St. Gallen, even though it seems as though it should be part of Canton Zürich. The main attraction of this small village is the **Swiss National Circus** and family Knie – who have operated this circus for four generations. With its headquarters firmly established here since 1919, the Circus also has a museum that provides insight into the history of this famed circus. Rapperswil is also home to a three-towered Castle that looks as though it came right out of *The Wizard of Oz*. Built in the 13th century, this castle sits above Rapperswil and gives good views of the city, Lake Zürich, and the Glarus Alps. The castle is home to the **Polenmuseum**, which covers Polish history through displays and documents. You can reach it by a series of steps beginning in the town square. There is also a deer park attached to the Castle with over a dozen animals, commemorating a legend dealing with the founding of the village.

THE LEGEND OF THE DEER

The legend says that when the original count and countess of Rapperswil went hunting one day, they chased a doe into a cave on the side of a hill. Upon entering the cave, the countess discovered the doe protecting two young fawns. She took pity upon the animals and demanded that their lives be spared. Later, while the count and countess were resting in the shade, the doe came forward and laid her head in the countess' lap as thanks for having spared her family's lives. The count took this as a sign from heaven and brought the three animals back to the village. later building his castle upon the spot where the doe and her youngsters had been hiding.

Also of note in this village is the **Heimatmuseum**, a small local museum featuring Roman relics, art and weapons housed in a 15th-century structure. Rapperswil also has three public rose gardens near the Capuchin Monastery, containing 15,000 rose bushes. You'll also want to take a stroll on the **Wooden Bridge**, which has carried people across the lake for centuries. Now built of stone on the original site, it has become a dam. In April 2001, a new timber bridge that reaches between Rapperswil and Hurden was opened.

■ Information Sources

Tourist Office

The Rapperswil Tourist Office can answer a wide array of questions about hotel reservations, and offer tours, maps and boat tickets. They are open from April to October, 10 am-5 pm and from November to March, 1-5 pm. Fischmarktplatz 1, Postfach 1006, CH-8640 Rapperswil. ☎ 55-220-5757, fax 55-220-5750.

■ Zoo

The Kinderzoo provides a chance for adults and children to pet and feed rhinos, elephants, camels, zebras and many other animals. A playground, pony and camel rides and animal shows complete the experience. The Kinderzoo was founded in 1962 through the efforts of Fredy and Rolf Knie of the Swiss National Circus (Zirkus Knie). Open from the middle of March to October, daily from 9 am-6 pm, Sunday and holidays from 9 am-7 pm. Adults 10Sfr, children four-16, 4.5Sfr. Oberseestrasse, CH-8640 Rapperswil. ☎ 55-220-6760.

■ Museums

The Circus Museum of family Knie. Open April-October, 10 am-5 pm, November-March, 1-5 pm. Admission is 4Sfr for adults and 2Sfr for kids three-12. Fischmarktplatz 1, CH-8640 Rapperswil. ☎ 55-220-5757.

The **Polenmuseum** is inside Schloss Rapperswil at Postfach 1251, CH-8640 Rapperswil. Open April-October, 1-5 pm, November, December, March from 2-5 pm, January-February, by appointment. ☎ 55-210-1862, fax 55-210-0662.

Canton Appenzell Ausserrhoden (AR)

■ At a Glance

 This is the larger of the two half-cantons of Appenzeller Land. Located entirely within the canton of St. Gallen, this half-canton of **Appenzell Ausserrhoden** encompasses 94 square miles (243 square km), and is home to 53,200 German-speaking natives, who are predominately Protestant.

Forty percent of these Appenzeller inhabitants (from 20 municipalities) work in the manufacturing, construction and energy supply fields. Another 18% work in the tourist industry. Locals are often quoted as saying that the entire Appenzell canton, embedded as it is in the canton of St. Gallen, is like a "five-franc piece in a cow patty." Just over one-half of this area is used for agriculture.

Founded in 1513 as the 13th member of the Swiss Confederation, this canton is one of the most unusual in terms of shape, reaching from the Austrian border and the **Bodensee** to the North, while wrapping around sister half-canton Appenzell Innerrhoden to Mt. Santis at the far south. The Alpstein chain of three mountains contains one of the best-known areas for walking in Eastern Switzerland, and in this canton trekking and hiking up hillsides is a great pastime. Following along with the Appenzell sense of humor, a visitor will find trails and walking paths clearly marked with themes – ranging from the "health path," to the "joke path," to the "metro path," etc. It makes for added fun along the way.

The region between Lake Constance (the Bodensee) and the hills of Canton Appenzell Ausserrhoden are known as the **Vorderland**. Health and hiking are the two main features of interest in this area, which allows countless vantage spots from which to view the surrounding areas of southern Germany and eastern Austria. The Vorderland is seen as very traditional by many Appenzellers, with many *Kurhäuser* (spas) in the area.

In order to give each Appenzeller canton an equal share in the holding of their *Landsgemeinde* – a traditional, annual assembly of citizens for open-air elections which is held on the last Sunday in April – the two Appenzell cantons each hold the assembly in alternating years.

The standing, bipedal black bear – which appears on the canton's coat of arms – represents the Abbey of St. Gallen. The name Appenzell derives from the Latin "abbatis cella," or "abbey cell," because the region was once home to colonies of the St. Gallen Abbey.

Heiden

This is one of the main towns of Canton Appenzell Ausserrhoden and for many years was considered one of the premiere health centers in Switzerland. During the second half of the 19th century, a health resort focusing on fresh air and whey-therapy was centered here. During the late 1990s, there has been a revival of that tradition, and visitors will find numerous health spas and treatment centers here.

■ Information Sources

Tourist Office

The **Appenzellerland Tourismus AR** is at Bahnhofstrasse 2, Heiden CH-9410. ☎ 71-898-3300 or 71-898-3301, fax 71-898-3309. This is also the tourist office for the city of Heiden. This office provides maps and information, and will also be able to arrange a wellness/spa package in conjunction with the local Health Hotels – a definite must for any weary hiker or traveler.

Post Office

The Heiden post office is at Kirchplatz 5, and is open from 7:30 am to noon and 1:30 to 5 pm Monday through Friday, Saturdays from 8 am to noon. ☎ 71-891-1124, fax 71-891-1323.

Codes

The abbreviation for Canton Appenzell Ausserrhoden is AR. The **area code** is 71, and the **postal code** is CH-9410.

Health Care

You couldn't be in a better spot in Switzerland for the latest in health care services, alternative medicines, and natural therapies and health spas than in the Appenzell Assuerrhoden canton. Located here are the **Health Office for Appenzell Ausserrhoden** and the **Institute for Intergrative Medicine** in Heiden, a not-for-profit organization specializing in the promotion of integration between conventional and homeopathic medicines.

HOBGOBLINS

On December 13 and again on January 13 (deemed "Old New Year's Eve" by the locals), men, boys and sometimes young girls participate in a **"Hobgoblin Celebration."** These **"Chlause"** (hobgoblins) stroll about through the Appenzell countryside and villages, ornately costumed. This tradition can be traced back to a debate concerning the calendar in the 16th century, when Pope Gregory II wanted to move New Year's Eve by 13 days. The Protestants of Ausserrhodes, however, did not yield to the Pope's wishes. These hobgoblins are reported to be based on a demonic cult that merged with fertility and vegetation cults near Urnäsch, in the valley of Schwägalp. This wandering of the hobgoblins is strictly a male-dominated event, although there are female figures portrayed throughout the processions. Bell ringing and yodeling are trademarks of the hobgoblins, who jaunt about wishing everyone a Happy New Year.

"Ugly" hobgoblins wear scary masks and clothing made out of foliage, straw, hay and other vegetation. These are presumed to be the figures of the original cult. The "beautiful" hobgoblins came into being around the start of the 19th century and are contained in groups of six, with one front roller (Rolli), four bell hobgoblins, and a back "Rolli." Either the front or back roller wears a woman's costume and sports a large wheel-shaped bonnet on his head. Around his waist is a leather strap with 13 round bells, called "Rollen." The bell hobgoblins in the middle of this group wear bells on straps across both shoulders, and their headdresses depict Appenzell country life. The "wood and nature" hobgoblins (which came into existence just 200 years ago) wear costumes and masks made of natural materials that are transformed into intricate designs, often using nuts, seeds and tiny Alpine flowers.

■ Getting Around

As in its sister half-canton, the best way to see Appenzell Ausserrhoden is by foot, cable car or railway.

■ Adventures

On Foot

There are many hikes you can take throughout this region. The best place to start is at the Tourist Office in Heiden, where you can ask for a "Wandervorschläge," or walking map, which offers detailed path information. Options for hikes range from easy strolls through grassy meadows to strenuous overnight treks. Trails often wind up and down mountains and around hills. The upper regions often stay snow-covered for a good portion of the year. It is recommended that tourists hike in small groups, but definitely never alone, and for the tougher treks, it is often wise to hire an experienced guide who is familiar with the area. If you decide to go it alone, however, always inform someone of your destination and when you plan to return.

By Rail

 The **Rorschach-Heiden Bergbahn** was established in 1875, and allows a nostalgic trip from Heiden to the edge of the Bodensee in Rorschach, offering a panoramic view of this great lake at a very slow pace. The driver of this steam-operated contraption encourages passengers to pick flowers along the way. Established in 1872, the Bergbahn Rheineck-Walzenhausen is another way to grab a scenic view of this region. Fares are 9-15Sfr and the train departs from Heiden daily at 11:20 am and 2:30 pm. You can find information on both of these lines at Postfach 247, CH-9410 Heiden. ☎ 71-891-1852, fax 71-891-6921.

On Water

 You can find several indoor **swimming pools** that are open year-round in Appenzell Ausserrhoden. Call first for available pool hours and fees. Hallenbad Bucher in Speicher, at ☎ 71-344-1811, **Hallenbad Klinik** in Gais at ☎ 71-793-6633 or the at the **Sportzentrum** (Sportscenter) in Herisau at ☎ 71-351-5176.

There are also outside public pools in this canton. Again, it is wise to phone for pool times and fees, if any. In Heiden, ☎ 71-891-1223. In Rehetobel, ☎ 71-877-1167. At Sonnenberg in Herisau, ☎ 71-351-6143. In Teufen, ☎ 71-333-1403. In Gais, ☎ 71-793-1545. In Waldstatt, ☎ 71-351-4771, and in Walzenhausenn, ☎ 71-888-7018.

■ Other Activities

Bowling

You can find a rare bowling alley at **Hotel Heiden**, ☎ 71-891-9111.

Tennis

 There are several public tennis courts in the canton, and all require reservation. **Heiden** tennis courts(three outside courts, two indoor courts), ☎ 79-436-3340. **Herisau** tennis courts (three outside courts), ☎ 71-351-6740. **Speicher** tennis courts (four outside courts, two inside courts), ☎ 71-344-3153.

Saunas

Gasthaus Falken, Gais, ☎ 71-793-1296. **Heilbad Unterrechstein**, Heiden, ☎ 71-891-2191. **Hotel Heiden**, ☎ 71-891-9111. **Hotel Herisau**,

☎ 71-354-8383. **Hotel Walzenhausen**, ☎ 71-886-2121. **Kurhaus Sunnermatt**, Heiden, ☎ 71-891-8888. **Kurhotel Seeblick**, Wienacht, ☎ 71-891-3141.

Gym & Fitness Centers

 Body and Soul, Herisau, ☎ 71-352-2479. **Bodyfit**, Heiden, ☎ 71-891-1434. **Fit & Fun**, Trogen, ☎ 71-787-1828. **No Limit**, Herisau, ☎ 71-352-5277. **Sport und Fitness Center**, Heiden, ☎ 71-891-4014. **Sportzentrum**, Herisau, ☎ 71-351-5176.

Therapeutic & Health Spas

These are very popular in this region, and range from medium-priced resorts, to the very expensive. In all cases, phone and inquire about rates.

The **Heilbad Spa Unterrechstein**, offering warm waters with a high mineral content and various types of therapies, is one of the best you'll find on the planet. ☎ 71-891-2191. Bad Gonten, Gontenbad, ☎ 71-794-1124.

Hotel Heiden offers water temperatures of 91° F (33° C). ☎ 71-891-9111.

Hotel Walzenhausen has temperatures of 82° F (28° C). ☎ 71-886-2121.

Kurhotel Seeblick in Wienacht offers temperatures of 90° F (32° C). ☎ 71-891-3141.

■ Museums

Henry Dunant is memorialized in a museum of the same name. This founder of the Red Cross lived in Heiden from 1887 to 1910. The museum is open April through October, Tuesday through Saturday from 1:30-4:30 pm and on Sundays year 'round from 10 am to noon and from 1:30 to 4:30 pm. There is also a free guided tour on Sundays at 10:30 am. From November through March, the museum is open on Wednesdays and Saturdays from 1:30 to 4:30 pm, and a free guided tour is provided the first Sunday of each month during this time at 10:30 am. Asylstrasse 2, CH-9410 Heiden. ☎/fax71-891-4404.

Heiden's Historical Museum and Natural History Museum are both worth a quick look. The Historical Museum was established exactly 150 years after a terrible fire had destroyed much of the village, and gives a decent historical overview of this region. Many displays of weapons, clocks, embroidery works and household utensils can be found here, sure to delight any history buff. The Natural History Museum offers collections of butterflies, birds, rabbits and exotic animals, as well as seasonal displays.

Both museums are open April-October on Sundays from 10 am to noon and from 2-4 pm, Wednesdays from 2-4 pm and Fridays from 10 am to noon. From June through September these museums are also open on

Saturdays from 2-4 pm. From November through March, they are open on Sundays at 2-4 pm. Bahnhofstrasse 2, CH-9410 Heiden. ☎ 71-898-3301, fax 71-898-3309.

Ortsmuseum Wolfhalden is a unique little museum just slightly north of Heiden in Wolfhalden, and celebrates "the wolf waste dumps." You'll find this odd museum in the middle of the village, across from the church. This 1682-built double house recalls the conditions of the people who once inhabited it, and is dedicated to the weavers and farmers who once worked in the village. Open May through October from 10 am to noon daily for a fee of 2Sfr. ☎ 71-891-2142.

■ Where to Stay

Heilbad Unterrechstein is one of the top hotels and health spas in Canton Appenzell Asserrhoden, and one of the most expensive ($$$-$$$$). It offers every therapy known to man, including massages, hot baths, saunas, and vegetarian meals. Postfach 131, CH-9410 Heiden. ☎ 71-891-2191, fax 71-891-2181.

HOTEL PRICE CHART	
$	30-75Sfr ($20-$49)
$$	76-205Sfr ($50-$109)
$$$	206-299Sfr ($110-$200)
$$$$	300Sfr+ ($200+)

Hotel Heiden is another top-rated hotel/health spa that overlooks the Bodensee, providing all of the pleasures to rejuvenate the soul and spirit, including alternative and traditional medicinal practices. ($$$-$$$$). Seeallee 8, CH-9410, Heiden. ☎/fax 71-898-1515.

Hotel Kurhaus Sunnematt is a family-run hotel/health spa whose motto is "Begin the day with a smile." Offering short, individually styled stays with a healthy focus at mid-range prices. ($$-$$$). Bahnhofstrasse 19, CH-9410 Heiden. ☎ 71-898-8888, fax 71-898-8889.

Hotel Linde offers traditional bath-therapies, complemented by exceptional cuisine. Suitable for large groups and seminars of up to 120 people. ($$-$$$). Poststrasse 11, CH-9410 Heiden. ☎ 71-891-1414, fax 71-891-5365.

Apparthotel Krone is a combination of mini-apartments and a hotel. Offering all modern amenities, this expensive ($$$$) and renowned inn is one of the most beautiful buildings in Heiden. Dorfplatz 9, CH-9410 Heiden. ☎ 71-891-1127, fax 71-891-3505.

Hotel Hirschen offers friendly and bright rooms suitable for families and large groups with traditional Appenzeller charm. The restaurant here also has a fine reputation. ($-$$). Werdstrasse 26, CH-9410 Heiden. ☎ 71-891-1044, fax 71-891-2868.

Hotel Park is owned and operated by the Heimeliger family and has beautiful and modest accommodations with balconies and views of the lake. ($-$$). Find them at Seeallee 5, CH-9410 Heiden. ☎/fax 71-891-1121.

Hotel Walhalla offers beautiful rooms in a cozy atmosphere, with a nice garden restaurant, and good wine collection. Badstrasse 5, CH-9410 Heiden, ☎ 71-891-1206, fax 71-891-6428.

Apparthotel Santé is a reasonably-priced ($$) hotel with modern and simple furnishings, only a short distance from the train station. Quiet. Bahnhofstrasse 15, CH-9410, Heiden. ☎/fax 71/891-1277.

■ Where to Eat

Restaurant Badhof, Pizzeria has a stunning ambiance and excellent fare at reasonable prices. A great place for romantics. ($-$$$). Open daily from 11 am to 2 pm, and 5-11 pm. Closed Wednesdays. Im Bad 6, CH-9410 Heiden. ☎ 71-891-2730.

DINING PRICE CHART	
Prices based on a typical entrée, per person, and do not include beverage.	
$	15-25Sfr ($10-$16)
$$	26-45Sfr ($17-$29)
$$$	46-70Sfr ($30-$47)
$$$$	71Sfr+ ($47+)

Restaurant Häädlerstube is a great place for groups, serving regional fare at inexpensive prices. Open daily, year-round from 9 am to 10 pm. Inside the Hotel Kurhaus Sunnematt at Bahnhofstrasse 19, CH-9410 Heiden. ($$). ☎ 71-898-8877.

Restaurant Löwen Apéro Bar features charming, upbeat and modern surroundings for a good meal and drinks. Open Monday through Thursday from 3 pm to midnight, Friday and Saturday from 3 pm to 2 am. Closed Sundays. ($$-$$$). Poststrasse 12, CH-9410 Heiden. ☎ 71-891-1439.

Restaurant Park Pizzeria is beautifully-decorated with a great ambience that is exceeded only by the fine food. Italian and vegetarian specialties, plus great pizza. ($$-$$$). Seeallee 5, CH-9410 Heiden. ☎ 71-891-1121.

Herisau

This is the capital of Appenzell Ausserrhoden and the largest city of this canton, with nearly 16,000 people residing here. Named "Alpine City of the Year for 2003," Herisau is a great example of where agriculture and industry meet in a jointly prosperous union. The city has a well-developed infrastructure complete with culture, good schools and industries, teamed with a high respect for the surrounding Appenzeller hinterland.

Hotel Bäen/Speiserestaurant-Bistro is a charming and beautiful hotel and restaurant all rolled into one package. Operated by the Knechtle family, with a homey atmosphere and real Swiss charm. Find them at Alpsteinstrasse 1, CH-9100 Herisau. ☎ 71-351-1716.

Hotel Herisau is clean, comfortable and affordable ($$). Near the train station at Bahnhofstrasse 14, CH-9102 Herisau. ☎ 71-354-8383, fax 71-354-8380, www.hotelherisau.ch.

Stein

Stein is a small town just north of Waldstatt, and offers two nice side-tours, including the **Schaukäserei** (Cheese Dairy). You can call ahead to reserve a guided tour of the dairy (for 45Sfr), where you'll be taken by an expert hostess through the cheese production process. You can view the cheese-makers at work daily from 9 am to 2 pm, and the dairy itself is open from 9 am to 7 pm, May through October, and 9 am to 6 pm from November through April. Find this unique treat at Dorf 711, CH-9063, Stein. ☎ 71-368-5070, fax 71-368-5075, www.showcheese.ch.

The Appenzeller Folklore Museum in Stein features one of the most important collections of paintings in Switzerland. If you're into handy works of any kind, than this spot is a must-see. There are 19th-century embroidery machines and weaving looms, as well as folk art, farmer's crafts and other exhibitions, which change frequently. Open Monday-Saturday from 10 am-noon, and from 1:30 to 5 pm, and on Sundays and holidays from 10 am to 5 pm. Dorf, CH-9063, Stein. ☎ 71-368-5056, fax 71-368-5055.

Urnäsch

The town of Urnäsch, at the western edge of this canton, is known for its festivities, and holds various galas throughout the year. **Appenzell String Music Day** is usually in late April (26th in 2003) in Urnäsch. This is a great treat for music lovers, and provides a taste of Appenzeller music, with 15 local restaurants featuring traditional live music, food, and traditional Appenzeller clothing.

Appenzeller Brauchtumsmuseum is the "Museum of Appenzell Customs," and includes exhibitions on dairy-farming wagons, farming crafts such as saddle and harness makers, local customs, embroidery works and the like. Open daily from April 1 to November 1, 1:30 to 5 pm, and in the winter, by request. Am Dorfplatz, CH-9107 Urnäsch. ☎ 71-364-2322 or at 71-364-1487 in the wintertime.

Teufen

This is a small village between Appenzell and St. Gallen, well known as the home to the **Grubenmann Collection**, a profile of architectural works by the famous Grubenmann family, builders who lived in Teufen and who worked as carpentry architects and engineers during the 18th century. Plans, models and drawings of wooden bridges, church tops, and other architectural delights are featured. Open every Saturday from 2 to 4 pm and on the first Sunday of every month from 10 am to noon. Dorf 7, CH-9053, Teufen. ☎/fax 71-333-2066.

*The village of Wald in the Appenzell region,
with Mount Saentis in the background*

Canton Appenzell Innerrhoden (AI)

■ At a Glance

The smaller half of the Appenzell canton, **Appenzell Innerrhoden** (Inner Rhodes) is home to just 15,000 German-speaking citizens, most of whom are Roman Catholic. Appenzell Innerrhoden is 66 square miles (172 square km), of which 58% is agricultural, and, like **Appenzell Ausserrhoden**, was founded in 1513. The people are known for their distinct sense of humor, called a "gifteln." It is the smallest Swiss canton within the Federation, and has only six municipalities. Over one-third of the population works in tourism, while another third works in the construction and energy industries.

Life was recorded in this area as early as the Ice Age, or 30,000 BC. The **Wildkirchli Caves** of the area show signs of life from this era, which was then settled by the abbots of St. Gallen in the valley basin where this city originated. These abbots formed the economic and religious center; together with the Mauritius Church, they helped to found the city in 1071. Appenzell joined Switzerland in 1513 as the 13th canton, before splitting into two half-cantons in 1597. Geographically, this three-chained mountain area is probably the best-known in Eastern Switzerland, and offers a wide array of walking and hiking paths and adventures.

Both half-cantons are also known for their dedication to folklore, though this smaller canton tends to preserve its traditions a bit more than her larger, sister canton. While many of the Swiss consider the residents to be the "hillbillies" of their country, this unique spirit and holding on to old traditions is what draws visitors to explore this area. In fact, it is not unusual to see the locals dressed in traditional Swiss apparel, which for the men means rakish earrings and no shoes (in the summertime). The women wear dresses adorned with intricate lace and embroidery works. The Appenzeller cantons are also famous for their cheeses, their exquisite embroidery, and the artwork on their buildings.

The annual assembly of citizens for open-air elections – the **"Landsgemeinde"** – is held in alternating years in the Appenzell cantons. The people of the two cantons vote on political issues and elect representatives for their cantonal government. The voting starts at noon and lasts for about two hours, with many different festivals being held in conjunction with the Landsgemeinde, both before and after the actual voting takes place. In 2003, the Landsgemeinde was held on April 27 in Appenzell; in 2004, it will be held in Appenzell Ausserrhoden.

The strutting, bipedal black bear – which appears on the canton's **coat of arms** – represents the Abbey of St. Gallen. The name Appenzell is reflective of the Latin "abbatis cella," or "abbey cell," because the region was once home to colonies of the St. Gallen Abbey.

Appenzell

This is the main town of Appenzell Innerrhoden, just 12 miles (20 km) south of St. Gallen and 785 feet (239 m) above sea level. This picturesque village has everything you'd expect from a Swiss town rich in tradition: cobblestone streets, rustic painted motifs on the buildings, local vendors, and an overwhelming sense of history. The main street, Hauptgasse, is car-free and thus allows ample strolling and is a great spot to people-watch. The local bus ride from St. Gallen to Appenzell is particularly fun, because it gives you a relaxing tour of tiny villages along the route. For schedules, call ☎ 71-227-3737. If you're driving, go toward St. Gallen, then drive south to Teufen, then south again to Appenzell. There are signs everywhere, so it is easy to find this quaint town. There is a train that leaves Zürich for Appenzell, but it is slow and takes nearly two hours to reach the town.

Up until the 1920s, hand embroidery was the major industry in this region. Very little industry settled here due to the fact that there were few railroads or major roadways. Craftsmen thus abound in this area – carpenters, painters, harness makers and goldsmiths can be found here. The town of Appenzell was burned to the ground on March 18, 1560, with only the parish church and Gothic choir and its crypt surviving. People often say that Appenzell is where "life is still true."

■ Information Sources

Tourist Office

The Appenzell Tourist Office is at Hauptgasse 4, and is open Monday-Friday from 9 am to noon, and from 2 pm to 6 pm. On Saturdays and Sundays the office is open from 10 am to noon and from 2 pm to 5 pm. ☎ 71-788-9641, fax 71-788-9650, www.ai@appenzell.ch. For cantonal information, go to Marktgasse 2, 9050 Appenzell. ☎ 71-788-9311, fax 71-788-9339.

Post Office

Poststrasse 9. Open Monday-Friday, 7:30 am-noon, and from 1:30-6 pm Saturday from 8 am-noon. ☎ 71-787-1360, fax 71-787-3963, www.post.ch.

Codes

The abbreviation for Canton Appenzell Innerrhoden is AR. The **area code** is 71, and the **postal code** is CH-9050.

Train Station

 This is right across from the post office and offers bike rentals and money changing.

■ Getting Around

 The best way to see this half-canton is on foot, by cable car or railway. The Appenzell Railway will take you on a leisurely ride from Gossau or St. Gallen through much of Appenzeller land in a very relaxed fashion. For train information, ☎ 71-354-5060; www.appenzellerbahnen.ch. **Walking or hiking** throughout the countryside and through the cobblestone streets of many of the little towns and villages that dot the landscape are also great ways to experience Appenzellerland. Still another unique way to visit this area is to take the postal bus from St. Gallen to Appenzell. Some of these bright yellow buses are doubled-decked, seating 90 people, and offer a different kind of trip throughout every nook and cranny of this canton. ☎ 71-228-4444 for information; www.post.ch.

■ Adventures

On Foot

 One of the most spectacular walks is to visit **Mount Säntis** via Wasserrauen and Schwägalp. Trains leave hourly from Appenzell to Wasserrauen. The walk from Wasserrauen to Schwägalp can take you up to six hours or slightly less, so wear comfortable shoes or hiking boots. This is a great walk and is also a good excuse for a picnic.

"Barfuss durchs Appenzellerland" is an easy, two-hour walking trip through grassy meadows from Appenzell to Gonten. You can get a map for this stroll from the Appenzell Tourist Office or take the 10-minute train ride from Appenzell to Gonten for a one-way walking trip back to Appenzell. If you do the round-trip walk, you can stop at the Gonton Hotel, which provides services for resting and washing your feet (for 2Sfr only), and you can also take in a light lunch at the hotel's restaurant ($-$$) before heading back.

The Kapellenweg Hike is a five-hour trip of medium difficulty. From the Appenzell train station you'll cross underneath the tracks and then veer to your left, before taking a right at the next major intersection. Here begins the trail, and you'll see brown "Kapellenweg" signs indicating that.

From Wasserrauen, just south of Appenzell, take the cable car up to **Ebernalp**. Here you can walk the crest of the ridge to the Säntis. You can also venture from Wasserrauen into the narrow valley of **Seealpsee**, the location for the annual yodeling of Mass of August 15. Here you can rest your feet at the Bergggasthaus Forelle, on the shores of the Seealpsee ($). ☎ 71-799-1188, fax 71-799-1596 (open April-October).

From behind Seealpsee you can take a more demanding two-hour hike up to **Meglisalp**, which also sports a Berggasthaus ($) that is open from May-October. ☎ 71-799-1128. This tiny village features a lively folklore festival in late July.

On Snow

Bobsledding is offered at **Luftseilbahn in Jakobsbad-Kronberg.** It is open daily from 8:30 am to 5 pm and lifts take you to the top every 30 minutes. The Kronberg is a family-oriented mountain in the high valley of Gonten. The resort also offers summer bobsledding for the whole family on a 1,000-meter-long course, which traverses the mountainside. The Berggasthaus offers an outdoor eating plateau, overlooking the area, while the hotel offers clean, modest accomodations at reasonable prices ($-$$).

Tennis, Squash & Billiards

Tennis is a popular sport in Appenzell and the surrounding areas. For information in Appenzell, call ☎ 71-787-3922. If you prefer **billiards**, ☎ 71-787-3922 in Appenzell. If you're looking for a place to work out, then check out **Appenzell's Fitness-Center,** ☎ 71-787-1828.

Sauna

If you want to heat up tired muscles after a long hiking trek, there are an abundance of saunas in Appenzell. The following locations offer sauna facilities: **Hallenschwimmbad Appenzell** at ☎ 71-787-3535, the **Hotel Kaubad** at ☎ 71-787-4844, the **Hotel Lowen** sauna at ☎ 71-788-8787, or the **Romantikhotel Santis**, at ☎ 71-788-1111.

Swimming

If it's swimming you prefer, then take a dip in one of these two indoor pools: the **Hallenbad Appenzell** at ☎ 71-787-3535 or the **Hotel Kaubad** at ☎ 71-787-4844. If you prefer an outdoor pool, then call ☎ 71-787-1474 for Appenzell's open-air pool.

■ Sightseeing

There is much to see in this tiny area, with the nearby towns of **Jakobsbad**, **Weissbad** and **Brülisau** only minutes away. However, the sights are more in the way of natural beauty and geographic features, as opposed to rousing nightlife. This is definitely more of a place for nature lovers.

No visit to Appenzell Innerrhoden would be complete without a trip to **Mount Säntis**, the highest peak in the Alpstein massif, at 8,209 feet (2,463 m). On a clear day Säntis offers you a superb panoramic view of the mountains of eastern Switzerland, including the Grisons, the Bernese Alps, Lake Constance and Lake Zürich. To get there, drive nine miles (14 km) west from Appenzell, following the signs for Schwägalp via Urnäsch, and take the Santis Schwebebahn to the peak. The cable car costs 33Sfr round-trip and departs at 30 minute intervals for a 10-minute ride, on a year-round basis. For information, ☎ 71-365-6565; www.saentisbahn.ch.

Once here, you can hike over to **Ebenalp**, which has hourly connections back to Appenzell. Be sure to wear proper hiking shoes or boots for this trip, which takes three to four hours. However, if you like to ski or want to spend more than a day here, you can stay at the **Scwägalp-Säntis**, a charming chalet that is a short walk from the Säntis ski resort ($$). ☎ 71-365-6600, fax 71-365-6601.

Landmarks & Historic Sites

For a fun hike, venture to **Ebenalp** (the top station), only four miles (six km) from Appenzell, where you can stroll at an elevation of 5,400 feet (1,620 m). Here you can visit the **Wildkirchli** – a chapel grotto that was home to hermits from the 17th to the 19th centuries, and where the earliest archeological signs of human life in Switzerland can be found. Drive or hike to **Wasserrauen**, where the road ends, and then take a cable car (which departs every 45 minutes) for a 12-minute ride to the summit of Ebenalp. From here, the walk is only 30 minutes down to the caves of Wildkirchli. The round-trip cost is 22Sfr. For information ☎ 71-799-1212.

You can also visit the oldest Inn or Gasthaus in the region while at Wildkirchli. **Berggasthaus Ascher** is 150 years old and one interior wall of this inn is part of the mountain slope wall. No showers, just dorm rooms, open May through October, but cheap at 25Sfr a night, breakfast included. ☎ 71-799-1142, fax 71-799-1856.

Museums

The **Museum Appenzell** features the history and culture of this half-canton, including traditional costumes, embroidery, other handiwork and folklore. Many exhibitions on site. Special arrangements can be made for adult or children's groups. This museum is open daily from April 1-November 1, 10 am to noon and 2-5 pm From November 2 to March, the museum is open Tuesday through Sunday, from 2-5 pm. Located at Hauptgasse 4, Appenzell (this is in the same spot as the Tourist Office). ☎ 71-88-9631, fax 71-788-9649.

The **Museum Liner** spotlights works of Swiss artists Carl August Liner (1871-1946) and Carl Walter Liner (1914-1997), as well as artwork from the 20th century and the present. Free admission with a Swiss museum pass. The museum is only 330 feet (100 m) from the train station at Unterrainstrasse 5. Open April through October, Tuesdays-Fridays from 2-5 pm, and on Saturdays and Sundays from 11 am to 5 pm. From November through March the museum is open from Tuesday through Saturday, 2-5 pm, and on Saturdays and Sundays from 11-5 pm.

Museum Im Blauen Haus is a unique blue house open 365 days a year, with an ever-changing-variety of artwork on display. Free admission and parking. Open Monday through Saturday from 9 am to 6 pm and on Sunday from 10 am to 5 pm. Located at Weissbadstrasse 33, Appenzell.

Parks & Gardens

 This small excursion is well worth your time if you like to hike or just laze in the sun, and is a bit cheaper and less crowded than more traditional spots. For flower enthusiasts, check out the **Alpengarten Hoher Kasten** from the middle of June to the middle of August. For information, contact Edi Moser at Schutzwiesstrasse 2, in Appenzell, or ☎/fax 71-787-2011. This alpine garden provides a good example of flora common to the Alps up to 16,000 feet (5,000 m).

■ Shopping

 The Appenzell region is well known for its cheeses and embroidery works. Be careful, however, as the growth in tourism has led to many fakes among the handmade souvenirs, so be sure to check that the tags don't say "made in China." There are two highly-regarded spots to find regional and authentic pieces, however. **Trachtenstube**, at Hauptgasse 23, specializes in traditional Appenzeller clothing and hand-embroidered handkerchiefs. When you go in the building, walk up to the second floor. This is where the locals shop for their necessities. ☎ 71-787-1606. **Margreiter** is just down the block at Hauptgasse 29 and carries a wide variety of embroidery products from local artisans. ☎ 71-787-3313.

If you love cheese, then check out **Mösler** at Hauptgasse 25, which offers a great variety of Appenzeller cheeses, which visitors may sample. ☎ 71-787-1317. Also, **Sutter**, at Marktstrasse 8, is another good source of regional and local cheeses. ☎ 71-787-1227.

■ Where to Stay

Hotel Romantic Säntis was originally built in 1835 and is right in the town center. This is a favorite among tourists. The rooms are filled with local antiques and the small restaurant provides regional fare. Ask for a room in the original part of the house for a real treat. Stefan and Catriona Heeb are fourth-generation owners of this beautiful inn, and are gracious hosts. ($$$). Open February to December, it accepts all major credit cards. Located at Landsgemeindeplatz 3, just over 400 yards (400 m) from the train station. ☎ 71-788-1111, fax 71-788-1110, www.romantikhotels.com/appenzell.

HOTEL PRICE CHART	
$	30-75Sfr ($20-$49)
$$	76-205Sfr ($50-$109)
$$$	206-299Sfr ($110-$200)
$$$$	300Sfr+ ($200+)

Hotel Appenzell. This modern hotel was built in 1983 and features a café and restaurant on the town's main square, just across from the Hotel Säntis. Owners Margrit and Leo Sutter are on hand to greet visitors and prepare meals in the hotel's fine restaurant, which is surprisingly inexpensive. An adjacent bakery is a constant temptation as the aroma filters over into the hotel. Open every month except November; all major credit cards. ($$). Am Landsgemenideplatz. ☎ 71-788-1515, fax 71-788-1551, www.hotel-appenzell.ch.

Hotel Hecht was built over 300 years ago and has been operated by the Knechtle family for over half a century. This is the largest hotel in Appenzell and offers small and comfortable rooms, situated just across the street from the Catholic Church in the center of town. The restaurant offers local fare at reasonable prices. ($$). Hauptgasse 9. ☎ 71-787-1025, fax 71-787-4783, www.hechtappenzell.com.

Hotel Löwen was built in 1780. This mid-priced hotel features embroidered linens, canopy beds and armoires in a cozy atmosphere. ($$). Hauptgasse 25. ☎ 71-787-2187, fax 71-787-2579.

Adler overlooks the Sitter River and provides commanding views, especially in the morning and evening hours. Hauptgass 1. ($$). ☎ 71-787-1389, fax 71-787-1365.

Freudenberg, though cheap ($), offers one of the best views of the town anywhere in the area. Built in 1969, it's just behind the train station on the hillside. This lovely little chalet has just seven rooms, a café and restaurant. ☎/fax 71-787-1240.

Hotel Hof, which also has a popular restaurant, offers 58 beds and 10 rooms in a dormitory-like setting for groups. Engelgasse 4. ☎ 71-787-2210, fax 71/787-5883.

Camping

Campingplatz Jakobsbad. The family Huber has owned and operated this peaceful campground in the high valley of Gonten, at the foot of the Kronbergs, in Jakobsbad, right between Appenzell and Urnäsch, since 1970. The campsite is just five minutes from the train station (Kronbergbahn). Paragliding, mountain biking, swimming, golf and miniature golf in the summer and ski driving and bobsledding in the wintertime can be found here. This is the place for serious and novice hikers alike.

Prices per night are 4Sfr for adults, 2.5Sf for children 6-16 years, kids under six are free. Dogs are allowed at 2Sfr each. Tents and campers are 6Sfr each, cars, 2 Sfr. Large RVs, 10Sfr, small RVs, 8Sfr. Motorcycles 2Sfr. Located at 9108 Gonten. ☎ 71-794-1131 or fax 71-794-1833, www.campingplatzjakobsbad.ch

Landgasthof & Camping Eischen. In the nearby town of **Kau**, just two miles (four km) west of Appenzell, you'll find a nice little inn with campsites and inexpensive dorms ($). Dogs are allowed on leashes, and this spot has facilities suitable for handicapped persons. Owner Alfred Inauen-Menzi takes reservations. CH-9050 Appenzell-Kau. ☎ 71-787-5030, fax 71-787-5660.

Hundsteinhütte, founded in 1959, is one of a number of rustic huts available to backpackers, hikers or budget tourists who opt for a different kind of night in the Alps. Sponsored by the Swiss Alpine Club and the Association of Swiss Hut Warders, each has a unique name. This Appenzeller hut literally means "Dog stone hut," and is at the far southern tip of this canton, offering 52 beds. The hut phone number is ☎ 71-799-1581, and the hut is open in May on the weekends, and from June until the end of October annually. To reserve a spot, phone Maria and Thomas Reiser, Sunnehugelweg 4, CH-9535 Wilen b. Will at ☎ 71-920-0737.

■ Where to Eat

Hof is a very popular hangout for locals and visitors alike, featuring cheese specialties such as käseschnitte and käsespatzli, as well as regional meats. Crowded, loud and lively, but tons of fun. All major credit cards accepted. Engelgasse 4. ☎ 71-787-2210. ($-$$).

Traube is a nice restaurant that is best visited in the summertime when you can sit out on the terrace. This is a real meat-

DINING PRICE CHART	
Prices based on a typical entrée, per person, and do not include beverage.	
$	15-25Sfr ($10-$16)
$$	26-45Sfr ($17-$29)
$$$	46-70Sfr ($30-$47)
$$$$	71Sfr+ ($47+)

and-potatoes joint (mainly pork), but also features fondue and Appenzeller chäshörnli – a local version of macaroni and cheese. Most items here are under 20Sfr. Closed on Mondays. Marktgasse 7. ☎ 71-787-1407. ($-$$).

Appenzell is a brightly lit favorite that offers vegetarian and healthier dishes (rare in the area), along with traditional regional fare. Try the Appenzeller hauptgasse, a mixture of pork, proscuitto and tomato au gratin. It's delicious. All major credit cards accepted. Landsgemeindeplatz. ☎ 71-787-4211, fax 71-788-1551. ($$-$$$).

Hotel Hecht Restaurant, established in 1650, is well-known for its excellent cuisine and wine. Fish, such as trout and pike, are the specialties, as is the cheese fondue. Located inside the hotel at Hauptgasse 9. All major credit cards accepted and reservations are recommended. ($-$$). ☎ 71-787-1025. Open daily from noon-2 pm and from 6:30-11:30 pm.

Offering a view of the main square is **Restaurant Santis**, on the first floor of the hotel of the same name. An ever-changing menu always includes delicious homemade noodles, and specialties include lamb and pork. ($$-$$$). Reservations are recommended, and all major credit cards are accepted. Landsgemeindeplatz. ☎ 71-788-111, fax 71-788-1110. ($$-$$$). Open daily from 11 am-2 pm and from 6:30 pm-11 pm. Closed January 15 to February 1.

Rössli is an inexpensive hangout frequented by the locals. Card games and gossip abound here. ($-$$). ☎ 71-787-1256. Closed Mondays and Tuesdays from the end of February to mid-March.

Bären is a fine little restaurant just three miles (five km) from Appenzell in Schlatt. It provides great views of the Alps. ($-$$).

The Cities of Brülisau & Hoher Kasten

A quick drive or hike southeast of the town of Appenzell is **Brülisau**. From here you can take a small trip well worth your time to **Hoher Kasten**, at the very edge of the Appenzell Innerrhoden canton. From Brülisau you can grab the **Luftseilbahn Hoher Kasten** to take the 10-minute ride up to the top of the peak, for 26Sfr round-trip. Once at the top, you can take Switzerland's first geological hike, an alpine footpath that allows wanderers a panoramic view, complete with 14 displays providing information on all geological features of the area. The lift leaves every half-hour. ☎ 71-799-1322 or fax 71-799-1466. luftseilbahn@hoherkasten.ch.

The **Berggasthaus Hoher Kasten** offers clean rooms at modest prices ($$), and the large restaurant specializes in traditional Appenzeller fare. You can enjoy your meals out on the terrace, which gives an outstanding view of the Rhine Valley, the Tiroler, and the Bodensee. This is a great spot to just relax, reflect, and escape from the tourists in Appenzell, especially in the summer months. It is operated by Frau Barbara Maissen and Herr Johnny Urben. ☎ 71-799-1117 or fax 71-799-1123.

Gonten

This tiny village, just four miles (six km) west of Appenzell, is home to the traditional wrestling festival held annually, known as the **Schwingfest**. (Schwingen means wrestling in German.) Check out the **Bären** in Gonten, a very cozy and excellent restaurant specializing in regional fare. ☎ 71-795-4010.

Gais

North and east of Appenzell, this little market village features an unyielding array of stunning buildings for those who love Baroque architecture.

Kau

This tiny town is a favorite for nature lovers and offers secluded spots to relax and hike. You can stay at the **Kaubad** ($$), which is quiet and cozy. ☎ 71-787-4844, fax 787-1553.

TRADITIONS

Old traditions die hard in Appenzell Innerrhoden. Farmers have moved their cattle from the lower pastures to the upper Alpine pastures for centuries in this tiny canton. The ascent usually begins from the end of May to the first week of June during the wee morning hours, and the descent runs from the end of August to the end of September in the late morning and afternoon. It is still treated as an occasion, with farmers, their families and helpers participating. Farmers usually dress in traditional Appenzeller costumes – bright red vests with gold or black pants – while their cows are adorned with flowered headwear and, in many cases, huge cowbells. Young boys often drive herds of Appenzeller goats in front of them, while at the end of the procession horsedrawn wagons carry pigs and equipment. Another tradition of the Appenzeller farming community is the Herdsmen's Ball or "Alpstobete." These lively summer dances focus on folk music and yodeling, and usually begin at noon and carry on until evening. They are typically held outside of an inn or restaurant.

Canton Graubünden (GR)

■ At a Glance

Graubünden – or The Grisons as it has come to be known in English – is the largest canton in Switzerland, the wildest, the most mountainous and the least populated. As such, for the purposes of this book it is designated as one of Switzerland's seven regions. Covering 2,744 square miles (7,106 square km), Graubünden has 185,700 German-speaking, mostly Protestant inhabitants, who reside in 212 towns and villages in this rural canton. Over 32% of the native Swiss here work in the tourist industry, while 26% work at industrial, energy or construction occupations. The canton – of which 30% is used for agriculture – became part of the Swiss Federation in 1803. It lies at the far eastern edge of the country, flanked by the cantons of St. Gallen and Glarus to the northwest, and by cantons Uri and Ticino to the west and south. It is this land that inspired the book *Heidi* and is home to the Swiss Grand Canyon, as well as to such outstanding winter resorts as St. Moritz, Davos and Arosa.

Graubünden is made up of 39 districts that represent century-old traditions. In some areas you'll find the traditional Landsgemeinde every two years, where citizens gather in an open-air setting to debate and cast votes for district judges and heads of cantonal parliaments.

The canton of Graubünden first gained notoriety in 1864, when crafty St. Moritz Hotel owner Johannes Badrutt concocted a wild publicity scheme to lure British tourists. When they arrived, Badrutt told them that, if they enjoyed their stay in his region, he'd cover their travel expenses, and that they could stay as long as they liked – at his expense. He also promised to pay their travel expenses if they were not happy with his hotel and the area. The response was tremendous, and that is how St. Moritz became the elite resort it is today.

The people of Graubünden, in contrast with their wild surroundings, are highly conservative. In fact, they were the last people in the civilized world to ban cars on their roads, not allowing them in until 1925.

Graubünden is home to the **Swiss National Park**, which can be found in the region known as the **Lower Engadine**. This canton is a hiker's paradise with over 6,500 miles (10,500 km) of walking paths – quiet, unspoiled and beautiful – epitomizing Alpine splendor at its finest. The "wanderwegs" are simple footpaths, while the "bergwegs" are mountain paths. Wanderwegs can be attempted by anyone of any age, while the bergwegs are for intermediate to experienced hikers who use proper gear and appropriate hiking shoes. Mountain huts abound throughout this area and provide a unique overnight stay.

Graubünden has over 615 lakes and rivers – including the **Inn** and the **Rhine** – and water sports such as sailing and windsurfing are quite popular, although no motorboats are allowed. In addition, 930 miles (1,500 km) of downhill ski slopes and 539 miles (868 km) of cross-country ski paths criss-cross the 937 peaks and 150 valleys. **Piz Buin** at 10,867 feet (3,133 m) is the tallest peak in the northern region, while **Piz Bernina**, at 13,307 feet (4,057 m) is the highest mountain in the entire canton.

There are 38 camping grounds in Graubünden. This is truly Switzerland's "great outdoors," and is the starting point for many train trips, including the **Bernina Express**, the **Heidi Express** and the **Palm Express**. There are over 14 mountain passes in Graubünden, including the Julier Pass, which has been used by the general public as an open pass since the 15th century. Prior to that it had been used by the ancient Romans and others.

The whole canton shuts down during May and June when the locals take a break and enjoy their own vacations. To stay overnight at any of the hotspots like St. Moritz or Davos, you must make a reservation well in advance. You can also expect outrageous prices for everything from ski rental to simple meals in most of these areas. However, this is also the best region for families traveling with children, as there are many child-friendly accommodations in Graubünden that offer kids' meals, playgrounds and sitting services.

ROMANSH

This ancient language is still taught in the Graubünden schools, even though only 25% of the people of this canton speak it. Romansh developed through influences from all of the Romance languages, but came primarily from Latin. In Graubünden, there are five dialects – due to the fact that there were isolated valleys whose inhabitants at one time never ventured far from home. This makes the language especially difficult, even for those who can speak it. The name of Graubünden, for instance, is "Grischun" in Romansh – a reminder of the Grey League, one of the three leagues, or popular associations, that united in 1471 to resist and eventually throw off the feudal oppression of the bishops and lords who nominally ruled the area.

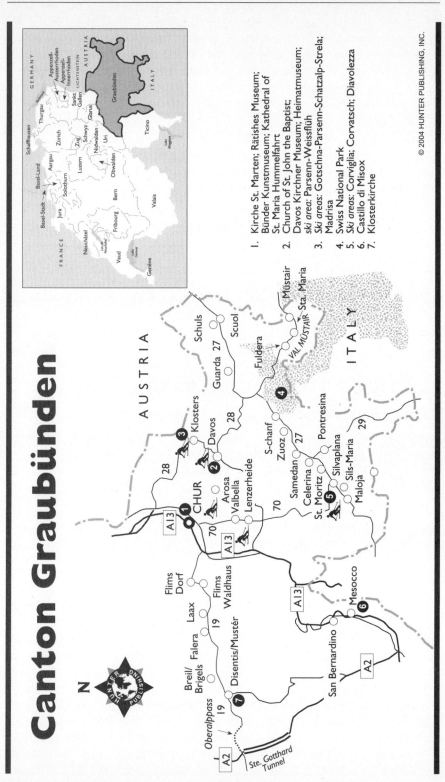

1. Kirche St. Marten; Rätishes Museum; Bünder Kunstmuseum; Kathedral of St. Maria Hummelfahrt
2. Church of St. John the Baptist; Davos Kirchner Museum; Heimatmuseum; *ski area*: Parsenn-Weissflüh
3. *Ski areas*: Gotschna-Parsenn-Schatzalp-Strela; Madrisa
4. Swiss National Park
5. *Ski areas*: Corviglia; Corvatsch; Diavolezza
6. Castillo di Misox
7. Klosterkirche

Canton Graubünden

The **coat of arms** of Graubünden represents the alliance of three leagues from the 14th and 15th centuries. The left side of the crest sports a black and white argent which represents the Grey League, who ruled the upper Rhine Basin, while at the bottom of the crest is a prancing ibex, representing the League of God's House. The right side of the shield represents the Ten Jurisdictions League as a cross of gold and blue, symbolizing the banner that flew in the Prätigau – the regions of Davos and Arosa.

The **Tourist Office of Canton Graubünden** is in Chur at Alexanderstrasse 24, on the second floor, and is a short, two-minute walk from the train station. ☎ 81-254-2424, fax 81-254-2400.

Chur

Chur is the capital of the canton of Graubünden and home to 32,000 citizens. The highlight of the town is the 12th-century **Cathedral** in the Altstadt (Old Town) district, believed to be Switzerland's oldest recorded settlement – at 5,000 years old. Chur is also well known for its spas and health centers, with 26 in or around the city. You'll also find Roman ruins, lots of cobblestone streets and narrow buildings, and a few good museums.

■ Information Sources

Tourist Offices

The **Chur Tourist Office** is at Grabenstrasse 5, CH-7000 Chur. ☎ 81-252-1818, fax 81-252-9076, www.chur.ch. **Budget travelers** can go to SSR Travel Services at Unteregasse, Chur, to find cheap accommodations and seasonal or weekly specials offered in the region. ☎ 81-252-9776.

Train Station

Chur is the main hub for most of the transportation in and out of Canton Graubünden. Besides travel services, you'll also find a currgency exchange (open from 7 am to 8 pm daily), a bike rental service (26Sfr daily), and luggage storage (5Sfr per day) and regular storage lockers (for 2Sfr per day).

This is also the meeting point for railways like the **Bernina Express**, which takes you from Chur to St. Moritz and then on to Tirano, Italy via the highest railway in the Alps. With its 70° grade, it is one of the steepest railway tracks in the world without cogwheels. The trip leaves Chur at 8:48 in the morning and arrives in Italy just in time for lunch at 12:40 pm. This is part of the **Rhätishe Bahn AG** (The Little Red One) line, at Bahnhofstrasse 25, CH-7002 Chur. ☎ 812-88-6100, fax 812-88-6101. This line also includes the **Glacier Express**, which whisks you from Chur to Zermatt in half a day, and the **Engadine Star**, which has a day-trip from

Chur to St. Moritz via the eastern region of Graubünden. You can also take the **Heidi Express**, which takes you from Chur to Tirano, Italy, and then buses you over to Lugano.

Post Office

Posttpost, right next to the train station. Open Monday-Friday, 7:30-noon, 1:30-6:30, Saturday from 8 am-noon. ☎ 81-256-3233, fax 81-256-3239.

Codes

The **area code** for Chur is 81, the **postal code** is CH-7000.

Internet Access

Rampa, at Tittwiesenstrasse 60, Chur, is open from 8 am-6:30 pm, daily, 12Sf per hour. ☎ 81-284-8928. Or you can head to The Street Café, which is a great little place to hang out at night. Open 9 am-midnight, 15Sfr per hour. Grabenstrasse 47, Chur. ☎ 81-253-7914.

Medical Services

A 24-hour emergency room can be found in Kantonsspital, Loestrasse 170. ☎ 81-256-6111. Otherwise, dial 117.

■ Getting Around

The best way to see Chur and the surrounding areas are either on foot, by rail or cable car, or on skis. The old part of Chur is mostly pedestrian only and, if you're driving, you'll find ample parking lots and garages. Chur is also a good starting point or base from which to explore the region, and rooms and eateries can be had here a bit cheaper than in the more-frequented tourist areas.

AUTHOR'S
PICK

Do as the Romans do... from Chur, drive toward the San Bernardino Pass and exit at Thusis, following the signs for the **Via Mala**, which in Italian means Bad Road. This is one of the oldest footpaths in Europe, used by the Romans and various traders, merchants and travelers for centuries. The trail itself is 3½ miles (six km) and runs alongside the Hinterrhein Gorge. Near the beginning of the gorge you can walk down the 300 steps (for 3Sfr) to view the old road and take in the spectacular scenery.

■ Adventures

On Foot

 If you're interested in hiking, you can take a cable car up to **Parpaner Rothorn** and choose from several of the walking paths that wind around the 9,397-foot (2,865-m) summit. The **Lenzerheide Tourist Office** can be very helpful. ☎ 81-385-1120, fax 81-385-1121.

On Snow

 Chur is not far from several ski areas. One of the least visited by foreigners are two linked resorts that are on opposite sides of the Heidsee – **Lenzerheide** and **Valbella**. Many Swiss from other regions of the country come here to learn how to ski. Don't expect the nightlife of Davos or St. Moritz, but do expect to find easy to moderate ski trails. Ski passes are slightly cheaper here: a one-day pass is 52Sfr for adults and 42Sfr for youths and seniors, while kids are 31Sfr. To get to either location is a 40-minute bus ride from Chur, or if you're driving you can take Highway 3 over the Julier Pass from Chur in the direction of St. Moritz.

Swimming/Tennis/Ice Skating

 These can all be done at **Obere Au Sportszentrum** in Chur. ☎ 81-254-4288.

Golf

 From Chur, the 27-hole **Domat-Ems golf course** is only a 15-minute ride and is best accessed by train or bus. You must make reservations. ☎ 81-633-3212.

■ Landmarks & Historic Sites

 Kirche St. Martin (St. Martin's Church) was destroyed by a fire in the eighth century and then rebuilt in the late 15th century. It is famous for its beautiful, stained-glass windows created by Graubünden artist Augusto Giacometti. Open daily from 8:30-11:30 am, and from 2-5 pm. Kirchgasse 12, Chur. ☎ 81-252-2292.

■ Museums

The Kathedrale of St. Maria Himmelfahrt (St. Mary of the Assumption), which dominates the city profile, was built in the 12th century with a mixture of Roman and Gothic influences, and contains the largest Gothic triptych in Switzerland. It is a dark and mysterious place and can be viewed only by appointment. You have to call ahead so that you can pick up the key to the Cathedral. Go to Hofstrasse 2, the first floor, to obtain the key. If you're not really into churches, skip this one, as it's a bit too dark and dreary to make a real impression. Open Monday-Saturday from 10-noon and 2-4 pm. ☎ 81-252-9257.

Rätishes Museum can be found in the 17th-century Buol Mansion and includes displays of Graubünden folklore and historical pieces relating to Chur. Open Tuesday-Sunday, from 10-noon, 2-5 pm. Cost is 5Sfr. Hofstrasse 1, Chur. ☎ 81-257-2889.

Bünder Kunstmuseum (Fine Arts Museum) displays works of 18th- to 20th-century artists who were either born or lived in Graubünden. Open Tuesday, Wednesday, Friday and Saturday from 10-noon, 2-5 pm, and on Thursdays from 10-noon, 2-8 pm. Cost is 6-10Sfr. Postplatz. ☎ 81-257-2868.

Speak Romansh? If you'd like to learn Romansh, you've come to the right village. Chur is home to The Lia Rumantscha, an organization dedicated to keeping this ancient language afloat. You can visit them at Obere Plessurstrasse 47, CH-7001 Chur. ☎ 81-252-4422, fax 81-252-8426.

■ Shopping

Chur's main street is auto-free, and a wide array of shops can be found here. It is worth a few hours browsing through this area and sampling the various culinary delights of the region.

■ Where to Stay

Romantik Hotel Stern is a historic, 300-year-old inn with wood-beamed ceilings and a comfortable atmosphere. It's home to one of the best restaurants in town, in the heart of the Old Town. ($$). Reichgasse 11, CH-7000 Chur. ☎ 81-252-3555, fax 81-252-1915.

HOTEL PRICE CHART	
$	30-75Sfr ($20-$49)
$$	76-205Sfr ($50-$109)
$$$	206-299Sfr ($110-$200)
$$$$	300Sfr+ ($200+)

Hotel Drei Könige (Three Kings Hotel) is a 200-year-old comfortable and cozy hotel/bar/café just a few strides from the Tourist Office at Reichsgasse 18, CH-7000 Chur. ($$). ☎ 81-252-1725, fax 81-252-1726.

Hotel Zumfthaus zu Rebleuten is a 500-year-old structure with elegant, comfortable rooms, with lovely and elaborate woodworking on its façade. The restaurant isn't bad either. ($-$$). Kupfergasse 1, CH-7000 Chur. ☎ 81-252-1357, fax 81-257-1358.

Duc De Rohan is a cozy old manor with quality services and rooms. It also has sauna and swimming pool services. ($$). Masanserstrasse 44, CH-7000 Chur. ☎ 81-252-1022, fax 81-252-4537.

Hotel Franziskaner, in the Old Town, offers simple rooms at reasonable prices. Great for those traveling on a budget, hikers and students. ($-$$). Kupfergasse 18, CH-7000 Chur. ☎ 81-252-1261.

The local **Youth Hostel** is just eight miles (12 km) south in Valbella, offering dorm rooms for 24Sfr per night. Open June-October and December-April. ($).Via Sartons 41, Valbella. ☎ 81-384-1208, fax 81-384-4558.

Camping

Camp Au is next to the Chur Sportszentrum and is open year-round. 7Sfr per person, per night, and 6.2Sfr per tent. ☎ 81-284-2283.

■ Where to Eat

Hotel Stern offers a wide variety of regional fare in rustic surroundings and is open for both lunch and dinner. Try the excellent vegetarian menu or, for a treat, you and a companion can order from the Bünder Menu – a seven-course meal for two – at 152Sfr. A fun treat and the food is delicious. ($-$$$$). Reichsgasse 11, CH-7000 Chur. ☎ 81-252-3555, fax 81-252-1915.

DINING PRICE CHART	
Prices based on a typical entrée, per person, and do not include beverage.	
$	15-25Sfr ($10-$16)
$$	26-45Sfr ($17-$29)
$$$	46-70Sfr ($30-$47)
$$$$	71Sfr+ ($47+)

Speiserestaurant Zollhaus features a lower bar room known as the Bierschwemme, where meals are inexpensive. ($). The upper level – known as the Bündnerstube – is a bit more sophisticated. offering regional dishes and Chinese food. ($$). Malixesstrasse 1, CH-7000 Chur.

The Giger Bar is owned by the Swiss artist HR Giger, who designed the fiendish-looking creatures in the *Alien* movies. If you're a science fiction buff, then don't overlook this place. The atmosphere is low-key, but the design inside the bar is unique, even if the local clients are not. You'll find it behind the Migros Hobby Lobby at Comercialstrasse 23, CH-7000 Chur. ($-$$). Open 8 am-midnight, closed Sundays.

Valentino's Grill offers up tasty, cheap food and drinks. Great if you're on a budget, and great if you're not. ($). Untergasse 5, CH-7000 Chur. Open Mon-Friday from 11:30 am-1:45 pm, 5-10 pm, Saturdays from noon-midnight. ☎ 81-252-7322.

The **Migros Supermarket** at Gauggelistrasse 28 offers self-service dining in a clean and comfy setting for those on a budget.

Flims

Flims is another resort town that's more of a favorite among the Swiss than it is with foreigners. Situated in the heart of Graubünden, Flims is on the road between Chur and Andermatt. This well-known ski resort at 9,774 feet (2,890 m) is divided into two sectors – **Flims Dorf** and **Flims Waldhaus**. Flims Dorf is the larger and more urban of the two, and closer to the ski lifts. Flims Waldhaus is host to most of the hotels, but is closer to the surrounding woods and forests and a longer walk to the ski lifts. The slopes here are easy to intermediate, while more experienced skiers will opt for the difficult runs from Crap Sogn Gion to Laax Murschteg.

The Flims Tourist Office is in Flims Waldhaus. ☎ 81-920-9200, fax 81-920-9201. The **Post Office** is in Flims Dorf.

River rafting in the Vorderrhine Gorge, Switzerland's Grand Canyon

Known as the **Alpen Arena**, Flims connects with the nearby villages of **Laax** and **Falera** to make up the largest connected ski area in Graubünden. This Alpen Arena connects 137 miles (225 km) of easy to intermediate downhill ski runs, with 30 ski lifts and 25 miles (60 km) of cross-country tracks. Altitudes range up to 9,843 feet (3,608 m), and hikers in Flims will find a spider-web of 90+ miles (200 km) of trails that lead all the way to the Rhine Gorge.

Just two miles (3.2 km) away is the other third of the Alpen Arena known as **Falera**. There is an odd site in the middle of this tiny village known as the "26 menhirs." This is a bizarre arrangement of huge stones fixed in a geometric pattern that dates back to the time of Falera's settlement in 1500 BC.

■ Adventures

On Foot

 A walking path at the top of the Alpen Arena is known as **Naturlehpfad** and takes only two to three hours to complete. This circular route can be accessed via a chairlift and then cable car from Flims to Cassonsgrat, for 32Sfr.

THE ALPINE GRAND CANYON

Nearly 14,000 years ago the Rhine Glacier retreated and the northern side of the mountain, where Flims is today, fell. Thousands of tons of rocks, boulders and mud crashed to the valley floor, damming the Rhine. This phenomenon eventually led to the creation of the Vorderrhein Gorge, which many in Switzerland call the "Grand Canyon." Now a heavily forested area, the landscape has parted to allow the Rhine to meander and wind its way through these valleys, creating a hiker's and rafter's paradise found nowhere else in Switzerland. One of the best hiking trails in Switzerland pierces directly through the Gorge from Trin, which is easily accessed via public transportation from Chur. For information: www.alpinearena.ch, CH-7017 Flims, ☎ 81-920-9200.

On Snow

 For downhill ski lessons in Flims, contact the **Swiss Ski School** at ☎ 81-927-7181; for cross country instruction, contact the **Langlauf Center** at ☎ 81-635-1688. The **Snowboard Fahrschule of Flims** teaches both snowboarding and skiing.

Only three miles (4.8 km) south of Flims is the tiny village of **Laax**, a popular snowboarding base that makes up one-third of the Alpine Arena. The World Cup of Snowboarding is held in Laax each April and, in addition, you'll find a mountain-bike free-style park here. Contact the **Tacho School** for lesson sand excursions at ☎ 81-927-7171.

On Water

 You can experience easy to moderate river-rafting at its finest here in Flims. The **Swissraft** in Flims Waldhaus offers full- and half-day trips, ranging in cost from 100-145Sfr. This company also offers mountain biking excursions, hot-air balloon trips (Flims is home to the Flims Ballon Festival, held annually during the first week of October), paragliding and fishing expeditions. Contact Swissraft in Flims Waldhaus. ☎ 81-911-5250, fax 81-911-3090.

■ Where to Stay

 Park Hotels Waldhaus is great for families and those with kids. It is also a health and spa center surrounded by wooded grounds. ($$$-$$$$). ☎ 81-928-4848, fax 81-928-4858, www.park-hotels-waldhaus.ch.

HOTEL PRICE CHART	
$	30-75Sfr ($20-$49)
$$	76-205Sfr ($50-$109)
$$$	206-299Sfr ($110-$200)
$$$$	300Sfr+ ($200+)

Hotel Vorab is convenient and modern, just across from the Dorf Post Office. ($$$). It also has two restaurants, serving vegetarian and Italian cuisine. ☎ 81-911-1861, fax 81-911-4229.

Guardaval in Waldhaus offers spacious rooms, free parking and reasonable rates. ($-$$). ☎-911-1119, fax 81-911-1179.

Backpacker Hotel Gutveina is a cheap ($) place for hikers to bunk down. Located on Via Gutveina in Waldhaus. ☎/fax 81-911-2903.

Camping

 Camping in Flims can be found in **Prau**, as you head toward Laax, which is only five minutes from the Flim Tourist Office. It is open year-round. ☎ 81-911-1575.

■ Where to Eat

 Restaurant LeBarga is a high-class gourmet French restaurant. Great ambiance, with a piano bar and log fireplace. ($$-$$$). Open daily; reservations are suggested. CH-7018 Flims Waldhaus. ☎ 81-928-2828.

DINING PRICE CHART	
Prices based on a typical entrée, per person, and do not include beverage.	
$	15-25Sfr ($10-$16)
$$	26-45Sfr ($17-$29)
$$$	46-70Sfr ($30-$47)
$$$$	71Sfr+ ($47+)

Hotel Laaxerhof specializes in vegetarian and international dishes. Open daily. ($$-$$$). CH-7032 Laax Murschetg. ☎ 81-920-8200.

Muhbarak is the hot spot for great fondue. Open daily. ($-$$). CH-7032 Laax Murshetg. ☎ 81-927-9941.

Pizzeria Veneziana serves up homemade pizza and pastas at reasonable prices. Closed Wednesday. ($-$$). CH-7017 Flims Dorf. ☎ 81-911-0103.

The Crap Bar is a local hangout for snowboarders and snowboarders, and is right next to the mountain railway and the trendy **Granite Bar**. ($-$$). Open daily. CH-7032 Laax-Murschetg, ☎ 81-927-9945.

WWW.Keller is an Internet bar/restaurant is another hot spot for "Alpine surfers." Open daily. CH-7032 Laax Murschetg . ☎ 81-927-9945.

Grischuna is a good little spot for food, right between Flims Dorf and Flims Waldhaus. Reasonably priced and hearty dishes – check out the meat fondues. Open daily. ($-$$). CH-7018 Flims Waldhaus. ☎ 81-911-1139.

> **Good Value:** During the high season on Tuesdays and Thursdays, for 42Sfr, you'll get a lift ticket, toboggan, fondue or raclette and an aperitif at Foppa, an old wooden chalet with a lovely sun terrace, where you can sit and enjoy your goodies after a fun toboggan run. Try the tobogganing at night when the trail is lit up – it is great fun! Contact the Flims Tourist Office for reservations. ☎ 81-920-9200, fax 81-920-9201.

Arosa

Arosa is considered to be trendy and yet traditional, and has been a popular Alpine health resort village since 1883, after Dr. Otto Herwig-Hold decided to set up a tuberculosis sanitarium there. Located at the end of the **Upper Schanfigg Basin**, it is sheltered by the wind and is one of the sunniest places in Switzerland, with the sun shining an average of eight to 12 hours daily. Here you'll find over 25 miles (40 km) of winter hiking trails and six varying sled runs, as well as 15 ski lifts. You can even sled-ride at night, under a full moon, if you like. So that hikers and skiers don't interfere with one another, the village has placed the ski slopes on one side of the valley and the hiking trails on the other. Arosa itself consists of the long main street of **Poststrasse**, which is lined with shops and hotels. The village is basically car-free, but the village bus offers free services daily from all major points, including ski lifts, cable cars and the train station.

■ Information Sources

Tourist Office

The Arosa Tourist Office is at Poststrasse, CH-7050 Arosa. ☎ 81-378-7020, fax 81-378-7021. They can provide you with great free hiking maps for both winter and summer months, and also have sleds available for rent; they can help to arrange ski lessons as well. Also, they will help you with hotel accommodations, as it is wise to make reservations ahead of time if you plan to plant your skis here.

Aelplisee Lake on Arosa Alp

Train Station

The Arosa train station has a currency exchange (open Monday-Saturday, 6 am-9 pm, Sunday 6:30 am-9 pm), lockers for just 2Sfr, and bike rental for 21-27Sfr per day.

AUTHOR'S
PICK

For a nice day-trip (if you're not a skier), visit Arosa via train from Chur. The train – which provides spectacular scenery along the way – leaves every hour and costs 12Sfr.

Post Office

Arosa's post office is in the village center, just to the right of the train station, and, besides mail services, also offers **Internet access.**

Codes

Arosa's **postal code** is CH-7050, and the **area code** is 81.

Canton Graubünden

■ Adventures

On Foot

Hiking

 Hiking in Arosa is some of the best to be found in Switzerland. The Arosa Tourist Office can arrange a guide for you from June through October for only 12Sfr for a seven-nine-hour hike at various levels of experience. One easy and popular hike is called the "squirrel path" or **Eichhörnliweg**; it takes you from Arosa to the nearby quiet suburb of Maran via a gently sloping path through the connecting pastures between the two villages.

HIKING THE ALTEINBACH TRAIL

 If you want a fun trip made for the average hiker, then this one is for you. Be sure to bring a backpack with water, rain gear and lots of munchies, or better yet, have your significant other carry a well-stocked picnic basket. This trip is about five miles long (eight km) and can take several hours (or longer, with a picnic), and is just a good healthy hike for anyone.

At the entrance to the town of Arosa, follow the signs to the water treatment plant or simply ask how to find it. You'll follow the service road and it will eventually expand into a fairly wide walking path. Soon you'll find yourself walking parallel and south to the Wälschtobelbach River (on your left-hand side). Follow the path and you'll then come to a spot where you can either go left or right. You want to walk to the left over the Altein River via a wooden bridge and then minutes later you'll cross the river again on the same trail. Stay on this path and the Altein Waterfall will soon be in sight, and it is a spectacular one indeed. From here you'll continue your jaunt upward, eventually arriving at an open field. Continue on and you'll cross the Altein River once more until you reach the Alteinsee, a small lake, which is the perfect spot for your picnic. Here, you'll get some great views of the Valbellahorn at 7,654 feet (2,764 m). At this point it's another 1½ miles (2.4 km) to the Alteiner Furggli Pass at 7,400 feet (2,500 m).

Tennis/Squash/Fitness

 These are available year-round. The **Sunstar Park Hotel** has one tennis and one squash court. The **Robinson Club** has two indoor tennis courts and two indoor squash courts, while the **Sporthotel Valsana** has two indoor tennis courts. You can get information from the Arosa Tourist Office on swimming pools, saunas and whirlpools to fit your needs.

On the Water

Sunbathing is popular in the summer months, and tan seekers will find the Untersee's free public beach to their liking. Here you can also rent a pedal boat for only 12Sfr per hour. It's a fun way to relax, catch some rays, and get a tiny bit of exercise.

On Horseback

The **Fuhrhalterei** stables offer horseback riding for 30Sfr per hour on local trails. You must make a reservation at least one day in advance. The stables are just outside the village near the campground. Phone the Messner family at ☎ 81-377-4196.

In the Air

Ballooning

This is great here in the wintertime as well as in the summer. Contact balloon pilot Walter Vollenweider at ☎ 81-391-3714 for information regarding trips.

Hangliding

This sport is done all year as well, but only in good weather. Prices range from 180-200Sfr. You'll take off from the Weisshorn lift-off site and land in either Obersee or Molinis. Contact the **Gliding-Taxi Arosa Jogi**, Tandempilot at ☎ 70-499-8813.

On Snow & Ice

Downhill Skiing

In Arosa this covers the three peaks of the **Hörnli**, the **Weisshorn** and the **Brüggerhorn** – all above the tree line – and features easy and intermediate runs over mostly hilly terrain. Ski passes abound in Arosa – here you can buy morning, afternoon, day, multi-day and weekly passes at prices ranging from 50 to 400Sfr for adults, while children under 15 ski for half-price and seniors at a 15% discount. The eastern edge of Arosa tends to be the most popular for skiers, who take a cable car up to the Weisshorn at 8,704 feet (2,611 m), where they enjoy one of the most spectacular views in all of Switzerland. There are over 40 miles (64 km) of ski runs, and the **Swiss Ski School** is based here, with 100 instructors for all levels of skiers. Contact them at ☎ 81-377-1150 or call the Grison Association of Private Ski Instructor Arosa at 81-377-1556 for private lessons.

Cross-Country Skiing

This is done on **Maran, Pratschalp/Ochsenalp**, in the Isel and on the Obersee, where there are 15½ miles (25 km) of cross-country runs. It is now mandatory for all visitors to purchase a Cross-Country Ski Pass, in order to help support and maintain the long-distance ski runs found here; it includes free use of all long distance runs in Arosa and, in some cases, free bus rides in the area. Runs vary in difficulty and from one to five miles in length. Passes range in price from 5 to 90SFr and can be purchased at any ski school or equipment store, or at the Tourist Office and on the Isla-Bus. **The Geeser Cross-Country Ski School** can help to advise you and provide rental equipment. ☎ 81-377-2215.

Sledding

Most of the sled runs are free in Arosa and the majority are three miles (4.8 km) long. Try the **Tschuggenhütte** for starters. To reach the starting point you must take a chairlift from Innerarosa-Tushuggen or with the Arosa-Weisshorn cable car to the Mittelstation. Next, you can try the **Prätschli-Scheiterböden-Obersee**. Although this run is also used by walkers and horse-drawn sleighs, it is worth trying, especially because it is floodlit throughout the season. Rent sleds from **Stivetta Sled Rental** at CH-7050 Arosa, ☎ 81-377-2181. You can pick up the train in Arosa to get to the tops of these runs; call the **Arosa Bergbahnen AG** at ☎ 81-378-8484.

Snowshoe Hiking

Hunters and travelers traversed this land for centuries on snowshoes. Hiking trips are easy to organize and moonlight hikes have become very popular in the last few years. This is an easy sport to get into, because there is really nothing you need to know other than how to strap on your snowshoes! Weekly guided hikes are available: The **Easy Trapper** is held every Monday from 1:45 to 3:45 pm and is a light walk, requiring little exertion. The **Prätsch Trail** hike takes place on Tuesdays and Thursdays from 1:45 to 4:45 and is a bit more taxing, but anyone in decent shape should be able to handle this walk. For information, contact **Geeser Snowshoe & Cross-Country Center** at ☎ 81-377-2215.

Curling

This is one of Arosa's traditional winter sports. If you'd like to try it, there are weekly introductory courses on the open-air ice-rink. For information, ☎ 81-377-1745. You can also try Bavarian curling, which is played on a natural ice-rink in Innerarosa until March. ☎ 81-377-2930.

Ice Skating & Hockey

 You can do either one from the middle of December until the middle of April at the ice-rink at Obersee. Natural rinks are also available in Innerarose and at Hof Maran. ☎ 81-377-1745 for information.

Horse Racing

 If you like watching horse racing in the snow, then check out Arosa's local "snow track." This half-mile oval on the frozen Obersee is host to flat racing (thoroughbreds), harness racing (Standardbreds) and steeplechase (racing over fences), as well as **Skikjoring** – which was first held here in 1917. Harness racing was introduced in 1922, and the races are usually held in either January or February. **Pferdesport-Verein Arosa** (Arosa Horse Sport Association), CH-7050 Arosa. Contact president Peter Luscher at ☎ 81-377-3141, fax 81-377-2310, or vice-president Marth Hebeisen at ☎ 81-377-1539, for information.

■ Where to Stay

Hotels

 Arosa Kulm Hotel & Alpine Spa, a five-star luxury hotel, offers the best of everything for winter and summer sports enthusiasts, as well as a beauty and health spa. One of the oldest (1882) and highest-altitude hotels in Arosa, it is situated at the edge of the village, sur-

HOTEL PRICE CHART	
$	30-75Sfr ($20-$49)
$$	76-205Sfr ($50-$109)
$$$	206-299Sfr ($110-$200)
$$$$	300Sfr+ ($200+)

rounded by a sunlit southern slope. Activities for families with children abound – such as the Lollipop Children's Holiday Program. There are six great restaurants and three bars. Babysitting services, sauna, massage as well. ($$$-$$$$). Free outside parking and a parking garage (15Sfr daily). Innere Poststrasse, CH-7050 Arosa. ☎ 81-378-8888, fax 81-378-8889.

Tschuggen Grand Hotel is one of the most prestigious hotels in Switzerland. Spacious modern rooms accommodate many of the world's rich and famous, with prices to match their pocketbooks. Four restaurants, bars, kindergarten, fitness room. ($$$-$$$$). Closed April 3-December 2. Parking available (30Sfr daily). CH-7050 Arosa. ☎ 81-378-9999, fax 81-378-9990, www.tschuggen.ch.

Arosa Bergbahnen is the local ski lift company. They operate two inns for skiers – the Haus Florentium and Haus Bellaval – and a ski-lift ticket is included when you rent a room from them. **Haus Florentium** is the larger of the two inns and is a former convent with 150 beds, lounges and a disco. Breakfast is included and dinner is cheap ($). Ski passes range from 150 to 480Sfr. During July and August, no ski packages are available and room prices drop to 30-39Sfr per night. This hotel is a bit off the beaten trail: to get here, walk down the cobblestone road from the tourist office and at the top of the road turn right, then left at the gravel path, then right again at the next path nearby. It sounds complicated but it's hard to miss, as a great number of skiers are heading either to or from this inn. **Haus Bellaval** is small and simple, with just basic rooms, but is above the train station for convenience. Prices range from 139 to 423Sfr; during the summer, prices fall to 40-53Sfr per night and include a lift pass for two hiking trails. ($-$$$$). ☎ 81-378-8423, fax 81-378-8443.

Waldhotel-National Hotel is off the beaten path, tranquil and secluded. The Waldhotel was originally a sanitorium, then a military hospital, and finally a hotel. Prices are determined by the view each room provides – with those facing south providing a view of Arosa and those facing north with a view of the forest. Restaurant, swimming pool, fitness room, massage. ($$-$$$). Closed April 20-June 26, and from September 14-December 5.

Golf & Sports Hotel Hof Maran is a charming hotel suitable for families and run by gracious hosts Marc and Astrid Lehmann. Gently situated in the palm of the valley, this facility has a wide array of packages available for both summer and winter sports. Two restaurants, bar, golf course. ($$-$$$$). CH-7050 Arosa. ☎ 81-378-5151, fax 81-378-5100.

Hotel Alpina looks like a traditional Swiss mountain chalet, complete with wood-carved hand railings, Swiss flags, and lots of wood beams. Comfy chairs, Alpine clocks and other furniture that you'd find in a Swiss country house can be had here. Moderately priced ($$-$$$), with a relaxed atmosphere. Restaurant and bar. Closed April to mid-June, and from November to December 6. CH-7050 Arosa. ☎ 81-377-1658, fax 81-377-3752.

Hotel Restaurant Obersee is near the Obersee and offers a homey, cozy atmosphere with all modern facilities at reasonable rates, and with packages available. Close to nearby lifts and walking trails, with tennis courts, and an ice and curling rink right beside the hotel. ($$-$$$$). The family Schemmekes works hard to greet all guests, and the excellent restaurant serves up Engadiner schnitzel, fresh fish, vegetarian and French specialties. CH-7050 Arosa. ☎ 81-377-1216, fax 81-377-4566.

Backpackers Chalet Arosa looks just like a Swiss chalet should. It offers rooms and package discounts. Only a short walk from the bus station on Hubelstrasse. ($-$$$). CH-7050 Arosa. ☎ 81-378-5252.

Pensions, Hostels, Huts & Camping

Pension Suveran is a great bargain in the typical style of a Swiss chalet – wooden, homey and quaint. No frills, but comfy and relaxing. Breakfast

Selma, in the Calanca Valley, near the Valle Mesolcina, Graubünden

Above: At Wildspitz, Canton Schwyz (see page 200)

Below: Muotatal, Canton Schwyz, seen from the Pragel (see page 211)

ake Walen (Walensee), bathing beach near Walenstadt, Canton St. Gallen (see page 91)

Footbridge over the Reuss River in Wassen, Canton Uri,
on the way to the Susten and Gotthard passes (see page 247)

is included and dinner is a mere 15Sfr. Open year-round except for November. ($-$$). ☎ 81-377-1969, fax 81-377-1975.

Naturfreundehaus Medergen is a Swiss mountain hut that is open from June-October, and from December-April. Reservations are required. Mattresses are provided, but bring a sleeping bag anyway. This hut is tricky to find, but the Arosa Tourist Office can help direct you. ($). ☎ 81-377-5215.

Ramozhütte is another mountain hut in a tricky spot and requires a two- to three-hour hike up through a valley south of Arosa. Discounted prices for SAC (Swiss Alpine Club – see page 25) members, but prices start at 24Sfr anyway ($). Reservations are strongly suggested. ☎ 81-252-4820.

The Arosa Youth Hostel has 160 beds and is open January 1-April 21, June 16-October 20, and from December 14-31. ($). Parking available. Hubelstrasse, CH-7050 Arosa. ☎ 81-377-1397, fax 81-377-1621.

Camping Arosa is open year-round in a small valley and offers basic services such as showers. Adults 8Sfr, children ages 6-12 5Sfr, tents 5Sfr. ☎ 81-377-1745, fax 81-377-3005.

■ Where to Eat

Zum Wohl Sein is one of the most famous eating establishments in Arosa and literally means "to your health." It has room for only 20 diners at a time, and owner/chef Beat Carduff prepares a seven-course meal that changes every night (Wednesday-Saturday). The décor is lovely, the wine list exhaustive, and the food outstanding. You've got to come here at least once in your lifetime. Reserva-

DINING PRICE CHART	
Prices based on a typical entrée, per person, and do not include beverage.	
$	15-25Sfr ($10-$16)
$$	26-45Sfr ($17-$29)
$$$	46-70Sfr ($30-$47)
$$$$	71Sfr+ ($47+)

tions required. ($$$$). Closed April 15-December 5. Located in Hotel Anita, Hohepromenade, CH-7050 Arosa. ☎ 81-377-1199, fax 81-377-3618.

The Weisshorngipfel provides light, exquisite fare cooked by owners Agi and Hans Tobler at the top of the Weisshorn. A beautiful outdoor seating terrace gives the visitor a great view of the area. Open November 30-April 22. ☎ 81-378-8402.

The Brüggerstuba is between the base and the top terminal of the cable railway to the Weisshorn. Delicious pastas and spirits by Urs Amstad and Christina Tschudi.. Open November 30-April 22. ☎ 81-378-84-25.

Tschuggernhütte is a cozy place with a huge outdoor terrace, where many families with children hang out. The restaurant includes a "cow's bar" and "Mountain Mac" café for smaller appetites. Run by Alain Balbinot and his team. Open from November 30-April 22. ☎ 81-378-8445.

Orelli's is a family restaurant with a great panoramic view of the area, serving up vegetarian and hearty regional fare. ($). Open daily, 7:30 am-9 pm. Closed May and November. Poststrasse. ☎ 81-377-1208.

Café Kaiser is a great pasta and dessert joint just south of Orelli's on Poststrasse. ($). ☎ 81-377-3454.

Davos

Davos is often referred to as the Global Village, and as Europe's highest-altitude city, has been a location well-known throughout history. The village originally obtained its freedom from Austria in 1649, then became famous as a place where people came for the treatment of tuberculosis in the 1860s. Robert Louis Stevenson completed his book *Treasure Island* here, and Thomas Mann used the Zauberberg as the setting for his novel *The Magic Mountain*. Arthur Conan Doyle, creator of Sherlock Holmes, skied and stayed in Davos as well. It has been one of Switzerland's hot spots for skiing for over a century. Davos is also well-known for ice skating, hosting the first world figure-skating championships in 1899, as well as European speed skating competitions.

There are two sectors to Davos – **Davos-Platz** and **Davos-Dorf** – which are connected by the Promenade Boulevard. Containing hotels, shops, restaurants and cafés, it stretches for 2½ miles (four km). Originally these were two separate villages, but during the 1970s they were connected and now together form one of the largest ski resort areas in Switzerland. The location of Davos within a high valley protects it from strong winds, which makes it an ideal location for summer and winter sports alike.

■ Information Sources

Tourist Offices

The Davos Tourist Office is at Promenade 67, CH-7270 Davos-Platz. There is also another smaller Tourist Office in Davos-Dorf, across from the train station. Both are open Monday-Friday from 8:30 am-6 pm, Saturdays from 8 am-5 pm. ☎ 81-415-2121, fax 81-415-2100.

Train Station

The Davos train station offer a currency exchange and luggage storage. Davos-Platz station is open Monday-Saturday from 4:50 am-9 pm, Sunday from 5:50 am-9 pm. Davos-Dorf station is open daily from 6:50 am-8 pm, and you can rent bikes here for 28Sfr daily.

Post Office

The main post office is in Davos-Platz at Promenade 43, open Monday-Friday from 7:45 am-6 pm, Saturday from 8 am-noon.

Codes

Davos-Platz **postal code** is CH-7270, Davos-Dorf's **postal code** is CH-7260, and the **area code** (in most cases) is 81.

Internet Access

Get connected at **Expert Roro** in Davos-Dorf for 12Sfr per hour. Open Monday 2-6 pm, Tuesday-Friday from 8:30 am-noon, 2-6:30 pm and Saturday from 8:30 am-noon and 2-5 pm. Promenade 123. ☎ 81-420-1111.

Medical Services

Dial 111 for emergencies.

■ Getting Around

Throughout Davos you'll see yellow and white buses traveling about, making stops at all the major hotels and eateries between Davos-Dorf and Davos-Platz. Buses stop every 10 minutes in the winter time from 7 am-11:20 pm; in the summertime they run every 20 minutes. The fare is 5Sfr. There are lots of lifts, cable cars and gondolas to take you to various ski areas as well. If you're driving, you'll find parking lots everywhere near Promenade, costing 1-2Sfr per hour. You can also park for free at the Kongresszentrum (Meeting Center).

■ Adventures

On Foot

Over 280 miles (450 km) of paths and trails surround Davos, allowing you to explore woods, mountains, streams, and outright gorgeous scenery. Each mountain maintains an open ski lift during the summer, to whisk you away to a desirable starting point.

The Davos Tourist Office can provide you with free maps and sites to visit during your hikes.

HIKING WITHOUT LUGGAGE

Davos, along with Arosa and Lenzerheide-Valbella, have combined to create a "Hiking without Luggage" tour – allowing hikers to wander from point to point without having to drag their luggage along. Four- and seven-day programs allow hikers to have their luggage taken to their next destination, with Davos being the most popular home base. Prices range from 270 to 525Sfr, and children ages 12-16 get a 30% discount, while those aged six-12 get a 50% discount. Kids under six-years-old are free. Hiking maps, breakfast, luggage transfers, and railway transfers are all included in the packages. For beginners, we suggest taking the route from Arosa to Davos, via Sapün. If you're an experienced hiker, you could opt for the more difficult route via Tritt. Both paths eventually lead to the Strela Pass, where you can either keep walking to Davos or take the railway down. Contact the Davos Tourist Office at ☎ 81-415-2121 for information.

The **Dürrboden-Fuorclas da Grialetsch Pass** is also a popular hike for tourists and the Swiss often come here with their families as well. At just five miles (eight km), it is a fairly easy hike and can take five hours or more, depending on how much you like to stop and take in the scenery, which at times is breathtaking. Buses leave four times a day for the nine-mile ride from Davos to the popular base parking lot/restaurant at Dürrboden. This trail is easy to follow and actually gets easier the higher you climb. You'll pass the Schwarhorn and the Radüner Rothorn early on in your jaunt before the trail veers to the left. Next, you'll come to the Furkasee, a small lake before the Fuorcla da Grialetsch Pass at 8,321 feet (2,537 m). Here you'll also find the **Grialetsch Hütte** and see the Vadret da Grialetsch glacier, on your right in the distance. The trail then splits into three sub-trails, which will eventually lead to a road where you can easily hail a bus back to Davos. However, it is much easier to just retrace your steps.

Another popular five-mile hike takes you from Davos-Platz to **Monstein**. From Davos-Platz, take bus #8 to the Sertig-Dörfli stop and follow the signs to the Fenezfurgga. This hike will also lead you past a waterfall and into a valley dividing the Hoch Duncan and the Alpihorn, before reaching Monstein. Here you can take a bus back to Davos or simply follow the trail back.

The **Panoramaweg** is a very easy level trail for almost any hiker and provides great views of the southern Alps. To begin, you can take the Panoramaweg stop on the **Parsenbahn**, which departs from near the Davos-Dorf station. The Parsenbahn is the highest funicular railway (8,731 feet, 2,662 m) in Switzerland. This walk will take about two hours.

The **Davos Tennis & Squash Center** has both indoor and outdoor courts and is open daily from 8 am-10 pm. Court rental is 26Sfr. In Davos-Platz at Clavadelerstrasse. ☎ 81-413-3131.

Golf Club Davos provides golfing at its finest, with full rental options. Green fees with a golf cart are 80-100Sfr, and clubs can be rented for 30Sfr. ☎ 81-416-5634.

On Water

Swimming

This is available in both the summer and winter at **Hawlbad**. Sauna facilities are also available and prices range from 6.5-13Sfr. Promenade. ☎ 81-413-6463.

On Snow & Ice

Skiing

Skiing is the main sport in Davos, which includes five large ski areas. **Parsenn-Weissflüh** is considered to be one of the best ski areas in Europe. The Parsennbahn railway will take you from Davos-Dorf to the **Weissflühjoch** at 8,740 feet (2,622 m), which is the entrance to the main ski area. Here you'll find all types of slopes and runs for any level of skier. You can take a cable car up to **Weissflühgipfl** at 9,260 feet (2,778 m), where more advanced skiers will try the northern Kublis run. **Parsenn** has long runs and scary vertical drops for intermediate and advanced skiers, while the **Jacobshorn** is more for beginners and for those who enjoy snowboarding.

Ski passes are available with many options. The **Davos/Klosters R.E.G.A. Ski Pass** includes access to five different ski regions within both Davos and Klosters, who share 200 miles (322 km) of snow and ski runs, with varied types of cable cars, railways, ski lifts and chairs, and gondolas. Prices range from 125Sfr for a two-day pass to 320Sfr for a seven-day pass. Children from six to 16 usually get a 35-40% reduced rate, while kids under five ride for free. **Cross-country skiers** will find 47 miles (76 km) of trails throughout Davos, including a night-lit trail.

The Swiss Ski School of Davos offers lessons for individuals and groups starting at 35Sfr. Promenade 157. ☎ 81-416-2454.

Skating

Ice skating takes place in Davos-Platz, on the largest natural ice rink in Europe, the **Natureisbahn.** The Davos Tourist Office manages the ice rink, which is usually open from December to February. There is also a huge man-made ice rink, and a few other smaller rinks throughout Davos-Platz. These are generally open daily from 10 am-4 pm, with admission prices of 5-10Sfr.

The **Davos Curling Club** provides two hours of instruction for 40Sfr. Promenade 46, Davos-Platz. ☎ 79-610-2454.

In the Air

The **Delta Flying School**, run by Hans Guler, offers instruction in hangliding for 100-150Sfr. CH-7270 Davos-Platz. ☎ 81-413-6043 or 79-357-2050, www.davos-sport.ch.

■ Landmarks & Historic Sites

Church of St. John the Baptist was first built in 1280, and then restored in 1481. You can find it at the east end of the train station in Davos-Platz on the Talstrasse. The **Rathaus** is attached to the church and dates from 1564. The **Church of St. Theodulus** is a 14th-century structure found in Davos-Dorf.

■ Museums

Davos Kirchner Museum features the work of artist Ernst Ludwig Kirchner, a German citizen who is known as the co-founder of the expressionist group "Die Brucke." Kirchner lived in Davos and later committed suicide. His work is known for its tension, sharp contrasting colors, and eroticism. 8Sfr for adults and 6Sfr for children, open from Christmas-Easter and mid-July to September, Tuesday-Sunday from 10 am-6 pm. Open the rest of the year from 2-6 pm, Tuesday-Sunday. Located at the Ernst Ludwig Kirchner Platz, Davos. ☎ 81-413-2202.

Heimatmuseum provides visitors with a history of Davos through special exhibitions and artifacts. Open June-October on Wednesday, Friday and Sunday from 4-6 pm. Located inside the **Altes Pfründhaus** at Museumstrasse 1. Adults 5Sfr, children 2Sfr. ☎ 81-416-2666.

■ Shopping

In Davos, shopping revolves around sports clothing and equipment, rather than Swiss souvenirs, although there are plenty of those to be found as well. All you have to do is stroll up and down the Promenade, and you'll find everything from chocolate to skis to oil paintings and watches. **Ettinger Sport** at Promenade 1053 is one of Davos-Dorf's best sports shop, ☎ 81-410-1212, while **Angerer Sport** on Promenade 49 in Davos-Platz is also good. ☎ 81-413-6672.

■ Where to Stay

Steigenberger Belvédère was built in 1875 and is one of the most famous resort hotels in the world. The inside is breathtakingly beautiful, with wood-carvings, fireplaces, beamed ceilings and gorgeous furniture. Closed from April 10-August

27 and from October 15-November 24. There are two restaurants, bar, sauna, swimming pool, tennis courts, babysitting services. Breakfast is included. ($$$$). Promenade 89, CH-7270 Davos-Platz. ☎ 800-223-5652 in the USA & Canada, ☎ 81-415-6000, fax 81-415-6001, www.steigenberger.ch.

HOTEL PRICE CHART	
$	30-75Sfr ($20-$49)
$$	76-205Sfr ($50-$109)
$$$	206-299Sfr ($110-$200)
$$$$	300Sfr+ ($200+)

Flüela Hotel has been operated by the Gredig family for over 100 years, and is elegant, stately and very comfortable. It's quiet and a great place for relaxation, with two restaurants, bar, sauna, Turkish bath and babysitting services. Closed April and May and October 7-November 24. ($$$$). Bahnhoffstasse 5, CH-7260 Davos-Dorf. ☎ 81-410-1717, 81-410-1718, www.fluela.ch.

Hotel Europe is right in the center of Davos-Platz, near the tourist office, the ice rink, a golf course and the Schatzalp-Strela funicular. Built in 1868, it is one of the oldest hotels in Davos, adorned with hunting trophies inside, and has spectacular views from the south-facing balconies. Three restaurants, three bars, tennis courts, swimming pool, fitness room, sauna, babysitting services. Breakfast included. ($$$-$$$$). Promenade 63, CH-7270 Davos-Platz. ☎ 81-413-5921, 81-413-1393.

Parsenn Sporthotel sits across the street from the Parsennbahn, near several ski lifts. Built in 1907, and renovated since then, it is the epitome of a Graubünden chalet on the exterior. Comfortable and cozy rooms with an in-house restaurant and bar. Closed Easter to early December. ($$-$$$$). Promenade 152, CH-7260 Davos-Dorf. ☎ 81-416-3232, fax 81-416-3867.

Zur Alte Post is pretty in pink and once served as the town's post office in the late 1600s. All of the 20 rooms are small but lovely and cozy, especially those that overlook the mountains. The hotel bar is a hangout favored by the locals, and the oldest of the inn's three antique dining rooms – Tavaasar Schtuba, featuring 16th-century woodwork – is open only during the winter months. Closed May, June, November. ($$-$$$$). Berlistutz 4, CH-7270 Davos-Platz. ☎ 81-413-5402, fax 81-413-5403.

Hotel Ochsen was built in 1900 and is close to the Jakobshorn cable car lift. It is clean, convenient, and well-kept, with large rooms, a restaurant and a bar. Great views of the Jakobshorn from the upper rooms. ($$-$$$$). Talstrasse 10, CH-7270 Davos-Platz. ☎ 81-413-5222, fax 81-413-7671.

Jacobshorn Ski Mountain Lodges. Three lodges catering to the young on this mountain offer rooms with ski lift packages (good only for this mountain). ($$-$$$$). Open November-May. Breakfast included. Prices for ski packages range from 110Sfr for a one-day, two-night stay to 600Sfr for a six-night, seven-day package. ☎ 81-414-9020, fax 81-414-9102 for reservations at all three lodges; www.fun-mountain.ch.

- **Bolgenschanze** is for those who want to ski all day and party all night. Located over a bar, with breakfast and dinner included. You must be at least 18 to stay here. Skistrasse 1.

- **Guest House Bolgenhof** is for those who want to relax, not party, after a day on the slopes. Breakfast and dinner included. Located above the Davos-Platz train station on Brämabüelstrasse.

- **Snowboarder's Palace** looks like a ski-lodge should look, and is right above the Davos-Platz Tourist Office on Oberestrasse 45-47.

Great Value: Just three miles (4.8 km) from Davos center is **Davos-Laret**, on the highway between Davos and Klosters. Here you'll find a terrific little hotel and restaurant with great rates and free transportation service to the Davos ski lifts in wintertime. **Hübli's Landhaus** provides 20 rooms, 14 with bathrooms, some of which are connected to the excellent restaurant via a tunnel. The restaurant enjoys one of the finest reputations throughout Switzerland. It was originally built over 100 years ago as a post office relay station. Owners Felix and Anne-Marie Hübli offer diners regional fare, which varies in accordance with the season. Very cozy, unique and relatively inexpensive. ($$-$$$). Reservations for rooms or dinner strongly recommended. To get there, drive two miles (3.2 km) north on Route 28, toward Klosters. Located on Kantonsstrasse, CH-7265 Davos-Laret. ☎ 81-417-1010, fax 81-417-1011.

Hotel Montana is a bit tattered inside, but provides decent lodgings year-round, and is right next to the train station in Davos-Dorf. ($-$$). Bahnofstrasse. ☎ 81-420-1880, fax 81-42-1881.

The Davos Youth Hostel Albula has 146 beds and is open year-round. Horlaubenstrasse 27, CH-7270, Davos Dorf. ($-$$). ☎ 81-360-1441, fax 81-360-1438, www.youthhostel.ch/davos.

Camping

There are two nice campgrounds in the Davos area. **TCS Camping and Caravan Färich** is near and divided by the Flüelabach creek in the midst of a thick forest of conifers. It offers 100 campsites, with all the modern conveniences, including washers and dryers, a kiosk and a restaurant. Open May-September and on request. Cost is 25-35Sfr per person. Sandstrasse 1, CH-7260 Davos Dorf. ☎ 81-416-1043, fax 81-420-1044.

Caravan and Mobilhome Rinerlodge has 30 sites for 26-32Sfr per person and is near the Rinerhorn Valley train station. There is also a bed and breakfast. Open June-October, and December-April. Operated by Ruedi Buhlmann. Bergbahnen Rinerhorn AG, CH-7277 Davos Glaris. ☎ 81-401-1252, fax 81-401-1314, www.rinerhorn.ch.

■ Where to Eat

Hübli's Landhaus (see previous page).

Dining at **Bünderstübli** is kind of like sitting down for lunch at a Swiss farmer's home. Large portions of hearty food in a rustic setting allow a visitor to feel right at home. Local fare is the specialty, including lots of differnt potato dishes. Just a really nice casual place to dine. You can order off the menu or request a four-course fixed dinner for 85Sfr. Reservations required. ($-$$$). Open Tuesday-Sunday from 11:30 am-2 pm, 5-11 pm. Closed May, June and November. Dischmastrasse 8, Davos-Dorf. ☎ 81-416-3393.

DINING PRICE CHART	
Prices based on a typical entrée, per person, and do not include beverage.	
$	15-25Sfr ($10-$16)
$$	26-45Sfr ($17-$29)
$$$	46-70Sfr ($30-$47)
$$$$	71Sfr+ ($47+)

The Vinikus is a very formal restaurant run by the cook David and wife/host Jutte Kempf. The food is excellent, and while dining you are able to view the main street of Davos and the mountains surrounding it. Specialties include homemade pastas and vegetarian dishes and rösti, as well as traditional Swiss meats dishes containing venison, steak, and veal. A very clean and proper atmosphere. Reservations required ($$-$$$$). Open Wednesday-Sunday from 11 am-2 pm and from 6-11 pm. Closed May, June. Promenade 119, Davos-Platz. ☎ 81-416-5979.

Bistro Gentiana et Café de Artistes is known for its 10 different types of fondue and for an unusual assortment of escargot dishes. Daily specials abound, including rich desserts and traditional Swiss fare such as dried beef. Reservations required ($-$$$). Open daily 11 am-11 pm. Closed Wednesday in the summer. Promenade 53, Davos-Platz. ☎ 81-413-4921.

At the **Röstizzeria** the décor is Japanese, but the food is definitely Swiss, specializing in Rösti and pizzas. ($-$$). Open daily 6-11 pm. Promenade 128 in Davos-Dorf. ☎ 81-416-3323.

Café Carlos serves up hamburgers, sandwiches and American dishes at inexpensive prices. ($). Open Tuesday-Saturday 10 am-3 am. Promenade 58, Davos-Platz. ☎ 81-413-1722.

Klosters

Founded in 1222, this 4,000-foot-high (1,219 m) **Prattigau Valley** village offers a quiet respite to Davos and St. Moritz. Where those two towns are sophisticated and cosmopoloan, Klosters is rural and down-to-earth. Only eight miles (13 km) north of Davos, Klosters has retained its Swiss charm by keeping its chalets intact. You'll see very few of the high-rise hotels here that have become commonplace in St. Moritz and Davos. The late Princess Diana visited here often, as do many Hollywood celebrities. Many of the streets here aren't well-marked, but it is fairly easy to get around on foot.

■ Information Sources

Tourist Office

 The Klosters Tourist Board is in the center of town and is open Monday-Saturday from 8:30 am-6 pm and on Sundays from 9:30-6:30 pm. Alte Bahnhofstrasse 6, CH-7250 Klosters, ☎ 81-410-2020, fax 81-410-2010, www.klosters.ch. They can provide you with maps, current weather conditions, and brochures on all of the snowboarding, skiing, and hiking areas nearby, and they can also give you a list of hotels.

Train Station

 There are two stations in Klosters – in **Klosters-Platz**, where most of the city action takes place, and in **Klosters-Dorf**, which is also home to the ski school and to a small neighborhood of locals, many of whom work at one of the resorts in the area. Klosters-Platz station has a currency exchange (open 6 am-8:30 pm daily), lockers (2Sfr), luggage storage (5Sfr daily) and scooter rental (19Sfr daily). For bike rentals, go to **Andrist Sport** at Gotschnastrasse. They rent bikes for 38Sfr daily, or 130Sfr per week. Open Monday-Friday, 8 am-noon, 2-6:30 pm, Saturdays 2-4 pm.

Post Office

 Klosters-Platz post office is at Bahnhofstrasse, CH-7250 Klosters. Open Monday-Friday, from 7:30 am-noon, 1:45-6:15 pm, Saturday from 8:30-noon. ☎ 81-422-1410, fax 81-422-3880. Klosters-Dorf Post Office is at Landstrasse, CH-7250 Klosters. Open Monday-Friday, 8 am-11 am, and 3-6 pm, Saturday from 8:30-11 am. ☎ 81-422-1430, fax 81-422-4095. Both are closed Sundays.

Codes

The **postal code** for Klosters-Platz is CH-7250, and 7252 for Klosters-Dorf. The **area code** for both is 81.

Internet Access

Internet services can be had at **Silyretta Parkhotel**, ☎ 81-423-3435 or at **Wunderlin Sport**, ☎ 81-422-1770.

■ Getting Around

The bus service in Klosters is excellent. It runs from the train station at Klosters-Dorf, to the ski lifts, and back again through town. Klosters is 27 miles (43 km) east of Chur and, if you're driving, you'll take Highway #3 to Lanquart, then head south on Route 28.

■ Adventures

On Foot

Winter Hiking Treks

Klosters offers 16 miles (26 km) of winter walking trails for visitors. Here are some of the most popular ones: **Klosters-Monbiel-Alp Garfiun** is an easy, 4.2-mile walk (7.2 km) that starts at the Sports Center parking lot. Follow the footpath along the Landquart River to the village of **Monbiel**. You can either re-trace your steps, catch a bus back to Klosters, or you can continue on for another two miles (3.5 km) to **Alp Garfiun**. Walk to Monbieler Schwendi or alongside the road to Alp Garfiun, where you'll find the tiny Garfiun alpine cabin for a soda or light meal.

From the top of the **Madrisa** area you have a choice of two fine winter walks. The easiest is to follow a well-marked trail which will take you 1½ miles (2.4 km) round-trip to the **Mässplatte**, where you'll get a great panoramic view of the **Prättigau Valley**. The other trail will lead you over a high-altitude path to the **Saaser Alp** and on to the **Zügenhüttli.** This 3.1-mile (5 km) trail has you climbing 1,344 feet (410 m) in altitude during a walk which should take two hours or less to complete. To get to Madrisa, take the **Madrisabahn** from Klosters-Dorf.

Klosters Tourism also offers a **Klosters Adventure Program** where visitors can experience a wide variety of adventure tours, such as mountain biking, glacier walks and canoe trips. Weekdays from mid-June to mid-October. ☎ 81-325-2444.

Canton Graubünden

Snowshoeing treks are available in Klosters with an experienced guide from the **Swiss Ski & Snowboard School Klosters** (above) at ☎ 81-410-2828. Treks range from daily to weekly, or the popular full-moon treks. There's a four-person minimum; rates start at 50Sfr for the night treks, and include snowshoe rental. Full-day, half-day and weekly trek rates available upon request.

On Snow & Ice

Skiing

Skiing is the main reason folks flock here: Klosters shares six ski areas with Davos for a total of 190 miles (300 km) of runs for skiers of all levels. The **Gotschna-Parsenn-Schatzalp-Strela** area has 26 ski lifts. Here you can also rent a toboggan at the Gotschna station to try the 2.1-mile toboggan run halfway up the mountain. One of the best runs begins at Parsenn and follows a well-groomed trail through snowfields, then dips into the forest, through vast pastures and into the town of Kublis. Here, after their seven-mile run, skiers stop for a hot drink at the train station while waiting to take the train back to Klosters.

The **Madrisa** skiing area has eight lifts with 29 miles (47 km) of runs, and is also a great site for families with kids. For nighttime skiers, the **Selfranga** lift is open every Friday night from 8-10 pm for 8Sfr.

There are many public and private ski schools in Klosters. The **Swiss Ski & Snowboard School Klosters** offers individual and private lessons for first-timers. Bahnhofstrasse 4, CH-7250 Klosters. ☎ 81-410-2828, fax 81-410-2829. The **Swiss Ski & Snowboard School Saas** offers instruction in both disciplines at Landstrasse 15, CH-7252 Klosters-Dorf. ☎ 818-420-2233, fax 81-420-2230. **Boardriding Freeridecamps/Guiding** offers instruction and guided tours in snowboarding at Lehenweg 24, CH-7250 Klosters-Platz. ☎ 81-420-2662, fax 81-420-2660.

If it's **cross-country skiing** you're interested in, then check out the folks at the **Nordic Skischool Klosters**, in Bardill Sport AG, at Landstrasse 185, CH-7250 Klosters-Platz. ☎ 81-422-1040, fax 81-422-5587. For trail condition updates, ☎ 81-415-2133 or 81-410-2020

Ice Sports

Ice hockey, **skating** and **curling** are available at the **Klosters Sports Center**. You can rent ice skates here. The Center is open late October through mid-March, with weekly free classes for curling and ice hockey. It is open Friday evenings for a night skate. Rink time costs 2-4Sfr for skating, and 20Sfr per hour for hockey practice. Call ☎ 81-410-2131 for information regarding skating and curling, or for hockey practice rink availability. Skate rental costs 5Sfr, slider rental 5Sfr, and hockey stick rental 7Sfr.

In the Air

 Hangliding is quite popular here, and in Klosters you can learn to glide safely at the **Grischa Flying School**, with rates starting at 90Sfr for a trial day, and up to 150Sfr for a passenger flight. Contact Stefan Holenstein, CH-7250 Klosters-Platz. ☎ 81-422-2070 or 79-336-1919.

On Horseback

 Horseback riding and sleigh rides are available in Klosters. Packages include riding and skiing holidays for youngsters and adults alike. There are also daily guided treks to Alp Garfiun and the Schifer mountain resort. Reservations required. Contact Jörg Marugg-Waldburger, CH-7252 Klosters-Dorf. ☎ 81-422-14634 or 79-409-7493. Horse-drawn sleigh rides are provided by local farmers – family Flütsch at ☎ 81-422-1873 or 79-405-9029; Johannes Marugg at ☎ 81-422-2429 or 79-611-4287; Rudolph Roffler at ☎ 81-422-1566.

■ Shopping

 You'll find a lot of sport shops here, catering to skiers and hikers mostly. In **Klosters-Platz** try **Gotschna-Sport** at Alte Bahnhofstrasse, ☎ 81-422-1197 – they carry nearly everything you'll need to wander or hike. So will **Bardill Sport** at Landstrasse 185, ☎ 81-422-1040. Also check out **Wunderlin Sport** at Landstrasse 201, ☎ 81-422-1270, for hiking gear, and **H. Obrist** at Doggilochstrasse 31 for biking needs, ☎ 81-422-1212. In **Klosters-Dorf** there's **Albeina Sport**, at Landstrasse 26, ☎ 81-422-3959, for skiing and hiking stuff, and the **Laser Bike Shop** at Bahnhofplatz, ☎ 81-422-3942.

■ Where to Stay

Hotels

 Romantik Hotel Chesa Grischuna and its **Chalet Grischuna** is just as well-known for its excellent restaurant as it is for its hotel. Located in the center of Klosters-Platz, it has antique furniture, wooden ceiling beams and sloping floors. Owned by the Guler

HOTEL PRICE CHART	
$	30-75Sfr ($20-$49)
$$	76-205Sfr ($50-$109)
$$$	206-299Sfr ($110-$200)
$$$$	300Sfr+ ($200+)

family and run with a real homey atmosphere and caring attention to the details of its clients. Closed mid-October to mid-December, and from the end of May to mid-July. ($$$-$$$$). Bahnhofstrasse 12, CH-7250 Klosters-Platz. ☎ 81-422-2222, fax 81-422-2225.

Piz Buin Hotel is a chalet of the highest order and one of the most elegant in Klosters. Smack in the middle of the village, this hotel is close to the skiing and hiking areas of Parsenn. Rooms are rented by the week in the winter. With restaurant, bar, swimming pool, fitness room, sauna, massage. ($$$$). Closed mid-April to late June, mid-October to early December. Alte Bahnhofstrasse 1, CH-7250 Klosters. ☎ 81-423-3333, fax 81-423-3334.

Hotel Pardenn is an elegant resort that blends traditional Swiss hospitality and modern charm in a beautiful setting. You'll find something for everyone here. Two restaurants, bar, swimming pool, fitness room, sauna, massage. ($$$$). Closed early April to late June, mid-September to mid-December. Monbielerstrasse CH-7250 Klosters-Platz. ☎ 81-422-1141, fax 81-422-4006.

Hotel Albeinia is a beautiful Swiss chalet situated in a prime spot in Klosters-Dorf, designed in the original rustic style of the Graubünden canton, allowing for undisturbed views of the surrounding mountain countryside. Only a three-minute walk from the train station, with free bus service to various ski centers in the winter. Beautifully decorated with three restaurants and a bar. ($$-$$$). CH-7252 Klosteres-Dorf. ☎ 81-423-2100, fax 81-423-2121.

Bad Serneus Kur and Sporthotel is 3½ miles (5.6 km) north and downhill from Klosters in the suburb of Bad Serneus. It offers a cozy, clean setting at inexpensive prices. You can ski here from Klosters if you like, and in summer there are plenty of places to hike nearby. A good value for your buck. Restaurant, sauna, swimming pool and massage. Closed early April to mid-May, and from late October to late December. ($$$). CH-7250 Klosters. ☎ 81-422-1444, fax 81-42-2251.

Hotel Rustico is over 100 years old and right in the center of Klosters-Platz. The staff is personable and helpful, complementing the homey atmosphere. The cozy rooms have all modern conveniences. Weekly reservations are required from early to mid-December, early to late January, and mid-March to early April. The hotel also offers ski packages that include lift passes, ski rental and instruction. The restaurant is excellent, and breakfast is included. ($$-$$$). Closed June, November. CH-7250 Klosters-Platz. ☎ 81-422-1212, fax 81-422-5355.

The **Jugendberge Soldanella** is a beautiful chalet where guests are treated like family. Only a 10-minute walk from the Klosters-Platz train station, this hostel offers a serene reading room and a stone terrace with great views of the Madrisa. Rooms for singles and families, with 84 beds. ($-$$). Reception is open from 7-10 am, 5-10 pm. Closed Easter to early July and from mid-October to mid-December. Talstrasse 73. ☎ 81-422-1316, fax 81-422-5209, www.youthhostel.ch/klosters.

Schweizerhaus is a clean and cozy place to rest your head that is close to the Klosters-Dorf train station and to the Madrisa ski lift. ($-$$). Closed May, June, November. ☎ 81-422-1481.

Mountain Huts

The mountain hut **Silverttahütte** has 85 spots to bunk down, and is open March to April and from July to October. From Klosters, take the bus to Monbiel and walk to Alop Sardasca up to Galtürtälli, about a five-hour trek. For reservations contact Philip Werlen and Gerlinde Haas, Bova CH-7432 Zillis ☎ 81-630-7007, 79-628-4841 or 81-422-1306, www.sac-stgallen.ch.

Fergenhütte is another smaller mountain hut offering 24 beds. It can be found high about Praettigau in the Kloster Alps, on the south slope of the Fergenhorn. Start at Monbiel and from here walk to Saljan or Obergarfiun and the hut. A good two- to three-hour walk, popular with families. Contact Seraina and Norbert Gruber-Strecher for reservations. Aeujerstrasse 15, CH-7250 Klosters-Platz. ☎ 81-422-5488, fax 81-413-4962.

■ Where to Eat

Chesa Grischuna is probably the finest restaurant in Klosters, with a gourmet menu sure to delight any diner. Reservations required. Closed mid-October to mid-December, and from the end of May to mid-July. ($$-$$$$). Bahnhofstrasse 12, CH-7250 Klosters-Platz. ☎ 81-422-2222, fax 81-422-2225.

DINING PRICE CHART	
Prices based on a typical entrée, per person, and do not include beverage.	
$	15-25Sfr ($10-$16)
$$	26-45Sfr ($17-$29)
$$$	46-70Sfr ($30-$47)
$$$$	71Sfr+ ($47+)

Walserstube is an old farmhouse, set in traditional Graubünden style, and right in the middle of Klosters-Platz. Over the years it has played host to a long-list of who's-who, including Prince Andrew and the Hollywood A-list. Fish, Scottish lamb, lobster, duck and fresh greens are generously prepared and presented in this gourmet setting. It's *the* place to be in town for food and people watching. ($$-$$$$). Reservations required in the high season. Open daily from 11:30 am-2 pm, 6-11 pm. Closed late April to mid-June, late October to early December. Located in the Walserhof Hotel, CH-7250 Klosters-Platz. ☎ 81-410-2929, fax 81-710-2939.

Hotel Sport Klosters offers three unique dining areas sure to please any taste. The **Bünderstübli** provides a romantic, cozy setting featuring local specialties, including fish and meat fondues, complemented by an extensive fine wine list. Reasonable prices ($$) and hearty fare. The **Panorama room** offers seating for small and large groups in a more formal setting and buffets are served here in the winter, allowing a great view of the surrounding landscape. ($$-$$$). The **Panorama Terrace** has great views for lunch, overlooking a children's zoo and playground, with the Alps in the background. ($-$$). Landstrasse, CH-7250 Klosters-Platz. ☎ 81-423-3030, fax 81-423-3040.

Chesa Selfranga is a reasonably priced, family-friendly restaurant with a cozy attitude, specializing in fondue, calf's liver, rosti, and other Swiss traditions. Reservations strongly suggested. ($$). Selfrangastrasse 40, CH-7250 Klosters-Platz. ☎ 81-422-1255.

Albeina Dorfstube has a sunny terrace for breakfasts, lunch and fine dinners, featuring Swiss regional fare and a nice salad bar. The attached **Dörfji Bar** features live music during the week, and **Alberto's Pizzeria** – at the valley station of the Madrisa Mountain Cableway – serves excellent pizzas. ($-$$$). Located in the Hotel Albeina, CH-7252 Klosters-Dorf. ☎ 81-423-2100, fax 81-423-2121.

Berghaus Erika provides diners with a simple setting in classic Swiss style. Simple and hearty regional dishes are served here. ($-$$). Schlappin CH-7252 Klosters-Dorf. ☎ 81-422-1117.

Gasthaus Casann offers traditional Swiss food at inexpensive prices. Open Monday-Friday from 8 am-12:30 pm, Saturdays 8 am-6 pm. Closed November ($). Landstrasse 171, Klosters-Dorf. ☎ 81-422-1229, fax 81-422-6278.

St. Moritz

This is perhaps the best-known resort in the world, catering to the "50 and over" crowd, and globe-trotting jet setters. That's not to say that younger people can't or don't visit St. Moritz – they do – but just not to the extent that older tourists do. Fashion, nightlife, restaurants, bars, fine boutiques, sports, health spas and more are all to be found in St. Moritz. The list of things to do is endless and could fill an entire guidebook.

The village is actually made up of two separate sections connected by a single thoroughfare – Via dal Bagn – **St. Moritz Dorf** (containing all the hotels, restaurants, shops, etc.) and **St. Moritz Bad** (the less hectic area on the southwest side of the lakeshore). St. Moritz is at the upper end of the valley known as **Engadina**. Meaning "The valley of the river Inn," Engadina is a region in Graubünden whose river has its sources beginning in the north-south mountain passes of Maloja. The sun shines an average of 322 days per year in St. Moritz, which sits at 5,823 feet elevation (1,775 m). The weather here is very dry, but never hot, due to the high elevation. In addition to snow sports and summer hiking, St. Moritz is also a cultural haven, with many artistic venues sponsoring gallery exhibitions in the summertime. The orchestra performs free concerts throughout the summer at the Bädersall or in the park.

■ Information Sources

Tourist Office

The St. Moritz Tourist Office is at Via Maistra 12, and is open Monday-Saturday from 8 am-6 pm, Sunday from 4-6 pm during the high season, and Monday-Friday from 9 am-noon, 2-6 pm, Saturday from 9 am-1 pm in the off-season. ☎ 81-837-3333, fax 81-837-3366, www.stmoritz.ch. The Tourist Office also offers **taxi** service from their location.

Train Station

St. Moritz is 46 miles (74 km) southeast of Chur, and 50 miles (80 km) south of Davos, easily reached by trains via Chur, which takes about two hours. For rail information, ☎ 900-300-300.

Post Offices

The St. Moritz post office is at Via Serlas 23 and is open from 7:45 am-noon, and from 1:45-6:15 pm Monday-Friday, and on Saturdays from 8:30-noon. ☎ 81-833-0388, fax 81-837-6790. The St. Moritz Bad post office is at via Rosatsch 12 and is open from 8:30-11 am, 1:45-6 pm Monday-Friday, Saturdays from 8:30 am-noon. ☎ 81-833-3093, fax 81-833-9218.

Codes

The **postal code** for St. Moritz and St. Moritz Bad is CH-7500; the **area code** is 81.

Internet Access

Check out **Bobby's American Pub** (20Sfr per hour). You can also access the Internet for free at the post office, but there is usually a very long wait.

Medical Services

Phone 911 for emergencies. The **Galerie Apotheke** is the local pharmacy, at Via de Bagn. Open Monday-Friday, from 8 am-noon, 2-6:30 pm and on Saturdays from 8 am-noon, 2-5 pm. ☎ 81-833-7292.

■ Getting Around

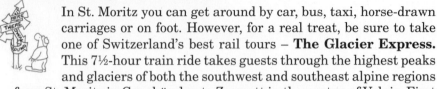

In St. Moritz you can get around by car, bus, taxi, horse-drawn carriages or on foot. However, for a real treat, be sure to take one of Switzerland's best rail tours – **The Glacier Express.** This 7½-hour train ride takes guests through the highest peaks and glaciers of both the southwest and southeast alpine regions – from St. Moritz in Graubünden to Zermatt in the canton of Valais. First opened in 1928, the Glacier Express tunnels through the eight-mile-long Furka mountain at one point, and also traverses 291 bridges and 91 viaducts on its journey. Reservations are strongly suggested and required for the restaurant cars. Fares start at 150Sfr for second class and 240Sfr for first class; however those holding a Swiss Rail Pass will have their fare covered in full. Eurailpass holders will be responsible for half-price fares in both classes. ☎ 81-833-5912 or contact the Swiss National Tourist Office at ☎ 212-757-5944.

■ Adventures

On Foot

Hiking

Piz Nair offers great views of the Upper Engadina valley and lakes. Take the funicular to **Corviglia** and then a cable car to the top. From here, you can walk to the summit. You can also take a 3½-hour walk that will bring you back to St. Moritz-Dorf. From Piz Nair, follow the path downward to **Survetta Pass** (8,578 feet, 2,625 m). Here, the trail will veer to the left and you'll come to the Lac Survetta, a good spot for a rest and a picnic. Continue down, walking parallel to a stream through pastures and lovely Alpine fields. The stream soon turns into a waterfall, and just past this spot the trail will veer left again, and

The Roseg Valley, with Piz Roseg

then proceed sharply upward. Soon the trail widens out, allowing great views of the Surlej village, Piz Corvatsch and Lake Silvaplana. The path will lead you back to St. Moritz-Dorf.

From Murtel to Fuorcia Surlej: You can also take a rather easy walk (3½ hours) from the intermediate station of **Murtel** on the way up to Piz Corvatsh. Take the cable car from the base at Fuorcia Surlej to Murtel, and walk to the pass, where you'll get a lovely view of Bernina Massif. From here, you can walk back to Fuorcia Surlej by following a rocky path. You'll be able to see the lakes of St. Mortiz, Silvaplana, Champfer and Sils on your hike.

For a strenuous and popular hike, try walking to the **Chamanna Coaz Refuge** from Fuorcia Surlej; allow yourself at least five hours. The trail is well-marked as it winds around the mountain slope, giving you plenty of great views to take in, including waterfalls, streams and the Piz Roseg. About two hours into your walk you'll come to the Chamanna Coaz Refuge, looking out upon the Roseg and Sella Glaciers. From here, you'll retrace your steps for approximately 15 minutes before you encounter a turn to the right, toward Puntraschigna (Pontresina). This part of the trail is the most difficult, steep and stoney. You'll soon come to Lake Vadret. Follow the stream on down to a small hotel where the trail ends. From here you can take a carriage ride back to Pontresina and then catch the bus back to Fuorcia Surlej or St. Moritz.

Also worth a try is the hike up the Roseg River Valley to the **Tschierva Hütte** and the **Coaz Hütte.** Be prepared – this is an all-day hike or an

Biking near Lake Silvaplana

Canton Graubünden

overnight excursion if you like. You can take a bus to begin the trail at the village of Pontresina. You walk from town, following the signs for Hotel Roseg; you can walk on either the right or left side of the river – both offer easy paths. Just prior to reaching Hotel Roseg, the path veers off to the left toward the Tschierva Hütte. The path remains relatively flat for nearly half a mile, then begins to climb steeply. You'll see the Roseg Glacier, the Tschierva Glacier and Piz Roseg and the Hütte, eventually reached by walking between the lateral moraine and the hillside. At 8,439 feet (2,573 m), the Tschierva Hütte offers hikers a great spot to rest. Meals and dorm rooms are provided on a first-come, first-served basis. You can also climb above the Hütte for even more spectacular views of the area, and here you are sure to see chamois – especially in the evening and early morning hours. From the Tschierva Hütte, you can then walk back down to the Hotel Roseg junction, where you have several options. Here, the trail on the left will take you up to the Coaz Hütte, where you'll get great views of the Roseg Glacier. From there, retrace your steps down until you come to a fork in the road. Walk to the left (the right takes you back to Hotel Roseg) and you'll soon be at Fuorcia Surlej. From here, you can go through the pass and walk the remaining five miles (eight km) back to St. Moritz.

THE IBEX PATH

For another fun way to see Swiss wildlife in action, try the path from **Muottas Muragl to Piz Languard**, a five-mile hike that should take you around eight hours to complete. This is a great way to catch a glimpse of an ibex or two (somewhat similar to a mountain goat). From St. Moritz you can the take the bus to Pontresina and then hike up or take a chairlift to Punt Muragl. From there, you can hike up to the Muottas Muragl, where you pick up the Ibex Path, toward Piz Languard. From the Languard chairlift station follow the path signs saying Piz Languard. The trail climbs a bit before crossing the stream and then entering a nature preserve. A little farther on you'll encounter a fork in the road. Veer left, and you'll finally reach the Berghaus Piz Languard, a 10,699-foot-high hut and restaurant (3,262 m). You can then walk past the hut and on up to the summit, which is another 204 feet (62 m) higher. On your way down, instead of backtracking, consider taking the path to Via da Fain, which eventually leads you to the road south of Pontresina. You can walk back to the village on parallel trails near the road, or catch one of the buses along the way. The best times to view the ibex are August and September. They are protected in Switzerland and are unafraid of humans for the most part.

The Rhaetische Bahn near the Morteratsch station of the Bernina Railway.

The **Morteratsch to Boval Hütte** trail is another fun excursion that begins from Pontresina. Expect to be walking for five hours or so. From Pontresina you can walk or drive five miles (eight km) south to the Morteratsch railroad station. From here, there is parking available for your car since you begin your trek in front of the station, at the gated service road. Stay on this path until the glacier trail veers to the left and walk until you come to the base of the glacier, for some commanding views. From here, retrace your steps until you come back to the original fork in the road, and continue up the main trail. You climb steeply for about half a mile before the path levels out again. The trail continues to climb until it reaches the Boval Hütte at 8,184 feet (2,495 m). Here you can relax with a picnic or get lunch from the hut-keeper, while enjoying views of the Pers and Morteratsch Glacier, among others. You'll also see the Piz Boval (behind the hut), the Piz Bernina, the Piz Bellavista, the Piz Cambrena and Piz Palü.

Other Sports

Tennis and **squash** can be played at the **Corviglia Tennis Center** in St. Moritz-Bad. Here you'll find indoor and outdoor courts. You can rent rackets and balls here, and tennis court costs start at 25Sfr per hour (summer) up to 46Sfr (winter). Squash courts range from 20 to 26Sfr for 45 minutes, depending on the season. ☎ 81-833-1500.

Golf is available at Samedan, 4½ miles (7.2 km) south of St. Moritz in the valley, from late May to early October, 7 am-7 pm, later hours in July and

August. Green fees are 95Sfr per day and you can rent clubs for 35Sfr daily. For information, contact the **Samedan/St. Moritz Golfplatz** at ☎ 81-852-5226.

On Water

Windsurfing has become one of St. Moritz's most popular summer sports. You can rent equipment for 35Sfr for two hours. If you need lessons, they can be had for 265Sfr for 10 sessions. Call the **Windsurfschule St. Moritz** at ☎ 81-828-9229 or 81-833-4449.

The **fishing** season in St. Moritz runs from mid-May to mid-September. You must be 16 or older to purchase the mandatory fishing license, which costs 84Sfr for one day, or 245Sfr for a week on one of the 25 lakes in the region. ☎ 81-833-6752.

On Wheels

St. Moritz is also a great spot for the serious **mountain biker**, with 75 miles (120 km) of bike trails in and around town, plus another 200 miles (354 km) in the surrounding areas. Check out the **Van D'Vina Trail.** Information and maps are available at the Tourist Office.

On Snow

Skiing

In addition to glitter and glamour, skiing is what St. Moritz is all about. As the host of the 2003 Alpine Ski World Championships and the spot for the world's oldest ski school (1927), St. Moritz continues to attract the world's best downhill skiers. The **St. Moritz** and **Suvretta Ski Schools** are both arms of the Swiss Ski School and have more than 300 instructors in the area. ☎ 81-833-8090 in St. Moritz or 81-833-3332 in Suvretta.

There are three basic sectors of the St. Moritz skiing area – **Corviglia, Corvatsch** and **Diavolezza.** St. Moritz is host to the base mountain of Corviglia – to get there you take a funicular from the town center or from **Suvretta** up to the **Piz Nair Massif** (10,029 feet, 2,087 m). The ski area over Piz Nair Massif is a good beginner's mountain – it contains 50 miles (80 km) of pistes and 23 chairlifts. It is often crowded with beginners, however, and those electing to stay at the Suvretta Hotel have their own beginner lift. Corvatsch is on the other side of the valley and can be accessed from **Sils Maria** and **Surlej. Piz Corvatsch** (10,837 feet, 3,303 m) has 40 miles (64 km) of intermediate runs over slightly rougher terrain than Piz Nair. Diavolezza (9,755 feet, 2,978 m) has 30 miles (48 km) of runs for the experienced skier and is accessed by either train or bus. Up here **Piz Lagalb** (9,708 feet, 2,959 m) offers 18 miles (29 km) of pistes

*The Landwasser Viaduct near Filisur
on the Albula rail line*

with the best intermediate skiing to be found in the area. **Muottas Muragli** (8,048 feet, 2,453 m), reached by funicular, has five miles (eight km) of intermediate pistes. All of these slopes provide the charm, atmosphere and sun that you'd expect to find in this Alpine winter paradise. All mountains can be skied via a single lift pass, and prices begin at 58Sfr for a one-day pass. ☎ 81-830-0000, www.skiengadin.ch.

The two most popular areas for **cross-country skiing** around St. Moritz are **Silvaplana** and **Pontresina**, offering 100 miles (161 km) of trails. Group instruction is available on Monday, Wednesday and Friday from 11 am-1 pm, costing 35Sfr for a half-day lesson. You can also take a group trek for 45Sfr. Contact the **Schweizer Langlaufschule St. Moritz** at ☎ 81-833-6233.

Other Winter Sports

Snowboarding is done at Piz Nair at Corviglia. Here you'll find four half-pipes and a trail through a border crossing into Italy.

Try **curling** at the **Al Parc Rink** on Via Maistra. If you want to take lessons, your first 40 minutes are free; after that it will cost 45 Sfr for another 45 minutes. ☎ 81-833-4588 for information.

Bobsledding is available at the **Olympic Bobsled Run**. It's pricey at 200Sfr, but you get a certificate stating you accomplished the task, plus a drink and photo of your excursion. Via Maistra. ☎ 81-830-0200.

St. Moritz's most famous **toboggan** run begins at **Muottas Muragli** – this 2.6-mile (4.2 km) run is accessed by a funicular from Punt Muragl, 2.2 miles (3.5 km) north of St. Moritz. If you're a hard-core tobogganer, you can stay at **Muottas Muragli's Berghotel**, at the start of the run, which has modest rooms with shared baths. ($$-$$$). ☎ 81-842-8232, fax 81-842-8290. **Preda-Bergün** is another famous 3.1-mile (5 km) toboggan run. This one takes you from the Preda station through the **Albula Pass** to Bergün. From here, you can take the RHB train back to the start. This run is open day and night with lighted runs, www.berguen.ch. St. Moritz's **Cresta Run** is meant for pros. You can find information about this scary toboggan run at the Tourist Office.

The abbreviation RHB stands for the Rorschach-Heiden-Bergbahn (Rorschach-Heiden-Mountain train), a rack-railway between the villages of Rorschach and Heiden in the canton of St. Gallen. For the Bergbahn Rheineck-Walzenhausen, with mountain train service between the villages of Rheineck and Walzenhausen, the abbreviation is RhW.

On Horseback

Horseback riding can be done at the **Reithalle** year-round, only a 10-minute walk from the center of St. Moritz. Rides vary from 55Sfr (one-half hour in an arena) to 140 Sfr for a three-hour, half-day tour of the nearby countryside, forest and mountains. Via Ludains 3, St. Moritz.

WHITE TURF

One of St. Moritz's top attractions takes place in February on the St. Moritzersee, when up to 30,000 of the elite, rich and famous congregate to experience horse racing on the "White Turf." Trotters from throughout Europe come together to compete on three consecutive afternoons. Sleigh runners are substituted for the standard bike wheels on the sulkies, allowing these diagonally gaited specialists and their snow-suit-clad drivers to glide over the snow with grace. Thoroughbred races are also held, and the jockeys don ski masks and goggles beneath their helmets, as their mounts kick up clouds of snow. One of the highlights of these competitions is the traditional **Skikjoring** race, where upwards of a dozen horses tow skiers 1.625 miles (2.6 km) for a sought-after trophy. Horse racing was first organized in Switzerland in 1872, and the first races were held on the St. Moritzersee in 1906.

Besides racing amid the spectacular surroundings, fine art and excellent cuisine can be enjoyed on these White Turf days. You can also take a ride in a horse-drawn sleigh, and witness various horse exhibitions in between races. In 2003, for instance, a four-horse Roman battle chariot was galloped past the crowd, and a Hungarian stagecoach pulled by five horses had the driver standing on the backs of the horses, as he guided them in front of the stands at a dead-run.

There are countless gourmet food stands throughout the area during this time. Local hotels also offer up their specialties. Badrutt's Palace Hotel offers Champagne and pasta truffles; Hotel Schweizerhof has tartar and salmon sandwiches; Hotel Steffani serves up Chinese dishes; Hotel Monopol puts forth great-tasting risotto; and Hotel Margna serves traditional Swiss raclette. The Hotel Hauser offers the best-tasting coffee and cakes in town, and the local butcher shop Heuberger sizzles with its grilled sausages. Prices range from inexpensive to outrageous, and there is something for everyone here. Swing, jazz, Caribbean rhythms, pop, and gospel and local groups all perform at various times, on two separate stages.

Temperatures are far below freezing during this time, so the frozen lake is hardy enough to accommodate both the horses and the cars that are parked there. The 100th Anniversary of the White Turf will take place in 2006, so this is something you definitely don't want to miss. Make your reservations way in advance. Seats in the stands range from 15-48Sfr. For reservations, ☎ 848-800-800, or you can reserve online at www.ticketcorner.ch. For further information contact the White Turf Racing Association, Via Mulin 4, CH-7500, St. Moritz. ☎ 81-833-8460, fax 81-833-1062, www.whiteturf.com.

Spas

St. Moritz is also known as a "spa" town – in fact one section is known as **St. Moritz-Bad** (bath). Here you'll find physical therapies, mineral baths, and various other alpine therapies. The **Health Spa Center**, opened in 1976, features carbonic baths, among other hot water treatments, beginning at 35Sfr. If you present proof of payment for one of St. Moritz's hotels, you'll get a substantial discount. ☎ 81-833-3062.

■ Museums

The **Engadine Museum** provides visitors with a history of St. Moritz and the Engadina Valley. Architecture, antiques and regional furniture are featured. (5SFr). Open June to October, Monday-Friday from 9 am-noon, 2-5 pm, Sunday from 10 am-noon. From December to April, Monday-Friday, 10 am-noon, 2-5 pm, Sunday from 10 am-noon. Closed May, November. Via dal Bagn 39. CH-7500 St. Moritz. ☎ 81-833-4333.

Segantini Museum features the works of artist Giovanni Segantini, who lived in Maloja of Engadina during the latter part of the 19th century until his death in 1899. (3-10Sfr). Open Tuesday to Sunday from 10 am-noon, 3-6 pm. Closed late October, November, May.

■ Shopping

You're sure to be overwhelmed by the number of designer boutiques and shops in St. Moritz. International and elegant, there is something for all tastes here, catering to the wealthy and ultra-wealthy. Versace, Prada, Bucherer and the like are found both on the street and in the fancier hotels, along with a wide array of sport shops.

■ Where to Stay

Badrutt's Palace is on a hilltop overlooking St. Moritz in the Rosatch Mountain Range. This is a very elegant and traditional winter and summer resort, opened by the Badrutt family in 1896. It's a good resort for families with children, and has a wide vari-

HOTEL PRICE CHART	
$	30-75Sfr ($20-$49)
$$	76-205Sfr ($50-$109)
$$$	206-299Sfr ($110-$200)
$$$$	300Sfr+ ($200+)

ety of activities, including fishing, horseback riding, sauna, carriage rides, an 18-hole golf course nearby, ice skating, an indoor squash court and 40 miles (64 km) of ski runs. There is also a 2½-mile running path around Lake St. Moritz. There are designer boutiques, gourmet restaurants and a disco. ($$$$). Located at via Chasellas 1, St. Moritz. ☎ 81-837-1000, fax 81-837-2999. Toll-free in the US at 800-223-6800, www.badruttspalace.com.

Kulm Hotel is made up of three buildings constructed in the 18h and 19th centuries. The oldest, built in 1760, was the first building in Switzerland to have electricity (in 1878) and was the site of the 1928 and 1948 Olympics. This is an amazing venue that has huge rooms with marble bathrooms and all amenities, including three restaurants. It is also here that you'll find St. Moritz's curling rinks. ($$$$). Closed mid-April to June and mid-September to mid-December. Via Veglia 18 Dorf, CH-7500 St. Moritz. In the USA & Canada, ☎ 800-223-5695; in Switzerland ☎ 81-836-8000, fax 81-836-8001, www.kulmhotel-stmoritz.ch.

Meierei Landgasthof is across the lake from St. Moritz, and provides a great view of the city. This inn was built in the 17th century for a bishop who owned a farm on the property. Now it has become a popular stop for hikers looking for a hearty meal on the outdoor terrace. Offering just seven rooms, the inn is as well known for its homey atmosphere as for its restaurant, and is only a 20-minute walk from downtown St. Moritz and St. Moritz-Bad. You can get to either locale via paths that wind around the lake. A great out-of-the-way spot. ($$$$). Open December-April and June to October. Via Dimiej 52, CH-7500 St. Moritz. ☎ 81-833-8838 or 81-833-2060.

Carlton Hotel was originally built in 1913 for the last czar of Russia, Nicholas II. Includes every amenity you can think of. It has marble bathrooms and luxurious bedrooms. Need we say more? ($$$$). Closed early April-mid June, mid-September to early December. ☎ 81-836-7000, fax 81-836-7001, www.carlton-stmoritz.ch.

Hotel Eden, an elegant and friendly inn, is in the center of St. Moritz, and is family-owned and -operated. Antiques and wood fixtures are found throughout. Be sure to sample the exquisite breakfast, where the buffet is presented on an antique sleigh. ($$$-$$$$). Open December to mid-April and from mid-June to mid-October. Via Veglia 12, CH-7500 St. Moritz. ☎ 81-833-6161, fax 81-833-9191.

Suvretta House was built in 1912 on a plateau about a mile from the center of St. Moritz. It has a pair of medieval towers that make it hard to miss, and spacious rooms set in classic Alpine style. It offers guests a private ski lift and has a feel of isolation that you can't find in the city center. A good value by St. Moritz standards. ($$$-$$$$). Closed from early April to late June and early September to mid-December. Two restaurants, two bars, swimming pool, golf, tennis courts, sauna, ice rink, playground, massage, babysitting. Via Chasellas 1, CH-7500, St. Moritz. ☎ 81-836-3636, fax 81-836-3737, www.suvrettahouse.ch.

Hotel Languard has the kind of atmosphere you'd expect to find in the Appenzeller countryside. Owned and operated by the Giovanni Trivella family, it has only 22 rooms, but provides a quiet alternative to the hustle-bustle of the city. The rooms are large and contain lots of wood and antiques, with great views of the lake and surrounding mountains. ($$$-$$$$). Open June-October and December-April. Via Veglia 14, CH-7500 St. Moritz. ☎ 81-833-3137, fax 81-833-4546.

Minotel Soldanella is a few minutes walk from the city center and features an 18-hole golf course nearby and tennis courts next to the wooded mountainside. Comfortable rooms and a good restaurant, just slightly off the beaten path. ($$$-$$$$). Closed late March-late May, mid-October to mid-December. Via Somplaz 17, CH-7500 St. Moritz. ☎ 81-830-8500, fax 81-833-2337, www.minotel.com/hotel/ch170.

Posthotel was built in 1908 and is in the heart of the city. With its huge fireplace, it offers a cozy and comfortable retreat from the big crowds of the city, and is a good value for your pocketbook. There are two separate sections to the hotel, but they are connected by a covered walkway. ($$-$$$$). Closed mid-April to mid-May, and from mid-October to mid-

Canton Graubünden

December. Via dal Vout 3 Dorf, CH-7500 St. Moritz. ☎ 81-832-2121, fax 81-833-8973, www.posthotel-stmoritz.ch.

Hotel Waldhaus am See is run by hosts Helen and Claudio Bernasconi-Mettier and offers guests a castle-like setting with fantastic views of the lake. Comfortable rooms and three tasty restaurants. ($$-$$$$). Via Dimiej 6 CH-7500 St. Moritz. ☎ 81-833-7676, fax 81-833-8877, www.waldhaus-am-see.ch.

Hotel National was built over 100 years ago and retains much of the charm of that time. Small, clean rooms with a classy little restaurant that serves up good Italian, Swiss and French fair. ($$-$$$). Closed mid-April to May, mid-October to November. Via de l'Ova Cotschna 1, CH-7500 St. Moritz. ☎ 81-833-3274, 81-833-3275.

St. Moritz Bad Youth Hostel Stille is just one mile from the city center on the east side of the St. Moritz Sports Arena, and on the south side of St. Moritzersee. This hostel is open year-round. There are 192 beds and prices start at 43Sfr. ($-$$). Via Surpunt 60, CH-7500. St. Moritz Bad. ☎ 81-833-3969, fax 81-833-8046, www.youthhostel.ch/st.moritz.

Camping

Camping can be found at at **Olympiaschanze**, just a half-mile southwest of St. Moritz Bad. Open June to September. Contact Roberto Christen at ☎ 81-833-4090, fax 81-834-4069, www.campingtcs.ch.

■ Where to Eat

Chesa Veglia is a swanky restaurant owned by the Palace Hotel that features three separate dining levels, and caters to the gourmet crowd. The **Chadafo Grill**, which is open only in the winter, is known for cooking dishes over a wood fire while you watch. The **Patrizier-Stube** focuses on regional fare year-round, and the **Hayhoft** features excellent pizzas in a less-than-

DINING PRICE CHART	
Prices based on a typical entrée, per person, and do not include beverage.	
$	15-25Sfr ($10-$16)
$$	26-45Sfr ($17-$29)
$$$	46-70Sfr ($30-$47)
$$$$	71Sfr+ ($47+)

formal setting. The structure was built in 1658 and is one of the few Engadina homes still left in town. Excellent eats at excellently high prices, with a wide variety of international dishes. ($$$-$$$$). Reservations required; open daily from 11:30 am-3 pm, 6:30 pm-midnight. Via Veglia 2, CH-7500 St. Moritz. ☎ 81-837-2800.

Restaurant Le Relais has served meals to the rich and famous, including Hollywood types, kings, queens and shahs. Luxurious at every step, it requires men to wear suits for dinner, in a setting that specializes in caviar, oysters, and gourmet meals. ($$$-$$$$). Located in Badrutt's Palace

Hotel on Via Serlas 27. Reservations required; open daily from 12:15-3 pm, 7:30-11 pm. Closed early April-late June, mid-September-mid-December. ☎ 81-837-1010.

Across the lake from St. Moritz is **Meierei Landgasthof**. This popular stop once fed Picasso and the Shah of Iran, among others. The homey atmosphere and local fare have made it popular among locals and visitors alike. It also offers seven guest rooms. ($-$$$). Open December-April and June to October. Via Dimiej 52, CH-7500 St. Moritz. ☎ 81-833-8838 or 81-833-2060.

A pricey little hangout at the top of Corviglia, **La Marmite** is reached by riding the funicular. The place for caviar, wine, spirits and other delights; it also has a cafeteria that caters to skiers. Reservations recommended. ($$-$$$). Open daily from 8:30 am-5:30 pm. Closed mid-April to mid-December. ☎ 81-833-6355.

With excellent pasta, fish and grilled meats from throughout the region, **Veltlinerkeller** is a great place for a very good meal at reasonable prices. Reservations required. Open daily from noon-3 pm, 6-11:30 pm. ($-$$). Via dal Bagn 11, CH-7500 St. Moritz. ☎ 81-833-4009.

Restaurant Engadinia is best-known for its excellent pizza and fondue. ($-$$). Open Monday to Saturday from 8:30 am-11 pm. Closed Sunday. Plazza da Scoula 10, CH-7500 St. Moritz. ☎ 81-833-3265.

Restaurant Hauser has many different dishes for all tastes at reasonable prices. ($-$$). Open daily from 7:30 am-11 pm Sonneplatz, CH-7500 St. Moritz. ☎ 81-833-4402.

Try **Boccalino** for great wood-oven pizzas. ($-$$). Via dal Bagn 6, CH-7500 St. Moritz. ☎ 81-832-1111.

 After Hours is a 24-hour grocery store at Via Maistra 2, CH-7500 St. Moritz. ☎ 81-834-9900.

Pontresina

Four miles (6.4 km) southeast of St. Moritz on Highway 29, this is the base for some of the best hiking trails and mountaineering found in the area. It also offers access to all of the major ski sites as it is halfway between Diavolezza and Corviglia. Because of the close proximity to St.Moritz, sports buses run back and forth between the two villages every half-hour from 7:30 am to 6:30 pm.

■ Information Sources

Tourist Office

 The **Pontresina Tourist Office** can offer free maps and information, and is open daily Monday-Friday from 8:30 am-noon, 2-6 pm. ☎ 81-842-6488, fax 81-842-7996, www.pontresina.com.

*The **Pontresina Bergsteigerschule** (Mountaineering School) can be contacted here at ☎ 81-838-8333 for a four-hour hike onto the Morteratsch Glacier.*

■ Where to Stay

Hotels

There are a number of very nice hotels to stay at in Pontresina, but the best by far is the **Grand Hotel Kronenhof**, which has been owned and operated by the same family since the mid-1800s. Cozy and hospitable, this ho-tel has two restaurants (including the

HOTEL PRICE CHART	
$	30-75Sfr ($20-$49)
$$	76-205Sfr ($50-$109)
$$$	206-299Sfr ($110-$200)
$$$$	300Sfr+ ($200+)

excellent **Kronenstübli**, ($$-$$$), two bars, tennis courts, bowling and an ice-skating rink, among other amenities. ($$$$). Closed late March-late June, October to mid-December. CH-7540 Pontresina. ☎ 81-842-0111, fax 81-842-6066.

The Hotel Schweizerhof is a huge hotel with one of the best restau-rants in town. (the **Hof Restaurant**, $$-$$$, which serves up generous regional dishes). Built in 1910, it has been renovated several times but still retains a lot of Swiss charm and atmosphere. Good-sized rooms and a friendly staff. ($$$$). Closed mid-April to mid-June, mid-October to early December. CH-7540 Pontresina. ☎ 81-842-0131, fax 81-842-7988.

The Hotel Garni Chesa Mulin in Pontresina stretches your dollar a lit-tle further than the Kronenhof or the Schweizerhof. A rustic interior com-plemented by a gracious staff makes you feel right at home in this centrally located inn. ($$$). Closed May and November. CH-7504 Pontresina. ☎ 81-838-8200, fax 81-838-8230.

Hostel

The Pontresina Youth Hostel "Tolais" is at the Langlaufzentrum and is open from mid-December to April 1, and from late June to late October. CH-7504 Pontresina. ☎ 81-842-7223, fax 81-842-7031, www.youthhostel.ch/pontresina.

Camping

Try the **Plauns Campground**, open summer and winter in a beautiful setting that allows gorgeous views of the valley and surrounding mountains. A great little retreat with all of life's modern conveniences. ($). Reservations recommended. Con-tact Albert Brulisauer at ☎ 81-842-6285, fax 81-834-5136.

■ Where to Eat

 In addition to the excellent restaurants in the Hotels Schweizerhof and Kronenhof (see above), **Restaurant Locanda** specializes in traditional Swiss fondue and raclettes at reasonable prices ($-$$), as well as other hearty dishes featuring meat, fish and sausages. Located inside the Hotel Bernia. Reservations recommended. Open daily, 9 am-midnight. Closed mid-April to June 1, early October to mid-December. ☎ 81-838-8686.

The Berninastrasse & Poschiavo Valley

The Berninastrasse begins just slightly north of St. Moritz and descends through the Poschiavo Valley into Tirano, Italy, linking the Engadina Valley to the Valtellina in Italy. This can be a fun little road trip if you're driving, with plenty of interesting stops along the way. You can also take the Berninabahn, which runs year-round and is the highest railway in Europe that doesn't use racks. This is especially advisable in the winter, when the Bernina Pass tends to be blocked with snow.

South of Pontresina you'll find some great walks from **Diavolezza** via the west side of the **Berninastrasse.** For years the former refuge of Diavolezza, at 9,754 feet (2,973 m) has been the starting spot for one of Europe's most spectacular glacier runs. The cable car takes you up in about 10 minutes and from the Diavolezza restaurant you can view all of the surrounding peaks in all of their splendor, including the Piz Pallu, the Piz Bellavista, the Piz Zupas, Crast Aguzza, Piz Bernina, and Piz Morteratsch. From here, you can take an easy walk to **Munt Pers**, at 10,522 feet (3,207 m). Just follow the signs right outside the Diavolezza restaurant – this walk should take you about 1½ hours and will allow for an even more gorgeous view of the area. Starting at the same base point, on the eastern side of the Berninastrasse, you can take a cablecar up to **Piz Lagalb**, where you'll find equally outstanding views of the nearby mountain ranges.

When you reach the **Bernina Pass** at 7,638 feet (2,328 m), you'll have clear views of the Cambrena glacier and peak. If you continue to follow the Berninastrasse south, you'll come to the tiny village of **Alp Grüm**, then wind your way down through the valley, criss-crossing back and forth before reaching **Poschiavo**, a modest little village that has the early 16th-century church of San Vittore. Just south of here lies the **Poschiavo Lake**, a great spot for picnics and watersports. At the end of the lake you'll find the village of **Miralago**, whose name means "look at the lake."

AUTHOR'S PICK

From Miralago, you'll get one of the prettiest views in all of Switzerland. With the mountains reflected in the lake's crystal blue waters, it's a perfect romantic spot for couples.

Silvaplana

Silvaplana is just four miles (6.4 km) southwest of St. Moritz along highway 27, sitated on the shore of Lake Silvaplana, at the base of Piz Corvatsch and the south end of the **Julier Pass**. As with some of the other villages in the area, there are no street names, but an abundance of signs pointing to hotels, restaurants and shops.

■ Information Sources

Tourist Office

The Silvaplana Tourist Office, which is open from 8:30 am-noon, and from 1:30-6:30 pm most days, can help provide you with directions, maps and information. ☎ 81-838-6000, 81-838-6009.

Internet Access

You can access the Internet in **Hotel Julier**, at the left of the Tourist Office for 10Sfr per hour, 7:30 am-2 pm daily.

■ Adventures

Most of the action in Silvaplana takes place on the lake, near the campground on the shores. It was in this tiny village that the sports of **kitesurfing** and **kitesailing** was invented. These involves changing the sail on your windsurfer to a kite. In the winter it is done on the frozen lake. The **Sportzentrum Mulets** or the **Drachen Atelier** in the city center can arrange kitesurfing for you at ☎ 81-828-9767, fax 81-828-9771, www.kitesailing.ch. **Windsurfing** is extremely popular here as well. Each August, Silvaplana plays host to the nine-day Engadine Wind Festival, which includes a freestyle competition and the Swiss and European championships of windsurfing. For rental information, contact **Windsurfers**, at the campground, ☎/fax 81-828-9229. For winter or summer sports and hikes, take the **Corvatsch Bergbahn** up to Piz Corvatsch. ☎ 81-838-7373 for departure times. For ski instruction in the winter months, **The Corvatsch Skischule**, at ☎ 81-828-8684, charges 89Sfr for a one-hour private lesson.

■ Where to Stay

Hotel Albana, with its beamed ceilings and cozy atmosphere, is one of the best places to stay in the area.

HOTEL PRICE CHART	
$	30-75Sfr ($20-$49)
$$	76-205Sfr ($50-$109)
$$$	206-299Sfr ($110-$200)
$$$$	300Sfr+ ($200+)

Rooms are very comfortable and those with balconies are especially romantic. ($$$-$$$$). CH-7513 Silvaplana. ☎ 81-828-9292, fax 81-828-8181.

Hotel Chesa Grusaida is very popular among the ski crowd, and provides small but comfortable accommodations in a rustic Swiss setting. ($$-$$$). Closed May to mid-June, late October to mid-December. CH-7513 Silvaplana. ☎ 81-828-8292, fax 81-828-9409.

Camping

Camping in Silvaplana takes place along the shores of the lake, with Frau and Herr Wyss as your hosts. Open mid-May to mid-October. ($).CH-7513 Silvaplana. ☎ 81-828-8492, fax 81-833-5413.

■ Where to Eat

The two best places to eat in Silvaplana are in the Hotel Albana. **La Gourmet** offers gourmet-type meals for the discriminating diner in a slightly formal setting ($$-$$$), while **Spunta Grishun** ($$) serves regional dishes in a modest, relaxed dining area. Reservations are recommended for both. ☎ 81-828-9292.

Sils

Sils is a quiet little village, known for its relaxing hikes in the summer and its skiing in the winter. Actually, Sils is made up of two sister cities known as Sils-Baselgia and Sils-Maria, which are connected through a thin sliver of land between the two lakes of Silvaplana and Silser. Located on the Silsersee just a mile south of Silvaplana, the **Furtschellas** cable car connects you to Silvaplana's slopes in the winter. Here you can also visit **Friedrich Nietzsche's** house, halfway between the post office and tourist office on Sils' main road. The famous philosopher spent his summers here during the 1880s.

Canton Graubünden

■ Information Sources

Tourist Office

 The Sils **Tourist Office** can provide you with hiking and skiing maps, and has Internet access for only 6Sfr per hour. Open daily, Monday-Friday from 8:30 am-6 pm, Saturday from 9 am-noon, 4-6 pm. ☎ 81-838-5050, fax 81-838-5059.

■ Where to Stay

 Check out **Hotel Margna** in **Sils-Baselgia**. This was originally a private home, built in 1817 between the two lakes. This prime location is near countless hiking and cross-country ski trails. The hotel hosts a grill restaurant with a grand fireplace, a second dining area and a fondue restaurant in the basement. The hotel also has its own six-hole golf course. ($$$$). CH-7515 Sils-Baselgia. ☎ 81-838-4747, fax 81-838-4748.

In Sils-Maria you can stay at the charming **Hotel Pensiun Privata**, on the same small piece of land between the two lakes as Hotel Margna. Here you'll find the prices a bit more reasonable. ($$$). On the hotel grounds are trails leading up to the mountains and surrounding meadows. Fresh flowers are in every room, and the restaurant offers a four-course menu with excellent fare. Breakfast and dinner are included in some rates. CH-7514 Sils-Maria. ☎ 81-826-5247, fax 81-826-6183.

The Sils Youth Hostel is open from April 1 to the end of October, with 40 beds. CH-7411 Sils im Domlescg. ☎ 81-651-1518, www.youthhostel.ch/sils.

Maloja

This is four miles (6.4 km) southwest of Silvaplana on Highway 27, at the edge of the Silsersee, and is home to only 310 people. However, in the summertime this little village overflows with hikers, fishermen and nature lovers and the Maloja Pass provides a connection between the Inn and Mera valleys. When here, take a walk to **Belvedere Castle**, where you'll get a great view of the Bergell Mountains on one side, and the Engadina mountains on the other side.

■ Information Sources

Tourist Office

 The Maloja **Tourist Office**, at ☎ 81-824-3188, fax 81-824-3637, can provide you with maps of the many hiking trails in the area.

■ Adventures on Foot

 For a nice relaxing five-hour hike, begin at **Promontogno**. This is the village directly on the main road, while the neighboring village of Bondo lies a little farther away, near the mouth of the valley downstream. From Promontogno you can either walk or take a bus to **Soglio**. At the right of the bus stop follow the signs to Casaccia and Panoramico. The trail is well marked and will bring you near mountain streams and numerous impressive waterfalls. The path will then enter a dense forest and bring you to a beautiful meadow, before you reach the hamlet of **Vicosoprano**. From here, you'll continue on along the main road before you reach

A farmer's wife at Soglio, with the Sciora Mountains in the background

the path again. Ignore the power lines here as you'll soon return to peace and quiet, and stay on the path, which will eventually bring you to **Casaccia**, not far from the Maloja Pass.

For an easy day-long hike that takes you through nine towns from Maloja to Castasegna near the Italian border, grab a map at the Bregaglia Tourist Office. It will also show you the historical places of interest along the way.

■ Where to Stay

 There are only four hotels in Maloja. All offer free parking, a restaurant or small café, and in most instances breakfast is included with an overnight stay.

Hotels

Scweizerhaus & Postli is a traditional and trendy inn that is home to a gourmet restaurant, fondue grill and pizzeria. The rooms are comfy, with

Canton Graubünden

all amenities. ($$$-$$$$). ☎ 81-838-2828, fax 81-838-2829, www.maloja-schweizerhaus.ch.

HOTEL PRICE CHART	
$	30-75Sfr ($20-$49)
$$	76-205Sfr ($50-$109)
$$$	206-299Sfr ($110-$200)
$$$$	300Sfr+ ($200+)

The Hotel Longhin offers a family atmosphere with all the modern comforts, and a very good restaurant that serves up a wide array of international fare. ($$-$$$). ☎ 81-824-3131, fax 81-824-3677, www.hotel-longhin.ch.

Hotel Maloja Kulm offers traditional Graubünden hospitality in a quality setting at the south end of the village. ($$-$$$). The restaurant specializes in regional dishes. A good spot for families with children. ☎ 81-824-3105, fax 81-8248-3466.

Sporthotel is centrally located, and has good rooms, catering to the ski and adventure sports crowd. The fine restaurant specializes in regional cooking and includes a large bar, with an outdoor terraces. ($$-$$$). ☎ 81-824-3126, fax 81-824-3490.

Hostels & Mountain Huts

 The Maloja Youth Hostel has 54 beds and is open from January 1 to mid-March, from late June to mid-October, and from mid- to late December. Hauptstrasse, CH-7516 Maloja. ($-$$). ☎ 81-833-3239, fax 81-833-3575, www.youthhostel.ch/malajoa.

The Forno Mountainhut, at 8,442 feet elevation (2,574 m), is open from mid-March to mid-May, and from the end of June to the end of September. It is a 3½-hour hike from Maloja, and is a great spot for relaxing and taking photos. Contact Roberto Costa for reservations at ☎ 81-842-6130, or call the hut directly during the season at 81-824-3182.

Camping

 Campground Curtinac is open from early June to late September, and offers 95 camping sites, with easy access to nearby amenities, on the shoes of the lake. Contact Max Pittin at CH-7516 Maloja. ☎ 81-824-3181, www.campingtcs.ch.

Bregaglia Valley Hikes: from the Maloja Pass, along the region southwest on highway 27 between Switzerland and Italy is what is known as the **Val Bregaglia.** This is great hiking country. You can get information and maps at the **Bregaglia Tourist Office**, in the town of Stampa, between Gorgonovo and Promontogno on Highway 27. Phone ☎ 81-822-1555, fax 81-822-1644, www.bregaglia.ch.

Samedan & Celerina

Samedan and Celerina are just two miles (3.2 km) northeast of St. Moritz on Route 27 and are usually considered suburbs of the great resort. These smaller villages offer a great spot for hiking excursions, and the **Samedan Tourist Office** will provide you with maps and free information at ☎ 81-852-5404, www.samedan.ch. Celerina lies at the base of the ridge that separates the Samedan Basin from the upper levels of the Engadina lakes. It lies on the Inn River and, with its old stone houses adorned by sgraffito designs, it offers a quiet respite from St. Moritz. For information, contact the **Celerina Tourist Office** at ☎ 81-830-0011, fax 81-830-0019, www.celerina.ch. Both villages offer ski lifts and ice-skating rinks, as well as lots of trails for hiking. You can hire a horse-drawn carriage here to carry you to St. Moritz, or you can take guided tours through the Swiss National Park via the Tourist Offices. You'll also want to visit the **San Gian** church, which is an easy landmark to spot in the valley, sitting on a lone mound at the east end of Celerina. Inside, you'll find frescos and a painted ceiling from the 15th century.

■ Where to Stay

Check out the **Hotel Chesa Quadratscha** in Samedan. Built in the 19th century, it was once a private home that has been converted into a hotel. Beautiful rooms with generous views. ($$$$). Closed mid-April to mid-June and from mid-October to mid-December. CH-7503

HOTEL PRICE CHART	
$	30-75Sfr ($20-$49)
$$	76-205Sfr ($50-$109)
$$$	206-299Sfr ($110-$200)
$$$$	300Sfr+ ($200+)

Samedan. ☎ 81-852-4257. In Celerina, you'll find the expensive **Cresta Palace Hotel**, an inn with rustic furnishings that is over 100 years old. ($$$$). Hauptstrasse, CH-7505 Celerina. ☎ 81-836-5656, fax 81-836-5657, www.crestapalace.ch.

For more modestly priced lodgings, go to the **Hotel Misani** down the street. Open all year, this inn has one of the finest restaurants in the area. Nice, cozy rooms at reasonable prices. ($$$). Hauptstasse, CH-7505 Celerina. ☎ 81-833-3314, fax 81-833-0797.

■ Where to Eat

For dining out, look no further than the **Arvenstübli/ Stuvetta**, in the Hotel Quadratscha in Samedan. Fish, wild game and grilled meats are the specialties served in this quaint restaurant, which features two combined dining areas. Excellent meals daily from noon-2 pm and 6-11:30 pm. Closed late April to early June, mid-October to mid-December. Reservations are recommended. ($$-$$$). ☎ 81-852-4257.

Zuoz

Zuoz can be found 12 miles (19 km) northeast of St. Moritz on Route 27 and is easily accessed by train and auto. Located right on the Inn River, it was once the center of the Engadina world, and is today one of the best examples of Engadina lifestyles in the area. Nearly all of the 1,200 residents speak Romansh. On the main square you'll find the famous, privately-owned **Planta House** – a combination of two structures in traditional Engadina style – with white stucco and tiny windows. Because it's a mini-resort town, you'll find skiing, horseback riding, and a ski school. The Zuoz **Tourist Office** is on Via Maistra and is open Monday-Friday from 9 am-noon, 3-6 pm. ☎ 81-854-1510. For the local ski school, ☎ 81-850-1717.

■ Where to Stay

In Zuoz you can stay at the **Posthotel Engiadina**, a hard-to-miss inn because of the color – an off-pink hue. Built over 125 years ago, the hotel was originally used as a postal stop, and is now home to two of the best restaurants in the area. It has cozier rooms than the outdoor façade would suggest, with all modern amenities. ($$). Closed April-May, mid-October to mid-December. CH-7524 Zuoz. ☎ 81-854-1021, fax 81-854-3303, www.hotelengiadina.ch.

S-Chanf

S-Chanf is just slightly northeast of Zuoz, and is one of the entrances to the Swiss National Park, which in the winter doubles as a cross-country ski area. The S-Chanf **Tourist Office** is on Via Maistra. ☎ 81-854-2255, fax 81-850-1765.

■ Where to Stay

Here you'll find the **Hotel Scaletta**, a real charmer and a bargain. Built in 1624, this structure was originally used as a midway point for people traveling on horseback through the Engadina passes. Set only a few steps from the village church, Hotel Scaletta is hard to miss – beautiful, stately and open year-round. The restaurant serves up hearty regional fare at reasonable prices. ($$). Via Maistra 52, CH-7525 S-Chanf. ☎ 81-854-0304, fax 81-884-0506, www.hotelscaletta.ch.

Guarda

Another tiny village set in the lower part of the valley Engadina just off of Highway 27. Guarda sits at 5,413 feet above sea level (1,650 m) and, despite its remote location, has seen a revival in recent years. Narrow roads and restored houses with traditional paintings help to make this little village a wanderer's delight. It's close to the Swiss National Park and a great hideaway from the crowds during the high season. It was here that a remake of the movie *Heidi* was filmed.

■ Switzerland's National Park

 The Swiss National Park was founded on Swiss Independence Day, August 1, 1914, and was one of the first national parks in Europe. This is the only national park in Switzerland. One-third of the park is Alpine forests, another third is Alpine meadows, and the rest is mountains. Located in the very east end of Switzerland, the park is a protected sanctuary where nature is left to its own with very little interference. You'll find the visitor center and park headquarters at the entrance, near the village of **Zernez** – where you can also see the white houses of Engadina, found nowhere else in Switzerland. The walls of these houses are nearly three feet thick, in order to protect the inhabitants from the brutally cold winters (when tempratures get down to -20°F). Likewise, the towns of **Scuol** and **Guarda** are just to the north of the park, with **S-Chanf** at the far northwest edge. The south edge of the park presses up against the Italian border.

You can get to the park by a number of routes. If you're coming from outside of the Grabünden canton, you can take the **Ratische Bahn**, which will bring you to Zernez. From other points you can pick up one of the Swiss postal buses which routinely skirt around the parameter, traversing the three major border roads. All make stops at Zernez, and access to the park is free.

You'll travel through the park on the **Ofenpass** – the only road within the entire park – either in your own vehicle or via bus, which leaves from Zernez. Walking on the Ofenpass is highly discouraged by park rangers – the road is narrow and there is heavy traffic. The buses stop at the nine parking lots within the park, where you can begin and end treks of various lengths. Once in the park, you'll travel on foot throughout its 105 square miles (273 square km), with a host of treks awaiting hikers of all levels.

There is no camping here, and the park is closed from November-May. Also, picking flowers or plants is strictly forbidden, and rangers patrol the park religiously. June and July are the best times to observe the Alpine flowers and birds, while September is the best month to see the ibex, chamois and deer. There are no campfires, mini-stoves, pets or bikes allowed, and visitors are responsible for their own waste disposal. Visitors are forbidden to walk anywhere except on marked trails, and hunting or disturbing the wildlife or plant life is punishable by a 500Sfr fine. For information, contact the Swiss National Park, CH-7530 Zernez. ☎ 81-856-1282, fax 81-856-1740, www.nationalpark.ch.

Hikes

The park is more hilly than mountainous for the most part, with altitudes from 4,592 feet to 10,496 feet (1,400-3,200 m) above sea level. Many of the hikes send trekkers above the tree lines, so appropriate footwear, warm clothing, and rain gear should be carried in a backpack at all times. Also, it is a good idea to include a small first aid kit, sunglasses, maps, munchies and water, along with your other provisions. Below you'll find a few of the most popular hikes of varying difficulties.

It's a five-hour hike from Zernez to the Chamanna Cluozza (five miles/eight km) for a night's rest at 6,175 feet (1,882 m), and then another four hours (4½ miles/7.2 km) the following day from here to the **Vallun Chafuol**, the next parking lot (P3). This is a fairly strenuous hike, through a coniferous forest with alpine grass at your feet, followed by long, steep, rocky sections on the trail, but it is a great way to see chamois, marmots and golden eagles.

Another fun route suitable for any hiker is from **Stabelchod-Val dal Botsch-Val da Stabelchod-Stabelchod**. This trail is a 4.4-mile circular hike, with some steep and rocky sections, and takes about four hours to complete without stops. You'll begin at parking lot eight (P8) – Stabelchod – and follow the trail to P7. From here you'll hike upward to Val dal Botsch and onward to the rest area at **Margunet** – probably the toughest part of the journey due to the increase in elevation (+1,456 feet/444 m) from Stabelchod). From here you can then descend through Val da Stabelchod back to either Stabelchod (P8) or parking lot nine (P9) – though no bus stops here. Be on the lookout for chamois, stags, marmots and bearded vultures.

If you only have an afternoon to spend in the park, then try this short hike to **Alp la Schera**, where you can bring a picnic lunch. You'll get a fine view into Italy and may catch a glimmer of a golden eagle cruising on the Alpine wind. There are actually three trails to Alp la Schera. You can begin at parking lot four (P4) – Punt la Drossa, near the entrance to the Livigno, Italy tunnel. Or you can start at parking lot five (P5) or parking lot six (P6) – Il Fuorn, near the hotel Il Fuorn. Or start at parking lot nine (P9), known as Buffalora. If you use the bus system, you can combine any of these trails to avoid retracing your steps. This four-mile trail is basically very easy, with a few steep sections, and takes about three hours to complete up to a high point of 6,925 feet (2,111 m). At Alp la Schera, you'll find a small hut where you can hang out and enjoy a picnic lunch, or just enjoy the view over the waters of Lake Livigno, Italy.

Hiking to **Alp Grimmels** is another easy, popular hike for young and old, and features a nice, even 4½-miles (7.2 km) trail that takes about three hours to complete. Expect to see a lot of marmots throughout the grassy meadows and near the forests. Great scenery abounds and this is a fun hike for any sunny day. There are three trails that circle around en route to Alp Grimmels. You can start at parking lot P1-Champlönch, which takes you through the valley of Champlönch, or you can access the trail by P2, P3, P5, and P6. Again, using the bus you don't have to retrace your steps back to the original starting point.

For those who want a bit more of a challenge, try this excursion to **Alp Trupchun** via the town of S-Chanf in the Inn Valley. From the town, you'll head east for 1.2 miles (1.9 km) on the road marked Varusch/National Park until the road ends. Follow the trail over across the Ova da Varusch stream and continue to the Varusch hut, where a number of trails come together. You can either stay at this elevation or climb upward, where you'll encounter great views as the trail winds into the park. Here is where you will likely see marmots stuffing their cheeks with various plants. Once at the 6,669-foot (2,040 m) summit, you can either walk back the way you came or continue on the trail to **Fuorcla Trupchun Pass** into Italy.

For a really fun and challenging hike, take the route from S-Chanf to Zernez (a 15-mile trek) via the **Fuorcla Val Sassa Pass**. Head out from S-Chanf to the Varusch hut, over the Ova da Varusch stream. When the trails converge, take the trail to the left (if you went straight you'd be heading on to Alp Trupchun). This trail then crosses the **Muschauns** stream over a hardy-looking wooden bridge once and then back again before it begins to climb steadily upward, before finally reaching the Fuorcla Val Sassa, a 9,731-foot (2,857-m) pass. This trail is hard to follow in the winter time, so beware. Follow the trail through a forest and three miles (4.8 km) past the Fuorcla Val Sassa you should find yourself at the Chamanna Cluozza, where you can spend the night, or continue on down through the fields and meadows. The trail will cross the Spol River and eventually reaches the Ofenpass just outside of Zernez.

■ Staying Overnight in the Park

Hotel Meisser fits in perfectly with her surroundings in Guarda. This 17th-century renovated farmhouse provides the perfect picture of an Engadina structure – with its baskets of fresh flowers, antiques and ambiance. There are actually two parts to this hotel, a main house and a newly converted farmhouse just across the street. Owners Kathrine and Ralf Meisser are gracious and accommodating hosts. Open May to November and December to April. CH-7545, Guarda. ($$-$$$). ☎ 81-862-2132, fax 81-862-2480.

HOTEL PRICE CHART	
$	30-75Sfr ($20-$49)
$$	76-205Sfr ($50-$109)
$$$	206-299Sfr ($110-$200)
$$$$	300Sfr+ ($200+)

You can also stay in the **Chamanna Cluozza** – a mountain chalet with rooms of varying sizes accommodating up to 68 people. It's situated in the midst of the Cluozza Valley. Built in 1910, this log cabin was renovated completely in 1993, with dormitories holding 44 beds, and the rest in private rooms. Reservations are required from late June to mid-October (☎ 81-856-1235), and at other times through hut wardens Dumeng and Claudia Duschletta (☎ 81-856-1689, fax 81-856-1686).

The Hotel & Restaurant Il Fuorn is right on the Ofenpass with bus service to the door at parking lot six (P6). Built in the early 20th century, this hotel is near the start of several lovely hikes. Run by the Denoth-Grass family, this sprawling inn – decorated in traditional Engadina style – has 60 beds in private rooms and a dormitory to accommodate 20 people at mid-range prices. ($$-$$$). ☎ 81-856-1226.

 Camping sites are available in the nearby towns of Zernez, Susch, Scuol, Tschierv, Mustair, Sta. Maria in Münstertal and Cinuos-Chel. No camping or pitching of tents is allowed anywhere in the National Park.

Schuls

A small village in the lower part of the valley Engadina, at an elevation of 4,081 feet (1,244 m) on Highway 27. While the main street is a lively part of this modern town, closer to the river you'll find traditional houses and a quieter section of the village worth a stroll. The **Schloss Tarasp** is also found here, a stunning medieval castle and fortress situated on the top of a hill in the Tasna Valley. Schuls is also the home station for the "Rätische Bahn" (RHB) and is close to the entrance of the Swiss National Park. The Schuls (Scuol) **Tourist Office** is in the center of town, ☎ 81-861-2222, fax 81-861-2223, and will provide you with free maps of local, easy hikes.

Schuls is home to many health spas, including the **Engadin Bad Scuol**, in the town center on the main street. ☎ 81-861-2000. Here you'll find the first Roman-Irish baths, where you'll soak for several hours before you get a stimulating massage with soap and brushes, all the while gazing at the mountains in front of you. You'll also want to check out whitewater rafting expeditions on the River Inn. You can pay 100Sfr for a half-day trek or 150SF for a whole day. **Swissraft Engadine** is in Schuls. ☎ 81-911-5250.

■ Camping

Camping Gurlaina lies across from the village on the Inn River and is open year-round, and is one of the best camp-grounds we found, in terms of conveniences. Contact Janett Flurin at Gurlaina, CH-7550 Scuol. ($). ☎ 81-864-1501, fax 81-864-0760.

The Val Müstair Region

The Val Müstair region is at the end of the Ofenpass, in the far southeastern foot of Graubünden; its name means "cathedral valley." The surrounding mountains reach as high as 9,840 feet (3,000 m). In this area of six villages, the road signs are almost all in German and Italian. Traveling south on the Ofenpass (Highway 28), you'll first encounter **Tschierv**, **Fuldera**, **Lü**, **Valchava**, **Sta. Maria im Münstertal**, and, finally, **Müstair**. From here, there are many gorgeous hikes at all levels. The countryside is especially beautiful. The Val Müstair **Tourist Office** is in Tschierv, CH-7532. ☎ 81-850-3929, fax 81-850-3930.

■ Tschierv

Tschierv, at 5,435 feet (2,284 m) above sea level is the first village along highway 28 in the Val Müstair region, and its Romansh name literally means "a place to view." It is from here that you'll first catch a glimpse of Italy's famous Ortler, just across the border at 12,808 feet (3,905 m). Tschierv is the center for all winter sports and an ideal place to begin any hikes.

Where to Stay & Eat

Hotel Staila-Sternen is beautiful, charming, quaint and extremely reasonable. ($$-$$$). Home to three distinct restaurants, this is a great place to settle in for a night or two. Definitely worth a visit! Restaurants Arvenstube, Speiserestaurant, and Bankettsall are all delightful, and each specializes in various types of dishes.7532 Tschierv. ☎ 81-858-5551, fax 81-858-5142.

Hotel Garni Turettas is another extremely charming and reasonable place to plop your head in Tschierv. The rooms are spotless and quaint, and the restaurant and café both serve up hearty dishes. ($$). CH-7532 Tschierv. ☎/fax 81-858-5852.

Gasthaus "La Vopa" was originally built in 1678 and is beautiful and typical of the Val Müstair region design – very pretty white stucco-like exterior, with red designs and accents. Inside, you'll find simple, plain rooms with rustic charm. ($$). CH-7532 Tschierv. ☎ 81-858-6248, fax 81-858-3650.

HOTEL PRICE CHART	
$	30-75Sfr ($20-$49)
$$	76-205Sfr ($50-$109)
$$$	206-299Sfr ($110-$200)
$$$$	300Sfr+ ($200+)

Hotel Süsom-Givè sits at just over 7,000 feet (2,100 m), facing the Ortler, and provides travelers with clean rooms and a panoramic restaurant. There is access to the local ski area, Minschuns, and it's a hiker's paradise. They host many of the rowdier travelers. ($$-$$$). CH-7532 Pass dal Fuorn-Tschierv. ☎ 81-858-5182, fax 81-858-6171.

Camping

Campground Staila is in the middle of Tschierv and is close to hotels, restaurants, and shopping. There is also a heated pool, tennis courts and a children's playground next to the campground, which campers may use free of charge. ($). CH-7535 Tschierv. ☎ 81-858-5628.

The **TCS Campground** ($) offers year-round places to stake your tent. Contact Mario Gross for camping information and reservations. CH-7532 Tschierv. ☎ 81-858-5628.

■ Fuldera

At 5,379 feet (1,640 m), this is just beyond Tschierv, and is a simple little farming village just west of the main road, encased in the valley by a shrowd of dark green conifers. The houses here are distinguished by the sgraffito decorations native to this valley, and the carpentry work here is noted throughout Switzerland. Here you can escape with easy walks through the forest. The **Tourist Office** in the town center will help you with maps and information.

Where to Stay & Eat

The village hotel, **Landgasthof Staila**, offers clean rooms, and their restaurant serves regional specialties such as steinpilzrisotto. Staila is run by the Wymann family – mother and daughter attend the hotel guests, while son and father handle the restaurant duties. The restaurant serves up tasty regional fare and the wine cellar is an added treat. A great value for your money in a beautiful setting, both inside and out. ($$-$$$$). Available for singles, families and groups. CH-7533 Fuldera. ☎ 81-858-5160, fax 81-858-5021.

■ Lü & Luesai

Both of these small villages are just south of Fuldera, and you can access Lü from the road to Luesai. Luesai is home to only 70 inhabitants, and is car-free – you have to park your auto in a tiny lot just outside of the village – which is situated on a mountainside and is highlighted by the late-medieval Evangelist church.

Just past Luesai and below Fuldera is the village of Lü, which is accessible by car. It is also easy to just walk to Lü on foot from Tschierv. This little town is a hiker's paradise and is home to some lovely Alpine flowers and fauna, including orchids, hyacinths and butterflies galore.

Where to Stay

You can bunk down in the **Pension Hirschen** with the Felix family in Lü. Clean, comfortable rooms in spotless surroundings at very reasonable rates in a traditional Swiss setting. ($$). CH-7534 Lü. ☎ 81-858-5181, fax 81-858-5103.

Where to Eat

Wirtin – the only restaurant to be found in the tiny village of Luesai – offers up superb fare, including apples with vanilla sauce and native Buendner barley soup, for which it is well known.

■ Valchava

Just to the west of Highway 28, Valchava offers visitors more fine examples of the regional houses of Val Müst at 4,723 feet (1,440 m). Built on the side of the valley, Valchava is home to the **Chasa Jaura**, a valley museum established in 1973 that highlights the lifestyle and crafts of the people of this region. You'll also find the 15th-century **St. Martin church** here, with its Baroque tower in the middle of the village.

Where to Stay

Hotel Central La Fainera is the pride of owner Maggi Schnitzer, and offers simple, clean rooms with many amenities at fair prices. ($$-$$$).CH-7535 Valchava. ☎ 81-858-5161, fax 81-858-5816.

■ Sta. Maria im Münstertal

This is a small village at the far-eastern edge of Val Müstair on Highway 28. Located at 4,454 feet (1,358 m) in a rural valley, it is the last stop before the tiny town of Müstair on the road which then crosses the boarder into the Italian valley town of Taufers. It is also the meeting point of two important roads in this region. The north/south road branches in the middle of the village and, heading south, leads to the Umbrailpass into Italy, while the east/west route is the Ofenpass. The north/south road is usually closed in the wintertime.

The Engadina houses are typically stone, white-washed homes with ornate sgraffito decorations that include various religious or historic mottos and scenes. The town church, which was built in 1513, has an external wall with an impressive medieval mural. The town is also known for its exceptional handwoven products dating back to that same time. Hotels in this town are noted for their excellent cuisine, and glacier skiing can be undertaken year-round at Italy's Stilfser, just a 45-minute ride south on the Umbrail Pass. If you're camping contact Clara Hoffmann at **Camping Sta. Maria** for reservations at ☎ 81-858-7133, fax 81-858-5079.

Where to Stay & Eat

Hotel Alpina has been run by the same family for four generations, and appears more Italian in color and structure than Swiss on the outside. On the inside, however, you'll find a beautiful inn with classic Swiss comforts in a spotless setting. Very reasonable and the restaurant food is outstanding. ($-$$). 7536 St. Maria. ☎ 81-858-5117, fax 81-858-5697.

Crusch Alba has been operated by seven generations of the same family and was erected in the 15th century. The beautiful white façade is highlighted with blooming flower boxes in every window, and the rooms come will all of the modern amenities. The adjoining **Buendnerstube** provides guests with regional specialties, and the former kitchen, now used as a lounge, contains antique baking devices. ($-$$). 7536 St. Maria. ☎ 81-858-5106, fax 81-858-6149.

The local **youth hostel** has 62 beds. Open from January 1 to mid-March, from mid-May to late October, and from mid- to late December. ($-$$). Chasa Plaz, CH-7536, Sta. Maria im Münstertal. ☎ 81-858-5052, fax 81-858-5496, www.youthhostel.ch/sta.maria.

If you're camping, contact Clara Hoffmann at **Camping Sta. Maria** for reservations at ☎ 81-858-7133, fax 81-858-5079.

■ Müstair

Müstair is situated at 4,090 feet (1,247 m) and is the last village before the Italian border. The village, home to 830 inhabitants, got its name from the Latin word for monastery (monasterium) and is the largest village in the area. The huge **St. Johannes monastery** in town hails from the eighth century, and contains medieval frescos not to be missed if you're a church buff. It is still inhabited by Benedictine nuns today. Wintertime here is great for cross-country skiers, who can enjoy four miles (6.5 km) of well-groomed trails.

Where to Stay & Eat

Hotel Liun provides guests with spa and "wellness holiday" packages that include hay baths, massages and guided walking tours – for 770Sfr. A huge, handsome building that is hard to miss, run by the Caratsch-Oswald family. ($$-$$$). CH-7537 Müstair. ☎ 81-858-5154, fax 81-858-6293.

Hotel Chavalatsch is beautiful and in the town center on the Hauptstrasse. Quaint, with clean and modern rooms. The restaurant offers regional specialties in an attractive pine-paneled setting; breakfasts here are hearty and filling. There is very good value here for the money. ($-$$). CH-7537 Müstair. ☎ 81-858-5732, fax 81-858-5350.

Hotel Tschierv-Hirschen is at Plaz Grond, with classy, romantic accommodations, as well as excellent cuisine in their restaurant. ($$-$$$). CH-7537 Müstair. ☎ 81-858-5152, fax 81-858-5474.

Hotel Chasa Chalavaina was built in 1499 and retains all of the rustic charm of this tiny Swiss village. Jon Fasser is your attentive host in this simple and clean inn. ($-$$). CH-7537 Müstair. ☎ 81-858-5468.

Müstair, with the Benedictine monastery of St. John the Baptist, founded in 780-90

Canton Graubünden

Camping

 This is available at **Clenga**, run by Sibylla and Hans Rolli, at the far west edge of the village. The grounds are open from May 1 through the end of October. Reservations are requested at ☎ 81-858-5410, fax 81-858-5422.

Southwestern Graubünden

The San Bernardino Pass is the route from the southwesternmost area of Graubünden canton leading north to Chur. If you're traveling south on Highway 13, known as the San Bernardino Pass, then Roveredo is one of the last villages in the canton before you enter the sunny lower valley of the canton of Ticino, and the large city of Bellinzona. Though it's only 120 miles (193 km) by car from Roveredo to Chur, you can take a whole day to make the journey or several, depending upon whether you want to stop for some overnight hiking trips or just enjoy the scenery. You can travel either via the main highway or on the older route, which runs parallel to the highway. Beware in the wintertime, however, as the San Bernardino Pass can be covered with snow.

THE SAN BERNARDINO PASS

At 6,773 feet (2,065 m), the pass was used by the Romans, who no doubt took advantage of its location. Located between the Mesolcina Valley and the Rhine Valley, the Romans christened the pass *Mons Avium*, which means "bird mountain" in Latin. The symbol of San Bernardino today is called "Pizzo Uccello," which means the same thing in Italian. The name of the village of San Bernardino was originally Gualdo de Gauareida, until 1400 when it was renamed for the Saint who lived there. During the early 1600s a chaplain's house was built to house two monks, who were to see that the pass remained open at all times, and to provide lodging for travelers. This house still exists today. In 1823 the road was constructed and in 1860 excavations discovered the remains of Roman wooden baths. Both the new road and these excavations helped to stimulate the area economically. Wealthy people began to come to San Bernardino to seek out therapeutic remedies from the waters here. However, the two world wars put this area in a kind of standstill for many years, and it wasn't until 1967 that San Bernardino began to experience a rise in tourism once again. This was mainly due to the construction of the San Bernardino tunnel-highway, which allows cars and trains to pass quickly from one side of the mountain range to the other.

On the Susten Pass near the Steingletscher (see page 247)

Above: The Tell Chapel on Lake Uri (see page 241)

Below: The revolving restaurant at the Atanserhorn, with a view of the Nidwalden Alps (see pages 249-50)

On the way up to the Stanserhorn, with the Pilatus in the background (see page 250)

On main Highway 13, you'll travel north from the village of Roveredo up to Mesocco, leaving the Mediterranean fields along the way. There are a number of small villages along this route, which justify a stop or two, just for the scenery – especially at the **Buffalora Waterfall**, a double waterfall that will be on the west side of the road between Lostallo and Soazza. If you want to stay overnight, you can do so in Soazza, at the **Al Cacciatore Inn** – a pink hotel on the southern side of the village. Comfortable and cozy lodgings. ($$-$$$). ☎ 91-831-1820, fax 91-831-1979.

At Mesocco, stop to visit the ruins of the **Castello di Misox**, before continuing on to the village of San Bernardino, which will take you through some fun twisting and turning if you're driving. Huge boulders, stones and rocks litter the area around San Bernardino. The Pass connects the Moesa River – a tributary of the Ticino – with the Po and Upper Inner Rhine Valley, known as the Hinerrhein. You'll see glaciers here, including the Zapportgletscher and the Rheinquelhorn.

■ Where to Stay & Eat

Brocco e Posta, situated in the center of town, is moderately priced and comfortable, with a swimming pool and sauna. ($$). ☎ 91-832-1105, fax 91-832-1342.

HOTEL PRICE CHART	
$	30-75Sfr ($20-$49)
$$	76-205Sfr ($50-$109)
$$$	206-299Sfr ($110-$200)
$$$$	300Sfr+ ($200+)

Hotel Bellevue looks like a typical Swiss chalet and is a good spot for families with kids. Located in the center of the village, with rustic charm and modern facilities. ($$). ☎ 91-832-1126, fax 91-832-1797.

Hotel Suisse is another family-oriented inn in the village center, and is home to a splendid restaurant that specializes in Italian and international dishes at very reasonable rates. ($$). ☎ 91-832-1662, fax 91-832-1197.

Youth Hostel San Bernardino is in a new building in town, with 148 beds in rooms for two, four, six, or eight persons. Adults 30Sfr, kids and teens 25Sfr per night. ☎ 91-827-1765, fax 91-827-3566.

When you are in San Bernardino, you might want to take a hike out to the **Zapporthütte**, at 7,465 feet (2,276 m), just northwest of the menacing Zapporthorn (10,338 feet, 3,152 m). This small mountain hut is great for skiers or photographers and hikers, and contains 35 beds. You can begin your trek at the parking lot on the north side of the San Bernardino Pass. For reservations, contact Anita Götte at CH-7414 Fürstenau. ☎ 81-651-1937 or on the hut phone at ☎ 81-664-1496.

■ Excursions

When you leave San Bernardino, you'll travel eastward (Highway 13) up through the towns of **Splügen** and **Sufers**, from where you can hike to the **Cufercalhütte**, at 7,822 feet (2,385 m), which lies to the west, at the south of the Safiental mountain ridge, and offers 30 beds. To reserve a spot, contact Hans Ullius at ☎ 81-252-8717, fax 81-253-3055. At **Avers-Roffla**, the **Rofflaschlucht** will be on the western side of the road just before you reach Andeer, and is one of the most impressive waterfalls in Switzerland.

For a nice little side-trip, you can hike southward, following the signs to **Innerferrera**, via the **Averserrhein Valley**. The Averserrhein is a tributary of the Hinterrhein, and makes it way through this beautiful valley encompassed by imposing massifs. This road will bring you all the way south to the tiny border village of **Campsut**, near the Italian boarder, and to the town of **Cröt**, where the road branches out in two directions. In Crot you'll find the **Avers-Cresta**, a pretty little white church set on the hillside. The road eventually ends at Stettli, and you can simply retrace your steps.

Once you return to Highway 13, you'll continue on to **Andeer**, where you'll travel through dense woods before the road bends north. Upon reaching the town of Zillis, you could stop to view the **Kirche St. Martin**. The ceiling inside is considered to be one of the most valuable works of Ro-

Obermutten, above the Albula Pass, between Thusis and Tiefencastel

manesque artists found anywhere in Switzerland, and is believed to have been finished in the 12th century. From here, you can walk or drive to the tiny village of **Mathon**, which sits on the slopes of **Piz Beverin** overlooking the Schons valley. **Via Mala** is further north, just off the highway, and here you can take a nice hike down to the Rhine riverbed (via 345 steps).

The town of **Thusis** is farther north and in the valley, below the ruins of a castle and church – known as the **Hohenrätien** – that were destroyed in the 15th century. At Thusis you can also travel east, then slightly north and you'll come to Davos, or you can stay on Highway 13, which will bring you into Chur. If you opt for the eastern route, you have two more options which will take you to St. Moritz – the **Julier** and **Albula Passes**.

The Julier Pass road begins at the north in the village of **Tiefencastel**, a little town residing in the Albula Valley, and then continues southward through the **Oberhalbstein** region, before finally ending in Silvaplana.

The Albula Pass road begins in **Alvaneu-Bad** at the north, and runs parallel with the **Albula River**. If you stop in **Bergün/Bravuogn** along the way, you can take a railway up to **Chants** and hike to the surrounding glaciers or out to the **Keschhütte**, at 8,610 feet (2,625 m). This charming hut has 92 beds and is open year-round. The hut phone is ☎ 81-407-1134, or call Daniel Gianelli in Davos at ☎ 81-413-4647. The road will wind and twist through Preda and eventually end at **La Punt**, just north of St. Moritz, and south of Zuoz on Route 27. From here, you could also hike to the beautiful **Chamanna d'Es-chahütte**, on the south slope of Piz Kesch. With 50 beds, it is open from mid-March to late April, and from late June to mid-October. ☎ 81-854-1755 or 81-833-4338 for reservations.

Western Graubünden & the Oberalp Pass Road

The western portion of this canton will find you traveling on Route 19 westbound from Chur through the Vorderrhein Valley on a road known as the Oberalp Pass, since it will eventually lead you over into the canton of Uri and the town of Andermatt. The village of **Versam** is a nice little place to visit, as it provides splendid views of the Vorab summits on the far side of the ravine. **Ilanz** is a 14th-century village, which also warrants a stop. This town is known as the former capital of the original "Grey League" of Graubünden. From here you can go to either **Vals** or **Vrin** for more breathtaking views of the surrounding Alps. The village of **Trun** is known as the home of the abbots of Disentis, whose massive **Ligia Grischa** was built in 1674 to house the abbots. The structure is open to visitors, and is a delight to those who enjoy Baroque architecture.

■ Disentis/Mustér

Disentis/Mustér offers visitors a fine network of ski lifts and hiking trails, and is the capital of the Upper Graubünden and Oberland valleys. The town was established in the Middle Ages by the St. Benedict monks, and here you'll find one of the oldest Benedictine abbeys in Switzerland, dating back to the eighth century. The **Klosterkirche** (abbey church) was built in the late 17th century and is easily recognizable with its two bulbous towers and double-tiered windows. From here, you can also travel southward through the **Val Medel**, which will give you more beautiful views of the surrounding areas and quickly bring you into the canton of Ticino. The Disentis-Sedrun **Tourist Office** can help you find a hotel, and provide hiking and skiing maps of the area. CH-7188 Sedrun. ☎ 81-920-4030, fax 81-920-4039.

From Disentis/Muster, it is 19 miles (30 km) to Andermatt (Canton Uri) via the Oberalp Pass. This pass is typically blocked by snow in the winter (November-May), but if you're driving, a train will take you and your car through from the town of Sedrun. In the summer it is worth parking your car in Sedrun, Selva or Tschamut and exploring the area on foot.

A steamer of the Lake Lucerne fleet at the landing near the railroad station

Central Switzerland

Central Switzerland is made up of cantons **Lucerne**, **Zug**, **Schwyz**, **Glarus**, **Uri**, and the half-cantons of **Nidwalden** and **Obwalden**. Known as the "Cradle of the Confederation," the founding cantons of Schwyz, Glarus and Uri offer an insight into the history of Switzerland from the beginning – dating back to 1291 when representatives of these three came together on the Rütli

Meadow at the northern end of Lake Uri. This area is also referred to as "Inner Switzerland" and is a good starting point for many journeys – via rail, auto or ship. Both Lake Lucerne and Lake Uri offer abundant ship excursions, and you'll find numerous cycling and hiking trails throughout the region. Likewise, cantons Zug, Nidwalden and Oberwalden are interconnected by highways, secondary roads and rail service – making travel through the region a simple matter. The vast canton of Lucerne, excluding the city of Lucerne itself, contains many excellent spots for picnics and walking excursions.

Canton Lucerne (LU)

■ At A Glance

The canton of Lucerne (spelled Luzern in German) appears as the heart of Switzerland on the map – wedged firmly between the cantons of Bern, Aargau, Zug, Schwyz and Obwalden. It is the ninth-largest canton in terms of land mass (925 square miles/2,405 square km), and the seventh largest in terms of population, with 357,400 residents, who are primarily German-speaking Roman Catholics. The northern end of the canton is relatively flat and home to many small farms. The southern end is more rolling and heavily forested, and is a great spot for scenic hikes and relaxing walks.

The **coat of arms** for Lucerne is a simple blue and white pattern similar to that of canton Zürich's shield. The shield is split down the middle vertically, with blue on the left and stark white on the right.

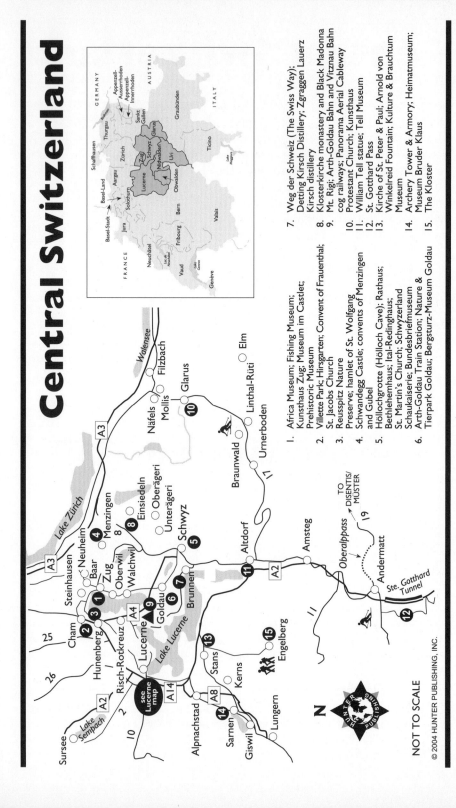

Central Switzerland

1. Africa Museum; Fishing Museum; Kunsthaus Zug; Museum im Castlet; Prehistoric Museum
2. Villette Park; Hirsgarten; Convent of Frauenthal; St. Jacobs Church
3. Reuspitz Nature Preserve; hamlet of St. Wolfgang
4. Schwandegg Castle; convents of Menzingen and Gubel
5. Höllochgrotte (Hölloch Cave); Rathaus; Bethlehemhaus; Ital-Redinghaus; St. Martin's Church; Schwyzerland Schaukaiserie; Bundesbriefmuseum
6. Arth-Goldau Train Station; Nature & Tierpark Goldau; Bergsturz-Museum Goldau
7. Weg der Schweiz (The Swiss Way); Detting Kirsch Distillery; Zgraggen Lauerz Kirsch distillery
8. Klosterkirche monastery and Black Madonna
9. Mt. Rigi; Arth-Goldau Bahn and Vitznau Bahn cog railways; Panorama Aerial Cableway
10. Protestant Church; Kunsthaus
11. William Tell statue; Tell Museum
12. St. Gotthard Pass
13. Kirche of St. Peter & Paul; Arnold von Winkelreid Fountain; Kulture & Brauchtum Museum
14. Archery Tower & Armory; Heimatmuseum; Museum Bruder Klaus
15. The Kloster

NOT TO SCALE

Lucerne

The capital city of the canton is home to 180,000 inhabitants, making it Switzerland's eighth-largest city by population. It is also one of the most popular tourist destinations in Switzerland, for good reason. Tourism began in this city as early as 1845, when the first major hotel opened. More soon followed, and a number of ports and a long promenade along the Vierwaldstätersee (Lake Lucerne) now allows visitors to take a peaceful stroll near one of Switzerland's loveliest lakes. The historic Old Town is split by the Reuss River and empties into Lake Lucerne just past the Chapel Bridge near the main train station.

■ Information Sources

Tourist Offices

Lucerne Tourism Ltd. is in the main train station, at Zentralstrasse 5, CH-6002 Lucerne. ☎ 41-227-1717, fax 41-227-1718, www.luzern.org. It is open Monday-Friday from 8:30 am-6 pm, Saturday from 9 am-6 pm and Sunday from 9 am-1 pm. The tourist office for central Switzerland (Zentralschweiz Tourismus) is on Alpenstrasse 1, CH-6002 Lucerne. ☎ 41-418-4080, fax 41-418-4081.

AUTHOR'S
PICK

*For **hotel reservations** in central Switzerland, call Zentralschweiz Tourismus at ☎ 41-318-4141, fax 41-318-4140. You can purchase a **museum pass** for 29Sfr at either of the above tourist offices that allows free entrance for one month into all of Lucerne's museums.*

Train Station

If you're into train stations, then you'll love Lucerne's ultra-modern one, with its huge overhead glass atrium and many shops. It's great fun to peruse through the two levels of the station, offering everything from freshly cut flowers to fresh baked goods, chocolates and souvenirs, as well as toiletries. This is also the junction of Switzerland's four major train lines, and you can get to any destination in Europe from here. You can rent bikes here for 27Sfr per day, from 7 am-7:45 pm daily. For rail service information, ☎ 90-03-0300.

Post Office

The main post office in Lucerne is at Bahnhofplatz 4, CH-6001 Lucerne. Open Monday-Friday from 7:30 am-6:30 pm, Saturday from 8 am-noon. ☎ 41-229-9523, fax 41-210-0301.

Lucerne

1. Kornmarkt (Corn Market);
   Altes Rathaus (Town Hall)
2. Kapellbrücke (Chapel Bridge) and
   Wasserturm (Water Tower)
3. Spreuerbrücke
4. Lucerne Naturmuseum
5. Train Station; Tourist Office
6. Jesuit Church
7. Culture & Congress Center;
   Neues Kunstmuseum (Fine Arts Museum)
8. Picasso Museum
9. Vehrkershaus (Swiss Transport Museum)
10. Richard Wagner Museum
11. Historiches Museum
12. Bourbaki-Panorama
13. Löwendenkmal (Lion Monument)
14. Gletschergarten
15. Musegg Wall

1000 FEET
303 METERS

© 2004 HUNTER PUBLISHING, INC.

TO 9

TO 10

ADLIGENSWILERSTR.
ZINGGENSTORSTR.
HALDENSTRASSE
NATIONALQUAI

Lake Lucerne
(Viernaldstättersee)

INSELQUAI

BAHNHOFPLATZ

7

5

ZENTRALSTRASSE

SCHWEIZERHOFQUAI

LÖWENSTRASSE
ALPENSTR.

12

DENKMALSTR.

14 13

ZURICHSTRASSE

FLUHMATTSTRASSE

SEEBRÜCKE

HERTENSTEINSTRASSE

BERGSTRASSE

BRAMBERGSTRASSE

BAHNHOFSTRASSE

PILATUSSTRASSE

HIRSCHMATTSTRASSE

MURBACHERSTRASSE

1
2
8

PHATUSSTRASSE

FRIEDBERGSTRASSE

BRAMBERSTRASSE

MUSEGGSTRASSE

LÖWENGRABEN

REUSSBRÜCKE

6

STATE HOUSE

15

ST.KARLI-QUAI

3 11

4

BASELSTRASSE

HIRSCHENGRABEN

BRUCHSTRASSE

KLOSTER

Northern walkup to the covered bridge at Lucerne, with the ancient water tower

Codes

The **area code** for Lucerne is 41 and the **post codes** range from 6000 to 6016.

Internet Access

This can be had at **Café-Bar Parterre**, daily from 7 am-12:30 am, Sunday and holidays from 9-12:30 am. Mythenstrasse 7, CH-6002 Lucerne.

Medical Services

Lucerne has an excellent reputation for medical services. The **Lucerne Cantonal Hospital** can be reached at ☎ 41-205-1111, and **emergency service** is available in the city at ☎ 41-211-1414 or via the national emergency service number of ☎ 144. For **children's** emergency service for dial ☎ 41-205-3166 and for **poison** information call ☎ 41-251-5151. For **police** dial ☎ 117 and for **fire** ☎ 118.

■ Getting Around

Lucerne's Old Town is car-free, so you can get around only on foot. The rest of the city can be explored on a bike or by car. But the main part of Lucerne that you'll want to visit is the Old Town, and it is easily visited in a few hours time on foot.

Central Switzerland

The Lucerne Tourist Office sponsors daily **city walks** from May 1-October 31 at 9:45 am. The walk features an English guide for the two-hour journey and costs 16Sfr. From November 1 to April 30 the walk is available on Wednesday and Saturday only. You may also want to purchase a **Tell Pass** from the tourist office if you plan on traveling via boat, mountain train or postal bus throughout the canton of Lucerne. The prices range from 135 to 184Sfr for two to five days of travel from April through October. You'll also want to grab a Junior Card that offers free travel for kids under the age of 16 if they are traveling with an adult.

■ Adventures

On Foot

 The 7,000-foot (2,134-m) mountain of **Pilatus** can be reached via the world's steepest cogwheel railway on a four- to five-hour journey. You can purchase tickets for the trip through the Lucerne Tourist Office or from the Pilatus Bahnen, Schlossweg 1, CH-6010 Lucerne. ☎ 41-329-1111, fax 41-329-1112. For information on weather atop Pilatus, ☎ 41-329-1129.

To visit the 10,000-foot (2,380-m) **Titlis** mountain, the highest point in central Switzerland, you can take the first revolving aerial cable car in the world that provides you with an exhilarating 360-degree panoramic view. From Lucerne you take the train for an hour to the village of Engelberg. From here you board a cable car for the 45-minute ride to one of the most breathtaking Alpine glacier crevasses in all of Europe. You can purchase tickets from the Lucerne Tourist Office or from Titlis Rotair, CH-6391 Engelberg. ☎ 41-639-5050, fax 41-639-5060. For the Titlis station and weather information, ☎ 41-639-5061.

Mount Rigi is known as the "Queen of the Mountains" and deservedly so. It is where Europe's first cogwheel mountain train was built and operated, and at the top there are 13 mountain lakes and spectacular views. For a great five-hour journey, take the Rigi-Kulm excursion, which is a combination of cogwheel railway train, cable car and boat trip on Lake Lucerne. You can purchase tickets at the Lucerne Tourist Office or through Mt. Rigi Railways, CH-6356 Rigi Kaltbad. ☎ 41-397-1128, fax 41-397-1982.

On Water

 You can rent pedal, motor and sailboats through **Marina Charter** from April through October. Alpenquai 13, CH-6010 Lucerne. ☎ 41-360-7944. If you want to go swimming in Lake Lucerne, then check out **Lido,** on Lidostrasse, CH-6002 Lucerne. ☎ 41-370-3806. Swimming times vary according to weather and lake conditions. You can rent windsurfing equipment or schedule lessons through **Dobler & Ingold,** on Alpenquai 13, CH-6010 Lucerne. ☎ 41-360-8244.

Golf

 Lucerne has its own 18-hole public golf course. Call ahead to schedule a tee time at the **Lucerne Golf Club**. ☎ 41-420-9798.

■ Sightseeing in Lucerne

 There are a great number of historic squares and fountains in the Old Town of Lucerne. The main square is the **Kornmarkt** (Corn Market, the site of the old grain market) that today includes such tourist sites as the Town Hall.

Landmarks & Historic Sites

Altes Rathaus (Town Hall) was first used in 1606 and today continues to be the home of the Lucerne city council. You'll find this historic building on the Rathausquai at the north end of the Rathaus-Steg (Town Hall Bridge).

The **Kapelbrücke** (Chapel Bridge) and its **Wasserturm** (Water Tower) is a landmark of Lucerne and was painstakingly restored after a tragic fire destroyed most of it in 1993. It was originally the oldest (built in 1333) roofed wooden bridge in Europe, and contains a series of paintings on each section of its ceiling beams. Also, midway across the bridge you'll find a Wasserturm (water tower) and a small souvenir shop. The reconstruction of the bridge cost $2.1 million and it was reopened for foot traffic in spring 1994. It is wheelchair-accessible.

The **Spreuerbrücke** (Mills Bridge) was built in 1407 and later restored in the late 1800s. It's narrower than its sister Chapel Bridge. It also includes a series of paintings on its interior walls that depict the 14th-century European plague. between the Geissmatt and Reuss Bridges.

 The **Musegg Wall**, left, is an 860-yard-long (786-m) fortress wall that was built from 1350 to 1408 and features nine distinct towers: the Nölli Tower (Guild Hall and Archive of the Safran Guild), the Männli Tower, the Luegisland Tower, the Wacht Tower, the Zyt Tower, with a clock dating from 1535, the Schirmer Tower with its gate, the Pulver Tower, the Allenwinden Tower and the Dächli Tower. The wall forms the northern half of the Old Town and was originally part of a wall that encompassed the city during the 14th and 15th centuries.

The Bourbaki-Panorama is a series of wrap-around paintings created by 19th-century artist Edouard Castres. The painting is of various battles fought in Switzerland. Admission is 6Sfr. Open daily from 9 am-6 pm. Lowenplatz 11, CH-6000 Lucerne. ☎ 41-412-3030, fax 41-412-3031.

The Jesuit Church (Jesuitenkirche) is a beautiful Baroque church that sits on the Ruess River, with a pair of lovely green onion domes set upon

Central Switzerland

imposing towers. This church was built between 1666 and 1673 in dedication to St. Franz Xazer and the two towers were completed in 1893. Open daily from 6 am-6:30 pm. On the Bahnhofstrasse just west of the Rathaus-Steg. CH-6004 Lucerne. ☎ 41-210-0756.

Museums

The **Neues Kunstmuseum** (Fine Arts Museum) is a collection of contemporary art and 19th-century Swiss landscapes. Open Tuesday-Sunday from 10 am-5 pm, on Wednesdays from 10 am-8 pm. You can find this museum inside Lucerne's Kultur and Konngress Zentrum (Culture & Congress Center), just east of the Bahnhofplatz. Admission is 10Sfr for adults, 8Sfr for kids or students. Europlatz 1, CH-6000 Lucerne. ☎ 41-226-7800.

The **Picasso Museum** is just west of Chapel Bridge at the Rathausquai on the north side of the Reuss River. This was home to the famous painter and contains a variety of his work, plus over 100 photographs of the artist. Admission is 6Sfr. Open from 10 am-6 pm. Am-Rhyn-Haus, Furrengasse 21, CH-6004 Lucerne. ☎ 41-410-3533, fax 41-410-1773.

The **Vehrkershaus** (Swiss Transport Museum) is the largest museum dedicated to transportation in Europe, and is home to an IMAX theater. Admission is 21Sfr. Open daily, 9 am-6 pm from April-November, 10 am-5 pm from November-March. Lidostrasse 5, CH-6006 Lucerne. ☎ 84-885-2020, fax 41-375-7500. ☎ 41-375-7575 for the IMAX theater.

The **Richard Wagner Museum** is at the site where the composer lived from 1866 to 1872. You'll see his musical instruments and personal items. It's on the lake, two miles from the city center, and can be reached by driving south on the frontage road parallel to the lake. In summer, motorboats leave every hour from in front of the railway station (rail passes are valid for the trip). Or you can take buses 6, 7 or 8. Admission is 5Sfr. Open Tuesday-Sunday from 10 am-noon, 2-5 pm, closed Monday. Richard Wagner Weg 27, CH-6016 Lucerne. ☎ 41-360-2370.

Historiches Museum is in a 1567 armory that displays weapons, flags, sculptures and scenes from Swiss life throughout the ages. Admission is 6Sfr. Open Tuesday-Friday from 10 am-noon, 2-5 pm, weekends from 10 am-5 pm. Closed Monday. Pfistergasse 24, CH-6000 Lucerne. ☎ 41-228-5424, fax 41-228-5418.

The Lucerne Naturmuseum displays scenes from local natural history. Admission is 6Sfr. Open Tuesday-Friday from 10 am-noon, 2-5 pm, weekends from 10 am-5 pm. Closed Monday. Kasernenplatz, CH-6003 Lucerne. ☎ 41-228-5411, fax 41-228-5406.

Parks & Gardens

Lucerne's main city garden is known as the **Gletschergarten** (Glacier Garden), also home to the Lion Monument, just to the east of Zürichstrasse on the north side of Old Town. The **Löwendenkmal** (Lion Monument) is a beautiful stone memorial – the oldest preserved figure monument in Switzerland – and was carved in memory of the 786 Swiss men who perished while defending Louis XIV and Marie Antoinette in the Tuileries attack of 1792. The Glacier Garden was created by the runoff waters from nearby glaciers, and includes a mirror maze built for the 1896 Paris Exhibition. Admission is 9Sfr. Open daily from 9 am-6 pm, April-October, and from 10 am-5 pm, November-March. Denkmalstrasse 4, CH-6006 Lucerne. ☎ 41-410-4340, fax 41-410-4310. www.gletschgarten.ch.

TAKE A TRIP TO SURSEE

While in Lucerne, it is worth your time to visit the lakeside village of **Sursee,** at the northwest corner of the **Sempachersee** (Lake Sempach). Known as the "golden village," Sursee has a delightful Old Town, with its historical buildings carefully restored over the past 25 years to their original dark golden colors. You'll find many old buildings and churches from the Middle Ages, as well as a wide variety of cafés and shops run by local artisans. The Sursee Tourist Office is at Parkweg 5, CH-6210 Sursee, ☎ 41-921-1977, fax 41-921-0108, and can provide you with maps of the city. There are also plenty of hiking and walking paths around the lake, and a number of opportunities for watersports such as windsurfing, sailing and boating.

You can also take a wonderful one- to two-hour train ride on the **Sursee-Triengen-Bahn**, a historic steam locomotive that makes a wide circle around the village, with  various stops for photo opportunities. There is a dining car, and a bar car available as well. You can get information on times through the tourist office or contact the office for the Sursee-Triengen-Bahn at Postfach 182, CH-6210 Sursee. ☎ 41-921-4030, fax 41-921-4284.

If you want to stay overnight and enjoy a meal, check out the following inns. The **Hotel Bellevue** at the Lake is a beautiful medieval hotel with gorgeous views of the lake and Alps. Near the sports center, it includes a bar and excellent in-house restaurant. The outside of the hotel is quite beautiful, with stucco walls and capped roofs. ($$-$$$). The restaurant is open Tuesday-Sunday from 8 am-midnight, and closed Monday. Bellevueweg 7, CH-6210 Sursee. ☎ 41-925-8110, fax 41-925-8111. The **Hotel Hirschen** is a small, family-run inn that is beautiful and quaint on the outside and just as lovely inside. Leonard Wust and his family have carefully maintained this historic building, which also has a gourmet restaurant serving wonderful meals in all price ranges ($-$$$$). With its warm atmosphere, this hotel feels more like a home. ($$-$$$). Open year round. CH-6210 Sursee. ☎ 41-921-1048, fax 41-921-2709.

■ Shopping

There are lots of shops on the **Kapellgasee** in Old Town, and outside this area you'll find that the city is typical of a large European city with its shops, malls and outlets. Two Swiss chain department stores (**Globus**, on Pilatusstrasse 4, ☎ 41-227-0707, and **Manor**, on Weggisgasse 5, ☎ 41-419-7699) both offer less pricey souvenirs as well as clothes, home items and toiletries. For embroidered and lace goods, look to **Neff**, at Löwenstrasse 10, ☎ 41-410-1965, or **Sturzennegger**, on Schwanenplatz 7, ☎ 41-410-1958. For gifts, Lucerne-made handicrafts and souvenirs, check out **Ordning & Reda**, on Hertensteinstrasse 3, ☎ 41-410-9506; **Casa Grande**, on Grendelgasse 6, ☎ 41-418-6071; or **Schmid-Linder** on Denkmalstrasse 9, ☎ 41-410-4346. The finest watch and jewelry shop is **Bucherer**, on Schwanenplatz 5, ☎ 41-369-770, and for sporting equipment and clothing look to **Bannwart Sport AG**, at Weggisgasse 14, ☎ 41-410-4538.

■ Where to Stay

Romantik Hotel Wilden Mann is one of the most unusual and pleasant finds in the city. A Lucerne landmark since 1517, this charming inn was originally a group of small houses. Here, each room has been individually decorated with fine detail. Antiques and works of

HOTEL PRICE CHART	
$	30-75Sfr ($20-$49)
$$	76-205Sfr ($50-$109)
$$$	206-299Sfr ($110-$200)
$$$$	300Sfr+ ($200+)

art can be found throughout this splendid inn, which also features three dining areas. One is a fine French restaurant, the second is the relaxed Swiss-style **Burgerstube**, and the third is an outdoor garden terrace for summer dining. Open year-round and run by hosts Ursula and Charles Zimmermann. ($$$-$$$$+). Bahnhofstrasse 30, CH-6000 Lucerne. ☎ 41-210-1666, fax 41-210-1629.

Hotel Ambassador is one of the finest in Lucerne, on one the most active squares in town. Within walking distance of the Lion Monument, the lake, casino and shopping. Offers all modern amenities, parking and a shopping center. ($$$-$$$$). Open year-round, this hotel is a quick five- to 10-minute walk from the train station. Pets are allowed. Zürichstrasse 3, CH-6004 Lucerne. ☎ 41-418-8100, fax 41-418-8190, www.ambassador.ch.

Hotel Krone is in the heart of Lucerne's Old Town and features a beautiful outside façade in traditional Swiss style, while the interior offers all modern amenities. Breakfast is included, and a warm family atmosphere is apparent in the small touches found throughout this inn. ($$$-$$$$). Weinmarkt 12, CH-6004 Lucerne. ☎ 41-419-4400, fax 41-419-4490.

Hotel des Balances has a stunning riverside location along the shores of the Reuss River that dates back to 1200; it's very near to the local fish and wine market (Weinmarkt Square). This four-star hotel offers all modern amenities in lovely, large rooms and provides wonderful views of the lake and mountains. Within walking distance of all the hotspots of Lucerne's Old Town. Features a splendid restaurant, **Rotes Gatter**, that serves gourmet dishes. ($$$-$$$$). Weinmarkt, CH-6000 Lucerne. ☎ 41-418-2828, fax 41-418-2838.

National Hotel was first built in 1870, and was the original base of Cesar Ritz, who eventually designed and built the world famous Ritz luxury hotels that are so well known today. This hotel has a massive façade that takes up a good portion of the promenade along the lakeside and is hard to miss. There is a snappy piano bar, restaurant and all modern amenities. ($$$-$$$$). Haldenstrasse 4, CH-6003 Lucerne. ☎ 41-419-0909, fax 41-419-0910.

Des Alpes is in the heart of Old Town on the river, and has large, homey rooms in a splendid location with great views of Lucerne, the Alps and the lake. A good deal for the money. ($$-$$$). Rathausquai 5, CH-6003 Lucerne. ☎ 41-410-5825, fax 41-410-7451.

The **Löwengraben** is a former jail that is now home to a funky hotel. The 51 rooms are situated atop restaurants and a bar, which adds to the uniqueness of this lively spot. ($$).Löwengraben 18, CH-6004 Lucerne. ☎ 41-417-1212, fax 41-417-1211, www.lowengraben.ch.

Hotel Alpha is in a quiet yet central spot in Lucerne, a quick walk to the bus stop, and a 10-minute walk to the railway station and the lake. Contains a nice small library and two community TV rooms. The rooms are small, but comfortable and very clean. Dogs are allowed and breakfast is included in the rates. Open year-round. ($-$$). Zahringerstrasse 24, CH-6003 Lucerne. ☎ 41-240-4280, fax 41-240-9131.

The **Youth Hostel** in Lucerne is open year-round and contains 194 beds just north of Old Town, on the shores of the Rotsee (Red Lake). They have all types of rooms for singles, couples and groups. This is one of the best Youth Hostels in Switzerland. ($-$$). Am Rotsee, Sedelstrasse 12, CH-6004 Lucerne. ☎ 41-420-8800, fax 41-420-5616, www.youthhostel.ch/luzern.

Camping

 Camping is available at the **Lido Campsite**, open March-October. ($). Lidostrasse, CH-6004 Lucerne. ☎ 41-370-2146, fax 41-370-2145.

■ Where to Eat

The **Old Swiss House** has been tempting tourists since 1859 with its Swiss and French cuisine. The half-timbered house has stained-glass windows, huge oak doors and wooden stairways, and the walls are adorned with beautiful oil paintings. It is well known throughout the city for its fancy Wienerschnitzel, calf's liver and veal. Open Tuesday-Sunday from 11:30 am-midnight. Reservations recommended. ($$$-$$$$). Löwenplatz 4, CH-6004 Lucerne. ☎ 41-410-6171.

DINING PRICE CHART	
Prices based on a typical entrée, per person, and do not include beverage.	
$	15-25Sfr ($10-$16)
$$	26-45Sfr ($17-$29)
$$$	46-70Sfr ($30-$47)
$$$$	71Sfr+ ($47+)

Scala Restaurant features a 1920s Art Deco design with beautiful views of the Alps and Lake. The menu ranges from à la carte to fresh pasta dishes, and the meals are carefully prepared. ($$-$$$). Located in the Hotel Montana, open daily. Adligenwilerstrasse 22, CH-6004 Lucerne. ☎ 41-410-6565, fax 41-410-6676.

Restaurant Spatz has a great winter garden terrace (enclosed in glass) so that you can view the goings-on year-round. The menu offers meat, fish and vegetables, with the house special being the "Luzerner Kügelipastetli." ($$-$$$). Located in Hotel Spatz. Obergrundstrasse 103, CH-6005 Lucerne. ☎ 41-310-6348, fax 41-310-1084.

Mr. Pickwick Pub is in Hotel Pickwick and serves up an authentic English breakfast all day long, as well as all types of sandwiches, burgers and Irish stew. Only 600 yards from the train station on the banks of the Reuss River in Old Town, with a great view of the "Kapell-bridge." Open Monday-Sunday from 11:30 am-midnight. ($-$$). The hotel has good, simple rooms at reasonable rates, and pets are welcome here. Rathausquai 6, CH-6004 Lucerne. ☎ 41-410-5927.

Canton Zug (ZG)

■ At a Glance

The canton of Zug is set on the shores of Lake Zug, surrounded by the Alpine foothills and green, rolling pastures. Lake Zug is the sixth-largest lake in Switzerland – running north and south for nine miles (14.5 km), and is divided by the Kiemen peninsula. The canton sits snugly in between four cantons – with Lucerne and Aargau to the west and northwest, while Zürich is on the northern side and Schwyz meanders along the southern border. The cities of Zürich and Lucerne are each only 30 minutes away by car or train.

The population of this canton has doubled in size since 1960 and is home today to some 98,000 German-speaking citizens who are mostly Roman Catholic. This increase in population has been in response to the growth of international trade and industries within Canton Zug. Electronic technology is one of the largest industrial sectors in the canton. The growth of both population and industry was initially spurred by low taxes here. However, 45% of the canton is still used for agricultural purposes.

Zug is thought to have first been established in 858 as a trading post for the Gotthard route. Then, in 1315, a fierce battle (the Battle of Morgarten) took place between the Confederates and the Habsburgs on the shores of the tiny Agerisee, which lies east of Lake Zug beyond the Zugerberg. Zug than joined the Swiss Confederation in 1352 – the seventh canton to do so – along with Glarus. Today there are 11 distinguishable communities within Canton Zug. Oberaegeri, Unteraegeri, Menzingen and Neuheim make up the mountain regions of the canton, while Stadt Zug (city of Zug), Baar, Steinhausen, Cham, Huenenberg and Walchwil comprise the valley regions around the area of Lake Zug. Zug is the largest municipality in terms of population, followed by Baar and Cham.

The **coat of arms** is shows a blue horizontal bar that cuts through the middle of the otherwise white shield.

The City of Zug

Founded in 1803,Stadt Zug is the capital of the canton and home to 22,314 citizens. The main attraction of this town is the *Altstadt*, where many of the buildings are 500 years old or more, and the streets are mostly auto-free. You'll want to take in the 1557 **Zytturm** (clocktower) in Kolinplatz, the medieval village center. The shields just below the clockface represent the first eight cantons to join the Swiss confederation, while the blue and white tiles above it show the cantonal colors. The **fountain** here was dedicated to **Wolfgang Kolin**, who bore the flag when the Swiss army was defeated in the 1422 Battle of Arbedo.

*You will notice an abundance of cherry trees in Zug, and the **Zuger kirschtorte**, a delightfully sinful combination of fresh cherries, almonds, pastry and cherry brandy, is found in most Zug restaurants and cafés.*

*Zug's medieval town center, with the Zytturm (clocktower)
and St. Oswald Church*

■ Information Sources

Tourist Office

 The Tourist Office of Canton Zug is at Alpenstrasse 16 in Stadt Zug. They provide information, maps, tours and weekend excursions for the entire canton. There are a variety of hikes and specialized walking tours that can be arranged through this office. CH-6304 Zug. ☎ 41-711-0078, fax 41-710-7920, www.zug-tourismus.ch.

Train Station

 Zug's train station is less than half a mile north from the village center and offers **bike rental** and a **currency exchange**. Bikes are available for rent at no charge from May to October, in Zug, Baar and Cham. From this station, you can connect to virtually any spot in Switzerland via rail.

Post Office

 The Zug post office is at Postplatz 1 and is open Monday through Friday from 7:30 am to 6:30 pm, Saturday from 8 am to noon. ☎ 41-729-5252, fax 41-729-5255.

Codes

The **area code** for Zug is 41, and the **postal code**s are CH-6300 or CH-6301 (Zug), CH-6302 (Zug 2, Baarerstrasse), CH-6303 (Zug 3, Herti), CH-6304 (Zug 4, Bahnhof), and CH-6305d (Zug 5, Annahme).

Media

 The *Neue Zuger Zeitung* is published daily, Monday through Saturday, and provides cantonal and city news. The *Zuger Presse* is published three times a week while the *Zuger Woche* is published every Wednesday and is free. *Radio Sunshine* is the main radio station for the canton, at 94.2FM.

■ Getting Around

 There are 347 miles (559 km) of hiking trails throughout the canton, and most are suitable for families and older folks. You'll find countless bike and mountain biking trails through this canton. Zug's *Altstadt* is best explored on foot, and boat trips abound at Lake Zug's Schiffsstaion.

■ Adventures

On Foot

 For **guided walking tours** of Stadt Zug's old city, contact Pauline Hruza at ☎ 41-780-3105. Industrial educational tours, which give you a profile of Zug's history up to the present, can be arranged through the **Verein Industriepfad Lorze**, CH-6304 Zug. ☎ 41-729-4069.

Known as one of the "Seven Wonders of Switzerland," the **Höllgrotten**, or Hell Caves are a great excursion for a rainy day. These unique, dripstone caves are near the town of Baar. You'll see stalagmites, stalactites, ponds and unusual rock formations. The walk through the caves can be as long or as short as you want to make it, but on average it takes slightly less than an hour. You can either walk to the caves via a path from the Baar train station or hike, drive or ride a bike from Zug. Admission is 5-9Sfr. There is also a small restaurant (☎ 41-761-6605; closed Monday) at the caves. Höllgrotten, CH-6340 Baar. ☎ 41-761-8370, fax 41-760-3620.

The **Zugerberg** is a small mountain by Alpine standards, at just 3,241 feet (988 m), but offers impressive views of various mountain ranges in a panoramic setting. Take Bus #11 or drive to Schöneg and grab the funicular to the top. There are a number of hikes you can take from here:

There's a two-hour hike from **Zugerberg to Walchwil**. From the summit, follow the signs along the trail as it twists and winds near the

Lotenbach stream. The path will then turn and lead you through a forest, the Girwald, and into the Dietschwand (an old farm road) as you continue toward Lake Zug. You'll eventually be on the Vorderbergstrasse (literally, the Front Mountain Street) and pass the St. Ann chapel coming into Walchwil. From here, you can take a boat or bus back to Zugerberg.

For a more demanding hike (not recommended for seniors or kids), try the trail from **Zugerberg to Sildspitz**, which will take up to seven hours. Leaving from Zugerberg, you follow the trail south at a fairly even level, until you come to where you'll climb up to **Wildspitz**, at 4,800 feet (1,580 m), the highest point in Zug. Here you'll enjoy impressive views of the Gripen montain range. You can either retrace your steps or head back around the Agerisee (Lake Ageri) toward Unterägeri.

There are also three round-trip walks for families and seniors that are easy, and named after animals: the fox (2½ hours), the rabbit (two hours), and the deer (four hours). All of these begin at the Zugerberg mountain station.

On Water

On both the Zugersee and the Agerisee you'll find many boating possibilities, including the rental of **pedaloes**, **rowboats**, and **fishing boats**, as well as boat excursions on both lakes. **Surfing** and **sailing** lessons are also available. For Lake Zug, contact the **Immensee Surfing School** at ☎ 41-780-8217 or the **Zug Surfing School** at the TCS Campingplatz in Zug at ☎ 41-780-2666. For the Agerisee, contact **Sailing School Agerisee** at Waldhofstrasse 6, CH-6314 Unter, ☎ 41-750-5735, fax 41-750-5733. Open Tuesday through Sunday, noon-8 pm.

Golf

Golf is available at Minigolf Zug – behind the main post office – from May to October, Monday through Saturday, 2-7 pm, and on Sundays, 10 am-7 pm. During July and August, it is open until 10 pm. at am Löberensteig, CH-6300 Zug. ☎ 41-170-2235.

Winter Sports

Zug is home to tobogganing, ice-skating, cross-country skiing, snowshoe hiking, and winter hiking.

Tobogganning/Sledding

The Zugerberg mountain railway offers sleds and toboggans for rent, and the night toboggan ride from the summit to the base is particularly exciting. Contact the **Talstation Schonegg** at ☎ 41-711-5376 for information and times. Lift prices typically run from 5Sfr for two hours to 10 Sfr for five hours of sledding time.

Skating

There are two ice rinks in Zug: the **Eishalle Herti** at General-Guisanstrasse 4, CH-6300 Zug, ☎ 41-725-3131, and the **Eissportvereing Zug** at General-Guisanstrasse 2, CH-6300 Zug, ☎ 41-725-3100.

Cross-Country & Downhill Skiing

Cross-country tracks abound on the Zugerberg, and the paths in the nearby villages of Ägerital and in Menzingen are well-prepared and available for nighttime ski runs. Downhill skiing is available on the Zugerberg; it is low-key and great for families with children.

Snowshoe Hiking

Check out **Kaktus-Outdoor** for rental, trekking sticks, and avalanche sensors at Baarerstrasse 49, CH-6300 Zug, ☎ 41-710-2261. They also specialize in organized snowshoe hiking trips for groups of all ages.

Curling

The **Zug Curling Club** welcomes all visitors to learn this unique sport. Contact Alice Haslimann at ☎ 76-372-3999 for information. Curling is usually done in one of Zug's two indoor ice rinks.

■ Museums

Zug's **Africa Museum** presents masks andv carvings from Central Africa. Open Monday to Friday, from 8:30-11:30 am, 2-5:30 pm, Saturday and Sunday by request. St. Oswaldgasse 17, CH-6300 Zug. ☎ 41-711-0417.

The **Fishing Museum** features an exhibition about fishing methods and examples of fishing gear from the past and present. Fischereiverein, CH-6300 Zug. ☎ 41-769-0610.

Kunsthaus Zug was established in 1990 and has collections by contemporary and 20th century artists. Admission is 8Sfr for adults, 6Sfr for students and kids. Open Tuesday through Friday from noon-6 pm, Saturday and Sunday from 10 am-5 pm. Dorfstrasse 27, CH-6300 Zug. ☎ 41-725-3344, fax 41-725-3345.

Museum im Castlet is a 13th-century castle that displays historical relics from the city and canton of Zug. Kirchenstrasse 11, CH-6300 Zug. ☎ 41-728-3297.

The **Prehistoric Museum** shows archeological finds from Canton Zug. Admission is 5Sfr for adults, 2Sfr for kids. Open Tuesday through Sunday from 2-5 pm, closed Monday. Hofstrasse 15, CH-6300 Zug. ☎ 41-728-2880, fax 41-728-2881.

The German-Swiss Bee Keeping Association has a display inside the Hotel Rosenberg on the art of bee keeping, including bee anatomy and beeswax production.

■ Shopping

At Zug's **Landsgermeindeplatz** you'll find a variety of restaurants, cafés and shops that cater to tourists.

■ Where to Stay

Hotels

Hotel Löwen am See sits right on the banks of Lake Zug and offers all modern amenities in a charming and comfortable atmosphere. ($$$). Landsgemeindeplatz 1, CH-6301 Zug. ☎ 41-725-2222, fax 41-725-2200.

HOTEL PRICE CHART	
$	30-75Sfr ($20-$49)
$$	76-205Sfr ($50-$109)
$$$	206-299Sfr ($110-$200)
$$$$	300Sfr+ ($200+)

Hotel Ochsen Zug was once host to Goethe and French King Louis Philipp. This 16th-century inn has modern comforts combined with an old-world setting. The in-house restaurant offers Swiss, international and seasonal specialties, along with a fine wine list. ($$-$$$). Kolinplatz 11, CH-6300 Zug. ☎ 41-729-3232, fax 41-729-3222.

Hotel Restaurant Guggital is a 10-minute walk from the train station, on and above the Zug See in a beautiful, quiet location. An in-house restaurant features Swiss, seasonal and vegetarian dishes. ($$-$$$). Zugerbergstrasse 46, CH-6300 Zug. ☎41-711-2821, fax 41-710-1443.

Hotel Zugertor was built in 1897 and is lovingly maintained by Heinz and Anita Rickenbach. Near the train station, it includes a good, in-house restaurant that serves up Swiss, seasonal, and vegetarian specialties. ($$). Baarstrasse 97, CH-6302 Zug. ☎ 41-729-3838, fax 41-711-3203.

Yellow, **das Zuger Lagerschiff** is a former cruise ship that has been converted into a floating dormitory with a sundeck and on-board restaurant. Reservations required. ($$-$$$). Open April to October. CH-6300 Zug. ☎ 41-727-6180, 41-727-6172, www.msyellow.ch.

Hostel

Jugendherberg Zug offers 92 beds near the city center on Allmendstrasse 8 at Sportstadium Herti. ($). Open March to September. CH-6300 Zug. ☎ 41-711-5354, fax 41-710-5121.

Campground & Mountain Hut

Campground Bruggli is open from April to October on the Chamer Fussweg 36, CH-6300 Zug. ☎ 41-741-8422, fax 41-741-8430.

Mountain Hut Sustlihütte is open from the end of June to November and has room for 83 people. Contact Giorgio and Brigitte Ruele for reservations and information. Bellevueweg 38, CH-6300 Zug. ☎ 41-711-5843.

■ Where to Eat

Gasthaus Rathauskeller specializes in gourmet regional dishes, French, international and seasonal cuisine. in the village center near the boat docks. ($$-$$$). Open Tuesday through Saturday from 11:30 am-2:30 pm, 6:30-10:30 pm. Closed Sunday, Monday. Ober-Altstadt 1, CH-6301 Zug. ☎ 41-711-0058, fax 41-710-4977.

DINING PRICE CHART	
Prices based on a typical entrée, per person, and do not include beverage.	
$	15-25Sfr ($10-$16)
$$	26-45Sfr ($17-$29)
$$$	46-70Sfr ($30-$47)
$$$$	71Sfr+ ($47+)

Hecht Am See is the pride of Zug's Altstadt, as this restaurant has been here since 1435. Fresh fish and game are the specialties and the desserts are delicious. near the lake in the town center. ($-$$$$). Open daily, 11:30 am-3 pm, 5:30-11 pm. Fischmarkt 2, CH-6300 Zug. ☎ 41-711-0193, fax 41-729-8130.

Aklin Restaurant has been a Zug favorite for 216 years (since 1787). In the heart of the old city, it features seasonal dishes. Open daily except for Sundays. ($-$$$$). Kolinplatz 10, CH-6300 Zug. ☎ 41-711-1866, fax 41-711-0750.

Café Pizzeria Platzmühle serves fish, pizza, Italian and vegetarian fare at inexpensive prices. Open daily from 7-midnight (closed Wednesdays during the winter). ($-$$). Landsegemeindeplatz 2, CH-6300 Zug. ☎ 41-711-6550, fax 41-711-6575.

Fischerstube (Fisherman's Lounge) features good hearty Swiss food at reasonable prices. ($-$$). Unter-Altstadt 12, CH-6300 Zug. ☎ 41-711-2010, fax 41-711-2298.

Weinstube Zur Taube Tabeen La Paloma is a wine lounge housed in a 500-year-old structure, between the Casino and Fishmarket. This unique and reasonably priced restaurant specializes in Spanish cuisine. ($-$$). Open Tuesday through Saturday from 11 am-2 pm, 5-midnight. Closed Sunday and Monday. Unter-Altstadt 26, CH-6300 Zug. ☎ 41-711-3266.

Baar

Baar is the second-largest town in Canton Zug, just two miles (3.2 km) north of Stadt Zug, with 19,024 citizens. The highlight of this area is the **Hollgrotten** (Hell Caves) and the **Baarburg**, a wooded hilltop in the nearby village of Baar that, according to local legend, contains the remains of the prehistoric village – although this has never been proven. There are many cycling and hiking paths around Baar as well, including the **Baar-Kappel Cultural-Historical Path**. This begins at the Baar train station, and brings you alongside the Lorze River and many historical sights. This is a good hike for seniors and those with cultural interests.

The Baar **Tourist Office** is at Leihgasse 2, CH-6340 Baar. ☎ 41-761-1568, fax 41-760-3620, www.baar.ch. **Bikes** are available for rent for free from May to October at the **train station**, and you can make reservations at ☎ 41-761-3335. For information and rental of in-line skates, as well as maps, contact the **Baar Skating Hall** at ☎ 41-760-8877.

■ Where to Stay & Eat

The **Hotel Ibis** is in the city center and is open year-round. Their restaurant offers Swiss and international fare at reasonable prices. ($$). Clean, comfortable and quiet. Bahnhofstrasse 15, CH-6340 Baar. ☎ 41-766-7600, fax 41-766-7676.

Baarburg is a tiny, simple and clean inn with eight rooms, and only accepts cash as payment. Pets are permitted. ($-$$). Marktgasse 14, CH-6340 Baar. ☎/fax 41-761-1733.

The **Dörfli Restaurant** serves up meat specialties as well as regional fare in hearty portions. Open Monday through Saturday from 8:30 am-midnight, Sunday from 9 am-9 pm. ($-$$). Dorfstrasse 7, CH-6319 Gemeinde Baar. ☎ 41-710-1535.

Cham

Cham is the third-largest town in Canton Zug and is home to 13,200 residents. Three miles (4.8 km) west of Zug, Cham is also the oldest settlement in the canton, set on the northwest edge of Lake Zug. Highlights of this city include the **Villette Park**, the **Hirsgarten**, the **Convent of Frauenthal** and **St. Jacobs Church**. Hiking and cycling trails can be found throughout this area. The Cham **Tourist Office** is in the Cham **train station**, where you can also rent bikes for free from May to October. CH-6330 Cham. ☎ 41-780-3222, fax 41-781-4386, www.cham.ch.

■ Where to Stay & Eat

The **Hotel-Restaurant Lorze** is in the village center and is a handicapped-accessible facility with 26 rooms, which are nicely decorated and clean, with all modern amenities. The restaurant offers seasonal and international cuisine. Open daily except Sunday. ($$-$$$). Dorfplatz 1, CH-6330 Cham. ☎ 41-780-4050, fax 41-780-4555.

Hotel Bahnhof is a beautiful Swiss chalet close to the Villettepark in the city center by the lake. Bike trails and miniature golf is nearby as well. This inn only has 10 rooms, but all are charmingly decorated. The in-house restaurant offers a wide range of dishes, including Swiss, international, vegetarian, organic and seasonal fare. ($$). Bahnhofstrasse 2, CH-6330 Cham. ☎ 41-785-5050, fax 41-785-5055.

A **farm stay** is available at Annemarie Gretener-Villiger's farm in Cham. A 10-person dormitory, kitchen, bathroom and shower can be had for 30Sfr per day per person. Bring your own sleeping bag. Families with two kids are 75Sfr, with three kids, 85Sfr. Breakfast is available on the premises, and horseback riding tours can be arranged here as well. Baregg, CH-6330 Cham. ☎ 41-780-0264, fax 41-783-2588.

The restaurant **Vino e Cucina** serves northern Italian dishes, pizza and international fare at reasonable prices ($-$$). Closed Sunday. In the town center at Dorfplatz 1, CH-6330 Cham. ☎ 41-780-4050, fax 41-780-4555.

Wirtschaft Schiess offers good hearty food and seasonal specialties at reasonable prices. ($-$$). Open Monday through Thursday from 9 am-2 pm, 5 pm-midnight, Friday from 9 am-midnight. Closed Saturday and Sunday. Schulhausstrasse 12, CH-6330 Cham. ☎ 41-780-1187, fax 41-780-1175.

Hünenberg

This tiny village nestled in the Alpine foothills between the Reuss River and Lake Zug is home to 7,072 inhabitants. The **Reusspitz Nature Preserve** and the town center are popular attractions, but the pride of the locals is the hamlet of **St. Wolfgang** on the outskirts of the village and its Gothic church, which dates back to 1475. For information and hiking information, contact Einwohnergemeinde Hünenberg. Charmerstrasse 11, CH-6331 Hünenberg. ☎ 41-784-4444, fax 41-784-4499.

Menzingen

Menzingen is known as the "pearl of the mountainside," and is home to 4,109 people. This little village is made up of farmhouses and is a hiker's paradise. Here, you'll also find the **Schwandegg Castle** and the **Menzingen and Gubel convents**. Contact Verkehrsbüro Menzingen at Neudorfstrasse 6, CH-6313 Menzingen. ☎ 41-755-1301, fax 41-755-1814.

■ Where to Stay & Eat

For a unique place to bunk, try the **Gasthaus Gubel**, which sits atop Menzingen's highest moraine and offers terrific hikes throughout. Maintained by the family Ruckli-Rogenmoser. ($-$$). Auf dem Gubel, CH-6313 Menzingen. ☎ 41-755-1142. You can also try the **Hotel-Restaurant Ochsen**, an inn in the town square that has a beautiful outdoor terrace and a fine restaurant. Excellent wine list as well. Ten rooms, all handicapped-accessible. Breakfast is included. ($$). Neudorfstrasse 11, CH-6313 Menzingen. ☎/fax 41-755-1388.

Neuheim

Neuheim has only 1,905 inhabitants (the smallest population in the canton) and is a peaceful and relaxing village far away from the hustle and bustle of bigger cities. Sitting on the moraine between the Sihl and Lorze rivers, Neuheim offers great hiking opportunities. For information contact Gemeindeverwaltung Neuheim, Dorfplatz 5, CH-6345 Neuheim. ☎41-757-2130, fax 41-757-2140.

Oberägeri

Oberägeri is known as the "sun terrace of Zugerland," and sits along the shores of the Agerisee. Home to 4,551 residents, it provides visitors with great hiking paths, biking trails and boat excursions. The streets here are filled with more bikes than cars. Contact the Verkehrsburgo Agerisee (**Tourist Office**), at Postfach, CH-6315 Oberägeri. ☎ 41-750-2414, fax 41-750-2443.

■ Where to Stay & Eat

If you're looking to stay overnight here, then check out the **Morgarten Oberägeri**, a beautiful inn at the shores of Agerisee. This is a great place for families with small children, and includes a kid's playground, two bowling alleys, and a surfing school. Make your reservations early, however, as there are only 10 rooms, all very modern and clean. The in-house restaurant offers Swiss, seasonal and vegetarian dishes. ($-$$). Am Aegerisee, Sattelstrasse 1, CH-6315. Morgarent-Oberägeri. ☎ 41-750-1291, fax 41-750-5949.

Risch-Rotkreuz

R isch-Rotkreuz is comprised of the villages of Risch, Rotkreuz, Buonas and Holzhaüsern. This area has an extensive network of hiking and biking trails around Lake Zug, the Reuss River and the Steintobel up to the Michaelskreuz – a beautiful chapel that offers marvelous views of the area and is the starting point for various walking paths. Home to some 7,119 people, Risch-Rotkreuz is another great place to escape to if you're tired of the tourist scene. Verkehrsbüro Risch-Rotkreuz (**Tourist Office**), CH-6343 Rotkreuz. ☎ 41-790-1116, fax 41-790-2220.

Steinhausen

T his is a tiny village with 8,696 citizens that is home to the **Don Bosco Church** – unique in the fact that it houses both a Catholic and a Protestant church. There is also a tiny lake within the beautiful Steinhausen woods. Contact Gemeindeverwaltung Steinhausen (**Tourist Office**), Bahnhofstrasse 3, CH-6312 Steinhausen. ☎ 41-748-1111, fax41-741-3181.

■ Where to Stay & Eat

You can stay at the **Bergrestaurant Wildspitz**, a large home suitable for singles and small groups, but you must bring a sleeping bag. The in-house restaurant is open Wednesday-Sunday, mornings to 5 pm. ($). Rossbergstrasse, CH-6416 Steinerberg. ☎ 41-832-1139, fax 41-832-0939.

Unterägeri

A town of 7,043 inhabitants, Unterägeri also sits on the shores of Lake Ageri, and offers swimming, sailing, surfing and rowing. Hiking trails abound here, including the famous **Panorama Route**, the **Industriepfad Lorze**, and others. Contact the Verkehrsbüro Ägerisee (**Tourist Office**) at Postfach, CH-6315 Oberägeri. ☎ 41-750-2414, fax 41-750-2443. There is a good **campground** here on Wildrunnenstrasse 81, CH-6314 Unterageri. ☎ 41-750-3928, fax 41-750-5021.

Walchwil

This town, with 3,171 inhabitants, sits directly at the foot of the Rossberg mountain, and is often referred to as the "Riviera of Central Switzerland," due to its mild climate throughout most of the year. Here you'll find typical Zug farmhouses, vineyards, a distillery, cheese dairy and a fish-breeding center. Verkehrsbüro Walchwil (**Tourist Office**) is at Dorfstrasse 2, CH-6318 Walchwil. ☎ 41-758-2939, fax 41-758-1321.

■ Where to Stay

A good place to stay here is the **Zuger Alpi**, a summer inn with cheap, bare rooms. ($). Zugerberg, CH-6318 Walchwil. ☎ 41-758-1143. Or, you can bunk down at the **Stiftun Jugendhause Wilchwilerberg**, a mountain house that offers space for up to 25 people at inexpensive rates ($). To get there, you have to walk from the Voderbergstrasse in Walchwil to the Zugerberg upper station, then to the hut. This is about a one-hour hike, with great views and splendid trails.

The Landwasser viaduct with the Rhaetische Bahn railway near Filasur on the Albula route

Canton Schwyz (SZ)

■ At a Glance

The canton of Schwyz became one of the founding members of the Swiss federation on August 1, 1291, along with cantons Uri and Unterwalden, when they united against surrounding aggressive factions atop the Rütli mountain. This initial union paved the way for the Switzerland we know today.

Schwyz is just to the east of Lake Lucerne and south of Lake Zürich and the Obersee, covering an area of 563 square miles (1,464 square km). Schwyz's boundries touch the cantons of Zug, Zürich, and St. Gallen to the north, with Canton Glarus along its eastern side, and Canton Uri on the south. To the east, Canton Schwyz lies north of Lake Lucerne at several points, and then caresses the edges of the Zugersee on that lake's southwestern shores. Within Schwyz you'll find the spectacular **Etzel Waterfall**, with a 330-foot (100 m) drop near the Hurden Peninsula that divides the Obersee from the upper portion of Lake Zürich. On the western edge, you'll find the ever-popular **Rigi-Kulm**, a great spot for photographing the region from its panoramic peak. In the middle of the canton sits **Einsiedeln**, just to the west of the Sihlsee, while farther east still is the tiny, beautiful **Wagitaler See**, nestled in the Alps.

With 131,400 German-speaking, mostly Roman Catholic residents, Schwyz is 17th in terms of population figures among the 26 cantons. There are 30 main municipalities within Schwyz, and about 41% of the land is used for agriculture. Over one-third of the population works in the energy, construction and manufacturing sectors, while about a quarter works in the service and tourism industries.

The coat of arms of Canton Schwyz was originally plain red, and was later changed to represent the national coat of arms for all of Switzerland seen today. The arms are based on the original arms and banner of the canton from 1481. The cross first appeared on the red background in 1729, and this shield was officially noted in 1815, but the official size of the white cross was not decided until 1963.

Schwyz

The city of Schwyz sits at the foot of the **Mythen Peaks**, slightly east of Lake Lucerne and Lake Lauerzer, along main Highway 4 and is the capital city of the canton. This city is home to 114,000 "Schwyzers." It was here, after the battle of Morgarten in 1315, that the name for Switzerland came into being, when it was changed from Helvetia to Schweiz (in German). The old part of the city has a rich history, and the town houses here are famous throughout the country. It is also in Schwyz that the historical archives of the founding of Switzerland are housed.

■ Information Sources

Tourist Offices

For the town of Schwyz, go to Tourismbüro Schwyz (Tourist Office), Bahnhofstrasse 4 (beside the train station), CH-6430 Schwyz. Open Monday-Friday, 7:15 am-noon, 1-5 pm, Saturday from 8:30 am-noon. There is also a Tourist Office inside the post office, open Monday-Friday from 7:30 am-noon, 1:30-6:30 pm, Saturday from 8-11 am. Postelle Schwyz at Oberer Steisteg 14. ☎ 41-810-1991, fax 41-819-3488.

Train Station

The train station for Schwyz is 1.2 miles (1.9 km) west of the Schwyz village center in the suburb of Seewen. You can get there from Schwyz by taking any Schwyz Post bus.

Post Office

The Schwyz post office is open 7:30 am-noon, 1:30-6:30 pm, Monday-Friday, and on Saturday from 8 am to noon. Postfach, CH-6340 Schwyz. ☎ 41-811-2710, fax 41-811-1406.

Codes

The **postal code** for Schwyz is CH-6340, and the **area code** is 41.

■ Getting Around

The best way to see Schwyz is on foot. The town itself can be a little difficult to get in and out of by car, and most of the natives use buses to get around locally. The closest train station is 1.2 miles (1.9 km) west in Seewen.

■ Adventures

On Foot

Hiking abounds in this area of Switzerland in the summertime, and you'll definitely want to hike to the **Ibergeregg Pass.** Beginning in Schwyz, you'll travel southeast to Rickenbachstrasse and continue on, over winding and twisting roads. The road will suddenly become very steep, and will be a hard, heart-pumping climb until you reach the Ibergeregg Pass at 4,613 feet (1,406 m).

You'll also want to check out the **Frontalpstock** at 6,306 feet (1,922 m). To get there walk 10 minutes south on the secondary road from Schwyz to the town of **Ibach**. From here, continue south to Morschach where you can take a funicular up to Stoos, and from there another lift up to Fronalpstock.

For another hike, travel from Schwyz southeast two miles (3.2 km) through the **Muota Valley** to **Schlatti**. Once here, grab the funicular for the 10-minute climb up to **Stoos** at 4,200 feet (1,280 m). From here, you can follow a number of excellent footpaths in the summer, while in the winter skiing abounds throughout this area.

You can also walk to **Rickenbach**, a small village just a mile southeast of Schwyz. Here, take the cable car to the upper station of the **Rotenfluh** at 5,135 feet (1,565 m) for some excellent panoramic views of the area.

You also might want to check out the **Swiss Holiday Park** (especially if you're traveling with children) just a few miles south on main Highway 4 from Schwyz in Morschach. This is a water-park, spa, and sun-bathing spot, with various activities such as thermal baths and a fitness center suitable for the whole family. CH-6443, Morschach. ☎ 41-825-5050, fax 41-825-5060.

In the winter, many of the hiking paths serve as cross-country ski routes, and downhill skiing can be found here as well. The local tourist boards provide information and maps of the areas.

■ Sightseeing

You'll want to spend some time walking along the shores of **Lake Lauerzer** on the western side of Schywz. This tiny lake is bordered by beautiful mountain flowers and is best visited on the west and south shores. An ugly rock quarry on the eastern edges takes away from the beauty of this otherwise glorious spot.

Another must-see is the **Höllochgrotte** (Hölloch Cave). This is the largest cave in Europe and was first discovered in 1949. While there are 91 miles (146 km) of galleries to be found here, only a half-mile can be explored by the public. The inside of the cave is like something out of a *Lord of the Rings* movie, with bizarre and eerie rock formations. To get there, take the **Muotatal Road** south to the **Hinteral**, then cross the river and go left (northeast) up a steep road to **Stalden**. You can park your car here (if you drove) at the **Gasthaus zur Höllgrotte**.

Landmarks & Historic Sites

The **Rathaus** (town hall) was built in the 17th century and was later (1891) decorated with murals on its outside depicting various aspects of Swiss history. Inside, the hall is adorned with stained-glass windows and ornate woodworking. It's in the village center square, at Hauptplatz 1. Tours are Monday-Friday, from 10 am to 3 pm. ☎ 41-81-4505.

On the northwestern edge of the Hauptplatz, you'll find the **Bethlehemhaus**, which is the oldest wooden house in Switzerland, dating back to 1287. It has very small rooms with low ceilings that make you wonder about the size of the people who occupied it at the time. It is next to the equally impressive **Ital-Redinghaus**, which features antique objects, ornate wood paneling and stunning stained glass from the 17th and 18th centuries. They are both open May to October, Tuesday-Friday, from 2-5 pm, Saturday and Sunday from 10 am-noon, 2-5 pm. Closed on Mondays, and November through April. Located at Rickenbachstrasee 24 & 26.

St. Martin's Church, which is filled with 18th-century Baroque frescos and decorations, is also in the village square across from the Rathaus. You'll also want to visit the **Schwyzerland Schaukaiserie**, found at the back of the train station. Here you'll see how cheese is made and prepared in various stages. Admission is free, and the factory is open Tuesday-Saturday from 9 am-6 pm.

Museums

The **Bundesbriefmuseum** contains the original documents of the Swiss Federation. Erected in 1934, this building has a Danioth fresco on its façade, and the inside contains a Clénin fresco entitled "the Oath." The pacts of alliance of the original eight cantons are contained here, as is the Bundesbrief from the pact of 1291, and the Morgartenbrief from the pact of 1315. Admission is 4Sfr. Open May to October, Tuesday-Friday from 9-11:30 am, 1:30-5 pm, Saturday and Sunday from 9 am-5 pm; November to April, Tuesday-Friday, from 9-11:30 am and 1:30-5 pm, Saturday and Sunday from 1:30-5 pm; closed Monday. Bahnhofstrasse 20. ☎ 41-819-2064, www.sz.ch/kultur.

THE SWISS ARMY KNIFE

 The history of Swiss Army knives began in Canton Schwyz in 1884, when a poor young Swiss man, Carl Elsener, founded the Swiss Cutlers' Association. Elsener – from the small town of Ibach, just 10 minutes south of Schwyz – had seen a need for reliable pocket knives and army blades, but was undercut by a German competitor in 1893 and nearly lost his entire investment. But he enlisted the help of family members, and in 1897 produced a light pocketknife, which he had patented. These first knives grew in popularity, and soon Elsener began providing the Swiss army with knives.

The name Victorinox sprang from two ideas – Elsener had named his Ibach factory Victoria, in honor of his mother and, when stainless steel was introduced in 1921 as INOX, Elsener decided to combine the two names. The name Victorinox was later given official status by both the Swiss and American armies. Today the same Ibach factory produces 34,000 Swiss Army knives a day, in all shapes and sizes. The factory has an on-site store that sells knives at discount factory prices. In Ibach at Schmiedgasse 57. Open Monday-Friday, 7:30 am-noon, 1:15-6 pm, Saturday from 8 am-3 pm.

■ Where to Stay

Hotel Restaurant Wysses Rössli offers large, clean rooms in a charming atmosphere. ($$). The in-house restaurant is excellent, and serves up regional fish and other Swiss specialties at reasonable ($$) prices. Both are open seven days a week. Am Hauptplatz. CH-6430 Schwyz. ☎ 41-811-1922, fax 41-811-1046.

HOTEL PRICE CHART	
$	30-75Sfr ($20-$49)
$$	76-205Sfr ($50-$109)
$$$	206-299Sfr ($110-$200)
$$$$	300Sfr+ ($200+)

Gasthaus Schwyzer Stubli offers nice, quiet rooms ($$) and windows adorned with flowers. The in-house restaurant ($) serves hearty Swiss fare, but is closed Monday and Tuesday. Ridestrasse 3, CH-6430. ☎ 41-811-1066, fax 41-811-8067.

Hotel Engel is near St. Martin's Church on the Schulgasse and offers cheap rooms, some with balconies. ($). Breakfast can be had for only 5-6Sfr. CH-6430 Schwyz. ☎ 41-811-1242.

Hirschen Hotel is a cozy old inn full of Swiss charm and simplicity. ($-$). Hinterdorfstrasse 14. CH-6430 Schwyz. ☎ 41-811-1276.

Youth Hostel Rotschuo has 96 beds and is seven miles (11.3 km) west of Schwyz. Open March 1-November 30. ($). CH-6442 Gersau . ☎ 41-828-1277, fax 41-828-1263.

■ Where to Eat

Sternen, behind the Postplatz bus stop, has good pizzas and pastas at cheap prices. ($). Closed Monday. Zeughausstrasse 6, CH-6430 Schwyz.

The Ratskeller serves good hearty food in generous portions. ($-$$). Strehlgasse 3, CH-6430 Schwyz. Closed Sunday and Monday. ☎ 41-811-1087.

Goldau

This tiny village near Highway 4 just east of the Rigi offers a good base from which to begin many hikes.

■ Information Sources

Tourist Office

The Schwyz Tourist Office (cantonal) is found here at Postfach 525, CH-6410 Goldau. ☎ 41-855-5950, fax 41-855-5951, www.schwyz-tourismus.ch.

Post Office

The Goldau post office is at Bahnhofstrasse 3, CH-6410, and is open from 7:30 am-noon, 2-6 pm Monday-Friday, and Saturdays from 8-11:30 am.

Train Station

Arth-Goldau train station is one of the most famous in all of Switzerland. Work first began on the station in 1882 and it was finally completed in 1897, allowing connections throughout the country. This station prompted a boom of construction activity throughout the region, and brought many people to Goldau and surrounding towns and villages, seeking work at planned hotels and multi-family buildings. One hundred years after work first began on the Arth-Goldau station, the entire facility was renovated and a signal tower was added. The inside was modernized to allow operators to control the traffic of inbound and outbound trains electronically. Arth-Goldau thus became the most important north-south (Basel-Zürich to Ticino) traffic junction for not only Switzerland but for all of Europe. Inside the station today you'll find the **Bahnofbuffet** restaurant, which is well worth a stop. The whole station combines modern conveniences with an aura of yesteryear that makes this train stop worth a walk-through, even if you're not traveling in or out of it. For information, contact the **Verkehrs und Informationsbüro** at Rathausplatz 3, CH-6415 Arth am See, ☎ 41-855-4242, or the **Informationbüro** at the Schwyzer Kantonalbank at Parkstrasse 1 in Goldau, ☎ 41-855-3182.

■ Adventures

On Foot

A good hike is from Goldau to the **Rigi-Scheidegg**. You'll follow the narrow, winding road 2½ miles (four km) to Kräbel Station and then take the cable car up to Scheidegg, at 5,268 feet (1,665 m). From here, you can climb to the summit of Rigi-Scheidegg for great panoramic views of the area.

■ Sightseeing

Nature & Tierpark Goldau was founded in 1925 and features many species of Swiss and European animals, including chamois, bears, wolves, marmots, foxes and wildcats. There is also a self-serve restaurant within the park (☎ 41-855-2786). Admission is 14 Sfr for adults,12Sfr for seniors, and 9Sfr for kids six to 11-years-old. Open November 1-March 31 from 9 am-5 pm, April 1-October 31, Monday-Friday from 9 am-6 pm, Saturday, Sunday and holidays from 9 am-7 pm. PO Box 161, CH-6410 Goldau. ☎ 41-855-1510, fax 41-855-1520.

Right next to the entrance of the **Tierpark** is the **Bergsturz-Museum Goldau**, worth a quick visit. Built in 1956, this tiny museum features information about landslides in the region. Admission is 2Sfr. Open April-October daily from 1:30-5 pm. Postfach 104, CH-6410 Goldau. ☎ 79-478-1105, fax 41-859-1601.

■ Where to Stay

Hotel Restaurant Rössli features cheese fondue and other Swiss goodies at its restaurant, while the rooms are clean and comfortable with modern facilities. You can stay and eat here for reasonable prices. ($-$$). Located just five minutes from the train station, and breakfast is normally included in the rates. Gotthardstrasse 29, CH-6410 Goldau. ☎ 41-855-1319, fax 41-855-4602.

HOTEL PRICE CHART	
$	30-75Sfr ($20-$49)
$$	76-205Sfr ($50-$109)
$$$	206-299Sfr ($110-$200)
$$$$	300Sfr+ ($200+)

Camping

The **Bernerhöhe** campground is open year round in Goldau and has 20 camping sites for tourists. Contact Bruno Gwerder for reservations. ($). CH-6410 Goldau. ☎ 41-855-1887, fax 41-855-5970.

Central Switzerland

■ Where to Eat

Restaurant Gotthard is an elegant dining room that features daily specials of the seasons. Open year-round except for Thursdays. Excellent fare. ($$). Parkstrasse 21, CH-6410 Goldau. ☎ 41-855-1462.

DINING PRICE CHART	
Prices based on a typical entrée, per person, and do not include beverage.	
$	15-25Sfr ($10-$16)
$$	26-45Sfr ($17-$29)
$$$	46-70Sfr ($30-$47)
$$$$	71Sfr+ ($47+)

Gasthaus Bauernhof is a charming farmhouse that serves up regional and Swiss fare in hearty portions. ($-$$). Gotthardstrasse 18, CH-6410 Goldau. ☎ 41-855-1213.

Restaurant Goldauerhof serves good, hearty meals, including burgers and local and regional fare such as lamb and pig roasts. Closed Thursday. ($-$$). Bahnhofstrasse 10, CH-6410 Goldau. ☎ 41-855-1177.

Restaurant Schönegg Goldau is a bright and cheery restaurant that features a nice wine list. Closed Monday. ($-$$). Open Tuesday-Saturday from 10:30 am-midnight, and on Sunday from 10:30 am-8 pm. Schönegg 34, CH-6410 Goldau. ☎ 41-855-2353.

Bären Restaurant Pizzeria da Toni is a good little pizzeria in a cozy setting. ($). Centralstrasse 3, CH-6410 Goldau. ☎ 41-855-5252.

Brunnen

Brunnen is at the meeting point between the Vierwaldstättersee and the Urnersee and is one of the top resort spots in the region. It is also a high-traffic water port between the cantons of Schwyz and Uri. It was in Brunnen that the three cantons of Uri, Schwyz and Unterwalden (Obwalden and Nidwalden) joined together on December 9, 1315 after the victory at Morgarten. Home to 7,200 residents, it is also the starting and ending point for the well known **Swiss Trail** around Lake Uri, which leads you to many historic sites and through beautiful scenery. This resort town has more visitors than any other city within Canton Schwyz, and is a popular place for nature lovers, with over 35 miles (56 km) of walking trails and hikes.

■ Information Sources

Tourist Office

The Brunnen Tourist Office is open Monday-Friday, from 8:30 am-noon, 1:30-6 pm at Bahnhofstrasse 32, CH-6440, Brunnen. ☎ 41-825-0040, fax 41-825-0049. The office offers guided walking tours of Brunnen, including visits to all of the chapels, and a guided tour of the convent. Costs vary according to the type of tours taken.

Post Office

 The Brunnen post office is open Monday-Friday, from 7:30 am-noon, 1:45-6 pm, Saturday from 8-11:30 am Parkstrasse 1, CH-6440, Brunnen. ☎ 41-820-1010, fax 41-820-4077.

■ Adventures

On Foot

 Weg der Schweiz (The Swiss Way) begins and ends in Brunnen. It was inaugurated in 1991, during the 700th anniversary of the Swiss Confederation. The walk takes you 21.7 miles (35 km) through the cantons of Schwyz and Uri around the Urnersee, passing through eight communities. The trail is divided into separate sections, according to the canton it travels through, and most parts are suitable for families, seniors and even wheelchair-bound travelers. You'll find numerous picnic spots and places for a campfires along the way. For maps and information, contact the **Interessengruppe Pro Weg der Schweiz** at Postfach 684, CH-6440 Brunnen. ☎ 41-825-0046, fax 41-825-0049. You can also call their Wandertelephone at ☎ 41-871-1033, or their Weatherphone at ☎ 41-820-1534.

The **Urmiberg cable car** in Brunnen is open from November 1 to March 31, Wednesdays-Sundays, leaving every half-hour from 9 am to 6 pm. From April 1-May 31, it begins at 8 am, following the same weekly schedule. From June 1-October 31, it operates seven days a week from 8 am to 6 pm, except on Monday and Sunday, when it goes from 8 am to 7 pm. Prices start at 11Sfr. To get there, travel west on the road leaving Brunnen on the north side of Lake Lucerne toward Gersau; it's about half-way in between these two villages on Highway 2B. You can travel to the top to sit out on the panoramic deck of **Restaurant Timpelweid**, where you'll find hearty Swiss fare and great views of the Alps. CH-6440 Brunnen. ☎/fax 41-820-1405.

On Water

 Boat trips on **Lake Lucerne** are very popular and will take you from Brunnen to Schillerstein, Rütli, Tellskapelle, and Füelen in round-trip fashion. You'll have many options once on-board, including full-day and half-day trips that may include a lunch, snacks or a drink. Some include stops at restaurants on-shore. One popular trip is the excursion to **Rigi**. You'll take the ship to **Vitznau** and then board the cog railway up to Rigi-Kulm, where you can stay, hike or enjoy the splendid views while sipping a hot drink. You can then retrace your steps or take another cog railway to Goldau, before coming back to Brunnen. This trip typically costs around 60Sfr. Prices for most of the boat trips start at 17Sfr, and you can make reservations at the Tourist Office.

Rowing excursions are available as well via the Brunnen Tourist Office. For instance, you can embark at Brunnen and row to Rütli to visit the history museum there, then hike to Treib for a lunch at the historic restaurant, finally returning to Brunnen via ship.

■ Landmarks & Historic Sites

The **Detting Kirsch Distillery** offers guided tours through its distillery and includes a tasting of their traditional Kirsch brandies. For groups up to 15 people, the total cost is 150Sfr, and 15 Sfr for each individual thereafter. There is another distillery at **Zgraggen Lauerz**. This one also offers guided tours, at 10Sfr per person for groups of up to 15 people. Here, you'll watch a slide show on the evolution of the Kirsch distillery process, entitled *From the Cherry to the Kirsch*. The Brunnen Tourist Office can help get you included in a scheduled tour of these facilities.

■ Where to Stay

Seehotel Waldstätterhof Brunnen sits on the shores of Lake Lucerne, and is behind a large park, with great views of the Alps. Huge, traditional and stately, this hotel with 100 rooms has played host to the rich and famous over the years, including Queen Victoria of

HOTEL PRICE CHART	
$	30-75Sfr ($20-$49)
$$	76-205Sfr ($50-$109)
$$$	206-299Sfr ($110-$200)
$$$$	300Sfr+ ($200+)

England, Winston Churchill, the first George Bush and Hermann Hesse. ($$$-$$$$). Includes two restaurants (see *Where to Eat*), along with a bar and terrace café. Located on the Waldstätterquai, CH-6440 Brunnen. ☎ 41-825-0606, fax 41-825-0600.

Hotel Bellevue Au Lac is a three-star, beautiful and stately hotel on Lake Lucerne with spectacular views of the Rutli, Schillerstein and Trieb. Modern facilities and many rooms come with balconies. ($$$). Axenstrasse 2, CH-6440 Brunnen. ☎ 41-820-1318, fax 41-820-3889.

Hotel Elite is the perfect hotel for hikes and other excursions as it is centrally located within the village. The in-house restaurant is famous throughout the country (see *Where to Eat*). ($$$). Axenstrasse 1, CH-6440 Brunnen. ☎ 41-820-1024, fax 41-820-5565.

Hotel Gotthard Garni is in the center of town, just a stone's throw from the lake, and near the train station and forest. ($$). Am Leewasser 1, CH-6446 Brunnen. ☎ 41-825-4060, fax 41-825-4061.

Weisses Rossli is a charming little inn that was once visited by Louis II of Bavaria and, as a result, contains five frescos created in his honor. ($$). Bahnhofstrasse 8, CH-6446 Brunnen. ☎ 41-820-1022, fax 41-825-1122.

Schmid und Alfa is on the lakeshore and is a clean and comfortable spot with great views of the lake and surrounding mountains. ($$). The restaurant is well known for its excellent cuisine. Open March to October. ☎ 41-820-1882, fax 41-820-1131.

Camping

There are two campsites in Brunnen. **The Hopfreben** is open from the end of April to the end of September and offers 150 tourist plots. Contact George Stirnimann for reservations (strongly requested). ($). CH-6440 Brunnen. ☎ 41-820-1873, fax 41-820-1479. **The Urmiberg** campground is open April 1-October 31 with 80 plots for guests. Maurus Betschart takes reservations. ($). CH-6440 Brunnen. ☎ 41-820-3327.

■ Where to Eat

Restaurant Elite is a definite must if you're staying overnight in Brunnen. The fish is always fresh from the Urnersee, and the preparations are wonderful. Also, the restaurant features a nice buffet breakfast – served until 11:30 am – that is delicious and plentiful. ($$-$$$). Axenstrasse 1, CH-6440 Brunnen. ☎ 41-820-1024, fax 41-820-5565.

DINING PRICE CHART	
Prices based on a typical entrée, per person, and do not include beverage.	
$	15-25Sfr ($10-$16)
$$	26-45Sfr ($17-$29)
$$$	46-70Sfr ($30-$47)
$$$$	71Sfr+ ($47+)

Seehotel Waldstätterhof Brunnen is home to a pair of grand restaurants (the elegant **Rôtisserie** and the rustic **Sust-Stube**), along with a bar and terrace café. The Rôtisserie serves up international cuisine, including seasonal specialties, with a generous wine list and numerous cheese offerings. ($$-$$$). Open daily, from 11:30 am-2 pm, 6:30 pm-midnight. The Sust-Stube offers simple, hearty meals, with monthly specials. ($-$$$). Open daily, 8 am-midnight. The lakeside terrace and boulevard café seats up to 270 people, and it provides one of the loveliest views of Lake Lucerne found anywhere. Open from early spring to late autumn daily, 9 am-9 pm, A hearty Sunday brunch is served each week from 9:30 am to 2 pm at Sfr39.50 per person. There is something for everyone here. Located on the Waldstätterquai, CH-6440 Brunnen. ☎ 41-825-0606, fax 41-825-0600.

Restaurant-Hotel Ochsen Brunnen has been in the same family for four generations and is the oldest house in Brunnen, having been built in 1740. Beautiful and charming, it also offers hotel rooms at reasonable

Central Switzerland

prices ($$), with modern amenities. The restaurant is known for its historical rendition of regional specialties, preparing meals and dishes from medieval times. Bahnhofstrasse 18, Postfach 454, CH-6440 Brunnen. ☎ 41-820-1159, fax 41-820-5566.

Einsiedeln

Einsiedeln is in the north of the canton, just west of the Sihlsee, and is 18 miles (29 km) northeast of Schwyz. It is just 3.1 miles (five km) east off of Highway 8. This town is well known for its 18th-century **monastery**, which was originally built in 934 by Otto I and Duchess Reglinde of Swabia. Einsiedeln's main street runs along the huge façade of this Benedictine Abbey. The monastery's famous **Black Madonna** has been on display for over 1,000 years, and has miraculously escaped destruction on more than one occasion. During Napoleon's era, the French leader tried to steal the Black Madonna away when his armies took over the church, but the Swiss had already moved the sacred figure to Austria for hiding. Today you'll see the Black Madonna within its own black marble chapel at the western end of the church.

There are 14 separate drinking fountains at the front of the monastery, and tradition calls for visitors to drink from each, for good luck.

■ Information Sources

Tourist Office

The Tourist Office of Region Einsiedeln is at Hauptstrasse 85, CH-8840 Einsiedeln. ☎ 55-418-4488, fax 55-418-4480.

Post Office

The Einsiedeln post office is at Bahnhofplatz 3, Postfach 417. It is open Monday-Friday, from 7:30-noon, 1:30-6 pm, Saturday from 8-11:30 am. CH-8840, Einsiedeln. ☎ 55-418-4412, fax 55-418-4410.

■ Landmarks & Historic Sites

The **Klosterkirche** (Abbey Church), shown at left, was built in 1719-1735 and is a popular example of the Vorarlberg Baroque style of architecture. The outside is flanked by two tall towers while the inside is extremely spacious, with domes and ornately decorated panels, aisles and

naves. Frescos and stucco designs are also found throughout. The Grosser Saal (Great Abbey Hall) is on the second floor of the monastery and was built in the 18th century. Art exhibitions are held here on a regular basis.

MIRACULOUS DEDICATION

Einsiedeln is also home to the Miraculous Dedication, a religious celebration held every year on September 14. In addition, every five to 10 years nearly 700 citizens get together and are led by the local monks in a rendition of *Das Grosse Weltheater (The Great World Drama)* in front of the church. It was first celebrated in Spain in 1685, and the next performance is set for the summer of 2006.

■ Where to Stay

Gasthaus Meinradsberg is a smoke-free inn, offering clean rooms at very reasonable rates, which include breakfast. ($-$$). The restaurant specializes in fresh fish from Lake Zürich, lamb, and a tasty home-made apple and orange punch. Julgenweidstrasse 3, CH-8440 Einsiedeln. ☎ 55-418-8197, fax 55-418-8198.

HOTEL PRICE CHART	
$	30-75Sfr ($20-$49)
$$	76-205Sfr ($50-$109)
$$$	206-299Sfr ($110-$200)
$$$$	300Sfr+ ($200+)

Hotel Restaurant Sonne has nice, simple rooms and a good in-house pizza parlor and sun terrace. ($-$$). Klosterplatz. CH-8440 Einsiedeln. ☎ 41-412-2821, fax 41-412-4145.

Hotel National has just six beds, but is clean and cheap ($). Located near the train station at Hauptstrasse 18, CH-8440 Einsiedeln. ☎ 41-412-2616.

Camping

This is available on the eastern side of the Silhsee at **Grüene Aff** in Willerzell. Open year-round, with 20 tourist spots. ($). Contact Alois Ochsner at CH-8846 Willerzell. ☎ 41-412-4131.

■ Where to Eat

"**Zur Glocke Restaurant** serves up great burgers and fantastic desserts in a beautifully paneled dining room. Open 11 am-midnight daily. ($-$$). Hauptstrasse 73, CH-8440 Einsiedeln. ☎ 55-422-1216, fax 55-422-1217.

Landgasthof Heidenbühl has cheap, hearty meals. ($). Located across the train station tracks. ☎ 41-412-4221.

Rigi

Rigi is the stuff legends are made of, and many a traveler has spent the night atop this majestic mountain to watch the sun come up over the Alps on the summit of Rigi-Kulm – its highest point at 5,896 feet (1,799 m). This mountain is surrounded on virtually all sides by water – the lakes of Lucerne, Zug and Lauerz have it nearly embedded on an island of sorts, pinched in between cantons Schwyz, Lucerne, Zug and Unterwalden.

■ Information Sources

The **Mt. Rigi Tourist Board** is at Rigi-Kaltbad and can assist you with hiking maps, railway times and hotel information. CH-6356 Rigi Kaltbad. ☎ 41-397-1128, fax 41-397-1982.

■ Getting Here

You can access Rigi by a number of different routes. If you're driving, you can either take the A1 Highway from Bern or the A2 highway from Basel from the west or, if you're traveling from the east, take A1 (Highway 4) from Schwyz-stadt and Gotthard or A14 from Zürich & Chur. By train, there are many direct and fast train connections to Arth-Goldau, and via boat, you can access Rigi from Lucerne to Weggis or Vitznau.

There are two cog railways that operate year-round up to Rigi, either the **Arth-Goldau Bahn** or the **Vitznau Bahn**. The Vitznau Bahn was built in 1871 and was the world's first mountain railway, stretching from Lake Lucerne to the top of Rigi. The Arth-Goldau Bahn reaches the Rigi summit from the opposite side of the mountain. The **Panorama Aerial Cableway** travels from Weggis to Rigi-Kaltbad on a daily basis at half-hour intervals. Check local timetables for specific times. **Mt. Rigi Railways**, CH-6354 **Vitznau**. ☎ 41-399-8787, fax 41-399-8700. For weather information, ☎ 41-399-8770. If you're in Weggis, then contact the **Mt. Rigi Railways** there at CH-6353 **Weggis**. ☎ 41-390-1844, fax 41-390-2610.

■ Adventures

On Foot

You'll find hikes, hikes and more hikes in Rigi! Rigi offers some 62 miles (100 km) of hiking and footpaths that are auto-free in some of the most gorgeous areas of Switzerland. Here you'll find walkers, strollers, serious hikers, and picnickers enjoying the beautiful scenery. Unless otherwise noted, these hiking paths and trails can all be accessed via cog railways from Vitznau to Rigi Kaltbad, by cable car from Weggis to Rigi Kaltbad or via Arth-Goldau to Rigi First.

The Rigi Höhenweg is an easy 6.2-mile hike that is suitable for almost anyone, and will take anywhere from three to four hours. The hike begins at the Rigi-Kulm station, where you'll follow the well-marked footpath on Rigi's north side, crossing the train tracks at the Rigi-Staffel station at 5,257 feet (1,603 m). From here, follow the signs of the "Gratweg" until you reach Chänzeli at 4,801 feet (1,464 m). Continue downward to Lake Lucerne and the train station of Rigi Kaltbad, then past this tiny town until you pass a light wooded area. Continue on to the Felsenweg and the path will veer right as you walk across the mountainside to the Schild at 4,769 feet (1,454 m). The path will wind around a bit through the crests of these mountains, which is actually the old Scheidegg-Bahn railway route that is no longer in service. You'll come to the **Berggasthus**, a cheap ($) spot for overnight lodging (☎ 41-85500127) and, once past this, the trail continues through a small tunnel before reaching a tiny valley. Here you'll see a sign at Hinter Dosser; continue on, turning left into a pasture. The trail then meanders to the right before you reach the plateau of Rigi-Scheidegg at 5,438 feet (1,658 m). From here, walk on along the footpath until you come to the station of Kräbel-Scheidegg. You can either take the cable car back down or walk down (another hour) to the Geshwänd-Burggeist chairlift station.

The Kulmhütte Path takes you from Rigi Kaltbad to the Kulmhütte at 5,497 feet (1,676 m) and is a 4½- to five-hour hike. From Rigi Kaltbad, follow the signs to **Felsenkapelle** (the chapel within the rocks), and continue on this idyllic nature path to **Rigi Känzeli**, which provides fantastic views of Lake Lucerne and the Bürgenstock. The path will climb slightly up to **Rigi Staffelhöhe** at 5,804 feet (1,550 m), level out a bit and then climb some more through pastures and woods before you come to the Kulmhütte. From here you can continue on to the Schochenhütte, the Tribhütte, and finally to Ständli. After these points the path will bring you to Rigi First, and then on back to Rigi Kaltbad.

The Staffelhohe Path leads you from Rigi Kaltbad, traveling along the Kaltbad Path to Rigi First and typically takes from one to two hours. It is suitable for almost anyone. Look behind the hotel at Rigi First to find the rest of the path as it climbs slowly upward through an Alpine meadow at the base of the Rostock, facing the Rigi Railway tracks. Continue on up to the Staffelhöhe at 5,084 feet (1,550 m) and on to Rigi Kaltbad.

The walk from **Rigi Kaltbad to Küssnacht** will take you two to three hours, depending upon how long you stop to enjoy the scenery. From Rigi Kaltbad, walk on the footpath to the famous lookout point of **Känzeli** and then continue north, all the while descending slightly before coming to **Alp Rab** at 3,686 feet (1,124 m). From here, continue on downward

Central Switzerland

through the forest, passing Chürzboden and the Altruedisegg before the trail becomes somewhat flat. Continue onward to Seebodenalp, where you can take a cable car to Küssnacht. From here you can either retrace your steps or catch a bus back to Weggis, Vitznau or Arth-Goldau.

The Lake Path (Seeway) offers great views of the snow-topped mountains of Uri, Unterwalden and the Bernese Oberland, as well as Lake Lucerne. It should take you two to three hours. Again, just follow the well-marked path from Rigi Kaltbad to Rigi First along the defunct Rigi Scheidegg tracks. Continue on to the Felsenweg until you reach the Rigi Scheidegg tracks again, and then veer right toward Unterstetten. You'll cross a bridge and ascend to the Rotbalmegg at 4,778 feet (1,457 m). From here, the path will descend over the Glettialp to Hinterbergen, where you can catch a cable car back to Vitznau.

Walking from **Rigi Kulm** to **Rotstock** takes about two hours and is mostly a downhill hike. From Rigi Kulm, follow the path downward to Rigi Staffel, and then ascend to the Rotstock at 5,441 feet (1,659 m). Continue down through a lovely Alpine meadow to Rigi First, before the now-level path returns you to Rigi Kaltbad.

To get to **Rigi Klösterli** from **Rigi Kulm** will take you about 1½ hours, and it's a fairly easy hike for almost anyone. From Rigi Kulm, walk past the old rail depot through lovely Alpine meadows, down to the Kulmhütte. Continue on along the "Kulmgrat" or mountain ridge pathway to the Schochenhütte, and turn right. The path will then lead to the Alp Trib before continuing over a small bridge to the Hotel Des Alpes, before leading to a wide open path as you approach the Rigi Klösterli at 4,270 feet (1,302 m).

On Rigi mountain, with the Pilatus in the background

Canton Glarus (GL)

■ At a Glance

 Canton Glarus – in the east central portion of Switzerland – is approximately 424 square miles (1,102 square km) sandwiched in between the cantons of St. Gallen to the north and east, Schwyz to the west, and Uri and Graubünden to the south. Also known as "Glarnerland," this canton is home to two beautiful lakes, the **Walensee** and the **Klöntalersee**, perfect for hiking, water sports and camping excursions. One of the oldest cantons in Switzerland (founded in 1352), it is home to some 39,000 German-speaking, primarily Protestant citizens in 29 municipalities, who still participate in the Landsgemeinde, or open-air democracy forums for governmental elections and laws. It is the 10th-smallest canton in terms of landmass, and the fifth-smallest in terms of population in Switzerland. However, it is the eighth largest (21%) in terms of foreign citizens, probably due to the fact that there are many small factories here. Some 34% of the citizens of Canton Glarus are employed in manufacturing or industry.

You'll also find the river **Linth** here, which has helped to produce hydroelectric power for over 200 years. There are many factories, such as dye-works and weaving operations, that continue to use this form of energy.

 *Glarus is also home to **Schabzieger** cheese – a cone-shaped herbal and skim milk cheese made only here and which can be preserved for lengthy periods of time. Also of note are the famous Glarus fruit tarts, known better as "**Glarner Pasteten**."*

Glarus contains over 186 miles (299 km) of well-marked hiking paths, ranging from easy walking trails to intermediate and difficult mountain excursions. There are also a variety of mountain bike routes here. The mountain ranges of this canton provide breathtaking treks up to the **Glärnisch** (at 7,651 feet/2,333 m) or **Tödi** (at 11,847 feet/3,612 feet the tallest in the canton), and there are also gondolas and chairlifts that will take you up to beautiful Alpine pastures.

The **coat of arms** for Canton Glarus is represented by St. Fridolin, who is the patron saint of this district. St. Fridolin stands erect, holding a golden staff in his right hand, with a red Bible in his left hand, against a red background.

Glarus

The capital city of this canton is the village of the same name. Glarus, home to some 6,000 citizens, is found in a deep ravine at the foot of the **Vorder Glärnisch Cliffs.** The city was rebuilt in 1861 after a fire rampaged through and destroyed most of it. Since that time the Landesgemeinde (an open-air public election and meeting to decide on the laws) has met on the first Sunday in May each year in the Zaunplatz.

■ Information Sources

Tourist Office

The Glarnerland Tourist Office is in the town of Niederurnen at Raststatte A3, CH-8867 Niederurnen. ☎ 55-610-2125, fax 55-610-2826. However, the Tourist Office for **Glarus Stadt** is in the Glarus train station at CH-8750 Glarus. Open July-October, Monday-Friday from 9 am-noon, 2-6 pm; Saturday from 9 am-noon, 2-4:30 pm and Sunday from 9 am-1 pm. From November-July, Monday-Friday from 9 am-noon, 2-5 pm. ☎ 55-650-2090, fax 55-650-2091.

Post Office

The post office is open year-round, Monday-Friday, from 7:30 am-6 pm, Saturday from 7:30 am-noon. Schweizerhofstrasse 10, CH-8750 Glarus. ☎ 55-646-5205, fax 55-640-4093.

Codes

The **postal code** for Glarus is CH-8750 and the **area code** is 55.

■ Sightseeing

You'll want to visit the double-towered **Protestant Church** that was erected in 1866, and the **Kunsthaus**, which contains works from 19th- and 20th-century Swiss artists. The church was previously a religious center for both Protestants and Catholics, and features renditions from both the Gothic and Roman periods. It was the first type to represent the neo-Romanesque style in Switzerland. Beginning in the sixth century, many churches throughout Europe were designed in the shape of a Latin cross. There are other churches in Switzerland with Latin cross basilicas, but none with double towers. This one has two symmetrical towers on either side of the entrance, while behind them is a stunning, long off-white basilica. Open daily from 10 am-4 pm.

■ Shopping

The center of Glarus offers up small shops and traditional wares, including some handwoven linens and handkerchiefs from the local textile factories. The area is definitely worth a stroll.

■ Where to Stay

Hotel Restaurant Roessli is a medium-sized hotel with lots of family charm that features very nice rooms with basic amenities at reasonable rates. ($$). Glarnischstrasse 12, CH-8750 Glarus. ☎ 55-640-1646, fax 55-640-8060.

HOTEL PRICE CHART	
$	30-75Sfr ($20-$49)
$$	76-205Sfr ($50-$109)
$$$	206-299Sfr ($110-$200)
$$$$	300Sfr+ ($200+)

Berggasthaus Schwammhöhe is a beautiful, rustic, cabin-like hotel/restaurant in the rural area of Glarus, just a 15-minute walk from the train station, with stunning views of the Klöntalersee. Open daily from April through November. Small functional rooms, and some which are handicap-accessible, with a sun terrace and restaurant. ($-$$$). Im Klöntal, CH-8750 Glarus. ☎ 55-640-2817, fax 55-640-4117.

Camping

This is available on the shores of the **Klöntalersee at** Im Vorauen, which is open from May 1- September 30 in a very quiet area. The campsite is handicapped-friendly and offers over 100 spots for visitors. ($). Im Vorauen, CH-8750 Klöntal. ☎ 55-640-4859. **Güntlenau** is open from May 1-Septmber 30 with 60 tourist spots. ($). CH-8750 Klöntal. ☎ 55-640-4408.

■ Where to Eat

Wirtschaft Sonnegg features classical fine dining in a romantic, stylish atmosphere. Has one of the finest wine cellars in all of Glarnerland. ($$-$$$).Open daily, parking available. Beim Sonnenhügel , CH-8750 Glarus. ☎ 55-640-1192.

CITY Café-Restaurant & Bar is the place if you're young and single or even if you're older and pretty hip. Lots of color and ambiance, in the heart of the city on the Rathausplatz. Here you can drink coffee, or eat hearty meals, while listening to various bands. Open daily from 7 am until, on the weekends, around 2 am. ($-$$). Bahnhofstrasse 18, CH-8750 Glarus. ☎ 55-640-1365, fax 55-640-7650.

Brauerei Glarus features a charming, wood-paneled room that can feed up to 80 people. Specialties include burgers on the grill and other meats. ($-$$). Open 5 am-midnight, Tuesday-Sunday. Closed Monday. Wirtschaft zur alten Brauerei, CH-8750 Glarus. ☎ 55-640-6891, fax 55-640-6991.

Pizzeria Restaurant Gartenwirtschaft features pizzas, salads and traditional Italian desserts at reasonable prices. ($-$$). Open daily from 10 am-2 pm, 5-11 pm; Sunday from 5-11 pm. Closed Wednesday. Abläschstrasse 15, CH-8750 Glarus. ☎ 55-640-2307, fax 55-650-1661.

Restaurant Erlengarten features vegetarian dishes at reasonable prices. ($-$$). Closed Monday and Tuesday. Auf Erlen 24, CH-8750 Glarus. ☎ 55-640-2291, fax 55-640-4560.

Braunwald

Braunwald (Brown Forest) is considered to be the home of mountaineering in Switzerland, as the Swiss Alpine Club built the first shelter in 1863 on the **Tödi Massif**, at 11,858 feet (3,615 m). It is also an auto-free resort village with only 500 citizens, which makes it particularly attractive to hikers and bikers. Deemed the "Sun terrace of Glarnerland," Braunwald is only 70 minutes south of Zürich in the southernmost region of Glarnerland, sitting high above the Linth Valley at 4,264 feet (1,300 m) in what is considered to be the sunniest spot in Canton Glarus. From here you can easily view the Glarner Alps: Ortstock, Tödi, Biferten and Hausstock. To get here you have to take the **Braunwaldbahn**, which leaves every half-hour from Linthal, a 90-minute ride on the funicular.

■ Information Sources

Tourist Office

The Tourist Office is great for offering ideas and specials on where to sleep or eat. They can also provide you with a computer list of vacant apartment rentals. Braunwald Tourismus, CH-8784 Braunwald. ☎ 55-653-6586, fax 55-653-6586, www.braunwald.ch.

■ Adventures

On Foot

Braunwald features 31 miles (50 km) of well-marked trails and hiking paths, with gondolas and chairlifts ready to whisk you away to panoramic restaurants.

Above: St-Ursanne on the Doubs River in Canton Jura (see page 293)

Below: A funicular from Muelenen station to the Niesen on Lake Thun (see page 332)

Berne – view of the Old Town with the Nydegg Church on the left, the Cathedral in the background and the Swiss Parliament Building on the right (see page 309)

On Snow

 In Braunwald you'll want to ski the **Bächital**. It has all levels of slopes, with 20 miles (32 km) of courses, two gondolas, three chairlifts and two ski lifts. Snowboarding is also popular here and you can rent skis and snowboards as well. Cross-country enthusiasts will find two miles (3.2 km) of well-groomed trails, and you can winter hike on 11 miles (17.6 km) of wonderful trails. For lessons, contact the **Ski & Snowboard School Braunwald**, CH-8784 Braunwald. ☎ 55-643-1261 or ☎ 79-215-2125. For equipment rental, contact **Kessler Sport** in Braunwald at ☎ 55-643-2222.

■ Where to Stay

 Fairy-Tale Hotel Bellevue Braunwald opened in 1907 as the "Grand Hotel" and has housed the crowned heads of European society since that time, as well as sports enthusiasts from around the globe. Now, the hotel caters to families with children and makes every ef-

HOTEL PRICE CHART	
$	30-75Sfr ($20-$49)
$$	76-205Sfr ($50-$109)
$$$	206-299Sfr ($110-$200)
$$$$	300Sfr+ ($200+)

fort to accommodate visitors of all ages. All amenities can be found, including an indoor pool, whirlpool, solarium, sauna, massage, billiards, children's menu, daycare, and a high-altitude clinic with a live-in doctor. Dogs are welcome as well for only 8Sfr per day. Expensive, but well worth it. ($$$$). CH-8784 Braunwald. ☎ 55-643-3030, fax 55-643-1000.

The Panorama Hotel Waldhaus is another luxury resort hotel, with its own golf course, indoor swimming pool and sauna. Not as kid-suitable as the Fairy-Tale Hotel Bellevue, but nice for couples and romantics. ($$-$$$). CH-8784 Braunwald. ☎ 55-653-6262, fax 55-653-6263.

Hotel Cristal is family-run, comfortable and very affordable. Lots of amenities in traditional Swiss fashion with modern conveniences. ($$-$$$). CH-8784 Braunwald. ☎ 55-643-1045, fax 55-643-1244.

Youth Hostel Im Gyseneggli sports 82 beds and is open from December 31-January 4, and January 4-October 20. ($). CH-8784 Braunwald. ☎ 55-643-1356, fax 55-643-2435.

■ Where to Eat

 Spieserestaurant Uhu has been run by the Meier family since 1962, and features seasonal specialties from Glarus. Tasty and affordable. ($$-$$$). CH-8784 Braunwald. ☎ 55-643-1736, fax 55-643-2730.

Chämistube is at the Bergstation Grotzenbüel at 5,116 feet (1,560 m) and features a huge sun terrace, a snow bar and a children's playground (open in summer only). For reservations and information, contact Moni or Rolf Schweizer at ☎ 55-643-3528 or 55-643-3284. This couple also runs the **Seblengrat Restaurant**, near the Bergstation Seblen at 6,248 feet (1,905 m), catering to skiers and snowboarders. Open December to April.

Elm

Elm is a beautiful little village lying at the end of the Sernf valley and is mostly overlooked by foreign tourists. Home to 760 residents, it has excellent hiking and skiing trails, and houses the Elmer mineral water plant. Just over 35% of the inhabitants here are employed in agriculture, a very high percentage at a time when many of the younger Swiss are abandoning their mountain and farm lives for the lure of the bigger cities. The dark wooden houses in the village center of Elm date back to the 17th century, and have twice received awards (in 1975 and 1981) from the Swiss Heritage Society for their excellent preservation.

Martinsloch, or Martin's Hole, Elm is well-known by astronomers, for its a natural phenomenon that occurs eight days before the astronomical start of spring, and eight days after the beginning of autumn. At this time the sun shines through Martin's Hole – a large gap in the top of Tschingelhorn Mountain – directly onto the village's only church.

The **Tourist Office**, Elm Tourismus is inside the Vekehrsbüro Elm, CH-8767 Elm. ☎ 55-642-6067, fax 55-642-6061, www.elm.ch.

■ Adventures
On Foot

Visitors to Elm can retrace the great Russian general Suvorov's footsteps along a well-marked trail, and visit the house he stayed in, as well as the Swiss Army's modern tank firing range at the end of the valley. Suvorov and his troups stopped in Elm in 1799 before retreating from Napoleon's forces on the Panixer Pass.

On Snow

Elm is one of Switzerland's best-kept skiing secrets, especially if you don't like the hustle-bustle of big crowds and lots of excitement. The village recently installed a new ski lift that gets skiers to the slopes quicker and more directly. Also, you can take lessons here from one of Switzerland's most celebrated downhill skiers, three-time Olympic champion **Vreni Schneider**. A native of Elm, Schneider returned to her hometown after winning 55 championships and three Olympic gold medals.

■ Where to Stay

Hotels

Hotel Sardona is a four-star hotel that is best suited for families with children. Includes 66 rooms with a nice restaurant at surprisingly affordable rates and features a sauna, bowling, kids playroom, and billiards. ($$). CH-8767 Elm ☎ 55-642-6868, fax 55-642-6869.

Gasthaus Sonne is a simple and clean little inn with 10 rooms. ($-$$). CH-8767 Elm. ☎ 55-642-1232, fax 55-642-1938.

Hostels & Mountain Huts

Alp Camperdun Alphüttli is on the outskirts of Elm and offers three rooms, with four-six beds in each. ($). Contact Streiff Hansruedi. Unterdorf, CH-8767 Elm. ☎ 55-642-1910, fax 55-642-2545.

Alp Bergli **Panoramahütte** in Rietboden and Alp Bergli Unterstafel **Loch** in Matt are two Alpine huts not far from Elm that are open from June 1 to September 30. The former has 45 sleeping spots, while the latter offers 25 places to bunk down for the night. ($). Contact Marti Heinrich for reservations. CH-8766 Matt. ☎/fax 55-642-1492.

Niederenalphütte is a 1½-hour hike from Elm, near the village of Mollis. Open from June 1 to mid-October on Saturday and Sunday, with 20 sleeping spots. Contact Kasper and Irene Hefti for reservations. ($). Allmeindstrasse 21, CH-8753 Mollis. ☎ 55-612-2466.

■ Where to Eat

Suworow-Cheller Elm provides a unique and dark atmosphere in a cave-like setting and features hot and cold specialty drinks and coffees, desserts and Swiss fare such as various types of cheese fondues and raclettes. ($-$$). Open Saturday and Sunday from 4 pm, and Monday, Tuesday and Friday from 5 pm. Closed Wednesday and Thursday. CH-8767 Elm. ☎ 55-642-1731, fax 55-642-5301.

Pizzeria Bar Sternen is the local pizza restaurant/bar/hangout spot. Good pizzas and pasta. ($-$$). Obmoos, CH-8767 Elm. ☎/fax 55-642-2338.

Filzbach & the Kerenzerberg Range

Filzbach is a tiny village above the Walensee on the Kerenzerberg Mountain range. It contains the remains of a Roman watch tower built in 15 BC. Here you can try bungee jumping, the summer toboggan run, or rock and mountain climbing. There are also many easy mountain paths, as well as difficult hiking trails for all levels of wanderers.

■ Culinary Journey

Take a hike or a biking excursion along the **Goat's Highway** to learn about and sample the production of goat's cheese. This "Highway" takes you in between three mountain inns (Alpenrösli, Fronalpstock and Froni) on the **Mullern** and **Fronalp**. The well-marked path gives information about goat milk production – from the types of grasses and clover the goats feed on, to the actual cheese making process. Full- and half-day outings are available, on foot or via bicycle. You'll begin at the mountain station of the Filzbach railway known as **Habergschwänd**, and traverse alpine meadows until you reach **Ennenda**, just east of Glarus, or you can begin in Ennenda and travel in the opposite direction.

High above the Walensee on the Flumserberg,
with the Churfirsten range in the distance

Berggasthaus Alpenrösli is in **Mullern** at 3,936 feet (1,200 m) and offers extremely charming rooms at great rates ($-$$) and a fine restaurant ($-$$) with outstanding views. The restaurant serves up all types of fondues, as well as burgers and international fare. Mullern, CH-8753 Mollis. ☎ 55-612-1284, fax 55-612-3872.

Berggasthaus Frontalpstockhaus at 4,428 feet (1,350 m) offers outstanding views at very reasonable rates ($-$$) for its rooms. Clean and charming. Run by Bruno and Franzi Reich-Dreher. Closed Wednesday and Thursday. Fonalp, CH-8753 Mollis. ☎ 55-612-1022.

Berggasthaus Fronalp is a beautiful Swiss chalet that was built in 1917, offering 16 rooms with beds for up to 60 people. Reasonable ($-$$), with great views. Run by the Menzi family. Postfach 61, CH-8753 Mollis. ☎ 55-612-1012, fax 55-612-1001.

■ Adventures

Sportbahnen Filzbach AG is the place to go to rent scooters or to try your luck on the summer toboggan run. The more adventurous will want to try **climbing** up and roping down a 196-foot (60 m) rock face. For another exciting feat, try **Tyrolien**, where you're suspended above a mountain stream on a single rope. Both of these tests are done with the help of experienced guides. (Cost is 75Sfr per person.) Bring good footwear. Talstation, CH-8757 Filzbach, ☎ 55-614-1268, 55-614-1065.

■ Where to Stay

Hostel

If you want to bunk down up here, the local youth hostel, **Lihn**, is probably your best choice. Located in the Blaukreuz Kurs and Ferienzentrum, it offers 50 beds, and is open year round, except from December 13-24 annually. ($). CH-8757 Filzbach. ☎ 55-614-1342, fax 55-614-1707.

Camping

This is available at **Campingplatz Gäsi**, in a forest on the shores of Lake Weesen. No electricity, but this campground has a nice beach and a children's playground. Suitable for tents only, with camp-fire spots. Facilities are suitable for the handicapped. ($). Open April-September. CH-8872 Weesen. ☎ 55-610-1357.

Näfels

The sister cities of Näfels and Mollis are north of Glarus and just slightly southwest of the **Kerenzerberg Range**. In Näfels you'll find the **Sportzentrum Glarner Unterland** or SGU-Linth-Arena, a huge sports complex that features everything from tennis, beach-volleyball and an indoor shooting range to sauna and massage. This fitness center also includes a nice restaurant and overnight accommodations. ($-$$$). Rooms are clean and functional without being fancy. SGU-Linth-Arena, CH-8752 Näfels. ☎ 55-612-1509, fax 55-612-29623.

Linthal-Rüti

This is at the far southwestern portion of Canton Glarus, on Highway 17, just before you pass (traveling west) into the canton of Uri. This town sits at the foot of the Tödi mountain, an ideal departure base for hiking and walking excursions. There are also five mountain huts in the area, and a number of small hotels. The Linthal-Rüti Tourist Office will assist you with hiking maps and in finding suitable accommodations. CH-8783 Linthal. ☎ 55-643-3917.

Urnerboden

Urnerboden is the largest and one of the most beautiful Alps in Switzerland. Home to only 56 people, Urnerboden erected a cable railway to the Fisetengrat in 2001. In the summertime over 1,200 cows are brought to graze here, and nearly 700 more are found on the nearby mountains of Gemsfairenalp and Fiseten. Cross-country skiing, ice climbing, downhill skiing, dog-sledding, hiking and biking are all found on the Urnerboden. During the winter Urnerboden can only be reached from within the canton of Glarus, since the Klausenpass, shown above, is closed at this time. In the summer you can reach Urnerboden via Altdorf (Canton Uri) over the Klausenpass by train or bus.

■ Information Sources

Tourist Office

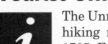

The Unrnerboden Tourist Office can provide you with detailed hiking maps of the area. CH-8751 Urnerboden. ☎ 55-643-1705. For cross-country and downhill ski information, contact the Urnerboden Ski Association at ☎ 55-643-2131. For dog-sledding excursions, ☎ 55-643-1416 or 79-338-2735.

■ Where to Stay & Eat

There are only a few places to stay and eat in Urnerboden:

Gasthuas Sonne features a large sun terrace with 26 clean and comfy rooms. The in-house restaurant serves up home-made traditional Swiss and international fare, and features a nice wine list. ($$). Open year-round, with plenty of parking. CH-8751 Urnerboden. ☎ 55-643-1512, fax 55-643-1579.

Gasthof Urnerboden offers comfortable, relaxing rooms and an excellent restaurant that is open year-round. Suitable for families as well as large or small groups. ($$). ☎ 55-643-1416, fax 55-643-2082.

Restaurant Alpenrosli serves homemade Swiss fare in a cozy and romantic atmosphere provided by the Herger family. ($-$$). Open during the summer season only. ($-$$). ☎ 55-643-1214.

The Suworow House in Elm, a stone building dating from 1748, served as quarters for the Russian general in 1799 during the Napoleanic Wars

The paddle steamer Unterwalden *near Fluelen on Lake Uri, a side branch of Lake Lucerne*

Canton Uri (UR)

■ At a Glance

Uri sits south and slightly east of the Lake Lucerne, encompassing 415 mountainous square miles (1,079 square km), with the cantons of Schwyz and Glarus to the north and northeast respectively. To the west is the canton of Graubünden, to the south Ticino, and on the western side are the cantons of Valais, Bern, Obwalden and Nidwalden. Uri is virtually cut off from all other cantons, with the exception of its old partners, which were the original members of this landlocked nation. As one of the founding cantons from 1291, Uri residents united with the citizens of Schwyz and Glarus to form an Alliance against all oppressors, which eventually grew into the 26-canton country known today as Switzerland. Home to some 36,000 German-speaking Roman Catholics, Uri is well known for the **Gotthard Pass** and **Gotthard Railway**, the **Devil's Bridge**, and the **Sustenpass**. It is here that you'll also find the beautiful **Urnersee** (Lake Urner), the **Rütli Meadow**, the majestic **Dammastock Mountain** and the **Reuss River**.

The **coat of arms** for Uri shows a bull with a red ring through its nostrils and its red tongue sticking out. The black head of the bull contrasts sharply with the bright gold background.

Altdorf

Altdorf is the capital of Canton Uri, and was home to William Tell for many years. It is, in fact, the town where Tell supposedly shot the apple off his son's head. Altdorf is often overlooked by tourists, and is visited by the Swiss for short historical vacations. It is just two miles (3.2 km) south of the Urnersee at Flüelen on main Highway 4, west of the Klausenpass on Highway 17, and north of Amsteg and Andermatt. Altdorf is also a popular spot for bikers.

■ Information Sources

Tourist Office

The Tourist Office for Canton Uri and the city of Aldorf is in Altdorf, in the Tellspielhaus on Schutzengasse 11. Postfach, CH-6460 Altdorf. Here you can grab some good bike touring and hiking maps. Open Monday-Friday from 9-11:30 am, 1:30-

5:30 pm, and on Saturday from 9-11:30 am. ☎ 41-872-0450, fax 41-872-0451.

Post Office

The post office is at Bahnhofstrasse 9, CH-6460 Altdorf. ☎ 41-870-2185, fax 41-870-5318. Hours are Monday-Friday, 7:30 am-noon, 1:45-6:15 pm, Saturday from 8 am-noon.

Codes

The **area code** for Altdorf is 41 and the **postal code** is CH-6460.

■ Getting Around

Getting around in Altdorf is most fun done on a bike or a motor scooter. You can rent bikes at the Altdorf train station (☎ 41-870-1008). Mountain bikes, scooters and motorcycles can be rented from **Mototreff**, at Fluelerstrasse 20, CH-6460 Altdorf. ☎ 41-870-9737. **Zweirad Affentranger** also rents mountain bikes and/or motorbikes at Gotthardstrasse 53, CH-6460 Altdorf. ☎ 41-870-1315. Bike rental is available at the nearby train station in Flüelen as well at ☎ 41-870-1093.

■ Adventures

On Foot

Just over a mile southeast of Altdorf is the tiny village of **Bürgeln**, the home-village of William Tell, which is easily accessed on foot, by car or by bus. Here, you'll find the **Tell Museum**, left, with historical papers and exhibits on Tell. Open from May to mid-October, daily from 10-11:30 am, 1:30-5 pm; July through August from 9:30 am-5 pm daily. Cost is 5Sfr per person. Postplatz in Burglen. ☎ 41-870-4155.

■ Landmarks & Historic Sites

The **Willam Tell statue**, made famous on a postage stamp, stands regally in front of Altdorf's 19th-century town hall. The Tell memorial was built by Richard Kissling in 1895. The adjoining tower dates from the Middle Ages.

Rütli Meadow is one of the best places to visit in all of Switzerland from a historical standpoint. It was here that the members of cantons Uri, Schwyz, and Unterwalden are recorded as meeting in 1307 to re-establish their 1291 Oath of Eternal Alliance or Oath of Everlasting League – as it is sometimes referred to – in the forming of Switzerland. On the eastern shores of the Urnersee, at the base of Axen Mountain, is found the Tellsplatte – the ledge that William Tell jumped onto when he escaped from Gessler's ship. You'll also find a tiny church here (shown above), complete with frescos depicting Tell's actions. It was originally built at the beginning of the 16th century, but was restored in 1881 when the murals were painted. During World War II, Swiss Commander-in-Chief General Guisan called a meeting of soldiers here to reaffirm their alliance to Switzerland. To get here, you can either travel via ship from Lucerne or take the Axenstrasse south from Schwyz or north from Altdorf. The Rütli Meadow itself is on the western shores of the Urnersee or Lake Uri.

■ Where to Stay

Goldener Schlüssel (the Golden Key) is a family-run historic inn smack in the center of town and dates back to the 19th-century. Original paintings and homemade accessories give this inn a welcoming atmosphere. Rates include breakfast. ($$-$$$). The in-house restaurant is one of the best in town for traditional Uri and Swiss dishes. Schützengasse 9, CH-6460 Altdorf. ☎ 41-871-1002, fax 41-871-1167.

Hotel Höfli provides very clean and comfortable rooms at reasonable rates. ($$). Attractive, with an affable staff. The in-house pizzeria is open from 7 am to midnight daily, except for Tuesday

Hotel and restaurant Zum Schlüssel

and Wednesday when it closes at 5 pm Hellgasse, CH-6460 Altdorf. ☎ 41-875-0275, fax 41-875-0295.

Hotel Bahnhof looks more like a private residence than a hotel. It has small but clean and comfortable rooms, each with a sink. The batrooms are communal. ($-$$). Rates include breakfast. CH-6460 Altdorf. ☎ 41-870-1032.

The Gadenhaus Beim Rütli is the local Youth Hostel in nearby Seelisberg. Offering 25 beds, this hostel is open from April 8-October 31. ($). CH-6377 Seelisberg. ☎ 41-820-1562, fax 41-820-1550.

◼ Where to Eat

Restaurant Bar Lehnhof is one of the top restaurants in the area, featuring great pastas and regional as well as international fare. There are many fine wines and spirits to choose from, as well as some very fancy desserts. ($-$$$). Open Tuesday, Wednesday and Thursday from 11 am-2 pm, 5 pm-midnight; Friday 11 am-2 pm, 5 pm-2 am, Saturday from 11 am to 2 am. Closed Sunday and Monday. Lehnplatz 18, CH-6460 Altdorf. ☎ 41-870-1229.

DINING PRICE CHART	
Prices based on a typical entrée, per person, and do not include beverage.	
$	15-25Sfr ($10-$16)
$$	26-45Sfr ($17-$29)
$$$	46-70Sfr ($30-$47)
$$$$	71Sfr+ ($47+)

Hotel Restaurant Wilhelm Tell features Italian dishes, pizza and seasonal fare at reasonable prices. Hearty portions in a swanky, comfortable and lively atmosphere. Open 10 am-midnight daily Tuesday-Sunday. Closed Monday. Tellsgasse 27, CH-6460 Altdorf. ☎ 41-870-1030.

THE LEGEND OF WILLIAM TELL

William Tell is considered to be the hero of Swiss independence. As a legendary Swiss patriot, Tell refused to salute the Austrian-born governor of Canton Uri, Hermann Gessler. When this happened Gessler ordered Tell to shoot an arrow through an apple set upon the head of Tell's young son. Tell performed the feat without fear, but told Gessler that if he were to kill his son, then he would kill Gessler as well. Gessler imprisoned Tell, whereupon Tell escaped and eventually killed Gessler. Tell is thus credited with helping the Swiss to rebel against their Austrian rulers, and helping to spark the Swiss into unification. Richard Kissling's monument to Tell in Uri's capital city of Altdorf remains one of the most photographed monuments in Switzerland.

Amsteg

If you travel south only nine miles (14.5 km) on main Highway 2 from Altdorf you'll come to the village of Amsteg, which is at the western edge of the Maderanertal valley. From here, you'll be able to see the St. Gotthard Railway in the distance to the south. There is no tourist office here, but the Altdorf Tourist Office can help you out with anything you'll need in Amsteg. There is also no train service here, and most folks go to Erstfeld (located between Amsteg and Altdorf), then either walk to Amsteg or take one of the many shuttle buses. Many visitors to Amsteg use this small village as a base for walking or hiking excursions, and the village is also considered to be the north/south stop on the St. Gotthard route.

THE ST. GOTTHARD PASS

This is one of the most memorable of all Alpine passes. At 6,914 feet (2,108 m) above sea level, the St. Gotthard Pass was first crossed in the 13th century, allowing travel from Italy on up into Germany and beyond. In fact, the old cobblestone road that was part of the original pass can still be seen today. It is a great path to wander on, avoiding many of the tourists. You can hike for three hours to Airolo, or take alternate routes through Val Canaria to Airolo that will take about six hours. If you want to bunk down for the night, the **Albergo Ospizio San Gottardo** (Hotel St. Gotthard) is at the start of the trail. They are reasonably priced ($-$$), and you can stay here from June 1 through the end of October. CH-6780, Airolo. ☎ 91-869-1235, fax 91-869-1811. Be sure to check out the **Museo Nazionale del San Gottardo** as well, which shows the history of the St. Gotthard Pass through displays and slide shows. Open May-October, from 9 am-6 pm daily. Cost is 8Sfr per person. It wasn't until 1775 that a wagon first was able to cross the pass, and then nearly another 100 years before work began on a railway track underneath the pass. The train ride offers spectacular views, and takes you through the mountain at one point for nearly 20 minutes.

A visit to Amsteg would not be complete without at least one overnight stay in the **Hotel Stern und Post**. This rustic inn has been managed by the Tresch family since the early part of the 18th century. It is famous for once having housed the then privately owned Swiss Postal Route stop. It was also able to stable over 400 horses, which were used for transporting mail and supplies over the St. Gotthard Pass. Lots of the original charm remains today, and it is lovingly maintained throughout. All rooms feature high ceilings and ornate windows. The in-house restaurant has a private cellar with many fine wines and the cuisine is second-to-none. There is no finer hotel anywhere in this area. Rates for the hotel include breakfast ($$-$$$) and 14 of the 20 rooms come with private baths; the rest have sinks with running water only. Closed January to mid-March. CH-6774 Amsteg. ☎ 41-883-1440, fax 41-883-0261.

 In 1980 the St. Gotthard road tunnel was completed and, at 10.1 miles (16.3 km), is the longest road tunnel in the world. Beware of traveling on this road during bad weather, however, as it often has horrible traffic jams in both directions.

■ Adventures

On Foot

 If you travel east two miles (3.2 km) on the local road out of Amsteg, you'll come to the little village of **Bristen** at 2,615 feet (797 m) in the Maderanertal Alpine Valley that feeds on the Kärstelenbach River. In Bristen, grab the cable car up to the Golzernsee at 4,626 feet (1,410 m) and follow the well-marked path for a splendid 2½-hour round-trip hike. The Golzernsee is a small lake situated along the northern slopes of the Maderanertal and at the top you'll find the **Hotel Schweizer Alpenclub**, which is often used by experienced hikers and mountain climbers as a base for many excursions. Alternatively, you can hike from the Golzernsee to the **Windgällenhütte** (☎ 41-885-1088). For overnight accommodations in Bristen, check out the **Gasthaus Wehrebrücke** ($) at ☎ 41-883-1119 or the **Gasthaus Alpenblick** ($-$$) at ☎ 41-883-1240. Both small inns' rates include breakfast. The Alpenblick is a bit more sophisticated than the Wehrebrücke, but both offer clean, ample rooms.

The "Fourcla da Cavardiras" Hike

For an exciting hike of medium difficulty, you'll want to try the walk from Platten to Disentis/Mustér. Known as the Fourcla da Cavardiras in Romansh, this walk connects the cantons of Uri and Graubünden in a hike which can be as short as one day or as long as three. Total walking time ranges from 12 to 14 hours. Wear a good pair of hiking shoes and stock up on water and munchies. Not recommended for seniors or families with very small children.

To begin, take the Golzen cable car to the lower station of Platten and follow the road up the valley until it turns into a dirt road. You'll soon come to the glacial waters of the Chärsterlenbach, and on the south side of the trail and south of these waters will be the **Berggasthaus Legni**, which is open mid-May through late October. It features dorm beds and little else. ($). ☎ 41-883-1143. Continue on the trail on the north side of the

Chärsterlenbach through a few configurations of fir trees. After 1½ hours, you'll reach **Balmenschachen**, a small stop where you can rest. From here, follow the trail along the riverside and eventually the road will reappear and lead you to **Guferen**. Continue on over a small footbridge as you pass a wider path on your north (left) side. If you'd like, you can go up to the Balmenegg at this point to the **Berghotel Maderanertal**, with its comfortable rooms. ($). The hotel serves hearty breakfasts and is open from mid-June to mid-October. ☎ 41-883-1122.

Continue along the south side of the Chärsterlenbach for another hour and the path will cross itself several times as it continues to climb steeply. The trail is fixed by steel plates at some spots and, after approximately 1½ hours, you'll arrive at the **Hinterbalmhütte**. This hut is open year-round but has an attendant only from June to mid-October. It offers beds without breakfast but does have kitchen facilities where you can prepare your own meals. ($). ☎ 41-883-1939. You've now traveled about four hours and can bunk here overnight if you like, as this is a good resting point for the remainder of your journey.

From the Hinterbalmhütte, follow the path along the Brunnital's picturesque grassy slopes. You'll come to a stone footbridge near a beautiful waterfall and the path will soon bring you to a lovely Alpine meadow. From here, cross back over the stream onto the eastern slope which begins to gently slope upwards. The path here becomes rocky, but it is well-marked and eventually leads you to a natural plateau, which is a good spot for a picnic. Continue upward until you reach the Brunnifirn Glacier and follow the arrows until the mountain hut comes into view. The path will veer left over the Uri-Graubünden border, and just past this cantonal separation is the **Camona da Cavardiras hut**. This hut is also open year-round, but is attended only from early July through early September. It features dorm beds without breakfast ($), but offers great views. ☎ 81-947-5747. This part of the hike should have taken about 3½ hours.

The next part of your hike will take the longest – anywhere from four to five hours. From the Camona da Cavardiras, follow the path down a rocky incline across a small snowfield to the grassy basin of the Val Cavardiras. A well-marked, graded trail follows alongside the northern banks of a small creek, careening up and down until you eventually reach Alp Sura after about two hours. Continue on as the path winds its way through thickets and Alpine pastures, crossing back and forth over the creek on a variety of small stone bridges. The path becomes dirt again nearing the Alp Cavrein-Sut as you enter the Russein Valley. The trail will take you to a bridge and then veer right onto a road that runs parallel with the river. You'll pass the Barcuns hydroelectric reservoir and a small forest before reaching the Punt Gronda, a small bridge-plateau on the Trun-Disentis Road. From here, walk west and cross the Russein creek through a covered wooden bridge and just past here you'll see a postbus stop. If you like, you can continue onward, following the signs reading "Senda Sursilvana" by the railroad tracks. Follow this trail marked with yellow diamond-shaped symbols through a few pastures and wooded areas before reaching the village of **Disla**. You can leave the main road and follow a country path past the old church and farmhouses that will eventually bring you to Disentis.

Andermatt

Andermatt is at the southernmost tip of Canton Uri, and is the meeting point of the St. Gotthard, Oberalp and Furka Passes. It is situated high in the Urseren Valley and is the main village of the region. However, in the winter it can sometimes become a dead-end resort because the St. Gotthard road and rail tunnels bypass it in both directions, and there are no adjoining ski areas or resort villages. It offers great hiking opportunities, as well as cross-country skiing and fantastic mountain biking excursions. Along with its nearby sister cites of Hospental and Realp, Andermatt features 34 ski lifts and just over 100 miles (161 km) of pistes, as well as 12.4 miles (20 km) of cross-country runs between Andermatt and Realp.

■ Information Sources

Tourist Office

The Andermatt Tourist Office is at Gotthardstrasse 2, CH-6490 Andermatt. ☎ 41-887-1454, fax 41-887-0185.

Post Office

The Andermatt post office is at Gotthardstrasse 24, CH-6490 Andermatt, and is open Monday-Friday, from 8:15 am-noon, 2-5:45 pm, and on Saturday from 8:15-11 am. ☎ 41-887-1258, fax 41-887-1736.

Codes

The **postal code** for Andermatt is CH-6490 and the **area code** is 41.

■ Adventures

On Foot

Andermatt is a good village for walking and was formerly one of Switzerland's main training centers for Alpine troops. The charm and dignity of its cobblestone streets reveals little of the military influence here, however, and there are plenty of shops and cafés to keep one busy for an afternoon. Don't expect a lot of sunshine in the village center, though, since the mountains overshadow most of the village.

On Snow

At either end of the village are two main ski areas, while the little towns of Hospental and Realp each provide less popular, smaller ski areas. The skiing here is not for the faint of heart, and Andermatt has long been popular with the local Swiss communities. The Gemsstock has a treacherous vertical drop and off-piste skiing suitable for experienced skiers or those with a guide only; most beginners truck over to the Grossboden area. The Snow Hot Line gives information, but in German only at ☎ 41-887-0181.

On Wheels

Biking is very popular here, and the **Snow Limit** shop at Gotthardstrasse 41 rents bikes and other summer and winter sports equipment. CH-6490, Andermatt. ☎ 41-887-0614. Also check out **Christen Sport** for biking equipment, on Gotthardstrasse 55, CH-6490 Andermatt. ☎ 41-887-1251.

A RECOMMENDED ROAD TRIP

One of the best trips you can make by car is a three-pass, round-trip route beginning and ending at Wassen. **The Susten Road** travels from Wassen through the Meiental and over the Susten Pass tunnel at 7,297 feet (2,295 m), before descending into the Gadmen valley, and the village of Innertkirchen.

The Grimsel Road links the Bernese Oberland with the Upper Valais and the Furka. Beginning in Innertkirchen, it twists through forests and Alpine meadows in the Hasli Valley and climbs to Handegg, where the terrain becomes pure rock, eventually reaching the Grimsel Pass at 7,013 feet (2,138 m). From this high point, you'll descend to Gletsch at 5,784 feet (1,763 m).

The Furka Pass Road is a 20-mile jaunt from Gletsch to Andermatt that can take you up to 2½ hours via auto. It is the most exhausting part of your journey in terms of driving, but will offer one of the most spectacular scenic trips anywhere in Switzerland. It is also especially fun if you enjoy driving around hairpin turns continuously for an extended period of time. The top of the Furka Pass, at 7,976 feet (2,432 m), is unequalled for its raw natural beauty.

■ Where to Stay

Hotel Drei Könige und Post (Three Kings) was first erected in 1234 and has housed some very famous guests, including Goethe in 1775. This is a beautifully decorated Swiss chalet, inside and out, with paneled bedrooms, some with balconies. ($$-$$$). The old

HOTEL PRICE CHART	
$	30-75Sfr ($20-$49)
$$	76-205Sfr ($50-$109)
$$$	206-299Sfr ($110-$200)
$$$$	300Sfr+ ($200+)

inn is well worth an overnight stay. Many amenities. Closed in May and from November 1-December 15 annually. Gotthardstrasse 69, CH-6490 Andermatt. ☎ 41-887-0001, fax 41-887-1666.

Hotel Aurora is a family-owned and -operated inn, overflowing with warmth and charm. Clean, comfortable rooms in traditional Swiss style. ($$). Rates include breakfast. Closed May and November. CH-6490 Andermatt. ☎ 41-887-1661, fax 41-887-0089.

The family **Danioth** offers 26 spots for "Sleeping in the Straw" at their farm ($). ☎ 41-887-1627, fax 41-887-1622.

Hospental Youth Hostel has 65 beds available from January 12-October 31. Gotthardstrasse, CH-6493 Hospental. ☎ 41-887-0401, fax 41-887-0902.

■ Where to Eat

Hotel/Restaurant Metropol & La Curva specializes in classical Swiss and international fare. The atmosphere is elegant and the menu first class. ($$-$$$). The hotel also sports a fun bar, La Curva, that features over 100 types of cocktails in a romantic setting. Open daily from 6 pm to whenever. Gotthardstrasse 43, CH-6490 Andermatt. ☎ 41-887-1575, fax 41-887-1923.

DINING PRICE CHART	
Prices based on a typical entrée, per person, and do not include beverage.	
$	15-25Sfr ($10-$16)
$$	26-45Sfr ($17-$29)
$$$	46-70Sfr ($30-$47)
$$$$	71Sfr+ ($47+)

Bahnhofbuffet serves up grilled dishes, pastas, fish, meat and Swiss favorites such as rösti in a fun, upbeat setting – old railway cars from the Andermatt/Zermatt lines. The desserts are also mouth-watering. ($-$$). Open 6 am- 8 pm daily. CH-6490 Andermatt. ☎ 41-888-0050, fax 41-888-0054.

Restaurant Kronen is in the hotel of the same name and features Alpine treats that are prepared with natural and organic ingredients, for a light and healthy meal. Complemented by a fine wine list. ($-$$). Gotthardstrasse 64, CH-6490 Andermatt. ☎ 41-887-0088, fax 41-887-1838.

Canton Nidwalden (NW)

■ At a Glance

 The half-canton of Nidwalden ("lower forest") is encompassed on the south and west sides by its sister half-canton of Obwalden ("upper forest") in the middle of Switzerland. The northern side leans up against the shores of the Vierwaldstättersee-Sud (literally, "four-forest-cities-lake-south"), while the east edge pushes up against the mountain ridges of Canton Uri. The landmass of Nidwalden – which makes up 107 square miles (278 square km) – stretches along the valley of the Aa River nearly to the peak of Titlis and is home to 38,000 German-speaking residents, mainly Roman Catholics, most of whom work in the tourism and service industries. Established in 1291, Nidwalden is the fourth-smallest canton in terms of people in Switzerland. About 38% of this canton is used for agriculture.

The **coat of arms** of Nidwalden was first developed for the unified canton of Unterwalden in 1478. After the split of the canton into the two half-cantons of Obwalden and Nidwalden, a new set of arms was needed for Nidwalden, as Obwalden kept the old crest with a few revisions. Today Nidwalden's crest shows the white keys of St. Peter back-to-back over a solid red background.

Stans

Stans sits at the south end of the Vierwaldstättersee, and at the northern end of Canton Nidwalden, for which it is the capital city. Stans is best-known for its close proximity to the **Stanserhorn** (6,232 feet, 1,900 m). The village, which is typically quiet and neat, begins just behind the train station, runs from the Bahnhofstrasse onto Dorfplatz. It has cobblestone streets and narrow alleyways, with one of the prettiest little central squares found anywhere.

■ Information Sources

Tourist Office

 The Tourist Office of Stans and the Vierwaldstättersee-Süd is above the Stans train station, and is open Monday-Friday, from 9-11:30 am and from 2:30-5:30 pm. They have hiking and biking maps and can provide you with information for the entire Nidwalden area. You can also rent bikes here. Bahnhofplatz 4, CH-6370 Stans. ☎ 41-610-8833, fax 41-610-8866.

Post Office

The Stans post office is open Monday-Friday from 7:30 am-6:15 pm, Saturdays from 8 am-noon. Bahnhofplatz 3, CH-6370 Stans. ☎ 41-618-3111, fax 41-618-3112.

Codes

The **postal code** for Stans is CH-6370; the **area code** is 41.

■ Adventures

On Foot & Rail

Take a ride up the old cog railway to the summit of the **Stanserhorn**, where you'll find a terrace restaurant and many hiking trails. You can walk back down to Stans via a pleasant path that should take about 3½ hours or, as an alternative route, follow the steeper path to the village of **Wirzweli**, a 2½-hour hike.

■ Landmarks & Historic Sites

The Stans **Kirche of St. Peter & Paul**, left, is easy to spot as the Romanesque bell tower looms boldly above the rest of the buildings in the village center (Dorfplatz). Built in the 16th century, the Baroque interior is a stark contrast of black and white marbles, with beautiful frescos. At one time this was the only church in the entire canton, and it was continuously expanded

The **Arnold von Winkelried Fountain** is just outside the church and was dedicated in 1865 to this native of Stans who is credited with helping the Swiss army during the 1386 Battle of Sempach. History says that Winkelried diverted the attention of the Austrian army to himself, and thus, gave his comrades the opportunity to gain an advantage over their enemies and eventually win the war.

■ Museums

The **Kulture & Brauchtum Museum** features a 16th-century altar within its tiny chapel. It also has displays about September 1798, when the French invaded and fought with the Stans mountain people.

■ Where to Stay

Hotel Engel, shown on the following page, provides 40 charming accommodations at reasonable rates in this gorgeous building in the village center. Breakfast is included, and generous helpings of good food are served here. ($$). Dorfplatz 1, CH-6370 Stans. ☎ 41-619-1010, fax 41-619-1011

HOTEL PRICE CHART	
$	30-75Sfr ($20-$49)
$$	76-205Sfr ($50-$109)
$$$	206-299Sfr ($110-$200)
$$$$	300Sfr+ ($200+)

Hotel Linde is centrally located, with 17 rustic accommodations in traditional Swiss style, but with modern amenities. Breakfast included. Also home to an excellent gourmet restaurant. ($$). Dorfplatz 7, CH-6370 Stans. ☎ 41-619-0930, fax 41-619-0948.

Hotel Stanserhof provides 30 clean rooms suitable for individuals or groups and is home to a nice little bar. CH-6370 Stans. ☎ 41-619-7171, fax 41-619-7172.

Farm Stays

"Sleeping in straw" stays are available at two farms in Stans. You'll find the farm of **M & W Waser-Küttel** near the Oberdorf train station, just outside of Stans to the east, about a one-mile hike. ($). Göhren, CH-6370 Oberdorf. ☎ 41-610-5027.

In Stans you can stay with **M & P Wasser-Lussi** at Buchserstrasse 50, CH-6370 Stans, from May-October. They have room for up to 10 people and breakfast is included with your stay. They can provide service taxi service as well. ($). ☎ 41-610-6558.

■ Where to Eat

Rosenburg-Höfli serves up seasonal and regional dishes. ($-$$). Seating for up to 50 people; closed Monday and Tuesday. CH-6370 Stans. ☎ 41-610-2461.

DINING PRICE CHART	
Prices based on a typical entrée, per person, and do not include beverage.	
$	15-25Sfr ($10-$16)
$$	26-45Sfr ($17-$29)
$$$	46-70Sfr ($30-$47)
$$$$	71Sfr+ ($47+)

Wilhelm Tell features weekly specialties of the region, including their remarkable cheeses. Seating for up to 80 people. ($-$$). Closed Thursdays. CH-6370 Stans. ☎ 41-610-5503.

Allmendhuisli features specialties from Nidwalden. ($-$$). Open Monday-Friday until 6 pm, closed weekends. CH-6370 Stans. ☎ 41-610-1237.

Bistro 54 features French cuisine. ($$). Closed Saturday and Sunday. CH-6370 Stans. ☎ 41-611-0223.

Buffet LSE has seats for 12 people and serves burgers and the like. ($). Closed Saturdays only. Bahnhofplatz 4, CH-6370 Stans. ☎ 41-610-2821.

Pizzeria da Max serves pizzas, pasta, and salads. Closed Monday. ($). CH-6370 Stans. ☎ 41-610-5358.

Hotel Engel, Stans

Canton Obwalden (OW)

■ At a Glance

The half-canton of Obwalden is made up of two areas smack dab in the middle of Switzerland, just south of Lake Lucerne, with their sister half-canton of Nidwalden (NW) between both and circling the smaller portion of Obwalden. Established in 1291, Obwalden means "upper forest," and is home to some 33,000 German-speaking inhabitants who are primarily Roman Catholic. The combined half-cantons are known as "Unterwald," and are made up of 159 square miles (413 square km) of land, 38% of which is used as farmland. The larger portion of Obwalden – known as the Sarneraatal region – is divided by Highway 8, which runs north and south, and includes a number of mountain passes through six municipalities. The smaller portion holds the resort town of Engelberg, which sits at the foot of the snow-clad Titlis. This half-canton is also one of the three founding cantons of Switzerland, and is the second smallest canton in terms of population.

The **coat of arms** reveals the key of St. Peter set on a red and white horizontal background. Obwalden and its sister half-canton of Nidwalden were originally part of Canton Unterwalden, whose arms were a shield of red and silver divided horizontally. When Unterwalden was divided, Obwalden took the old crest, while Nidwalden was given a variation on the original – a double key instead of the original single key.

Sarnen

This is the capital of Obwalden and, as its largest city, is home to 9,500 residents. It's situated at the north end of Lake Sarnen in the region of Obwalden. The Melchtal Alps tower over the city. Sarnen is known for its charming countryside, tradespeople, crafts and folklore. The city contains cobblestone streets and beautiful fountains, adorned with flowers in the summertime. The Altstadt is especially nice for walking, and here you'll find the Baroque Town Hall, the St. Andreas monastery (a female parish of the "Sarner-Jesuskind") and St. Peter church.

The former city hall, in the village square, contains the "white book," which is the oldest record of the establishment of the Swiss confederation. During the last Sunday in April, voters gather in the village center to hold their traditional (since 1616) open-air elections. There are a number of attractions within Sarnen that you'll catch sight of when walking, including the stone houses and the village well, which dates back to 1604. Each Saturday morning, from May through October, a fine market takes place on the village square. If you're there in March, check out the Easter market, and, if visiting in November, be sure to catch the Christmas market (Weihnachtsmarkt).

■ Information Sources

Tourist Office

The Sarnen Tourist Office offers packages for hikers and skiers. Hofstrasse 2, CH-6060 Sarnen. ☎ 41-666-5040, fax 41-666-5045.

Post Office

The Sarnen post office is at Lindenhof 6, CH-6060 Sarnen 1. ☎ 41-660-1566, fax 41-660-0477. Open Monday-Friday from 7:30 am-noon, 1:45-6:30 pm, Saturday from 8 am-noon.

Train Station

The Sarnen Bahnhof (train station) contains a currency exchange that is open daily until 11:30 pm. ☎ 51-227-2980.

Codes

The **area code** for Sarnen is 41; the **postal code** is CH-6060.

Internet Access

You can access the Internet in Sarnen at two of the **Obwaldner Kantonal Banks**. One is in the center of Sarnen and the other is at Bahnhofstrasse 2, with varying rates.

*On rainy days you can visit the **Sarnen Cantonal Library**, in the Grundacherhaus. Here you'll find over 50,000 books in all languages. Open Monday-Friday from 1:30-6 pm. ☎ 41-660-1396.*

■ Getting Around

This is easy on foot, by bike, or by car. If you need a taxi, you can call **Ernst Taxi** at ☎ 41-660-1313 or find him at the Bahnhof Standplatz.

■ Adventures

On Foot

There are a great number of easy hikes out of Sarnen. One of the most popular is to Flüeli Ranft and back. Here the path will take you through a beautiful meadow and forest, with a slight incline, to the Lourdesgrotte. From here, you'll walk to the Melcha Ravine, then pass over a high bridge to the Fluei. Simply retrace your steps for this three-hour hike.

Another easy two-hour hike is to Alpnach. Here you'll walk along the Sarneraa to the protected Wichelsee where you can see various waterfowl. The path then leads you into a forest and to Alpnach. For hiking maps of various difficulties, consult the Sarnen Tourist Office.

On Water

Windsurfing

Contact the **House of Surf**, Tellikurve, Alpnachstad, for lessons and equipment rental at ☎ 79-445-1212. For the **Lungerersee Surf School No Limit**, ☎ 55 79-677-4020.

Fishing

You can fish on the banks of the **Lungerer**, **Sarnersee** and **Alpnachersee** from April 1 to mid-October without a permit. Maps for rivers and lakes can be found at the Tourist Office or at the Fishery Administration in Sarnen, at Village Square 4. ☎ 41-666-6383.

On Wheels

Mountain Biking

Mountain biking treks can be arranged through **Velohandlung Zeno Britschgi** at ☎ 41-660-6070, or at the Sarnen Bahnhof (train station) at 51-227-2980.

Go-Karting

For indoor and outdoor go-cart racing and a host of other fun-to-do things, go to the **Kart-Center Kägiswil**. Open Tuesday-Friday from 5-11:30 pm, Saturday from 1:30 pm-midnight, Sunday from 1:30-8 pm. Kernserstrasse 6, CH-6056 Kagiswil. ☎ 41-662-0766, fax 41-662-0765.

On Snow

 Sarnen is a great spot for skiing and snowboarding over the **Melchsee Frutt**, the **Moerlialp**, **Lungern Schöenbüel**, the **Hasliberg**, and the **Klewenalp**, among others. All are accessible by mountain railways, cable cars and gondolas. To rent equipment, contact **Huwyler Sport**, Poststrasse 7, CH-6060 Sarnen. ☎41-660-2585.

The **Glaubenberg**, or "Mountain of Belief," contains one of Europe's finest cross-country skiing sites at 4,500 feet (1,372 m) – the Langis – with 25 miles (40 km) of trails. You can take instruction from the **Swiss Cross-Country Ski School**, with advance reservations, and rent equipment. Contact them at ☎ 41-675-1146.

In the Air

Paragliding

 Go to **High Adventure AG**, at Stanserstrasse 107, CH-6064 Kerns, ☎ 41-662-0175, or to **Kiwi & H1Z Passagierfluge**, CH-6064 Kerns, ☎ 41-660-5471.

Hasliberg, above Meiringen in the Haslital

On Horseback

You can ride at the **Reitsportzentrum Sand**, Aecherlistrasse 15, CH-6064 Kerns. ☎41-660-2766.

Other Sports

For a wide array of sports, including skiing, dog-sledding, cross-country skiing, biking, skating, canyoning, and windsurfing, contact **Obwalden Erlebnis-Sport**, Brünigstrasse 131, CH-6061 Sarnen. ☎ 41-662-0993, fax 41-662-0994.

Fitness & Tennis

Clubs for tennis and fitness are popular in Sarnen. Check out **Top Gym** for aerobics, open Monday-Friday, from 9 am-9 pm, Saturday from 9 am-1 pm. Industriestrasse 4, CH-6060 Sarnen. ☎ 41-660-7730.

The local **Tennis & Fitness Center** is open daily from 8 am to 10 pm and offers sauna, a solarium and tennis, squash and badminton courts. ☎ 41-660-6222. The **Kurhaus am Sarnersee** offers whirlpool, light therapies, a fitness room and sauna. Open daily at Voranmeldung. ☎ 41-666-7466. **Sun For Fun** is a solarium at Tuplenweg 2, open Monday-Sunday from 7:30 am-10 pm.

Miniature Golf

You can play from April to October at the **International Norm** in Seefeld, Sarnen. ☎ 41-661-0346, fax 660-3146.

Billiards

If you enjoy billiards, the check out the **Billiard und Spiel-Center**, open daily from 10 am-midnight. Brünigstrasse 135, CH-6060 Sarnen. ☎ 41-660-5235.

■ Landmarks & Historic Sites

The **Archery Tower & Armory**, with its arched gables, was erected in 1752 by Ignaz Imfeld, and sits atop a hill overlooking Sarnen.

■ Museums

Heimatmuseum (Folk Museum) exhibits prehistoric and early Christian art, as well as Roman wares, weapons and uniforms from the 16th to the 19th centuries. Religious art, paintings, sculptures, and an Alpine hut

Central Switzerland

replica can be found here as well. Open mid-April to late November, Monday-Saturday, from 2-5 pm, and by appointment.

Museum Bruder Klaus provides a permanent exhibition of the life of 15th-century St. Niklaus von Flüe and of 19th-century writer Heinrich Federer in a beautiful Baroque setting. Open from the end of March to early November, Tuesday-Sunday from 9:30 am-noon and from 2-5 pm. Dorfstrasse 4, CH-6072 Sachseln. ☎ 41-660-5583.

■ Shopping

There are many shops full of local crafts in Sarnen, and a stroll up the main cobblestone street is worth your time. There are also local bakeries and cafés to visit, featuring regional cakes and cookies sure to satisfy any traveler's palate.

■ Where to Stay & Eat

Hotel Krone is a huge Swiss chalet. Rooms come with many amenities. ($$$). Brunjigstrasse 130, CH-6060 Sarnen. ☎ 41-666-0909, fax 41-666-0910.

HOTEL PRICE CHART	
$	30-75Sfr ($20-$49)
$$	76-205Sfr ($50-$109)
$$$	206-299Sfr ($110-$200)
$$$$	300Sfr+ ($200+)

The **Krone Restaurant**, in the Krone Hotel, has an international kitchen specializing in vegetarian dishes. The hotel also contains a Chinese and a French restaurant. ($$-$$$). Closed Mondays and Tuesdays. Brunjigstrasse 130, CH-6060 Sarnen. ☎ 41-666-0909, fax 41-666-0910.

Hotel Metzgern is in the historic Dorfplatz. The restaurant specializes in fish and vegetarian fare. ($$). Dorfplatz 5, CH-6060 Sarnen. ☎ 41-660-1124, fax 41-660-1217.

Obwaldner Hof is a small hotel near the train station, with a garden restaurant and children's playground. Owned and operated by the family Amstad-Niederberger. Clean and charming. ($$). Brünigstrasse 151, CH-6060 Sarnen. ☎ 41-660-1817, fax 41-661-0817.

Garni Peterhof is a small inn with a good restaurant specializing in fresh garden fare and rösti. ($$). Bergstrasse 2, CH-6060 Sarnen. ☎ 41-660-1238, fax 41-660-9340.

Hotel Mühle has six simple, clean rooms with charming atmosphere. The restaurant features a garden terrace and serves up regional cakes, burgers and other hearty foods. ($-$$). Giglenstrasse 2, CH-6060 Sarnen. ☎ 41-660-1336.

Q-Die Beiz specializes in homemade pastas, fine wines and over 20 malt liquors. ($-$$). Closed Sundays, Mondays. ☎ 41-662-1515.

Camping

 Camping Lido Sarnen provides grounds open year-round that are close to the surfing school, shops and restaurants. ($).Reservations are requested. ☎ 41-660-1866, fax 41-662-0866.

Alpnachstad & the Alpnach Region

Although the Alpnach area is the northernmost section of Canton Oberwalden, it is at the lowest elevation of the six municipalities in the Sarneraatal region – standing at just 1,525 feet (465 m). At the top of Alpnach, just over the cantonal boundry (between Oberwalden and Lucerne), lies the magnificent **Pilatus**, at 7,000 feet (2,129 m), while the **Tomlishorn** sits slightly west of Pilatus at 6,979 feet (2,121 m). The eastern portion of this region is made up of thick forests, while the tiny Alpnachersee sits at the south end.

■ Alpnachstad

Within the Alpnach region there are a few tiny villages that dot the landscape, the largest of which is Alpnachstad. This small village dates back to the time of the Romans, and artifacts from that era have been found on the banks of the Alpnachersee.

Today, Alpnach is known as the main helicopter base for the Swiss Air Force.

Contact the Alpnach Tourismus (**Tourist Office**) in Alpnachstad for hiking maps, help with hotels and information. Bahnhofplatz 6, CH-6053 Alpnachstad. ☎ 41-670-1244, fax 41-670-1355.

THE PILATUSBAHN

The Pilatusbahn first began running back and forth between Pilatus and Alpnachstad in 1889. It was then and is now the steepest rack railway in the world, with a 48% gradient. A rack railway involves the combination of a locomotive cogwheel and a toothed "rack rail," which makes it possible for the train to handle steep inclines. It took three years and 600 Italian immigrant workers to complete the railway and at the time cost two million Swiss francs to build. Call ☎ 41-329-1111, fax 41-329-1112 for information and schedules.

Central Switzerland

Adventures

On Foot

Hiking trips abound in this area, and are especially fun on Pilatus. Here are two which should delight any hiking enthusiast. **Alpnachstad-Aemisgen-Pilatus** is a nine- to 10-hour round-trip hike, so it's best to begin in the morning. Walk from Alpnachstad, following the path through forests, where the trail will begin to ascend steeply. The path will follow the Pilatusbahn track somewhat, and connect at Aemisgen. Stay on the trail and you'll eventually come to the Alpine meadow of Mattalp, in the summer filled with Alpine flowers, before eventually reaching Pilatus. The second hike is a five-hour jaunt that takes you from **Lütoldsmatt-Oberwaldnerfräkmünt-Pilatus**. This is a very easy trail, with the exception of the path from Chilchsteinen to Pilatus. For the most part, this trail flattens out through lush meadows. If you want a bit more stress in your life, then opt for the extension from Chilchsteinen to the Matthorn. For information and maps, ☎ 41-670-1244.

By Rail

A fun trip for any traveler is to take the **Brünig Railway** from the northern village of Alpnachstad to the southernmost village of Lungern. The train first began running this route back in 1888. You'll pass through the cities of Alpnach Dorf, Sarnen, Sachslen, Giswil, Kaiserstuhl, and finally to Lungern, passing the lakes of Wichel, Sarnen and Lungern along the route. It's a great way to view this section of Obwalden – taking you past the forests, meadows, rivers and majestic mountain ranges. To make reservations, contact the SBB at Güterstrasse 3, Postfach 4267, CH-6002 Lucerne. ☎ 51-227-3085, fax 51-227-3133.

Where to Stay & Eat

On Pilatus

If you'd like to stay on the mountain itself, then you'll have several options. **Hotel Pilatus Bellevue**, at the top of Pilatus, provides visitors with imposing views of the Alps and Lake Lucerne. All amenities are available and the restaurant serves up fondue and other regional specialties from mid-April until mid-November in its Panoramic Restaurant. Includes a Snow Bar and sun terraces. ($$). ☎ 41-670-1255, fax 41-670-2635.

Hotel Pilatus Kulm was built in 1900 and is a charming Swiss hotel that offers clean rooms with spectacular views in good weather. Includes breakfast at very reasonable rates. The restaurant, called **Swiss Express**, offers regional fare, including fondue, in a fun atmosphere. ($). ☎ 41-670-1255, fax 41-670-2635.

You can also dine at **Restaurant Fräkmüntegg**. At 4,650 feet (1,418 m), it's the starting point for many great Alpine hikes and offers a 100-seat dining area and sun terrace. Closed on Monday and Tuesday from late November to late April, but open otherwise when the gondolas from Kriens to Frakmuntegg are running. ☎/fax 41-329-1177. **Restaurant Krienseregg**, at 3,375 feet (1,029 m), offers a 35-seat dining area and sundeck. Open from the first of May to the end of November, when the gondolas from Kriens to Frakmuntegg are running. Bergrestaurant Krienseregg. ☎ 41-329-1155.

Alpnachstad

Hotel Rössli is family-owned and -operated and provides charming rooms in clean, fashionable Swiss style at reasonable rates ($$). Contact the family Moll for information. CH-6053 Alpnachstad. ☎ 41-672-9070, fax 41-672-9072.

Hotel Garni Sternen offers guests Internet hook-ups in a clean and comfortable setting just two minutes from the train station. Family Jöri-Röthlin runs this reasonable and beautiful inn. ($$). CH-6053 Alpnachstad. ☎ 41-627-7070, fax 41-672-7071.

Hotel Alpenrösli is close to the train station and to the boat landings, and features a unique Mexican café/bar on the premises. Extremely reasonable. ($-$$). Contact Lisa Britschgi at CH-6053 Alpnachstad. ☎ 41-670-1193, fax 41-670-2937.

Restaurant Chalet Alpnachstad is at the base of the railway up to Pilatus. Closed from mid-November to May 1. ($). Inexpensive, hearty food.

Camping

 Camping Bachmattli offers close proximity to the Pilatusbahn, restaurants, shopping and swimming, and is open from April 1 to mid-October annually. ($). Contact Martin and Margrit Iten at CH-6053 Alpnachstad. ☎ 41-671-0703, fax 41-671-0731, www.bachmattli.ch.

The Sachseln Region

The Sachseln region is the fifth-largest of the Obwaldener municipalities, divided into the two main villages of Sachseln and Flüeli-Ranft. Sachseln lies on the shores of the **Sarnersee** at 1,590 feet (485 m), and was founded in the 12th century. It remained primarily a farming community until the late 20th century. In August of 1997, a storm dumped hundreds of thousands of gallons of water over the village, devastating most of it and causing millions of Swiss francs worth of damage. Houses and hotels were evacuated and business were shut down for days, and many of the local roads were washed away.

Around Lake Sarnen you can find hiking paths, fishing, rowing, canoeing, paragliding, bike paths, horseback riding, tennis, volleyball and climbing. The **Sachseln/Flüeli-Ranft Tourist Office** can help with reservations, maps and directions. CH-6072 Sachseln. ☎ 41-660-2655, fax 41-660-9451.

One of the grandest spots to overnight in this region is the **Hotel Belvoir**, situated on Lake Sarnen. It is very close to the slopes of Lungern-Schoenbuehl and Melchsee-Frutt for winter sports and summer hikes. Clean, comfortable rooms with all amenities, an excellent restaurant (gourmet buffet, fondue, Swiss specialties) with a sun terrace and disco make this hotel a fun stop on your tour. Very reasonable rates. ($-$$). Run by the Zumstein family. Bruenigstrasse 5, CH-6072-Sachseln. ☎ 41-666-7676, fax 41-666-7677.

You can camp at the excellent **Sachseln-Ewil Campgrounds**. This huge and well-placed campground has 100 plots for permanent and temporary visitors. ($). Close to hiking trails and fishing. Contact Albert Von Moos at CH-6072 Sachseln. ☎ 41-666-3270, fax 41-666-3279.

 **St. Nicholas** was originally born Nicholas Lowenbrugger in Flüeli, near Sachseln, in 1417, and later became known as Nicholas of Flüe. The son of an affluent Swiss farmer, Nicholas lived a pretty normal life, marrying and fathering 10 children. At the age of 50, however, he was said to be transformed forever after hearing an inner voice that told him to "leave all he had and put his life into God's hands." So Nicholas did just that on October 16, 1467 and lived out the rest of his life as a hermit. It was during this time that he acquired the name of "Brother Klaus." He settled in Basel, but was then instructed by his inner voice to travel to Ranft, where he lived for the next 20 years. He was sought out by the people in various communities for his counsel. Brother Klaus was known for never forgetting a person's name, and never turned anyone away. When Switzerland was in the midst of a domestic dispute and near war in 1481, Nicholas was chosen as an arbitrator. He eventually passed away in 1487 on March 21, his 70th birthday, and was canonized by Pope Pius XII in 1947. A feast in his honor is celebrated every March 21 in Switzerland.

Kerns

Kerns is just slightly east of Sarnen and is a region known for its thick forests and beautiful walking paths suitable for families with children. Here you'll also find bike paths, fishing in streams and rivers, and playgrounds for the kids. Contact the **Kerns/Melchsee-Frutt Tourist Office** at CH-6064 Kerns. ☎ 41-660-7070, fax 41-660-7175. If you want a hearty hike, you can follow the road eastward out of Kerns to the Acherlipass into the sister canton of Nidwalden at 4,782 feet (1,458 m).

Giswil

This village is south of the Sarnersee and north of the Lungerersee on Highway 8 and is best-known for the skiing at Mörlialp, with five ski lifts, the Swiss Ski School, and well-groomed cross-country runs. In summer there are numerous fishing, sunbathing and swimming spots. This is a great place for families with kids who want to enjoy the beauty of Switzerland without St. Moritz prices. From Giswil you can follow the road west to Kleintell as it winds around to the Glaubenbüelenpass at 5,284 feet (1,611 m).

Contact the **Giswil/Morlialp Tourist Office** at CH-6074 Giswil. ☎ 41-675-1760, fax 41-675-1746. Camping is available at the **Giswil Sarnersee International Camping** site, with 100 sites for tourists. ($). Contact T. Fankhauser at CH-6074 Giswil. ☎ 41-675-2355, fax 41-675-2351. You can also travel seven miles (11.2 km) south to the town of Lungern and pitch your tent at the beautiful edge of the Obsee and its campgrounds there. **Obsee Camping** has 150 tourist plots in a gorgeous setting year-round that is close to everything. Call Klalus or Erika Burgi at CH-6078 Lungern. ☎ 41-678-1463, fax 41-678-2163.

Engelberg

The name means "Angel Mountain," and it's the main village in the Canton Obwalden region, at 3,280 feet (1,000 m). Originally a monastery village, today it's home to six mountain railways, ski lifts and numerous hotels and restaurants. It's hard to find a bad hotel or restaurant here. There is just one road in and out of the town (from either Lucerne, Stans or Dörfli), and it weaves through narrow valleys along the way. For the hiker, Engelberg provides the splendid Titlis, Spannörter and Uri Rotstock.

■ Information Sources

Tourist Offices

The **Engelberg Tourist Office** offers packages for hikers and skiers on Dorfstrasse, just around the corner from the train station, at CH-6390 Engelberg. ☎ 41-637-3737, fax 41-637-4156. You can also get information from the **Engelberg-Titlis**

Tourismus at ☎ 41-639-7777, fax 41-639-7766. Or contact the **Adventure Engelberg Tourist Center** at CH-6390 Engelberg. ☎ 41-639-5450.

Train Station

The train station is in the middle of Engelberg on Bahnhhofstrasse and is open daily from 7:30 am-midnight. Currency exchange and lockers are available here.

Post Office

The Engelberg post office is at Bahnhofstrasse 9, CH-6390. Open Monday-Friday, from 8 am-noon, 2-6 pm, Saturdays 8:30-11 am. ☎ 41-637-1153, fax 41-637-1939.

Codes

The **area code** for Engelberg is 41; the **postal code** is CH-6390.

■ Adventures

On Foot

A hiker's paradise, with the **Titlis** – at 10,627 feet (3,239 m) – being the prima donna of the area. To get there, take the cable car to **Trübsee**, which provides you with great views of the Engelberg village. Here you walk around this beautiful mountain lake, beginning to the right of the cable car exit, for a good 1½-hour hike. On the southwest side of the Trübsee you can take a chairlift to the **Joch Pass** at 7,241 feet (2,207 m) – which is home to some of the best mountain bike trails in Switzerland. You can also take a lift down to the lakes of Engstlensee, Tannen and Mechsee – where a variety of hiking trails can be found. To get to Titlis take the cable car farther up from Trübsee to Stand at 8,038 feet (2,450 m). Then take one of the unique revolving cable cars known as the "Rotair" up to the peak, where it is another 15-minute hike up to the viewing deck, and another 45 minutes up to summit. These are some sturdy hikes up, so be prepared with good hiking shoes, sunglasses and a raincoat in case of inclement weather. On the way back, you can hike to Trübsee via Stand on a well-marked path.

Two miles (3.2 km) east of Engelberg, you'll find the **Fürenalpbahn**, which takes you up to the Fürenalp, at 6,069 feet (1,850 m), allowing great views of the area. From the top of the Fürenalp station, walk to the right and you'll see a path that slopes slightly downward. You'll quickly come upon the **Abnet** village; head toward it through the midst of cows in the pastures on either side. Continue on until you get to the village of **Stäfeli**. Here you can either retrace your steps or follow an alternative path back to the Fürenalp station. This hike should take you three to four hours.

There are two mountain huts in the area: the **Rugghubelhütte** and the **Brunnihütte**. The Brunnihütte sits at 6,100 feet (1,860 m) and offers up 40 sleeping spots, with great panoramic views of the area. Contact Christian Wyss at ☎ 41-637-3732 for reservations. This hut can be reached by cable car and then by chairlift. The Rugghubelhütte offers accommodations for 100 people and is open from June to October. Sitting at 7,527 feet (2,295 m), this hut allows you to view wildlife in the surrounding areas. It's a 2½-hour hike from Ristis. Contact Fredi Schleiss Niderberger at ☎ 41-637-2064. To get there, follow the well-marked path from Engelberg to the local nature preserve and beyond to the hut, www.rugghubel.ch.

For another light jaunt, you can follow a narrow road north and then west and north again to the small village of **Schwand**. Here's a good spot for a picnic with the family that offers great views of the Titlis and surrounding mountains. Allow a couple of hours for this trip.

On Snow

Engelberg offers a wide variance in the ski slopes, though its skiing area is small compared to most Swiss resorts, with 26 lifts for 51 miles (82 km) of pistes. There are 25 miles (40 km) of cross-country ski runs heading toward the Trübsee. Contact the **Skischule Engelberg Titlis** at ☎ 41-639-5454. Snowshoe walking tours are available for 60Sfr with a guide, followed by fondue or raclettes later in the evening. Contact **Engelberg-Titlis Tourismus** at ☎ 41-639-7777. Snowboarding tours and lessons are also available.

Summer Adventures

Besides hiking, Engelberg offers kayaking, caving, glacial tours, bungee jumping, rock climbing, golf, downhill mountain biking, and paragliding. Contact **Engelberg-Titlis Tourismus** at ☎ 41-639-7777.

■ Landmarks & Historic Sites

The **Kloster St. Gallen** (see page 267) is a massive set of structures that were originally built in the 12th century, and are now home to a religious college. The Baroque church is home to one of the largest organs in Switzerland. Open year-round Tuesdays-Saturdays from 10 am-4 pm. Admission is 2.5Sfr.

■ Where to Stay in Engelberg

Hotel Waldegg is a four-star, gorgeous and stylish hotel set in the heart of Engelberg. Offers special rates for singles, doubles and families, with ski, gourmet meal and various packages

Central Switzerland

available. ($$-$$$$). Schwandstrasse 91, CH-6390 Engelberg. ☎ 41-637-1822, fax 41-637-4321.

Berghotel Trübsee-Hof sits at the central station of Titlis-Gondelbahn, in the middle of the Engelberg ski region. Beautiful and stately, with gracious accommodations and an excellent restaurant. ($$-$$$$). CH-6390 Engelberg/Trübsee. ☎ 41-637-1371, fax 41-637-3720.

Hotel Sonnwendhof is quite near to the Titlis tram station, and is a beautiful white stucco house with wood trim and wood paneling throughout. Comfortable, with a garden sun terrace, restaurant and bar. ($$-$$$). Gerschniweg 1, CH-6390 Engelberg. ☎ 41-637-4575, fax 637-4238.

Hotel Schweizerhof is a comfortable, three-star hotel in the village center that offers all amenities, including saunas, massages and facials. ($$-$$$$). Dorfstrasse 42, CH-6390 Engelberg. ☎ 41-637-1105, fax 41-637-4147.

Berghaus Youth Hostel houses 160 beds and is open from late November to mid-April, and from late May to late October. ($). Dorfstrasse 80, CH-6390 Engelberg. ☎ 41-637-1292, fax 41-637-4988, www.youthhostel.ch/engelberg.

Camping

Camping is at **Eienwäldli**, close to hiking trails and ski lifts with 150 permanent and 100 temporary spots. Contact Josef Bünter at CH-6390 Engelberg. ☎ 41-637-1949, fax 41-637-4423, www.eienwaldli.ch.

■ Where to Eat in Engelberg

Bergrestaurant Ristis-Brunni is open daily and is a great spot at 5,248 feet (1,600 m), only five minutes up the mountain via the Luftseilbahn cable car. Includes a banquet hall, an outdoor terrace and a large playground for children. Features regional and international dishes. ($-$$). CH-6390 Engelberg. ☎ 41-637-1483, fax 41-637-4485.

Restaurant Flüematt can be reached on foot from the Engelberg central train station in 45 minutes or via a small lift in three minutes. Sitting at 4,264 feet (1,300 m), the restaurant is typical of an Engelberg house (they are stacked among throngs of thick trees along a steep a mountainside, and are two to three stories high, with dark slanted roofs and white facades). This one serves up regional fare at reasonable rates. Run by the Paul Hurschler-Hacki family. ($-$$). Open daily. ☎ 41-637-1660.

Älplerbeizli Rigidalalp can be reached in 30 minutes by foot from Engelberg and serves up Engelberger fare, while diners overlook the valley and surrounding mountains. ($-$$). Contact family Werner Hurschler-Ulrich at ☎ 79-302-6543.

Restaurant Schwand can be reached from Engelberg in about an hour on foot. Open daily, and a favorite among hikers and skiers. ($-$$). Run by the family of Thomas Wallimann. ☎ 41-637-1392.

Most other restaurants in Engelberg are on the Dorfstrasse in the village center and offer a wide array of choices, from Chinese to Italian, Swiss, French or even Thai.

Kloster St. Gallen, Engelberg

Northern Switzerland

1. Town Hall; Juventuti School; Porte de France; Hotel Dieu
2. Old Town; Hotel de Ville (town hall); Chapelle du Vorbourg; Jurassic Art and History Museum
3. cheese factory
4. Kunsthaus Grénchen; Kultur-Historiches Museum Grénchen; Mudjibur Riding Hall
5. St-Ursen Cathedral; Baseltor; Rathaus; Zeltclockenturm; Mauritus Fountain; Jesuit Church; Krummer Turm; Solothurn Kunstmuseum; Altes Zeughaus; Bluemstein Historical Museum
6. Basel-Land Cantonal Museum; Dichtermuseum; Monteverdi Car Collection
7. Schuhmuseum
8. StadtKirch; Fountain of Justice
9. Kunstmuseum; Historiches Museum

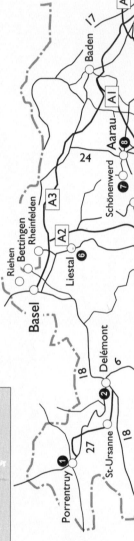

Northern Switzerland

This region is just north of Central Switzerland and west of Canton Zürich. It is home to the international city of **Basel** and to the cantons of **Basel-Stadt, Basel-Land, Jura, Solothurn** and **Aargau**. By using Basel as a base, you can travel easily throughout this region within five days or less. For horse enthusiasts, there's no finer place than

the village of **Saignelègier** in Canton Jura. Numerous horseback riding excursions and holidays are to be found here, and the National Horse Fair is held here annually. From Basel, you can travel either by car or trail to most destinations in this region in an hour or less. For cyclists, the Aare Bike Trail begins and ends in Canton Aargau, which is home to the village of Rheinfelden, famous for its saltwater health spas, and the health-resort village of Baden on the Limmat River. Solothurn's old city is perfect for rainy-day walks and shopping trips, as is the medieval village of Zofingen, in Canton Aargau. And you definitely won't want to miss the Roman ruins in the village of Liestal, just a short distance east of Basel's city center.

Basel itself is worth a few days of exploration. The city is a haven of museums, and the Old Town, with its numerous bridges and historic buildings, is enchanting and romantic. Basel is also a major junction for trains and highways connecting Switzerland with other European destinations.

Canton Basel-Stadt (BS)

Basel

■ At a Glance

Basel is Switzerland's third-largest city – encompassing 14 square miles (36 square km) – and, as a half-canton, borders the Jura Mountains, the German Black Forest and the French Vosges. It is often referred to as the "Gateway of Switzerland," and is well known for its chemical industries, the Rhine harbor and its **Fasnacht** celebration. Basel-Stadt is the meeting place for France, Germany and Switzerland, and influences of all three nations abound in this unique city, which is also the home of Switzerland's oldest university. Mostly Protestant, German-speaking citizens inhabit Basel-Stadt, which is the smallest canton in Switzerland. In terms of population the canton ranks 14th out of the 26 cantons, and it is home to the third-largest contingent of foreigners found anywhere in Switzerland, behind the cantons of Geneva and Ticino.

Basel dates back to 374 AD, when it was a Roman fortress. It joined the Swiss Confederation in 1501 and has become Switzerland's main artistic and cultural center. Home to over 40 museums and a dozen theaters, the town retains much of its medieval atmosphere, as reflected in the architecture of its buildings.

The city of Basel is split into two areas: **Grossbasel** (Greater Basel) and **Kleinbasel** (Lesser Basel). Grossbasel sits on the steep left side of the Rhine River, while Kleinbasel sits on the right bank. Six bridges link both parts of Basel together, and ferries run continuously back and forth. Grossbasel is the commercial and cultural center of the city, while Kleinbasel is the industrial and business arm. Grossbasel is focused on the Rhine, where visitors can stroll for hours along its banks or explore the cobblestone streets of the Old Town. The Rhine Harbor (Rheinhafen) is on the far northern side of the city, which is home to 162,800 residents, making it the third-largest city in Switzerland in terms of poulation.

This canton is also a "Sister State" to the US state of Massachusetts. The two formed an official partnership in June 2002 to help benefit each area's communities and residents in regard to technology, science and culture.

The cantonal **coat of arms** of Basel-Stadt reflects a black bishop's crosier on a white background, representing a time when the town was home to a prince-bishop.

■ Information Sources

Tourist Offices

The **Basel Tourismus** (Tourist Office) is open Monday-Friday, from 8:30 am to 6 pm, and on Saturday from 10 am to 4 pm. Closed Sunday. Schifflände 5, CH-4001 Grossbasel. ☎ 61-268-6868, fax 61-268-6870, www.baseltourismus.ch. There is a **City Information Center** at the SBB Bahnhof in Grossbasel. ☎ 61-271-3684.

Train Stations

Basel has one of the largest rail junctions within Europe. The SNCF train station is on the Centralbahnstrasse, as is the SBB (Schweizerische Bunesbahnen, ☎ 900-300-300) on the south side of the old town. The DB (Deutsch Bundesbahnen, ☎ 61-690-1111)

is on the other side of the Rhine on Richenstrasse in Kleinbasel. You can rent bikes at the SBB train station kiosk for 29Sfr daily with an ID. Open 7 am-midnight.

Post Office

The main post office in Basel is at Rudengasse 1, CH-4001. ☎ 61-266-1616, fax 61-266-1604. Hours are Monday-Friday, 7:30 am-6:30 pm, and Saturday, 7:30-noon. There are 28 branch offices throughout the half-canton.

Codes

The **area code** for Basel-Stadt is 61 and the **postal codes** range from CH-4001 to 4032.

Internet Access

Internet cafés abound in Basel-Stadt. You can let your fingers do the surfing at these following locations: **Domino**, on Steinenvorstadt 54, CH-4051 Basel. ☎ 61-271-7298. Open Monday-Thursday, from 11 am-midnight, Friday and Saturday from 11 am-1 am, and Sunday from 1 pm-midnight. **Jäggi Bücher**, at Greifengasse 3&5, CH-4058 Basel. ☎ 61-264-2694. Open Monday, Wednesday, Friday, 9 am-7 pm; Thursday, 9 am-8 pm; Saturday, 9 am-5 pm. **Beim Kundendienst**, at Greifengasse 22, CH-4058 Basel. ☎ 61-685-4618. Open Monday, Tuesday, Wednesday, Friday, 8:30 am-7 pm; Thursday, 8:30 am-9 pm; Saturday, 8 am-5 pm. **Mausklick** at Klingentalstrasse 7, CH-4057 Basel. ☎ 61-683-4183. Open Monday through Friday, 7:30 am-5 pm.

■ Getting Around

Public transportation is cheap in Basel, but beware of the taxis, as they are horribly expensive. You probably won't need to take a taxi anywhere, since the best way to see Basel is either on foot or by bicycle. The heart of the city is best explored on foot – especially since most of the main sites such as museums and shopping are contained in the historic district.

■ Adventures

On Foot

Though Basel is known for its culture and industry, you may be surprised to learn that the city has 744 miles (1,198 km) of dedicated walking trails on its perimeter. These well-marked paths allow for some great hikes. Take city bus #70 to Reigoldswil and then grab the Gondelbahn (cable car) up to the

Wasserfallen peak at 3,073 feet (937 m). From here you'll find paths branching out in all directions for relaxing and scenic hikes. For information, ☎ 61-941-1881.

The old part of Basel is unique and self-contained. Informative **walking tours** are available through Basel Tourismus, leaving from the Schifflände office. The tours cost only 15Sfr and are well worth it. They operate May through October, Monday-Saturday at 2:30 pm, and November through April on Saturdays only at 2:30 pm.

 *You can purchase a **Basel Card** at the tourist office. This card allows discounts and special rates at all museums and many restaurants, shops and art galleries. The cost starts at 25Sfr.*

■ Festivals

 Besides Fasnacht, Basel is home to festivals throughout the year, but two main ones are the **Vogel Gryff Volksfest** and the **Basel Art Fair**. The Vogel Gryff Volksfest occurs on January 13, 20 or 27, with the three main neighborhoods of the city depicted by their traditional symbols – a lion, a griffin and a "wild man from the woods." These three float down the Rhine on a raft and afterwards street celebrations and dancing take place. The Tourist Office or any hotel can tell you exactly when the festival will be occurring. The Basel Art Fair is held in mid-June and displays the works from over 1,000 artists worldwide. For information on the Art Fair, ☎ 61-686-2020.

Fasnacht is Basel-Stadt's annual carnival, and brings everyone into the streets for partying, singing and dancing on the Monday following Ash Wednesday. At exactly four in the morning, all the lights of the city are turned off and thousands of people gather with masks, drums and pipes for a procession through the city. This is the Swiss version of Mardi Gras, bursting with people, many of whom don masks, and music in a wild celebration for three days and nights.

FOODS OF FASNACHT

Fasnacht gets its name from the start of Lent, when fasting is to take place. However, there is little fasting going on during Fasnacht. In fact, you can find food specialties all over Basel-Stadt during this carnival. For instance, **Fasnachtskiechli** is a kind of powdered pancake that has a sugar icing. Or you can try the famed **Zwiebelwähe** – onion pie. **Mehlsuppe** is a traditional Fasnacht flour gruel; and for dessert you're sure to be served a **lenten pie** spiced with aniseed.

■ Sightseeing

Sightseeing here begins with the **Rheinbrücke**, Basel's Middle Rhine Bridge, and one of its most historic sites. The original bridge was built in 1225 of wood and was later replaced with stone during the early 1900s. You'll also want to visit the **Rathaus** (Town Hall) that was built to honor the city's joining of the Swiss Federation in 1501. It hovers over the marketplace and, with its bright red façade and fancy frescos, it's hard to miss. The **Marktplatz** is the place to be every morning beginning at 6 am. Here vendors of all kinds come to sell their wares, everything from fruits, vegetables, roasted nuts, to housewares, clothing and electronics. Up a bit on the northwest side of the city from the Marktplatz is the **Fischmarkt** (Fish Market) Square, whose fountain once served as a holding tank for the day's fresh catches.

Landmarks & Historic Sites

The Basler Zoologischer Garten was founded in 1874 and is one of the best zoos anywhere. Just a few minutes walk from the central train station, this zoo encompasses 26 acres in the middle of the city and is famous for breeding a variety of endangered species. A must-see! Open daily, 10 am-5 pm. Admission is 5Sfr for adults and 3Sfr for students, free for kids 15 and under. Binningerstrasse 40, CH-4001 Basel. ☎ 61-205-8600.

The Münster (Cathedral), at left, has evolved from a ninth-century Carolingian church into the imposing structure seen today in the middle of **Münsterplatz Square** in Grossbasel. Many additions and alterations have been made to the cathedral over the centuries, and it is a sight not to be missed in Basel. It features a beautifully restored doorway, known as St. Gallus Doorway, originally built in the 12th century. Open from Easter to mid-October, Monday-Friday from 10 am to 6 pm, Saturday, 10 am-noon and 2-5 pm, Sunday, 1-5 pm. Open from mid-October to Easter, Monday-Saturday, 10 am-noon, 2-4 pm, and on Sunday, 2-4 pm. Münsterplatz, CH-4002 Grossbasel.

The Beyeler Foundation has one of the top private contemporary art collections in the world, established through an endowment of Hildy and Ernst Beyeler. Located at Baselstrasse 101 in the nearby suburb of Riehen in the Berowerpark. Open daily, 10 am-6 pm. ☎ 61-645-9700.

Museums

The Kunstmuseum (Fine Arts Museum) is the oldest museum in Switzerland and features everything from Impressionists to classical and religious sketches and sculpture. Open Tuesday-Sunday from 10 am to 5 pm. Admission is 10Sfr for adults and 8Sfr for seniors and kids. St. Alban-Graben 15, CH-4001 Grossbasel. ☎ 61-206-6262.

Basel

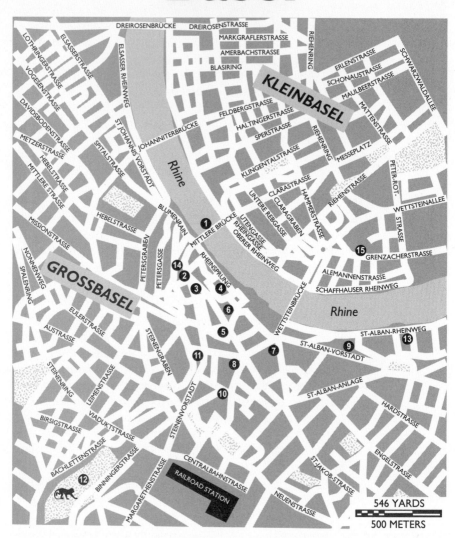

1. Mittlere Brücke (Middle Bridge)
2. Rathaus
3. Marktplatz
4. Natur Historiches Museum;
   Museum der Kulturen Basel
5. The Münster
6. Historiches Museum Baufüsserplatz
7. Kunstmuseum
8. Kunsthalle
9. Museum für Gegenwartskunst
10. Haus Zum Kirschgarten
11. Puppenhausmuseum (Doll House Museum)
12. Basler Zoologischer Garten
13. Schweizer Papiermuseum
14. Pharmazie-Historisches Museum
15. Jean Tinguely Museum

The Kunsthalle (Art Gallery) has been the premiere art hall for modern works in Basel since 1872. Open Tuesday, Thursday and Sunday from 11 am to 5 pm, and on Wednesday from 11 am to 8:30 pm. Admission is 9Sfr for adults, 6Sfr for seniors and kids. Steinenberg 7, CH-4001 Grossbasel. ☎ 61-206-9900.

Museum für Gegenwartskunst (Museum for Contemporary Art) features works by artists from 1960 to the present. Open Tuesday-Sunday from 11 am to 5 pm. Admission is 10Sfr for adults, 8Sfr for seniors and kids. Alban-Rheinweg 60, CH-4002 Basel. ☎ 61-272-8183.

Historisches Museum Barfüsserplatz is housed inside the Church of Barefoot Friars (Barfüsserkirche), a structure dating back to 1250. Inside you'll find many 15th-century tapestries, wooden sculptures, armor, and coins from throughout Basel's history. Open Wednesday-Monday, 10 am-5 pm. Admission is 5Sfr for adults and 3Sfr for students. Barfüsserplatz, CH-4001 Basel. ☎ 61-205-8600.

The Jean Tinguely Museum features the work of the Swiss sculptor Jean Tinguely, who passed away in 1991. The museum spotlights 70 mechanical sculptures by the artist. Admission is 8Sfr, 5Sfr for seniors and students. Free to kids 16 and under. Grenzacherstrasse 210, CH-4002 Basel. ☎ 61-681-9320.

Schweizer Papiermuseum und Museum für Schrift und Druck (Swiss Paper Museum & Museum for Writing & Printing) is a lovely medieval millhouse that demonstrates typesetting, bookmaking and papermaking.

Haus zum Kirschgarten features 18th- and 19th-century porcelain, timepieces and other historical items. Originally an 18th-century palace, it is now home to various rooms dedicated to specific eras in Basel history. Open Tuesday, Thursday, Friday and Sunday from 10 am to 5 pm, and Wednesday from 10 am to 8 pm, Saturday, 1-5 pm. Admission is 7Sfr, and the first Sunday of every month is free. Elisabethenstrasse 27-29, CH-4001 Grossbasel. ☎ 61-271-1333.

Naturhistorisches Museum (Natural History Museum) and **Museum der Kulturen Basel** (Basel Museum of Cultures). Both of these fine museums are contained under the same roof, and both contain excellent collections. Admission is 7Sfr and allows you access to both museums. Open Tuesday-Sunday, 10 am-5 pm. The first Sunday of the month admission is free. Augustinergasse 2, CH-4001 Grossbasel. ☎ 61-266-5500.

Puppenhaus Museum (Doll House Museum) features toys, dolls and teddy bears from the 18h and 19th centuries and is definitely worth a look, no matter what your taste in toys. Open Friday through Wednesday, 11 am-5 pm, Thursday from 11 am to 8 pm. Admission is 7Sfr. Steinenvorstadt 1, CH-4001 Grossbasel. ☎ 61-225-9595.

Pharmazie-Historisches Museum (Museum of Pharmaceutical History) spotlights one of Basel's oldest and most profitable professions, within the Zum Vorderen Sessle Haus. The numerous displays are interesting and profile many types of pharmacology through the ages. Open Tuesday-Friday, 10 am-6 pm, Saturday, 10 am-5 pm. Totengasslein 3, CH-4001 Grossbasel. ☎ 61-264-9111.

■ Shopping

Shopping takes place along the streets of **Gerbergasse**, **Freiestrasse and Steinenvorstadt**, with a wide variety of wares to choose from. Along the **Elisabethenstrasse** you'll find English-language books in many of the bookstores there.

If you're looking for Swiss and European handicrafts, linens and related items, such as handkerchiefs, doilies, bandanas and embroidery work, as well as Basel souvenirs, then check out these stores, all in Grossbasel:

- **Langenthal** (for fine linens, embroidered clothing, placemats, tableware accessories) on Gergergasse 26 (☎ 61-261-0900).
- **Seven Sisters** (unusual artsy products) on Spalenberg 38 (☎ 61-262-0980).
- **Brockenhaus Basel** (antiques, odds & ends) on Ochsengasse 12 (☎ 61-681-4366).
- **Schweitzer Heimatwerk** (handmade Swiss items and souvenirs) on Schneidergasse 2 (☎ 61-261-9178).
- **Caraco** (brand-name textiles) on Gerbergasse 77 (☎ 61-261-3577).
- **Johann Wanner** (world-famous for Christmas and nonseasonal decorations) on Spalenbergasse 14 (☎ 61-261-4826).
- **Roosens** (over 8,000 different types of buttons in all shapes, sizes and colors) on Grunpfahlgasse 8 (☎ 61-262-0168).
- **Zem Baselstab** (souvenirs and gifts) on Schnabelgasse 8 (☎ 61-261-1016).

For mainstay European items, such as shampoo, toothpaste, personal care products, housewares, toys and clothes, look to **Manor** on Greifengasse 22 in Grossbasel (☎ 61-685-4699) or to the **Globus** at Marktplatz 2 (☎ 61-268-4545). Also, a **Migros** in the SBB train station is open until 10 pm at the Centralbahnhofplatz in Grossbasel (☎ 61-279-9745); Migros is a grocery and convenience store chain found throughout Switzerland.

■ Where to Stay

 Drei König Hotel (Three Kings) is Europe's oldest hotel (1026) and was originally a coach stop, later expanded into a classy guest house. The in-house restaurant is extremely formal and serves up classic French fare. Expensive but worth it. ($$$$+). Blumerain 8, CH-4001 Basel. ☎ 61-260-5050, fax 61-260-5060.

HOTEL PRICE CHART	
$	30-75Sfr ($20-$49)
$$	76-205Sfr ($50-$109)
$$$	206-299Sfr ($110-$200)
$$$$	300Sfr+ ($200+)

Hotel Basel is in the Old Town and caters mostly to the business crowd. The rooms are stylish, and some have elegant marble bathrooms. Many amenities. ($$$-$$$$). Munegasse 12, CH-4001 Grossbasel. ☎ 61-264-6800, fax 61-264-6811.

Hotel Euler also caters to the business set and is home to a famous bar covered in red velvet and leather. Many amenities in clean and modern Swiss surroundings. ($$$-$$$$). Centralbahnhofplatz 14, CH-4002 Grossbasel. ☎ 61-275-8000, fax 61-275-8050.

Hohel Schweizerhof was built in 1864 and is one of the most beautiful inns in the city, complete with wrought-iron balconies overlooking a lovely park. Owned and operated by the Goetzinger family for over half a century, it has played home to such notables as Arturo Toscanini. The bedrooms are traditional Swiss with modern facilities at moderate prices that include breakfast. ($$-$$$). Centralbahnhofplatz 1, CH-4002 Basel. ☎ 61-271-2833, fax 61-271-2919.

Teufelhof Art Hotel was opened in 1989 by Monica and Dominique Thommy, who brought their love of art to the hotel and restaurant complex. Each room was created by a different artist. ($$-$$$). Leonhardsgraben 47, CH-4051 Basel. ☎ 61-261-1010, fax 61-261-1004.

Hotel Helvetica sits close to the SBB train station with ultra-modern rooms and two excellent eateries: the **Chez Alin** restaurant and the **Old Red Ox** bar. Rates include breakfast. ($$-$$$). Kuchengasse 13, CH-4051 Basel. ☎ 61-272-0688, fax 61-272-0688.

Hotel St. Gotthard is right across from the train station and has been run by the same family for over 75 years. One of the most friendly staffs anywhere in the city. A clean and comfortable spot to bunk down at reasonable rates. ($$-$$$$). Centralbahnhofstrasse 13, CH-4002. Basel. ☎ 61-225-1313, fax 61-225-1314.

Hotel Krafft am Rhein sits just across the Rhine from the Rathaus, with a beautiful terrace and rooms overlooking the river. Antiques abound throughout this inn, complete with Oriental rugs and works of art. ($$-$$$). Rheingasse 12, CH-4058 Basel. ☎ 61-690-9130, fax 61-690-9131.

The Basel Youth Hostel is one of the largest in Switzerland, offering 196 beds and a variety of rooms to choose from. Open February 1-December 21. ($-$$). St. Alban-Kirchrain 10, CH-4052 Basel. ☎ 61-272-0572, fax 61-272-0833.

■ Where to Eat

The Bruderholz-Stucki restaurant features the finest international cuisine in Basel in a very formal setting. Reservations are required. ($$$-$$$$). Closed Sunday and Monday. Bruderholzallee 42. CH-4001 Basel. ☎ 61-361-8222.

DINING PRICE CHART	
Prices based on a typical entrée, per person, and do not include beverage.	
$	15-25Sfr ($10-$16)
$$	26-45Sfr ($17-$29)
$$$	46-70Sfr ($30-$47)
$$$$	71Sfr+ ($47+)

Chez Donati features classic Italian fare. This restaurant is well-known for its hors d'oeuvres and classic atmosphere. ($$$-$$$$). Closed Sunday and Monday. St. Johanns-Vorstadt 48. CH-4001 Grossbasel. ☎ 61-322-0919.

La Rôtisserie des Rois is famous for its Rhine River terrace and its market-fresh dishes that change with the seasons. ($$$-$$$$). Located in the Hotel Drei Könige. Open daily from noon to 2:45 pm, and 7-11 pm. Blumerain 8, CH-4001 Basel. ☎ 61-260-5050, fax 61-260-5060.

Zum Goldenen Sterren dates back to 1421 and is one of the oldest restaurants in Switzerland. Here you'll find traditional Swiss and French cuisine featuring lamb, eel, trout, lobster and veal. ($$-$$$). Open daily, noon-2 pm, and 6-10 pm, St. Albanrheinweg 70, CH-4001 Basel. ☎ 61-272-1666.

Schlüsselzunft was once a 12th-century guild house and is now home to a tasty restaurant. Fish and venison are the specialties here, in season. ($$-$$$). Open Monday-Saturday, 11:30-3 pm, 6 pm-midnight. Freie Strasse 25, CH-4001 Basel. ☎ 61-261-2046.

L'Escargot is found in the main train station and features a combination of Swiss and French cuisine that is surprisingly good, given the location. ($$-$$$). Open Monday-Friday, 11 am-2 pm, 6-11 pm. Closed mid-July to mid-August and on Saturdays and Sundays. Centralbahnhofstrasse 14, CH-4001 Grossbasel. ☎ 61-295-3966.

Safran-Zunft serves tasty appetizers and outstanding soups at reasonable prices – the fixed-price lunch is only 25Sfr. This spot is famous for its "Bacchus" fondue, with veal as a key ingredient. ($$-$$$). Open July through August, Monday-Friday, 10 am-2 pm, 5 pm-midnight; September

to June, Monday through Saturday, 11:30 am-11 pm. Gerbergasse 11, CH-4001 Basel. ☎ 61-269-9494.

Kunsthall Restaurant features Italian and French fare in an artsy setting. ($$-$$$). Open daily, 11 am-2 pm, 6-10 pm. Steinenberg 7, CH-4001 Basel. ☎ 61-272-4233.

St. Alban-Eck serves up Swiss and French dishes in a cozy setting in the antique district not far from the Museum of Fine Arts. ($$-$$$). Closed Sunday and Saturday for lunch, otherwise open daily. St. Alban-Vorstadt 60, CH-4001 Grossbasel. ☎ 61-271-0320.

Brauereri Fischerstube is the local brewery, which specializes in ales and lagers. "Ueli Bier" is the house special and the restaurant features grilled and local dishes. ($$). Rheingasse 45, CH-4012 Kleinbasel. ☎ 61-692-6635.

Löwenzorn features traditional German, Swiss and Italian dishes as well as large steins of beer in a friendly, easygoing atmosphere. ($-$$). Closed Sundays only. Gemsberg 2, CH-4001 Grossbasel. ☎ 61-261-4213.

Café Pfalz is Grossbasel's best-kept secret, featuring vegetarian dishes, a salad and juice bar in a comfy, modern setting. ($-$$). Münsterberg 11, CH-4001 Grossbasel. ☎ 61-272-6511.

Besides Basel, there are only two other municipalities in this half-canton, Bettingen and Riehen, with both in the area known as **Wiesental**, in the north of the canton.

Riehen

This small village of 20,000 citizens sits on the German border, having joined the canton of Basel-Stadt in 1522. It can be easily reached from the city by taking Tram 6 or Bus 31 from Basel-Stadt. Riehen is home to the late Gothic St. Martin Church, a municipal museum and the country estates of Wenkenhof and Bäumlihof. There are many wineries to be found in this farming community as well, but most visitors come here to visit the Beyeler Foundation (see above).

Bettingen

Bettingen is a tiny village that is home to only 1,200 people. The village is split between the districts of **Dorf** (village) and **St. Chrischona** – the highest point in Canton Basel-Stadt, which rises to 1,712 feet (522 m). From this striking vantage point you can view the Jura, the Bernese Alps and the Santis. There is also an 820-foot (250 m) transmission tower here – Switzerland's tallest – but the views are spectacular even if you don't climb the tower. Another favorite spot is the Chrischona church, which looms boldly over the village and is home to the Protestant Pilgrims Mission and Clinic. Another unique feature of Bettingen is that it shares more of its border with Germany than it does with its homeland Switzerland.

Morcote, on Lake Lugano, along the North-South Cycling Route 3 from Basel over the Gotthard Pass to Chiasso

Canton Basel-Land (BL)

■ At a Glance

The canton of Basel-Land officially separated from the city of Basel in 1833 after a two-year civil war that occurred between 1831 and 1832. Home to around 264,000 German-speaking Protestant citizens, Basel-Land is made up of 165 square miles (429 square km) of narrow valleys and wooded hillsides that are mostly used for agriculture. Farms and small manufacturers call this corner canton home, as it is sandwiched in the far northwestern edge of Switzerland, between the cantons of Solothurn to the south and southwest and Aargau to the east. The countries of France (to the west) and Germany (to the north and east) also mesh borders with Basel-Land. Slightly over 26% of residents of this canton work in manufacturing or energy supply, while 29% are employed in tourism-related businesses.

This canton can be traversed in several days and offers a wealth of lovely landscapes within reach of Basel-Stadt. The Jura hills provide year-round views of the city and Rhine valley, with Germany's Black Forest to the northeast and France's Vosges to the northwest. Along the banks of the Rhine River sits **Augusta Raurica**, the oldest remains of a Roman colony found in Switzerland.

The **coat of arms** of Basel-Land represents the prince-bishop who once ruled over this area. A bishop's crosier facing east in bright red appears on the shield, against a white background, using the color scheme of the national flag.

Liestal

Liestal is the capital of Basel-Land, a well-preserved old village about nine miles (14.5 km) south of Basel-Stadt on Highway 12. It features cobblestone streets in a quaint setting and the village is famous for the ancient celebration of "**Chienbäse**," which falls shortly before Basel-Stadt's Fasnacht (usually in early to mid-March). The traditional Chienbäse dates back to the 16th century, and features locals dragging giant bonfires through the town on floats, while onlookers swing fiery torches made of pine branches over their heads. This, all through the narrow streets (mainly on the Rathausgasse) of Liestal, makes for a spectacular sight and is well worth a visit if you're in the area at the right time of the year (just before Basel-Stadt's Fasnacht).

■ Information Sources

Tourist Office

The Basel-Land Tourist Office is at Altmarktstrasse 96, CH-4410 Liestal. ☎ 61-927-6535, fax 61-927-6550.

Post Office

The Liestal post office is open Monday-Friday, from 7:30 am-6:15 pm, Saturday from 8 am to noon. Poststrasse 3, CH-4410 Liestal. ☎ 61-926-9444, fax 61-926-9445.

Codes

The **postal code** for Liestal is CH-4410 and the **area code** is 61.

■ Adventures

On Foot

Only seven miles (11 km) from Basel-Stadt, and six miles (9.6 km) north of Liestal, is Augusta Raurica, or **Rome on the Rhine** as it is known. Over 1,800 years ago this Roman town was home to some 20,000 people – native Celts and Mediterraneans. The site today features a large open-air archeological museum that is home to a well-preserved theater, a replica of a Roman house and a Roman farm animal park. Expect to spend an entire day here to take in the more than 20 exhibits. The grounds are free to the public, and admission to the Roman museum and Roman house is just 5Sfr. If you'd like a **guided tour** of the grounds and museum, you can make reservations through **Basel Tourismus**, Schifflande, CH-4001 Basel. ☎ 61-268-6832, fax 61-268-6870. Open daily, 10 am-5 pm. For information contact Römerstadt Augusta Raurica, Giebenacherstrasse 17, CH-4302 Augusta. ☎ 61-816-2222, fax 61-816-2261. To get here you can take any train from Basel to Augusta and it is a 10-minute walk to the Roman museum Or take bus #70 from Basel. For a fun **bike ride** to Rome on the Rhine, you can rent a bike at the Rheinfelden train station (reservation necessary at ☎ 51-229-3484), and explore the area via a 1.4-mile path through the ruins. In the summer you can take a boat from Basel-Stadt (Schifflände), or from Rheinfelden to Augst and then walk 15 minutes to the Roman Museum. ☎ 61-639-9507 for departure times. The entire trip from Basel to the ruins takes about 1½ hours. Last, but not least, you can walk from Liestal to Augst along well-marked pedestrian routes marked in yellow.

Hikes

There are two mountain huts worth a visit in Basel-Land if you're hiking, and the Basel Tourist Office can provide you with maps and information. The **Tierberglihütte** is reached by starting from the Steingletscher/ Sustenpass for a nice 3½-hour walk along a well-marked trail (with blue and white signs). The hut is open from July 1 to the end of September and offers 70 sleeping spots, and a nice kitchen, where the hut-warden often serves up tasty dishes at nominal prices. For information contact the Huettenwartin (hut warden) Trudi Imdorf at CH-3860 Meiringen. ☎ 33-971-6817, or ☎ 33-971-2782 at the hut.

The **Waldweldhütte** is a private hut from the Basel-Land Hut Club. From here you can take lovely walks throughout the Jura hills of Basel-Land. For an easy 1½-hour walk you can begin at the forest castle in Reigoldswil, southwest of Liesel. Here you'll find the well-marked trail, the "Ruchweg," up to the Waldweldhütte. The hut is open from Saturday afternoon at 2 pm until Sunday at 4 pm, when it is attended by a hut warden. There are 24 sleeping spots, but you must make arrangements with the hut warden to stay there. Contact Hans at Moosmattstrasse 3, CH-4416 Bubendorf. ☎ 61-931-2948.

■ Museums

The **Basel-Land Cantonal Museum** is in Liestal, at Zueghausplatch 28, CH-4410 Liestal, and includes a wide array of historical documents and displays spotlighting the history of the region. Admission is 7Sfr for adults, 5Sfr for kids under 16, students and seniors. Open Tuesday-Friday from 10 am-noon, 2-5 pm, Saturday and Sunday, 10 am-5 pm, closed Monday. ☎ 61-925-5986, fax 61-925-5088.

The **Dichtermuseum** (Writer's Museum) is open the first Saturday of every month, or by private arrangement. It features works and historical documents by Nobel Prize-winner Carl Spitteler, who was born in Liestal, and others. Located in the Rathaus, CH-4410 Liestal. ☎ 61-901-3978.

The **Monteverdi Car Collection** in nearby Binningen is a must for any auto enthusiast. This museum contains Europe's largest collection of model cars – 8,000 to be exact. Open daily from 1 to 5 pm, but you must make a reservation to visit. Oberwilerstrasse 20 CH-4102 Binningen. ☎ 61-421-4545, fax 61-421-4546.

■ Where to Stay

Hotel Engel is the largest of four inns in Liestal, with 80 beds, and caters more to the business crowd, but offers ample amenities in a modern setting. ($$-$$$). Kasernenstrasse 10, CH-4410 Liestal. ☎ 61-927-8080, fax 61-927-8081.

Hotel Bad Schauenburg, a 300-year-old inn, features a very nice gourmet restaurant and also caters to many business people. It's a clean and comfortable medium-sized hotel. ($$-$$$). CH-4410 Liestal. ☎ 61-906-2727, fax 61-906-2700.

Seiler's Radackerhof Hotel is a modest and clean, medium-sized inn that has good accommodations at reasonable rates. ($$). Rheinstrasse 93, CH-4410 Liestal. ☎ 61-901-3222.

Seiler's Gitterli Hotel has only 15 beds, but is a nice, cheap and clean spot to bunk down for the night. Simple, modest rooms. Located on Kasernenstrase 51, CH-4410 Liestal. ☎ 61-921-4188.

■ Where to Eat

Hotel Restaurant Bad Bubendorf is near Liestal and features an excellent restaurant in a large hotel. Swiss cuisine in hearty portions. ($$-$$$). Open daily until 11 pm, parking available, handicapped-accessible. Kantonstrasse 3, CH-4416 Bubendorf. ☎ 61-935-5555, fax 61-935-5566.

Restaurants Engel are three restaurants in the hotel of the same name, and feature everything from traditional international gourmet and Swiss cuisine to comfort foods in a variety of settings: formal, relaxed and bar-casual. ($$-$$$). Kasernenstrasse 10, CH-4410 Liestal. ☎ 61-927-8080, fax 61-927-8081.

Restaurant Murenberg features fish and seafood in an elegant setting. ($$-$$$$). Open daily until 10 pm, closed Wednesday and Thursday. Parking available. Krummackerstrasse 4, CH-4416 Bubendorf. ☎ 61-931-1454, fax 61-931-1846.

S'Chruz offers creative and traditional Swiss dishes at reasonable prices. Open daily until 11 pm, closed from Tuesday afternoon at 2 pm and all day Wednesday. ($-$$). Handicapped-accessible, and a good spot for non-smokers. Hintergasse 31, CH-4416 Bubendorf. ☎ 61-931-1737, fax 61-931-1998.

Top Stars Sportbar is a cheap little spot featuring snacks and light dishes and drinks. ($). Open daily until midnight. Rheinstrasse 4, CH-4410 Liestal. ☎ 61-921-5835, fax 61-921-5833.

Canton Jura (JU)

■ At a Glance

Canton Jura is the youngest of Swiss cantons, having joined the Swiss Federation as the 26th canton on January 1, 1979. Jura is comprised of three main districts that are home to 83 tiny communities: **Delémont** (the capital), **Porrentruy** (with the regions of Ajoie and Clos du Doubs) and **Les Franches Montagnes**. Formerly a part of the canton of Bern, the residents of this region decided in the late 1970s that they wanted to have their own canton, and by vote it was so granted. A long period of political unrest since the late 1940s between various factions in the region had necessitated the split. In the 18th century the area around the capital city of Delémont was the site of holiday retreats for the prince-bishops of Basel.

The northwestern and western side of the Jura canton borders France, while the extreme southwestern side slightly touches the canton of Neuchâtel. The entire south and southeastern side bump against Canton Bern, while on the northeastern side Jura borders Canton Solothurn. The canton has an enlongated, somewhat triangular shape of 519 square miles (1,349 square km), in which 69,400 French-speaking, mostly Roman Catholic citizens live. About 46% of the populace works in manufacturing, energy supply or construction, while only about 22% work in the tourism industry. It is one of the least populated cantons within Switzerland, ahead of only six other cantons in that regard and 50% of its land is used for agricultural purposes.

This canton is a great spot for those who enjoy horseback riding, as it offers over 125 miles (200 km) of well-groomed horse trails, as well as 930 miles (1,490 km) of hiking trails and cross-country ski trails.

The name "Jura" is a Celtic term, meaning "mountains of the forest."

The **Swiss Jura** are not like the rest of the Alps. There are long valleys, forests, and gently rolling hills. These low mountains (known as the **Franches-Montagnes** within this canton) extend 93 miles (149 km) northeast along the French and Swiss border, with the lowest peaks in the north near Basel and the higher peaks at the south near Lake Geneva. These flowing mountains cover the six cantons of Basel, Solothurn, Jura, Bern, Neuchâtel and Vaud, offering easy and uncomplicated walks compared with the more strenuous paths found in some of the other Swiss cantons such as Graubünden or Valais.

The **coat of arms** for Canton Jura represents the colors and arms of the former prince-bishops of Basel. The shield is split vertically, with horizontal "Swiss" red and white stripes on the right, and a set of red arms on the left against a plain white background.

Delémont

The capital city of Canton Jura, Delémont once belonged to the Dukes of Alsace, before being annexed to France in the 18th century. It was then given back to Switzerland in 1815 by the Congress of Vienna and made a district of Canton Bern, before becoming part of Canton Jura. The old town is particularly splendid, and retains its medieval atmosphere, with cobblestone streets, aged fountains and old-world charm. Home to 12,000 inhabitants, Delémont is easily accessed by train or car via Highway A16 and is in the middle of the eastern portion of Canton Jura.

■ Information Sources

Tourist Offices

The Delémont Tourist Office is small but efficient and is open Monday-Friday from 9 am-noon, 2-6:30 pm, Saturday from 9 am-noon, 2-4 pm. 12 Place de la Gare, CH-2800 Delémont. ☎ 32-422-9778. The cantonal tourist office (Jura Tourisme) is found at 6 Place du 23 Juin, CH-2350 Saignelégier. ☎ 90-112-3400. Here you'll find information about the more than 30 horseback riding centers throughout the canton, www.delemont.ch.

Train Station

Delémont's train station is across the street from the post office and provides a money exchange and bike rental. The money exchange office is open Monday-Saturday from 5:45 am-9:15 pm, Sunday from 6:30 am-9:15 pm.

Post Office

The Delémont post office is open Monday-Friday, from 7:30 am-6:15 pm, Saturday from 8:30 am-noon. Place de la Poste 4, CH-2800 Delémont. ☎ 2-421-3030, fax 32-421-3040. There is also a small branch office at St. Michel 2, CH-2800 Delémont. ☎ 32-421-3090, fax 32-421-3095. Open Monday-Friday from 7:30-11:45 am, 2-6 pm, Saturday from 8:30-11 am.

Codes

The Delémont **postal code** is CH-2800 and the **area code** is 32.

■ Getting Around

It is best to explore the town of Delémont on foot, and the same goes for the surrounding countryside with its multitude of hiking and walking trails. You can also rent horses at many of the local stables, usually starting at 25Sfr per hour. Bikes are another excellent way to see the area.

■ Adventures

On Foot

One of the top adventures in this region is the 112-mile **Jura High Route** that runs from Geneva to Basel over some of the highest points of the Swiss Jura. It is specially marked with yellow-red diamonds and takes 10+ days to complete. The Delémont Tourist Office can provide you with information and maps.

The **climbing and hang-gliding** school is a popular attraction in Delémont. For a full-day excursion (for adults 16 and up) that begins at 9 am at the Delémont train station, you can expect to pay 265Sfr. You have a morning coffee with guide and instructor Frédéric Lovis before heading out to a nearby slope, where you'll learn the art of hang-gliding. At noon you'll be treated to a farmer's lunch; afterward you'll work at climbing, either outdoors or indoors (if in bad weather). Climbing maestro Philippe Steulet will lead you to such spots as the Moutier Gorges at Le Vaferdeau or to the Rebeuvelier platform, where you will have a chance to hone your skills. You'll return to the Delémont train station just before 6 pm.

■ Sightseeing

Strolling through the Old Town is a must, and you won't be able to miss the Renaissance fountains or huge fortress gates and classical 18th-century structures. The town hall – **Hotel de Ville** – features a Baroque doorway and unique outdoor staircase.

If you're into cheese, than visit nearby **Moutier** in the canton of Bern, just 6½ miles (10.5 km) south of Delémont in the direction of La Chaux-de-Fonds. Here you'll find the factory that produces **Vacherin Mont d'Or** and **Tête-de-Moine** cheeses.

Landmarks & Historic Sites

Just a mile north of town is the **Chapelle du Vorbourg**, a tiny church that sits on a small wooded hill. Visitors are welcome, and masses are held on Sundays and holidays at 9:30 am.

Museums

The **Jurassic Art and History Museum** (Musée Jurassien d'Art et d'Histoire) features exhibitions and displays that focus on a contemporary view of Jura society, art and history. In the heart of the old town, the museum is housed in five interconnected buildings and also contains archeological finds, religious objects and furnishings from many eras. Admission is 6Sfr. Open Tuesday-Sunday, from 2-5 pm, other times for groups by appointment only. Guided tours are available as well. 12 Place de la Gare, CH-2800 Delémont. ☎ 32-422-8077.

■ Where to Stay

Hotel du Midi is a unique little out-of-the way stop that is a traveler's delight. With just four cozy and charming rooms, this is one spot you won't want to miss if you're anywhere in the region ($$). The restaurant is excellent and serves up hearty portions of regional

HOTEL PRICE CHART	
$	30-75Sfr ($20-$49)
$$	76-205Sfr ($50-$109)
$$$	206-299Sfr ($110-$200)
$$$$	300Sfr+ ($200+)

and international fare at reasonable prices, ($$). It's open daily except for Wednesday. 10 Place de la Gare, CH-2800 Delémont. ☎ 32-422-1777, fax 32-423-1989.

Le National Hotel in the heart of the old village offers 27 clean and comfortable rooms at reasonable rates ($$). Route de Bale 25, CH-2800 Delemont. ☎ 32-422-9622, fax 32-422-3912.

Delémont Youth Hostel has 80 beds and is open from early April to October 20. Handicapped-accessible and close to bike trails. ($). Route de Bale 185, CH-2800 Delémont. ☎ 32-422-2054, fax 32-422-8830, www.youthhostel.ch/delemont.

■ Where to Eat

Au Gros Pré serves up regional and traditional Swiss fare in an elegant setting. ($$-$$$). One of the best restaurants around. Route de Porrentruy, CH-2800 Delemont. ☎ 32-422-9033, fax 32-422-9036.

La Tournesol features traditional Swiss cuisine in a rustic and comfy setting. Friendly staff. ($-$$). Rue de l'Avenir 3, CH-2800 Delémont. ☎ 32-422-2477.

DINING PRICE CHART	
Prices based on a typical entrée, per person, and do not include beverage.	
$	15-25Sfr ($10-$16)
$$	26-45Sfr ($17-$29)
$$$	46-70Sfr ($30-$47)
$$$$	71Sfr+ ($47+)

Confiserie Tea Room Werth offers light snacks at reasonable prices ($-$$). Closed Monday. CH-2800 Delémont. ☎ 32-422-2823, fax 32-422-2824.

Porrentruy

Established in the 13th century, Porrentruy became home to prince-bishop Blarer at the start of the 16th century, who later founded a college here with an extensive library in the city. It is the second-largest city in Canton Jura and is situated on a Jurassic plateau near the French border at the far western edge of the canton and of Switzerland. The region surrounding Porrentruy is known as the "Orchard of the Jura," or Ajoie region, and features plum trees, underground caves, a prehistoric park and lovely fields, lakes and ponds. The city is home to nine schools and colleges, scattered among 18th-century buildings hugging the streets of the old village.

■ Information Sources

Tourist Office

The Porrentruy Tourist Office is in an old hospital, and will help with walking tours of the city. Open Monday-Friday from 9 am-noon, 2-6 pm; in July and August the office is also open on Saturday from 10 am-1 pm Grand Rue 5, CH-2900 Porrentruy. ☎ 32-466-5959.

Post Office

The Porrentruy post office is at Rue de Jura 6 and is open Monday-Friday from 7:30 am-noon, 1:45-6:15 pm, Saturday from 8:30-11:30 am. CH-2900 Porrentruy. ☎ 32-466-5505, fax 32-466-3305.

Market scene in Porrentruy

Codes

The **postal code** for Porrentruy is CH-2900 and the **area code** is 32.

■ Landmarks & Historic Sites

The **Porrentruy Town Hall** is an elegant Baroque building, at the village center, built in 1761-64. It houses a 1455 bell and a 1413 clock, whose inner workings date back to 1760. Nearby is the neo-classic **Juventuti School**, established in 1859. The building was renovated in 1995 and today houses the Repertory of cultural goods of Canton Jura. **The Porte de France** is an impressive 14th-century fortress and tower that you can climb up daily from 9-11:45 am, 1:30-6 pm. It provides an excellent view of the village.

Hotel Dieu features the work of Pierre-Francois Paris, who designed the Town Hall at Grand Rue 5. Inside you'll find a lovely double-tiered staircase. Restored in 1987, it is now home to the **Library for Young People** (open Tuesday-Friday from 2-6 pm, Saturday from 10 am-noon. ☎ 32-465-7891); the **public library** (open Tuesday-Friday from 3-6 pm, Saturday from 10 am-noon); the regional **Arts Center of Porrentruy**; the **Jura Tourist Office**; the **Game Library** and the **Hospital Museum**.

■ Where to Stay

Hotel De La Poste is small, but pleasant, cozy and quiet. Located in the heart of the Old Town. ($-$$). 15 Rue Malvoisins, CH-2900 Porrentruy. ☎ 32-466-1827.

Camping

Camping is available in Porrentruy at **Camping de l'Allaine**, with 12 spaces for visitors. ($). CH-2900, Porrentruy. ☎ 32-466-2240, fax 32-466-9332.

■ Where to Eat

Guillaume Tell features spectacular fondues and pastries, including a specialty cheesecake made every Friday morning. ($-$$). Grand Rue 36, CH-2900 Porrentruy. ☎ 32-466-1522.

The **Buffet de la Gare** is inside the train station and offers a surprisingly good buffet of local and international dishes. ($). Place de la Gare 4, CH-2900 Porrentruy. ☎ 32-466-2135.

The Monkey Bar Crêperie is a fun locale which serves up inexpensive crêpes and other reasonably priced French dishes. ($). Rue Pierre Péquignat 7, CH-2900 Porrentruy. ☎ 32-466-4888.

Nothern Switzerland

Carriage races at the Marché-Concours, national horse fair, in Saignelégier

Saignelégier

This town, alone in the middle of the south end of Canton Jura, is *the* place for horse enthusiasts, offering miles of riding paths and one of Switzerland's 11 racetracks. During the second week of August, the annual National Horse Fair is held – drawing crowds from throughout Switzerland, France and Germany. You can ride year-round, and also take sleigh and carriage rides at appropriate times of year. Many farms in the area offer riding packages and tours – some that include overnight accommodations and family packages suitable for small children.

■ Information Sources

Tourist Office

The Saignelégier Tourist Office for the canton sits across from the train station on Rue del la Gare and is open Monday-Friday from 9 am-noon, 2-6 pm, Saturday from 9 am-noon and during July and August on Sunday from 9 am-noon, 2-4 pm. ☎ 32-952-1952.

Post Office

 The Saignelégier post office is at Rue de la Gare 6 in the train station and is open Monday-Friday from 8 am-noon, 2-6 pm, Saturday from 8:30-10:30 am. CH-2350. ☎ 32-951-1165, fax 32-951-1644.

Codes

The **postal code** in Saignelégier is CH-2350 and the **area code** is 32.

■ Getting Around

 There is only one good way to see this tiny village – on foot. Otherwise, you'd buzz right through it via auto. You can rent bikes at the train station, but you must call well in advance to reserve one, as they are very popular once the snow is gone. In front of the local **Centre de Loisirs** sports center you'll find a helpful map outlining local hiking, cross-country ski, and biking trails – all of which are clearly marked with yellow signs throughout the region. Call ☎ 32-951-1755 for information regarding the sports center's amenities, which include an ice rink, swimming pool, weight room, and gym.

■ Adventures

On Horseback

 The **Manège de Saignelégier** offers horses for rent by the hour, ☎ 32-951-1755; while the **Jean-Louis Froidevaux Stable** offers carriage rides, ☎ 32-951-1067. You can also contact Viviane Auberson at the **Centre d'Equitation** at Tuilerie 1, CH-2350 Saignelégier. ☎ 32-951-1755, fax 32-951-3508, for information regarding riding lessons.

The **Saignelégier Racetrack** offers both harness racing and steeplechase for two days each year, during the popular **Marché Concours** over the second weekend in August. This is the largest national horse show in Switzerland and spotlights the only true Swiss breed – the **Freiberger** horse. Jumping contests as well as Roman chariot races are also held in a county-fair setting. The racetrack features a good restaurant and grass racing surface. Contact director Annick Kuhn for information at CH-2345 La-Chaux-des-Breuleux. ☎ 32-954-1059.

■ Where to Stay

 A very popular spot is the **Hotel/Café du Soleil**, a local hangout for artists, musicians and equestrians. The hotel only has seven rooms, but they're all clean, cozy and ample ($-$$) for an overnight stay. The café's vegetarian food is excellent, with fresh salads, and the live music adds a nice '60s touch. Across the street from the local equestrian hall. ($-$$). Closed Monday. Marché Concours 14, CH-2350 Saignelégier. ☎ 32-951-1688, fax 32-951-2295.

Hotel Bellevue offers 23 rooms in traditional, modern Swiss style, which are comfortable and clean. ($$). Gruere 13, CH-2900 Saignelégier. ☎ 32-951-1620, fax 32-951-1606.

Camping

This is available at either **Sous La Neuvevie** on the south side of Saignelégier from May-October, ☎ 32-951-1082, or at the nearby town of **Goumois** from April-September, ☎ 32-951-2707.

■ Where to Eat

Hotel du Doubs, in nearby Goumois, offers excellent regional and traditional Swiss cuisine. The food is better than the rooms here. ($-$$). ☎ 32-951-1323. Also in Goumois, you'll find **Le Theusseret**, a local spot in an old mill, specializing in excellent fresh-caught local fish. ($-$$). ☎ 32-951-1451.

St-Ursanne

St-Ursanne is south of Porrentruy in the territory known as **Clos de Doubs**, on the Doubs River. Here you'll find lots of opportunities for hiking, biking, fishing, canoeing and kayaking. The village is home to a 12th-century church – **la Collegial** – and offers some nice walks along the riverside, over the old stone bridge across the Doubs River. The main streets are Porte de St. Pierre on the east side and the Porte de St. Paul on the west side. The local **Tourist Office** is at 18 Rue du Quartier, and is open daily from March to October, 10 am-5 pm. ☎ 32-461-3716. They offer hiking and walking maps, as well as information regarding fishing and watersports. There are five nice inns in St-Ursanne, but, unless you're here for an overnight sporting occasion, this town is worth a day-trip only.

Solothurn, with the Hauptgasse in the historic center
and the façade of St. Ursen Cathedral (1763-77)

Canton Solothurn (SO)

■ At a Glance

Solothurn is probably the oddest-shaped canton in Switzerland. Its northwestern border touches France, while the rest of the canton snakes in between cantons Jura, Bern, Aargau, and Basel. As a result, you'll find a touch of almost everything and anything in this canton. There are hints of French influence, touches of Rome, and an overall lightheartedness in the people that suggests a multitude of international influences. It is said among the locals that there is no finer place to be during the fall months than in Solothurn, when the narrow passes of the Jura collide with the lovely colors sparked by the Aare River.

Slightly less than half (43%) of this canton's land is used for agriculture, and the population is made up of 241,635 German-speakers, mostly Roman-Catholics. Only about 21% of Solothurnians work in fields related to tourism, and most (about 41%) work in some type of industry or manufacturing business. Despite its odd shape, it has 126 municipalities within 490 square miles (1,270 square km).

Solothurn was the 11th canton to join the Swiss Federation in 1481. Strangely enough, the capital city of Solothurn has 11 churches, 11 chapels, 11 historic towers, and 11 historic fountains. Its most famous church – that of St. Ursen Cathedral (left) – has a divided staircase, each with 11 steps, 11 altars and 11 bells. It is the 11th-largest canton in terms of population.

Most of the populace of Solothurn resides in either the capital city of Solothurn, or in Olten or Grenchen. All of these towns offers sophistication, but with the ambiance of a small city.

The **coat of arms** of Solothurn is a simple shield, divided horizontally with "Swiss" red on the top and white on the bottom, and its appearance has not changed since Canton Solothurn joined Switzerland.

Solothurn

The capital city of the canton and Switzerland's finest Baroque city, it sits on both banks of the Aare River at the base of the last ridge of the Jura hills, known as the **Weissenstein**. Called "Soleure" in French,

Solothurn is considered the very classic essence of Baroque – with its narrow cobblestone streets and Celtic influences. It was once home to French ambassadors, and today is a thriving community with 20,000 citizens, and a variety of industries and people. To get here by car, exit northwest of main Highway One.

■ Information Sources

Tourist Office

The Solothurn Tourist Office is at Hauptgasse 69 on Kronenplatz, near the Cathedral and very near the train station. Open Monday-Friday from 8:30 am-noon, 1:30-6 pm, Saturday from 9 am-noon. ☎ 32-626-4646. They offer 1½-hour walking tours of the Altstadt from May-September on Saturdays at 2:30 pm. Cost is 5Sfr.

Train Station

Solothurn's train station is unusually grandiose and offers a wide array of services, including money exchange and bike rentals (open daily from 5 am-9 pm). Located on Hauptbahnhofstrasse. ☎ 32-621-3474.

Post Office

The main Solothurn post office is open Monday-Friday, 7:30 am to noon, 2-6 pm; Saturday from 9-11 am. Dornacherstrasse 40, CH-4501 Solothurn. ☎ 32-625-2970, fax 32-625-2975. There is also a large post office on Poststrasse 14 (CH-4502, ☎ 32-626-5400), open Monday-Friday from 7:30 am-6:30, Saturday from 8 am-noon.

Codes

The **postal codes** in Solothurn are CH-4500-4503 and the **area code** is 32.

■ Getting Around

As with most Swiss cities, Solothurn is best explored on foot. From the train station on Hauptbahnhofstrasse ("main train station street"), exit to your left and walk to the auto-free **Kreuzackerbrücke**, which leads you into Old Town.

■ Adventures

On Foot

The **Weissenstein** mountain ridge, at 4,211 feet (1,284 m), provides breathtaking views of the Swiss Mittelland, the Juran and the Bernese Alps. You can hike to the ridge by leaving from the center of Solothurn via the corner of Wengisteinstrasse and Verenawegstrasse, following the signs to the top, which should take about two hours. Or you can grab a train in Solothurn that takes you to Oberdorf. From here, you can either hike or take a chairlift to the top, where you'll find the **Weissenstein Hotel** (☎ 32-622-0264, fax 32-623-8947), great for an overnight stay or a gourmet meal. The chairlift hours of operation are from April-October, Monday-Friday, 8:30 am-6 pm, Saturday and Sunday, 8 am-6 pm; in July and August on Fridays from 8:30 am to 9:30 pm; from November-March, Monday-Friday, 9 am-5 pm, Saturday from 8 am to 5 pm. A round-trip ticket costs 19Sfr. There are numerous walks you can take along the mountain crest.

For a nice **four-hour hike**, you can walk from Balmberg to Grenchenberg via Weissenstein. This is a very picturesque hike that provides stunning views of the Jura, Schweizer Mittelland and the Aare Valley. From the Balmberg bus station, follow the red hiking trail signs toward Weissenstein. Just before reaching Weissenstein, veer to the right and then left as the trail begins to ascend the **Höhenweg**. Continue on toward **Häsenmatt**, along the "Hammer Trail." After 1½ hours, you should reach the restaurant at Weissenstein. Continue on the trail towards Häsenmatt and Grenchenberg. After another hour, you should come to the Häsenmatt summit at 4,736 feet. From here, the trail will descend in the direction of **Müren**, near the restaurant Althüsli. Once in the village of Müren, follow the signs to **Oberer Grenchenberg**. When you reach the Restaurant Oberer Grenchenberg, follow the trail to **Unterer Grenchenberg**. At the Restaurant Unterer Grenchenberg you can grab a bus back to Grenchen.

From the south side of the city on the Aare's north bank, you can begin a good two-hour hike west that will bring you to the village of **Altreu**. Since 1948, this has been home to one of the largest stork colonies in the world. Regeneration of the white storks in Switzerland was the brainchild of one Max Bloesch, who began the process by purchasing storks from Algeria. The massive stork colony is now the pride of this tiny village.

■ Landmarks & Historic Sites

The **St. Ursen Kathedral** (1762-73) is one of the highlights of the town of Solothurn. This Italian-designed cathedral sits at the entrance to the old town, just inside the Basel Gate on Baselstrasse, two blocks from the river. It has an impressive green tower with inscriptions referring to Solothurn's patron martyr saints, Ursus and Victor. You can visit the interior of the cathedral daily, 8 am-noon, 2-7 pm (from October-Easter to 6 pm).

Just a few steps eastward is the 1508 original gate to the city, known as the **Baseltor,** and directly across from the Arsenal is the **Rathaus,** built in the 15th and 17th centuries. It features a stunning Renaissance doorway with double Russian towers. The **Marktplatz** is close by and has a 12th-century **Zeitclockenturm** (Clock Tower) – one of Solothurn's oldest structures. There is also a rustic sundial from 1545 in the middle of the building. The **Mauritus Fountain** here is decorated in gold and red (see figure at left). A few steps away is the **Jesuit Church,** with a beautiful stucco interior that dates to 1680. You'll have to look a bit to find it, however, as its unpretentious exterior belies the beauty inside.

On the southern bank of the Aare sits the **Krummer Turm** (Twisted Tower), which dates back to 1460. This odd configuration of stone near the Romandie pier appears ready to fall over at any minute, but has been steadfast for over 450 years.

■ Museums

The **Solothurn Kunstmuseum** (Museum of Fine Art) displays works by 19th- and 20th-century artists, as well as many of the old masters. Open Tuesday-Saturday from 10 am-noon and 2-5 pm; Thursday until 9 pm; Sunday from 10 am-5 pm. Admission is free. Werkhofstrasse 30, CH-4501 Solothurn. ☎ 32-622-2307.

Just a few steps northwest of the church is the **Altes Zeughaus** (Old Arsenal), housing the largest collection of arms and armory anywhere in Europe. Features include over 400 suits of armor and a Nazi tank from World War II. Open from May-October, Tuesday through Sunday from 10 am-noon, 2-5 pm; November-April, Tuesday through Friday from 2-5 pm, Saturday and Sunday from 10 am-noon, 2-5 pm. Admission is 6Sfr. Zeughausplatz 1, CH-4502 Solothurn. ☎ 32-623-3528.

The **Bluemstein Historical Museum** is northwest of the town center in an 18th-century building contained in a small park. Here you'll find historical costumes, ceramics, furniture, tapestries and musical instruments from various periods in Solothurn's rich Baroque history. Bluemensteinweg. CH-4501 Solothurn.

■ Where to Stay

Hotel Krone is the hot spot in town and features a good central spot near the clock tower. The rooms are huge, clean and have lots of atmosphere. Napoleon's wife Josephine stayed here in 1811. ($$$). Hauptgasse 64, CH-4501 Solothurn. ☎ 32-622-4412, fax 32-626-4445.

The Tour Rouge Inn dates back to 1100 and has been used as a hotel since 1840. From an architectural standpoint, this has to be one of the most interesting hotels in the world, as its rooms twist and wind through a labyrinth of narrow hallways. Extremely clean rooms set in traditional Swiss décor. ($$). A good bargain. Rates include breakfast. Hauptgasse 42, CH-4500 Solothurn. ☎ 32-622-9621, fax 32-622-9865.

Hotel Baseltor offers just six comfy rooms, so make your reservations early at this popular spot. ($$) Hauptgasse 79, CH-4501 Solothurn. ☎ 32-622-3422, fax 32-622-1879.

Zunfthaus zur Wirthen is a former guildhouse, built entirely of wood, and offers large rooms, some with bathrooms, some with sinks only. ($$). Conveniently located at Hauptgasse 41. CH-4501 Solothurn. ☎ 32-626-2848, fax 32-626-2858.

Hotel Kreuz is cheap but clean, with shared bathrooms, and is a hangout for many backpackers. ($-$$). Kreuzgasse 4, CH-4501 Solothurn. ☎ 32-622-2020, fax 32-621-5232.

Youth Hostel Solothurn Am Land is one of the best in Switzerland – modern and clean – inside a 17th-century building. ($). Open January 11-November 17. Landhausquai 23, CH-4501Solothurn. ☎ 32-623-1706, fax 32-623-1639.

■ Where to Eat

Zum Alten Stephan is one of the finest and oldest restaurants in the area and is housed in a building that is over 1,000 years old. There are two separate restaurants here, on two different floors, both with varying menus and dining options. Upstairs ($$$-$$$$) offers a gourmet-like setting and cuisine, while the downstairs ($-$$) is more traditional and relaxed. Downstairs is open daily from 11 am-midnight; upstairs is open Tuesday-Saturday from 11 am-2 pm, 5 pm-midnight. Friedhofplatz 10, CH-4502 Solothurn. ☎ 32-622-1109.

Manora is a self-service restaurant in the Manor department store, just off the Marktplatz. Great fresh salads and fresh-cooked meals at reasonable prices. ($-$$). Open Monday-Friday from 9 am-6:30 pm, Thursday until 9 pm, Saturday from 8 am-5 pm.

Rust, on the Marktplatz, is *the* place to stop for *Solothurner Kuchen,* a tart comprised of nuts and whipped cream on a biscuit. Stop here for an afternoon snack and a great cup of traditional Swiss coffee.

Olten

The city of Olten leans against the banks of the Aare River at the eastern edge of the canton, and is an important railroad junction within Switzerland. This pleasant little spot – with 19,000 citizens – has a nice old town that is worth an afternoon stroll. The wooden covered Alte Brücke (Old Bridge) is auto-free and leads into the Altstadt. You might want to visit Olten's **Kunstmuseum** (Fine Arts Museum), featuring paintings and art works from 19th and 20th century artists, or the **Historisches Museum** on Konradstrasse that has displays relating to regional history.

Just three miles (4.8 km) southeast of the town center is the **Säli-Schlössli**. You can hike or drive here, via the Sälistrasse. The road twists and turns as it climbs steadily up to the ruins of **Wartburg**, in Muttenz (see left), where you'll find a small castle and fire-watching tower that was the responsibility of the Säli family for over 300 years. The views up here allow the visitor to observe Olten, the Aare Valley and the surrounding hills.

Grenchen

Grenchen is at the far-western edge of the canton and often touted as the "industrial town in the countryside." Grenchen sits just between the Jura mountain range and the Aare River valley. For years this town has been home to watch factories and more recently to high-precision technologies such as engineering and machine manufacturers. Grenchen is also home to a canoeing complex on the Aare River, and provides visitors with well-maintained hiking paths and cross-country ski trails.

The **Kunsthaus Grenchen** features fine contemporary art. Open daily from 2-5 pm, closed Monday. Freiestrasse 2, CH-2540 Grenchen. ☎ 32-652-5022, fax 32-652-5003. Also, the **Kultur-Historisches Museum Grenchen** offers insight into local history through the ages. Located at Abstye 3, CH-2540 Grenchen. ☎ 32-652-0979. **Horseback riding** enthusiasts will want to visit the **Mudjibur Riding Hall** of Grenchen. This stable offers group rides at reasonable rates. Contact owners Cordelia Weber or Jenny Fahrni at Dählenstrasse 44 CH-2540 Grenchen. ☎ 79-344-3279. There is also a **golf course** here, at Bellevuestrasse 30, CH-2540 Grenchen. ☎ 32-652-8561. For **canoeing**, contact the **Kanu-Club Grenchen** at Archstrasse 107-109, CH-2540 Grenchen. ☎ 32-652-3303.

Canton Aargau (AG)

■ At a Glance

Canton Aargau is home to 564,200 inhabitants, making it the fourth-largest canton in terms of population, behind Zürich, Bern and Vaud. The majority of these residents are German-speaking Protestants who work in the energy, manufacturing, supply or construction industries – making up about 40% of the workforce. Another 28% work in tourism. According to the locals, however, there are no "Aargau people," meaning that each of the three districts tend to align more closely with other cantons than they do with their own. For instance, the Freiamt district tends to relate closely with the Catholic, central area of Switzerland, while the eastern side – particularly near Baden – is more oriented toward Zürich than toward Aargau's capital city Aarau. As a result, the Frick Valley is often overlooked by many in its northern Jura Mountain location on the Rhine.

Part of the reason for these divided loyalties dates back centuries to when the area now known as Canton Aargau belonged to Freiamt (the land of the Count of Baden), the former Austrian region of Fricktal-Rheinfelden, and the Bernese Aargau. It became part of the Swiss Federation in 1803, making it one of the youngest cantons, as it celebrates its 200-year anniversary in 2003.

The name Aargau (Argovia) means the "country of the Aare," and this region is the least mountainous of any in Switzerland. This 870-square-mile area is home not only to the Aare River, but to the Rhine, Limmat and Reuss as well. Besides these gently flowing rivers, the Hallwilersee (Lake Hallwil) and over 1,000 miles (1,610 km) of hiking and biking trails are sure to delight any wanderer. Aargau faces the German border to the north, Canton Zürich directly east, and Canton Zug southeast. To the south sits the canton of Lucerne, while on the western side it bumps borders with Solothurn and Basel-Land.

The **coat of arms** of Aargau is split vertically, with a blue panel on the right-hand side and a black panel on the left. Three white stars in the center of the blue panel represent the three districts which form this canton, while three wavey, horizontal white lines over the black panel represent the Aare River, which flows through Canton Aargau.

Aarau

Aarau is the capital city of Canton Aargau, home to 16,000 people, in the area of Switzerland known as the **"Schweizer Mittelland,"** or

Swiss Middleland. The city sits on the River Aare, just south of the Jura slopes at the western edge of the canton. It was originally founded in 1240 by the Counts of Kyburg, then handed over to the Habsburgs, before coming under Bernese rule in 1415. Today, this well-preserved city features many decorated houses throughout, especially in the Altstadt (Old Town). Here you'll find lots of good walks, as well as throughout the Aare Valley and surrounding Jura and Mittelland hills. It is a city bustling with business and commerce – one of the wealthiest in Switzerland – with many machine and textile industries based here.

■ Information Sources

Tourist Office

 The cantonal Tourist Office is in the fine village of Zofingen, in the southwesternmost region of Aargau. **Aargau Tourismus**, Postfach, CH-4800 Zofingen. ☎ 62-746-2053, fax 62-746-2041. The **Aarau Tourist Office** (Aarau Info Verkehrsburo) is at Graben 42, CH-5001 Aarau. ☎ 62-824-7624, fax 62-824-7750.

Post Office

 The Aarau post office is open Monday-Friday, from 7:30 am-6:30 pm, Saturday from 8 am-noon. Bahnhofstrasse 67, CH-5001 Aarau. ☎ 62-835-6822, fax 835-6819.

Codes

The **postal codes** in Aarau are CH-5000, 5001, 5003, and 5004. The phone **area code** is 62.

■ Getting Around

 The best way to see Aarau is on foot. As you walk through the old town's narrow streets, you'll find frescoed houses with wrought-iron railings and beautifully painted facades. At the extreme western edge of the city you'll find the **Stadtkirch** (Parish Church), which is highlighted by a 17th-century bell tower. In the nearby square is the **Fountain of Justice**, dating back to 1643. The **Oberer Turm** (Clock Tower) in the city center has parts that date back to 1270, though most of the clock hails from the 16th century.

■ Adventures:

On Foot

Three miles (4.8 km) southwest of Aarau on the Olten road, just outside of the village of **Schönenwerd**, is the **Schuhmuseum**, the Bally Shoe Museum. It was here that Bally's first workshops were opened. Features include exhibits, the history of shoe-making, and books relating to shoe crafts.

On Wheels

The Aare Bike Trail is part of Switzerland's 2,050 miles (3,300 km) of cycling trails – the country has nine trails in total, each with its own name. The Aare Trail provides the cyclist with varying degrees of difficulty (easy to medium) as well as good scenery and typically takes six-eight days to complete. Most people start out in **Meiringen** (in Canton Bern, among the highest of the Bernese Alps) and end up in Aarau for this 155-mile trek. The point of the journey is to follow the movement of the Aare River over the land it has influenced for so many years. From Meiringen, the trail moves past the **Brienz Lake**, past the **Giessbach Waterfalls** and **Iseltwald** to **Interlaken** (19 miles/30 km). From Interlaken, the trail will then climb up to **Beatenberg** and a spectacular panoramic route, before slowly taking you back down to the city of **Thun**, another 19 miles (30 km). Eighteen miles (29 km) farther north on the route is **Bern** and between Switzerland's capital city and Thun you'll encounter the wide, sweeping **Aare Valley**. The trail passes right through the middle of Bern, past the famed Clock Tower and out of town again past the Aare River, past **Aarburg** towards **Biel**, another 31 miles (50 km) ahead. From Biel, the Aare Trail brings you parallel with the Aare River once more on your way (21 miles/34 km) to **Solothurn.** The trail then winds and sweeps through old villages and tiny towns as it meanders through **Olten**, before bringing you up to Aarau (37 miles/59 km between Solothurn and Aarau).

This trip is suitable for families as well as individual cyclists of all levels, and can be complemented with cable car and ship rides to either shorten or lengthen your journey. The Swiss Tourist Office can provide information and maps for you, and there are also US-based travel agencies that specialize in this type of excursion. **Adventure Sport Holidays** in Massachusetts offers a seven-day ride during the summer months starting at $1,405, offering hotels and meals along the way. Contact them at 815 North Road, Westfield, MA 01085. ☎ 800-628-9655.

■ Where to Stay

Hotel Aarauerhof is comfortable and clean, and offers all modern amenities in classic Swiss style, with a business atmosphere. Located very close to the train station ($$$-$$$$). Their restaurant features gourmet, international fare. Bahnhofstrasse 68, CH-5001 Aarau. ☎ 62-837-8300, fax 62-837-8400, www.bestwestern.ch/aarauerhof.

HOTEL PRICE CHART	
$	30-75Sfr ($20-$49)
$$	76-205Sfr ($50-$109)
$$$	206-299Sfr ($110-$200)
$$$$	300Sfr+ ($200+)

■ Where to Eat

El Camino Zunftstube features traditional Swiss dishes with a Mexican flare. Pricey, and reservations are recommended ($$$-$$$$). Pelzgasse 19, CH-5000 Aarau. ☎ 62-822-3677.

DINING PRICE CHART	
Prices based on a typical entrée, per person, and do not include beverage.	
$	15-25Sfr ($10-$16)
$$	26-45Sfr ($17-$29)
$$$	46-70Sfr ($30-$47)
$$$$	71Sfr+ ($47+)

Restaurant Graben has a friendly and charming staff that serves up traditional Swiss fare at reasonable prices ($$-$$$). Good hearty meals. Graben 36, CH-5000 Aarau. ☎ 62-822-3222.

Restaurant Weinberg features wine and beer, as well as regional, diverse dishes from Portugal ($$-$$$). Erlinsbacherstrasse 2, CH-5000 Aarau. ☎/fax 62-822-3434.

Baden

Even though Aarau is the capital, Baden is perhaps the best-known city in Canton Aargau, sitting on the eastern side of the canton, near Zürich. This town of 16,000 lies on the banks of the **Limmat River**, at the foot of the last of the Jura and is well known world-wide as a top electromechanical engineering center. For centuries, Baden has also been known for its health spas, known in Roman times as "Aquae Helvetia," and was the country's top resort during the Middle Ages. It is said that Casanova visited this spa in 1760 in search of young females bathing naked in the waters. There are 19 sulfur springs here, and many people come to relieve symptoms of rheumatoid arthritis and other medical ailments in the 118°F degree waters. Quite honestly, there are few reasons to visit Baden other than to take in the waters, but that's why most people come here in the first place.

The train station splits Baden into two sections; you can find the Old Town to the south, and the spas to the north, in the lower region of the

Limmat, known as the **Kurgebiet** (Cure District). The two main thoroughfares are known as Badstrasse (Bath Street) and Baderstrasse, and connect these two districts. The **Baden Tourist Office**, just a few steps north of the train station offers free guided tours of Baden on Monday at 2 pm, and is very helpful and friendly. They can provide you with maps of the town, and information regarding local hotels and spas. Open Monday-Friday from 8:30 am-noon, 2-6 pm, Saturday from 10 am-noon. ☎ 56-222-5318, www.baden-schweiz.ch.

Most hotels in Baden favor long stays and, while not expensive, many require a week, since most people tend to stay in the city for at least that amount of time while seeking treatment at the spas. Therefore, if you're looking for an inexpensive alternative that doesn't require more than one night, check out **Baden's Youth Hostel**. Open from March 16-December 24, this clean hostel features 83 beds and a restaurant ($). Located on Kanalstrasse 7, CH-5400 Baden. ☎ 56-221-6736, fax 56-221-7660.

There is also a unique hostel in nearby **Brugg**, just a bit northwest of Baden. "**Schlössli Altenburg**" features 52 beds inside a romantic castle, right on the Aare River, only 15 minutes from the Old City of Brugg. This hostel also has a children's playground and a covered area outside for lounging or picnics. The medieval town of Brugg features an original campsite of the Roman Legions, as well as the ancestral seat of the Habsburg family, and the Brunegg Castle. Open year-round ($). Im Hof 11, CH-5200 Brugg. ☎ 56-441-1020, fax 56-442-3820.

Zofingen

Zofingen is one of the most delightful little villages you'll find anywhere in Switzerland. Pretty, quiet and unpretentious – Zofingen is the perfect spot to lose yourself and blend in with the locals. The cobblestone streets and narrow walkways are a delight, as are the cafés, bakeries, flower shops and local businesses. In fact, the town motto is appropriately "a city you'll fall in love with and stay." The Zofingen **Tourist Office** (Verkehrsbüro der Stadt Zofingen) is at Marktgasse 10, CH-4800 Zofingen, and is open Monday-Friday from 9 am-noon, 2-6 pm, Saturday from 9 am-noon. ☎ 62-745-0005, fax 62-745-0002.

Zofingen sits on Highway 2 at the far-western edge of Canton Aargau, between Olten and Lucerne. In fact, if you'd like a nice, easy three-hour hike, try walking from Zofingen to Olten along the well-marked path. It brings you to the train station in Olten, where you can catch a quick ride back to Zofingen, or simply retrace your steps. Along the way you'll pass the Wildpark Mühlitäli, and the Sälischlössli.

The **Modelfluggruppe Zofingen** (Model Airplane Club of Zofingen) has been around for 33 years and features events nearly every week from May through October. For information, contact Club President Heinz Gisler at Höhenweg 6, CH-4812 Mühletal. ☎ 62-752-1645.

■ Where to Stay

There are five good hotels in Zofingen's Altstadt or old city to choose from: **Hotel Krone** (at Hauptgasse 94, ☎ 63-751-1144, fax 63-751-1205), **Hotel Sternen** (Sternengasse 4, ☎ 63-751-3066, fax 63-752-2737), and **Hotel Raben** (Hauptgasse 27, ☎ 62-751-8180) all offer inexpensive clean rooms ($-$$). **Hotel Zofingen** (Kirchplatz 30, ☎ 62-745-0300, fax 62-745-0399) and **Hotel Engel Garni** (Engelgasse 4, ☎ 62-751-5050, fax 62-751-9966) offer a bit more fancy accommodations, still at reasonable rates ($$-$$$).

There is a **youth hostel** in town, at General Guisanstrasse 10, that has 58 sleeping spots. This hostel is open from the end of February to December 15 annually. ($). CH-4800 Zofingen. ☎ 62-752-2303, fax 62-752-2316, www.youthhostel.ch/zofingen.

■ Where to Eat

Be sure to check out the **Schmeidstube** for local Swiss favorites, especially for dinner. ($$-$$$). Storchengasse 6, CH-4800 Zofingen. ☎ 62-751-1058, fax 62-751-1860. For outstanding pizza at reasonable prices ($-$$), check out the **Pizzeria Kirchplatz La Lupa** at Kirchplatz 10, CH-4800 Zofingen. ☎ 62-751-1236. For an afternoon coffee and a bit of pastry, cake or strudel, stop in at the **Oberstadt Café**, at Hauptgasse 110, CH-4800 Zofingen. ☎ 62-751-0700. It features traditional homemade Swiss favorites.

Rheinfelden

This small village of just 7,000 inhabitants sits quietly on the left bank of the Rhine River facing the Black Forest in the uppermost northwestern portion of the canton, and features two indoor saltwater spas. The waters here have some of the highest concentrations of salt found anywhere in Europe. The town features 15th-century walls and towers, and it is well worth a trip on the Rhine via one of the many ships that come to call here from Basel. The Rheinfelden **Tourist Office** is at Am Zähringerplatz, CH-4310 Rheinfelden. ☎ 61-833-0525, fax 61-833-0529. It is open Monday-Friday from 9 am-noon, 1:30-5:30 pm.

Canton Bern (BE)

The Canton of Bern covers some 2,659 square miles, making it second in size only to Canton Graubünden. Thus, because of its size and for the purposes of this book, this canton stands alone as one of the seven regions of Switzerland. Canton Bern is also the second-largest in terms of population after Canton Zürich – with nearly one million citizens. Curiously, Canton Bern ranks only 22nd in the number of foreigners living here, suggesting that, like Zürich, this is truly a Swiss region. This canton is, like the central region, touches no foreign borders. To the north sit cantons Jura, Solothurn, Basel and Aargau, while to the east you'll find Lucerene, Obwalden and Uri. In the south, the cantonal border collides with Canton Valais and on the west side are cantons Vaud, Fribourg and Neuchâtel.

Bern contains most of the country's best-known tourist sites, and is divided into two geographical areas: the **Bernese Oberland** (the southern part of the canton), and the **Bernese Mittleland** (middle and northern half of the canton).

The Bernese Mittleland is a relatively flat region that sits in a valley plain between the Jura mountains and the Alps in the northern part of the canton. It is home to the cantonal capital and the Swiss national capital of Bern, as well as other small towns and villages such as **Burgdorf, Biel-Bienne** and **Langnau** – famous for its Emmentaler cheese. In the capital of Bern, you'll see many historic sites such as the Bear Pits, the Clock Tower and the cobblestoned Old Town. From the city of Bern it is an easy drive to the nearby villages of Langenthal or Sumiswald, where you can shop for the finest Swiss porcelain or linens and go swimming, hiking and biking.

The Bernese Oberland, south of the Mittleland, stretches from **Gstaad** on the western side to the **Susten Pass** on the eastern side, and includes the famed city of **Interlaken** and the **Jungfrau Region** – home to some of Switzerland's most alluring Alpine scenery. Here you'll enjoy a wide array of both summer and winter sports, as well as adventure activities. Besides the resort villages of Grindelwald and Gstaad, you'll also find lakes Thun and Brienz, shadowed by the imposing Alps at the far south. For exploring the Oberland, it is best to use Interlaken as your base, before embarking out to the nearby regions. If you are driving, and also want to experience Switzerland by rail, then you're in luck. The Oberland is well-

Canton Bern

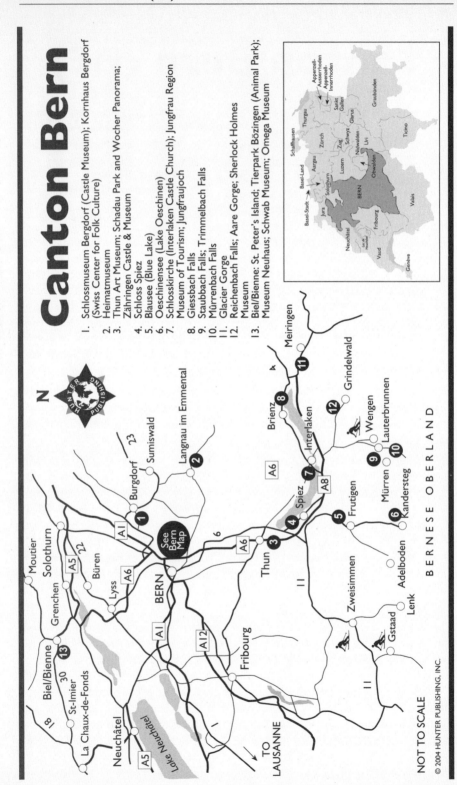

Canton Bern

1. Schlossmuseum Bergdorf (Castle Museum); Kornhaus Bergdorf (Swiss Center for Folk Culture)
2. Heimatmuseum
3. Thun Art Museum; Schadau Park and Wocher Panorama; Zähringen Castle & Museum
4. Schloss Spiez
5. Blausee (Blue Lake)
6. Oeschinensee (Lake Oeschinen)
7. Schlosskirche (Interlaken Castle Church); Jungfrau Region Museum of Tourism; Jungfraujoch
8. Giessbach Falls
9. Staubbach Falls; Trimmelbach Falls
10. Mürrenbach Falls
11. Glacier Gorge
12. Reichenbach Falls; Aare Gorge; Sherlock Holmes Museum
13. Biel/Bienne: St. Peter's Island; Tierpark Bözingen (Animal Park); Museum Neuhaus; Schwab Museum; Omega Museum

NOT TO SCALE

The **Aare River** wraps around Bern like a quiet serpent, encompassing the old town in all of its architectural splendor. Bern is also known as the "City of Fountains" and has over 100 fountains throughout its streets, with 11 that are particularly noteworthy. These feature figures from history and most were built in the mid-16th century.

On Tuesdays and Saturdays throughout the year, a visitor will find various markets throughout the city, selling everything from fruits and vegetables, to meats, flowers and household goods. One market you won't want to miss is the **"Zibelemarkt"** (Onion Market), which takes place on the fourth Monday in November, where the onion is honored in every way.

Bern is also the home of the delicious Toblerone chocolate; Theodor Tobler patented his recipe here in 1909.

Bern is an ideal starting point for journeys elsewhere in Switzerland or throughout Europe. It is a home base for the high-speed TGV train and is also easily accessed by major highways. From Bern you can take a four-hour ride on the TGV and reach Paris in time for lunch, spend the afternoon at the Louvre and be home by midnight the same day. Better yet, use Bern as your base and go to Paris for the whole weekend. You can get to any destination within Switzerland from Bern's outstanding, modern train station. Even if you aren't planning any type of rail excursion, exploring Bern's train station is worth a quick stroll.

■ Information Sources

Tourist Offices

Bern Tourismus, the Tourist Office, is in the main train station and is open daily from June-September 30, 9 am-8:30 am. From October to the end of May it is open from 9 am-6:30 pm, Monday-Saturday, Sunday from 10 am-5 pm. Bahnhof, CH-3001 Bern. ☎ 31-328-1212, fax 31-328-1277, www.bernetourism.ch. For hotel reservations only, call Bern's "Hotelline" at ☎ 31-328-1210 or you can book online at the above web address.

There is also a Bern Tourist office at the Bärengraben (Bear Pits) that is open Monday-Friday from 9 am-6 pm, June to end of September. From March until the end of May, and during the month of October, the office is open Monday-Friday, 10 am-3 pm. From November 1 to the end of Februaryis, it's open Friday, Saturday and Sunday from 11 am-3 pm.

For information on the entire Swiss Mittelland, contact the **Schweizer Mittelland Tourismus** at Postfach, CH-3001 Bern. ☎ 31-328-1228, fax 31-311-1222.

Train Station

The Bern train station offers money exchange on the lower level, open 6:15 am-9:45 pm daily from June 1-mid-October, and from 6:15 am-8:45 pm, mid-October to the end of May. This is a major junction for all trains traveling east/west/north and south throughout Europe. You'll have no problem making a connection to any major city in Bern, which also offers TGV (high-speed train) service to Paris on a daily basis. For bike rental, be sure to phone ahead to ☎ 51-220-2374. For rail information, ☎ 90-030-0300.

Post Office

There are numerous branch post offices in Bern, but the main office is located at Schanzenstrasse 4 CH-3001 Bern. The hours are Monday-Friday from 7:30 am-6:30 pm and on Saturday from 7:30-noon. ☎ 31-386-6111, fax 31-386-6112.

Codes

The **area code** for Bern is 31 and the **postal code**s range from 3000 to 3032.

Internet Access

Internet access is available at the **Staufacher Book Shop** for 10Sfr per hour, at Neuengasse 25, CH-3001 Bern. ☎ 31-311-2411.

Police, Fire & Medical Care

Dial ☎ 117 for the **national police** or call Bern's police station directly at ☎ 31-321-2121. The **emergency fire** number is ☎ 118, ☎ 144 for an **ambulance**, or ☎ 31-311-2211 for an **emergency doctor or dentist**. Bern's **University Hospital** on Fribourgstrasse can be reached at ☎ 31-632-2111. For **drugstore** needs, got to the Central-Apotheke Volz & Company, located right near the Clock Tower on Zeitglockenlaub 2, CH-3001 Bern. ☎ 31-311-4115. They speak English and are open from 7:45 am to 6:30 pm weekdays, Saturday from 7:45 am-4 pm.

■ Getting Around

This is best done on foot. If you're driving and want to explore Bern for a day, then we recommend parking just before and north of the Nydeggbrucke (Nydegg Bridge) before it crosses the river Aare at the entrance to the old village, and across from the Bear Pits. This is a good starting point for walking through Bern, and will give you a nice view of the city as you stroll across the bridge and up the slightly-inclined

Gerechtigkeitsgasse before you reach the famous Clock Tower. You can reach Bern by train from virtually any point in Switzerland or Europe. The train station is at the western end of the old village, and is close to all shopping and tourist sites.

■ Adventures

On Foot & On Wheels

 The Tourist Office also offers guided walking tours and tours by coach bus. **Walking tours** cost 14Sfr. per person and are offered June through September at 11 am daily. Two-hour **coach tours** depart daily from April 1 through the end of October at 2 pm for 25Sfr, and on Saturdays as well from November 1 through the end of March at 2 pm. Reservations are strongly suggested for both excursions.

If you've never experienced riding in a **Swiss Postauto Bus**, the Bern Tourist Office offers excursions to nearby **Aarburg** for only 24.80Sfr. Allow yourself a day or half a day at least, as the bus leaves Bern once an hour and takes you over the Seeland plain and on to the Jura heights and the medieval village of Aarburg. Here you'll have to time stroll through this tiny village or wander along one of the many scenic hiking trails.

If you're **driving**, it's worth your time to take a little side-trip to **Gurten**. Leave Bern on the southeast side of the old town and follow the signs to the village of Wabern, just two miles away. There is a parking lot here for the funicular, which will take you on a five-minute ride to the summit of Gurten at 2,825 feet (861 m). The **Gurten-Kulm Hotel** stands at the summit offering great views of Bern and the surrounding area. You can have lunch or dinner on the outdoor terrace of the hotel, and there is also a miniature railway here, which the kids should love. There are good walking trails here, suitable for anyone, that bring you to other spots overlooking the city and the Bernese Alps.

On Water

 There are a variety of ways to explore Bern, and one of the most unusual that we've found is via **raft**. The Tourist Office offers 1½-hour guided tours from June through the end of September, daily and upon request, from 5 to 6:30 pm. The cost is 35Sfr per person, and it is an excellent way to see Bern's sandstone bridges and flower-adorned buildings. You must make a reservation with the Tourist Office.

Summer Sports

 Bern is a great place for summer excursions such as swimming, biking and walking, but offers little outside the immediate city in the winter. There are 155 miles of hiking trails and the Tourist Office has excellent maps for exploring the region. Bern has an indoor **public swimming pool** (Hirschengraben Pool), that is open daily from 8 am-9 pm, and also offers **Turkish baths**

and sauna. Closed July and August. Admission is 6.5Sfr to the pool and 15Sfr to the sauna. Maulbeerstrasse 14, CH-3014 Bern. ☎ 31-381-3656. For **cycling trips**, the Tourist Office and train station both offer maps of the area's 1,860 miles of biking trails. If you're a **golf** addict, you can play at the **Golf and Country Club**, 11 miles west of Bern in Blumisberg, provided you bring your golf club card from home. ☎ 26-496-3438.

■ Sightseeing

This is best done on foot. There is so much to see here that walking should be mandatory for any visitor. Also, because the Old Town is so contained, you can see most of the village easily in a day or less.

Landmarks & Historic Sites

The **Bear Pits (Bärengraben)** celebrate the symbol of Bern – the Bear. You can view the bears in their oval pits during the summer from 8 am-5:30 pm and during the winter from 9 am-4 pm. Free. Located at the eastern edge of the Old Town, just south of the Nydegg bridge.

The **Clock Tower (Zeitglockenturm)** at left is one of Bern's finest prizes – the timekeeping mechanism dates back to the 16th century. It is located between Kramgasse and Marktgasse, and is very hard to miss. The Tourist Office offers one-hour guided tours of the tower for only 8Sfr and they are well worth it. From inside the tower you get a very different perspective of Bern. Open daily from May 1-October 31 at 4:30, and from July 1-August 31 at 11:30 am and 4:30 pm.

The **Prison Tower (Käfigturm)** stands at the western edge of the city and was originally built in 1256 and used until 1344. The present tower was built in 1641-43 as a prison, and was used as such until 1897. You'll find it on the Bärenplatz at Spitalgasse.

The **Einstein House** was home to Nobel prize winner Albert Einstein from 1903 to 1905. Admission is 3Sfr for adults, 2Sfr for students and children. Open Tuesday-Friday from 10 am-5 pm, Saturday and Sunday from 10 am-4 pm. Closed Monday. Kramgasse 49, Postfach 638, CH-3008 Bern. ☎ 31-312-0091, fax 31-312-0041.

The **Bundeshaus** is Bern's Federal Palace, and is home to Switzerland's Parliament. Built in 1902, the structure contains beautiful stained-glass windows and has a glass dome that depicts the Swiss cantons. Located on the Bundesplatz, where a flower market is held each Tuesday and Saturday from 7 am-noon. Admission to the Bundeshaus is free and tours are given on the hour, Monday-Saturday, 9-11 am and 2-4 pm. Hours on Sunday are 10 and 11 am, or 2 and 3 pm, except when Parliament is in session. ☎ 31-322-8522.

The **Dählhölzli Tierpark (Zoo)** features over 2,000 European animals in a delightful setting on the banks of the Aare river just slightly south of the Old Town. Admission is 7Sfr for adults, 3Sfr for children six to 16 and free for kids under age six. Open daily from April-September 30, 9 am-5 pm.

Museums

The **Kunstmuseum (Museum of Fine Arts)** contains a wide array of artwork spawning eight centuries and includes over 3,000 paintings and sculptures, as well as 48,000 drawings, lithographs, photographs, videos and films. It is probably best-known for having the largest collection of Paul Klee, the Swiss artist born in 1879. Admission is 7Sfr for adults, 5Sfr for seniors. Open Tuesday from 10 am-9 pm, Wednesday-Sunday, 10 am-5 pm. Closed Monday. Hodlerstrasse 8-12, CH-3011 Bern. ☎ 31-328-0944, fax 31-328-0955.

The Natural History Museum has a marvelous collection of Alpine minerals, rocks and stones, and various displays of the earth's geological wonders. One of the top attractions at this museum is "Barry" the famous St. Bernard dog, who is stuffed for all eternity. Open Monday, 2-5 pm, Tuesday, Thursday and Friday, 9 am-5 pm, Wednesday, 9 am-6 pm, Saturday and Sunday, 10 am-5 pm. Admission is 7Sfr, kids 16 and under free. Bernastrasse 15, CH-3005 Bern. ☎ 31-350-7111, fax 31-350-7499.

The Historical Museum of Bern features the history of Bern in varying displays, as well as influences by the Celts and Romans. There are artifacts from the tombs of ancient Egypt, Asian and Oceanic art, and Burgundian tapestries. Open Tuesday-Sunday from 10 am-5 pm, Wednesday from 10 am-8 pm. Closed Monday. Admission is 13Sfr for adults, 8Sfr for seniors and 4Sfr for children six-16. Helvetiaplatz 5, CH-3005 Bern. ☎ 31-350-7711, fax 31-350-7799.

The Museum for Communication contains the world's largest stamp collection. Unique and worth a visit. Located just south of the Old Town on Helvetiastrasse. To get there, cross the Kirchenfeldbrücke (bridge) and walk south until you come to Helvetiaplatz, where the road splits. Walk along the Thunstrasse for a short block and the museum will be halfway down on the next block, the first street on your right. Helvetiastrasse 16, Postfach 278, CH-3006 Bern. ☎ 31-357-5555, fax 31-357-5599.

The Swiss Alpine Museum first opened in 1905 and is a showcase of Alpine nature, including displays on geology, glaciers, weather, flora and fauna, as well as human exploration of the Alps. Open Monday from 2-5 pm, Tuesday-Saturday from 10 am-5 pm. Admission is 8Sfr for adults, 5Sfr for seniors and 2Sfr for kids ages six-16. Helvetiaplatz 4, CH-3005 Bern. ☎ 31-351-0434, fax 31-351-0751.

The Swiss Rifle Museum has all types of rifles, from the flintlock to the modern firearm, with displays from the 16th century to the present. Ad-

Canton Bern

mission is free. Open Tuesday-Saturday from 2-5 pm, Sunday from 10 am-noon, 2-5 pm. Closed Monday. Bernastrasse 5, CH-3005 Bern. ☎ 31-351-0127, fax 31-351-0804.

The Collection of Classical Antiquities features over 200 casts and original arts and crafts from ancient Greece, Rome and the Middle East. Admission is free. Open Wednesday from 6-8 pm or by appointment. Hallerstrasse 12, CH-3012 Bern. ☎ 31-631-8992, fax 31-631-4905.

Swiss Federal Archives is the historical center of the federal government and the keeper of all federal and historical documents. There is a public reading room, where periodicals and various publications can be viewed. Admission is free. Open Monday-Thursday from 9 am-5:30 pm, Friday from 9 am-3:30 pm. Archivstrasse 24, CH-3003 Bern. ☎ 31-322-8989, fax 31-322-7823.

Salvation Army Museum & Archives honors this organization and has displays depicting its development in Switzerland from its birth to the present day. Admission is free. Open Tuesday-Thursday from 9 am-noon, 2-5 pm and by appointment. Laupenstrgasse 5, CH-3008 Bern. ☎ 31-388-0591, fax 31-388-0595.

State Archive of Bern collects and preserves all important documents from the canton of Bern, and makes these documents available to the public in a reading room. Admission is free. Open Tuesday-Thursday from 8 am-noon, 1-5 pm, Friday from 8 am-noon, 1-3:30 pm. Closed Monday. Falkenplatz 4, CH-3012 Bern. ☎ 31-633-5101, fax 31-633-5102.

■ Parks & Gardens

Bern's **Botanical Garden** contains over 6,000 species of plants and vegetation spread over more than two acres and in seven greenhouses. Open Monday-Friday from 8 am-6 pm, Saturday and Sunday from 8 am-5 pm. The greenhouses are open daily from 8 am-5 pm. Admission is free. Wheelchair-accessible. Altenbergrain 21, CH-3011 Bern. ☎ 31-631-4944, www.botanischergarten.ch.

Elfenau & Municipal Gardens is an 18th-century country manor that contains a tropical greenhouse in a picturesque setting high above the Aare River. Admission is free. Open daily from 8:30 am-5 pm. Wheelchair-accessible. Elfenauweg 94, CH-3006 Bern. ☎ 31-352-0713, fax 31-352-6549.

■ Shopping

Bern is a perfect spot for shopping at any time of the year, with its over four miles of covered arcades. You'll find everything from designer ware such as Gucci, Fendi and Rolex, to locally owned artisan shops, second-hand book stores and department stores. Most businesses are open Monday from 2-6:30 pm, Tuesday, Wednesday and Friday from 8:15 am-6:30 pm, and on Thursday from 8:15 am-9 pm. Also on Saturday from 8:15 am-4 pm. Most are closed Sunday.

If you're looking for a fine **Swiss Army Knife**, then check out **Messer-Klôtzli**, on Rathausgasse 84, near the Clock Tower. Here you'll find one of the largest selections of knives (over 1,000!), professional kitchen-wares, tools and Wenger watches (☎ 31-311-0080). You can also walk to **Swiss Plaza**, which sells Swiss Army Knives, souvenirs and watches at Kramgasse 75 (☎ 31-311-5616, fax 31-311-8465).

For the best **Swiss chocolates** go to **Abegglen** at Spitalgasse 36 (☎ 31-311-2111) or to **Beeler** at Spitalgasse 29 (☎ 31-311-2808, fax 31-312-5303). Sometimes you can find better deals on all types of Swiss chocolate at **Merkur**, located at Spitalgasse 2 (☎ 31-311-0425, fax 31-318-4386).

For unusual miniature **porcelain** items, go to **Chramere 76**, an underground shop just a few steps south of the Clock Tower at Kramgasse 76, (☎ 31-311-0865, fax 31-311-1475).

Traditional and historical renditions of Swiss **glass** art can be found at **Art In Martin**, at Klösterlistutz 10 (☎/fax 31-331-4266).

Department stores are popular in Bern and feature everything from clothing to house wares, Swatches and jewelry. Look to **Globus**, at Spitalgasse 17-21 (☎ 31-313-4040, fax 31-313-4088); **Migros** at Marktgasse 46 (☎ 31-310-3232, fax 31-310-3215); **Loeb AG** at Spitalgasse 47-51 (☎ 31-320-7111, fax 31-312-1788); or **EPA AG** at Marktgasse 24 (☎ 31-311-2422, fax 31-311-3004).

Canton Bern

PORCELAIN

A good side-trip is to visit the small Swiss farming village of Langenthal. This is a great little farm village typical of the Mittlelland and one that is rarely visited by tourists. It is also the home to an outstanding porcelain factory – with some of the most unusual porcelain to be found anywhere in the world. The **Porzellanfabrik** produces unique china and porcelain sold in some of the finer shops throughout Switzerland, but at the factory you'll get rock bottom prices. The specialty is their BOPLA! line, which features unique geometric designs, animals, planes and circus animals. The factory is open Monday-Friday from 9 am-noon, 1:30-6 pm, Saturday from 9 am-3 pm, closed Sunday. Bleienbachstrasse, CH-4900 Langenthal. ☎ 62-919-0404, fax 62-919-0505. Be sure to drive three miles outside of town on the northeast road to St. Urban and you'll see a former Cistercian abbey, now used as a psychiatric clinic. Known as the **Klosterkirche**, it was built in the Baroque style of the 18th century, and two symmetrical towers highlight this magnificent structure.

■ Where to Stay in Bern

Hotel Bellevue Palace offers outstanding accommodations in the heart of Bern, next to the Parliament Building. With a dramatic entry and many majestic rooms, this hotel is known to cater to royalty and celebrities in grand style. Home to three restaurants, a bar,

HOTEL PRICE CHART	
$	30-75Sfr ($20-$49)
$$	76-205Sfr ($50-$109)
$$$	206-299Sfr ($110-$200)
$$$$	300Sfr+ ($200+)

and a large terrace. ($$$$+). Kochergasse 3-5, CH-3001 Bern. ☎ 31-320-4545, fax 31-311-4743, www.bellevue-palace.ch.

Hotel Schweizerhof is smaller than the Hotel Bellevue Palace but has many amenities, including a private artwork and antiques collection. Located next to Bahnhof Platz and within walking distance of all major points of interest. ($$$-$$$$). Its **Restaurant Schultheissenstube** features gourmet dining. ($$$-$$$$). Open 11:30 am-3 pm, 5:30 pm-midnight, closed weekends. **Jack's Brasserie** is more casual and is open daily from 6 am-midnight ($-$$). The **Arcady Bar** is under the arcades outside, open daily from 10 am-whenever, with live piano music beginning daily at 5 pm. Bahnhofplatz 11, CH-3001 Bern. ☎ 31-326 –8080, fax 31-326-8090, www.schweizerhof-bern.ch.

Hôtel City am Bahnhof is an extremely modern hotel in the heart of Bern, across from the train station, near the Bern arcades. Very hip and trendy. ($$$). Bahnhofplatz, CH-3011 Bern. ☎ 31-311-5377, fax 31-311-0636.

Gasthof Linde Stettlen (Lime Tree Hotel) is on the outskirts of town, and offers a more bed-and-breakfast type of atmosphere in traditional Swiss cleanliness and charm. Route 59, CH-3066 Stettlen am Bern. ($$). ☎ 31-931-8586, fax 31-931-5503, www.linde-stettlen.ch.

Hotel Restaurant Jardin is a well-located and very casual hotel with a lovely yellow exterior close to old town and the railway station, also only two minutes from the Bern-Wankdorf highway exit. It is the closest hotel-restaurant to the "BEA-Expo" sports and exhibition grounds. ($$). Militärstrasse 38, CH-3014 Bern. ☎ 31-333-0117, fax 31-333-0943, www.hotel-jardin.ch

Hotel Goldener Schlüssel is a comfortable hotel in the center of old town, with a cozy restaurant (open 364 days a year) and provides convenience and value a stone's throw from the Aare River. It has a gorgeous exterior and well-lit interior. ($$). Rathausgasse 72, CH-3011 Bern. ☎ 31-311-0216, fax 31-311-5688, www.goldener-schluessel.ch.

Pension Marthahaus offers inexpensive rooms with lots of features including free use of bicycles, Internet access, and children's beds. The renovated guesthouse, from the turn of the last century, has 40 rooms in a quiet location with some rooms facing an inner courtyard. Car parking 10Sfr per day (on request). ($). Wyttenbachstrasse 22a, CH-3013 Bern. ☎ 31-332-4135, fax 31-333-3386, www.marthahaus.ch.

The **Bern Youth Hostel** is very large and offers 156 beds for weary heads. Open January 1-7, January 21-December 31. ($). Weihergasse 4, CH-3005 Bern. ☎ 31-311-6316, fax 31-312-5240.

■ Where to Eat in Bern

HONEY CAKES

AUTHOR'S PICK

For the finest Berner Lebkuchen (honey cakes decorated with the famous Bern bears) check out **Confiserie Eichenberger**. Owner Daniel Eichenberger has operated his pastry shop for over 42 years, and has become famous for producing these lovely, tasty cakes. They come in all sizes and make great gifts to bring home, as they are easy to carry and pack. They are similar in texture to our gingerbread cookies, and are more like them than a traditional "cake." Eichenberger produces over three tons of these cakes annually, and also manufactures and markets over 15 tons of chocolate. At his pastry shop you'll also find a tea room that serves up delicious light snacks, pastries, cookies, cakes and tortes. Here, you can sample a small Berner Lebkuchen along with a great cup of Swiss coffee. ($-$$). Bahnhofplatz 5, CH-3001 Bern. ☎ 31-311-3325.

Café Moléson offers fine dining featuring Swiss, French and international cuisine, with house specialties such as beef and fish. A fine wine list and dessert tray complement every meal. Located minutes from the Parliament, the interior is wood-paneled, with privately owned art. ($$$-$$$$). Open Monday-Friday from 11:30 am-2:30 pm, 5-11:30 pm. Aarburgergassse 24, CH-3011 Bern. ☎ 31-311-4463, www.moleson-bern.ch.

DINING PRICE CHART	
Prices based on a typical entrée, per person, and do not include beverage.	
$	15-25Sfr ($10-$16)
$$	26-45Sfr ($17-$29)
$$$	46-70Sfr ($30-$47)
$$$$	71Sfr+ ($47+)

Restaurant Brasserie Anker is Bern's premiere rösti café. (Rösti is a one-dish potato casserole loaded with vegetables, veal, pork or cheese.) This local favorite seats 35, serves "good plain cooking" and has Egger beer on tap. Near the Zytglogge (Clock Tower). Open Monday-Thursday, 9 am-11:30 pm, Friday and Saturday, 9 am-noon, Sunday, 9:30 am-6 pm. ($-$$$). Kornhausplatz 16, CH-3007 Bern. ☎ 31-311-1113, fax 31-311-1171.

A local favorite just steps from the Clock Tower is **Restaurant Harmonie**, a very traditional restaurant (wood paneling and white tablecloths) that features such traditional fare as cheese fondue and other Swiss specialties. Owned and operated by the same family since 1915. A good friendly staff. ($$-$$$). Open daily from 8 am-11:30 pm. Closed Saturday and Sunday. Hotelgasse 3, CH-3011 Bern. ☎ 31-313-1141, www.harmonie.ch.

Spaghetti Factory serves a wide selection of Italian favorites in an upbeat, lively atmosphere. The help is gracious and friendly and the portions are hearty at reasonable rates. Open daily from 11 am-1 pm. ($-$$). Kornhausplatz 7, CH-3006 Bern. ☎ 31-312-5455, www.spaghettifactory.ch.

Hotel-Restaurant Ador has good à la carte goodies and describes itself as "small but stylish." It's only a five-minute walk from the main train station and is right next door to the Bern-Forsthaus autobahn connection. ($-$$). Laupenstrasse 15, Postfach CH-3001 Bern. ☎ 31-388-0111, fax 31-388-0110.

Restaurant Dählhölzli offers a good vegetarian menu for solo travelers or families with kids. Swiss cuisine is also available. ($-$$). Tierparkweg 2, CH-3005 Bern. ☎ 31-351-1894, fax 31-351-7141.

Burgdorf

This is just to the north and slightly east of Bern. Situated at the entrance to the Emmental Valley, it has a massive 12th-century brick castle that was built by the Dukes of Zähringen, with a museum (Schlossmuseum Bergdorf) in its three square towers.

■ Information Sources

Tourist Office

The **Burgdorf Tourist Office** is open Monday-Friday from 7 am-8 pm, weekends from 8 am-6 pm. Bahnhofstrasse 44, CH-3400 Burgdorf. ☎ 34-423-6905.

Train Station

The Burgdorf train station has money exchange, Western Union, bike rentals and storage lockers available. Their office is open Monday-Friday from 5:30 am-8:30 pm, Saturday from 6 am-7 pm, Sunday from 6:30 am-8 pm. ☎ 51-220-6515.

Codes

The **postal code** for Burgdorf is CH-3400 and the **area code** is 34.

■ Museums

The **Schlossmuseum Burgdorf (Burgdorf Castle Museum)** has been housed in the Zahringen Castle for over 100 years. The dukes of the family Zahringen who originally built this castle in the 12th century were responsible for the founding of Bern, Fribourg, Murten and Burgdorf, and the history of this family and the Emmental region is traced within the museum. The Knight's Hall displays Emmental clothing, furniture, porcelain and musical instruments and artifacts of Johann Pestalozzi, who lived and worked here from 1799-1804. There is also a good view from the top of the castle tower of Burgdorf and the Bernese Alps. Admission is 5Sfr. Open April-November, Monday-Saturday from 2-5 pm, Sunday from 11-5 pm; November-March on Sundays from 11 am-5 pm. ☎ 34-423-0214.

Kornhaus Bergdorf (Swiss Center for Folk Culture) displays Swiss costumes, musical instruments, folklore documents and a yodeling room. Temporary displays are changed every few months and with the seasons. Admission is 10Sfr. Open November-March, Tuesday-Friday from 1:30-5 pm, Saturday and Sunday from 10 am-5 pm, mid-March to October, Tuesday-Friday from 10 am-12:30 pm, 1:30-5 pm, Saturday and Sunday from 10 am-5 pm. Kornhausgasse, CH-3400. ☎ 34-423-1010.

■ Where to Stay

The **Stadthaus** was built in 1745 and was originally the Town Hall of Burgdorf. Today it is luxury personified, and features sophisticated rooms with all amenities. The excellent in-house restaurant, **La Pendule**, has an extensive wine list and a private "cigar and whiskey" room. Member of Small Luxury Hotels of the World. ($$$-$$$$). Kirchbuhl 2, CH-3402 Burgdorf. ☎ 34-428-8000, fax 34-428-8008, www.stadthaus.ch.

Berchtold is a modern hotel located in the heart of Burgdorf's shopping district, just one minute from the train station. Some of the rooms can access a rooftop terrace, and the in-house restaurant offers Mediterranean dishes in a semi-formal setting. There is a nice bar here as well. ($$-$$$). Bahnhofstrasse 90, CH-3401 Burgdorf. ☎ 34-428-8428, fax 34-428-8484.

■ Where to Eat

Restaurant Da Gino Chin Chin is a combination of Italian and Chinese that serves tasty pizzas, spaghetti, tortellini, gnocchi, rice dishes and other typical Asian fare. The wine list is extensive, with Italian, Swiss and French wines. ($-$$). Open Monday from 10 am-2 pm, Tuesday-Thursday from 8 am-2 pm, 5-

11:30 pm, Friday and Saturday, 8 am-2 pm, 5 pm-12:30 am. Ruetschelengasse 17, CH-3400 Burgdorf. ☎ 34-422-1470.

Gasthof Emmenhof serves a wide array of French fare, specializing in fish, lamb, duck, soups and cheeses. The husband-and-wife team of Werner and Margit Schuerch prepare each dish themselves in a relaxed and lovely setting. ($$). Kirchbergstrasse 70, CH-3400 Burgdorf. ☎ 34-422-2275, fax 34-423-4629.

Restaurant Gasthaus was built in the 17th century and today serves up light dishes, apertifs and coffees in a café and garden terrace. ($$). Wynigenstrasse 13, CH-3400 Burgdorf. ☎ 34-428-8200, fax 34-428-8228.

Sumiswald

Sumiswald is a lovely little Swiss village with wooden houses that have large facades and double-tiered windows. They sit close together, with immense, overhanging roofs. The gables are often ornately painted with bright colors and designs. You'll find this small village – home to just 1,000 inhabitants – on Road 23, about 10 miles east of Burgdorf. It lies in a sunny green valley amidst gently rolling hills and shady fir woods that are perfect for hiking and cycling excursions. For various tours throughout the Emmentaler Valley, go to **Emmental Tours AG**, located at Lutoldstrasse 4, CH-3453 Sumiswald. ☎ 34-431-2161, fax 34-431-3370.

■ Where to Stay & Eat

Hotel-Restaurant Bären is a charming and beautiful country inn in the village center. The in-house restaurant has a generous wine list and traditional Swiss cuisine. Breakfast is included in rates. ($$). Closed December only. Marktgasse 1, CH-3454 Sumiswald. ☎ 34-431-1022, fax 34-431-2324, www.baren-sumiswald.ch.

For good hearty meals, look to **Restaurant Griesbach** in the village center. Meals are served in traditional Emmental style and portions are generous. ($-$$). Griesbach 768, CH-3454 Sumiswald. ☎ 34-431-1153, fax 34-431-1110.

Langnau im Emmental

This is a picturesque village that sits on the banks of a small tributary of the Emme River, and is known for its famous cheese and forestry industry. The village itself is pretty quiet, but the two tourist offices can provide you with maps of the local walking trails, of which there are many.

The Langnau **Tourist Office** is at Dorfmuhle 22, CH-3550 Langnau. ☎ 34-409-9595, fax 34-409-9598. It is open 8 am-noon, 1-6 pm, Monday-Thursday; Friday from 1-9 pm, Saturday, 9 am-4 pm. The regional tourist office, Pro Emmental is also very helpful with maps and sites of the area. Open Monday-Friday from 8 am-noon, 1:15-5:30 pm. Schlossstrasse 3, CH-3550 Langnau im Emmental. ☎ 34-402-4252, fax 34-402-5667, www.emmental.ch.

Langnau's **Heimatmuseum (Local Museum)** spotlights traditional tools, crafts, furniture and the history of the area. It is in a massive chalet and is open only from April-October, Tuesday-Sunday from 1:30-6 pm, although private tours can be arranged by calling ahead. Admission is 4Sfr. Located on the Barenplatz 2A, CH-3550 Langnau im Emmental. ☎ 34-402-1819.

■ Where to Stay & Eat

Hotel Hirschen is a huge, traditional inn that practically takes over the village center in Langnau. Clean and comfortable with all modern amenities but with a rustic Swiss charm. Most rooms are bright and airy and feature pretty woodwork, lace curtains and comfortable beds. ($$). The elegant à la carte restaurant (closed Monday only) serves up seasonal specialties at reasonable rates ($-$$$), and has a good selection of wines. Dorfstrasse, CH-3550 Langnau. ☎ 34-402-1517, fax 34-402-5623.

Hotel Restaurant Da Luca is near the train station and offers nine rooms. ($-$$). The in-house restaurant is a fine pizzeria that also serves pastas and local favorites. Open daily. Bahnhofstrasse 5, CH-3550 Langnau. ☎ 34-402-1495, fax 34-402-6336.

The best restaurant in the region is probably the **Gasthof zum Goldenen Löwen (House of the Gold Lion)**. Set in Emmentaler style, this gorgeous restaurant features daily fish specialties that will tempt any palate, and a good wine list. Open Monday-Friday, 8 am-11:30 pm, Saturday, 5 pm-12:30 am, closed Sunday. Guterstrasse 9, CH-3550 Langnau. ☎ 34-402-6555, fax 34-402-1196.

The local **youth hostel** features 24 rooms for rock-bottom rates ($) all year long, except for February and October, when they are closed. Mooseggstrasse 32, CH-3550 Langnau. ☎ 34-402-4526, www.youththostel.ch/langnau.

Biel-Bienne

Biel-Bienne is actually only one town, but shares a bilingual name (Biel in French, Bienne in German). One-third of the 60,000 citizens speak French and the other two-thirds speak German. All the street signs here are in both languages. This town is known as the hub of watchmaking in

Canton Bern, and is a very busy and somewhat sophisticated city. Both Rolex and the Omega watch factories are based here. The upper old village is worth a stroll, as many of the old historical buildings are well preserved. You'll find Biel-Bienne at the northern end of Lake Biel, at the northwestern side of this canton, on Highway 6.

Biel-Bienne offers a rich historic center, complete with fountains, impressive flower-adorned buildings and a 15th-century Gothic church. The Jura mountains are in easy reach, via a funicular, and the lake port is a great spot to embark on scenic river and lake cruises. There are also a variety of walking and cycling paths throughout the city and around the lake. The famed "Vegetable Route" takes you through the nearby quiet farming pastures, with signed panels along the way to give you highlights of the vegetation growing there. Biel-Bienne is also a good base from which to visit the nearby villages of St. Imier, Moutier and Lyss.

■ Information Sources

Tourist Office

The **Biel-Bienne Tourist Office** is just in front of the train station at Place de la Gare, and is open from 8 am-noon, 1:30-6 pm, Monday-Friday, and from 9 am-3 pm on Saturday. ☎ 32-322-7575, fax 32-322-7757.

Post Office

The Biel-Bienne main post office is across from the train station at Place de la Gare, CH-2501 Biel-Bienne. ☎ 32-321-1840, fax 32-322-3720. Open Monday-Friday from 7:30 am-6:30 pm, Saturday, from 7:30 am-noon.

Codes

The **postal code** for Biel-Bienne is CH-2500 and the **area code** is 32.

■ Getting Around

This is best done on foot as part of the old town is pedestrian-only. For trips around the lake, we recommend renting a bike at the train station for the day.

■ Adventures

These center around the lake, and you'll either find a wide array of water sports, or hiking, walking and bike trips along the lakeshore. A great outdoor adventure service is **Outdoor Experience**, at Postfach 3155, CH-2500 Biel-Bienne. They offer all types of summer and winter adventure sports, such as bungee jumping, bike touring, canyoning, snowboarding, skiing, river rafting, kitesurfing and the like. ☎ 32-331-3732 or 79-357-9257, fax 32-331-3733.

Adventures On Water

 If you want to go diving in the Bielersee, then go to **About Diving AG**, at Elfenaustrasse 3, CH-2500 Biel-Bienne, for lessons and trips. ☎ 32-325-3666, fax 32-325-3669. For boat rentals/pedal boats, check out **Neptun Boat Service** at Neuenburgstrasse 168, CH-2500 Biel-Bienne. ☎ 32-323-9348. Swimming is available at many stops along the lake for free.

Adventures On Wheels

 You can rent bikes at the train station for 30Sfr daily. ☎ 51-226-2281. Also, the **Bike Station** offers bikes, mountain bikes, roller skates and in-line skates for rent. Open daily from 9 am-7 pm. Uferweg 5, CH-2560 Nidau-Biel. ☎ 32-333-2525, fax 32-333-2526.

■ Landmarks & Historic Sites

 While in Biel-Bienne be sure not to miss **St. Peter's Island**, a wildlife sanctuary at the southwest end of Lake Biel that is a haven for wild birds, and exotic flora. There is an 11th-century monastery on the grounds that was once home to Jean-Jacques Rousseau and can be visited. You can walk to St. Peter's Island via a natural bridge that links it to the mainland or, better yet, you can take the one-hour boat trip from Biel for only 8.5Sfr.

Tierpark Bözingen (Bözingen Animal Park) is a small free zoo that is open year-round, with free admission. Handicapped-accessible. Located on Zollhausstrasse, CH-2500 Biel-Bienne. ☎ 32-342-5917.

■ Museums

Museum Neuhaus is the local art and history museum. Open Tuesday-Sunday from 11 am-5 pm, Wednesday from 11 am-7 pm. Closed Monday. Admission is 7Sfr for adults, 5Sfr for seniors and students; kids under 16 free. ☎ 32-328-7030, fax 32-328-7035.

The Schwab Museum was named after the 19th-century colonel who discovered the remains of the ancient lake-dwelling people of this region. It features archeological finds from the area. Open Tuesday-Saturday from 10 am-noon, 2-5 pm, and on Sunday from 11 am-5 pm. Admission is 5Sfr. Seevorstadt 50, CH-2500 Biel-Bienne. ☎ 32-322-7603, fax 32-323-3768.

The **Omega Museum** provides an insight into this watch manufacturer's history. Open by request, and admission is free. Stampflistrasse 96, CH-2500 Biel-Bienne. ☎ 32-344-9211, fax 32-343-9329.

■ Where to Stay

Hotel Elite is over 70 years old and one of the finest hotels in the city, with attractive, modern and spacious rooms. ($$$-$$$$). There is also a fine dining restaurant, **Amphitryon**, with market-fresh cuisine, and an outdoor café (**Baramundo**) and bar. Bahnhofstrasse 14, CH-2502 Biel-Bienne. ☎ 32-328-7777, fax 32-328-7770.

Hotel Baren is near the Old Town and offers spacious and simple rooms at reasonable rates. ($$). This hotel is also home to a pizzeria that is open daily. Nidaugasse 22, CH-2500 Bienne. ☎ 32-322-4573, fax 32-322-9157.

Hotel de la Poste is an inexpensive, small hotel that is very functional and clean. ($-$$). There are single and double rooms with community showers on each floor. The in-house restaurant serves up hearty Swiss fare at inexpensive rates ($-$$), and is closed Sunday. Guterstrasse 3, CH-2500 Bienne. ☎ 32-322-2544.

Camping

Camping is available at four sites on the southern end of Lake Biel. Local trains will bring you within walking distance of these sites at 30-minute intervals on a daily basis. Open from Easter through October. ($). ☎ 32-397-1345.

■ Where to Eat

Restaurant Falker offers an old-world atmosphere, serving Swiss favorites, sandwiches and chicken wings. ($-$$). Bahnhofstrasse, CH-2502 Biel-Bienne. ☎ 32-322-4761.

Gottstatterhaus creates seasonal cuisine and fresh fish at reasonable prices. ($$). Neuenburgstrasse 18, CH-2500 Biel-Bienne. ☎ 32-322-4052.

Pinocchio is famed for its pizzas, pasta and salads in a rustic pizzeria setting. ($-$$). Nidaugasse 22, CH-2500 Biel-Bienne. ☎ 32-322-4573, fax 32-322-9157.

Moutier

Moutier is just north of Biel-Bienne on local road 30 and sits at the foot of the Jura Mountains. Modern and clean, it offers many sporting venues, including two soccer fields, fitness centers, a public pool, skating

Above: Oberhofen Castle (12th century) on Lake Thun, with Eiger, Moench and Jungfrau as the backdrop (see page 330)

Below: On the Allmendhubel Trail above Muerren, with Eiger, Moench and Jungfrau behind (see page 355)

*On the Grosse Scheidegg, above Grindelwald,
with Moench and Eiger behind (see page 361)*

Above: Susten Pass, Uri, with the village of Meien in the background (see page 366)

Below: St.-Saphorin, in the wine-growing area of Lavaux on Lake Geneva (see page 383)

The Aletsch forest, Canton Valais, at the foot of Europe's longest glacier (see page 443)

rink, tennis courts, and man-made climbing walls. Founded in 650, it was first made into a university village by German monks and today is a quiet little city that offers the modern conveniences of a larger city, without the congestion of either heavy traffic or people. It is also considered part of the Jura-Bern watchmaking valley.

The Jura Bernois **Tourist Office** is at Avenue de la Gare 9, CH-2740 Moutier. ☎ 32-494-5343, fax 32-493-6156. They can provide you with local hiking and climbing maps and advise you on walking trails too. Horseback riding is popular here. For organized rides or rides in a coach, contact **Manege Gafner** at CH-2740 Moutier. ☎ 32-493-1717. Hot-air ballooning and hang-gliding trips can also be arranged through the tourist office.

■ Where to Stay & Eat

Hôtel du Cheval Blanc, a family-run inn, once housed the great German writer Goethe in October of 1779. ($$). The rooms are clean and comfortable. CH-2740 Moutier. ☎ 32-493-1044, fax 32-493-4421.

Hotel-Restaurant des Gorges offers pizzas, pastas and grilled fare at reasonable rates ($-$$), with most foods cooked over a wood fire. Open daily until 11:30 pm. The hotel provides clean, comfortable rooms with breakfast included in the rates. ($$). CH-2740 Moutier. ☎ 32-493-1669, fax 32-493-4959, www.htl.ch/hoteldesgorges.

Hotel-Restaurant Moutier is a country restaurant specializing in cold dishes, rösti, cheese plates, homemade breads and grilled dishes. ($-$$). The hotel has clean, functional rooms. ($-$$) CH-2740 Moutier. ☎ 32-493-1771.

The Clown Restaurant is a combination of a fine dining room and a brewery that serves locally caught fish and seasonal dishes. ($-$$$). Open daily until 11:30 pm, closed Tuesday. CH-2740 Moutier. ☎ 32-493-7414.

Restaurant Loetschberg dishes out hearty portions of Swiss seasonal specialties in a family setting. Open until 11:30 pm nightly, closed Tuesday. ($-$$). CH-2740 Moutier. ☎ 32-493-4443.

Café Bären is an upbeat coffee house that provides live jazz music and serves light snacks. Open until 2:30 am on Friday and Saturday nights. Closed Tuesday. ($). CH-2740 Moutier. ☎ 32-493-1863.

St. Imier

This town is in a valley, west of Biel-Bienne on Road 30 and is home to a grand 11th-century Gothic church, which has been restored over the centuries and includes frescos and other artwork from the 13th and 15th centuries. The town is a popular spot for rock climbers and hiking enthusiasts, and it's here that you will find Mount Crosin, which has the largest wind-operated power park in Switzerland, utilizing modern windmills to produce electricity. The Jura Bernois **Tourisme Office** is at Rue du Marche 6, CH-2610 Saint-Imier. ☎ 32-941-2663, fax 32-941-1435.

■ Where to Stay & Eat

 Hotel Erguel offers comfortable rooms at reasonable rates ($$) and features a good in-house restaurant that serves up game meats and traditional fare à la carte. CH-2610 St. Imier. ☎ 32-941-2264.

The Green Wood Inn is set high on Mount Crosin above St. Imier and features comfy rooms near the "Natural Path" walking trail. From here, you can catch biking paths and have direct access to the ski pistes. ($$). CH-2610 Mount-Crosin. ☎ 32-944-1455.

Pizzeria Fountain features pizzas cooked over a wooden fire, as well as pastas, salads and grilled dishes. The ice cream here is the best in the region. ($-$$). Located in the Fountain Hotel. CH-2610 St. Imier. ☎ 32-941-2956.

Lyss

Lyss is just off Highway 6, south of Biel-Bienne and north of Bern. It is a very typical Swiss town of 11,000 people, and is worth visiting for a couple of hours to get a feel for what life is like in an average town. There is a small **Tourist Office** at Hirschenplatz 1, CH-3250. ☎ 32-387-0087, fax 32-387-0085. They can provide you with a map and historical information on the town. The history of Lyss traces back to the seventh century. For hundreds of years it was a farming village that garnered its power via water mills. Throughout the village and in the area you'll see many "mill" signs that date back to these times. Life in this town centers around the **Hirschenplatz**, where you'll find a lovely shopping mall and many local shops and bakeries; it is worth an afternoon stroll.

The Bernese Oberland: Western Region

Thun

Thun is the northernmost city in the Bernese Oberland, sitting at the northern edge of Lake Thun (Thuner See) on Highway 8. The Old Town is best-known for its unique walking path along the busy **Obere Hauptgasse** (literally Upper Main Road), where visitors walk on the flowered terraces that are actually the roofs of the shops below. Home to some 41,039 citizens, Thun has a polished look and feel to it, and the gorgeous views of the Alps looming over Lake Thun only add to the picture-postcard setting.

■ Information Sources

Tourist Office

The **Thun Tourist Office** is on Bahnhofstrasse 2, right near the train station, and offers bike rental, money exchange and lockers. CH-3600 Thun. ☎ 33-222-2340, fax 33-222-8323.

Post Office

The main post office in Thun is at Panoramastrasse 1, Bahnhofplatz, CH-3601 Thun. ☎ 33-224-8841, fax 33-224-8851. Hours are Monday-Friday from 7:30 am-7 pm, Saturday from 7:30 am-noon.

Codes

The **postal code** for Thun is CH-3600 and the **area code** is 33.

■ Landmarks & Historic Sites

Sitting high above Thun is the **Zähringen Castle & Museum**, shown at left. It contains a collection of regional history artifacts and documents. Weapons, uniforms and medieval objects from the 18th and 19th centuries are on display. The castle was built in 1911 and provides wonderful views of Thun and the countryside from its towers. To get here, you walk up a covered stairway from the medieval Rathausplatz (Town Square) in the Old Village. Open daily from April-October, 9 am-6 pm, November to March from 10 am-4 pm. Admission is 6Sfr for adults, 2Sfr for kids. ☎ 33-223-2001.

■ Museums

The Thun Art Museum is housed in the former Thunerhof – a stylish hotel – and is also home to the city's administrative offices. This museum features works from mostly Swiss artists of the 20th century, with special emphasis on those who have hailed from Canton Bern and the Bernese Oberland. Etchings, paintings and statues, as well as graphic arts and drawings are found here. Located at Hofstettenstrasse 14, CH-3602 Thun. ☎ 33-225-8420, fax 33-225-8906.

On the grounds of the heavily forested **Schadau Park** you'll find the **Wocher Panorama**, sponsored by the Thun Art Museum. This piece was created from 1809 to 1814 by artist Marquard Wocher (1760-1830) and is a circular picture of Thun. It is the oldest panoramic painting in the world.

Just two miles north of Thun is the country village of **Steffisburg**, *where you'll find a relaxing swimming pool/aquatic park that also contains a winding water slide and children's pool. It's an ideal spot for families with children who need a break from sightseeing in the cities. There is a good restaurant on the premises, and parking for cars, motorcycles and RVs. Open from mid-May to mid-September, 7 am-7 or 8 pm (depending on the weather). Admission is 4.5Sfr for adults, 2Sfr for children ages six-16. For further information, call the* **AquaParc** *at ☎ 33-439-4353.*

■ Adventures

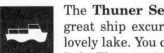

The **Thuner See (Lake Thun)** is where you'll find many great ship excursions that cross back and forth across this lovely lake. You can drive completely around the lake as well. Lake Thun is 13 miles long and two miles wide, and was originally connected to Lake Brienz, which is to the east, on the other side of Interlaken. However, so much sediment was deposited from the run-off of the Lutschine River that it eventually divided the two bodies of water. From April-October ships leave from Thun almost hourly to Interlaken West, Spiez and other destinations. Prices start at 35.60Sfr. **Lake Brienz** is smaller than Lake Thun at just nine miles long and two miles wide. It is often overlooked by tourists in favor of the activities on Lake Thun, but is favored by vacationing Swiss.

■ Where to Stay

Hotel Krone is a beautiful inn – originally built in 1590 – that features a beautiful outside tower, and a terrace that overlooks the Aare River in the heart of Old Town. Quiet, with modern, charming rooms. ($$-$$$). It has a pair of restaurants, **Wong-Kun**, with Chinese food, and **Le Bistro**, serving French cuisine. Only half a mile from the train station. Rathausplatz 2, CH-3600 Thun. ☎ 33-227-8888, fax 33-227-8890.

HOTEL PRICE CHART	
$	30-75Sfr ($20-$49)
$$	76-205Sfr ($50-$109)
$$$	206-299Sfr ($110-$200)
$$$$	300Sfr+ ($200+)

Freienhof is a four-star hotel right on Lake Thun in Old Town. It features all modern amenities in a sophisticated atmosphere and is open year round. The international restaurant – Giardino – specializes in locally caught fish and regional dishes. ($$-$$$). Freienhofgasse 3, CH-3600 Thun. ☎ 33-227-5050, fax 33-227-5055.

Seepark Kongress Hotel is a first-class hotel on the shores of Lake Thun, ultra-modern and spacious. It caters to a business clientele. ($$-$$$). The in-house restaurant, **La Voile**, serves a wide range of international dishes ($-$$$) in a relaxed, semi-formal atmosphere. Seestrasse 47, CH-3602 Thun. ☎ 33-226-1212, fax 33-226-1510, www.seepark.ch.

Hotel Alpha is modern and offers first-class comforts at the edge of the Old Town, with impressive views of the Bernese Alps and Lake Thun. The in-house restaurant features Mediterranean fare. Located only five minutes from the Thun-Sud exit on Highway 6. ($$-$$$). Breakfast is included in rates. Eisenbahnstrasse 1, CH-3604 Thun. ☎ 33-334-7347, fax 33-334-7348.

Emmental was originally built in 1898 and continues to charm guests with beautiful rooms that include all modern amenities. The sun terrace offers outdoor dining, and international bands perform live here on a weekly basis. Reasonable rates. ($$). Bernstrasse 2, CH-3600 Thun. ☎ 33-222-0120, fax 33-222-0130, www.essenundtrinken.ch.

■ Where to Eat

Restaurant Holiday is the pride of French chef Jacky Levy, who painstakingly prepares regional and French dishes for his guests. A generous wine list complements your meal. ($$-$$$). Located in the Holiday Hotel, Gwattsrasse 1, CH-3604 Thun. ☎ 33-334-6767, fax 33-336-5704.

DINING PRICE CHART	
Prices based on a typical entrée, per person, and do not include beverage.	
$	15-25Sfr ($10-$16)
$$	26-45Sfr ($17-$29)
$$$	46-70Sfr ($30-$47)
$$$$	71Sfr+ ($47+)

Spiez

Spiez is a tiny town on the south shore of Lake Thun at the foot of the Niesen Mountain and makes a good base for summer excursions. The village is just south of Thun on Highway 8 and is only 11 miles north of Interlaken. Its main attraction is its huge lakeshore castle – **Schloss Spiez**, shown at left – an 11th-century structure containing a 1,000-year-old Norman church. The castle is closed from late October through early April. Otherwise it's open Monday, 2-5 pm, Tuesday-Sunday, 10 am-6 pm. ☎ 33-654-1506.

From Spiez you can travel southwest along road 11 to Zweisimmen, where this junction leads to the resorts of Gstaad or Lenk. Or you can go straight south along the Kanderstrasse (secondary road), which soon splits at Frutigen and then heads to either Adelboden in the west, or Kandersteg in the south. If you continue around Lake Thun on Highway 8, you'll come to Interlaken in about 30 minutes.

■ Where to Stay & Eat

Seegarten-Marina is a gorgeous, stately hotel by the lake that has lovely rooms with excellent views of the countryside and the Alps. The in-house restaurant/pizzeria serves up tasty homemade pizzas, and à la carte fare with fish specialties at reasonable rates. ($-$$$). The restaurant is open from 11:30 am to 10:30 pm nightly, and the pizzeria is open from 5-10:30 pm nightly. The hotel bar – **Piratenbar** – is open daily from 5 pm to midnight. Schachenstrasse 3, CH-3700 Spiez. ☎ 33-655-6767, fax 33-655-6765.

Aqua Welle is fine hotel in a quiet spot on the Spiez Bay landing, with great views of the Lake and Alps. The hotel contains a swimming pool, sailing school and many opportunities for long hikes and romantic walks. There is also a sun-bathing beach for guests. The in-house restaurant serves Italian and Chinese dishes. ($$). Seestrasse 67, Schiffstation, CH-3700 Spiez. ☎ 33-654-4044, fax 33-654-7675.

Hotel Des Alpes is in the heart of Spiez and offers excellent views of Lake Thun and the Alps. ($-$$). A good base for hiking excursions. Seestrasse 38, Postfach 221, CH-3700 Spiez. ☎ 33-654-3354, fax 33-654-8850, www.desalpes.ch.

Bellevue is a small, family-run inn that offers modern and comfortable rooms, close to hiking and biking trails. ($-$$). Seestrasse 36, CH-3700 Spiez. ☎ 33-654-8464, fax 33-654-8448, www.bellevue-spiez.ch.

Zweisimmen

The town sits along Highway 11, at the junction of the road that continues west to Gstaad and the alternative road south, which ends at Lenk. Zweisimmen is set in the midst of meadows and attracts many guests during the summer months, but it is considered primarily a winter resort village. It contains 19 miles of cross-country ski trails, as well as dog sledding and toboggan runs. During the winter months a cable car takes visitors to the high-altitude plateau of **Sparenmoos**, with 22 downhill ski lifts and 155 miles (250 km) of pistes.

The **Zweisimmen Tourist Office** is at Thunstrasse 8, CH-3770 Zweisimmen. ☎ 33-722-1133, fax 33-722-2585. Here you can grab maps of the region for summer and winter hiking trips, and get information on local hotels and ski conditions.

■ Where to Stay

If you're looking to stay overnight, your best bet is to bunk down in the **Sporthotel Krone**, in the heart of the village, minutes from the town grocery, bank, post office and train station. The style is that of a traditional Swiss chalet and rooms are clean and comfortable. ($-$$). Lenkstrasse 4, CH-3770. ☎ 33-722-1715, fax 33-722-3155.

Gstaad

Gstaad is five miles southwest of Zweisimmen, just south of the village of Saanen on the Saanenstrasse, and is one of Switzerland's top ski resorts. The village is considered to be the dividing line between the German- and French-speaking areas of southern Switzerland, although neither really seems to dominate the area. Obviously, people who visit Gstaad are really more interested in skiing than in any lingual disputes. The village is enhanced by chalet-style housing, and is yet another home of rich and famous jet-setting clients such as Elizabeth Taylor, Julie Andrews, Sting, Prince Rainier and Roger Moore – to name just a few.

The village is wedged between glaciers, mountain lakes and mountain plateaus. Centuries ago, Gstaad was a junction where traders changed horses on the route across the Bernese Oberland. The railways changed all that, and the village soon became a winter playground, and a home and schooling center for the children of royalty from throughout Europe. You'll find a few street signs scattered here and there, but there are other

Saanen resort in the Bernese Oberland offers 60 modern ski lifts, 155 miles (250 km) of downhill pistes and 62 miles (100 km) of cross-country ski trails

signs directing you toward restaurants and hotels, so getting around here isn't a problem.

■ Information Sources

Tourist Office

The **Gstaad-Saanen Tourist Office** is open from July to August, Monday-Friday, 8:30 am-6:30 pm, Saturday, 9 am-6 pm, Sunday, 10 am-5 pm. September-June, the hours are Monday-Friday, 8:30 am-noon, 2-6 pm, Saturday, 9 am-noon. Promenade, CH-3780 Gstaad. ☎ 33-748-8181, fax 33-748-8133, www.gstaad.ch.

Post Office

The Gstaad post office is found on the Bahnhofplatz 778, CH-3780 Gstaad. Hours are Monday-Friday from 8 am-noon, 2-6 pm; Saturday from 8:30-11 am. ☎ 33-744-2003, fax 33-744-5479.

Codes

The **postal code** for Gstaad is CH-3780 and the **area code** is 33.

■ Getting Around

Getting around is best done on foot or skis, or via cable car, chairlift or gondola.

■ Adventures

On Snow

Skiing

This is the main attraction in Gstaad. Along with the sister re-sort areas of Saanen, St. Stephan, Saanen-Moser and Schonried, it's is known to many visitors as "Saanenland." The four valleys that make up this region are criss-crossed by 70 funiculars, gondolas and chairlifts that offer access to 155 miles (250 km) of downhill slopes and 30 miles (48 km) of cross-country pistes.

GET A PASS

AUTHOR'S
PICK

Your best bet if you like to ski and plan on spending time here is to get the **Ski Gstaad Pass**, which can be purchased at any of the resort's funicular stations. This all-inclusive pass varies in price, but you can ex-pect to pay around 100Sfr for two days, up to 200Sfr for five days and about 280Sfr for seven days. The pass is also of-fered to children and varies in price according to the age of the child and the length of stay. The **Eggli-La Vide Manette Pass** is your other option, but it is sold only as a one-day pass for 50Sfr, offering limited access throughout this area.

The **Gstaad Swiss Ski School** offers lessons in downhill skiing, cross-country and snowboarding; it also has mountain guides available. ☎ 33-744-1865.

Other Sports

Alpinzentrum Gstaad offers snow sport instruction and mountain guides for all types of trekking in the winter months. ☎ 33-748-4030. **Experience Gstaad** also has winter trekking, ice and rock climbing, and guides for off-trail skiing. (☎ 33-744-8800). If you're really in great shape, seeking the ultimate test in outdoor adventures, then call **Beats Adventure Tours** at ☎ 33-744-1521. Horseback lessons and riding excursions are available through **Rietzentrum Gstaad**. ☎ 33-744-2460. Tennis lessons and courts are available at **Pro Tennis Gstaad**, ☎ 33-744-1090, with three indoor and four outdoor courts available for play. For badminton, you'll want to go to the **Gstaad Tenniscenter**. ☎ 33-744-1090. Reservations are required.

For bungee jumping, contact **Jumping Keller**. ☎ 33-744-8800, fax 33-744-8801.

■ Shopping

Shopping abounds in Gstaad, and includes everything you'd expect from a resort catering to a royal clientele. The main shopping street is the **Hauptstrasse**, where you'll find every designer name known to man, such as Valentino, Gucci, Rolex, DKNY and the like. Otherwise, you can visit the upscale boutiques and salons found in the Palace Hotel for the priciest of goods.

For souvenirs, look to **Bazar Ryf** on the Bahnhofstrasse (☎ 33-744-1633). For fine stationery and souvenirs, go to **Cadnau on Promenade** (☎ 33-744-1492, fax 33-744-4678) or to **Potpourri-BodyWell** on Gstaaderhof (☎ 33-744-2223). For baked goods, check out **Bäckerei Brand**, Hauptstrasse (☎ 33-744-1185) and, for fine chocolates, pralines, truffles and other mouth-watering fare, go to **Early Beck** on the Promenade (☎ 33-748-7048, fax 33-748-7049).

■ Where to Stay

Palace Hotel Gstaad is the premiere landmark hotel in the village. Built in 1912, it has corner towers and a medieval façade. This is where you'll find Hollywood royalty as well as European queens, kings and princes. It contains the finest in fitness centers, restaurants, tennis courts, bars, cafés, shops and discos. Each room has been carefully decorated and meticulously maintained. Nothing is left to chance. Be sure to ask for a room facing south, however, as the northern ones overlook the unspectactular parking lot. If you've got unlimited funds, this is the place to be. ($$$$+). Rooms start at 790Sfr in the wintertime, and a suite goes for 2,200Sfr. Prices are slightly lower in the summer, but only slightly. All modern amenities, free parking and the rates include breakfast (thank goodness!). CH-3780 Gstaad. In the USA you can call toll-free at ☎ 1-800-223-6800; otherwise ☎ 33-748-5050.

Hotel Le Grand Chalet sits on a hilltop just a few minutes from Gstaad's center, and provides visitors with grandiose views of the surrounding Alps. The 20 rooms and four suites are all very spacious and feature all modern conveniences with sophisticated Swiss charm. ($$$$). The in-house restaurant and cozy bar are divided by a see-through stone fireplace. This is a great base for hikes, walking trails and cycling excursions. The hotel also includes a gym, sauna, and heated swimming pool. CH-3780 Gstaad. ☎ 33-748-7676, fax 33-748-7677, www.grandchalet.ch.

Hotel Olden is a beautiful chalet that caters to the rich and famous in this ski resort village. Besides outstanding, well-equipped, modern rooms, the hotel contains two fine restaurants with superb local specialties, a cozy bar with a large fireplace, and an outside terrace and private sunbathing deck. Pets are accepted. ($$$$). Closed from mid-April to mid-May. CH-3780 Gstaad. ☎ 33-744-3444, fax 33-744-6164.

Posthotel Rössli is one of the oldest hotels in town, and one of the most atmospheric. Very cozy and cheery, it features all modern amenities, and is a popular spot where the locals hang out in the pub and elaborate restaurant. As an added treat, on a weekly basis, mountain guide and ski instructor Ruedi Widmer offers walks and grill parties in the summer or skiing treks in the winter at no extra charge to hotel guests. ($$$-$$$$). CH-3780 Gstaad. ☎ 33-748-4242, fax 33-748-4243, www.posthotelroessli.ch.

Hotel Alphorn sits at the base of the Wispile cable car. This small chalet was built in 1970 and then remodeled in 1992. It contains 30 comfy, clean rooms and a ski shop. ($$). Steigstrasse, CH-3780 Gstaad. ☎ 33-748-3434, fax 33-748-4546.

The local **youth hostel** – known as **Chalet Rüblihorn** – is in nearby Saanen, with 72 sleeping spots for weary travelers. Open from mid-December to mid-March, and from late May to late October. ($). CH-3792 Saanen-Gstaad. ☎ 33-744-1343, fax 33-744-5542, www.youthhostel.ch/saanen.

There are also two **mountain huts** in the Gstaad area: the **Wildhornhütte**, which offers 100 sleeping spaces, ☎ 33-733-2382, and the **Wildstrubelhütten**, with 70 spots to bunk down, ☎ 33-744-3339. The Gstaad Tourist Office can provide you with maps for reaching both of these huts.

■ Where to Eat

If you visit Gstaad, then you've got to eat at the **Chesery**, considered one of the top restaurants in Switzerland. You'll dine amidst pink marbled floors, polished wooded walls, and fancy white linens on some of the finest cuisine in the world. The menu changes daily and could include fresh Maine lobster, Scottish lamb, Italian truffles or Grecian octopus. The menu includes fixed-price options for both lunch ($$$) and dinner ($$$$), or you can order à la carte. Reservations are required. Open Tuesday-Sunday from 11:30 am-2:30 pm, 7 pm-midnight. Closed mid-October to mid-December, Easter to mid-June and in the winter for lunch from Tuesday through Friday. Lauenenstrasse, CH-3780 Gstaad. ☎ 33-744-2451.

The Palace Hotel has three elegant dining rooms, requiring formal attire, and offering the finest in service. Appetizers such as the finest caviar and foie gras are served, and entrées can include venison, duck, pastas, beef, lamb and veal. The dessert trays are especially delightful and beautifully prepared. Reservations are required, and a three-course fixed-price lunch ($$$$) and five-course fixed-price dinner ($$$$) are offered as well as à la carte menus. Open daily from 12:30-2:30 pm and from 7:30-10:30 pm. Closed from late March to mid-June and from mid-September to late December. Located in the Palace Hotel, CH-3780 Gstaad. ☎ 33-748-5000.

Restaurant Bernerhof is an international pub-style eatery in the hotel of the same name. This is a great spot for families or those traveling with children, as the menu is extremely diverse, offering everything from standard Swiss fare to seasonal and regional specialties, as well as freshly made pastas, fondues and Asian delights. Reservations are recommended. Open daily from 11:30 am-2:30 pm, 6:30-10:30 pm. Closed late November to December 1. ($-$$$). Fixed-price menus for both lunch ($$) and dinner ($$$), as well as à la carte. In the Hotel Bernerhof, CH-3780 Gstaad. ☎ 33-748-8844.

Ristorante Rialto specializes in fine Italian cuisine, with the freshest of salads and pastas found anywhere in Gstaad. Seasonal specials highlight the tempting menu, which includes Mediterranean delicacies such as sea bass and octopus. Reservations are recommended. ($$-$$$). Open Monday-Saturday from noon-2 pm, 8:30-11:30 pm, Sunday from noon-2 pm. Closed on Mondays during May, June and November. Located in the village center on the Promenade. CH-3780 Gstaad. ☎ 33-744-3474.

Posthotel Rössli is in the heart of Gstaad's shopping district, and has delighted shoppers for 150 years with its rustic interior and hearty portions of steaming schnitzels, fondues and pastas. You'll find fresh salads here too. ($-$$). This spot is a long-time favorite among the locals. Open daily from 11:30 am-2:30 pm, 4:30-10 pm. Hauptstrasse 1, CH-3780 Gstaad. ☎ 33-748-4242.

Lenk

Lenk is a great little resort village in the heart of the Simmental region, on the secondary road that runs south from Zweisimmen off main Highway 11. Although not as famous as nearby Gstaad, Lenk offers a wide array of spa hotels, fitness centers, skiing, hiking and horseback riding excursions – without the crowds or overwhelming prices of Gstaad. The village is split by the Simme River and sits atop the Simmental Mountain Range.

■ Information Sources

Tourist Office

The **Lenk Tourist Office** is open Monday-Friday from 9 am-noon, 2-5 pm. Rawylstrasse, CH-3775 Lenk. ☎ 33-733-3131, fax 33-733-2027.

Post Office

The Lenk post office is open Monday-Friday, 8 am-noon, 2-5 pm, Saturday from 8 am-noon. Kronenplatz, CH-3775 Lenk. ☎ 33-733-1005, fax 33-733-3101.

Codes

The **postal code** in Lenk is CH-3775 and the **area code** is 33.

■ Getting Around

This is easily done on foot in Lenk, as the village is small and split by the Simme River, with the post and tourist offices on the north side, and the train station and sports and riding centers on the south side.

■ Adventures

Adventures abound in this resort village and many can be arranged through the Tourist Office. For instance, if you'd like to go **fishing** on the nearby Iffigsee (Lake Iffig), you'll have to purchase a permit (5Sfr per day) from the Tourist Office. They can also arrange for you to visit an **Alpine cheese factory** (Alpkäsereibesichtigung, ☎ 33-733-2020), and provide you with maps for **hiking and walking** excursions. There are 10 easy walks in Lenk, which take up to 1½ hours and are suitable for anyone. In addition, there are four hikes of medium difficulty and five for experienced hikers only.

For badminton, go to the **Reit und Sportzentrum**, located next to the Hotel Simmehof. ☎ 33-736-3434. You can also take **riding** lessons or go on riding excursions throughout the area. ☎ 33-733-3025 for the riding stable.

For **tennis**, contact Lenk's public tennis center, which offers six courts and a snack bar. Open Monday-Saturday, 7 am-9 pm, Sunday from 7 am-7 pm. ☎ 33-733-2204.

You can play **miniature golf** at the Hotel Tenne, daily from 10 am to sunset. ☎ 33-733-2221.

The **Trainingcenter Lenk** offers a wide range of fitness programs, massage and physio-therapies. ☎ 33-733-3366, fax 33-733-3377.

Lenk also has an **aquatic center** with indoor and outdoor pools, a children's pool, sauna and bistro. Open Monday, Thursday and Friday from 10 am-8 pm, Tuesday from 1:30-8 pm, Wednesday from 10 am-9:30 pm, Saturday from 1:30-8 pm and Sunday from 10 am-8 pm. ☎ 33-733-1901.

■ Where to Stay & Eat

Lenkerhof Alpine Resort is a large, first-class hotel that specializes in wellness treatments such as sulphur and salt pools, bio-sauna light therapies, herbal saunas, steam baths, and various types of massages. The spa also includes a beauty salon, an aerobics pavilion and fitness park. The rooms are beautifully decorated and modern. ($$$-$$$$). PO Box 241, CH-3775 Lenk Im Simmental. ☎ 33-736-3636, fax 33-736-3637.

Hotel Simmehof is a beautiful, modern hotel and wellness center that is great for families with children. It features pools, saunas, whirlpools and four fantastic dining rooms: the **Walliserstube** (formal international dining), the **Simmerstube** (casual Swiss dining), the **Tessiner Grotto** (elegant haute cuisine) and the **Bünderstube** (casual international cooking). ($$-$$$$). CH-3775 Lenk Im Simmental. ☎ 33-736-3434, fax 33-736-3436.

Wildstrubel is a lovely Swiss chalet offering modern rooms, a sauna, solarium, and a restaurant sun terrace and beautiful garden. Rates include breakfast ($$). CH-3775 Lenk im Simmental. ☎ 33-736-3111, fax 33-733-3151.

Frutigen

Frutigen is south of Spiez, along the Engstligental Mountain Range at the junction of the Kander and Engstligenbach rivers. From this spot you can travel either southwest to Adelboden or southeast to Kandersteg. Frutigen is known for its spectacular waterfalls and unusual rock formations. The strong waters from the two conjoining rivers have eroded the rocks and stones near many of the waterfalls and make for some of the most beautiful scenery in Switzerland. Ever industrious, the Swiss have placed numerous walkways, stairs and stone paths and railings around these areas to allow visitors close access. The small information office here can provide you with maps and directions to all of the hiking trails and waterfalls. ☎ 33-672-5200.

NATURAL WONDER

While in Frutigen, be sure to take a half-day to visit the small but deep **Blausee (Blue Lake)**, a privately owned lake slightly north of Frutigen. Boat rides, a trout nursery and picnic areas are available for 5Sfr per person from May-November, from 9 am-6 pm daily. The rest of the year it is open at no charge for walks. ☎ 33-671-1641.

Adelboden

A delboden is nine miles southwest of Frutigen and is a popular summer and winter resort. The village sits in a sunny spot at the peak of the Engstligentals and is home to some 3,600 residents. It offers hiking excursions in the summer and plenty of snow sport activities in the winter. There are over 135 miles (217 km) of walking, hiking and snow sports paths in this area.

■ Information Sources

Tourist Office

The **Adelboden Tourist Office** is open Monday-Friday from 8:30 am-noon, 2-6 pm, Saturday from 8:30 am-noon, 2-5 pm, Sunday from 9 am-noon. Dorfstrasse 23, CH-3715 Adelboden. ☎ 33-673-8080, fax 33-673-8092.

Codes

The **postal code** for Adelboden is CH-3715 and the **area code** is 33.

■ Getting Around

This is best done on foot or on a bike. The village is a mecca of hotels and shops, and there are a great many footpaths just outside the village for exploring. You can also travel throughout the area on one of the many "**Bergbahnen**" (mountain trains). One popular trip is to ride the **Adelboden-Lenk Bergbahnen** from each of these two resort villages. CH-3715 Adelboden. ☎ 33-673-3500, fax 33-673-3535.

■ Adventures

On Foot

In the summer you can follow the **Vitaparcours Fitness Trail** to keep in (or get in) shape. This path is open to the public and serves as a downhill ski slope in the winter months. The **Adelboden Flower Path** offers a 1½-mile walk along the Hahenmosspass that features a wide variety of flowers, each with its own identifying marker. The flowers are in bloom from May until October.

The **Adelboden Forest Trail** takes you round-trip for two to three hours and features 13 information boards and a picnic area, leading you through some stunning mountain scenery and sunny meadows. The **Aeugi-Lowa Klettersteig** (climbing path) takes you from the Hahenmosspass to the

Engstligenalp and has some very steep climbs, but can be done by amateur mountaineers. From May to October only.

The **Vogellisi Path** is a two-hour hike that starts out from the Berglager (halfway between Adelboden and nearby Silleren) and takes you through meadows, past mountain streams and offers beautiful views of the area before reaching the top station of the Adelboden-Silleren-Bahn. You can either ride the train from here or retrace your steps. Open May to October. Information and maps available at the tourist office for all of the above trails.

In Water

The **Gruebi outdoor swimming park** offers an adult and children's pool, as well as an ice rink, beach volleyball yard and playground. Admission is 7Sfr for adults, 4Sfr for kids. CH-3715 Adelboden. ☎ 33-673-1520, fax 33-673-8092.

On Wheels

There are over 20 marked and maintained bike trails in and around Adelboden, with treks through the Hahnenmoos Pass or to Lake Thun, for bikers at all levels. Bike maps are available through the tourist office.

On Snow

Cross-country skiing is very popular in Adelboden. If you need lessons, look to **Swiss Snowsports School Adelboden**. ☎ 33-673-8090.

On Ice

Curling is available at the local Curling Club, and lessons start at 40Sfr, while a game will cost you 15Sfr per person. The rink is available from 10 am-noon and 2-4 pm for curling games. Call Adelboden's **Curling Club** at ☎ 33-673-1777, fax 33-673-1761. **Ice skating** and **hockey** can be found at the **Kunsteiszentrum**, open from October 5-December 20, daily from 10 am-noon, 1:30-5 pm; from December 21-October 4, daily from 10 am-5 pm, Wednesday nights from 8-10 pm. Admission si 7Sfr for adults and 4Sfr for kids. You can also rent ice skates here. ☎ 33-673-8080, fax 33-673-8092.

■ Where to Stay

The **Parkhotel Bellevue & Spa** is a charming wellness hotel near the village center in a quiet spot on a hill overlooking Adelboden. The hotel features a private park, sunbathing terrace, pools, whirlpools, fitness center, and a host of beauty and massage treatments. The staff is gracious and hospitable and the atmosphere modern and relaxing. Packages for weeklong or weekend stays are available. ($$$-$$$$). CH-3715 Adelboden. ☎ 33-673-8000, fax 33-673-8001.

Adler Sporthotel is a family-run inn in the heart of Adelboden across from the church, and near the bus station. It's also close to the cable cars and retail shops. The rooms are furnished in rustic pinewood, with all modern amenities, and the Aqua wellness center includes whirlpools, sauna, steam baths, massage and solarium. There is also a special section for children, as well as billiards, darts and Ping-Pong. The in-house restaurant features local and French cuisine in hearty, well-prepared portions. ($$-$$$). Dorfstrasse 19, CH-3715 Adelboden. ☎ 33-673-4141, fax 33-673-4239.

Berghotel Engstligenalp is a large, sprawling chalet that sits on a lovely plateau surrounding by mountains, outside of the village center. It is a three-minute walk to the cable car station Unter-dem-Berg Engstligenalp, and a five-minute walk to the ski lifts. This is a popular spot for cross-country skiers and snowboarders in the winter, and for hikers and mountain climbers in the summer. It's is also a great spot for families traveling with children, as the area around the hotel is open and free from traffic. The hotel offers dorms as well as private rooms. ($-$$$). CH-3715 Adelboden. ☎ 33-673-2291, fax 33-673-4691.

■ Where to Eat

 La Tosca creates Italian specialties in a sophisticated and formal atmosphere. Open from 6-10 pm daily. Closed Wednesday and Thursday. ($$$). Dorfstrasse 7, CH-3715 Adelboden. ☎ 33-673-8383, fax 33-673-8380.

DINING PRICE CHART	
Prices based on a typical entrée, per person, and do not include beverage.	
$	15-25Sfr ($10-$16)
$$	26-45Sfr ($17-$29)
$$$	46-70Sfr ($30-$47)
$$$$	71Sfr+ ($47+)

Pizzeria Bodehüttli Pension has a wonderful panoramic view. It's part of the Bodehüttli Pension, perched on the mountainside. The pizzas and Italian dishes are tasty, as is the traditional Swiss food. ($$). Pets are welcome. Open daily. Closed Monday. Obere Bodenstrasse 6, CH-3715 Adelboden. ☎ 33-673-3700, fax 33-673-3703.

For a truly enjoyable meal in traditional Swiss style, go to **Restaurant Hohliebe-Stübli**, just across from the village on the other side of the valley. Meals are served in a rustic, pine-enhanced setting and casual atmosphere. A great spot for large families with kids and handicapped persons. ($-$$). The portions are hearty and the atmosphere is warm and homey. Hohliebeweg 17, Postfach 225, CH-3715 Adelboden. ☎/fax 33-673-1069.

Kandersteg

This lies at the north entrance to the Lötschberg Tunnel, just eight miles south of Frutigen on the Kanderstegstrasse. This tunnel links Canton Bern to Canton Valais and the Rhône Valley, taking cars through the Lötschenberg in just 15 minutes. You drive your car onto a train, which is open on the sides, with a canopy on the top. The cost is 25Sfr, and you stay inside your car throughout the journey.

In the late 1700s this village was a cattle-trading center and eventually became a tourist resort some 150 years later. The village sits at the foot of the Blümlisalp mountain chain and is spread out over 2½ miles, so it is rarely crowded. You won't find many street names in this village, but there are plenty of directional signs to guide you on your way through the area. The Blümlisalp (at 12,018 feet/3,700 m) and the Doldenhorn (at 11,949 feet/3,600 m) tower over this lovely area and the Oeschinensee is one spot that should not be missed.

The Kandersteg **Tourist Office** is open Monday-Friday from 8 am-noon, 2-6 pm. Hauptstrasse, CH-3718 Kandersteg. ☎ 33-675-8080.

■ Getting Around

This is easily done on foot or bike during the summer months, and in the winter on skis or via snow taxis.

■ Adventures

On Foot

No visit to Kandersteg would be complete without a hike to the **Oeschinensee (Lake Oeschinen)**, at 5,176 feet (1,578 m) above the village on a sunny plateau, surrounded by the peaks of the Blümlisalps. The walk up to the lake can be steep in spots, but not difficult overall and takes from 1½ to 2 hours. There is also a chairlift to the top of the Oeschinen station that costs 12Sfr one-way or 18Sfr round-trip. It is really much better to walk, however.

On Snow

Kandersteg has eight miles of downhill ski runs, and 47 miles of cross-country ski paths that double as hiking trails in the summer. There are eight ski lifts and most of the runs here are suitable for beginners to medium skiers. Rates for ski passes are relatively cheap by Swiss standards. A two-day adult pass is 62Sfr, a five-day pass is 135Sfr and a seven-day pass is 185Sfr. Seniors and children receive discounts depending on their ages and whether they are traveling with other adults or families.

■ Where to Stay & Eat

The Royal Park Hotel has been operated and owned by the Rikli family for over 100 years and is one of the finest hotels in the Bernese Oberland. This four-story hotel has spacious rooms and is lavishly decorated with antiques and Victorian furniture, with modern, completely updated baths. This is a great spot for horseback riding and the hotel stable offers a wide choice of steeds to suit any level of equestrian. But the hotel also requires that you ride in proper attire, so be sure to bring your boots and breeches along. You can also take boat excursions with either a sailing or motorized vessel on nearby Lake Thun. The hotel has tennis courts, a fitness center, two pools, Jacuzzi, bike rental and massage. ($$$$-$$$$+). You'll also find four outstanding restaurants with all types of cuisine, and a romantic bar in the hotel. CH-3718 Kandersteg. In the USA ☎ 1-800-874-4002, otherwise ☎ 33-675-8888, fax 33-675-8880.

Ruedihaus is a lovely little chalet in a quiet meadow just west of the village center. Built in 1753, this tiny inn with only nine rooms has antiques throughout and the beds have handmade quilts and dainty linens. One in-house restaurant, **Käse und Wystuben**, serves an all-Swiss menu that includes fondues, salads, sausages and homemade desserts. The other in-house eatery (**Biedermeier**) is more formal and specializes in meat dishes. There is also a small café on the premises with light fare. ($$-$$$). CH-3718. ☎ 33-675-8181, fax 33-675-8185.

Hotel Victoria-Ritter is a combination of two inns. First built in 1789, the original building was the Ritter Coach House, named after the local Ritter family. In 1912, the larger Victoria House was added on. This is a good hotel for families with children as it offers kindergarten and babysitting services. There are two tennis courts on the grounds as well. ($$). Closed from mid-October to mid-December. CH-3718 Kandersteg. ☎ 33-675-8000, fax 33-675-8100.

The Bernese Oberland: Eastern Region

Interlaken

Interlaken and the Jungfrau Region are in the Bernese Oberland, the southernmost region of Canton Bern. Known as the "capital" of the Bernese Oberland, Interlaken is home to some 15,000 inhabitants, and sits at the foot of the impressive trio of the Eiger, Mönch and Jungfrau mountains, in between the Thun and Brienz lakes. The region around Interlaken is known locally as the "Bodeli," a combination of three political communities: Interlaken, Unterseen and Matten.

■ Information Sources

Tourist Offices

The **Interlaken Tourist Office** is at Postfach 369, Hoheweg 37, CH-3800 Interlaken. It is open from July to mid-September, Monday-Friday from 8 am-6:30 pm, Saturday from 8 am-5 pm, Sunday from 10 am-noon, 5-7 pm. Hours vary at other times of year. ☎ 33-826-5300, fax 33-826-5375. This office will provide you with maps and details of the various hikes available throughout Interlaken and the surrounding area.

Berner Oberland Tourismus is open from 7:30 am-noon, 1-5:30 pm Monday-Friday, on the first floor of Jungfraustrasse 38. CH-3800 Interlaken. ☎ 33-823-0808, fax 33-823-0330. Here you can purchase the **Bernese Oberland Regionalpass**, valid for either seven days (three days of unlimited free travel, four days of travel at 50% reduction) or 15 days (five days of unlimited travel, 10 days at 50% reduction) on all bus, rail, and boat excursions throughout the Bernese Oberland. Good May through October.

Train Stations

There are two train stations in Interlaken. **Interlaken West** offers money exchange (Monday-Sunday from 7 am-8 pm) and bike rental. **Interlaken Ost** (East) has money exchange (Monday-Sunday from 6 am-8 pm). Here you can purchase the Jungfrau Railway Pass, good for travel within the Jungfrau Region, including the Wengen-Mannlichen Aerial Cableway, the Grindelwald-First Mountain Transport Company and the Grindelwald-Mannlichen Aerial

Condola Cableway. This pass allows for unlimited travel on all off these railways for five consecutive days.

Post Office

The Interlaken post office is open Monday-Friday from 7:45 am-noon, 1:30-6:15 pm, Saturday from 8:30 am-noon. Marktgasse 1, CH-3800 Interlaken. ☎ 33-224-8950.

Codes

The **postal code** is CH-3800 and the **area code** is 33.

Internet Access

This is available at **Buddy's Pub Hotel Splendid**, Rosenstrasse, CH-3800 Interlaken, ☎ 33-822-6922, at Hotel Artos, Alpenstrasse 45, CH-3800 Interlaken, ☎ 33-828-8844, or at **Backpackers Villa Sonnenhof**, Alpenstrasse, CH-3800 Interlaken, ☎ 33-826-7171.

Medical Services

Medical services in Interlaken are available at ☎ 33-823-2323 and the regional hospital is at Weissenaustrasse 27.

■ Getting Around

This is easily done on foot or by bike. Driving is very easy here and there are plenty of public parking places, with the streets well-marked. The **Höheweg** is the main street that winds and twists through the city; most major sites can be found on or just off this main thoroughfare.

■ Landmarks & Historic Sites

Interlaken Castle-Church (Schlosskirche) was originally an Augustinian monastery that was founded in 1133, before being used as a private castle in 1745. Today it is used as a business office. You'll find it at the end of the Höhematte, Interlaken's 35-acre public park that sits along the Höheweg.

■ Museums

The Jungfrau Region Museum of Tourism traces the history of tourism throughout the area from 1800 to the present and includes displays of trains, mountaineers and early snow sports. Admission is 5Sfr. Open Tuesday-Sunday, 2-5 pm, May to mid-October. Oberegasse 26, CH-3800 Interlaken. ☎ 33-822-9839.

Jungfraujoch with Sphinx

■ Shopping

Shopping abounds on the Höheweg and near Interlaken West station. You can find all kinds of arts, crafts and Swiss hand-made linens, doilies and handkerchiefs. For the best of all these and more, look to **Boutique Edelweiss** at Höheweg 26 (☎ 33-823-8060) or **Heimatwerk Interlaken** at Höheweg 115 (☎ 33-823-1653). In addition, at both of these spots you can purchase Swiss Army knives, wood carvings, T-shirts and ot

■ Adventures

Interlaken has almost any type of sport for any enthusiast, and both winter and summer activities are available for all ages. Most tourists also come to Interlaken to trek to the southernmost portion of the Bernese Oberland. The area consists of a seemingly endless series of mountains, highlighted by the **Jungfrau** at 13,638 feet (4,158 m), the **Mönch** at 13,445 feet (4,099 m) and the **Eiger** at 13,022 feet (3,970 m).

Harder Kulm is Interlaken's own mountain that sits above the city from the north, sandwiched in between Lakes Thun and Brienz. From this 4,337-foot (1,822-m) mountain top you'll get a bird's-eye view of the

Jungfrau region and marvelous panoramic opportunities. The restaurant on the summit offers visitors folk dancing and music on Friday nights, from June through September. The funicular leaves from near the Interlaken East station, on the north side of the Beaurivage Bridge. A round-trip ticket costs 21Sfr. The train leaves daily from 9:10 am to 6:30 pm every 30 minutes, June through September.

THE TOP OF EUROPE

The Jungfraujoch – known as the "Top of Europe" – summits at 13,638 feet (4,158 m). Adventurers and tourists have been traveling to the top of this mighty peak ever since the **Jungfraubahn** was first placed in service in 1912. Excursions to the top of the Jungfraujoch and the highest railway station in the world (at 11,400 feet/3,476 m) are not to be missed, even if you're scared of heights. There are five modern restaurants at the station and another terrace and observation center, **The Sphinx**, shown above, that you can get to via an elevator. It will whisk you another 364 feet (111 m) skyward. There is also an **Ice Palace** on the station plateau, and a scientific research station. During good weather, you can take skiing lessons and go dog sledding here. You may feel a bit dizzy or lightheaded after you reach the station, but the small kiosk in the reception area offers coffee and chocolates to help you adjust to the altitude.

Trains leave once a day from Interlaken West, stopping at Interlaken East, Wilderswil, Lauterbrunnen, Wengen and the Kleine Scheidegg. The return trip takes you back down to Interlaken via Grindelwald. Cost for a round-trip ticket is 162Sfr, and trains depart daily at 7:45 am, with the last train down from the Jungfraujoch at 6 pm. This is a trip that is a lot of fun no matter what time of year you are visiting, although in the winter you may have to deal with limited visibility. When the weather is clear, the views from the Jungfraujoch cannot be defined with mere words. On clear days you can see as far as Germany and France, and the surrounding scenery is spectacular. Jungfraubahnen, Harderstrasse 14, CH-3800 Interlaken. ☎ 33-828-7233, fax 33-828-7264. For Jungfraujoch weather information, ☎ 33-855-1022.

Other Activities

Beach volleyball takes place at the Thunersee in Interlaken. For information, ☎ 33-822-9330.

Bowling is popular in Interlaken and the surrounding area. It's available at Piz Paz Pizzeria, Bahnhofstrasse 1, CH-3800 Interlaken. ☎/fax 33-822-2533.

The Interlaken Paragliding School offers lessons for would-be gliders at Postfach 455, CH-3800 Interlaken. ☎ 33-822-0428, fax 33-822-0426.

For inline **skating gear**, look to **Action Sport Landolt Ag**, located on Gsteigstrasse 12, CH-3800 Matten-Interlaken. ☎ 33-821-1001, fax 33-821-1002.

Rock climbing is available through **Swiss Alpine Guides**, at Postfach 29, CH-3800 Matten-Interlaken. ☎ 33-823-4100, ☎/fax 33-823-4101.

You can play **tennis** at **Interlaken's Sport Center**, Hoheweg 53, CH-3800 Interlaken. ☎ 33-826-0000, fax 33-826-0001.

Zorbing is available through the **Alpin Center**, in nearby Wilderswil at CH-3812. ☎ 33-823-5523, fax 33-823-5513.

On Water

For rafting trips, as well as bungee jumping, canyoning, climbing, glacier hiking, hydrospeeding, paragliding, mountain biking, moutaineering, skydiving, and mountain trekking, contact **Swissraft** on Jungfraustrasse 72, CH-3800 Interlaken. ☎ 33-823-0210, fax 33-823-0501.

For **fishing** on Lake Thun, contact the Interlaken Tourist Office.

Boat rentals/pedal boats can be had at the **Hang Loose Water Sports Center**, on the Thunersee in Interlaken. ☎ 79-233-5228. They also offer water skiing and wind surfing trips.

Cruises are available on Lake Thun or Lake Brienz through the Interlaken Tourist Office. You can take full- or half-day excursions on one of the many lake steamers available. There are evening cruises available as well. Cruises depart at Interlaken Ost for Lake Brienz or Interlaken West for Lake Thun.

On Wheels

Bikes are available for rent at both Interlaken train stations. At Interlaken West, ☎ 33-826-4748; at Interlaken East, ☎ 33-828-7319.

In the Air

You can enjoy spectacular views from above in either a helicopter or small plane, via either **Scenic Air AG** (☎ 33-826-7717) or **Bohag** (☎ 33-828-9010), both in Interlaken.

COGWHEEL TRAIN TRIPS

 The last stop on the way up to the Jungfraujoch is at the **Kleine Scheidegg**, at 6,762 feet (2,062 m). Here you'll also greet the north wall of the mighty **Eiger**. This is still a busy meeting point today for mountain farms bringing and taking their cattle to Alpine pastures. Also, it is a grand start for many serious hikers and amateur walkers alike. Mountaineers converge here in preparation for their ascent of the Eiger. Another trip not to be missed from Interlaken is to the **Schynige Platte** at 6,445 feet (1,964 m). This is considered by many serious mountain trekkers to be the best vantage point from which to view the Eiger, Mönch and Jungfrau. From here you can take a number of hiking trails suitable for families, kids and seniors. At this wide-open plateau you'll also have access to the **Alpine Botanical Garden**, which features over 500 species of mountain flora, including the coveted Edelweiss. Cogwheel trains run from 7:30 am-6 pm daily for the 50-minute trip from late May to late October. The cost is 56Sfr round-trip or 32Sfr for a one-way ticket. For information on these excursions, contact the Interlaken Tourist Office, or call the Jungfraubahnen at ☎ 33-828-7233.

Grindelwaldblick Hotel on the Kleine Scheidegg, with the Wetterhorn at right

■ Where to Stay

Grand Hotel Beau-Rivage is set in a quiet spot between the Höheweg and the Aare River, close to the Interlaken East train station, and is a landmark in Interlaken. This luxury hotel is a good starting point for all types of excursions and adventures and the rooms are modern and clean, many with terrific views of the Jungfrau and the Aare River. There are two in-house restaurants, a bar, pool and health club. ($$$$). Höheweg 211, CH-3800 Interlaken. In North America, ☎ 1-800-447-7462, otherwise ☎ 33-821-6272, fax 33-823-2847, www.beau-rivage-interlaken.ch.

Victoria-Jungfrau Grand Hotel & Spa has been the pride of Interlaken since 1865, and has been home to guests such as Samuel Clemens (Mark Twain) and the King of Siam. You'll find this magnificent hotel right in the heart of Interlaken, with 216 rooms of various shapes and and sizes. Everything about this place speaks of luxury. ($$$$-$$$$+). Includes two restaurants, two bars, tennis courts, pool, spa, and sauna. Höheweg 41, CH-3800 Interlaken. In North America ☎ 1-800-223-6800, otherwise ☎ 33-828-2828, fax 33-828-2880, www.victoria-jungfrau.ch.

Hotel Chalet-Oberland is located in the heart of the city, featuring 150 rooms – all spacious, clean and modern. A good base for hiking trips, and close to shopping. ($$$). Postgasse 1, CH-3800 Interlaken. ☎ 33-827-8787, fax 33-827-8770.

Hotel Alplodge caters to backpackers and has 20 rooms with 70 beds. All rooms are non-smoking and have wash basins; many have showers and bathrooms in the rooms. There are community showers and toilets on each floor as well. Lockers and Internet access are available in this hotel, and you can rent bed linens here for 2Sfr. ($-$$). Marktgasse 59, CH-3800 Interlaken. ☎ 33-822-4748, fax 33-823-2098.

The Interlaken Youth Hostel is just one mile east of the Interlaken East train station in the suburb of Bönigen and has 150 beds, with all sizes of rooms. It is open year-round and has a wide array of facilities nearby. ($). Aareweg 21, Am See, CH-3806 Bönigen. ☎ 33-822-4353, fax 33-823-3058, www.youthhostel.ch/boenigen.

■ Where to Eat

Il Bellini is in the Metropole Hotel, specializing in Italian and international fare in a formal setting of pink and green pastels. Everything is delicately prepared and served in a quiet, intimate style. Reservations are recommended. The prices are surprisingly reasonable. ($$-$$$$). Open daily from 11:30-2 pm and from 6:30-10 pm. Höheweg 37, CH-3800 Interlaken. ☎ 33-828-6666.

Restaurant-Hotel Bären serves Swiss specialties on their lovely outdoor dining terrace and street café. Open daily from 11:30 am-2 pm, 5:30-

10 pm. Closed October-June. ($$-$$$). Marktgasse 19, CH-3800 Interlaken. ☎ 33-822-7676, fax 33-822-2855.

Aare Café specializes in Swiss dishes served up in hearty portions throughout the summer months, from 8 am-9 pm, Monday-Thursday; Friday and Saturday until 11 pm. ($$). Strandbadstrasse 15, CH-3800 Interlaken. ☎ 33-823-1333, fax 33-823-1337.

Brienz

Directly east of Interlaken is Lake Brienz. At just nine miles long and two miles wide, it is the smaller of the two Oberland bodies of water (the other is Lake Thun). Most Europeans tend to make this their holiday destination of choice, as opposed to the more crowded Thunersee (Lake Thun). The village of Brienz sits at the north end of the lake, across from the **Giessbach Falls** – a spectacular waterfall that can be reached via funicular for 5Sfr for adults and 2.5Sfr for kids. You have to take a boat to reach the funicular, and you'll find this boat at the lakeshore pier in the center of Brienz. The trip takes two to three hours and is worth it. **The Brienz Tourist Office** (CH-3855 Brienz) can provide you with information, schedules and tickets. ☎ 33-952-8080, fax 33-952-8088.

You also might want to visit the **Brienzer Rothorn** at 7,700 feet, which provides you with super views of the Bernese Alps and Lake Brienz. The cogwheel railway trip costs 66Sfr per person and this entire excursion lasts two to three hours. The train runs up to 10 times daily from June to October. Again, look to the Brienz Tourist Office for tickets and times.

Brienzer Rothorn in the Bernese Oberland, accessible via the steam-powered cog railway from Brienz

You can also travel around Lake Brienz on a steamer. There are six ships to accommodate any journey; the most popular is a three-hour trip that takes you from Interlaken East to

Canton Bern

Iseltwald, Giessbach, Brienz and then back to Interlaken East, starting at 30Sfr. This trip is also worth a half-day of your time. ☎ 33-334-5211 for information.

The village of Brienz is famous for woodcarving. If you'd like to try your hand at it, carver Paul Fuchs will teach you how to carve a revered Brienzer cow. You can make a reservation with the Tourist Office or call Fuchs directly at ☎ 33-951-1418. His shop is in Hofstetten, between Brienz and Ballenberg, on Scheidweg 19D. The cost is 22Sfr for a one-hour lesson.

Iseltwald on Brienzersee

Lauterbrunnen

This village is six miles south of Interlaken at 2,612 feet (1,100 m) and is easily accessed from either Interlaken train station. The village offers chalets and large parking areas for visitors traveling to the resort villages of either Wengen to the east or Murren to the south. From here you can grab the trains heading for the Jungfraujoch or the Schilthorn. You'll find the hotel rates a bit cheaper in Lauterbrunnen than in other nearby resort villages, and this is a good base for walking trips.

There are many spectacular waterfalls throughout the length of the Lauterbrunnen Valley, including the **Staubbachfälle (Staubbach Falls)** and the **Trümmelbachfälle (Trümmelbach Falls)**. The former are lighted at night and make for a grand sight, while the latter are found inside the Jungfrau Mountain itself – a result of glacier waters from the higher peaks of the Jungfrau. They can be accessed by an underground train. These spots are easily reached from the village, and the paths and walkways are clearly marked to bring you to the falls. Entrance to the underground falls costs 10Sfr. You can visit them from April-June and from September to November, daily, 9 am-5 pm, during July and August, 8 am-6 pm. Closed December-March. ☎ 33-855-3232.

■ Where to Stay

If you want to stay overnight in Lauterbrunnen, look to the **Hotel Silberhorn**, a family-owned and operated inn, next to the cogwheel railway that takes you to Mürren. This rustic inn is set in a garden, with 30 pine-paneled rooms and a lovely sun terrace. The casual in-house restaurant serves Swiss favorites such as fondue, raclette and rösti. ($$). CH-3822 Lauterbrunnen. ☎ 33-855-1471, fax 33-855-4213, www.silberhorn.com.

Mürren

Mürren is seven miles south of Lauterbrunnen in a sunny spot atop the Lauterbrunnen valley at 5,361 feet (2,252 m). It is easily reached from both Interlaken train stations, and is the main stop on the way to the Schilthorn and Piz Gloria. It serves as a good base for many hiking excursions and doubles as a ski resort in the winter. From Interlaken you can take the one-hour train ride to Lauterbrunnen, and then grab the cogwheel train up to Mürren. This is an auto-free village, and can be reached only via the cogwheel train. Besides skiing and hiking, most tourists visit Mürren to take the cable-car ride up to the **Schilthorn**, a mountain made famous in the James Bond flick *On Her Majesty's Secret Service*. There are no streets in Mürren, but there are plenty of directional signs everywhere to help you find your way. Things can get a bit pricey here, since all supplies and materials have to be hauled up by a cable car or helicopter.

The **Tourist Office** is in the Sportzentrum, found in the middle of the village, and is open Monday-Friday from 9 am-noon, 2-6:30 pm and on the weekends from 2-6:30 pm. ☎ 33-856-8686.

■ Adventures

Often overlooked by tourists is Mürren's own **Mürren-Allmendhubel Cableway**. You'll find the station at the northern edge of the village, and for only 14Sfr the cable will whisk you up to the Allmendhubel at 5,723 feet (1,745 m). This is a delightful spot in the summer, when the area is covered with wild Alpine flowers over the green, hilly plateau. You can stroll throughout the area, have a picnic or dine in the restaurant here.

re grand, and on a sunny day you will have a panoramic view
terbrunnen Valley and the surrounding Alps. The cable car
from 8 am-5 pm. ☎ 33-823-1444.

zentrum has facilities for tennis, squash, curling, swimming,
ice skating and hockey. There is also a playground, snack bar and lounge
on the premises. It is open Monday-Friday from 9 am-noon, 2-6 pm and on
the weekends from 2-6 pm. It shares the same phone number as the Tourist Office. You'll find dozens of downhill ski runs throughout the area and
a 7½-mile cross-country track, accessed by railway from Mürren. Ski
passes range from 52Sfr for a one-day pass to 236Sfr for a seven-day pass.

The Schilthorn

At 9,742 feet (4,093 m), this is the major attraction of this area. From
Lauterbrunnen you can take a rack railway to the Schilthornbahn base
station at Stechelberg, next to the gorgeous **Mürrenbachfalle
(Mürrenbach Falls)** in the valley just south of Mürren. You can also
take the Lauterbrunnen-Mürren funicular and railway to Mürren, via
Grutschlp and Winteregg, before grabbing the Schilthornbahn. Murren is
actually the second stop the Schilthornbahn makes on its four-stop journey (the first stop from the Schilthornbahn base station is at
Gimmelwald, the third is at Birg, and the fourth is the Schilthorn summit). The top station features a unique revolving restaurant, known as
Piz Gloria, which allows fantastic 360-degree panoramic views of the
surrounding Alps. Be sure to allow time for a meal in this unique restaurant – the selections change with the seasons, and the salads are crisp

*The Schilthorn with the revolving restaurant Piz Gloria and in the background
the Eiger, Moench, Jungfrau and Gletscherhorn*

and fresh. And if you are an ice cream lover, be sure to order the "007" dessert – five scoops of various types of ice cream smothered with fresh fruits. (\$-\$\$). ☎ 33-856-2140. There is also a trendy pub – the **James Bond Bar** – at the summit. It was here that scenes from the movie *On Her Majesty's Secret Service* were filmed. The round-trip cost from the Shilthornbahn base station at Stechelberg costs 87Sfr per person during the summer months, with reduced rates in the winter season, while the round-trip cost from Mürren is 60Sfr. ☎ 33-856-2141. You can also make your reservations in Interlaken at Schilthornbahn AG, Höheweg 2, CH-3800 Interlaken. ☎ 33-823-1444, fax 33-823-2449, www.schilthorn.ch.

> *Be sure to check the weather forecast for the summit if you're visiting the Schilthorn in the winter, as snow conditions can put a big damper on your journey. You may ascend to the top on a seemingly clear winter day, only to have a severe snowstorm interrupt your meal in the Piz Gloria, and force a quick return trip back down the mountain.*

■ Where to Stay & Eat

The Hotel Eiger is one of the oldest chalets in Mürren, having been built in the 1920s, and the atmosphere throughout is warm and cheery, with great views from most of the rooms. This place reeks of traditional Alpine hospitality, and is just across the street from the Lauterbrunnen cable car station. Rates include breakfast. (\$\$\$-\$\$\$\$). Many modern amenities throughout, including a pool, sauna, bar and fitness center. The in-house restaurant – the **Eigerstübli** – is the best in Mürren, serving the finest in traditional Swiss favorites. The desserts are especially delightful, and reservations are highly recommended. (\$\$-\$\$\$\$). Open daily from 11:30 am-2 pm, 6-9 pm. The restaurant is closed from Easter to mid-June and from mid-September to mid-December. The Hotel Eiger, CH-3825 Mürren. ☎ 33-856-5454, fax 33-856-5456, www.muerren.ch/eiger.

The Bellevue-Crystal is a typical Alpine ski chalet, catering to skiers and snow enthusiasts. All of the 17 pine-paneled rooms have small balconies and modern bathrooms. (\$\$-\$\$\$). The in-house restaurant is warm and friendly, and specializes in good hot dishes during the winter months. Closed from Easter to early June. CH-3825 Mürren. ☎ 33-855-1401, fax 33-855-1490, www.muerren.ch/bellevue.

Hotel Blumental is another traditional Swiss chalet, in the heart of the village, with very reasonable rates for this area. (\$\$). The 16 rooms are attractive, with wood paneling and tidy bathrooms, and some have private balconies. During the summer months you can enjoy your breakfast or supper on the outside dining terrace. Rates include breakfast. CH-3825 Mürren. ☎ 33-855-3638.

Wengen

Wengen sits at 4,180 feet (1,274 m), three miles (4.8 km) northeast of Murren, 16 miles south of Interlaken, a 30-minute train ride from Lauterbrunnen, via cog railway. It is known for its superb hiking trails and peaceful surroundings, with the Eiger, Monch and Jungfrau sheltering this auto-free village. To get here, take the Interlaken East train to Wengen for 12Sfr. Trains depart every 45 minutes from 6:30 am to 11:30 pm daily. There are few street names here, and you'll find the **Tourist Office** in the center of the village. It is open Monday-Friday, from 9 am-noon, 2-5 pm, and on Saturday from 8:30-11:30 am.

Wengen is well known for its skiing pistes, 155 miles (250 km) of downhill runs and seven miles of cross-country trails, which you'll find throughout the area and on the many plateaus and ridges of the Mannlichen, Kleine Scheidegg and Eigergletscher. Ski passes start at 52Sfr for a day pass up to 278Sfr for a seven-day pass. There are endless well-marked hiking trails here as well, allowing even amateurs a chance to hike through some of the Bernese Oberland's most spectacular scenery.

■ Adventures

On Foot

 One of the classic hikes here is from Wengen to the Kleine Scheidegg, a relatively easy 2½-hour journey. The path starts in Wengen, not far from the Tourist Office on a well-marked path, and takes you along the terrace at the base of the Männlichen, before leading you through some forests and Alpine meadows. The trail leads gently upwards to the Wengernalp and to the slopes of the Lauberhorn and the Kleine Scheidegg. From here, it's an easy walk to the Männlichen plateau or to the Eiger Glacier, and the scenery is breathtaking.

A Cable Ride

 No trip to Wengen would be complete without a ride on the **Luftseilbah Wengen-Männlichen** (LWM) aerial cableway, which takes visitors to the top of the Männlichen at 7,317 feet (2,230 m). This gorgeous spot is renowned as one of the best panoramic sun terraces of the Jungfrau region as it rises between the Lauterbrunnen and Lütschen valleys. From here, there are endless hiking possibilities and during the winter months the area between the Männlichen and the Kleine Scheidegg is a haven for skiers and snowboarders. LWM, CH-3823 Wengen. ☎ 33-855-2933, fax 33-855-3510. The Tourist Office in Wengen can provide you with an excellent hiking map, which outlines 22 hikes of varying difficulties from one hour up to 3½ hours.

■ Where to Stay & Eat

 Hotel Silberhorn is a luxury hotel with 61 pine-paneled, immaculate rooms. The bathrooms all have heated floors to warm cold toes on frosty winter nights. Be sure to ask for a room in the old wing of the building, as these rooms are more charming and rustic. There are two outstanding in-house restaurants – one is a formal dining room, the other, a casual eatery. ($$$-$$$$). CH-3823 Wengen. ☎ 33-856-5131, fax 33-855-2244, www.silberhorn.ch.

Hotel Eiger is just behind the train station but is surprisingly quiet. The 33 rooms are clean, spacious and all come with balconies. ($$$-$$$$). The in-house restaurant – **The Arvenstube** – is one of the best in Wengen and presents Bernese favorites such as veal, beef and mushrooms and various types of fondues. ($$-$$$). Open daily from 11 am-2 pm, 6-9 pm (closed May only). In North America ☎ 1-800-528-1234, otherwise ☎ 33-856-0505, fax 33-855-1030, www.eigerhotel.ch.

Grindelwald

Grindelwald lies 14 miles (23 km) south of Interlaken at 3,445 feet (1,050 m) and is a popular summer and winter resort – sandwiched in between the north face of the Eiger and the less-imposing Wetterhorn. It is the only major village that can be reached by car, and thus is often more crowded than some of its surrounding, auto-free neighbors. This "glacier village" has every level of walk or sport for almost anyone, and most places are handicapped-accessible.

The **Grindelwald Tourist Office** is in the center of the village, just north of the train station on the main promenade. CH-3818 Grindelwald. ☎ 33-854-1212, fax 33-854-1210. Ask for a free visitor's card, which offers many reductions for hotel services, restaurants, shops, trains and ski passes. The office is closed from mid-September to mid-October; times vary during the rest of the year, so call first. www.grindelwald.ch.

Guided tours of Grindelwald are available through the Tourist Office every Wednesday from late June until mid-September and are free of charge with a visitor's card or 20Sfr without one. There is a short tour from 10 am-noon and a longer tour from 1:30-4:30 pm. You need to book a reservation one day in advance by calling ☎ 33-854-1212.

Other tours available through the Tourist Office include an Alpine Wildlife Excursion to the Grosse Scheidegg, and a trip to an Alpine dairy farm.

You can also purchase a regional Berner Oberland Pass that is good for excursions by train, boat, bus and cable car in the entire region. A seven-day pass costs 195Sfr and a 15-day pass costs 240Sfr. Available at the Tourist Office.

The Grindelwald **post office** is next to the train station and is open from 8 am-noon, 1:45-6 pm, Monday-Friday. Saturday it is open from 8-11 am. Beim Bahnhof, CH-3818 Grindelwald. ☎ 33-853-1306, fax 33-853-1601.

■ Getting Around

This is easy on foot, bike or by car. If you are driving from Interlaken, travel south on the Wilderswil secondary road to Grindelwald. There are signs everywhere leading you to this village.

■ Adventures

Summer Sports

The Grindelwald Sportzentrum offers a variety of activities for all members of the family. The complex has an indoor pool with a sunbathing area and a children's wading pool and includes a sauna, solarium, steam-bath and outdoor terrace, as well as badminton, table tennis and a fitness room. Ice hockey in both the summer and winter is possible, as well as curling and ice skating. There is also a game room, Internet café, and restaurant on the premises. Hauptstrasse, CH-3818 Grindelwald. ☎ 33-854-1230, fax 33-854-1238.

GLACIER GORGE

A fun hike from Grindelwald is to visit the Glacier Gorge, only 35 minutes from the village center. There is a 6Sfr per adult entry fee onto the wooden walkway that leads you around and through this spectacular natural wonder of gushing waters and close rock walls that face one another at slanted angles. Follow the signs from Grindelwald. The walkway is open from mid-May to early July, 10 am-5 pm; from mid-July to late August, 9 am-6 pm; and from late August to mid-October, 10 am-5 pm. After visiting the Gorge, you can dine at the nearby **Hotel-Restaurant Gletscherschlucht**, or stay overnight if you choose. This is a family-owned and -operated inn that is open daily until midnight. ($-$$). ☎ 33-853-6050, fax 33-853-6051.

Grindelwald Sports provides lessons and excursions at various price ranges for a number of adventure and traditional sports, including mountaineering, glacier hiking, rock climbing, and canyoning. CH-3818 Grindelwald. ☎ 33-854-1290, fax 33-854-1295.

Paragliding trips and lessons are available at **Paragliding Grindelwald**. Prices start at 160Sfr for tandem flights. ☎ 79-779-9000, fax 33-853-4788, www.paragliding-grindelwald.ch.

Helicopter rides are available for 180Sfr per person per 20 minutes through **Air-Glaciers SA**. They take you from Grindelwald to Lauterbrunnen and back. CH-3822 Lauterbrunnen. ☎ 33-856-0560.

Mountain biking excursions are available through the Tourist Office at ☎ 33-854-1212. The cost is 71Sfr and the trip takes you round-trip from Grindelwald to First and Bort.

Winter Sports

The **Grindelwald Ski and Mountain Sports School** offers ski and snowboarding lessons for all levels and ages. Schweizer Schnee und Bergsportschule, CH-3818 Grindelwald. ☎ 33-854-1280, fax 33-854-1295.

For private snowboarding and ski lessons, go to the **Swiss Snowboard School** (SSBS), Buri Sport Grindelwald, CH-3818. ☎ 33-853-3353.

MOUNTAIN TRIPS FROM GRINDELWALD

A popular trip from Grindelwald is to take the bubble car gondola to the First Mountain, at 7,113 feet (2,169 m). You'll stop at the two tiny villages of Bort and Grindd along the way, before reaching the plateau at First, where the **Bergrestaurant** (Mountain Restaurant) has a large menu of international fare in a casual setting. There are many walks in the First region, with over 60 miles of trails that are also suitable for handicapped persons. Bergbhanen Grindelwald-First AG, Postfach 11, CH-3818 Grindelwald. ☎ 33-854-5050, fax 33-854-5035.

Another excursion from Grindelwald is to visit the **Grosse Scheidegg** at 6,434 feet (1,962 m). This pass is reachable via foot (three hours) or by bus (50 minutes) and, again, you'll find numerous walks here. In fact, it is a fun trip to take the bus up and walk back to Grindelwald. **Grindelwald Bus**, CH-3818 Grindelwald. ☎ 33-854-1616, fax 33-854-1610.

You can also take the **Grindelwald-Männlichen Gondola Cableway** (GGM) up to the Männlichen. This is the longest gondola cableway in Europe, stretching nearly five miles in the sky from Grindelwald to the mighty Männlichen. GGM, CH-3818 Grindelwald. ☎ 33-854-8080, fax 33-854-8088.

■ Where to Stay

Hotel Kreuz & Post is in the main square of the village and features rustic furnishings and 18th-century antiques in a contemporary atmosphere. Balconies are included with most of the rooms, which provide spectacular views of the surrounding mountains. ($$$-$$$$). This is a first-class operation on all levels. CH-3818 Grindelwald. ☎ 33-854-5492, fax 33-854-5499, www.grindelwald.ch/kreuz-post.

HOTEL PRICE CHART	
$	30-75Sfr ($20-$49)
$$	76-205Sfr ($50-$109)
$$$	206-299Sfr ($110-$200)
$$$$	300Sfr+ ($200+)

Jungfrau-Lodge Swiss Mountain Hotel. This combination of two hotels was first built in 1903 (the Jungfrau) and 1972 (the Crystal) and are across the street from one another. Only three minutes from the train station, both feature immaculate, comfy rooms and pleasant sun terraces. ($-$$$). CH-3818 Grindelwald. ☎ 33-854-4141, fax 33-854-4142, www.jungfraulodge.ch.

Hotel Restaurant Steinbock was originally a pub that dates back to 1798, before becoming a hotel in the following century. It was completely renovated in 1992 by the Ponzio family – who are famous throughout Switzerland for their pizza. Rates include breakfast. This hotel is very close to the main ski lift of the village, and this is also a good base for many walking excursions. The ski bus stop for the Klein Scheidegg/Mannlichen is located right beside this lodge. ($$-$$$). The attached **Gruppa Bar** offers up a wide array of tasty hot and cold drinks. Dorfstrasse, CH-3818 Grindelwald. ☎ 33-853-8989, fax 33-853-8998, www.steinbock-grindelwald.ch.

Hotel Alpenhof is at the base of the ski runs. This charming chalet features a fine in-house eatery specializing in fresh vegetables grown nearby as well as traditional Swiss favorites. There are some great views of the Alps from this locale. ($$-$$$). CH-3818 Grindelwald. ☎ 36-853-5270.

The Oberland Inn is a charming little Swiss chalet that offers spacious apartments for one to four people. Located between the train and bus stations and the sports center. Parking available in the back. ($$-$$$). CH-3818 Grindelwald. ☎ 33-853-1019.

Stalden Inn is ideal for families with children. Family-owned and -run, this Swiss chalet is only five minutes from the village center and serves up hearty Swiss fare at its in-house restaurant. This is a good base for hiking, walking and skiing excursions. ($$-$$$). CH-3818 Grindelwald. ☎ 33-853-1112, fax 33-853-31101.

The Bellevue Bed & Breakfast is in the heart of Grindelwald and offers rustic and clean accommodations at very reasonable rates. ($$). Tuftli, CH-3818 Grindelwald. ☎ 33-853-1234, fax 33-853-1143.

The Grindelwald Youth Hostel offers 125 beds, and is just a little over half a mile from the village center, just north of the post office and train station. Open year-round, except from November 1 to December 13. ($-$$). Weid 12, Terrassenweg, CH-3818 Grindelwald. ☎ 33-853-1009, fax 33-853-5029, www.youthhostel.ch/grindelwald.

Camping

This is available at the **Eigernordwand Campground**, in a quiet and sunny spot at the foot of the north face of the Eiger, only four minutes from Grindelwald's city center, and only a five-minute walk to the base stations of Grund, Kleine Scheidegg, Jungrfraujoch and Männlichen. ($). Close to all major ski lifts. CH-3818 Grindelwald. ☎ 33-853-1242, fax 33-853-5042, www.eigernordwand.ch.

Camping is also available just outside of Grindelwald at **Camping Gletscherdorf**. Hosts Daniel and Ursula Harder offer seasonal and free plots from May 1-October 20; the rest of the year is reserved for members only. The campgrounds are in a quiet spot down from the Eiger, and feature hot water and showers for free, washers and dryers, a convenience store and camper station. Close to nearby activities and many foot and hiking paths. Dogs or pets of any kind are not allowed. ($). CH-3818 Grindelwald. ☎ 33-853-1429, fax 33-853-3129.

Sleeping in the straw is available at the charming home of the Wyss family farm. Located underneath the north face of the Eiger, and only three miles (4.8 km) from Grindelwald in a beautiful location close to many walking and hiking paths. The family will pick you up at the train station if you call ahead, and can accommodate up to 15 individuals or 30 people in a group. Just bring your sleeping back and be prepared for a wonderful experience, anytime from the middle of June until the end of September. Reservations strongly suggested. Hagibodmen, Wärgistal, CH-3818 Grindelwald. ☎ 33-853-3739.

Mountain Huts

If it's mountain huts you desire, then look no further than Grindelwald and the surrounding region. There are five in this area alone worth checking out.

The **Waldspitzhütte** is a recently renovated hut and restaurant in the middle of the First hiking area. It is a 2½-hour hike from Grindelwald or a one-hour walk from the First station. Breakfast is included in the rates. ($). CH-3818 Grindelwald. ☎ 33-853-1861.

The **Glecksteinhütte** is a large stone hut located on the sunny terrace of the upper Grindelwald glacier. ($). CH-3818 Grindelwald. ☎ 33-853-1140, fax 33-853-2569.

The **Stieregg** is a cozy mountain restaurant and hut that offers 10 dorm rooms and good views of the Alps. Prices ($) include breakfast and dinner is available upon request. An easy one-hour walk from the Pfingstegg. CH-3818 Grindelwald. ☎ 33-853-1766.

An easy 45-minute walk from the Jungfraujoch, the **Mönchjochhütte** is a good base for mountaineering and skiing excursions throughout the region of the Mönch, Eiger and Jungfrau. CH-3816 Lütschental. ☎ 33-971-3472, fax 33-853-6235.

The clean and functional **Männdlenen-Weberhütte** is a 3½-hour hike from First station, and a 2½-hour hike from the Schynige Platte. This hut offers a combination dinner and overnight stay with a night-time meal of raclettes and potatoes, and a hearty breakfast. ($-$$). CH-3815 Zweilütschinen. ☎ 33-853-4464.

The Grindelwald Tourist office can provide you with maps to and from the huts. If you want to see some outstanding scenery, and don't mind sparse accommodations, then staying in a mountain hut is definitely worth a try.

■ Where to Eat

Restaurant Francais, in the Hotel Belvedere, offers live piano music nightly and is considered one of the finest dining spots in Grindelwald. Lamb, fish and fowl dishes are the specialties, and there is also a spectacular buffet and a lengthy international wine list. ($$-$$$). Open daily from noon to 2 pm, 6:45 to 9 pm. CH-3818 Grindelwald. ☎ 33-854-5757.

DINING PRICE CHART	
Prices based on a typical entrée, per person, and do not include beverage.	
$	15-25Sfr ($10-$16)
$$	26-45Sfr ($17-$29)
$$$	46-70Sfr ($30-$47)
$$$$	71Sfr+ ($47+)

Sportzentrum Restaurant features an outdoor-like dining area, complete with natural trees set into the floor and located in the sports center at the heart of this resort village. From the restaurant, you'll have a good view of the ice hockey rink and the indoor swimming pool. Light dishes and snacks are served, as well as traditional Swiss fare, such as cheese fondue and wiener schnitzel. ($-$$). Open daily from 7:30 am to 11:30 pm. CH-3818 Grindelwald. ☎ 33-853-3277.

Memory is a family-style eatery in the Eiger Hotel, well known for its potato and cheese dishes. There are seven different types of rösti served here, as well as a delicious potato and meat garlic soup. ($$). CH-3818 Grindelwald. ☎ 33-854-3131.

Oinkel Tom's Hütte is set across from the Firstbahn in a country A-frame cabin. The owner creates his own fresh pizzas with a large iron baking oven for all in the restaurant to see. The large salads and homemade desserts are outstanding, and this unique pizzeria also features a surprisingly large international wine list. ($-$$). CH-3818 Grindelwald. ☎ 33-853-5239.

Meiringen

The is a small village of Meiringen was the backdrop for Sherlock Holmes' final excursion at the Reichenbach Falls in the story *The Final Problem*. A great hiking base, it sits at the junction of three Swiss passes – the Grimsel, Susten and Brunig – in the Häsli Valley. The village is eight miles east of Brienz on Highway 8, alongside the Aare River. It is reknowned for its meringue dessert, which was supposedly invented in this village. You'll find over 185 miles (298 km) of marked hiking trails and walking paths here and 37 miles (60 km) of downhill ski slopes

The **Meiringen Tourist Office** is in the center of town, across from the train station and is open Monday-Friday, from September-June, 8 am-noon, 2-6 pm, Saturday from 8 am-noon. In July and August the office is open Monday-Friday from 8 am-6 p.m, Saturday from 8 am-noon, 4-6 pm. ☎ 33-972-5050, fax 33-972-5055, www.meiringenhasliberg.ch.

■ Adventures

The **Reichenbach Falls** are one of the main reasons to visit Meiringen, especially if you're not into meringue. These falls are the point at which the rivers of the Rosenlaui Valley join, and they can be reached by a funicular that leaves every 10 minutes daily from mid-May to mid-September, 8:15-11:45 am and from 1-6 pm. The funicular takes you up 2,779 feet (1,168 m) above the falls and provides outstanding views along railed terraces. The cost is 7Sfr for adults and 3.5Sfr for children. For more information, ☎ 33-971-4048.

In Sir Arthur Conan-Doyle's The Final Problem, *detective Sherlock Holmes and his arch-enemy Professor Moriarty both plunged into the swirling waters of the Reichenbach Falls.*

The **Aare Gorge** is another natural wonder close to Meiringen. The Aare River has made this gorge into a work of art by sculpting it with its harsh waters over the centuries. To get there, take the Grimsel-Susten road and follow the signs. The gorge is open daily from May to October, 10 am-5 pm, and in July and August from 8 am-6 pm. Cost is 6Sfr for adults and 3.5Sfr for children.

A popular hike is to walk the 15 miles (24 km) from Meiringen to Grindelwald, which can take anywhere from six to 10 hours, depending on how fast you walk. The Tourist Office can provide you with maps, and advise you on weather conditions in the winter months.

The Three Passes (Grimsel, Furka & Susten)

To visit these three major passes of the Bernese Oberland, you can use Meiringen as a base village. The **Grimsel Pass**, at 7,103 feet (2,984 m) is south of Meiringen on Highway 6, just before you get to the village of Gletsch. From this pass you can view the Galenstock mountain summit, the lovely Grimselsee (Lake Grimsel) and the Rhone Glacier. When you reach Gletsch, if you then travel east on Road 19, via foot or auto, you will pass over the **Furka Pass** at 7,975 feet (3,350 m), toward the village of Andermatt. You can stop at the **Hôtel Furkablick** (☎ 41-887-0499) to get views of the mighty Galenstock up-close from this vantage point, or enjoy an overnight stay or hearty meal in the restaurant. The Furka Pass is the highest point on the shelf of Alpine ridges that separate the cantons of Bern, Valais and Graubünden. The **Susten Pass** is due east of Meiringen on Road 11 and reaches its highest point of 7,411 feet (3,114 m) above the quarter-mile tunnel on the pass (which is at 7,296 feet/3,065 m). It is easy to walk to the top of the pass, as there is a car park at the west end of the tunnel, or you can drive through it, but you'll miss the spectacular views from the top of the pass. There are massive glacier deposits to be seen here and grand views of the Bernese Alps.

■ Museums

If you're a big Sherlock Holmes fan, you can visit the **Sherlock Holmes Museum** in Meiringen, located in the center of the village. You'll find a replica of Holmes' living room at 221B Baker Street. Admission is 3.8Sfr. Open May-September, Tuesday through Sunday from 1:30-6 pm; October through April, Wednesday-Sunday from 4:30-6:30 pm. Bahnhofstrasse 26, CH-3658 Meiringen. ☎ 33-971-4221.

■ Where to Stay & Eat

 Wellness und Spa-Hotel Beatus is an outdoor adventure spa that features a variety of treatments and amenities, including an indoor pool, sauna, salon, massage, solarium, rowboats, pedal boats, water skiing, golf and hiking excursions. The hotel is just 15 minutes from Interlaken and Thun. ($$$$). CH-3658 Meiringen. ☎ 33-252-8181, fax 33-251-3676, www.beatus.ch.

Hotel Victoria Meiringen is relatively new (built in 1999), only two minutes from the village center, train station and bus station. Rooms are modern, tidy and cheery. You'll also find a solarium, children's playground, underground parking, in-house doctor, florist and baby-sitting service. Small pets are permitted. ($$$-$$$$). Bahnhofplatz 9, CH-3860 Meiringen. ☎ 33-966-3400.

Hotel Meiringen is an elegant small hotel that offers modern rooms with a family-like atmosphere. Close to all sports and adventures, including hiking, climbing, biking, tennis, paragliding, skiing, and snowboarding. Features an indoor and outdoor swimming pool, as well as tennis courts. ($$-$$$). The in-house restaurant, **Bahnhöfli**, serves up international fare at reasonable rates. CH-3860 Meiringen. ☎ 33-972-1212, fax 33-972-1219.

Alpine Sherpa Hotel has 60 clean and cheery rooms. The hotel also features a giant stone fireplace, a sauna, solarium, whirlpool and a large roof-top terrace. This family-owned and -operated inn has a beautiful and unique façade, and also includes two restaurants, a "Sherpa" bar, and a disco. Breakfast is included in the rates. ($$-$$$). Bahnhofstrasse 3, CH-3860 Meiringen. ☎ 33-972-5252, fax 33-972-5200.

Sporthotel Sherlock Holmes is a three-star hotel with a warm atmosphere and a gracious staff. It caters to backpackers, hikers, skiers and families. Nearly all of the 55 rooms in this unpretentious hotel look over the Reichenbach Falls. There is an indoor pool on the top floor of this inn. You'll find an in-house restaurant, a health club, sauna, billiards, table tennis and a bar. The rooms are clean and bright. Packages are available that include ski lift tickets, a four-course dinner and access to the swimming pool and sauna, starting at Sfr138. ($$). Rates include breakfast. Alpbachallee 3, CH-3860 Meiringen. ☎ 33-972-9889, fax 33-972-9888.

The Susten Pass, in the Gadmertal

*The Escaliers du Marché in Lausanne lead from the Palud Place
up to the cathedral of Notre-Dame*

Lake Geneva & Western Switzerland

This area is made up of cantons **Neuchâtel**, **Fribourg**, **Vaud** and **Geneva**, and is in the far-southwestern corner of Switzerland. It includes the lakes of Geneva and Neuchâtel and is home to some of the most impressive vineyards found anywhere in Europe. If you've flown into Geneva, then you'll find that this international city is a great base from which to begin your travels. Lake Geneva, shaped like a cucumber, is easily distinguished by its high-shooting Jet d'Eau fountain and the stately hotels amassed along its

Western Switzerland

lakeshore. The French call Switzerland's largest body of water Lac Léman, and you can catch any number of ships sailing over to France and the many little lakeside villages that dot the shoreline there.

From Geneva, you can drive along Lake Geneva north on Highway 1 to the lakeside town of Lausanne and then continue north on the same highway until you reach Yverdon-les-Bains, before exploring the rest of the French-speaking canton of Neuchâtel. Otherwise, you can travel north and then east along the perimeter of Lake Geneva, stopping in Vevey for a day or two. If you're traveling from Bern, it's an easy trip south on Highway 12 to the city of Fribourg, before journeying farther south to Vevey.

Canton Geneva (GE)

■ At a Glance

There are 425,400 people in the canton of Geneva (also known as Genève or Genf), making it the sixth largest canton in terms of population. However, only five other cantons are smaller than Geneva in terms of actual land mass – as this canton encompasses just 109 square miles (283 square km). Most of the locals speak French, and the majority of residents are Protestant. Also, nearly 40% of the

Lake Geneva & Western Switzerland

2 MILES

3.2 KM

N

FRANCE

Biel/Bienne
La Chaux-de-Fonds
Le Locle
Cernier
La Sagne
Valangin
Les Ponts de-Martel
Coffrane
Travers
Boudry
Colombier
Neuchâtel
Môtiers
Ste Croix
Lake Neuchâtel
Avenches
Yverdon-les-Bains
Payerne
Vallorbe
Fribourg
La Sarraz
Châtel-St-Denis
Bulle
Lausanne
Gruyères
Broc
Morges
Corsier-sur-Vevey
Lake Geneva
Vevey
Montreux
Château d'Oex
Nyon
See Geneva Map
Aigle
Les Diablerets
Geneva

© 2004 HUNTER PUBLISHING, INC.

1. Montreux Jazz Festival; Château de Chillon
2. Food Museum; Historical Museum of Vevey; Musée Suisse du Jeu (Museum of Games)
3. International Museum of Wine Labels; Museum of Viticulture & Wine
4. Artisan & Folklore Museum of the Old Highlands; Le Châlet
5. Castle of Morges and Vaud Military Museum
6. Musée Suisse du Cheval
7. stalagmite and stalactite caves; underground military fort; Iron & Railway Museum
8. Centre International de Méchanique d'Art
9. Centre Thermal; Pestalozzi Château; Science Fiction Museum; Modemuseum (Museum of Clothing)
10. Abbey Church
11. Aventicum (Roman city remains) and Roman Museum; Institut Equestre National Avenches
12. Hotel DuPeyrou; Collegial Church; Les Halles Square; Château; Tour des Prisons;

Château du Vaumarcus; Neuchâtel Museum of Art & History; Museum of Ethnography; Natural History Museum of Neuchâtel; Dürrenmatt Center; Botanical Garden; Jardin de Senteurs; Latenium museum; Le Landeron medieval village
13. Military and Painted Fabric Museum
14. Château & Museum at Valangin
15. Agricultural Museum
16. Museum of Firemen; Farming Professions Park
17. Tour de Pierre (Stone Tower); Areuse Museum; Musée de la Vigne et du Vin
18. Musée International d'Horlogerie
19. St. Nicholas's Cathedral; Eglise des Cordeliers; Town Hall; Fribourg Museum of Art & History; Fri-Art Fribourg; Gutenberg Museum; Fribourg Brewery & Beer Museum; Museum of Natural History; Swiss Museum of Sewing Machines; Fribourg Museum of Puppets
20. La Maison de Gruyères cheese factory

residents of this canton are foreigners – the largest number in any one canton within Switzerland – making Geneva and its capital city a land of international sophistication and a grand mixture of cultures.

Located in the Rhône Valley between the Jura mountains and the Alps, Geneva is situated at the southwestern edge of Lake Geneva or Lac Leman – as it is commonly referred to in French. The focus of this canton centers around the capital city of the same name, which is one of the largest European centers of tourism. The canton itself joined the Swiss federation in 1815 and at the time was one of the major banking centers in Europe, a title it still holds today.

Geneva has a long and storied history – beginning with Julius Caesar's visit in 58 BC and leading up to the forming of the League of Nations in 1919. The canton also was home to Jean Henri Dunant, famed for founding the International Red Cross in 1864. Over the years it has been a haven for writers and artists, including such notables as Mary Shelley, Richard Wagner, Franz Liszt, Victor Hugo, Alexandre Dumas and Lord Byron.

This is also one of Switzerland's major (third-largest) wine-growing regions – home to 3,700 acres (1,500 hectares) of vineyards. In the small village of Satigny, you'll find the largest wine-growing community in Switzerland. The countryside surrounding Geneva is full of rich, fertile soil that is near-perfect for grape growing. This countryside also is home to forests, small streams and rivers – making it ideal for bicycle outings, horseback riding, or romantic walks.

The **coat of arms** for Canton Genève is comprised of a split shield with a gold key on a red background on the right-hand side, and half a black eagle against a gold background on the left side. The eagle and the key both represent Geneva's status prior to the Reformation. The half-eagle represents Geneva as half-imperial, while the key symbol shows this land was a bishopric.

Geneva

This is Switzerland's second largest city (behind Zürich), with 178,900 residents, and is heavily influenced by its French neighbors to the west and south. Here you'll find the quintessence or haute école of everything Switzerland stands for in the new century: beauty, wealth, education, international relations and culture, not to mention romantic scenery at its finest. Geneva is easily reached by train or car, and is the home to Switzerland's second major airport. Nearly 400,000 people live in or around the Geneva city area.

The city has been known as a traditional meeting spot for over 2,000 years, and its international role is heightened by the fact that its foreign population comes from 157 different nations worldwide. During the 16th and 17th centuries, Protestants who were being persecuted in their own countries fled to Geneva in droves as it was well-known as a safe haven for refugees. Today Geneva – often referred to as the City of Peace – is home to over 200 international governmental and non-governmental offices and headquarters, including the Office of the United Nations.

Geneva is also renowned as a research, scientific and university center of Europe. The first academy was founded here in 1559 by Calvin, and today it is home to the **European Center of Nuclear Research** (CERN), among other institutions. In addition, Geneva has over 30 museums and private galleries, all of which contain prestigious private and public displays of art work, historical documents and cultural highlights. Geneva offers a diverse variety of cultural and sporting events such as classical music concerts, open-air movies on the lakeshore, as well as various trade fairs. Annually Geneva is home to the Inventions and New Techniques Fair, a rousing Automobile Show, an International Book and Press Fair and the High Watchmaking Fair.

The city is divided by Lake Geneva and the Rhône River into two areas: the Right Bank and the Left Bank. The **Left Bank** (Rive Gauche) is home to the **Vieille Ville**, or Old Town, and features cobblestone streets, wrought-iron balconies, a host of sidewalk cafés and eateries, and a hearty helping of shops and local stores. A visitor often can get lost just wandering through the streets, which are reminiscent of Paris at times, due to the overwhelming French influence here. The main avenue, or **Grand Rue** features homes dating from the 15th to 18th centuries and meanders uphill until it reaches the famed **Place du Bourg-de-Four** – one of Geneva's most popular squares. Lakeside – along the quai Gustave-Ador – you'll find the **English Garden** (Jardin Anglais), the **Flower Clock**, and the public parks **Parc LaGrange** and **Parc des Eaux-Vives**. The Rues Basses or "lower streets" of the Left Bank are the major shopping streets of Geneva. Here you'll find designer wares as well as local artisans.

The **Right Bank** (Rive Droite), on the north side of Lake Geneva, has been the home of watchmakers and jewelers since the 18th century. It has many public parks (Parc de L'Ariana, Jardin Botanique, Parc La Perle du Lac, Park Mon-Repos) and tree-lined walking paths along the Rhône River. The **quai Woodrow Wilson** runs along the lakeside and then becomes **quai du Mont-Blanc** – an area of many prestigious hotels and international meeting sites. Eventually this lakeside avenue veers left around Lake Geneva, at pont du Mont-Blanc, before veering left again with the beginning of the Left Bank at the Jardin Anglais.

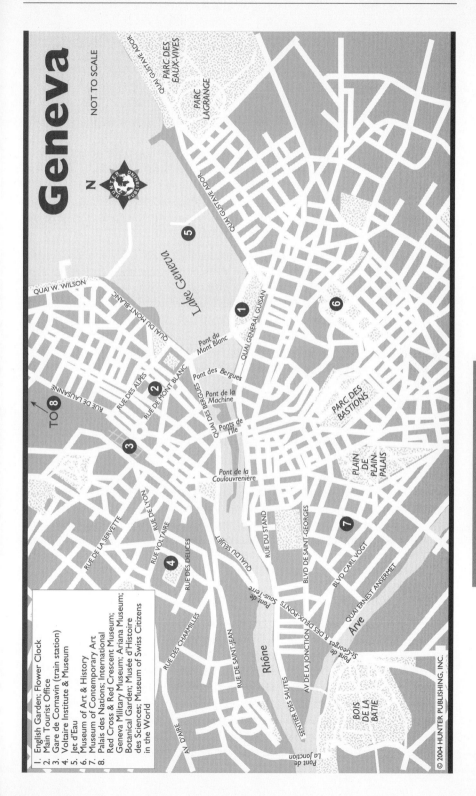

Geneva

NOT TO SCALE

N

Lake Geneva

PARC DES
EAUX-VIVES

PARC
LAGRANGE

QUAI GUSTAVE ADOR

QUAI W. WILSON

Pont du
Mont Blanc

QUAI GÉNÉRAL GUISAN

Pont des Bergues

Pont de la
Machine

Ponts de
l'Île

Pont de la
Coulouvrenière

RUE DES ALPES

RUE DE MONT BLANC

QUAI DES BERGUES

RUE DE LAUSANNE

TO 8

RUE DE LA SERVETTE

RUE DE LYON

RUE VOLTAIRE

RUE DES DÉLICES

RUE DES CHARMILLES

RUE DE SAINT-JEAN

AV. D'AIRE

SENTIER DES SAULES

QUAI DU SEUJET

Pont de
Sous-Terre

Rhône

Pont de
La Jonction

AV DE LA JONCTION

Pont de
St-Georges

R DES DEUX-PONTS

QUAI ERNEST ANSERMET

Arve

BOIS
DE LA
BÂTIE

BLVD CARL VOGT

BLVD DE SAINT-GEORGES

RUE DU STAND

PLAIN
DE
PLAIN-
PALAIS

PARC DES
BASTIONS

1
2
3
4
5
6
7

1. English Garden; Flower Clock
2. Main Tourist Office
3. Gare de Cornavin (train station)
4. Voltaire Institute & Museum
5. Jet d'Eau
6. Museum of Art & History
7. Museum of Contemporary Art
8. Palais des Nations; International
   Red Cross & Red Crescent Museum;
   Geneva Military Museum; Ariana Museum;
   Botanical Garden; Musée d'Histoire
   des Sciences; Museum of Swiss Citizens
   in the World

© 2004 HUNTER PUBLISHING, INC.

Lake Geneva & the West

One aspect of Geneva that is hard to miss is the Genevois' love of food. In fact, Geneva is home to more restaurants per capita (over 1,100 in total) than any other major city in the world – including Manhattan. A visitor will also note that the Genevois serve an unusual proponderance of organ meat dishes, known as "abats." Everything from blood pudding – "boudin noir" – to pickled pigs feet are popular and commonplace here.

You'll find that many hotels in Geneva cater to the rich and famous. This city by the lake does not have many of the more personal, family-run establishments found elsewhere in Switzerland.

Every August the city comes alive with **Les Fêtes de Genève** – a 10-day festival that features fireworks set to music over the lake. In December, the **Escalade** is celebrated, a festival commemorating a battle that took place on December 11th in 1602 between the Savoyards and the Genevois. For this, locals don costumes for a parade that makes its way slowly through Geneva's Old Town.

■ Information Sources

Tourist Offices

There is a small branch office in the train station, but Geneva's main tourist office (**Office du Tourisme de Genève**) is at 3 Rue du Mont-Blanc, CH-1201. ☎ 22-909-7000, fax 22-909-7011. The office is open mid-June to mid-September, Monday-Friday from 9 am-6 pm, and on Saturday and Sunday from 8 am-5 pm. From mid-September to mid-June the office is open Monday-Saturday from 9 am-6 pm. The office will provide you with free walking maps of the city and also offers an English audio-guided tour that you can rent for 10Sfr. This two-hour tour comes with a cassette player, map, and earphones, covering most of Geneva's highlights.

Train Station

The Geneva train station (Gare Cornavin) offers a money exchange (open 6:45 am-9:30 pm daily), and bike rental office. From here you can catch the super-fast TGV to Paris for just 80SFr one-way, second class. The TGV departs five times daily and is a great way to see Paris for a few days if you have limited time. You can also catch trains going to any major city within Europe from this station, and it also has a direct link from the Geneva-Cointrin Airport (☎ 22-717-7111), with trains leaving every 10 to 20 minutes to the city center from 5:30 to midnight daily. The seven-minute trip costs just 5Sfr in sec-

Above: Lake Lugano, with Monte San Salvatore (see pages 468-71)

Below: Madonna del Sasso, high above Locarno in Orselina (see pages 481-83)

Ascona on Lake Maggiore (see pages 483-86)

ond-class. If you opt for a taxi from the airport be prepared to shell out at least 30Sfr. A bus ride will cost only 2.5Sfr.

Post Office

Geneva's main post office is at Rue des Gares, CH-1211 Geneva. ☎ 22-739-2111. Open Monday-Friday from 8 am-10:45 pm, Saturday from 8 am-10 pm, Sunday from noon-8 pm. Fax, telephone and telegraph services are offered here. The other main post office is found at 18 Rue du Mont-Blanc, with similar hours.

Codes

The **area code** for Geneva is 22, and the **postal code**s are CH-1201-1211.

Internet Access

You can access the Internet at the **Funet Discount Internet Café**, close to the train station. Open Monday-Friday, from 9 am-9:30 pm, weekends from noon-9:30 am. 44 Rue de Lasusanne, CH-1201 Geneva. ☎ 22-738-5000. Or at **Club Video Rom**, at 19 Rue des Alpes, CH-1201 Geneva. ☎ 22-731-4748. It is open from 11 am to midnight daily for 5Sfr per hour. The **Placette Department Store** also has Internet access on its fourth floor for 10Sfr per hour.

Media

English-language news services: WRG (88.4 FM) features news in English, and **Radio 74** (88.8 FM) offers BBC news. *The International Herald Tribune* is available in most major hotels, as is *The New York Times*, *The Wall Street Journal* and *SA Today*, as well as French, Italian and British papers. Nearly all hotels offer English-language channels, including **CNN**, and major stations such as **ABC/NBC/CBS**.

The American Library on 3 Rue du Monthoux features English-language books and provides a free guide to Geneva in English. Open daily except for Monday. ☎ 22-732-8097. **The ELM Bookstore** features a large assortment of English-language books at 3 Rue Versonnex, Eaux-Vives, CH-1211 Geneva. ☎ 22-736-0945.

Medical Services

Medical services abound in Geneva, and many doctors speak English. For emergencies, ☎ 111 or 144 for an ambulance, or contact the **Cantonal Hospital**, 24 Rue Micheli du Crest at ☎ 22-372-3311. The **Medico Chirurgicale**, 21 Rue de Chantepoulet is a private clinic that is open 24/7. ☎ 22-731-2120. Dental services are available at **Servette Clinic**, 60 Avenue Wendt. Open 8 am-7 pm, Monday-Friday. ☎ 22-733-9800. For other emergencies, the national number of 117 for police, and 118 for the fire department.

■ Getting Here & Getting Around

This is best done on foot. The town is a virtual plethora of winding streets and roads, which can be confusing if you're driving. Geneva is easily reached by traveling south on Highway 1 from Lausanne, and you can get there on any train from virtually any spot in Europe, as it is a popular crossroad destination. You can also arrive in Geneva or leave via ship. Daily steamers arrive from and leave for other ports, such as Lausanne, Montreaux or Vevey, as well as French ports on the southern side of Lake Geneva. For ship and boat excursions, ☎ 22-312-5223. It must be noted here that Geneva is less than ideal for biking – there is a lot of traffic and many of the streets are steep and unpaved.

■ Sightseeing

A highlight is the **Palais des Nations**, the second-largest complex in Europe after Versailles. In 1936, the League of Nations switched its meeting site from the Palais Wilson to the Palais des Nations until they disbanded in 1946. After the United Nations was formed that same year in San Francisco, the Palais des Nations was deemed the headquarters for the European branch of the United Nations. Tour times vary so be sure to call ahead. Open July-August daily, 9 am-6 pm, September-June daily, 10 am-noon, 2-5 pm. Admission is 8.5Sfr for adults, 6.5Sfr for students, 4Sfr for children five and under. Parc de l'Ariana 14, Avenue de la Paix. CH-1211 Geneva. ☎ 22-907-4896.

Landmarks & Historic Sites

The **Flower Clock** (L'Horloge Fleurie) was erected in 1955 to pay tribute to the Swiss watchmaking industry. This accurate clock is made up of 6,500 flowers and plants. It is at quai du General Guisan and pont du Mont-Blanc and is especially beautiful in the summer.

The **Jet d'Eau** is Europe's tallest fountain, shooting some 460 feet (140 m) into the air. This attraction is hard to miss, as it is in the middle of Lake Geneva, and shoots water into the air from April to September. Built in 1891, it underwent renovation in 1951 and is called "jeddo" by the Genevese.

Museums

The **International Red Cross** and **Red Crescent Museum** features audio-visuals that depict humanitarian kindness. Artifacts, records and papers from prisoners of war are also displayed, as are disaster relief kits.

The museum has guided tours and brochures in English. Open Wednesday-Monday from 10 am-5 pm. Admission is 10Sfr. 17 Avenue de la Paix, International Area, CH-1201 Geneva. ☎ 22-748-9525, www.icrc.org.

The **Geneva Military Museum** presents weapons, uniforms and papers on the Swiss military. Admission is free. Open February-March on Saturday, Sunday from 2-5 pm; April-December, Wednesday-Friday, 2-5 pm, Saturday from 2-6 pm, Sunday from 10 am-noon, 2-6 pm. Closed from late December to late January. 18 Chemin de l'Impératrice, International Area, CH-1201 Geneva. ☎ 22-734-4875.

Museum of Swiss Citizens in the World (Musée des Suisses dans le Monde) is housed in a dark and dank 19th-century château and chronicles the accomplishments of the Swiss throughout the ages, including artists, military, explorers, bankers, inventors and others. Admission is 5Sfr. Open January-March, Wednesday-Sunday from 10 am-noon, 2-5 pm; April-December, Tuesday-Sunday from 10 am-noon, 2-6 pm. 18 Chemin de l'Impératrice, International Area, CH-1201 Geneva. ☎ 22-734-9021.

The **Ariana Museum** is housed in a fancy 1884 Italian mansion that features an overwhelming collection of ceramics and glassware from throughout the ages, and from all over the world. Open Wednesday-Monday, 10 am-5 pm. 10 Avenue de la Paix, International Area, CH-1201 Geneva. ☎ 22-418-5450.

The **Musée d'Histoire des Sciences** (Museum of the History of Science) features microscopes, sundials and barometers. Unique and interesting, with free admission. Open daily, except Tuesday, 10 am-5 pm. 128 Rue de Lausanne, CH-1201 Geneva. ☎ 22-418-5060.

Voltaire Institute & Museum is in the same spot where the great writer Voltaire lived from 1755 to 1760, and at various times after those years. Included are manuscripts, letters, documents, and furniture. Admission is free. Open Monday-Friday from 2-5 pm. 25 Rue des Délices, CH-1211 Geneva. ☎ 22-344-7133.

Museum of Art & History displays artistic works, armor, pottery, furniture, glass works and paintings from throughout history. Admission is free. Open Tuesday-Sunday from 10 am-5 pm. 2 Rue Charles-Galland, CH-1201 Geneva. ☎ 22-418-2600.

Museum of Contemporary Art first opened in 1994 and shows artwork from 1960 to the present, with over 1,000 pieces on display. Admission is 8Sfr for adults, 6Sfr for kids 13-18, kids under 12 free. Open Tuesday from noon-9 pm, Wednesday-Sunday from noon-6 pm. 10 Rue des Vieux-Grenadiers, CH-1201 Geneva. ☎ 22-320-6122.

Parks & Gardens

The **Jardin Botanique** (Botanical Garden) was built in 1902 and includes a small zoo, greenhouses, an Alpine garden and various exhibits on 69 acres of beauty. Admission is free. Open daily May-September, 8 am-7:30 pm; October-April, 9:30 am-5 pm.

Parc LaGrange is the site of the first Geneva Convention on August 11, 1864 and actually dates back to Roman times. The park now hosts two theaters and is home to many concerts and performances year-round, especially in the summer months. Located at Gustave-Ador, Eaux-Vives.

■ Adventures

On Foot

There are countless walking and jogging paths along the quais and in many of Geneva's parks. The **Parc Mon-Repos** and **Parc Bertrand** offer some of the best jogging paths.

On Water

Look for *Le Neptune* on quai Gustave-Ador, a barge built in 1904 and restored in 1970 that today is used for daily sailing excursions on Lake Geneva. ☎ 22-736-4804. For regular lake cruises that feature half- and full-day boat trips along the lake with several ports of call, there are several companies from which to choose. The **Mouettes Genevoises Navigation** specializes in small boats of 100 people or fewer that traverse the lake and the Rhône River, with guides in English and French. You'll find them at 8 quai du Mont-Blanc. The **Compagnie Generale de Navigation** (CGN) offers tours of an hour up to full-day tours that include lunch in dining rooms with white linen tablecloths. They are at quai Mont-Blanc, ☎ 22-312-5223.

Geneva Beach, at Port Noir, is a great spot for swimming, and admission is 7Sfr daily from 9 am-7 pm. ☎ 22-736-2482.

*If you're visiting Geneva in early June, be sure to catch the **Bol d'Or** – an annual sailing regatta that has been held annually for over 50 years. It features over 600 boats in a spectacular water and sailing festival.*

On Snow

A trip to Geneva would not be complete without a trip up to **Mont Blanc** – Europe's highest mountain and the topper of the French Alps. **Key Tours S.A.** can arrange for an all-day trip, with prices starting at 88Sfr per person (48Sfr for children). You'll travel to Chamonix by bus and then board a cable-car for ascent to the summit at 12,610 feet (3,844 m). The bus usually leaves by 8:30 am and returns around 6 pm, with lunch included, and an English-speaking guide. You'll find Key Tours at 7 Rue des Alpes, CH-1211 Geneva. ☎ 22-731-4140. If you're looking for skiing excursions, most people travel across the border to France.

Other Sports

 The **Silhouette Health & Fitness Club** is close to all of the major hotels on the Right Bank and offers a fitness room with weights and exercise machines, plus all types of exercise classes. Rates start at 20Sfr per hour. Open Monday-Friday, 9 am-9 pm, weekends from 10 am to 5 pm. 4 Rue Thalberg, CH-1201 Geneva. ☎ 22-732-7740.

The **Golf Club de Genève** offers an 18-hole course (open March-December, Tuesday-Sunday, 8:30 am-12:30 pm, 2-6 pm). You must call ahead, however, as they typically offer playing rights to those who are members of a golf club in their own country. Fees start at 150Sfr for the 18 holes. ☎ 22-707-4800. For **tennis**, check out **Le New Sporting Club**, which offers both indoor and outdoor courts. ☎ 22-774-1514. The **Patinoire de Noel** at Place du Rhône on the Left Bank is a free outdoor **ice skating rink** from December-March. The **Patinoire des Vernets** at 4-6 Rue Hans-Wilsdorf is an indoor ice rink that offers equipment rental, lessons and rink time, Tuesday-Saturday from October-March. ☎ 22-418-4022.

■ Shopping

 Geneva is a shopping paradise, featuring everything from the finest boutiques to small markets that offer wares from local artisans. Most shops are open Monday-Friday from 8 am-6:30 pm, and Saturday from 8 am-5 pm Often, on Thursday night, the stores will stay open until 8 or 9 pm. You'll find some of the most unusual shops in the old part of Geneva – harness makers, antique dealers, and many of the local craftspeople. Very few shops in Geneva offer inexpensive items, however, especially on the Rue du Rhône and the Grand Rue. There is no finer city than Geneva for buying **watches**. Here you'll find the prestigious **Bucherer**, at 45 Rue du Rhône, ☎ 22-319-6266; **Patek Philippe**, 41 Rue du Rhône, ☎ 22-781-3448; and **Piaget**, 40 Rue du Rhône, ☎ 22-817-0200 – all in the Centre Ville (center of town). Fine jewelry shops such as Cartier, Bulgari, and Chopard are also found in this area.

■ Where to Stay in Geneva

 Hôtel Beau Rivage was built in 1865 and retains the upscale Victorian ambiance that has made it a favorite among royalty for decades. This fancy overnighter has played host to many celebrities over the years, including Richard Wagner and Sarah Bernhardt. All modern amenities can be found here, amidst the classic, plush surroundings. The rooms are spacious and feature beautiful marble bathrooms. ($$$$+). 13 quai du Mont-Blanc, CH-1201 Geneva. ☎ 22-716-6666, fax 22-716-6060, www.beau-rivage.ch.

Lake Geneva & the West

Des Bergues is an elegant, sprawling four-story hotel adorned with chandeliers and marble baths. Expensive, plush and elegant, with two of the best dining rooms in Geneva: Le Pavillon and L'Amphitryon. ($$$$+). 33 quai des Bergues, CH-2111 Geneva. ☎ 22-908-7000, fax 22-908-7090, www.hotelbergues.com.

Noga Hilton International Geneva, one of my favorites, is the largest hotel in Switzerland, sitting on the edge of the lake. From here you can walk to almost everywhere in the city. All first-class rooms are very large, with marble baths, and most offer Internet hookups. Home to two great restaurants: **Le Cygne** and **Le Tse-Yang**. ($$$$+). 19 quai du Mont-Blanc, CH-1201 Geneva. ☎ 22-909-9081, fax 22-908-9090. In the USA, ☎ 1-800-445-8667.

Hôtel de la Paix was designed by an Italian and owned by Sardinia in its early years. Very fancy, but less haughty than some of its higher-priced rivals. ($$$$). 11 quai du Mont-Blanc, CH-1201 Geneva. ☎ 22-909-6000, fax 22-909-6001. In the USA, ☎ 1-800-223-6800.

Hôtel du Midi sits in the center of Geneva and is close to everything. The outside décor is somewhat plain, but the rooms are very clean and comfortable and the staff is friendly. The rates include breakfast. ($$$-$$$$). 4 place Chevelu, CH-1211 Geneva. ☎ 22-544-1500, fax 22-731-0020.

Strasbourg-Geneva was built in 1900 and sits near the main train station. This is one of the few hotels in Geneva that is run by a local family. Clean. Room sizes vary. Breakfast is included in the rates. ($$$). 10 Rue J-J-Pradier, CH-1201 Geneva. ☎ 22-906-5800, fax 22-728-4208. In the USA, ☎ 1-800-528-1234.

Edelweiss Manotel features a cozy ambiance and Alpine décor that is charming and oh-so-Swiss. It is a picture-perfect Swiss hotel and is reasonably priced. The restaurant is fun and lively, and rates include a hearty breakfast. ($$-$$$). 2 place de Navigation, CH-1201 Geneva. ☎ 22-544-5151, fax 22-544-5199.

Hotel Ibis is great for backpackers and train travelers, as it accommodates people 24/7. Only a five-minute walk from the train station. ($$). 10 Rue Voltaire, St. Gervais, CH-1201 Geneva. ☎ 22-338-2020, fax 22-338-2030.

The Geneva **Youth Hostel** is one of the largest in Switzerland, offering 334 sleeping spots for weary travelers. ($-$$). You'll find it at 30 Rue Rothschild, CH-1202 Geneva. ☎ 22-732-6260, fax 22-738-3987, www.youthhostel.ch/geneve.

■ Where to Eat in Geneva

Le Cygne is in the Noga Hilton, and features an international array of cuisine sure to dazzle your palate. The beautiful view of Mont Blanc enhances the meal, which also includes a cart of delicious desserts. Expensive ($$$-$$$$), but well worth every delicious bite! Reservations required; open daily noon-2 pm, 7-10:30 pm. 19 quai du Mont-Blanc, CH-1201 Geneva. ☎ 22-908-9085.

Restaurant Robert caters to an upscale crowd, but the ambiance and staff are very friendly and somewhat casual in this fashionable eatery. Pasta and fish are the specialties, and the wine list features unusual choices. ($$$-$$$$). 10 Rue Pierre-Fatio, CH-1201 Geneva. ☎ 22-311-8033.

Le Perle du Lac is just as its name suggests, a pearl from the lake. Serving up fresh-caught trout, sea bass and other lake fish, this restaurant also features good seasonal and international dishes, and a lengthy wine list that features mostly French wines. The flowered terrace overlooks Lake Geneva, with splendid views of Mont Blanc. ($$$-$$$$). Open Tuesday-Sunday, noon-2 pm, 7:30-10 pm. Closed Mondays and during January. 128 Rue de Lausanne, International Area, CH-1211 Geneva. ☎ 22-909-1020.

Le Neptune features some of Geneva's finest seafood in a grandiose setting of floral arrangements, beautiful frescos and paintings. The menu changes weekly in accordance with the local catch and the dishes are lovely in both appearance and taste. This place also features delightful pasta and a very nice rack of Scottish lamb. ($$$-$$$$). Open Monday-Friday from noon-2 pm, 7:30-10 pm. Reservations required. Located in the Hôtel Mandarin Oriental du Rhône, 1 quai Turrettini, CH-1211 Geneva. ☎ 22-909-0006.

La Mère Royaume features French dishes in one of the oldest restaurants of Geneva, and is named after a woman who poured a pot of hot stew on a soldier and then smashed him in the head with the steel bowl in 1602. Despite the name, the restaurant serves up pristinely prepared dishes such as lamb, venison, shrimp and fresh-caught fish. You'll also find such Swiss favorites as raclette and fondue. Reservations required. ($$$-$$$$). Open Monday-Friday from noon-2 pm, 7-10:30 pm; Saturday from 7-10:30 pm. 9 Rue de Corps-Saints, CH-1201 Geneva. ☎ 22-732-7080.

Chez Jacky is a trendy spot hailed for its innovative dishes. It attracts a wide array of customers and has reasonable rates. ($$-$$$). Open Monday-Friday from 11 am-2 pm, 6:30-11 pm. Closed early January and for three weeks in August. 9-11 Rue Necker, CH-1211 Geneva. ☎ 22-732-8680.

Patara serves up the finest Thai food found anywhere in Geneva, in the Beau-Rivage Hotel. If you're a vegetarian, then you won't want to miss this spot, where you'll also find huge prawns, succulent sea bass, and other Thai specialties. ($$-$$$). Open Monday-Friday from noon-3 pm, 7 pm-midnight. Reservations recommended. 13 quai du Mont-Blanc, CH-1201 Geneva. ☎ 22-731-5566.

Café du Centre is a mainstay in Geneva, having been established here in 1871. Lively and energetic, it offers up a variety of dishes that include fresh fish, meat, and seasonal fare. This is also a great place for families with kids, and features a fixed-price lunch menu for 19.5Sfr. Open daily from 7 am-midnight. ($-$$). Reservations recommended. 5 place du Molard, CH-1211 Geneva. ☎ 22-311-8586.

Pizzeria da Paolo is the best pizzeria in Geneva with the best prices. The setting is very homey and cozy, and features 20 different kinds of pizza, as well as pastas, salads and soups. Reservations are recommended. Open daily from 11:45 am-2 pm, 6:45-11 pm. ($-$$). 3 rue du Lac, CH-1201 Geneva. ☎ 22-736-3049.

Café-Restaurant Papon has been in operation since the 17th century and is one of Geneva's best kept secrets. This tearoom and restaurant is a great place to grab a bite of food, or relax after an afternoon of shopping. It is also a good spot for people watching. ($). 1 Rue Henri-Faxy, CH-1211 Geneva. ☎ 22-311-5428.

Aigle in Canton Vaud – the castle dates from the 15th century and is the home of the Vaud Wine Museum

Canton Vaud (VD)

■ At A Glance

 Established as part of the Swiss Federation in 1803, the Canton of Vaud is home to the vineyards of the Lavaux, the Castle of Chillon, and the sun-blazed slopes of Lake Geneva. As Switzerland's fourth-largest canton in terms of land, it encompasses 2,018 square miles (5,247 square km), with 626,200 residents who are mostly French-speaking Roman Catholics, making it the third-largest canton in terms of population (behind Zürich and Bern). Nearly 27% of the inhabitants of this canton are foreigners, and most have chosen to settle in the lakeside towns around Lake Geneva. The name Vaud is pronounced *Voh* in French and *Waddt* in German, although few visitors even recognize the name of this canton. Most foreigners and locals alike tend to think of this area as the "Lake Geneva region," a somewhat sour note among many Vaudois.

Vaud is at the far southwestern end of Switzerland, just north of Canton Geneva and just south of cantons Neuchâtel and Fribourg. At the far eastern tip, it briefly collides with Canton Bern, while at the south and southeast sides it borders Canton Valais. Directly south, Lake Geneva gently laps against the shores of Vaud. It is central Europe's largest lake, covering 225 square miles (585 square km). The Jura mountains flank its western side, while the Alps own a good part of the southeastern portion of the canton. The middle area is relatively flat, and is part of the region known as the Mittleland.

The **coat of arms** for Vaud features the motto *Liberté et Patrie* in gold on the upper half of the shield, set against a white background. The bottom half of the shield is a solid bright green. The motto was adopted when Vaud joined Switzerland and the green represents the founding of the Lemanic Republic in 1798.

Central & Eastern Vaud

Lausanne

As Switzerland's fifth-largest city, with 125,000 residents, Lausanne dates back to the Roman era, when the then-rulers used this outpost as a stop along the route from Italy to Gaul when they trudged through the St. Bernard Pass. Since that time, it has evolved into one of Switzerland's most eclectic cities, with one of its liveliest art communities. It has been the International Olympic Committee headquarters since 1915, and is also the home of Switzerland's highest court of appeals – the Tribunal Fédéral. Lausanne is also heralded for its outstanding universities and technological institutes. It is on Highway N1, just 40 miles (64 km) northeast of Geneva.

■ Information Sources

Tourist Offices

The **Office du Tourisme du Canton de Vaud** is at 60 Avenue d'Ouchy, CH-1006 Lausanne. ☎ 21-613-2626, fax 21-613-2610, www.lake-geneva-region.ch. The **Lausanne Tourist Office** is at 2 Avenue de Rhodaine, CH-1006 Lausanne. ☎ 21-613-7321, fax 21-616-8647. This office also offers **walking tours** of Lausanne from April to September. Call ahead to see when their English guides are available. Consult www.lausanne-tourisme.ch.

The **Office des Vins Vaudois** offers free maps of vineyard walks in the region, including stops where you can sample the wines. They can also provide you with the *Guide du Vignoble Vaudois* that includes suggested alternative walks. Contact the office at 6 Chemin de la Vuachere, CH-1005, Lausanne. ☎ 21-729-6161.

For hiking and walking excursions, contact the **Vaudois Association of Trekkers and Hill Climbers**, at 23 Grand St.-Jean, CH-1003 Lausanne. ☎ 21-323-1084. They will help you plan itineraries and provide you with detailed maps.

Train Station

The local train station is known as the Gare CFF de Lausanne and offers baggage service, storage, money exchange and bike rental. The train information office is open Monday-Friday from 8 am-7 pm daily, and Saturday from 8 am-5 pm on 1 Place de la Gare, CH-1000 Lausanne. ☎ 51-224-2162.

Post Office

There are 25 post office branches in Lausanne, but for convenience, the post office nearest the train station is the best. Located at Avenue de la Gare 43, CH-1000 Lausanne. It is open 7:30 am-6:30, Monday-Friday, and on Saturday from 8 am-noon. ☎ 21-344-3513, fax 21-344-3005.

Codes

The **postal codes** in Lausanne range from CH-1000 to 1026, and the phone **area code** is 21.

Lausanne

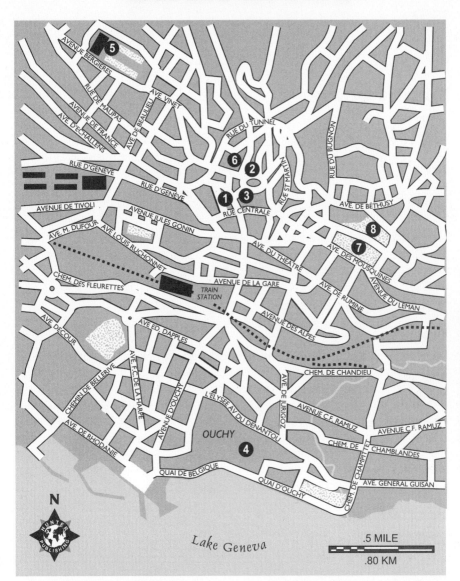

N

.5 MILE
.80 KM

Lake Geneva

Lake Geneva & the West

1. Place de la Palud; Hôtel de Ville
   (Town Hall); Fountain of Justice
2. Place de la Cathédrale; Lausanne Cathedral
3. History Museum of Lausanne
4. The Olympic Museum
5. Château de Beaulieu et L'Art Brut

6. Cantonal Museum of Fine Arts;
   Archaeological and Historical Museum;
   Zoological Museum; Paleontology Museum;
   Geology Museum
7. Mon Repos Park
8. Tribunal Fédéral

Internet Access

Access the Internet at **In Comm** for 15Sfr per hour. 32 Rue du Petit-Chène, CH-1000 Lausanne. ☎ 21-351-1191.

■ Getting Around

In Lausanne this is best done on foot, so be sure to bring comfortable walking or tennis shoes, because many of the streets in this cobblestone village are very steep, layered and inclined. There are a good many narrow streets and alleys still to be found in the close-knit buildings of the Old Town. The city does have a local tram available, but it is frightfully slow and you can usually beat it to any destination by walking.

*There are plenty of taxis in the city, but they are expensive, and we wouldn't recommend using them unless you have lots of luggage or are desperate. Contact **Taxibus** at ☎ 80-080-0312 or **Taxiphone** at ☎ 80-080-1802.*

■ Adventures

On Foot

You might want to walk to the nearby town of **St. Sulpice**, just a little under two miles (3.2 km) west of Lausanne along the shores of Lake Geneva. Here you'll find one of the finest 12th-century churches in Switzerland, the **Église de St.-Sulpice** (Church of St.-Sulpice), built by the Cluny Abbey monks from Burgundy. It became a private residence in the 16th century and for years was home to monks. Today it serves as the stage for local classical music performances. The walk there and back along the lakeshore provides absolutely stunning views and makes for a nice lazy afternoon stroll.

On Water

Ship excursions abound throughout the Lake Geneva region, and many ships and ferries will bring you to the French side of the lake, where you can visit such neat little villages as Yvoire or Evian-les-Bains. Many ships have half-day or full-day itineraries, leaving at various times throughout the day. Contact the **CGN** (Compagnie Générale de Navigation) at ☎ 21-614-6222 for information and reservations. Many of the ships come equipped with full restaurants or snack bars on board.

For **sailing** trips, rentals and classes, contact the **Ecole de Voile d'Ouchy** at ☎ 21-635-5887 or the **Ecole de Voile de Vidy** at ☎ 21-617-

9000. You can **rent boats** or pedal boats at the various stands located along the shoreline. For the best, look to the suburb of Ouchy at the Ste. C. Barke, Place du Vieux-Port, CH-1003 Lausanne-Ouchy. ☎ 21-616-0844.

Swimming in Lausanne is best done at the **Piscine de Montchoise**, (open May-August at 30 Avenue de Servan, ☎ 21-616-1062), which features a wave machine, or at **Bellerive Beach**, which has a lakefront beach as well as three pools and a self-serve restaurant. It's located in Ouchy at 23 Avenue de Rhodanie. ☎ 21-617-8131.

In the city center, **Mon-Repos** offers a covered swimming pool that is open from late August through the end of June. 4 Avenue du Tribunal-Fédéral. ☎ 21-323-4566.

Ice skating is available from October to March in a pair of Lausanne open-air ice rinks. **Patinoire de la Pontaise** (11 Route Plaines-du-Loup, ☎ 21-646-8163) and **Patinoire de Montchoisi** (30 Avenue du Servan, ☎ 21-616-1062) both offer skates for rent.

■ Sightseeing

You can begin with the **Place de la Palud** in the center of Lausanne's old village. The **Hôtel de Ville** (town hall), which dates back to the 17th century, has a beautiful façade and is the home of the Communal Council today. Here you'll also find the **Fountain of Justice**, an early 18th-century fountain, as well as an animated historical clock depicting scenes from the city.

Landmarks & Historic Sites

At the **Place de la Cathédrale** you'll see the **Lausanne Cathedral**, one of the finest medieval churches found anywhere. This cathedral – which dates to 1175 – looms some 500 feet (152 m) above the city, and features two towers, one of which can be climbed and has an observation deck. Admission to the cathedral is free, and it is only 2Sfr to climb up the tower. Services are still held Sunday mornings and visits are not allowed during this time. Open April-September, Monday-Friday from 8 am-6:30 pm, Saturday from 8:30 am-6 pm, Sunday from 2-7 pm. From October-March, it is open Monday-Friday, 7:30 am-6 pm, Saturday from 8:30 am-5 pm, Sunday from 2-5:30 pm.

Nearby is the **History Museum of Lausanne,** which was formerly a bishop's palace, and now features articles relating to Lausanne from throughout the centuries. Open Tuesday and Thursday from 11 am-6 pm, Friday, Saturday and Sunday from 11 am-5 pm. Admission is 4Sfr for

St-Saphorin, in the wine-growing area of Lavaux on Lake Geneva

adults and 2.5Sfr for children. 4 Place de la Cathedrale, CH-1000 Lausanne. ☎ 21-331-0353.

The Olympic Museum is home to the International Olympic Committee, and was opened in 1993 to honor the history of games. It features a coin and stamp collection, an Olympic Study Center, video and book libraries and commemorative artifacts. A must-see for any sports enthusiast. Open May-September from 9 am-6 pm (Thursdays until 8 pm); October-April, Tuesday-Sunday from 9 am-6 pm. Admission is 14Sfr for adults, 7Sfr for kids 10-18, free for kids nine and younger. 1 Quai d'Ouchy, CH-1006 Ouchy-Lausanne. ☎ 21-621-6511.

Château de Beaulieu et de L'Art Brut is housed in a château that dates from 1756. It's now home to a museum of modern art that displays artwork done by the mentally ill, the criminally insane and prisoners – all collected by artist Jean Dubuffet. This kind of art was christened "Art Brut" by Dubuffet and is bizarre and extreme, to say the least, but most interesting. Admission is 6Sfr for adults and 4Sfr for seniors, kids and students. Open Tuesday-Friday from 11 am-noon, 2-6 pm; Saturday and Sunday from 11 am-6 pm. 11 Avenue des Bergieres. CH-1003 Lausanne. ☎ 21-647-5435.

The **Roman Museum of Lausanne-Vidy** provides unique exhibits of Roman artifacts found in and around the Lausanne-Vidy-Ouchy region. This museum was once a private home and displays a variety of unique findings from a Roman settlement named Lousonna. Guided tours of the nearby archeological digs are held on the last Sunday of every month for only 3Sfr. Admission to the museum is 4Sfr. Open Tuesday and Thursday-Sunday from 11 am-6 pm; Wednesday from 11 am-8 pm. 24 Chemin du Bois-de-Vaus. CH-1005 Lausanne-Vidy. ☎ 21-625-1084.

The **Cantonal Museum of Fine Arts** features works of 19th-century French artists, including Degas, Matisse and Renoir, to name a few. This site is also home to Lausanne's **Archaeological and Historical Mu-**

seum, the **Zoological Museum**, the **Paleontology Museum** and the **Geology Museum**. Admission is 6Sfr for adults and 4Sfr for students and seniors. Free admission for kids under 16 years of age. Open Tuesday and Wednesday from 11 am-6 pm, Thursday from 11 am-8 pm, Friday, Saturday and Sunday from 11 am-5 pm. Located in the Palais de Ruminie, 6 place de la Riponne. CH-1000 Lausanne. ☎ 21-316-3445.

Parks & Gardens

Mon Repos Park on the eastern side of Lausanne features expertly manicured gardens, the Empire Villa and the Tribunal Fédéral – Switzerland's highest court.

■ Shopping

If you're a kid at heart, or if you're travelling with children, then you won't want to miss **Franz Carl Weber**, the ultimate Swiss toy store, at 23 rue de Bourg in the city center (☎ 21-320-1471). **Globus** is the local department store, at rue Centrale in the city center (☎ 21-342-9090), or you can scope out designer wares at **Bon Génie**, 10 Place St.-Francois in the city center (☎ 21-320-4811). For Vaudois items, there is no finer store than **Heidi's Shop**, at 22 Rue du Petit-Chêne. ☎ 21-320-5544.

■ Where to Stay

Beau-Rivage Palace is one of the finest hotels in Switzerland, and is set inside a 10-acre garden, filled with trees, hedges and sculptures. The original building was constructed in 1861 and additional rooms were added in 1908. It was in this hotel that the Treaty

HOTEL PRICE CHART	
$	30-75Sfr ($20-$49)
$$	76-205Sfr ($50-$109)
$$$	206-299Sfr ($110-$200)
$$$$	300Sfr+ ($200+)

of Lausanne was ratified in 1923 to settle disputes between World War I allies. The rooms are tastefully decorated with Oriental carpets and each has a private balcony overlooking the lake. All contain the finest of amenities, with outstanding room service. ($$$$). Three restaurants, fitness center, two pools, tennis courts and a pair of bars round out this beautiful hotel. 17-19 Place du Port, CH-1006 Lausanne. ☎ 21-613-3333, fax 21-613-3334, www.brp.ch. In the USA, ☎ 1-800-223-6800.

Hôtel Lausanne-Palace & Spa is set in a quiet location in the center of the city, with grand views of the Alps and Lake Geneva. Only a few steps away from the train station and from St.-Francois bus stop. Features three top restaurants (**La Table du Palace**, **Grand-Chêne** and **Côte Jardin**), as well as bars, a disco and lounges. ($$$-$$$$) This ultramodern hotel includes a beauty salon, fitness room, indoor swimming pool, massage, sauna, solarium, steam bath, whirlpool, and is handicapped-accessible. Rue du Grand-Chêne 7-9, CH-1003 Lausanne. ☎ 21-331-3131, fax 21-323-2571.

Hôtel Agora Fassbind S.A. offers 80 first-class rooms not far from the train station and lakeshore. Rooms are clean, comfortable and spacious, with all modern amenities. The in-house restaurant serves vegetarian fare as well as traditional Swiss dishes. This hotel is suitable for the handicapped and is in a quiet area. ($$$). Avenue du Rond-Point 9, CH-1006 Lausanne. ☎ 21-617-1211, fax 21-616-2605.

Hôtel Movenpick is in the suburb of Ouchy, only five minutes from Lausanne's city center, very close to the Olympic Stadium. The hotel is ultra-modern and right on the lakeshore, with three restaurants, a bar and a sun terrace. Great for families with children; those under 16 stay free in their parents' room. ($$). Avenue de Rhodanie 4, CH-1006 Ouchy – Lausanne. ☎ 21-612-7612, fax 21-612-7611.

Hôtel de la Paix has splendid views of the surroundings from all rooms, and features a good restaurant – **Le Café de la Paix** – and a lively after-hours pub, **Jacky's Bar**. Located minutes from the train station, this hotel is in the heart of the business and shopping districts. ($$). Avenue B-Constant 5, CH-1003 Lausanne ☎ 21-310-7171, fax 21-310-7172.

Hostellerie Les Chevreuils is a 100-year-old inn in a beautiful country setting in the Lausanne suburb of Vers-Chez-les-Blanc. Features include a nice garden terrace and two restaurants offering holistic cooking and traditional Swiss fare. ($$). Free parking and breakfast is included in rates. Kids three and under stay free in their parents' room. Route du Jorate 80, Vers-Chez-les-Blanc/Lausanne. ☎ 21-784-2021, fax 21-784-1545.

Hôtel-Restaurant Albatross Navigation sits perched on the lakeshore next to the yachting marina only two minutes from the Olympic Museum. Features an excellent restaurant with homemade and vegetarian dishes, with a terrace and garden dining area. Pets are welcome and kids 12 and under stay free in their parents' rooms. ($$). Avenue de La Harpe 49, CH-1006 Lausanne. ☎ 21-614-3800, fax 21-616-7080.

Hôtel du Boulevard is a tiny hotel only two minutes from the train station in the center of Lausanne. The rooms are quiet and tidy and some have kitchenettes. Ask about special rates for long stays. The in-house Italian restaurant, **Da Geppetto**, is one of the best in the city. ($$). Boulevard de Grancy 51, CH-1006 Lausanne. ☎ 21-614-2828, fax 21-614-2829.

Hôtel à la Chotte is a charming inn with just 14 rooms that is immaculate and gorgeous on the outside as well as the inside. Parking is free, pets are allowed, and the atmosphere is comfortable. Located in the Lausanne suburb of Romanel, this inn has a garden terrace dining area. ($-$$). Ch. du Village 19, CH-1032 Romanel-s-Lausanne. ☎ 21-646-1012, fax 21-684-5474.

Hôtel Pre-Fleuri is in nearby St. Sulpice and is a charming hotel with a spacious garden that is close to the University. The inn is surrounded by lovely flowers and is clean, tidy and comfortable. The in-house restaurant serves up gourmet fare and the staff is exceptionally friendly and gracious. Only three miles (4.8 km) from the Lausanne city center, they also offer free parking for guests. ($$). Rue du Centre 1, CH-1025 St.-Sulpice. ☎ 21-691-2021, fax 21-691-2020.

Pension ADA-Logements is a little bed & breakfast that caters to families and young travelers. Located in the city center, it offers parking for 3Sfr per day, and children under 12 stay for free in their parents' room. ($). Avenue de Tivoli 60, CH-1007 Lausanne. ☎ 21-625-7134, fax 21-625-7126.

The **Lausanne Youth Hostel** offers 240 beds ($) at Ch. Du Bois-de-Vaux 36, CH-1007 Lausanne. ☎ 21-626-0222, fax 21-626-0226, www.youthhostels.ch/lausanne.

■ Where to Eat

Café Beau-Rivage is one of the most elegant restaurants in Lausanne but, surprisingly, its prices are not as out-of-sight as one might expect. You'll dine on the lakeside terrace, adorned by flower containers overflowing with blooms year-round. The restaurant serves seafood, pasta, steaks and grilled fare, as well as many Swiss favorites. ($-$$$). The dining room becomes a piano bar after 7:30 pm nightly. The adjoining café is open from 11 am to 1 pm, Monday-Friday, and from 9 am to 1 am on the weekends. It serves light meals, snacks, coffees and desserts. ($-$$$). In the Beau-Rivage Palace, 17-19 Place du Port, CH-1006 Lausanne. ☎ 21-613-3333, fax 21-613-3334.

DINING PRICE CHART	
Prices based on a typical entrée, per person, and do not include beverage.	
$	15-25Sfr ($10-$16)
$$	26-45Sfr ($17-$29)
$$$	46-70Sfr ($30-$47)
$$$$	71Sfr+ ($47+)

La Grappe d'Or, a well-known Lausanne eatery, serves up French fare by world-renowned German chef Peter Baermann in a relaxed atmosphere. Dishes are carefully prepared and served under the supervision of Baermann's wife, Angelika, and include regional and seasonal specialties such as venison, fresh fish and seafood. The desserts are out of this world. ($$-$$$$). Reservations required. Open Monday-Friday for lunch and dinner. Saturday for dinner only, closed Sunday. 3 Cheneau de Bourg, CH-1000 Lausanne. ☎ 21-323-0760.

Not far from its parent restaurant above, **La Petite Grappe** is a lighthearted bistro that caters to the younger crowd of Lausanne, and features similar dishes to its older family member up the street. ($-$$$). Reservations required. Located at 15 Cheneau de Bourg, CH-1000 Lausanne. ☎ 21-311-8414.

A la Pomme de Pin is one of Lausanne's oldest wine pubs and features a wide array of dishes that will appeal to most palates, served between a fancy dining room and a casual café. Open for lunch and dinner Monday-Friday, Saturday for lunch only. Closed Sunday. ($-$$$). 11-13 Rue de la Mercerie, CH-1000 Lausanne. ☎ 21-323-4656.

Pinte Besson dates back to 1780 and is a favorite with the locals for its cheese and meat fondues, grilled steaks and typically Swiss fare. Hearty dishes at very reasonable prices. ($-$$). Open Monday-Friday from noon-2 pm, 6 pm-midnight, weekends from noon-2 pm. Closed during the month of August. 4 Rue de l'Ale, CH-1000 Lausanne. ☎ 21-312-7227.

Montreux

Montreux is often considered to be the most popular resort spot on Lake Geneva and is just 13 miles (21 km) southeast of Lausanne, or two miles (3.2 km) south of Vevey. This town of 20,000 residents extends some five miles (eight km) along the lake, with magnificent views of the surrounding Alps and beautiful green countryside. For centuries Montreux has attracted some of history's finest writers, artists and musicians, including Tolstoy, Byron, Nabokov, and Stravinsky, to name just a few. One of the main reasons to come here, aside from its annual music festivals, is to visit the Château de Chillon, a 12th-century castle that sits, literally, in the waters of Lake Geneva, and for many years served as a state prison. In fact, it was the basis for Lord Byron's poem *The Prisoner of Chillon*. The castle was originally built on the foundation of a Roman site by order of Duke Peter of Savoy. It is best to visit Chillon in the off-season if you really want to spend any time here enjoying the atmosphere; otherwise you'll be one of the many tourists who parade through the mighty structure in a long, stoic line. See next page for more details.

Montreux's Tourist Office is at 5 Rue de Theatre, CH-1821, Montreux. ☎ 21-962-8484, fax 21-963-7895, www.montreux.ch.

■ Music Festivals

The **Montreux Jazz Festival** is known worldwide. Held the first two weeks in July, it has free concerts during the day; evening concerts require tickets, which you can purchase via the UBS Bank ticket counters throughout Switzerland (☎ 84-880-0800) or from the Montreux Jazz Boutique at 100 Grand-Rue, CH-1821 Montreux. ☎ 21-961-1166. The festival has a website at www.montreuxjazz.com, or call festival reservations at ☎ 21-963-8282 for more information.

The **Montreux-Vevey Music Festival** is held from late August to the end of September annually and includes a wide array of classical music. For information on tickets and concert times, contact the Festival de Musique at 5 Rue de Théatre, Case Postale 162, CH-1820 Montreux. ☎ 21-966-8025, fax 21-963-2506, www.montreux-festival.com.

■ Historic Site

The **Château de Chillon** is open daily from April-September, 9 am-7 pm, and from November-February, 10 am-5 pm. Admission is 8.5Sfr. The castle is only two miles (3.2 km) south of Montreux, easily accessed on foot or by car. It was in Chillon that Geneva native Francois de Bonivard was imprisoned in the 16th century. He was held in the dungeon – which visitors can explore today – for six years, chained to one of the pillars there for preaching about the Reformation, which was strictly forbidden at the time. When the Bernese armies arrived in 1536, he was finally released. Chillon has been a source of inspiration for writers such as Lord Byron, Victor Hugo, Jean-Jacques Roussseau and oth-

Chillon Castle, on the shores of Lake Geneva

ers throughout the centuries. The castle is actually made up of 25 buildings that are joined together by three separate courtyards, the square tower and internal walls. There are four levels, including the still-intact underground vaults, the largest of which was occupied by Bonivard. The upper levels contain a banquet hall, apartments, a torture chamber, bedrooms and other living quarters. Chillon is both impressive and chilling at the same time, if one ponders its history, and is well worth a visit. Chillon Castle, CH-1820 Veytaux-Montreux. ☎ 21-963-3912, fax 21-963-8581.

■ Where to Stay

Hôtel Eden au Lac is a century-old hotel decorated with Louis 16th furniture; it retains much of its Victorian flavor. There are three restaurants and a public lounge area. **La Terrasse** and **Le Jardin** both offer fine dining, while **Le 1900** serves breakfast only, which is included in the rates. ($$$$). The views overlooking Lake Geneva are spectacular. Rue du Théatre 11, CH-1820 Montreux. ☎ 21-966-0800, fax 21-966-0900.

Le Montreux Palace is a luxury hotel on the shores of Lake Geneva that was originally built in 1906. This grand Art Nouveau and Neo-Baroque hotel offers all of the modern conveniences available today and features quality restaurants, a stunning wellness center and the most modern of guest facilities. ($$$$). 100 Grand Rue, CH-1820 Montreux. ☎ 21-962-1212, fax 21-962-1717.

Grand Hôtel Suisse et Majestic is across from the train station. This first-class hotel is just as its name suggests – and more so. Built in 1870, it was completely renovated in 1992 and each room has a private balcony. The staff is friendly and gracious and pets are allowed at no extra charge. Breakfast is included in the rates, and there is a nice snack bar and open-air restaurant. ($$$-$$$$). Avenue des Alpes 43, CH-1820 Montreux. ☎ 21-966-3333, fax 21-966-3000.

Royal Plaza is right on the shores of Lake Geneva, and features large rooms with all modern amenities. There are three restaurants, a bar, a fitness center and a swimming pool. ($$$-$$$$). Grand Rue 97. CH-1820 Montreux. ☎ 21-962-5050, fax 21-962-5151.

Hôtel Villa Toscane is a charming Art Nouveau hotel that was completely renovated in 1989, near the Auditorium Stravinsky and the Congress Center across from the lake promenade. This hotel features a grand sunbathing terrace, sauna, a fitness room and a solarium. The rooms come complete with all modern fixtures, and a variety of services are offered here. ($$-$$$$). Rue du Lac 2-8, CH-1820 Montreux. ☎ 21-963-8421, fax 21-963-8426.

Hôtel Helvétie is across from the casino in the heart of Montreux. Huge, modern and beautiful, it is perched near the lake promenade. Built in 1890, it features 19th-century characteristics throughout, and also has a rooftop garden. ($$-$$$$). Avenue du Casino 32, CH-1820 Montreux. ☎ 21-966-7777, fax 21-966-7700.

Golf-Hôtel René Capt is on the lakeshore, with a private garden, and provides splendid views of the Alps and of Chillon Castle. The in-house restaurant serves fine Swiss and French cuisine. ($$-$$$$). Bon-Port 35, CH-1820 Montreux. ☎ 21-966-2525, fax 21-963-0352.

The **Montreux Youth Hostel** is open from February 15 through November 15 and offers 112 beds and rooms of various types. Reservations are suggested. Near a variety of attractions, including hiking trails, tennis courts and the lake. Passage de l'Auberge 8, CH-1820 Montreux-Territet. ☎ 21-963-4934, fax 21-963-2729, www.youthhostels.ch/montreux.

Camping

This is available near the lakeshore in Villeneuve at **Les Horizons Bleus** campground. Open from April 1 to September 30, it offers spaces for tents and campers at a nominal fee. ($). Reservations required. ☎ 21-960-1547.

■ Where to Eat

New Space Metropolis is a restaurant, brewery and pizzeria all rolled into one and serving soups, salads, seafood and meat fondues, as well as pastas and pizzas. Located in the heart of Montreux, it is handicapped-accessible and has a sun terrace for dining. ($-$$). Mainsrasse 57, CH-1820 Montreux. ☎ 21-963-7558, fax 21-963-3906.

Le Museum was originally a 13th-century convent that now has three dining rooms and a large rustic fireplace. Specialties include grilled meats and Swiss favorites such as cheese and meat fondues. Open daily. Closed from December 25-January 1, July 25-August 15. ($-$$). 40 Rue de la Gare, CH-1820 Montreux. ☎ 21-963-1662.

Caveau des Vignerons is a unique spot set inside a cave, where you'll dine in candlelit bliss. Fondues and seasonal Swiss fare are the specialties, and the dessert tray is outstanding. ($-$$). Reservations are recommended. Open Monday-Friday from 9 am-midnight, Saturday from 3 pm-midnight. 30 Rue Industrielle, CH-1820 Montreux. ☎ 21-963-2570.

Coffee On the Lake is beside the Congress Center and has light international fare in a semi-formal setting. ($-$$$). Royal Plaza, Mainstrasse 97, CH-1820 Montreux. ☎ 21-962-5051, fax 21-962-5151.

Bar-Restaurant of the Earth serves fondues, veal, pigs feet, rösti and other Swiss favorites, as well as crocodile, ostrich, kangaroo, antelope, ox and horse for the avant-garde diner. ($-$$$). Open daily. Catholic Churchstrasse 3, CH-1820 Montreux. ☎ 21-963-2960, fax 21-963-2960.

Vevey

Vevey is just west of Montreux on the lake, and was the home of comedian Charlie Chaplin for 25 years, until his death on December 25, 1977. The famous silent screen genius is buried in the Corsier cemetery alongside his wife, Oona. Chaplin and his family originally settled in the Beau-Rivage hotel in 1953, before moving to Manoir de Ban, just north of Vevey in the village of Corsier.

In 1978, the coffin containing Chaplin's body was stolen from the cemetery by graverobbers, who demanded a ransom, but it was recovered three months later in a nearby cornfield. The coffin was returned and Chaplin's body was reburied, with his coffin this time encased in cement. In Vevey, there is a square named in Chaplin's honor and a statue in a nearby park of "The Little Tramp," overlooking Lake Geneva.

Vevey's **Tourist Office** can provide you with information regarding their **Vineyard Train** (Le Train de Vignes) that cruises the local vineyards, with tastings and tours of area cellars. Grande-Place 29, Case Postale 27, CH-1800, Vevey. ☎ 21-922-2020, fax 21-922-2024, www.vevey.ch.

Vevey is also the headquarters for chocolate manufacturing giant Nestle.

■ Museums

The **Food Museum** – owned and operated by Nestlé – offers social, scientific and historic perspectives on the subject. Open year-round, 10 am-noon, 2-5 pm; 10 am-5 pm during the summer months. Admission is 10Sfr. Quai Perdonnet, CH-1800 Vevey. ☎ 21-924-4111.

The **Historical Museum of Vevey** is housed in a 16th-century manor that contains art, weapons, furniture and wine-making equipment. On the first floor of the house, you'll find the Brotherhood of Winegrowers – the group that plans the celebration known as the Winegrowers Festival. (Held only every 25 years, it takes place next in 2024.) Admission is 4Sfr. Open March-October, Tuesday-Sunday from 10:30-noon, 2-5:30 pm; November-February, Tuesday-Sunday from 2-5:30 pm. 2 Rue du Château, CH-1800 Vevey. ☎ 21-921-0722.

The **Musée Suisse du Jeu** (The Museum of Games) celebrates some of life's most unusual games and brain-teasers, with many that you can participate in – although most are in French. Admission is 6Sfr for adults, 3Sfr for seniors, kids and students. Located in the Château de la Tour de Peilz just one mile east of Vevey on Route 9. Open Tuesday-Sunday from 2-6 pm. ☎ 21-944-4050.

■ Where to Stay

Hôtel de Bahyse dates back to 1700 and sits on the shores of Lake Geneva. Owned and operated by the same family for three generations, this inn, with a private garden, is decorated with rustic Swiss charm and offers all modern amenities. Just north west of Vevey in the village of Blonay, and close to many snow excursions, ski lifts and pistes, as well as a toboggan track. ($$$-$$$$). 11 Road of the Village, CH-1807 Blonay on Vevey. ☎ 21-943-1322, fax 21-943-4810.

Hôtel du Lac is centrally located in Vevey and has been housing guests since 1868. Quite a fancy spot, it has a lovely swimming pool and sunbathing terrace. ($$$$). Rue d'Italie 1, CH-1800 Vevey. ☎ 21-921-1041, fax 21-921-7508.

Hôtel Pavillon is a modern, chic hotel in the city center with air-conditioned rooms and a beautiful winter garden terrace, a traditional restaurant (**The Brasserie**) and a bar (**The Orient Express**). There is also a fitness and wellness center here. ($$$-$$$$). Place de la Gare, CH-1800 Vevey. ☎ 21-925-0404, fax 21-925-0400.

Hôtel de la Place is a quaint old inn that dates back to 1692 and features a nice café, fireplace and rustic interior. The rooms are small but functional, and each has a washbasin. Every floor has a communal shower and restroom. Great for families and romantics. ($-$$). Place du Temple 5, CH-1804 Vevey. ☎/fax 21-921-1287.

Hostellerie de Genève is a small hotel in the city center, near the lake and with an Italian restaurant. Rooms are small, but clean and comfortable. ($-$$). Place du Marché 11, CH-1800 Vevey. ☎ 21-921-4577, fax 21-921-3015.

Hôtel des Négociants is old hotel in Old Town, near the market square and the lake. ($$). Rooms are small but tidy. Rue du Conseil 27, CH-1800 Vevey. ☎ 21-922-7011, fax 21-921-3424.

■ Where to Eat

Restaurant Denis Martin is a local favorite and offers a sophisticated setting without pompous service. The waitstaff is friendly and the food is delicious. You'll find everyone from businessmen to winegrowers here year-round. Reservations required. ($-$$$). Closed Sunday and Monday. Located in the cellar of the Vevey Historical Museum at 2 Rue du Château, CH-1800 Vevey. ☎ 21-921-1210.

White Horse Pub offers scrumptious summer salads, pub dishes and daily specials. ($-$$). Simplonstrasse 33, CH-1800 Vevey. ☎ 21-921-0234.

The **Welcome Pub** features regional specialties, with a small garden terrace. ($$). Closed Sunday only. Town Square 29, CH-1800 Vevey. ☎ 21-921-2744.

Charly's Pub features salads, sandwiches, and grilled fare. ($-$$). Seestrasse 45, CH-1800 Vevey. ☎ 21-921-5006.

Aigle

The eastern portion of Vaud is often referred to as "**Les Alpes Vaudoises**" and, southbound along Highway 9, you'll first come to the village of Aigle – only 10 miles (16 km) south of Montreux. Here you'll find two museums devoted to winemaking next to one another: the Museum of Viticulture & Wine, and the International Museum of Wine Labels. Both are fascinating and worth a visit, especially given the fact that they're both housed in the beautifully maintained 12th-century **Castle of Aigle**, shown at left, once home to Bernese governors. It's set in the middle of a vast vineyard.

The **International Museum of Wine Labels** contains a collection of wine labels from over 50 nations, chronicling more than two centuries of wines. This museum sits atop the **Pointe du Paradise Wine Bar**, which looks out over local vineyards. Open April-June, September-October, Tuesday-Friday from 10 am-12:30 pm, 2-6 pm, Saturday from 9 am-noon. During July and August, it's open from Tuesday-Friday, 10 am-6 pm, Saturday from 9 am-noon. Admission is 4Sfr (9Sfr for both museums). Château d'Aigle, Maison de la Dimne, CH-1860 Aigle. ☎ 24-466-2130.

The **Museum of Viticulture & Wine** is located next door in the Château d'Aigle and exhibits old bottles, presses, wine-making tools and other artifacts of the wine-making process throughout the ages. A 9Sfr ticket allows entrance into both museums. Similar hours as the International Museum of Wine Labels. Château d'Aigle, CH-1860 Aigle. ☎ 24-466-2130.

Château d'Oex

The two main ski and winter sports areas of this region are Les Diablerets and Château d'Oex, both easily accessible from Aigle.

Château d'Oex is between Gstaad and Gruyères, 20 miles (32 km) northeast of Aigle on the Cole des Mosses Highway. At 3,280 feet (1,000 m), this village of 2,900 residents is a junction between the cantons of Vaud, Fribourg and Bern, and is well known as a winter sports playground and for its hot air ballooning endeavors. In the winter, many Swiss families come to this area with their children, as the majority of slopes are easy. There are 31 miles (50 km) of downhill runs, 19 miles (30 km) of cross-country ski runs reachable by 10 ski lifts, two chairlifts and one cable car. You'll also find a two-mile sled run here. A one-day pass costs only 33Sfr; a six-day pass is 166Sfr.

The **Château d'Oex Tourist Office** is in the village center, right below the clock tower. ☎ 26-924-2535, fax 26-924-3070.

■ Adventures

Winter Sports

For **ski lessons**, contact the local ski school at ☎ 26-924-6848. To rent ice skates contact **Planete Sports** at ☎ 26-924-4464; for snowshoes, call **Haute Pression Sports** at ☎ 26-924-5653.

Summer Sports

You can **swim** in Château d'Oex's open-air pool that also has a little restaurant. Admission is 6Sfr. ☎ 26-924-6234. For **mountain biking** excursions and bike rentals, contact **Palaz Bike** at ☎ 26-924-4251 or **Planete Sports** at ☎ 26-924-4464. You can choose from several **whitewater rafting** trips through **Rivières et Aventures**, Case Postale 68, CH-1837 Château d'Oex. ☎ 26-924-3424. If you want to experience **ballooning** over some of the most beautiful mountain ranges and countryside found anywhere, contact **Sky Event**, the local ballooning service, at ☎ 26-924-2520.

■ Sightseeing

There are two good little museums in Château d'Oex. The **Artisan & Folklore Museum of the Old Highlands** provides a detailed look at life in these Vaudois mountain villages. Exhibits include a farmer's house, a cheese maker's home, a carpenter's workshop, kitchens, furniture, ceramics, ironworks and artwork from the region. Open Tuesday, Thursday, Friday from 10 am-noon, 2-4:30 pm, Saturday and Sunday from 2-4:30 pm. Admission is 5Sfr. Grand-Rue, CH-1837 Château d'Oex. ☎ 26-924-6520.

Le Châlet is a mountain cheesemaker's house that has daily afternoon demonstrations of cheesemaking. Visitors can sit in the café and watch the entire process. There is an attached visitor's shop that sells local and regional crafts and cheese products as well. Admission is free. Open Tuesday-Sunday from 1:30 pm. CH-1837 Château d'Oex. ☎ 26-924-6677.

■ Where to Stay & Eat

The **Ermitage** is the most charming inn in this little village, featuring timbered and wooden ceilings, wood furnishings and 16 comfortable rooms, or four lovely suites. ($$-$$$). The sun terrace is perfect for hot air balloon watching and the in-house restaurant features a five-course gourmet meal with Swiss and Italian dishes. ($-$$$). There is also a playground for children and free parking for guests. CH-1837 Château d'Oex. ☎ 26-924-6003, fax 26-924-5076.

Hotel Buffet de la Gare is a lovely little café and restaurant located in the train station, serving regional and international fare at very reasonable prices. ($-$$).This is a popular spot to people-watch, and the food is surprisingly good. Reservations are recommended. ☎ 26-924-7717.

Les Diablerets

This is 12 miles (19 km) due east of Aigle, on a small, secondary road that will eventually lead you to Gstaad in Canton Bern. This tiny resort village sits at 3,806 feet (1,160 m) at the base of the 10,525-foot (3,209 m) Les Diablerets mountain and the 9,840-foot (3,000-m) glacier of the same name. Skiing and adventure sports are top priority here, with 18 lifts and six cable cars that bring snow bunnies to 75 miles (120 km) of downhill runs, 19 miles (30 km) of cross-country trails and four miles (6.4 km) of tobogganing trails. A one-day pass for the area, including a ride on the Glacier 3000 cable car, costs 52Sfr. Prices go up from there, with a six-day pass costing 264Sfr.

For snowshoeing, rock climbing, and dirt-bike excursions, as well as other adventurous tours, contact **Mountain Evasion**, at **Parc des Sports**, CH-1865 Les Diablerets. ☎ 24-492-1232. For hang-gliding, sledding, dirt biking, zorbing (rolling down a mountain in a plastic ball) and canyoning, see the folks at **Centre Paradventure**, Rue de la Gare, CH-1865 Les Diablerets. ☎ 24-492-2382.

The **Glacier 3000**, shown at left, is a high-altitude cable car that stretches from the Col du Pillon station (four miles/6.4 km outside of Les Diablerets) to the Scex-Rouge cliff. The views are awesome and the steep ride will take your breath away. At the top, you'll find a beautiful restaurant designed by architect Mario Botta. The cost is 49Sfr round-trip. Open from November to mid-April, daily from 9 am-4:30 pm; June and July, daily from 8:20 am-4:50 pm; August to October, daily from 9 am-4:50 pm. Closed from late April through May. ☎ 26-492-3377.

Hôtel Les Diablerets is a charming chalet that features clean, rustic rooms bursting with Alpine ambiance. The restaurant and café serve traditional Swiss fare. There is also a sauna, bar and parking lot on the premises. Open year-round, except for late April to June, and in October and November. ($$). Chemin du Vernex, CH-1865 Les Diablerets. ☎ 24-492-0909, fax 24-492-2391.

Auberge de la Poste has housed such guests as Stravinsky, David Bowie and Sting over the years in their seven-room inn. It's rustic and authentic, with wooden furnishings. The restaurant serves Swiss dishes in hearty portions and there is a homey feel throughout. ($$). Rue de la Gare, CH-1865 Les Diablerets. ☎ 24-492-3124, fax 24-492-1268.

Western Vaud

Morges

Morges is seven miles (11 km) west of Lausanne and 16 (26 km) east of Geneva on Highway N1 and is a great base for anyone wanting to explore Vaud's vineyards. It was also the home of screen legend Audrey Hepburn and was originally an important port and trade city centuries ago. Today its sophistication and chic ambiance is matched only by Geneva, and it is considered to be one of the major ports of call for the rich and famous, many of whom dock their yachts at Morges. The Morges **Tourist Office** is located at Rue du Château, CH-1110 Morges. ☎ 21-801-3233, fax 21-801-3130, www.morges.ch.

■ Adventures

On Wheels

Bike rides abound through this region, and there are a variety to choose from – beginning at the Morges train station. You can rent a bike here for 26-32Sfr per day and the Tourist Office will provide you with maps or help you design an itinerary all your own. One of the major bike paths is a 35-mile round-trip route from Morges to Begnins and back. It can take a whole day to complete the circuit if you stop and have a picnic or lunch; otherwise, the ride time is from 5½ to six hours. From Morges, you'll travel north to Bussy, then farther north to Apples, west to Ballens, and then finally Bière where you'll get spectacular views of Vaudois vineyards. From Bière, you head south past Gimel, eventually reaching the village of Begnins and the panoramic lookout post at Fechy. From here, you can ride down to the portside village of Gland and head north along the shore road back to Morges, via Rolle, Allaman and St.-Prex.

On Water

From May to September, you can catch the numerous steamers and ships that stop at Morges every day en route to Geneva, Lausanne or to the French side of Lake Geneva. Contact the **CGN** (Compagnie Générale de Navigation) at ☎ 84-881-1848 in Lausanne for schedules and reservations or in Geneva at ☎ 21-614-6200.

■ Landmarks & Historic Sites

The **Castle of Morges** was built in 1286 by Baron Louis of Savoy as a defense against the Bishop of Lausanne. It later (1536-1798) became the residence of a Bernese lord and much later was used as an arsenal for Vaud. Today it houses the Vaud Military Museum, which displays weapons and military uniforms of the 15th century to the present. Open February to June, and from September to mid-December, Tuesday-Friday from 10 am-noon, 1:30-5 pm; weekends from 10 am-5 pm and during July and August, Tuesday-Friday from 10 am-5 pm. Admission is 7Sfr per person. ☎ 21-804-8556.

■ Where to Stay & Eat

If you choose to bunk down in Morges for the night there are two pleasant inns. The first, the **Fleur du Lac** (Lake Flower), has 29 rooms – each of which is unique. All rooms face south, allowing for spectacular views of Lake Geneva, the Alps and Mont Blanc when the weather is clear. Rates are high, ($$$-$$$$), but well worth it. A group can stay for 470Sfr in a very good suite. The hotel also houses the best restaurant in this small village, a combination of seasonal Swiss and French cuisine that is delicately prepared at all times. ($$-$$$). There are over 250 wines to choose from in the dining room, which during the summer months becomes an outdoor terrace. Reservations required. There is also a smaller café on the premises that offers light fare at reasonable rates. ($-$$). Both are open daily from 11:30 am-2 pm, 5:30-10 pm. Quai Igor Stravinsky, Route de la Lausanne, CH-1110 Morges. ☎ 21-811-5811, fax 21-811-5888, www.fleurdulac.ch. Your other option is the splendid **Hôtel de Savoie,** located in Morges Old Town. This rustic inn offers 14 basic rooms, each with a private bath, phone and TV in a clean and unpretentious setting at very reasonable rates ($$), with a good breakfast included. The in-house restaurant (**de l'Union**) offers French fare with stunning pastries, grilled meats such as horse and lamb, plus side dishes of steamed veggies. ($-$$$). Open Monday-Saturday from 11:30 am-2:30 pm, 6:30-11 pm. Reservations recommended. 7 Grande-Rue, CH-1110 Morges. ☎ 21-801-2155.

Nyon

Nyon has been around since the days when Julius Ceasar used this lakeside village resort as a spot for his soldiers to rest. It's a great place for peaceful walks and to get away from the hustle and bustle of more cosmopolitan cities such as Geneva or Lausanne. It is about halfway between Geneva and Lausanne on Highway N1. The Nyon **Tourist Office** is at 7 Avenue Voillier, CH-1261 Nyon. ☎ 22-361-6261, fax 22-361-5396, www.nyon.ch.

Nyon is host to the **Paléo Festival**, a six-day international rock-and-roll concert held annually in late July. The festival takes place on a gigantic campground where five stages are set up, and it attracts over 200,000 people each year. Ticket prices range from 45Sfr on up and it is best to purchase them in advance, either by calling ☎ 22-361-0101 or via the Internet at www.paleo.ch.

■ Where to Stay & Eat

Château de Bonmont is five miles (eight km) northwest of Nyon in the tiny village of Chéserex. It was once a country estate that belonged to royalty, and features crystal chandeliers, beautiful wool tapestries, an 18-hole golf course, three tennis courts, a pool, sauna and massage. Horseback riding is also available, and there is a bar and in-house restaurant on the premises. ($$$-$$$$+). Open March-December. CH-1275 Chéserex. ☎ 22-369-9900, fax 22-369-9909, www.bonmont.ch.

The **Hotel des Alpes** is in a beautiful building in the heart of Nyon, set on a triangular corner close to the train station. The hotel offers free parking for guests and is handicapped-accessible. Built in 1905, it was renovated in 1996 and features two good restaurants: **Brasserie** and **Le Perdtemps**, both of which are open daily from 7 am-10 pm. ($-$$). Avenue Viollier 1, CH-1260 Nyon.

For a good dining experience in Nyon, try the **Auberge de Château**, a small local eatery with a lovely outside dining terrace that almost touches the Nyon Château. House specialties include veal (prepared five different ways) and game meats that are served primarily in the autumn months. Open year-round, but closed Wednesdays from October-April. ($$-$$$). 8 Place du Château, CH-1260 Nyon. ☎ 22-361-6312.

La Sarraz

This is a country village just slightly west off Highway 1 between the northern cities of Yverdon-les-Bains and Lausanne, in the watershed basins of the Rhône and Rhine rivers. This little village is often overlooked by tourists, but offers a large swimming complex (☎ 21-866-7979), horseback riding lessons in dressage, western and jumping (☎ 21-634-4871), a golf course (☎ 21-634-4871), and climbing expeditions (☎ 21-625-2555) from Magasin de Sports le Passe Montagne out of Lausanne. The local **Tourist Office** can be found at Grand-Rue 1, CH-1314 La Sarraz. ☎ 21-866-0229, fax 21-866-0227.

Lake Geneva & the West

For equine enthusiasts, this tiny village also contains a nice museum devoted to horses – the **Musée Suisse du Cheval**. This small museum – housed in a farmhouse that dates back to 1725 – was established in 1982 and features artwork, harnesses, saddles, carriages, rocking horses and sculptures depicting horses throughout the ages. In 1986 this museum was awarded the International Museum of the Year award by the European Arts Council. Open daily 1-5 pm, admission is 7Sfr for adults, 6Sfr for seniors and students, and 4Sfr for kids ages six-16. To get here, take Highway 1 (A1) toward Yverdon-les-Bains, exit at La Sarraz, and go to Avenue Château et dans le Bourg, where there is a parking lot. ☎ 21-866-6423, fax 21-866-1180.

■ Where to Stay

There are several hotels in La Sarraz. **Hôtel du Soleil Masetti Paolo** offers clean and comfortable lodgings, an Italian restaurant, café and bar in a country setting. ($$). Route de Cossonay 14, CH-1315 La Sarraz. ☎ 21-866-7139, fax 21-866-1020.

Hôtel de la Croix-Blanche is another option with 11 rooms, run by the Porchet family at Grand-Rue 22, CH-1315 La Sarraz. ☎ 21-866-7154, fax 21-866-7529.

Camping

There is a campground near the village, with modern conveniences and a parking lot, swimming pool, and on-site restaurant.

Vallorbe

Vallorbe sits next to the French border on the western edge of Canton Vaud, just off of Highway 9. It's known for its unique caves, the Iron Museum and an unusual military fort. The train station offers bike rental and money-changing services, and there is a small **Tourist Office** located nearby, just off the main street (Grand-Rue). ☎ 21-843-2583, fax 21-843-2262. Open daily from 9:30 am-noon and from 1:30-6 pm.

Just 1½ miles (2.4 km) southwest of Vallorbe's village center you'll find the **stalagmite and stalactite caves** that were formed by the Orbe River. You can walk there from Vallorbe; just follow the signs marked "Source Grottos," or, if driving, there's a free car lot just before you reach the caves. A one-hour guided tour costs 12SFr for adults, 6Sfr for children. The caves are open from May 1-November 1 annually, from 9:30 am-4:30 pm daily, and until 5:30 during the summer months.

To reach the **underground military fort at Pré-Giroud** will take you at least an hour on foot. There is a train that travels there as well, taking a little more than half an hour from Vallorbe. This underground military installation was built in 1937 to guard the Jourgne Pass and the Joux Valley route. On the outside it looks like a typical Swiss chalet, but underneath it has accommodations and quarters for over 130 people, including dorms, mess halls, a kitchen, and a medical facility with an operating room. Admission to this fascinating fort (which was never used during World War II), is 9Sfr for adults, 8Sfr for students, 5Sfr for children and includes a 75-minute guided tour in French. A written guide is available in English.

The **Iron & Railway Museum** features a natural forge, complete with a blacksmith hammering at his iron work, and a paddlewheel furnace driven by the Orbe River. You'll also find models of trains, with their Swiss routes and history. Admission is 9Sfr for adults, 8Sfr for students, 5Sfr for kids, and it's open daily from 9:30 am-noon and from 1:30-6 pm.

Sainte Croix

Sainte Croix is due west and north of Yverdon-les-Bains, almost at the border between Switzerland and France, and since the 19th century has been known for its music boxes. You'll find a museum devoted to the craft of making these intricate items, located in this tiny village of 4,500 inhabitants. The **Centre International de la Méchanique d'Art**, at Rue d'Industrie 2, is open Tuesday to Sunday, from 1:30-6 pm, with a 9Sfr admission cost for adults, 8Sfr for seniors and 7Sfr for kids. ☎ 24-454-2702, fax 24-454-321 for information.

Northern Vaud

Yverdon-les-Bains

This is at the far northern tip of Canton Vaud, along the southern shores of Lake Neuchâtel, and is primarily noted as a health resort. Considered to be the capital of northern Vaud, it has 24,000 inhabitants. Yverdon-les-Bains was once a Roman camp and remains have been found that date back beyond that era to 2800 BC. The village's main attraction is the Centre Thermal – thermal baths that the Romans used for medicinal purposes. Every day some 1,300 people come to this lakeside village to bathe in the mineral waters here.

■ Information Sources

Tourist Office

The **Office du Tourisme et du Thermalisme** is at Avenue de la Gare 1, CH-1401 Yverdon-les-Bains. ☎ 24-423-6290, fax 24-426-1122. Hours are from 8:30 am-noon and from 1:30-6 pm, Monday-Friday. On Saturday it is open from 9 am-noon.

Train Station

The local train station has bike rentals and a money exchange office that is open daily from 5:30 am-8:40 pm.

Post Office

There are three post offices in Yverdon-les-Bains, but the most convenient one is next to the train station at Avenue de la Gare, CH-1401 Yverdon-les-Bains. ☎ 24-424-2550, fax 24-424-2551. Hours are 7:30 am-6 pm, Monday-Friday. Saturday hours are from 8:30 am-noon.

Codes

The **postal code**s in Yverdon-les-Bains are CH-1400, 1401, 1402 and 1403; the **phone code** is 24.

Internet Access

For Internet access, you'll have to walk to Le Garage, an arcade with one computer at Rue de la Plaine 52, CH-1400 Yverdone-les-Bains. ☎ 24-426-0495.

■ Getting Around

The only ways to get around Yverdon-les-Bains are by bike or on foot, as the village's Old Town area is car-free.

■ Adventures

In the Water

You won't want to miss taking a dip in Yverdon-les-Bains' waters at **Centre Thermal**, located east of the Old Village center just off of the Avenue des Bains. Here you can test a number of treatments in one of the indoor or outdoor pools, get a massage or take a sauna or whirlpool treatment. Admission is 13Sfr to the pools, which are open Monday-Friday from **8 a**m-10 pm, and on the weekends and holidays from 9 am-8 pm. ☎ 24-426-1104, fax 24-423-0232.

■ Landmarks & Historic Sites

Yverdon-les-Bains is dominated by its castle, **Pestalozzi Château**, left, found in the center of town, Pestalozzi Platz. The château was originally owned by the Dukes of Savoy. It was later passed to the governors of Bern, and then became the home of the Pestalozzi Institute in 1805. Johann Pestalozzi was a famous European scholar and educator during the early 19th century and ran his school from here for 20 years. In 1912, it was modified into a library and small historical museum. You'll also find the **Hotel de Ville** (town hall), built in 1769-1773, in the main square of the village.

■ Museums

The **Science Fiction Museum** features books, magazines, photographs, comic books, films and videos, all devoted to the fantasy of science fiction. Open Tuesday-Sunday from 2-6 pm. ☎ 24-425-9310.

The **Museum of Clothing** (Modemuseum) displays thousands of articles of clothing and fashion accessories from 1850 to the present day. Open Tuesday-Sunday from 2-6 pm. ☎ 24-426-3164.

■ Where to Stay

Grand Hotel des Bains is an old castle that has been lovingly restored inside and out. It features private thermal baths and a beauty and health salon. ($$$-$$$$). Very swank rooms in a picturesque setting. 22 Avenue des Bains, CH-1401 Yverdon-les-Bains. ☎ 24-424-6464, fax 24-424-6465.

L'Ecusson Vaudois is in the old section of Yverdon-les-Bains and has a lively bar and pleasant eatery, along with nine rooms. Very close to all of the tourist sites, with reasonable rates ($$). Rooms are spacious, clean and lightly decorated. Rue de la Plaine 29, CH-14 Yverdon-les-Bains. ☎ 24-425-4015, fax 24-425-4015.

Hotel du Lac is a small and charming inn not far from the city center and only five minutes from the train station. Rooms are comfortable and clean. Offers free parking to guests and features traditional Swiss cuisine in their restaurant. ($$). Cygnes 25, CH-1400 Yverdon les Bains. ☎ 24-425-2307, fax 24-425-6636.

La Praire is a charming inn set on the edge of the Grand Parc and is only five minutes from the thermal baths. Open year-round, this inn is close to hiking trails and features tennis courts, a nice restaurant and all modern amenities. ($$-$$$). Avenue de Bains 9, CH-1400 Yverdon-les-Bains. ☎ 24-425-1919, fax 24-425-0079.

■ Where to Eat

Restaurant de la Plage offers a variety of fish specialties as well as great choices of Italian and French wines to complement your meal. ($-$$$). This French restaurant sits at the edge of Lake Neuchâtel and has a gorgeous view of the area and a playground for the kids. CH-1400 Yverdon-les-Bains. ☎ 24-425-3513, fax 24-426-4050.

Pizzeria L'Isle offers up 23 types of pizzas, as well as ox, duck, lamb, steak and various types of pastas. ($-$$$). Moulins 30, CH-1400 Yverdone-les-Bains. ☎ 24-425-2559, fax 24-426-3727.

Gift Camillo dishes up hearty portions of ox, pig, steaks, pastas and salads at reasonable prices. ($-$$). Moulins 10, CH-1400 Yverdon-les-Bains. ☎ 24-425-4282, fax 24-425-4229.

Payerne

This charming little village of just 7,000 residents sits in the far northern, snake-like section of the canton that lies between two portions of Canton Fribourg. The town got its name from a Roman family named Paterni who used to occupy this area. The highlight of the village is the **Abbey Church**, shown at left, which is probably one of the best examples of Romanesque architecture in all of Switzerland. It was founded in the 11th century and has impressive grey and golden blocks within its interior, along with beautiful 12th-century frescos. For tourist information, contact the Payerne **Tourist Bureau** at ☎ 26-660-6161.

From May to September, there are 170 camping spots available at the Payerne **campsite**, including a large swimming pool with diving boards and a water toboggan, a small football field and nearby tennis courts. There is also a refreshment bar and restaurant at the site. For standard accommodations, you'll want to try the **Hotel de la Gare,** a two-star hotel in the city center across from the train station that caters to families ($$). The hotel nightclub **Blue Lagoon** stays open very late every night. Rue de Temple 10, CH-1530 Payerne. ☎ 26-660-5621, fax 26-660-5660.

Avenches

Avenches is another small village, just to the north of Payerne. Home to just 2,000 residents, the village sits on a small hill and features a medieval castle and interesting old homes, which are actually part of the Roman settlement known as Aventicum. Just east of Avenches you can explore the excavated remains of this **Roman city**, which was at its height during the 1st and 2nd centuries. You'll find the remains of public baths, faint sections of the town walls, a theater, and a Corinthian column that is thought to have flanked a forum. There is also a small museum nearby that contains many other artifacts found at this site. Simply put, however, most Swiss come to Avenches to visit their nation's newest and largest equestrian facility, where both thoroughbred, steeplechase and harness racing take place during the year, as well as other equestrian disciplines, such as three-day events in dressage, show jumping and four-in-hand driving.

The **Avenches Tourist Office** is open from April to September, Monday-Friday from 8 am-noon, 1:30-5:30 pm; Saturday from 9 am-noon. Place de l'Eglise 3, CH-1580 Avenches. ☎ 26-675-1159, fax 26-675-3393.

Avenches' Roman Museum, located next to the excavations, features artifacts and historical finds from the ruins. Open March-September, Tuesday-Sunday from 10 am-noon, 1-5 pm, October-March, Tuesday-Sunday, 2-5 pm. Admission is 2Sfr. Avenue Jomini, CH-1580 Avenches.

Switzerland's newest racetrack is the **Institut Equestre National Avenches**, simply known to the locals as Avenches. Established in September 1999, this state-of-the-art equestrian facility features hurdle, steeplechase, flat racing and trotting. It has three main racing surfaces and four training surfaces, with 350 stalls. The complex also has a 400-foot (122-m) indoor arena with a viewing area/restaurant, bar, pressroom, and jumping paddock. The restaurant (**Le Paddock**) in the grandstand serves international fare overlooking the racetrack from a sun terrace, and also has an indoor dining area where you can watch jumpers perform in an indoor stadium. For information on racing times and dates, contact the IENA Secretariat at CH-1580 Avenches, ☎ 26-676-7676, fax 26-676-7677. For reservations in the dining room, ☎ 26-676-7671. This huge complex is hard to miss, located just off Highway A1 at the Avenches exit. You can see the complex from across the highway in either direction.

Lake Geneva & the West

*Place des Halles (Market Square) in Neuchâtel's old town center,
with buildings dating to the 16th century*

Canton Neuchâtel (NE)

■ At a Glance

Neuchâtel is renowned for its vineyards, lakes, green rolling hills, Jura Mountains and watchmaking. Not to be overlooked, either, is the French language spoken here. Many parents in the German-speaking areas of Switzerland send their children to Canton Neuchâtel to perfect the official second language of the country. Over 165,000 French-speaking, primarily Protestant citizens reside in Canton Neuchâtel, which joined the Swiss Federation in 1815, making it the second-youngest canton (along with Valais and Geneva). In terms of population, only six cantons have fewer inhabitants than Neuchâtel – Aargau, Glarus, Nidwalden, Uri, Obwalden, and Appenzell Innerrhoden.

The **River Doubs** officially separates the frontier between Switzerland and France on the western side of the canton, while Canton Vaud sits at the southern border, and cantons Jura and Bern are at the north and east. **Lake Neuchâtel** is the dividing line on the eastern side between cantons Bern, Fribourg and Vaud, and is connected to the Bieler See via the Zuhl-Kanal at the north end of the lake. In the upper northeast end of the canton is the Val de Ruz (Ruz Valley), while the Val de Travers (Travers Valley) is at the southern end.

Over the years Neuchâtel has become a favorite for vacationing Swiss and other Europeans who are on holiday, while it is often ignored by western tourists. Considered to be the cradle of the watchmaking industry in Europe, Neuchâtel began exporting its timepieces in the early 18th century. Today, "horology," as the craft is known, is still one of the most important industries of Canton Neuchâtel, along with the microtechnology and microelectronics industries.

Neuchâtel, while not a large canton – only 494

The River Doubs, near Les Brenets in the Neuchatel Jura

square miles (1,284 square km) – offers some of the most diverse and enlightening activities found anywhere in Switzerland. Ballooning, flying, horsebacking, hiking, wine-tasting and water sports abound here. In addition, there are a number of historic villages and towns worth exploring.

The **coat of arms** of Canton Neuchâtel is divided by three vertical panels of bright green on the left, white in the middle and red on the right, with a tiny white cross in the upper right hand corner, which symbolizes Neuchâtel's loyalty to Switzerland.

Neuchâtel

The capital of this canton of the same name is on the north shore of Lac de Neuchâtel, south of the Jura mountains on the east side of the canton. Ferries and motorboats criss-cross the lake daily, and the heart of the old city is on the lakeshore, just north of the harbor, where many 19th-century buildings can be seen. Just north of the city is the area known as Val-de-Ruz (Ruz Valley) that is a montage of fields and tiny villages.

■ Information Sources

Tourist Office

The main **Tourist Office for Neuchâtel** is the Tourisme Neuchâtelois at Hôtel des Postes, Case Postale 3176, CH-2001 Neuchâtel. ☎ 32-889-6890, fax 32-889-6296, www.neuchatel.ch.

Post Office

The Neuchâtel post office is open Monday-Friday from 7:30 am-5:30 pm year-round, Saturday from 8:30-noon. Hôtel des Postes, Avenue 1er Mars, CH-2001 Neuchâtel. ☎ 32-720-2601, fax 32-720-2619.

Codes

The **area code** for Neuchâtel is 32 and the **postal code**s are CH-2000, 2001 and 2003-2009.

■ Getting Around

This is best done on foot, or you can opt for a bike, which is available for rent at the train station. Lake Neuchâtel offers the opportunity for long walks or bike rides along the shoreline as well. Trains come in and out of Neuchâtel from throughout Europe on a regular basis, and this is also one of the stops for the TGV en route to Paris.

The Château and the Collegial Church on a hill overlooking Neuchâtel

■ Sightseeing

Guided tours of the entire city are available through the Neuchâtel Tourist Office. Most are done in groups of 25-30 people, with a group rate of 120Sfr. One of the most popular two-hour tours features the **Hotel DuPeyrou**, the **Collegial Church** and **Les Halles Square**. You can also visit the town via the **Tourist Train**, which provides visitors with a 45-minute ride through the Old Town. Daily during July and August; May, June and September on the weekends only. Admission is 6Sfr for adults and 3Sfr for kids. Reservations are made through the Tourist Office.

Wine Tasting takes place Monday through Friday from 9 am-noon, 1:30-5:30 pm at the **Caves du Vignoble Neuchâtel** (Neuchâtel Vineyards Wine Cellar). Contact the Tourist Office for information and reservations.

Landmarks & Historic Sites

The **Château**, left, dates from the 12th century and is now the home of the canton's government offices. Tours of 45 minutes are available free of charge during the following times: April 1-September 30, Monday-Friday at 10 am, 11 am, noon, 2, 3, and 4 pm; Saturday at 10 am, 11 am, 2, 3, and 4 pm; Sunday and holidays at 2, 3, and 4 pm. Château, CH-2000 Neuchâtel. ☎ 32-889-6001, fax 32-889-6071.

The **Tour des Prisons** (Prison Tower) provides a great panoramic view over Neuchâtel, the lake and the Alps. Open April 1-September 30 from 8 am-6 pm daily. Château, CH-2000 Neuchâtel. ☎ 32-717-7602.

Château de Vaumarcus was formerly known as the Château of 1,001 lives, and is situated on the shores of Lake Neuchâtel. This huge, walled fortress and castle dates from 1476 and is a definite must-see. It's now home to a restaurant, shops, a museum and a cultural center in the La Vaux valley. You can visit the Château upon request for 7.50Sfr for adults, 5Sfr for kids. ☎ 32-836-3636, fax 32-836-3637. Shops ☎ 32-836-3620. Winetasting is available upon request at ☎ 32-826-3636. The **Restaurant La Cour du Peintre** features exceptional gourmet cuisine for both lunch and dinner, with set menus or à la carte, and specializes in regional and international dishes. ($$-$$$). Open for breakfast, lunch and dinner, with varying times. Reservations are highly recommended. Château de Vaumarcus & Restaurant La Cour du Peintre. Cédric Gigon, CH-2028 Vaumarcus. ☎ 32-836-3610, fax 32-836-3637.

Museums

The **Neuchâtel Museum of Art & History** features 20 permanent and temporary exhibition rooms spotlighting traditional arts and their history. Open Tuesday-Sunday from 10 am-6 pm. Closed Monday. Wednesday free admission; otherwise adults 7Sfr, students and kids 4Sfr. Esplanade Leopold-Robert 1, CH-2000 Neuchâtel. ☎ 32-717-7925, fax 32-717-7929.

The **Museum of Ethnography** has permanent exhibitions of ancient Egypt and Tibet, among other cultures. Open Tuesday-Sunday from 10 am-5 pm. Closed Monday. Wednesday admission is free; otherwise adults 7Sfr, students and kids 4Sfr. Rue Saint-Nicolas 4, CH-2000 Neuchâtel. ☎ 32-718-1960, fax 32-718-1969.

The **Natural History Museum of Neuchâtel** features mammals and birds from throughout Switzerland. Open Tuesday-Sunday from 10 am-6 pm. Closed Monday. Wednesday admission is free; otherwise adults 6Sfr, students and kids 3 Sfr. Rue des Terreaux 14, CH-2000 Neuchâtel. ☎ 32-717-7960, fax 32-717-7969.

The **Dürrenmatt Center** is an exhibition center dedicated to literature and visual arts. Open Wednesday-Sunday from 11 am-5 pm, Thursday in the summer from 11 am-7 pm. Admission for adults is 8Sfr, kids 5Sfr. Chemin du Pertuis-du-Sault 74, CH-2000 Neuchâtel.

The **Military and Painted Fabric Museum** is housed in the Colombier Castle, in nearby Colombier, and features an outstanding collection of weapons, armor, clothing and artifacts from throughout history. Open March 1-November 1. Free 1½-hour guided tours are available Wednesday, Thursday, and Friday at 3 pm and on the first Sunday of each month at 2 pm and 3:30 pm.

The **Château & Museum at Valangin** features furnitures from the 17th and 18th centuries, as well as lace, weapons, paintings and engravings from the Neuchâtel area. Located just north of the city in the suburb of Valangin. Open year-round except from mid-December to mid-February, Tuesday-Sunday from 10 am-noon, 2-5 pm. Closed Friday afternoon and Monday. Admission is 5Sfr for adults and 3Sfr for students and kids. ☎ 32-857-2383.

On the west side of Neuchâtel is the tiny village of **Coffrane**, where you'll find a nice **Agricultural Museum**, depicting life on a typical 18th-century Neuchâtel farm. Free. Rue du Musée 30, CH-2207 Coffrane. ☎ 32-857-1512.

Farther northwest out of Neuchâtel is the town of **Cernier** that offers a fascinating **Museum of Firemen**. Exhibits include fire protection objects from the 19th century to the present. This free museum is definitely worth a visit. Open daily. Rue Frederic-Soguel, CH-2053 Cernier. ☎ 79-240-2900.

Also in Cernier is the **Farming Professions Park**, a free park dedicated to the cultivation of regional species and stock breeding, with emphasis on organic farming. Open 8 am-5 pm daily. Site de Cernier, Rue de l'Aurore, CH-2053 Cernier. ☎ 32-854-0540, fax 32-854-0541.

Just west of Cernier are the twin cities of **Chézard** and **Saint-Martin**, where you'll find a **pipe organ** manufacturer. Here you can view the construction, restoration, and assembly of pipe organs for free, but you must make a reservation. Grand-Rue 86, CH-2054 Chézard-Saint-Martin. ☎ 32-853-3121, fax 32-853-6880.

Just south of Neuchâtel, along Highway 5 near the lakeshore, is the picturesque village of **Boudry**, the birthplace of Philippe Suchard. Here you'll find the **Tour de Pierre** (Stone Tower), that now serves as a winetasting cellar, offering panoramic views of the area. Open May 1-October 31, Friday and Saturday from 5-8:30 pm, Sunday from 11 am-12:30 pm, 4:30-7 pm. Tour de Pierre, CH-2017 Boudry. ☎ 32-842-5916.

The **Areuse Museum**, named after the local river, features local history from the 19th century to the present. Open April 1-November 30, Tuesday-Sunday from 2-5:45 pm or by request. Admission is 3Sfr for adults, 2Sfr for kids. Avenue du College, CH-2017 Boudry. ☎ 32-846-1916.

For wine afficianados, the **Musée de la Vigne et du Vin** (Museum of Vines & Wine) can be found in the beautiful Château of Boudry, featuring a wine library and museum. Winetasting is possible by reservation only. Open Wednesday-Sunday from 2-6 pm. Closed Monday and Tuesday. Admission is 5Sfr for adults and 3Sfr for kids.

Parks & Gardens

 Neuchâtel's **Botanical Garden** is one of the prettiest gardens found anywhere in Europe. Free to the public unless you want a guide, and then it's only 5Sfr per person, per hour. Open April 1-September 30, from 9 am-8 pm, October 1-March 31 from 9 am-5 pm. The greenhouses are closed on Monday. Pertuis-du-Sault 58, CH-2000 Neuchâtel. ☎ 32-718-2350, fax 32-718-2357.

The **Jardin de Senteurs** (Garden of Scents) features over 1,000 aromatic and cultivated plants and is free to the public. Open April-October, Monday-Friday from 8:15 am-noon, 1:30-5 pm, Saturday from 8:15-11:45 am. Philippe Détraz, Châble 1, CH-2000 Neuchâtel. ☎ 32-753-2810, fax 32-753-2992.

GOOD VALUE TRIPS

Just north of Neuchâtel is the tiny suburb of **Hauterive**, which features a park and archeological museum known as the **Latenium**. Exhibits from the region include artifacts found under and around the lakes of Canton Neuchâtel, dating from Neanderthal times to the Middle Ages. Open year-round and handicapped-friendly. Tuesday-Sunday from 10 am-5 pm. Admission is 9Sfr for adults, 5Sfr for students and seniors, 4Sfr for kids ages 7-16. Espace Paul Vouga, CH-2068 Hauterive. ☎ 32-889-6910, fax 32-889-6286.

Farther north along Highway 5 is the small, walled and cobblestoned medieval village of **Le Landeron** – home to many small shops, cafés, restaurants and a modern art museum. The Town Hall museum features exhibits of Le Landeron history. This is an especially delightful little picturesque village that is ignored by many tourists. September is a great time to visit Le Landeron, when the village hosts its annual Antique Market.

At the far north end of Lake Neuchâtel is the port village of **Marin.** This simple village thrives on excursions such as hiking, biking, snowshoeing, canoeing, scuba diving, windsurfing, climbing and rafting – to name just a few. **Marin's Nature Excursions** can plan virtually any type of outdoor adventure that you can think of – at reasonable rates. Rue Fleur-de Lys, CH-2074 Marin. ☎ 32-753-0545, fax 79-679-4802. You'll also find the **Papilorama and Nocturama** in Marin, two domes containing two diverse tropical biospheres – one is home to nocturnal creatures such as bats, oppossums and raccoons, while the other features butterflies, birds, fish and lots of insects. Open April-September daily from 9 am-6 pm, October to March from 10 am-5 pm daily. Admission is 11Sfr. ☎ 32-753-4344.

■ Adventures

On Foot

Twenty different **one-day walks** are outlined in brochures that are available through the Neuchâtel Tourist Office. Also offered are **full-day excursions** via a 15-seat minibus, complete with a guide and meals for 98Sfr per person. Call ☎ 32-721-2100, fax 32-725-1111 for information. The **Time Path** gives the visitor an insight into evolution via a three-mile footpath, complete with a series of wooden signs and sculptures that trace the history of evolution. The path (free, year-round) is near the Botanic Garden and a booklet is available through the Tourist Office for 12Sfr.

In the Air

The **Neuchâtel Flying Club** offers flights over the three lakes, the Jura, the Alps and the entire canton. Prices vary depending on the type or length of flights, which can be experienced in a small plane or glider. Reservations required. Flights are made only in good weather. ☎ 32-841-3156, fax 32-841-1391. If you want to try ballooning, then contact **Captive Balloon** at ☎ 32-841-3156, fax 32-841-1391. Weather permitting, flights provide spectacular views of the city, lakes and surrounding countryside. Open daily from 9:30 am-midnight. Night flights from midnight to 2 am are available on Friday and Saturday nights and prices vary according to flight times and length. Reservations are required 48 hours in advance. ☎ 32-725-2800, fax 32-725-2802.

On the Water

Cruises on Switzerland's largest navigable stretch of water begin at the Port of Neuchâtel. Prices vary depending on the length and type of cruise. Port of Neuchâtel, CH-2000 Neuchâtel. ☎ 32-729-9600, fax 32-729-9601. **Public beaches** abound on the shores of Lake Neuchâtel, and you can also swim at the **Municipal Complex**'s indoor and outdoor pools at Nid du Cro, Route des Falaises 30, CH-2001 Neuchâtel. ☎ 32-722-6222.

On Wheels

There are 248 miles (397 km) of **bike paths** around Neuchâtel, and the Tourist Office can provide you with maps and routes for free. You can rent mountain bikes at the train station or at **Alilze**, Place du Septembre 12, CH-2001 Neuchâtel. ☎ 32-724-4090.

If you have a car, then you definitely won't want to miss the **Vue des Alpes**, a viewing area just north of Neuchâtel on Highway 20. The road

(13 km) from the city to this crest, which allows fantas-
...ps.

...as its own **indoor go-cart track**, open daily. Cost is
...utes. Monday-Thursday, 5 pm-midnight, Friday, 5 pm-1
...m 2 pm-1 am, Sunday and holidays from 2-8 pm. Rue de
...00 Neuchâtel. ☎ 32-730-3038, fax 79-449-4167.

On the Rails

The Transports Publics du Littoral Neuchâtelois offers the
only panoramic funicular ride in the Jura region. Built in
1910, this funicular links **Chaumont** to **La Coudre**, a small
suburb of Neuchâtel. The 13-minute ride to the top of the crest
of Chaumont is worth a visit. Chaumont rises 3,775 feet (1,150 m) above
Neuchâtel, and is the starting point for many hikes and walks throughout
the region. Open daily, admission is 9.20Sfr round-trip, 4.60Sfr for a one-
way ticket. Bikes are carried up free until noon each day. Place Godet,
Quai 5, CH-2001 Neuchâtel. ☎ 32-720-0600, fax 32-724-5134.

On Horseback

In nearby **Chaumont** you'll find the **Topeka Ranch**, where
you can ride Western-style on horseback or enjoy a stagecoach
ride, followed by an apertif. One- and two-day excursions either on horseback or on foot are also available, as are riding
lessons. The Ranch features a nice "Saloon" that specializes in fondue,
raclettes and barbecues upon request. Reservations are required. Prices
range from 15Sfr for kids pony rides, 40Sfr for a 1½-hour horseback ride
to 240Sfr for a two-day horseback excursion. Chemin du Grand Hôtel,
CH-2067 Chaumont. ☎ 32-753-2636.

■ Shopping

There are many little shops and cafés that offer chocolate,
pastries and the like in Neuchâtel. If it's souvenirs and trin-
kets you desire, then look no farther than **Magazin Caché**,
Rue du Saint-Honoré 2, CH-2001 Neuchâtel. ☎ 32-721-2022.

■ Where to Stay

Beau-Rivage is a 19th-century hotel that sits beside the lake
and offers the finest views of the area. Huge, luxurious bedrooms with cherry wood and rustic furnishings make this inn
a place not to be missed. ($$$$). The restaurant, with its seasonal specialties and fine wine list adds to the appeal of this unique inn.
The ambiance is old-world and spectacular. 1 Esplanade de Mont-Blanc,
CH-2001 Neuchâtel. ☎ 32-723-1515, fax 32-723-1616.

Le Maison du Prussien sits in the heart of the watchmaking area of Neuchâtel, on the lakeshore in an area that once belonged to Prussia (hence, the name). This ornate stone building features three floors, richly colored on the outside with blue and white shutters and gold trim. Inside, you'll find wooden ceilings, fireplaces and glamorous, modern bathrooms. ($$$-$$$$). Au Gor du Vauseyon, CH-2006 Neuchâtel. ☎ 32-730-5454, fax 32-730-2143.

■ Where to Eat

Le Cardinal Brasserie is one of the nicest cafés in Neuchâtel's Old Town, dating back to 1905. Fish and seafood are the seasonal specialties of the house, as are traditional Swiss dishes. Open daily. ($-$$$). 9 Rue du Syon, CH-2001 Neuchâtel. ☎ 32-725-1286.

La Maison des Halles features two restaurants: the top floor is formal and reserved, while the bottom level is more bar-like and relaxed. Both serve excellent cuisine, freshly caught local fish and other traditional Swiss favorites. ($-$$$$). Reservations recommended. Open daily (top level) from noon-2 pm, 7 pm-midnight; (bottom level) from 11 am-midnight. Rue du Trésor 4, CH-2001 Neuchâtel. ☎ 32-724-3141.

Du Marché is a lively and atmospheric eatery and bar, that offers hearty Swiss fare at reasonable rates. One floor above, you'll find a more formal dining area. ($-$$$). Place des Halles 4, CH-2000 Neuchâtel. ☎ 32-723-2330, fax 32-723-2333.

La Chaux-de-Fords

This town sits in a high valley in the Jura mountains, in the upper northwestern portion of Canton Neuchâtel. It is the birthplace of auto manufacturer Louis Chevrolet, the painter Leopold Robert, and the poet Blaise Cendrars. It is also home to the International Watch and Clock Museum and features a wide array of both summer and winter activities, sports and adventures.

■ Information Sources

Tourist Office

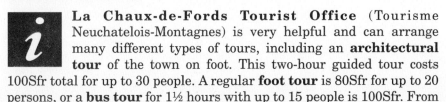

La Chaux-de-Fords Tourist Office (Tourisme Neuchatelois-Montagnes) is very helpful and can arrange many different types of tours, including an **architectural tour** of the town on foot. This two-hour guided tour costs 100Sfr total for up to 30 people. A regular **foot tour** is 80Sfr for up to 20 persons, or a **bus tour** for 1½ hours with up to 15 people is 100Sfr. From

Lake Geneva & the West

May-October, a two-hour **horse carriage tour** can be had, including a complete tour of the city and the Farming Museum. Cost is 15Sfr for adults and 7.5Sfr for kids. Espacite 1, CH-2302, La Chaux-de-Fords. ☎ 32-919-6895, fax 32-919-6297.

Post Office

La Chaux-de-Fords **post office** is open Monday-Friday from 7:30 am-noon, 1:30-6:30 pm, Saturday from 8 am-noon. Aveunue Leopold-Robert 63, CH-2301 La Chaux-de-Fords. ☎ 32-911-4171, fax 32-914-1159.

Codes

The **area code** for La Chaux-de-Fords is 32, and the **postal code** is CH-2300.

■ Adventures

In the Air

The **Aero Club of the Neuchâtel Mountains** features trips in a plane or glider over the three lakes, the Jura and the Alps, weather permitting. Open year-round; prices vary. Boulevard des Eplatures 56, CH-2300 La Chaux-de-Fords. Helicopter rides are available from **Helit Helicopters** year-round. Avenue Leopold-Robert 161, CH-2300 La Chaux-de-Fords. ☎ 32-926-6060, fax 32-926-5632.

On Snow & Ice

La Chaux-de-Fords features a variety of winter sports, including cross-country skiing, downhill skiing, sledding, tobogganing, illuminated ski trails for night-time skiing and indoor and outdoor ice rinks. The Tourist Office can provide you with maps and information of these activities.

■ Museums

Musée International d'Horlogerie (International Watchmaking Museum) features over 4,500 exhibits with 2,700 watches and 700 clocks. Open Tuesday-Sunday from 10 am-5 pm. Closed Monday. Admission is 8Sfr for adults, 4Sfr for seniors, students and kids. Rue des Musées 29, CH-2301, La Chaux-de-Fords. ☎ 32-967-6861, fax 32-967-6889.

Next door to the Watchmaking Museum in a 19th-century home is the **History Museum**, focusing on the people of La Chaux-de-Fords. Open Tuesday-Sunday from 10 am-5 pm. Admission is 5Sfr for adults, 3Sfr for kids. Free admission on Sunday until 1 pm. Rue des Musées 31, CH-2301 La Chaux-de-Fords. ☎ 32-913-5010, fax 32-913-4445.

The **Bell Foundry** features the ancient art of bell molding four days per week and casting twice weekly for free. Open Monday-Friday, 7 am-noon, 1:30-5 pm. Hôtel de Ville 26, CH-2300 La Chaux-de-Fords. ☎ 32-968-3943, fax 968-0564.

Musée des Beaux-Arts (Fine Art Museum) features artwork from Switzerland and around the world, including Van Gogh, Derain and Rouault. Open Tuesday-Sunday, 10 am-6 pm. Sunday admission is free; otherwise prices start at 6Sfr. Closed Monday. Rue des Musées 33, CH-2300 La Chaux-de-Fords. ☎ 32-913-0444, fax 32-913-6193.

The **Natural History Museum** profiles local and exotic fauna, as well as marine life. Closed Monday, open Tuesday-Saturday from 2-5 pm, Sunday from 10 am-noon, 2-5 pm. Admission is 5Sfr for adults, 3Sfr for kids. Avenue Léopold-Robert 63, CH-2300 La Chaux-de-Fords.

The **Museum of Farming and Handicrafts** is on a 17th-century farm, and shows what family life was like among watchmaking farmers. Lace making demonstrations are held on the first Sunday of each month. Admission is 5Sfr for adults, 3Sfr for kids. Open April-October, Tuesday-Saturday from 2-5 pm, Sunday from 10 am-noon, 2-5 pm. Closed Monday. November-February, open Wednesday, Saturday and Sunday from 2-5 pm. Crêtets 148, CH-2300 La Chaux-de-Fords. ☎ 32-926-7189.

■ Parks & Gardens

Bois du Petit Château is home to over 600 animals in a huge free public park that includes a zoo and a vivarium. Open daily from April 1-October 31, 8 am-7 pm; November-March 30, 8 am-5 pm. Rue Alexis-Marie Piaget, CH-2300 La Chaux-de-Fords.

■ Where to Stay

Grand Hotel Les Endroits features spacious, clean rooms in a quiet setting just outside the city center. Hearty meals are served at the in-house restaurant. ($$$-$$$$). 94 Boulevard des Endroits, CH-2300 La Chaux-de-Fonds. ☎ 32-925-0250, fax 32-925-0350.

Hotel du 1er Mars is simple and clean in the heart of old town. The restaurant features Swiss fare in generous portions. ($$). Rue du 1er Mars 7a, CH-2300 La Chaux-de-Fonds. ☎ 32-968-2832, fax 32-968-9022.

Fleur De Lys Hotel offers quiet rooms in a tranquil setting, with a hospitable staff. ($$$). 13 Avenue Leopold-Robert, CH-2300 La Chaux-de-Fonds. ☎ 32-913-3731, fax 32-913-5851.

La Chaux-de-Fonds Youth Hostel offers 80 beds from January 19 to November 24. ($). Rue du Doubs 34, CH-2300 La Chaux-de-Fonds. ☎ 32-968-4315, fax 32-968-2518, www.youthhostel.ch/chaux.de.fonds.

■ Where to Eat

Capucin au Gourmand features gourmet cuisine, including locally caught fresh fish and lobster. ($$$-$$$$). Reservations required. Charriere 125, CH-2300 La Chaux-de-Fonds. ☎ 32-968-1591.

Cercle Italien offers wood-oven pizzas, pasta and seafood at reasonable rates in a fun setting. ($$-$$$). Parc 43, CH-2300 La Chaux-de-Fonds. ☎ 32-913-1333.

The Nemrut Restaurant specializes in Turkish and vegetarian dishes. ($$-$$$). Daniel-Jeanrichard 14, CH-2300. ☎ 32-913-2048.

Le Locle

Le Locle is five miles (eight km) southwest of La Chaux-de-Fords on Highway 20 and is the "Second City" of watchmaking in this canton. The Le Locle Watchmaking Museum offers free 1½-hour guided tours on Sunday at 2:30 pm. Otherwise, admission is 7Sfr for adults, 4Sfr for kids and seniors. Open November 1-April 30, Tuesday-Sunday from 2-5 pm, May1-October 31, from 10 am-5 pm. Closed Monday. Route des Monts 65, CH-2400 Le Locle. ☎ 32-931-1680, fax 32-931-1670.

The Moulins Souterrains (Underground Mills) are underground caverns that contain a hydraulic factory. These have been in use since the 16th century and are a truly unique experience. Open May-October from 10 am-5 pm daily; November-April, Tuesday-Sunday from 2-5 pm. Admission is 9Sfr for adults, 6Sfr for kids. Le Col 23, CH-2400 Le Locle. ☎ 32-931-8989, fax 32-931-8915.

Le Locle Fine Arts Museum features paintings of Switzerland and the Jura region, as well as etchings and woodwork. Open Tuesday-Sunday from 2-5 pm. Admission is 6Sfr for adults, 3Sfr for seniors, students and kids. M.A.-Calame 6, CH-2400 Le Locle. ☎ 32-931-1333, fax 32-931-3257.

The Hôtel de Ville (Town Hall), left, features a beautiful interior and exterior with frescos and mosaics in classic Neo-Renaissance style. Open Monday-Friday from 7 am-noon, 2-5 pm. Free. ☎ 32-933-8400, fax 32-933-8401.

Only a few miles northwest of Le Locle is the Lake of Les Brenets and the spectacular Doubs Waterfall, a sight not to be missed. The Les Brenets Boat Company offers tours of all types, from April 1-October 31. Adults 11.5Sfr, kids 6.5Sfr. Le Pre du Lac, CH-2416 Le Brenets. ☎ 32-932-1414, fax 32-932-1717.

The **Agence Feel Concept** offers a variety of adventures, including canoe trips and "Tyrolienne" (crossing between cliffs), as well as food focus excursions. Prices vary according to the type and length of trip. Case Postal 565, CH-2400 Le Locle. ☎ 32-931-0865, fax 32-931-0919.

Les Ponts-de-Martel

Les Ponts-de-Martel is in the middle of the canton and provides a great spot for hiking and adventures. You won't want to miss the **Fromagerie Les Martel** (Cheese Dairy), that features a visitor's gallery and cheese tasting (4.5Sfr) or breakfast (12.5Sfr). Open daily from 8 am-noon, 5-7 pm. Major Benoit 25, CH-2316, Les Ponts-de-Martel.

You'll want to check out the **Green Trek Group**. They offer week-long or weekend trips of varying types in the countryside, including hiking with llamas, cycling, boating, horse-drawn carriage tours. Sleep in Indian teepees, tents, on straw or in dorms. All tours feature shower and bathroom facilities, with campfires and outdoor grills. Prices range from 499Sfr for adults for a week (399Sfr for kids) to weekend trips at 249Sfr for adults (195Sfr for kids six to 12-years old). Nathalie Guye, CH-2316, Le Ponts-de-Martel. ☎ 32-937-1516, fax 32-937-1532.

La Sagne

Southeast of Le Locle is the village of La Sagne, featuring **La Corbatière Equestrian Center**. Here you can take riding lessons or participate in riding holidays on horseback or in a carriage. Farm vacations are also available. Rides start at 25Sfr per hour. ☎ 32-913-4955. A nice little free **Regional Museum** can also be found in La Sagne, showing 20th-century objects and fauna of the region with an emphasis on local history. Open the first Sunday of each month from 1:30-5 pm. Le Crêt 103a, CH-2314 La Sagne. ☎ 32-931-8875.

A nice 1½-hour walk, known as the **Statues Route**, takes you from Les Petits-Ponts north up to La Sagne. This walk is steeply graded and a little challenging at points. For information, ☎ 32-919-6895, fax 32-919-6297.

Noiraigue

In the lower region of Canton Neuchâtel is the area known as the **Val-de-Travers**, better known to the locals as the "fée verte" or green valley. Traversed by the **Areuse River**, this lovely valley offers tiny villages that are perfect for long walks. At the upper end of the Val-de-Travers is the village of Noiraigue – the site of a guided walk known as the **Discovery**

Crossroad. Features include explanations on the forming of the Jura Mountain range, the Val-de-Travers, the Areuse gorges, as well as on the fauna and flora. These two-hour tours take place from April 1-October 20, every Sunday at 2 pm, meeting at the train station. Adults 12.5Sfr, kids 7.5Sfr, families (two adults, two-three kids) 35Sfr.

Travers

South of Noiraigue on Highway 10 is the village of Travers, home to an **Industrial Museum** that features a watchmaking and knitting workshop. Demonstrations daily at 11:30 am, May 1-October 20 for 7Sfr. The museum is free otherwise and is open daily from 9:30 am-5:30 pm. Site della Presta, CH-2105 Travers. ☎ 32-863-3010, fax 32-863-1925. **La Banderette Museum** in Travers features displays of local flora, fauna, geology, insects and minerals. Open May-October 15 on Sunday from 8 am-6 pm. ☎ 32-863-2284.

Travers is probably best-known for its **asphalt mines**, however, and features a restaurant known as the **Café des Mines** that offers ham cooked in asphalt. All visits are in the form of 1½-hour guided tours. Open April 1-October 20, daily from 10 am-2 pm; October 21-March 31, Sunday at 12 and 2 pm. Admission is 12.5Sfr for adults, 10Sfr for seniors and students, 7.5Sfr for kids ages 6-16. The Café is open April-October 20, from 9:30 am-5:30 pm.

Môtiers

Môtiers is a tiny village that is southeast off of Highway 10, south of Travers on a local road. This village is best-known as a one-time home of **Jean-Jacques Rousseau**. The museum in his name pays homage to the famous philosopher, who resided in Môtiers for three years. Open May-October on Tuesday, Thursday, Saturday and Sunday from 2-5 pm. Admission is 5Sfr. Rue Jean-Jacques Rousseau 2, CH-2122 Môtiers.

You'll also want to visit the **Regional Museum of History and Crafts** that recalls everyday life in the Val-de-Travers, from the 18th century to the present. Featured are the Chinese watchmakers, who came here and settled over 150 years ago. Open May-October, Tuesday, Thursday, Saturday and Sunday from 2-5 pm. Admission is 7Sfr for adults, 5Sfr for kids. Grand-Rue 14, CH-2112, Môtiers. ☎ 32-8611-3551.

The winetasting cellars of **Maulen & Cie**, **Le Prieure-St.-Pierre** are open Tuesday-Sunday from 10 am-noon, 3-6 pm. Visitors can experience the production of sparkling wines using the Champagne method. Admission is 7Sfr. ☎ 32-861-3961, fax 32-861-4364.

Le Bémont

At the far southwestern end of Canton Neuchâtel is the tiny village of Le Bémont, on a high plateau in the fold of the Jura mountains, just south of the **Lac de Tailléres**. The village – only half a mile from the French border – is situated on the Jura Highway, a road well-known to hikers, cyclists and cross-country skiers, and is a great base for panoramic walks and excursions. It is also a bird-watcher's paradise, and home to indigenous falcons. You can get here via auto or train, and just across from the wee train station is a very cute **youth hostel** that is suitable for families with children or the lone wanderer. The hostel is open from the end of January to mid-November annually and offers 93 beds. ($). CH-2877 Le Bémont. ☎ 32-951-1707, fax 32-951-2413, www.youthhostel.ch/bemont.

The Titlis Rotair cabins make a 360-degree rotation during their five-minute ascent from Engelberg to Klein Titlis (3028 m)

View of Fribourg through the Pont du Milieu

Canton Fribourg (FR)

Fribourg

■ At a Glance

Fribourg is best-known as the home to its Holstein cows – those black-and-white beauties that provide most of the agricultural folk in this region with their income. About 230,000 people reside in this mostly rural canton, which is 1,036 square miles (2,694 square km) of gently-rolling green hills, making it the eighth-largest canton in terms of land mass. In terms of population, it is the 12th-largest canton, comprised of mostly French-speaking Roman Catholics. Nearly 90% of the residents are natural-born citizens. Fribourg joined the Swiss Confederation in 1481 and has retained much of its medieval flavor, especially in the capital city of Fribourg.

With its green pastures and low-rolling hills, Canton Fribourg is excellent for walking, biking and hiking excursions and is often overlooked by tourists, except during the summer months, when many flock to the towns of Fribourg and Gruyère. Here you'll find the best fondue, made from the Gruyère cheese, as well as the traditional fall dish – *Kilbi*. The Fribourg feast, which takes place each autumn (in September), symbolizes the return of the Fribourgeoise cows from the upper Alpine pastures, and also features sweet smoked ham, lamb stew and a mixture of liquored pears.

The **coat of arms** of Fribourg represents the colors from the Dukes of Zähringen, who originally inhabited this area. The shield is split horizontally, with the top part painted black and the bottom section in white.

Fribourg old town center, with Saint Nicholas Cathedral

The capital city of **Fribourg** sports a great number of castles, churches and monasteries in a cobblestone village with quaint, narrow streets that sits along the shores of the Saane River. Founded in 1157, Fribourg is home to 42,000 inhabitants who enjoy lively Wednesday and Saturday mornings throughout the year, when a lively market is held near the village's town hall. Here you'll find fresh-baked goods, produce and local artisans selling handmade crafts. Most of the Old Town is on the west bank of the river.

■ Information Sources

Tourist Office

The **Fribourg Tourist Office** is open Monday-Friday, 9 am-12:30 pm, 1:30-6 pm; Saturday, 9 am-12:30 pm, 1:30-4 pm; Sunday, 9 am-12:30 pm. Closed from October-April on Saturday afternoons. Avenue de la Gare 1, CH-1700 Fribourg. The cantonal information numbers are ☎ 26-321-3175, fax 26-322-3527, and the town information numbers are ☎ 26-350-1111, fax 26-350-1112, www.fribourgtourism.ch. The train station is in the center of Old Town at Avenue de la Gare 1.

Post Office

There are nine post office branches in Fribourg, and one of the most convenient is near the train station at Avenue de Tivoli 3, CH-1701 Fribourg. ☎ 26-351-2655, fax 26-351-2656. It is open Monday-Friday, 7:30 am-6:30 pm, Saturday from 8 am to noon.

Codes

The **area code** for Fribourg is 26 and the **postal codes** are CH-1700-1709.

■ Getting Around

Getting around in Fribourg is best done on foot, as most of the streets are narrow, steep and cobblestone. If you're into fountains, then you'll love this city, as there are quite a few medieval fountains in the Old Town. Many of them are copies, as the originals have been relegated to the Museum of Art & History.

■ Adventures

On Foot

You'll want to get the view of Fribourg from the top of a small hill that overlooks the city and one which also offers a nice panoramic view of the countryside, with the Bernese Alps in the background. If you're lucky, on a very clear evening, you can even glimpse the southern Alps as well. To get here, you can either walk or take the local funicular that leaves hourly. You'll also pass a covered wooden bridge that dates back to 1580, known as the **Pont de Berne**.

You also might want to visit the **Schwarzsee** (Black Lake) while in Fribourg. This is an easy journey either by car, bike or on foot. It is 17 miles (27 km) south of Fribourg, and really makes for a nice bike ride in the summer. To get there, take the local road that travels southeast from Fribourg in the direction of Plaffeien. When you reach this village follow the signs to the village of Gypsera and the Schwarzsee (south). The scenery along this route is breathtaking.

On Snow

The **Alpes Fribourgeoises** (Fribourg Alps), as they are known, offer plenty of opportunities for downhill and cross-country skiing as well as snowboarding and sledding. The Schwarzee (Black Lake/Lac Noir in French) is 17 miles (27 km) south of Fribourg, offering three ski areas with eight lifts. You'll also find a short cross-country ski trail, and a skiing and snowboarding school. There are several nice peaks here ranging in height from 5,500 to 6,500 feet (1,677-1,980 m).

■ Sightseeing

The highlight in Fribourg is **St. Nicholas Cathedral**, a 15th-century church with an imposing bell tower that overlooks much of the city. Throughout this area you'll see excellent examples of Gothic houses and fountained squares. Slightly north of the Cathedral is the **Église des Cordeliers**, a church whose various parts were built from the 13th through the 18th centuries. Its famed Masters of the Carnation on the altar contains signatures of 15th-century artists who signed their names with a red or white carnation. For opening times, ☎ 26-347-1160.

Landmarks & Historic Sites

The **Town Hall of Fribourg** is a 16th-century structure that features an octagonal clock tower with motorized figures appearing every hour.

Museums

The **Fribourg Museum of Art & History** offers a rich collection of historical art objects dating from the city's early history to the present day. Housed in the Ratze Palace, this is home to the largest collection of Swiss sculptures from the early half of the 16th-century, and also includes works by Courbet, Marcello, Delacroix, Hodler, Crotti and Tinguely. Open Tuesday-Sunday, 11 am-6 pm, Thursday from 11 am to 8 pm. Rue de Morat 12, CH-1700 Fribourg. ☎ 26-305-5140.

Fri-Art Fribourg is the town's leading contemporary art center, presenting exhibits, displays and discussions by modern artists worldwide. Open Tuesday-Friday from 2 to 6 pm, Thursday from 8 to 10 pm, weekends from 2 to 5 pm. Petites-Rames 22, CH-1701 Fribourg. ☎ 26-323-2351.

The **Gutenberg Museum** is housed in a 700-year-old building, now opened as the Swiss Museum of Graphic Arts and Communication. The museum features displays documenting the history of the printing press, as well as possible future techniques. Open Wednesday-Sunday, 11 am-6 pm. Place Notre Dame 16, CH-1700 Fribourg. ☎ 26-347-3828.

The **Fribourg Brewery & Beer Museum** is housed in the former cellars of the Cardinal Brewery, featuring many antiquated objects related to brewing beer by traditional methods. The brewery adjoins the museum and provides insight into modern-day brewing and bottling methods. Admission by appointment only at Passage de Cardinal, CH-1700 Fribourg. ☎ 26-429-2211.

Museum of Natural History features permanent exhibitions of minerals, local wildlife, zoology, insects, and reptiles, as well as temporary displays on varying subjects. Open Monday-Sunday from 2 to 6 pm. Chemin du Musée 6, CH-1700 Fribourg. ☎ 26-300-9040.

The **Swiss Museum of Sewing Machines** is in the middle of the city, in a vault dating from the 12th century, and features sewing machines and other useful household objects from around the world. Open on the weekends only, upon request and appointment. Grand Rue 58, CH-1701 Fribourg. ☎ 26-475-2433.

The **Fribourg Museum of Puppets** features all types of puppets made from a variety of materials, and is in the center of town. Puppet shows are given at various times annually. Open on the weekends, 2-5 pm, or by request. Derrière-les-Jardins 2, CH-1701 Fribourg. ☎ 26-322-8513.

Shopping

Some of the best shopping spots are in and around the **Place de Tilleul** (Linden Square), the **Rue de Romont** and the **Rue de Lausanne**. Here you'll find local artisans as well as a few designer stores, and lots of cafés and coffee shops. **La Clef du Pays** features souvenirs from Fribourg. Rue eu Tilleul 1, CH-1701 Fribourg. ☎ 26-322-5120. You can also find such items at the **Office de Tourisme** (Tourist Office) at 1 Place du la Gare, CH-1700 Fribourg. ☎ 26-321-3175.

■ Where to Stay

The Golden Tulip is one of the best hotels in the city, near the train station and offering luxury rooms and suites, with a fine restaurant and private parking. Has good views of the old town and the Alps. ($$$-$$$$). Grand-Places 14, CH-1700 Fribourg. ☎ 26-351-9191, fax 26-351-9192, www.goldentulip.ch.

HOTEL PRICE CHART	
$	30-75Sfr ($20-$49)
$$	76-205Sfr ($50-$109)
$$$	206-299Sfr ($110-$200)
$$$$	300Sfr+ ($200+)

Au Parc Hotel is ultra-modern, clean and comfortable and features a French and Thai restaurant, a bar, disco and a shopping center. The rates include breakfast. ($$-$$$). The disco "Le Baccara" is open Tuesday-Saturday from 9:30 pm-4 am. Route de Villars 37, CH-1700 Fribourg. ☎ 26-429-5656, fax 26-429-5657, www.auparc-hotel.ch.

Duc Berthold is a first-class hotel in the heart of old town, next to the Cathedral. Housed in a historic building, this hotel features two restaurants (**L'Escargot** and **La Marmite**) and 36 modern rooms with all Swiss comforts. On-site parking, and breakfast included in rates. Dogs allowed. ($$-$$$). Rue des Bouchers 5, CH-1700 Fribourg. ☎ 26-350-8100, fax 26-350-8181.

Hotel Alpha is in the heart of the city, near the train station and the Fribourg University campus. Features private parking, a restaurant, bar, sauna, a cinema and fitness complex. The 27 rooms are clean and comfortable. This hotel is in a good location, and within walking distance of most of the city's tourist spots. ($$-$$$). Rue du Simplon 13, CH-1700 Fribourg. ☎ 26-322-7272, fax 26-323-1000.

My Lady's Manor is a nice little bed and breakfast in the small village of **Estavayer-le-Lac**, set on Lake Neuchâtel 14 miles (22 km) west of Fribourg. With only nine rooms, this gem features reasonable rates ($$) and terrific surroundings. The home was originally a mansion (built in 1910) and has been completely restored, set in a large garden surrounded by trees. Only a few minutes walk from the train station, the beach and bicycling and jogging trails. Route de la Gare, CH-1470 Estavayer-le-Lac. ☎ 26-664-2316, fax 26-663-1993.

Camping

Camping is available in nearby Marly, at **La Follaz Campground**, just south of the Fribourg center. Sitting on the riverbank, this campground is open from April to the end of September ($). ☎ 26-436-2495. **Campground Schiffenen** is north of the city in the village of Dudingen, and is open year-round ($-$$). ☎ 26-493-1917.

Lake Geneva & the West

■ Where to Eat

 Restaurant Acacia is in the nearby village of Marly, only two miles (3.2 km) from Fribourg's center. It has a handful of nice rooms should you decide to spend the night ($-$$). The restaurant features French fare and includes a nice sun terrace for outside dinning and a large brewery set in an informal atmosphere. ($-$$). Rte de la Gruyère 8, CH-1723 Marly. ☎ 26-430-0700, fax 26-430-0705.

DINING PRICE CHART	
Prices based on a typical entrée, per person, and do not include beverage.	
$	15-25Sfr ($10-$16)
$$	26-45Sfr ($17-$29)
$$$	46-70Sfr ($30-$47)
$$$$	71Sfr+ ($47+)

Gruyères

At the foot of the Moleson, this is one of the fine jewels of Switzerland. Best visited in the fall, winter or spring, when all the tourists are gone, Gruyères is home to one of the country's finest cheese-making factories. When mixed together with Vacherin – another style of cheese produced in Fribourg – the Gruyère cheese becomes the perfect fondue mixture. For centuries Gruyères belonged to a series of local counts, who took refuge in the giant castle here. The host of medieval houses and cobblestone walkways and lookout spots are especially fun.

If you visit Gruyères in the early summer, you'll be sure to catch the cow herders leading their droves of cattle to high Alpine pastures. The herders – known as *armaillis* – allow the cows to graze on the rich grasses found on the sunny mountain slopes until the fall months, when they make the annual pilgrimage back down to their winter quarters.

The **Gruyères Tourist Office** is in the town cen-

The medieval town of Gruyères is dominated by the castle, once home to the counts of Gruyères

ter, CH-1663 Gruyères. ☎ 26-921-1030, fax 26-921-3850, www.gru-
yeres.ch.

*Don't miss **La Maison de Gruyères** – the local
factory for Switzerland's famous cheese. They
produce 48 huge wheels of cheese (seen at left)
each day here, and can stock 7,000 cheese
wheels. Admission is 5Sfr per person. It's open
from 9 am to 7 pm (May-October), and from 9
am to 3 pm (October-May). You can watch the
cheese being made, with explanations in a
variety of languages. There is also a restaurant
and gift shop. Located just downhill from the
village of Gruyères, at Pringy-Gruyères, CH-
1662. ☎ 26-921-8400, fax 26-921-8401.*

■ Where to Stay

La Fleur de Lys hotel and restaurant was built in 1653 in the
heart of this medieval village. It was recently renovated to include all modern amenities, while the restaurant offers local
dishes, including trout from local lakes, fondue, raclette, cha-
let soup, and Alp macaroni, with a wide range of homemade desserts. ($$).
Very reasonable rates and a cozy, homey atmosphere prevail here. CH-
1663 Gruyères. ☎ 26-921-8282, fax 26-921-3605.

Six miles (9.6 km) outside of Gruyères and three miles (4.8 km) from Bulle
is **Hotel Chalet Les Colombettes**, set in the unpretentious countryside.
There are only 14 rooms here, but they are all ultra-modern, clean and
comfy. There is on-site free parking, a café (open 7:30 am-noon) and a res-
taurant (open 11:30 am-10:30 pm). They also offer currency exchange in
the hotel. ($$-$$$). CH-1628 Vuadems, Gruyères. ☎ 26-919-6063, fax 26-
919-6069. In the US, you can call ☎ 800-359-4827.

Hostellerie St.-Georges is a traditional inn in the center of Gruyères
that includes a bar, restaurants and functional and clean rooms. Near the
bus stop, this hotel is perfect for walking and hiking excursions. ($$). CH-
1663 Gruyères. ☎ 84-885-8757.

Hostellerie Des Chevaliers is charming and homey, offering splendid
views of the surrounding countryside. The rooms were individually decorated with lots of period and antique furniture. The in-house restaurant is
closed Sunday and Monday. ($$-$$$). CH-1663 Gruyères. ☎ 26-921-1933,
fax 26-921-2552.

■ Where to Eat

La Chalet Gruyères is one of the most popular spots in the village, featuring fondue, raclette with dry meat, cold and hot sandwiches, and delightful desserts such as fresh raspberries and Gruyères-made cream. There are three separate dining areas, one more formal and elegant than the other two. Be sure to try the Soupe de Châlet, a delightful mix of vegetable, Gruyères cream, and croutons. ($-$$). CH-1663 Gruyères. ☎ 26-921-3434, fax 26-921-3313.

Auberge de la Hall is in the heart of Gruyères and features all types of fondues, cheeses, trout and fruits with cream. Hosts Christian and Marie Chassot-Corboz serve up hearty dishes in a rustic and cozy setting at very reasonable prices ($-$$). CH-1663 Gruyères. ☎ 26-921-2178, fax 26-921-3313.

Bulle & Broc

Bulle is just east off of Highway 12, about three miles (4.8 km) northwest of Gruyères, while the sister city of Broc is about 1.2 miles (1.9 km) north. Broc, a tiny village, is known mainly as the headquarters of the **Nestlé-Cailers Chocolate Factory**. You can visit the factory from April to late October, Monday-Friday, by appointment only. ☎ 26-921-5151.

In Bulle you'll want to visit the **Musée Gruéirin**, a regional museum that features artwork, furniture, and religious artifacts. Open Tuesday-Saturday from 10 am-noon, 2-5 pm, Sunday and holidays from 2 to 5 pm. Admission is 5Sfr. The museum is behind the large, 13th-century castle in the middle of town.

You'll find nice accommodations at **Hotel Du Donnelier**, a family-run inn that offers two restaurants and a cellar bar, as well as 16 individualy decorated rooms. Breakfast is included in rates. ($-$$). Grand-Rue 31, CH-1630 Bulle. ☎ 26-912-7745, fax 26-912-3986. **Hotel Les Alpes**, in the city center is suitable for handicapped travelers and those journeying with pets. The rooms are spacious and a bit pricey for the area, however. ($$-$$$$). Rue Nicolas Glasson 3, CH-1630 Bulle. ☎ 26-912-9292, fax 26-912-9992. **Hotel Le Rallye** is an ultra-modern hotel in downtown Bulle, with all modern amenities and very reasonable rates ($$). Free parking for guests with spacious, comfortable rooms and a nice restaurant that serves up seasonal fare. Route de Riaz 8, CH-1630 Bulle. ☎ 26-919-8040, fax 26-919-8044.

Châtel-St-Denis

At the far southern tip of Canton Fribourg is Châtel-St-Denis, a wee village that is close to a wide array of activities, such as horseback riding, cross-country skiing, tennis, ice skating and a small zoo. If you like to camp, this is a great area and features a very nice campground – **Le Bivouac**, that sits high above Lake Geneva on the slopes of the lovely hills above Châtel-St-Denis. This campground has a swimming pool and kids' pool, a bar, sun-terrace, a self-service snack shop and a bakery, as well as a fitness circuit, jogging trails, showers, washing and drying facilities, and a mountain bike route. Contact the Fivaz family, owners at Camping Le Bivouac, Route des Paccots 21, CH-1618 Châtel-St-Denis. ☎ 21-948-7849, fax 21-948-7849.

If you're looking for fancier accommodations, then check out **Hotel Restoring Hermitage** at nearby Paccots, only minutes away from Châtel-St-Denis. The hotel has a brewery-restaurant and a nice bar-restaurant, as well as a fancier dining room and two separate smaller bars. Some rooms have Jacuzzis. ($$-$$$). A bit overpriced, but the ski lifts are only a few minutes walk from the hotel. CH-1619 Paccots. ☎ 21-948-3838, fax 21-948-3800.

A farmer accompanies his herd to the La Frasne Alp above Chatel-St-Denis

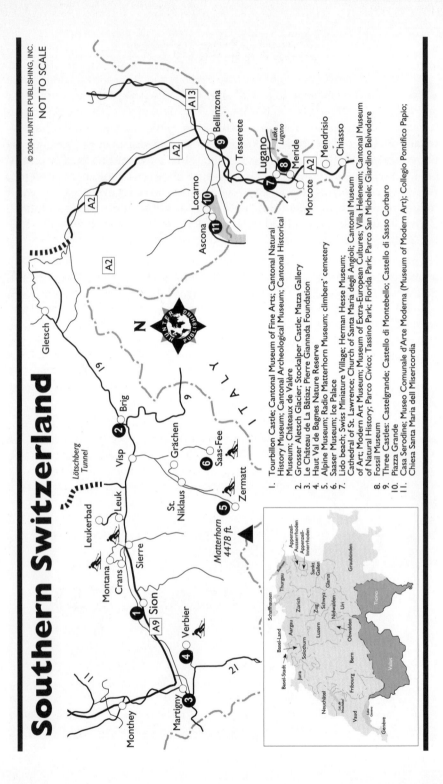

Southern Switzerland

Gletsch

Brig

Lötschberg
Tunnel

Visp

Leuk

Leukerbad

St.
Niklaus

Grächen

Saas-Fee

Montana
Crans

Sierre

Sion

Verbier

Martigny

Monthey

Matterhorn
4478 ft.

Zermatt

ITALY

Lugano

Lake
Lugano

Bellinzona

Tesserete

Locarno

Ascona

Mendrisio

Chiasso

Meride

Morcote

N

1. Tourbillon Castle; Cantonal Museum of Fine Arts; Cantonal Natural History Museum; Cantonal Archeological Museum; Cantonal Historical Museum; Châteaux de Valère
2. Grosser Aletsch Glacier; Stockalper Castle; Matza Gallery
3. Le Château de La Bâtiaz; Pierre Giannada Foundation
4. Haut Val de Bagnes Nature Reserve
5. Alpine Museum; Radio Matterhorn Museum; climbers' cemetery
6. Saaser Museum; Ice Palace
7. Lido beach; Swiss Miniature Village; Herman Hesse Museum; Cathedral of St. Lawrence; Church of Santa Maria degli Angioli; Cantonal Museum of Art; Modern Art Museum; Museum of Extra-European Cultures; Villa Heleneum; Cantonal Museum of Natural History; Parco Civico; Tassino Park; Florida Park; Parco San Michele; Giardino Belvedere
8. Three Castles: Castelgrande; Castello di Montebello; Castello di Sasso Corbaro
9. Piazza Grande
10. Casa Serodine; Museo Comunale d'Arte Moderna (Museum of Modern Art); Collegio Pontifico Papio;
11. Chiesa Santa Maria dell Misericordia

Southern Switzerland

The final region covered in this book contains the two southernmost cantons of **Valais** and **Ticino**. Though connected, both are vastly different in terms of geography, language and culture. Valais is home to some of Switzerland's best ski resorts, including the village of Zermatt, and the mighty Matterhorn.

Located on the western side of this region, Valais is literally one long valley that sits snugly in between the Bernese and Valais mountain ranges. You can drive through this region easily via Highway 9, which will take you from one edge of the canton to the other, or you can take a train from almost anywhere in Switzerland. One of the best drives ever is to go south from **Visp** on Highway 9 to the village of **Täsch**, park your car and then take the rack railway up to the auto-free village of Zermatt. The scenery is spectacular and the roads are just plain fun if you enjoy a bit of challenging driving.

The sister canton of Ticino at the eastern side of this region features palm trees, fruit groves and beautiful lakes. Here, Italian is the most popular language, and the atmosphere is laid-back and much more relaxed than in any other Swiss canton. Ticino is a mountainous area with attractive Alpine foothills, lakeside walking paths, and majestic peaks. Merlot is a very popular local wine, and the landscape and hills are dotted with tiny houses that are more reminiscent of neighboring Italy than of traditional Swiss chalets. It is here that you can travel through the St. Gotthard Pass or walk along the Strada Alta hiking trail

Canton Valais (VS)

■ At A Glance

The canton of Valais is perhaps best-known as the home of the ever-stunning Matterhorn – perhaps the most frequently photographed mountain in the world outside of Mt. Everest. Throughout this canton of 278,200 residents you'll also find lovely mineral collections, outstanding wines, and healthy hot springs and natural spa waters.

Valais joined the Swiss Confederation in 1815 and, as such, is one of the youngest and most rugged cantons. It is also the third-largest, behind Graubünden and Bern in terms of land mass at 3,240 square miles (8,424 square km). Nearly 40% of its residents work in the tourism industry, with French being the dominant language among these primarily Roman Catholic people, although you'll hear a good deal of Swiss-German and Swiss-Italian as well.

The coat of arms for Canton Valais is a lively display of red and white stars set against conflicting backgrounds. Split vertically, the right side is red with four white stars and the left side features four red stars against a white background. Running down the center are five stars split vertically with half white (on the right) and half red (on the left). These colors represent the Episcopal banner of Sion, while the 13 stars represent the 13 districts of this canton.

Sion

Sion, the capital of Canton Valais, is best-known for its castles, **Valére** and **Tourbillon**, whose mighty silhouettes hover over this village. "Sitten," as it known in German is also home to a host of vineyards and is a wine-making spot, with about 28,000 primarily French-speaking residents. Here you'll find more museums than any other city in Valais. Sion is also an especially nice town for walking.

■ Information Sources

Tourist Office

Sion Tourisme can be found at Place de la Planta, CH-1950 Sion. ☎ 27-327-7727, fax 27-327-7728. Hours are Monday-Friday from 8:30-6 pm, Saturday from 10 am-4 pm, Sunday 9 am-noon during July and August. Otherwise, the hours are Monday-Friday from 8:30 am-noon, 2-5:30 pm, Saturday from 9 am-noon. For cantonal information, contact **Valais Tourism**, Rue Pré-Fleuri 6, CH-1951 Sion. ☎ 27-327-3570, fax 27-327-3571, Swww.matterhornstate.com.

Train Station

The Sion train station is on the city's south side, at Cour de la Gare, and it offers bike rental and money exchange offices that are open daily.

Post Office

Sion's post office is open from 8 am-noon, 1:30-5:30 pm daily, Saturday from 8 am-noon. It is just slightly west of the train station on a tiny side street between Cour de la Gare and Avenue de France, across from the bus station.

Codes

The **postal code** in Sion is CH-1950 and the **area code** is 27.

■ Getting Around

Sion is best seen on foot. It's a lovely little village to explore, especially with the castle and the church looming impressively above.

■ Adventures

On Foot

There are numerous wine-tasting and vineyard trips to take in and around Sion. The Tourist Office can help you with arrangements and details.

You can play 18 holes of golf at the **Golf-Club de Sion** year-round during the week for 90Sfr, and on weekends for 100Sfr. Located at Route de Vissigen 150, CH-1950 Sion. ☎ 27-203-7900, fax 27-203-7901, www.golfclubsion.ch.

On Horseback

You can go horseback riding in Sion or take a group lesson at the **Manège de Tourbillon**, at Rue du Stade 52. An hour ride costs 30Sfr or a lesson in a group is 27Sfr. ☎ 27-203-3427 for information. The **Ranch des Maragnènes** also offers one-hour rides through the countryside starting at 24Sfr per hour, or a one-hour lesson for 20Sfr. Week-long excursions start at 450Sfr. Contact them at Route de Vex, CH-1950 Sion. ☎ 27-203-1313, www.ranch.ch.

In the Air

For airplane and helicopter trips over and around the Alps of Sion, Valais and Zermatt, contact **Air-Glaciers**, at Rte de l'Aéroport, CH-1951 Sion. ☎ 27-329-1415, fax 27-329-1429, www.air-glaciers.ch. Prices start at 268Sfr for one to five people in a plane and 344Sfr for one to four people in a helicopter. The **Groupe de Vol à Moteur**, at the Sion Airport, CH-1950 Sion, offers flights in planes (two people, 164Sfr) and helicopters (three people,

206Sfr). ☎/fax 27-323-5707, www.gvmsion.ch. **Helicoptère Service** at the Aéroport de Sion, CH-1950 Sion, offers flights around the Matterhorn from Sion for 164Sfr per person. ☎ 27-327-3060, fax 27-327-3061, www.heliservice.ch.

For parachuting and sky-diving, contact the **Para Club Valais**, at Case Postale 1061, CH-1951 Sion. Introductory jumps start at 250Sfr, and tandem jumps range from 300-350Sfr. ☎ 32-315-2885, fax 27-323-2497, www.pcv.ch.

In the Water

Scuba diving lessons are available from **Ecole de Plongée des Iles**, which offers outdoor and indoor pool instruction. Route des Iles 22, CH-1950 Sion. ☎ 27-323-0202.

On Snow

The **Sion Snowboarding School** offers lessons. Phone them at ☎ 27-327-7727 for costs and times.

Other Sports

If you enjoy inline skating, check out the **Sion Rollerpark** (Skatepark Tourbillon). ☎ 27-324-1262, fax 27-324-1288.

■ Landmarks & Historic Sites

The **Tourbillon Castle** sits high above Sion on the north side of the village. This medieval castle was first built in the 13th century and later destroyed by a fire in 1788. Its ruins are definitely impressive. Open from mid-March to mid-November, every day except Monday, from 10 am-6 pm. CH-1950. ☎ 27-606-4670. You also don't want to miss the **Tour des Sorciers** (Sorcerer's Tower), at Rue de la Tour – the last standing testament to the fortress walls that once surrounded this village. Open October-May, Tuesday-Sunday from 1-5 pm; June-September, Tuesday-Sunday from 1-6 pm. Admission is 3Sfr.

■ Museums

Museums in Sion are typically open every day except Monday. Information for all of them in Sion is at the **Valais Museum Information**, 15 Place de la Mjorie, CH-1950 Sion. ☎ 27-606-4670, fax 27-6060-4674.

The **Cantonal Museum of Fine Arts** features paintings and sculptures from late 19th- and 20th-century artists. Open every day except Monday from 10 am-noon, 2-6 pm. Admission is 5Sfr for adults and 2.5Sfr for kids. Place de la Majorie 15, CH-1950 Sion. ☎ 27-606-4670.

Cantonal Natural History Museum recently added a new room dedicated to large predators such as bears, wolves, bearded vultures, and lynxes. Open every day except Monday from 2-6 pm. Admission is 3Sfr for adults, 1.5Sfr for kids. Avenue de la Gare 42, CH-1950 Sion. ☎ 27-606-4670.

Cantonal Archeological Museum features displays of Valais during Roman times. Open every day except Monday from 10 am-noon, 2-6 pm. Admission is 4Sfr for adults, 2Sfr for kids. This museum also features a very interesting "Numismatics Room" that pays homage to both authentic and counterfeit coins. Rue de Châteaux 12, CH-1950 Sion. ☎ 27-606-4670.

Cantonal Historical Museum displays artifacts from the fourth to the 20th centuries. Open every day except Monday from 10 am-noon, 2-6 pm. Admission is 5Sfr for adults, 2.5Sfr for kids. Châteaux de Valère, CH-1950 Sion. ☎ 27-606-4670.

The huge fortress of **Châteaux de Valère** encompasses various buildings in addition to a church. The church contains the oldest playable organ in the world, built in the 14th century. You'll also find 15th- and 16th-century frescos inside. The church includes a small museum dedicated to its history. Open every day except Monday. Hours are from 10 am-noon, 2-6 pm. Admission to both is 6Sfr for adults, 4Sfr for kids. CH-1950 Sion.

■ Shopping

Between the **Rue de Conthey** and **Rue de Lausanne** you'll find a small shopping mall. Closer to the train station on Avenue de France is a huge **Migros** store with a self-service restaurant on the first floor, and almost anything you could want elsewhere throughout the store.

■ Where to Stay

Hotel Rhône sits on the outside of the Old Town and features 45 small rooms with very tidy bathrooms and spiffy furniture. Very reasonable rates ($$) with breakfast included. The hotel's restaurant serves hearty chow. 10 Rue du Scex, CH-1950 Sion. ☎ 27-322-8291, fax 27-323-1188.

Hotel Castel is on the road to Simplon on the northeastern side of Sion. If you want good views of the area, then this is the place to stay. ($$). 36 Rue du Scex, CH-1950 Sion. ☎ 27-322-9171, fax 27-322-5724.

There is a good **Youth Hostel** in Sion, offering 79 beds from February 2 to November 30 each year. ($). Located at Rue de l'Industrie 2, CH-1950 Sion. ☎ 27-323-7470, fax 27-323-7438, www.youthhostel.ch/sion.

■ Where to Eat

Le Jardin Gourmand is probably the best restaurant in town, and certainly serves the best Vaudoise dishes anywhere in the area. The restaurant is made up of three rooms that feature Victorian furniture, marble floors and wooden ceilings. Fine fish, seafood, filet and scrumptious desserts abound in this rare find. ($$-$$$$). Reservations recommended. Open year-round except for four weeks in July and August. Hours are Monday-Saturday from 11:30 am-2 pm, 7-10 pm. Near the train station at 22 Avenue de la Gare, CH-1950 Sion. ☎ 27-323-2310.

Au Chevel Blanc is in the heart of Old Town, and offers a comfortable atmosphere and hearty portions of Swiss favorites, as well as seasonal dishes such as venison and spaetzle. ($-$$). Open daily except for Sunday and Monday, and closed the last two weeks of December. 23 Rue du Grand-Pont, CH-1950 Sion. ☎ 27-322-1867.

Brig

Brig, a small village on Highway 9 at a junction on the eastern side of the canton, has for centuries been a trading stop between Switzerland and Italy. It is an ideal starting point for excursions to such spots as Zermatt, Saas-Fee, or Crans-Montana. Brig is considered to be the main town of Upper Valais, with a population of 11,800, and was an important village during Roman times because it was the start of the Simplon Pass. The village sits at the convergence of the Rhône and Saltine rivers and is also the junction for the roads to the Rhône Glacier and the Furka Pass.

■ Information Sources

Tourist Office

The **Brig Tourist Office** is at Postfach 688, CH-3900 Brig. Hours are Monday-Friday from 8:30 am-6 pm, Saturday from 9 am-1 pm. Closed Sunday. In July, August and September, the hours are Monday-Friday from 8:30-6 pm, Saturday from 9 am-6:15 pm and Sunday from 9 am-1 pm, ☎ 27-921-6030, fax 27-921-6031, www.brig.ch.

Train Station

From the Brig train station you can catch the **Glacier-Express**, which runs every day from Zermatt to St. Moritz via Brig (and vice versa). The trip takes approximately 7½ hours and leaves Zermatt starting at 8:10 am, with four trains daily in the summer, and one a day in the winter. For reservations and information, ☎ 27-922-8111, fax 27-922-8101. This is an important train stop for many travelers, and includes a train that carries cars and motorcycles through the Lötschberg Tunnel, from Goppenstein to Kandersteg (cost is 25Sfr) every 30 minutes from 6:10 am until 11: 10 daily. The trip takes only about 20 minutes and is a real treat if you've never traveled this way. You stay in your car and drive it directly onto the train. You will be inside the tunnel for about 12 minutes. There are grand views on both sides of the mountain when you first board the train and as you exit the tunnel. This is the shortest route between Canton Valais and Canton Bern and helps you to avoid an extra two hours of traveling by road around the mountain. This is the Brig-Spiez route, and there is also a Spiez-Locarno train that carries motor vehicles as well.

Brig is also the site of the 12.4-mile **Simplon Tunnel and Pass**, which brings you to Locarno in Canton Ticino. The cost is 50Sfr per rider and there are no vehicles allowed for this 2½-hour trip that stops in Domodossola, Italy for a change of trains.

If you are driving over the Simplon Pass, take care, especially in the winter months, as the roads are steep and winding, and at times can be treacherous.

Post Office

Brig's main post office is located in the train station on Bahnhofstrasse 1, CH-3900 Brig. Hours are 7:30 am-noon, 1:30-6:15, Monday-Friday. Open Saturday from 8-11 am. ☎ 27-921-6030, fax 27-921-6031. Inside the train station you also find a money exchange, lockers and bike rental.

Codes

The **postal code** in Brig is CH-3900 and the phone **code** is 27.

■ Adventures

On Foot

For a fun afternoon journey or half-day hike, consider going up to the **Grosser Aletsch Glacier** – the longest glacier in the Alps (16 miles long/26 km), which flows out of the Jungfrau in Canton Bern. From Brig, you can either drive (east on Highway 19) or take a local eastward train to the village of Fiesch. From here, you can take a gondola up to the Eggishorn at 9,489 feet (2,893 m), where you'll find the well-marked footpath with little effort. Follow the trail a bit north along the ridge before it becomes suddenly steep, then reverses back down a stoney slope. You'll come to an old farm road that suddenly turns westward and will bring you to the middle terminal of the gondola you came up on. Continue westward toward the village of Donnerstafel, past the Beemersee, at which point the trail veers around the small lake on the right side before continuing west again to the Blausee (Blue Lake). When you reach the Blausee, you can pass it on the north side and continue on along the ridge before it meanders south toward Rieder Furka, with a gondola station at the Riederalp. From here, you can ride the gondola down to Morel and catch a train or bus back to Brig, or you can simply walk, following the main road.

■ Landmarks & Historic Sites

 Brig's **Stockalper Castle** was built from granite and volcanic rock on Simplonstrasse and was formerly a private residence. This Baroque palace features three onion-shaped domes and a beautiful courtyard that shouldn't be missed. Open May 1-October 31, with guided tours at 10 and 11 am and 2, 3, 4 and 5 pm. During May and October, no tours at 5 pm. Admission is 5Sfr for adults and 2Sfr for kids. Postfach 688, CH-3900 Brig. ☎ 27-921-6030.

■ Museums

The **Matza Gallery** tells the story of the Simplon-Brig pass. Admission is free and the museum is open May 1-October 31, Tuesday-Sunday from 9:45 am-noon, 1:45-5 pm. Simplonausstellung, CH-3900 Brig. ☎ 27-921-6030.

■ Where to Stay

 Ambassador Brig is a good four-story hotel in the city center that features clean rooms at very reasonable rates. ($$). There are two dining rooms. One (**Cheminots**) is a small, cozy restaurant with wooden walls and ceilings and the other (**Jagerstube**) is a larger

HOTEL PRICE CHART	
$	30-75Sfr ($20-$49)
$$	76-205Sfr ($50-$109)
$$$	206-299Sfr ($110-$200)
$$$$	300Sfr+ ($200+)

dining area with a viewing window. Both are open from 9 am-11:30 pm daily. The hotel is family-owned and -run and is very quiet, but only a three-minute walk from the train station. Saflischstrasse 3, CH-3900 Brig. ☎ 27-922-9900, fax 27-922-9909, www.ambassador-brig.ch.

Hotel Garni Europe is very near the train station, offering easy access to the Zermatt Railway, the Furka-Oberalp Railway and the Glacier Express. The rooms are clean and tidy, and breakfast is included in the rates, which are very reasonable. ($$). Victoriastrasse 9, CH-3900 Brig. ☎ 27-923-1321, fax 27-923-1323.

■ Where to Eat

The **Walliser-Weinstube** (Valais Wine Cellar) is one of the best spots in town for traditional Valais and Swiss fare, served in hearty portions, with a good wine list and exceptional service. Very reasonable. ($-$$). Bahnhofstrasse 9, CH-3900 Brig. ☎ 27-923-1428.

DINING PRICE CHART	
Prices based on a typical entrée, per person, and do not include beverage.	
$	15-25Sfr ($10-$16)
$$	26-45Sfr ($17-$29)
$$$	46-70Sfr ($30-$47)
$$$$	71Sfr+ ($47+)

The **Schlosskeller** (Castle Cellar) features traditional Swiss cuisine in a lovely atmosphere, with good wines from the region. ($$). Alte Simplonstrasse 26, CH-3900 Brig. ☎ 27-923-3352, fax 27-923-6975.

The Brig train station features a surprisingly good buffet. **Zumthurm Odiolo** can be found at Bahnhofplatz 1, CH-3900 Brig. ($). Hours vary. ☎/fax 27-923-3522.

Martigny

This is considered to be the artistic capital of Canton Valais – and is home to the famous Pierre Gianadda Foundation (see page 445). In addition to an art gallery, the foundation is also home to the Gallo-Roman Museum and the Automobile Museum. This little village sits in the heart of the Alps at the southwestern edge of the canton on Highway 9, at the base of the St. Bernard Pass and is a good base for many excursions.

■ Information Sources

Tourist Office

The Martigny Tourist Office is at Place Centrale 9, CH-1920 Martigny. ☎ 27-721-2220, fax 27-721-2224. It is open from July-August, Monday-Friday, 9 am-noon, 1:30-6 pm, Saturday, 9 am-noon; May, June, September and October, also open on Saturday from 2-5 pm. They can provide you with maps of the area and for various hiking and walking trails throughout the region, including the Grand St. Bernard Pass and the Val de Bagnes.

Train Station

The train station is open Monday-Saturday from 6:30 am-8 pm, Sunday from 6:50 am-8 pm. You can rent bikes here from 5:45 am-8:45 pm, Monday-Saturday, and on Sunday, 6:15 am-8:45 pm. There is also a money exchange office that is open

Monday-Saturday from 5:45 am-8:45 pm and Sunday from 6:15 am-8:45 pm.

Post Office

The Martigny post office is open Monday-Friday from 7:30 pm-noon, 1:30-6:30 pm, Saturday from 8 am-noon. Avenue de la Gare 34, CH-1920 Martigny. ☎ 27-722-5120, fax 27-722-1229.

Codes

The **postal code** for Martigny is CH-1920 and the **area code** is 27.

Internet Access

The **Casino Bar/Café & Cinema** offers Internet access for 20Sfr an hour, daily until midnight. 17 Avenue de la Gare, CH-1920 Martigny.

■ Getting Around

This is easily done on foot, as there are really only two major streets – the Avenue de la Gare and Place Central, which you can easily traverse in an hour or two.

■ Adventures

On Foot

Just 10 minutes south of Martigny is where you'll find the **Trient Gorge** and the **Pissevache Waterfalls**. You can either walk or drive (head southwest out of Martigny on the local road, toward Trient) to the bridge that passes above the Trient River. This bridge was built in 1934 and connects a pair of 636-foot-high walls (193 m) on either side of the river. There is also a small path along the river shore. The river, rock walls and waterfalls are a spectacular sight, and this is a great spot for climbers and naturalists. The waterfalls have a drop of 374 feet (114 m). You can access them, the gorge and surroundings from 9 am-6:30 pm, May-October. Gorges du Trient, CH-1904 Vernayaz. ☎ 27-764-1613.

A popular nine-mile hike takes you from the nearby village of Bourg St. Pierre to **Cabane de Vélan** (Velan Cabin). Bourg St. Pierre (where Napoleon once stayed) is south of Martigny on the Grand St. Bernard Pass Road, and is shadowed by the **Grand Combin**, a 14,150-foot (4,314 m) glacier/mountain that sits imposingly at the border of Italy and Switzerland. You'll be following Le Valsorey river for most of the journey, which takes around seven hours round-trip.

From Bourg St. Pierre (at either the bus stop or a parking area), you'll find the well-marked trail just to the left of the Le Valsorey, which will criss-cross the old narrow farm road at various points. After 1.2 miles (1.9 km), you'll see a farmhouse where the road ends, and just a little farther up the trail you'll have to play hopscotch on some large rocks over the glacial stream. Beware, however, that after a rainstorm this tiny stream often becomes a wider river where the waters can be very strong. Soon after making this crossing, you come to a fork in the trail, and you'll want to veer right here to the Cabane de Velan. The left trail takes you to the Cabane de Valsorey, another mountain hut, but this definitely requires an overnight stay, and some parts of this trail are only suitable for very experienced hikers. You'll cross the stream on an old wooden bridge and then travel another 4.3 miles up a wide, mountain meadow along the mountainside before reaching the hut. To get back, you can simply retrace your steps. You'll find that many hikers come up here for an enjoyable day of picnicking and relaxation. In the high season, it is a very popular route, so be prepared for lots of other folks moving up and down the footpath.

Winetasting

You can do this at **Caves Orsat**, where they can accommodate up to 50 people. Route du Levant, CH-1920 Martigny. ☎ 27-722-2401, fax 27-722-9845. For smaller groups, your best bet is Eddy and Samuel Saudan, located at 1921 Martigny-Croix. ☎ 27-722-6477.

■ Landmarks & Historic Sites

The **Château de la Bâtiaz** is 13th-century fortress with a fancy round tower that is still impressive today. Open May 16-December 10, Thursdays from 6-11 pm, Friday and Saturday from 10 am-midnight, Sunday from 10 am-6 pm. Admission is free. Association du Château de la Bâtiaz, Rue des Moulins, CH-1920 Martigny. ☎ 27-723-5131, fax 27-723-5132, www.batiaz.ch.

■ Museums

The **Pierre Gianadda Foundation** was founded in 1978 and is built on the site of a sanctuary dating back to Roman times. It houses a Gallo-Roman museum, a vintage car museum and a sculpture garden, but is best-known for its art collections. The Roman artifacts lie in the shadow of Mont-Chemin and include ruins of an ancient Roman villa, public baths, latrines, temples and the Vivier Amphitheater, which has been fully restored. It now hosts open-air concerts and performances of all types. 59 Rue de Forum, CH-1920 Martigny. ☎ 27-722-3978.

■ Where to Stay

Hotel du Forum is a pleasant inn with 29 wood-paneled rooms. There are two very good restaurants housed here – one formal and another very informal café. ($-$$). Reservations suggested. 74 Avenue de Grand-Saint Bernard, CH-1920. ☎ 27-722-1841, fax 27-722-7925.

Camping

Camping and dorm rooms are available at **Les Neuvilles Campsite**, at 68 Route du Levant. You can rent rooms for 20Sfr or a four-person tent for up to 85Sfr. Clean site, with showers and hiking trails nearby. CH-1920 Martigny. ☎ 27-722-4544, fax 27-722-3544.

■ Where to Eat

Restaurant/Hotel des Trois Couronnes is one of Martigny's most popular spots, serving fine French cuisine at inexpensive to mid-range prices. ($-$$$). Open daily until 11:30 except for Sunday and Monday. 8 Place du Bourg, CH-1920 Martigny. ☎ 27-723-2114.

Verbier

Verbier is in the heart of the French-speaking part of the Valais Alps, and is set upon a high plateau – at 4,921 feet (1,500 m) – that offers exceptional views of the surrounding mountains. Since the city sits on the southwest shelf, it receives an overabundance of sunshine. This resort town is made up of mostly wooden chalets, and caters to the skiing crowd with a network of ski runs and nearly 100 lifts situated among four valleys. It is difficult to find a street sign or name anywhere in town – a common occurrence in many Valais villages. This area enjoys near-perfect snow conditions from November to April, allowing skiers and snowboarders of all levels to hone their skills here. One-third of the runs are classified as easy (blue), the other third are intermediate (red) and the rest are for experienced skiers only (black). The highest run tops out on the Mont-Fort Glacier at 10,824 feet (3,300 m). The village is 18 miles (29 km) east of Martigny. If you're driving, exit in the direction of Sembrancher. Via train, you have to go first to La Châble, and then transfer to a postal bus, or you can take a cable car directly up to Verbier from La Châble.

■ Information Sources

Tourist Office

Verbier-Bagnes Tourism, CH-1936 Verbier. ☎ 26-775-3888, fax 27-775-3889.

Post Office

The Verbier post office is open Monday-Saturday from 8 am-noon, Monday-Friday from 2-6 pm. Post de la Station, CH-1936 Verbier. ☎ 27-771-1046, fax 27-771-6615.

Codes

The **postal code** in Verbier is CH-1936 and the **area code** is 27.

■ Getting Around

This is very easy in Verbier, which has one of the best networks of ski lifts anywhere – with 46 that give access to 253 miles (405 km) of well-marked pistes. It also contains 12 gondolas, five cable cars, and 32 chairlifts. One-day lift tickets start at 58Sfr.

■ Adventures

On Foot

There are 12½ miles (20 km) of well-marked hiking trails in and around Verbier that are suitable for walking in all seasons. The Tourist Office can provide you with maps of Verbier and other regions in the area for free.

On Wheels

There are 150 miles (240 km) of biking trails in Verbier. **Jet Sports** (☎ 27-771-2067) and **Medran Sports** (☎ 27-771-6048) both offer equipment rental, excursion details and additional gear.

If you're driving, you might also want to visit the **Great St. Bernard Pass**, but only during the summer months. You can reach it by driving along the winding road east of Verbier toward Sembranchen. From this village, take road 21 and it will bring you to this historic pass in about an hour.

On Snow

Verbier is basically about skiing and snow sports. The **Swiss Ski School** has 170 instructors and offers group and private lessons. ☎ 27-775-3363. For information on skiing throughout the area, contact the **Televerbier S.A.**, which offers passes on more than 98 lifts throughout the four-valley region. ☎ 27-775-2511.

The **Bureau of Guides in the Maison du Sport** can provide you with ski and snowboarding lessons. ☎ 27-775-3363. If it's mountain trekking you're interested in, then check out either **La Fantastique** (offering hut-to-hut journeys, as well as rappelling and rock climbing excursions at ☎ 27-771-4141) or **No Limits Center** (for snowshoeing and cross-country ski touring at ☎ 27-771-7250).

Other Sports

Center Polysportif features swimming, tennis, squash, curling, a solarium, sauna and whirlpools, as well as a fitness center, and Internet café. (☎ 27-771-6601). There are two 18-hole golf courses in Verbier: **Les Moulins** (☎ 27-771-7693) and **Les Esserts** (☎ 27-771-5314).

■ Parks & Gardens

Verbier's **Haut Val de Bagnes Nature Reserve** is open from mid-May to early October and you can see a variety of plant and animal life here, including a wide range of Alpine flora such as edelweiss, lilies and orchids.

■ Shopping

Shopping in Verbier revolves around skiing and other sports, so don't be surprised to find a good variety of sporting goods and ski shops here. Many are located near the ski lifts or gondolas.

■ Where to Stay in Verbier

Hotel Rosalp is the best spot in town, a first-class hotel that features modern conveniences in a plush and atmospheric setting. There are only 18 rooms here, but they are all top of the line. This is also home to Verbier's best restaurant, **Roland Pierroz**. Breakfast is included in rates. Closed during the months of May, June, October, and November. ($$$$+). Rue de Medran, CH-1936 Verbier. ☎ 27-771-6323, fax 27-771-1059, www.relaischateaux.ch.rosalp.

Hotel Vanessa is a top-rated four-star hotel, the largest in Verbier,. Its huge modern rooms have balconies. Closed from April to June and from mid-October to early December. Includes a restaurant, bar, sauna, ja-cuzzi and baby-sitting services. ($$$$-$$$$+). Place Centrale, CH-1936 Verbier. ☎ 27-775-2800, fax 27-775-2888.

Hotel Catogne looks like a Swiss chalet, and offers a pleasant atmo-sphere, with simple, clean and comfortable rooms at reasonable rates. Rooms are not huge, but are charming. There is also an in-house restau-rant and bar. Closed for one month after Easter and from mid-November to mid-December. ($$$). Chemin de la Croix, CH-1936 Verbier. ☎ 27-771-6506, fax 27-771-5205.

■ Where to Eat

Roland Pierroz serves up the finest French food found any-where in the region at his premiere spot. The menu changes of-ten, but the meals are always an exquisite blend of fine meats and delicately prepared dishes. There are over 35 cheeses to choose from, and you won't find a finer dessert tray anywhere in Switzer-land. Located in the Hotel Rosalp. Reservations are required, and it's best to make them a few days in advance of your meal. Fixed-price menus start at 150Sfr. Open daily, noon-2 pm, 7-9:30 pm. ($$$-$$$$). Rue de Medran. CH-1936 Verbier. ☎ 27-771-6323.

La Caveau (The Cave) features a cozy, warm atmosphere above Verbier's main square. Here you'll find five varieties of fondue, grilled steaks, rösti, and other Valais delights. Very reasonable and just a really cool spot to hang out. The waitstaff doesn't care if you come just to have a drink and people-watch either. Reservations recommended. ($-$$). Place Centrale, CH-1936 Verbier. ☎ 27-771-2226.

Pizzeria Cheval is a real bargain in pricey Verbier. It offers up the best pizza in town in a rustic, wood-paneled setting that includes a sun ter-race. Besides pizza, they have great salads, pastas and steaks. ($-$$). Reservations recommended. Rue de Medran. CH-1936 Verbier. ☎ 27-771-2669.

Zermatt

This tiny, car-free village is set at the base of Switzerland's most spec-tacular mountain – **the Matterhorn**. It's also a world-famous resort town that for years has catered to the rich and famous. It has often been said that more Americans reside in Zermatt than do Swiss. This pictur-esque village first gained notice, however, when British explore Edward Whymper made a number of attempts to climb the Matterhorn from its Italian face. When Whymper then changed strategy and attempted the mountain from the base of Zermatt, he was finally successful on July 14, 1865 – becoming the first person to reach the summit of this impressive

The Gornergrat cog railway ascends from Zermatt to the Gornergrat Glacier, with the Matterhorn looming above

peak. He did, however, lose four of his fellow travelers during this process. Only three days after Whymper's ascent, an Italian explorer by the name of Jean-Antoine Carrel successfully ascended to Matterhorn's summit via the Italian side.

Zermatt is easily accessible by train from Brig or Visp, but I'd suggest you drive down through the scenic mountain passes and valleys to the base town of Tasch, where there is a large car park on the right-hand side of the road. You can park here for a nominal fee, and then board the cog railway for the ascent up to Zermatt. A round-trip ticket costs 14.8Sfr. To find your way around in Zermatt, look to the signs posted for hotels and restaurants, since you won't see a typical street sign here.

The best time to visit Zermatt, if you're not into skiing, is in early May. All the tourists and a good portion of the skiers have left by that time, and most of the shops are having sales, especially on tourist items such as T-shirts, handkerchiefs and even jewelry. You can find lots of bargains, even when it comes to hotel rates at this time.

Zermatt is home to some 5,600 residents – most of whom speak Swiss German, French, Italian and English with ease. The village has five doctors, one dentist, three pharmacies and, since 2000, its own television station that features live panoramic views of the various hiking and skiing areas.

You'll also be able to watch CNN and other English-language programs from your hotel, as well as movies and world news.

■ Information Sources

Tourist Office

 The **Zermatt Tourist Office** is on the Bahnhofplatz near the train station, and is open from mid-June to mid-October, Monday-Saturday from 8:30 am-6 pm, Sunday from 9:30 am-noon and 4-7 pm. At other times of the year, it is open Monday-Saturday from 8:30 am-noon, 1:30-6 pm. Info Zermatt, Haus Cheminots B, PO Box 424, CH-3920 Zermatt. ☎ 27-966-8100, fax 27-966-8101.

Early morning at the Riffelsee above Zermatt, with the Matterhorn in the distance

Post Office

 Zermatt's post office is open Monday-Friday, 8:30 am-noon, 1:45-6 pm, Saturday from 8:30-11 am. ☎ 27-967-1992, fax 27-967-5930.

Codes

The **postal code** for Zermatt is CH-3920 and the **area code** is 27.

■ Getting Around

 This is easy on foot, or you can take a horse-drawn carriage ride. An electric vehicle is provided by many of the hotels here to bring you, your skis and luggage to your hotel.

■ Adventures

On Foot

 There are a variety of hikes to Alpine huts throughout Zermatt. Your best bet is to contact the **Zermatt Alpine Center** at Postfach 403, CH-3920 Zermatt. ☎ 27-966-2460, fax 27-966-2469, alpincenter@zermatt.ch. They can provide you with itineraries, maps, suggestions and guides, and offer easy day tours for individuals, couples and groups, as well as hiking and treking tours for all levels of wanderers. They also have ice climbing, gorge-climbing adventures, snowshoe walks and indoor climbs.

A new hiking trail – the **Matterhorn Trail** – is being initiated as this book goes to press, adding to the already 248 miles (397 km) of extended hiking paths in and around the Zermatt area.

CLIMBING THE MIGHTY MATTERHORN

 This is a serious undertaking that should be attempted by experienced climbers only, in good physical condition and with an experienced guide at your side. If you are inexperienced, there are plenty of easier, kinder peaks to attempt in the area. However, if you've got the experience (rock climbing, walking with crampons, previous climbs), and want to have a once-in-a-lifetime experience, ascending the Matterhorn is for you. You will also need to spend at least 10 to 15 days in Zermatt acclimating to the area through daily hikes at high altitudes (3,280 to 4,920 feet/1,000 to 1,500 m). The best time to attempt the Matterhorn is from mid-July to mid-September. Your guide can pick a suitable date for you, based on weather and snow conditions. The mountain can be congested with climbers from the end of July through mid-August, so it is best to avoid these dates. The guide will arrange for a meeting spot the night before your ascent. Typically, the spot is the Matterhorn hut. The ascent attempt will begin early in the morning, usually no later than 4:30 or 5 am, and allowing four hours to reach the summit. Prepare for a similar time frame for the descent as well. Your best bet is to use the Zermatt Alpine Center mentioned above. They offer a one-to-one guide-client ascent trip, at a cost of 1,070Sfr per person.

On Snow

Zermatt offers skiing year-round, since most of the ski runs lie between 8,250 and 12,800 feet (2,515-3,900 m). The Rothorn, Stockhorn and Klein Matterhorn (Little Matterhorn) are for intermediate and experienced skiers; beginners have few options here. The **Klein Matterhorn** is reached by the highest cable gondola in Europe and features 20 miles (32 km) of pistes at the top. From here you can ski back down to Zermatt, or (and be sure to carry your passport) you can ski down the other side for lunch in Italy at Cervinia.

If you go for lunch on the Italian side, beware that you don't get shut out for the trip back, as lift times in Italy are not the same as in Switzerland.

In town, the **Zermatt Ski School** offers certified instruction and mountain guides, as well as tours at ☎ 27-966-2466. The **Alpine Center of Zermatt** can teach you all about mountaineering at their public facility. Rates vary. CH-3910 Zermatt. ☎ 27-966-2460, fax 27-966-2469, www.zermatt.ch/alpincenter.

If you think you'd like to try trekking over some of the most famous Alps on the back of a mule, then contact **Zermatt Mule Trekking's** Jacques Christinet at ☎ 79-285-6638 or 27-967-6459. A one-day trek costs 160Sfr per person, while a two- to three-hour trek costs 35Sfr.

On the Rails

No trip to Zermatt is complete without a ride on the Gornergrat rack railway. The **Gornergrat-Monte Rosa-Bahnen** first went into operation on August 20th, 1898, making the Alps accessible to all visitors for the first time. It provides excellent views of the Matterhorn and, at the top, you'll see the mighty mountain mirrored in the waters of the Riffelsee. You'll continue on to the summit station at 10,135 feet (3,090 m), and from here you can walk to the Gornergrat observatory, which is a rocky outpost that sits above the Gorner glacier. You'll get a sweeping panoramic view of the Alps from this point. You can walk back from the Gornergrat to Zermatt – on the way be sure to stop at the **Findel Glacier Restaurant** for either a hot or cool drink – depending on the weather conditions. Your walk will pass through the tiny resort village of **Findeln** at 7,102 feet (2,165 m), before bringing you back to Zermatt some 60 minutes later. For schedules and prices, contact the GGB Gornergrat-Monte Rose-Bahnen, Nordstrasse 20, CH-3900 Brig-Glis. ☎ 27-921-4111, fax 27-921-4119.

In late 2002 the new **Matterhorn-Express gondola-lift** was unveiled, featuring an eight-person left that travels from Zermatt to Schwarzee via Furi in just 12 minutes. It took seven months to complete the project, which cost 25 million Swiss francs and eliminated two previously stand-

The South

ing cable cars and one gondola along the route. The new lift was built to eliminate the bottlenecks of skiers at the Furi stop. This will also allow more visitors to the Schwarzsee area in the future, which is the traditional starting point for attempts to ascend the Matterhorn.

In the Air

Air-Zermatt can take you by helicopter for some stunning views of the Matterhorn for 195Sfr. Contact them at CH-3920 Zermatt. ☎ 27-966-8686, www.air-zermatt.ch.

■ Landmarks & Historic Sites

You'll want to visit the local **climbers' cemetery** in Zermatt. It's midway through the village just to the left of the main street, across the river and below the Parish church. Here you'll find many folks who tried, but never accomplished their goal of making it to the top of the Matterhorn. The gravestones are impressive in their statements honoring the mountain and the fallen explorers.

■ Museums

The **Alpine Museum** tells the history of mountaineering in Zermatt. Open daily in the summer from 10 am-noon, 4-6 pm; in the winter from 4:30-6:30 pm, Sunday-Friday (closed Saturday). Admission is 5Sfr for adults, 1Sfr for kids. Located behind the train station. CH-3920 Zermatt. ☎ 27-967-4100.

Radio Matterhorn Museum is open every day from 5-6:30 pm. Admission is 5Sfr for adults, 2.5Sfr for kids. Located on the Bahnhofstrasse, CH-3920 Zermatt. ☎ 27-967-4455, fax 27-967-5154.

■ Shopping

Most stores in Zermatt are open from 8:30 am-noon, 2-6:30 pm daily. If it's souvenirs you're searching for, than look no farther than **Zermatter Swiss Souvenirs** on Bahnhofplatz 6F, CH-3920 Zermatt. ☎ 27-967-1060, fax 27-967-1676. **Davis** (☎ 27-967-6070), **Perren Elfriede** (☎ 27-967-2463), **Rempfler Textil** (☎ 27-967-8400) and **WEGA** (☎ 27-967-2166) offer similar wares and all are located on the Bahnhofstrasse – Zermatt's main street (it travels the length of the village on the right side of the river if you're facing the Matterhorn). For Switzerland's best linens, try **Langenthal AG**, also on the Bahnhofstrasse. ☎ 27-967-1434.

For tempting baked goods, and the famous "Matterhorn chocolates" (tiny kiss-sized renditions of the Matterhorn), walk into **Hörnli** on the Bahnhofstrasse (☎ 27-967-4457) or the **Zellner** (☎ 27-967-1855).

■ Where to Stay

Hotel Alpenblick is one of the best-kept secrets in Zermatt and, if you ask for a corner room, you'll have stunning views of the Matterhorn from your private balcony and windows day and night. I've stayed here on three separate occasions and each time have experienced a quiet stay in a clean and comfortable room, with a spotless marble bathroom, not far from the ski lift area. The in-house restaurant features a hearty breakfast, and delightful lunches with fresh greens and homemade dishes served in a light and informal atmosphere. Reasonable rates and a very friendly staff make this a nice alternative to many of the pricer hotels in Zermatt. Located at the far end of the village, so for older travelers it might be necessary to take an electric taxi, although I brought my parents here (both in their mid-70s) and they had no trouble walking from the train station with their light luggage. ($$-$$$$). The Pannatier family are kind and gracious hosts. Oberdorfstrasse 106, CH-3920 Zermatt. ☎ 27-966-2600, fax 27-966-2605.

Hotel Mont Cervin is rated as one of the leading hotels in the world, and rightfully so. Right in the center of Zermatt, only five minutes from the train station, this hotel originally opened its doors in 1851, and in 1994 added the Residence across the street – a state-of-the-art building with 15 deluxe suites. Open from the end of November to the end of April and from mid-June to mid-October, this first-class hotel features all of the modern amenities you'd expect and is only a few minutes walk from shopping, restaurants and the mountain railways and gondolas. There are two restaurants – a dining area with à la carte services and weekly buffets that seats 240, and **Le Cervin Grill** that seats 95 and specializes in charcoal-grilled meat and fish. There is also a piano bar in the hotel. ($$$$-$$$$+). Bahnhofstrasse 31, CH-3920 Zermatt. ☎ 27-966-8888, fax 27-966-8899.

Hotel Bahnhof is very popular among hikers and mountaineers, as it has 12-bed dorms and showers on each floor. Prices ($-$$) don't include breakfast, but there is a small kitchen on the premises. Nothing fancy, but it's clean and the showers are hot. Directly across from the train station. CH-3920 Zermatt. ☎ 27-967-2406, fax 27-967-7216.

The **Zermatt Youth Hostel** offers 140 beds from January 1-April 15, and from May 31-December 31. They have a wide range of facilities with great views of the Matterhorn. ($). About a mile east of the train station at Winkelmatten, CH-3920 Zermatt. ☎ 27-967-2320, fax 27-967-5306.

Camping

This is available in and around Zermatt. At **Zermatt's campsite** (open June-September), you'll have to transport your equipment by train or taxi. Reservations recommended. ☎ 27-967-3921, matterhorn@campings.ch. There is also camping available at **Täsch** (☎ 27-967-3635), **Randa** (☎ 27-967-2555) and at **Grächen** (☎ 27-956-3202).

■ Where to Eat

 The Grill Room and **Stübli** are two of our favorite spots in Zermatt. This former farmhouse, located in the middle of town, is open year round, and offers a pair of delightful dining areas sure to please any picky palate. The Grill Room is a bit more formal, and has a fine selection of smoked fish, veal and fine foods prepared with either an Italian, French or German touch. The Stübli serves hearty portions of Swiss favorites in a more informal and atmospheric setting. Located in the Hotel Walliserhof on the Bahnhofstrasse. ($$-$$$). Reservations are recommended. Open daily from 11 am-2 pm, 7-11 pm. CH-3920 Zermatt. ☎ 27-966-6555.

Grillroom Stockhorn is one of the finest restaurants in town, and features a lovely fireplace in the dining area, along with wooden beams, stucco walls and a general rustic atmosphere. Courses range from Swiss favorites to pasta and grilled meats.The attached bar is equally delightful. ($$-$$$). Reservations are required. Open daily 11:30 am-1 pm, 6:30-10 pm. Closed May to mid-June, and from October to mid-November. Riedstrasse, CH-3920 Zermatt. ☎ 27-967-1747.

Le Gitan is another favorite, often booked weeks ahead in the high ski seasons. Small and comfortable, with a beautiful fireplace, this restaurant features Swiss and regional specialties, including venison and other game dishes. The lamb is considered to be the house specialty. Reservations required. ($-$$). Open daily from 6:30-10 pm in the Hotel Darioli on the Bahnhofstrasse. CH-3920 Zermatt. ☎ 27-968-1940.

For a great treat, check out **Elsie's Place**, a local hangout for skiers and snowboarders that serves great Irish coffee known throughout Zermatt. You can also dine there during the day and feast on such goodies as hot dogs, grilled cheese, BLTs and even caviar. ($-$$). Open daily from 11 am-2 am in the summer and from 4 pm-2 am in the winter. Located at Kirchplatz, this house is an original from 1879. ☎ 27-967-2431.

A quirky hangout for the funky-minded tourist is the **Brown Cow**, on the Bahnhofstrasse about midway through town. Here you'll find a very relaxed atmosphere, a bar and small café that serves up anything and everything – from burgers to hot soups, pasta and salads daily. The best part of this place is that the owner's dog gets to hang out and visit the patrons. ($-$$).

Saas-Fee

Saas-Fee is where many of the Swiss go for skiing, hoping to avoid the mass of crowds that tumble into the nearby resorts of Zermatt or Verbier. Here you'll find 13 peaks that loom up to 13,000 feet (4,000 m) or higher above this Alpine village. This car-free village provides an atmosphere of peace and the charm of an old-time resort with its wooden chalets, outdoor sun terraces, sidewalk cafés and delightful restaurants. Rightfully so, Saas-Fee is known as "the pearl of the Alps," and boasts the highest revolving restaurant in the world, as well as its largest ice pavilion.

Saas-Fee is one of the quietest ski resort villages you'll visit in Switzerland, and is definitely not a party town. Unlike St. Moritz or Verbier, Saas-Fee virtually falls asleep each night on the dot at 10 pm, and late-night noisemakers are typically fined 200Sfr or more!

■ Information Sources

Tourist Office

The Saas-Fee Tourist Office, ☎ 27-958-1858, fax 27-958-1860, is across from the bus station, and is open Monday-Friday from 8:30 am-noon, 2-6 pm; Saturday from 9 am-noon, 3-6 pm.

Post Office

At the bus station you'll find Saas-Fee's post office and lockers for luggage and backpacks.

Codes

The **postal code** for Saas-Fee is CH-3906 and the **area code** is 27.

Internet Access

For Internet access go to the **Hotel Dom** (☎ 27-957-2300), where you'll pay a rate of 20Sfr per hour.

■ Getting Around

This is only done on foot or by electric car since this village is auto-free. You can also grab a "horse taxi" or take an evening ride in one of the many carriages found throughout Saas-Fee. It is also important to note that there is no train service here – but you can get here by bus or by driving and parking your car at the entrance to the village for 13Sfr per day. Until 1951, Saas-Fee was accessible only on foot or by mule. The buses leave Brig, Visp and Stalden Saas every hour and the cost is 17.4Sfr for a one-way ticket.

■ Adventures

Summer Sports

Saas-Fee in the summer is a **hiker's** paradise, with over 174 miles (280 km) of hiking trails and foot paths suitable for all levels of wanderers. The tourist office organizes tours of the village, as well as of the mountains. Village tours meet every Monday at 5 pm at the tourist office, with talks in English about the history of vSaas-Fee and other interesting facts. Most of the hiking tours take place on Hannig (Saas-Fee's mountain). Every Friday at 2 pm, the tourist office features a 2½-hour hike from Hannig to the glacier lakes. ☎ 27-958-1858 for information. If you want to trek to a mountain, meet at the Metro Alpin station at 7:30 am for a fine 2½-hour hike to the Allalinhorn summit. The cost is 130Sfr per person. Call ☎ 27-957-4464 for a reservation.

Horse trekking excursions abound in Saas-Fee. Every Tuesday at 9 am riders meet at the Campground Kapelweg for a one- to three-hour trek. Cost is 80Sfr per person and reservations can be made through the tourist office (☎ 27-958-1858). On Wednesdays, the trek takes you to Kruezboden. For horseback riding in Sass-Grund, you'll pay 22Sfr for one hour. For a panoramic ride on Fridays from 1:30-4 pm, the cost is 40Sfr for adults and 30Sfr for kids. For romantics, you can take a carriage ride at dusk, on Wednesdays and Fridays at 8 pm. A minimum of four people is required at 17Sfr per person.

Guided **mountain bike tours** are available in Saas-Fee at 20Sfr for adults and 10Sfr for kids. ☎ 27-957-2825.

There is a good driving range in Saas-Fee for **golfers** and it is open daily from 8 am-7 pm at Kalbermatten. Prices start at 18Sfr. ☎ 27-957-2825. There is also a **miniature golf** course at the Valley Station Alpin Express, open June to the end of October, from 8:30 am-noon, 2-6 pm for 4Sfr per person.

Wine tasting takes place every Tuesday night at 8 pm at the Tourist Office for a fee of 20Sfr per person. Here you can sample wines of Valais, Vaud and Ticino.

The **Leisure Center Bielen and AquaWellness** is a huge, modern fitness center that is home to a pair of indoor tennis courts, badminton courts, a pool, sauna, steam baths, a whirlpool, ping-pong and billiards. Open 8 am-10 pm daily. Tennis lessons are available; ☎ 27-957-1606.

Winter Sports

 There are 62 miles (100 km) of ski slopes, a natural ice rink, winter walking trails and a sled run in Saas-Fee. You can cross-country ski on 14.3 miles (22.9 km) of runs between Saas-Almagell and Saas-Balen too. The **Saas-Fee Ski and Snowboarding School** provides lessons for all levels of snow bunnies. ☎ 27-957-2348, fax 27-957-2366. The **Eskimo Swiss Snowboard School** also offers lesson and equipment rental at ☎ 27-957-4904, fax 27-957-8124.

Winter walks on the Hannig, Saas-Fee's non-ski mountain, are very popular. There are 28.6 miles (45.7 km) of well-kept winter walking trails up here that stretch from Melchboden to Saas-Almagell. There is also a 3.1-mile **sledding** path that brings you back down to the base at Saas-Fee. You'll also find a nice **restaurant** on Hannig (☎ 27-957-1419, fax 27-957-2268).

Nightime sledding takes place every Tuesday and Thursday from Haning to Saas-Fee, starting at the Haning station, from 6-9 pm. The cost is 18Sfr per person, and sled rental is 8Sfr.

Saas-Fee's **mountaineering school** features tours for beginners and advanced climbers alike year-round. Contact **Mountain Life** for information at ☎ 27-957-4464. This company also features ice climbing excursions as well as gorge crossings between Saas-Fee and Saas Grund.

Dog sledding is available on request and dependent upon the snow conditions. Cost is 40Sfr for adults and 35Sfr for kids over 12. Contact the Tourist Office at ☎ 27-958-1858.

Walking with snowshoes to various mountain huts is a fun alternative to cross-country skiing, especially because once you reach the hut, you are able to enjoy a good Swiss meal or a tasty fondue. The Tourist Office arranges a walk every Thursday at 5:30 pm for 20Sfr per person, and reservations are required (☎ 27-958-1858). On Wednesday at 6 pm, you can take a similar walk with **Alpine Sport**. ☎ 27-957-3733 for reservations or **Cesar Sport** at ☎ 27-957-1416.

Snow tubing is the latest in adventure sports, as you tumble down the mountain in a giant plastic tube. The cost is 15Sfr per person, and you must register at the Tourist Office. Monday-Friday at 5 pm. ☎ 27-958-1858.

The South

■ Landmarks & Historic Sites

The **Ice Palace** is the world's largest ice pavilion, located on the Mittelallalin. The long gallery entrance to the pavilion can be reached via the Metro-Alpin rack railway. The inside of this ice castle is simply stunning and forever fascinating. Open daily. Admission is 7Sfr for adults, 3.5Sfr for adults. Eispavillon, CH-3960 Saas-Fee. ☎ 27-957-3560.

■ Museum

There is one little museum in Saas-Fee, the **Saaser Museum**, at left, which details the history of the village and its customs and traditions. Admission is 4Sfr and it's worth a rainy-day visit.

■ Where to Stay in Saas-Fee

Waldhotel Fletschhorn is one of the top hotels in Saas-Fee and offers ultra-modern rooms in a rustic setting. Many people come here just to enjoy the fine dining room that specializes in local dishes. ($$$$). CH-3906 Saas-Fee. ☎ 27-957-2131, fax 27-957-2187.

HOTEL PRICE CHART	
$	30-75Sfr ($20-$49)
$$	76-205Sfr ($50-$109)
$$$	206-299Sfr ($110-$200)
$$$$	300Sfr+ ($200+)

Ferienart Walliserhof has a complete wellness center, as well as an art gallery and an in-house waterfall. Located in the center of Saas-Fee, with great views of the village and surrounding mountains. Features four restaurants, a café, Internet access in all rooms and many amenities. ($$$$). CH-3806 Saas-Fee. ☎ 27-958-1900, fax 27-958-1905.

Beau-Site is a very elegant and stately hotel, with intimate rooms and tastefully decorated bathrooms. Also home to three restaurants, a café, bar, indoor pool, sauna, and hot tub. ($$$-$$$$). Postfach 135, CH-3906 Saas-Fee. ☎ 27-958-1560, fax 27-958-1656.

Hotel La Gorge is right next to the Alpin-Express cable car and provides the visitor with superior views of the glaciers and surrounding mountains. Rooms are tidy and clean, with modern amenities in this fine-looking Swiss chalet. ($$). CH-3906 Saas-Fee. ☎ 27-958-1680.

■ Where to Eat in Saas-Fee

Fletschhorn is an excellent restaurant on the northern edge of the village, with prix fixe meals ranging from 130Sfr and upwards. They also have à la carte service, which is more reasonable. ($$-$$$$). If you're really into cooking, than you can stay in the hotel here, and take cooking lessons from Fletschhorn's premiere chef, Irma Dutsch. Prices for the cooking lessons start at 280Sfr for two-day sessions and include your lodgings. Two- , three- and five-day packages are also available. CH-3906 Saas-Fee. ☎ 27-957-2131, fax 27-957-2187.

DINING PRICE CHART	
Prices based on a typical entrée, per person, and do not include beverage.	
$	15-25Sfr ($10-$16)
$$	26-45Sfr ($17-$29)
$$$	46-70Sfr ($30-$47)
$$$$	71Sfr+ ($47+)

Skihütte Restaurant serves good Valais dishes on a sunny terrace all year round. Close to the ski lifts, this restaurant is a great spot to people-watch during the daytime. ($-$$$). CH-3906 Saas-Fee. ☎ 27-958-9280.

La Ferme is right around the corner from the bus station/tourist office and has good vegetarian meals, as well as traditional Swiss favorites in hearty portions. ($-$$). This former agricultural house has farming tools hanging on the walls, and is open daily.

Monthey

Monthey is at the far western edge of the canton, along Highway 9 and is the first major city you reach when leaving France along Lake Geneva, or when heading from the north-west along the northern shores of this same land-locked lake. With just 15,000 inhabitants, this town is quaint, charming and quiet. This is also the home of Bolliger and Mabillard (B&M), who were once engineers at Giovanola Frères SA, a company that employs over 300 designers and engineers at its Monthey-based plant. B&M is the major designer of most major roller coasters, free-fall towers and assorted rides found throughout the world.

Monthey's **Office du Tourisme** is at Place Tübingen 5, CH-1870 Monthey. ☎ 24-471-1212, fax 24-471-1200. Monthey's **postal code** is CH-1870 and the **area code** is 24. The **Musée du Vieux Monthey** (Museum of Old Monthey) tells the history of the town throughout the ages. Admission is free, open upon request from the Tourist Office. CH-1870 Monthey. ☎ 24-471-2642. For overnight accommodations in Monthey, look no farther than **Hotel de la Gare**, near the train station and 15 minutes from the ski lifts. Hosts Pietro and Graziella Scalia offer a family-run inn with an in-house restaurant that serves hearty portions of local favorites. ($$). Avenue de la Gare 60, CH-1870 Monthey. ☎ 24-471-9393.

If you want to go **horseback riding** in this picturesque village, then **Manège de Monthey** is the place to go. For a one-hour excursion, the rates are 29Sfr for adults and 26Sfr for kids. A group riding lesson costs 29Sfr each. Route du Rhône, CH-1870 Monthey. ☎ 24-471-9468. Cross-country and downhill **skiing** is available at the nearby resort of **Les Giettes**. Call ☎ 24-475-7963, fax 24-475-7949 for information on both disciplines, and for snow-trekking and in-line skating at the Skatepark.

Leukerbad

This is the highest spa resort village in Europe and sits at 4,628 feet (1,410 m) near the Torrenthorn mountain, just north of the village of Leuk, between Sierre and Visp on Highway 9. Those seeking natural **spring and hot mineral waters** have been visiting Leukerbad for centuries to sample their medicinal and rejuvenating effects.

There are 42 miles (67 km) of downhill and cross-country **ski runs** in and around Leukerbad, reachable by the popular Torrent cable car. You'll also find the **Gemmi Pass** – a popular and historic crossing between the Berner Oberland and Lowe Valais regions that has been known to traders and travelers for hundreds of years. This pass can be easily crossed in a day by almost anyone.

However, the main reason to visit Leukerbad is for the **hot waters**. The **Burgerbad** is a multi-level spa that features indoor and outdoor pools, a solarium, sauna and exercise rooms. It is excellent for families with children, and costs 21Sfr per person to use the facilities. Open Sunday-Thursday from 8 am-8 pm, Friday and Saturday from 8 am-9 pm (☎ 27-470-1138). Leukerbad's other main resort is **Lindner Alpentherm**, which is statelier and caters more to an upscale clientele. It features a medical center, a shopping arcade, a beauty salon and pharmacy, and a juice bar. You won't see many children here, as those ages six and younger are not allowed. Open Monday-Thursday from 8 am-7 pm, Friday and Saturday from 8 am-8 pm. ☎ 27-472-7272.

Crans-Montana

These twin ski resort villages can be found northeast of Sion and slightly northwest of the village of Sierre off of Highway 9. To get here, you can drive eight miles (13 km) north from Sierre on a winding, twisty road that eventually makes its way to the village entrance. Otherwise, you can catch a bus or a funicular from Sierre to the villages (☎ 27-481-3355). The Tourist Office in Crans can help with hotel suggestions, hiking maps, itineraries, and general information at ☎ 27-485-0800. The Montana

Tourist Office can provide similar information at ☎ 27-485-0404. Both are open Monday-Friday from 8:30 am-noon, 2-5:30 pm; Saturday from 9:30-noon, 2-4 pm; Sunday from 9 am-noon. Both of these resorts sit majestically at 4,985 feet (1,520 m). Crans is the younger of the two villages and contains many half-timbered mountain chalets, while Montana tends to be just a bit quieter, older and more reserved. The latter is situated around Lake Grenon. Again, you'll find few street signs here, but most hotels and restaurants have signs leading you to their doors. During the summer months Crans-Montana becomes a golf junkie's paradise, while in the winter months, skiing takes precedence over anything else here. Hockey, skating, winter walking, sledding, and curling can also be done here.

Gletsch

This is a tiny resort village located 30 miles (48 km) northeast of Brig at the junction of Highways 9, 19 and 6. The base glacier of the Rhône River is here, offering grand views of the Bernese and Valais Alps. Close by are the **Furka** and **Grimsel Passes**, which you can drive over, or you can board the **Furka Cogwheel** steam train (☎ 84-800-0144) for a lovely, slow (1½ hours) ride up to the glacier summit.

Grächen & St. Niklaus

These are two little villages set high in the Valaisian Alps in the heart of the Zermatt Valley. Grächen is shown at left. They are well-known bases for numerous mountain hikes, and are quiet and quaint mountain spots that are still unspoiled by tourists – most of whom tend to just pass through on the way to Zermatt. For information, contact the Grächen **Tourist Office** at ☎ 27-955-6060, fax 27-956-3663, www.st-niklaus.ch, and the St. Niklaus Tourist Office at ☎ 27-955-6066, fax 27-956-2925, www.st-niklaus.ch.

Arcades at Piazza Riforma in the old town center of Lugano

Canton Ticino (TI)

■ At a Glance

As the fifth largest canton in Switzerland, Ticino is 1,085 square miles (2,821 square km) of alpine beauty, lakes, meadows and many other natural wonders. Located in the southern portion of Switzerland, Ticino is flanked by Canton Graubünden to the north and northeast, by Uri to the north, and by Valais to the west. Nearly the entire western portion of the canton, as well as the southern and half of the eastern side bumps frontiers with Italy. As a result, Ticino has become a region of transit – forever influenced by its geography, which offers surprisingly little in terms of natural resources overall. While the scenery is lovely, with countless lakes, streams and rivers, it has abundant stone, but little else. Ever resourceful, the people of Ticino – in the early history of this canton – became some of the world's finest and most respected masons. A vast number of fine architects have sprung from this region as well – the most famous being Mario Botta. Botta was born in 1943 and built the San Francisco Museum of Modern Art, as well as buildings in Paris and Venice. He is known for his bold, contemporary style. Not surprisingly, this canton is comprised of mostly Italian-speaking inhabitants, who are Roman Catholics. Ticino is also the only region in Switzerland that is entirely south of the Alps, and the only canton in which Italian is the official language. Just over 306,000 people reside here, making it the eighth largest canton in terms of population. In addition, Ticino is the second largest canton in terms of the number of foreigners who live here (27% of the cantonal population), behind Canton Geneva which has the most resident foreigners in all of Switzerland.

Because of its dual heritage, Canton Ticino offers some of the most diverse gastronomic choices anywhere in Switzerland. From the lake areas you'll be treated to locally caught fresh fish, and in the vast countryside you'll find hearty, home-cooked meals in one of the many *grotti* (taverns) that are usually off the beaten path. In addition, throughout this region you'll undoubtably be treated to one of the fine wines – usually from a variety of the Merlot grape that is grown on the slopes surrounding Lake Lugano. Well over six million bottles of wine are produced annually in Ticino.

Ticino is split geographically into two regions by the relatively small mountain range of Monte Ceneri, at the southern tip of the canton. This southern region – known as the **Sottoceneri** – encompasses all of that below the valley of Bellinzona (mainly Lugano), while the northern region is referred to as the **Sopraceneri** area, home to many valleys and the lakeside towns of Locarno and Asona. The Sopraceneri region tends to be mellower and less flashy than its southern counterpart of Sottoceneri and it's here that a visitor will come upon many small villages of only a few dozen people, tending to their small flocks of goats or quietly making their way through a valley or mountain path.

This canton also offers 1,240 miles (1,984 km) of well-marked foot paths – most of which are suited for families and children. The *Strada Alta*, the *Sentiero delle Meravigilie*, and the *Sentiero Basso* are just a few of the footpaths offered here, as well as the "Swiss Path," which passes through Ticino via Canton Graubünden and Italy.

As for the **coat of arms**, history tells us that in 1798 Ticino was defeated by Swiss confederates, and became a separate canton five years later (in 1803). Legend has it that on May 23 of that same year the local government decided that the cantonal colors would be red and blue, although the reason for this remains vague. Historians have long argued over what the symbolism of these colors is, with no real answer in sight. One theory is that they represented the two political parties of that time. The red was for the liberal party, while the blue represented the conservative party. Whatever the case, the shield has remained unchanged since 1803 – when Ticino joined the Swiss Federation – with the right side painted blue and the left side colored red.

The Sottoceneri Region

Lugano

Lugano sits at 892 feet (272 m) above sea level in the Sottoceneri region and offers the visitor a warm, relaxing climate with stunning scenery and vegetation. Here you'll find a full range of sporting excursions, such as hiking, skiing, walking and water sports. There are festivals of all kinds throughout the year in this region, where Italian culture and atmosphere mesh with Swiss charm, cleanliness and tradition. The city itself is situated around lakeside ports and village piazzas, many with extensive footpaths and gardens. In addition, the **Lake Lugano Region** is now the third largest banking area in Switzerland, and encompasses more than just Lugano and its nearby suburbs. **Ceresio**, **Malcantone**, **Valli di Lugano** and **Mendrisiotto** all come under this heading. This region sits at the crossroads between Switzerland and Italy.

Lugano is also the home to three outstanding mountains – each of which offers idyllic views and splendid hiking and walking opportunities. **Monte Bré**, **Monte San Salvatore**, and **Monte Generoso** each offer different vantage points from which to view the surrounding areas. Nature trails with well-marked signs designating native plant and tree species abound here.

■ Information Sources

Tourist Offices

The main Lugano Tourist Office is open from April through October, Monday-Friday from 9 am-6:30 pm, Saturday from 9 am-12:30 pm, 1:30-5 pm, Sunday from 10 am-3 pm. From November through March, it is open Monday-Friday from 9 am-noon, 1:30-5:30 pm. Palazzo Civico, CH-6901 Lugano. ☎ 91-913-3232, fax 91-922-7653, www.lugano-tourism.ch.

You'll also find two information offices, both in Lugano regional train stations. **Stazione FFS**, CH-6815 Melide, ☎ 91-649-6383, fax 91-649-5613; or **Piazzale Stazione**, CH-6950 Tesserete, ☎ 91-943-1888, fax 91-943-4212. The **Malcantone Tourist Office** is at CH-6987 Caslano, ☎ 91-606-2986, fax 91-606-5200, while the **Mendrisiotto & Basso Ceresio Tourist Office** is at CH-6850 Mendrisio, ☎ 91-646-5661, fax 91-646-3348.

Post Office

The main post office in Lugano is at Via della Posta 7, CH-6901. Hours are Monday-Friday 7:30 am-5:15 pm, Saturday from 8 am-noon. ☎ 91-807-8104, fax 91-923-1616. There are six other regional post offices in and around Lugano with similar hours: Paradiso CH-6902, Stazione CH-6903, Molino-Nuovo CH-6904, Cassarate CH-6906, Loreto CH-6907, Massagno CH-6908.

Codes

The **area code** for Lugano is 91 and the **postal code** is CH-6900.

Internet Access

Internet access can be had at **City Disc**, Via P Peri, for 10Sfr an hour. Open daily from noon to 9 pm.

■ Getting Around

You can get around the town of Lugano and the surrounding region by foot or by bike. The area has a vast network of footpaths and bike trails, all of which are clearly marked. The Tourist Office will be happy to provide you with walking excursion itineraries and maps of the area. You can rent bikes at the train station for 27Sfr daily, at ticket window one. ☎ 91-923-6691. **Monte San Salvatore** (2,992 feet/912 m), **Monte Generoso** (2,865 feet/873 m) and **Monte Bré** (3,061 feet/933 m) can all be reached by funiculars, bus or railway.

For information/train schedules/costs on each:

■ Monte San Salvatore, ☎ 91-985-2828, www.montesansalvatore.ch.

■ Monte Generoso, ☎ 91-648-1105, www.montegeneroso.ch.

■ Monte Bré, ☎ 91-971-3171, www.montebre.ch.

■ Adventures

On Foot

A popular hiking excursion in Lugano is a five-day trip known as the **Valli di Lugano hike** – a 40-mile, mountain-top trek that rarely drops below 4,920 feet (1,500 m) elevation. This walk offers great views over a well-marked path and, while long, is suitable for almost anyone who just loves to walk.

■ *Day One* (3½ hours walking time): **Astano-Monte Lema**. Take a bus or drive to Astano, an small village west of Lugano near the Italian border in the Malcantone region. From here, walk uphill toward the **Motto della Croce**. You pass through **la Forcolla** (at 3,667 feet/1,120 m), before coming to the crest of Monte Lema. You'll find a cross on the summit and a chairlift to **Miglieglia** – which features a small **restaurant**, great views and a place to bunk down if you choose.

■ *Day Two (four to five hours walking time):* **Monte Lema-Alpe Foppa**. You don't want to miss the sunrise, if the weather is good and clear. From Monte Lema, you'll be able to see the snow-capped peaks of the Matterhorn and Monte Rosa, which is a spectacular way to begin your day. Follow the path along the crest, to the rocky peak of **Breno** on the **Magno** summit. You'll see the villages of the Malcantone on the left, while on the right you'll find the Veddasca valley with its scattered tiny towns. Continue on to **Monte Gradiccioli**, and the trail will descend into the **Bassa di Indemini**, then climb upward once again to the summit of **Monte Tamaro**. Once you pass the **Motto Rotondo**, the trail heads down again to the **Alpe Foppa restaurant**, where it is possible to see ibex and chamois at the Alpine nature reserve.

■ *Day Three* (six hours walking time): **Alpe Foppa-Monte Bar Hut**. From Alpe Foppa, follow the path downward through some woods to the villages of **Rivera**, **Bironico** and **Camignolo**. At Camignolo, follow the signs posted to **Gola di Lago**, found behind the Camignolo cemetery. This path takes you through some peat bogs before reaching the crest line of the **Alpe di Davrosio**. Walk on to the Motto della Croce and the summit of **Caval Drossa**, at 5,352 feet (1,632 m). From here, you'll see Lugano, the lake, Monte Bré, Monte San Salvatore and the Denti della Vechhia, as well as the Magadino plain and Lake Maggiore. Walk on along the crest to

Monte Bar, where just below the summit is a fine **Alpine Mountain Hut** that features a large terrace.

■ *Day Four* (eight hours walking time): **Monte Bar Hut-Pairolo Hut**. Once you leave the hut, you'll follow the road south along the crest line around Monte Gazzirola. On your left are the slopes of Val Cavargna, and on the right are those of Val Colla. From here, continue on south to the summits of Fojorina and Oress, before arriving at the **Pairolo Alpine Mountain Hut**.

■ *Day Five* (five hours walking time): **Pairolo Hut-Gandria**. Follow the trail from the Pairolo Hut along the crest line to the village of Bre, at the south end of the trail, near the Italian border on Lake Lugano. From here you can return to Lugano via the funicular, by bus, by ship, or you can walk. Another fun option is to walk to the tiny lakeside village of **Gandria**, then take a boat back to Lugano.

A FUN DAY TRIP FROM LUGANO

Deemed the **"Floral Route"** by many locals, this one-day outing begins with a ride on the Monte San Salvatore funicular. Once you exit the cable car at the top, you'll find a path to the summit of San Salvatore near the restaurant. From just below the restaurant, the trail leads to Ciona, then on to **Carona**, which is home to four churches, all with many splendid paintings, frescos and stucco work. You then have two options from Carona. You can either visit the botanical gardens of San Grato, or you can follow the trail to the Baroque sanctuary of the Madonna d'Ongero, before heading downward to the village of **Morcote**, shown above, an ancient town on the shores of Lake Lugano. This tiny village, with its narrow streets and many "grottos" (small pubs offering light menu fare), is a delight to explore. You'll find great fresh fish and an abundance of little shops and cafés. From here, there is regular bus and ship service back to Lugano.

On Water

Lake Lugano provides a wide array of sporting and adventure options. The many lakeside ports and quays offer numerous boating (motorboats, paddleboats, cruise ships) excursions. The **Lake Lugano Navigation Company** runs daily trips around the lake with breakfast, lunch and dinner options. They can be found at most ports on the lake. There are also private trips via mahogany boats. Contact Gaetano and Mario Castelnuovo at ☎ 91-967-2013 or Arnoldo Mascetti at ☎ 79-686-2914 to arrange a custom outing.

You can rent sailboats at **Circolo Velico** by the hour. ☎ 91-972-6298. For water-skiing and windsurfing, contact the **Nautical Club of Lugano** at ☎ 91-649-6139. For diving and snorkeling, contact Lugano-Sub at ☎ 91-994-3740. The **Lido** is Lugano's most famous beach. Admission is 7Sfr for adults, 5Sfr for children six-14, and 1Sfr for kids under age six. Open daily from 9 am-7:30 pm in the summer.

■ Sightseeing in Lugano

You won't want to miss the **Swiss Miniature Village**, in the suburb of Melide, just a 10-minute train ride from Lugano's main station. This display accurately portrays Switzerland, complete with Alps such as the Jungfrau and the Matterhorn, and major cities like Zürich, Lausanne, Geneva, and Bern. A great way for kids to learn about the major sites and cities in Switzerland. Admission is 12Sfr for adults, 7Sfr for kids 15 and under. Open daily from 9 am-6 pm. Vian Cantonale, CH-6906 Melide-Lugano. ☎ 91-640-1060.

Hermann Hesse: If you're a fan, then you probably already know that the famed writer lived in Montagnola for 38 years. Since July 2, 1972 (the 120th anniversary of his death), the **Hermann Hesse Museum** in the walls of the **Tower of Casa Camuzzi** has celebrated his life and times. Admission is 6Sfr. Open March-October, Tuesday-Sunday from 10 am-12:30 pm, 2-6:30 pm; November-February on weekends, from 10 am-12:30 pm, 2-6:30 pm. ☎ 91-993-3770.

Landmarks & Historic Sites

The **Cathedral of St. Lawrence** is in the center of town and was built and rebuilt from the 13th to the 18th centuries, featuring Renaissance, Baroque and Romantic interiors and architecture. Located on the Via Cattedrale, in Old Town.

The **Church of Santa Maria degli Angioli** (Church of St. Mary of the Angels) is at Piazza Luini on the south side of the Old Town. This 15th-century church has beautiful frescos dating from that time by artist Bernardino Luini.

Museums

The **Cantonal Museum of Art** displays permanent works by Swiss, Swiss-Italian, and Italian 19th- and 20th-century artists, including sculptures and paintings. This is also the headquarters of the Swiss Photography Foundation, which holds exhibits here from time to time. Open Tuesday, 2-5 pm, Wednesday-Sunday from 10 am-5 pm. Admission is 7Sfr, temporary exhibits 3Sfr. Via Canova 10, CH-6900 Lugano (Old Town). ☎ 91-910-4780, www.museo-cantonal-arte.ch.

The **Modern Art Museum** is in the lakeside Villa Malpensata, a 19th-century mansion that was originally owned by the Foppa family of Lugano. It was then passed to local resident Antonia Caccia, who gave the villa to Lugano in 1893, on the condition that it be used as an art museum only. Open Tuesday-Sunday from 9 am-7 pm. Admission is 11Sfr. Riva Antonio Caccia 5. ☎ 994-4370.

The **Museum of Extra-European Cultures** can be found on the lakeshore of the public gardens of **Villa Heleneum**, a mansion on the road to Gandria between Cortivo and San Domenico, 2½ miles (four km) northwest of Lugano. This museum features three floors of varying exhibits and artifacts, including masks, ritual objects, musical instruments, and weapons from throughout Europe. It is also home to the Center for Ethnographic Studies and a library. Admission is 7Sfr for adults, 4Sfr for kids. Open Wednesday-Sunday from 10 am-5 pm. Via Cortivo 24, Lugano-Castagnola. ☎ 91-971-7353.

The **Cantonal Museum of Natural History** features plants, animals, minerals, rocks and fossils from throughout the Ticino region. It also contains a library with over 11,000 books on these subjects. This museum was founded in 1854, and was completely restored from 1976-1979. There are many permanent displays, as well as specialty exhibitions. Open Tuesday-Saturday from 9 am-noon, 2-5 pm. Admission is free. Via Cattaneo 4, Parco Civico. ☎ 91-911-5380.

The Fossil Museum, on the south side of Lake Lugano in the village of **Meride**, displays petrified relics from Monte San Giorgio, which looms above Meride. This small museum displays discoveries by teams of scientists from the Paleontology Institute of Zürich University. Included are remains of marine animals and fish, reptiles and invertebrates, along with some fossilized plants. To get there, drive south 10 minutes from Lake Lugano on main Highway 2 to Mendrisio, and from there travel west on the local road toward the Italian border and the village of Arzo, where you then turn right (north) to Meride. You'll also find the **Church of San Rocco** here, which dates back to 1578.

Parks & Gardens

 Parco Civico – Lugano's main public park – is one of the finest anywhere in Switzerland. In the center of Lugano, and bordered on one side by the lake and on the other by the **Cassarate River**, the park encompasses many acres of gardens, rare, tropical and regional trees and all types of plant species. Paths lead the visitor throughout the park, which also includes a large aviary and a small pasture for red and fallow deer.

The South

The **Tassino Park** is reminiscent of an English rose garden. Located on the slopes surrounding the bay of Lugano and Parco Civico, the Tassino offers huge manicured lawns and rose terraces containing 300 bushes and 80 types of roses, which bloom from May to late fall. To get here, walk from the train station and follow the signs to Paradiso. Once you come to the railroad crossing, cross the track and turn left onto a narrow lane leading into the park. Here, near the entrance, is an enclosure that is home to fallow and red deer, and wild mountain sheep.

The **Florida Park**, which spreads across the slopes between the village of Loreto and Lake Lugano, is small – just 3.2 square miles (8.3 square km) – but features some fine examples of Mediterranean and sub-tropical vegetation. There is also a giant chessboard, which anyone can use.

Parco San Michele lies on the slopes of **Monte Bré** at **Castagnola** in a seven square mile area that overlooks the lake. This park features romantic paths and beautiful palm trees, fountains and scupltures. To get here, you have to take the cable car from Cassarate. Also in this same area is the 12-square-mile **Parco degli Ulivi**, which lies beyond Castagnola, on the **Gandria Road.** This park leads the visitor down to the lakeside, featuring pre-Alpine flora, cypresses, laurels, rosemary and oleander.

Giardino Belvedere is a three-square-mile garden between Lugano and Paradisio, which features flowerbeds and trees of sub-tropical origin, as well as olives, magnolias, roses, palms and shrubs of all types. This garden is also the setting for a permanent collection of open-air works of art. Near Piazza Luini in Old Town.

■ Shopping

The **Franz Carl Weber Toy Store** is Switzerland's finest, and this is one of their largest outlets. Lots of toys, mechanical games, dolls, etc. Via Nassa 5. ☎ 91-923-5321. The **Münger**, at Via Luvini 4, sells some of the best chocolates and pastries in the region. ☎ 91-985-6943. **Bottega dell'Artigiano** has outstanding handicrafts from Canton Ticino. Via Canova 18. ☎ 91-922-8140. If you want to take home a Ticino wine, then stop in at **Bottegone del Vino**, at Magatti 3, CH-6900 Lugano. ☎ 91-922-7689. In nearby Mendrisio, you'll find **FoxTown** – a huge shopping outlet mall consisting of over 80 stores and shops, and a casino. There are local merchants here, as well as Nike, Bally, Gucci, Prada, Versace and others. FoxTown is open daily from 11 am-7 pm and includes a restaurant, snack bars and ample parking areas.

■ Where to Stay

Wellnesshotel Kurhaus Cademario is seven miles (11 km) outside of Lugano. This spa resort has outdoor and indoor pools, as well as sauna, fitness room, physiotherapy and treatments for all types of ailments. It's beautiful, clean and offers all types of sports, including archery, mountain biking, aerobics, gymnastics, dance, Tai Chi, escorted walks, and cricket, to name a few. Equipped with an on-site pharmacy, a medical lab, and an in-house dietician. There is an à la carte restaurant and piano bar. ($$$-$$$$+). CH-6936, Cademario. ☎ 91-610-5111, fax 91-610-5112.

Villa Sassa offers luxury at its finest in the heart of Lugano. Beautiful and first class all the way, it features a gourmet Mediterranean restaurant, a wellness center and a swimming pool. Close to everything, including shops and museums. ($$$$+). Via Tesserete 10, CH-6900 Lugano. ☎ 91-911-4111, fax 91-922-0545.

Hotel Lugano Dante is in central Lugano, close to the lake and train station, in an 18th-century building that was completely restored to its original state in 2001. If you like historic structures, than this is the hotel for you. Includes all modern amenities. ($$$-$$$$). Piazza Ciccaro 5, CH-6900 Lugano. ☎ 91-910-5700, fax 91-910-5777, www.luganodante.ch.

Tresa Bay Hotel is in the nearby suburb of Lugano, just five minutes from the Italian border. All modern rooms face the lakeside in this lovely inn, which includes a fitness and wellness center. Breakfast included in rates. There is a bar, pizzeria and an Italian restaurant. ($$$-$$$$). Via Lugano 19, CH-6988 Ponte Tresa. ☎ 91-611-2700, fax 91-611-2709.

Hotel Albatro is a high-rise hotel in the center of Lugano, but only a few minutes walk to Lake Lugano. Ultra-modern and elegant air-conditioned rooms with a swimming pool. ($$-$$$$). Features an Italian restaurant and bar. Via Clemente Maraini 8, CH-6907 Lugano. ☎ 91-921-0921, fax 91-921-0927.

Hotel Walter au Lac has been in business since 1888, and sits on the shores of Lake Lugano near the auto-free village center. All rooms face the lake, and all are equipped with modern amenities. ($$$). Piazza Rezzonico 7, CH-6900 Lugano. ☎ 91-922-7425, fax 91-922-4233, www.walteraulac.ch.

Hotel Cacciatori can be found in a quiet country setting surrounded by a chestnut grove. Features include two tennis courts and mountain bikes for guests. This is a wonderful sports-oriented hotel, and features many walking paths. Open year-round, except from mid-February to the end of March. ($$$). The in-house restaurant is well-known for its Ticino and Lombardi specialties, including an extensive collection of home-produced wines. CH-6936 Cademario. ☎ 91-605-2236, fax 91-604-5837, www.hotelcacciatori.ch.

Hotel Carlton Villa Moritz is in a quiet and sunny location on Lake Lugano with spectacular views of the Lake and surrounding mountains. The in-house restaurant features a sun terrace and garden, and there is a heated swimming pool on the premises. ($$-$$$). Via Cortivo 9, CH-6900 Lugano. ☎ 91-971-3812, fax 91-971-3814.

The South

Hotel Colibri is a family-run inn on **Monte Bré**. Great views and most rooms have balconies. Has a big swimming pool and a good in-house restaurant. Stay here for the views if nothing else. ($$-$$$). Via Bassone 7, CH-6974 Aldesago-Lugano. ☎ 91-971-4242, fax 91-971-9016.

Hotel Acquarello is a newly remodeled family hotel in the Cathedral Quarter. It's a short walk to the Lake and train station. ($$). Piazza Cioccaro 9, CH-6901 Lugano. ☎ 91-911-6868, fax 91-911-6869.

Hotel Dischma is a charming family-run inn with an amiable staff. Located near the Lake and bus station in the center of town. The in-house restaurant serves tasty dishes at reasonable prices. ($-$$). Vicolo Geretta 6, CH-6902 Lugano-Paradiso. ☎ 91-994-2131, fax 91-994-1503, www.hotel-dischma.ch.

Hotel Garni Domus has 30 cozy rooms in a high-rise building at the foot of Mount San Salvatore, only 150 feet (45 m) from the lake. Breakfast is included in the rates. ($-$$). Riva Paradiso 24a, CH-6900 Lugano. ☎ 91-994-3421, fax 91-994-0269.

Della Posta is a family-run inn in the heart of Lugano's hiking region. Includes a small swimming pool ($-$$). CH-6986 Novaggio. ☎ 91-606-1349, fax 91-606-7119.

Hotel Montarina sits in a large park near the train station and town center. Has a large swimming pool and caters to backpackers. ($-$$). Via Montarina 1, CH-6900 Lugano. ☎ 91-966-7272, fax 91-966-0017, www.montarina.ch.

Hotel Camelia is a simple and clean inn with cozy rooms. Near the train station. ($-$$). Via Sione 2, CH-6900 Lugano-Massagno. ☎/fax 91-966-3179.

Youth Hostel Lugano-Savosa offers 110 beds from mid-March through the end of October. A wide variety of overnight options are offered by this hostel, in a 10,000-square-mile park that includes a swimming pool and sundeck, Internet room and TV room. A good base for hikes and walking excursions. ($-$$). Via Cantonale 13, CH-6942 Lugano-Savosa. ☎ 91-966-2728, fax 91-968-2363.

Camping

This is available on Lugano's southwest side at **Eurocampo** ($) at ☎ 91-605-2114 or at **La Piodella** ($-$$) at ☎ 91-994-7788.

■ Where to Eat

Ai Giardini di Sassa is in hotel Villa Sassa and features the finest Mediterranean cuisine in Lugano. Specialties are complemented by a red Merlot produced locally. The outside dining terrace offers relaxing and romantic views of Lake Lugano.

($$-$$$$). Via Tesserete 10, CH-6900 Lugano. ☎ 91-911-4111, fax 91-922-0545.

Ristorante al Portone serves excellent Italian cuisine and some of the finest desserts found anywhere in the region. With fixed-price menus, the daily specials invariably include fresh-caught fish. ($$$-$$$$). Closed January 1-10 and from mid-July to mid-August. Via Cassarate 3, CH-6900 Lugano. ☎ 91-923-5511.

Restaurant Orologio serves a variety of pastas, along with home-grown veggies and regional favorites such as venison, scampi, pheasant and fresh fish. ($$-$$$). Open Monday-Saturday from noon-2:30, 7-10:30 pm. Via Nizzola 2, CH-6900 Lugano. ☎ 91-923-2338.

Panoramic Restaurant-Bar Casino Kursaal offers fine dining in a fancy outdoor setting; inside, trees grow up out of the wood floor. This restaurant and bar offers sushi, exquisite soups (zuppa), pastas, risotti and fish dishes, as well as fine Swiss wines from Vaud, Neuchâtel and Vallais. They also have a good selection of Italian, French, Spanish, Australian and American wines. Handicapped-accessible. ($-$$$). Open from noon-2:30 pm, 7 pm-midnight Monday-Saturday. Closed Sunday. The bar is open until 2 am on Friday and Saturday nights. Via Stauffacher 1, CH-6901 Lugano. ☎ 91-921-0203, www.extreme.ch.

Restaurant Lungolago is a piano bar and restaurant with quiet views of the lake in a romantic setting. Specialties include pastas, fish and meats, as well as seasonal dishes. ($-$$$$). Open 8:30 pm-1 am daily. Via Nassa 11, CH-6900 Lugano. ☎ 91-923-1233.

Osteria Del Portico is a charming little restaurant with pasta and fish specialties, plus good wines from Ticino, Italy and France. ($-$$). Open 8:30 pm-midnight Monday-Friday. Closed Saturday and Sunday. Corso Postalozzi 21A, CH-6900 Lugano. ☎ 91-921-0295, fax 91-923-9972.

The **Grotto dei Pescatori**, in the small village of Gandria, is reached only by boat. To get here, you have to board a boat (12Sfr round-trip) on Lake Lugano, and disembark at the Caprino/Grotto dei Pescatori stop. Inexpensive, hearty meals are served on a lakeside terrace in this simply decorated restaurant. Most dishes include pasta and fresh fish. ($-$$). Open Monday-Saturday from 11:30 am-11 pm. Reservations recommended. ☎ 91-923-9867.

Other Sites in the Sottoceneri Region

Tesserete is just a stone's throw north of Lugano in the region known as the "Valli di Lugano." This is a classic destination for families and is home to an annual carnival. There is a good hike around **Lake Origlio** that brings you to the church of **San Bernado** in Comano. The **Val Colla** offers jagged rocks known as the "Denti dell Vecchia" (old woman's teeth).

If you're looking for a resort atmosphere, then check out the **Origlio Hotel and Country Club**. Here you can experience horseback riding by the hour, day or week, as well as tennis and numerous spa options. This resort also features a children's playground, a large outside pool, solarium, fitness room, beauty salon, an indoor pool, a golf driving range, a park and numerous restaurants. First-class treatment all the way, and you should expect to pay for it. ($$$$-$$$$+). CH-6945 Origlio. ☎ 91-945-4646, fax 91-945-1031.

Morcote is a little village seven miles (11 km) south of Lugano via highway A4, or you can take one of the many ships that travel there on a regular basis. The **Morcote Tourist Office**, in the town center, can provide maps of the area. Open Monday-Friday from 8 am-12:30 pm, 1:30-6 pm, ☎ 91-996-1120. One reason to come to Morcote is if you're looking for a small hotel that is more like living with the locals than like a standard hotel. The **Hotel Rivabella** is away from the main part of town on the lake shore. It's an old Italian-style home, complete with flower boxes and comfortable, cozy and clean rooms at moderate prices. This is a family-run inn and the ambiance and views of the lake are well worth the extra little effort to get here. ($$). Rates include breakfast. Closed November to March. Via Cantonale, CH-6922 Morcote. ☎ 91-996-1314, fax 91-996-1652.

The villages of **Mendrisio**, **Basso Ceresio** and **Chiasso** all lie at the southern tip of Ticino, near the Italian border. This region is dominated by **Monte Generoso** – the highest peak (at 5,589 feet/1,704 m) in southern Switzerland. You can reach the top by taking the little cogwheel railway from **Capolago** for a 40-minute ride to the summit, where you'll find a nature trail. Throughout this region you'll see chestnut forests, and fields of tobacco and wheat.

Chiasso is a major stopping post for many travelers on their way either into or out of Italy. If you're looking for a reasonable spot to bunk down for the night, then try the **Mövenpick Albergo Touring Hotel**. Located in the center of town, this hotel is only 40 minutes from Milan and very near both the train station and the highway. It's great for families with kids and pets, as both stay overnight for free (kids under 16; pets can be any age!). The hotel has an indoor and outdoor pool, as well as tennis and a fitness center, and is near fishing and horseback riding areas, and backs up to some fine bicycling, jogging and hiking trails. ($$). Piazzo Indipendenza, CH-6830 Chiasso.

Motel Piccadily is right off of Highway A2 in Chiasso and is not fancy, but clean. The train station is behind this small inn. ($). No phones.

Hotel Conca Bella is near the Italian border in the small village of Vacallo, and features a fantastic kitchen and superb wine cellar. It is only five minutes to Lakes Como and Lugano from this inn, which offers nine cozy rooms that were completely remodeled in 2001. The restaurant, which serves fine Italian and French wines, is closed on Sunday and Monday. This small hotel offers a special romantic overnight stay for two that includes a gourmet dinner for 380Sfr. Otherwise, the rates are very reasonable ($$). Via Concabella 2, CH-6833 Vacallo. ☎ 91-697-5040, fax 91-683-7429.

There is a **youth hostel** in the village of **Figino** that offers 160 sleeping spots. It is open from mid-March to the end of October and is close to bike paths. ($) Via Casoro 2, CH-6918 Figino. ☎ 91-995-1151, fax 91-995-1070, www.youthhostel.ch/figino.

The Sopraceneri Region
Bellinzona

This is one of the first stops in Canton Ticino in the Sopraceneri region, if you're travelling from the north to the south, and is easily accessible by train or auto (via Highway 2 through the St. Gotthard Tunnel). Known as "la città dei castelli" (the city of castles), this village – as the capital of the canton – is believed to have Roman roots, since it sits along one of the most popular military and trade roads between Rome and northern Europe. It is a great base for exploring the other parts of this canton, and the village itself has castles, tree-lined streets and a relaxing old-world charm. Bellinzona is known for its medieval fortresses – **Castelgrande**, **Castello di Montebello** and **Castello di Sasso Corbaro**. The Saturday morning market takes place in the heart of Bellinzona's Old Town and is great fun. Weekly, from 7:30 am-noon, this part of the city becomes a popular spot for local vendors to offer their wares to the public. Here, you'll find fresh produce, handicrafts and clothing in all price ranges.

The Bellinzona **Tourist Office** is open Monday-Friday, from 8 am-6:30 pm, Saturday from 9 am-noon. Via dell Stazione, Piazza Civico, CH-6500 Bellinzona. ☎ 91-825-2131, fax 91-821-4120. The cantonal tourist office is also in Bellinzona at **Ticino Tourism**, Casella Postale 1441, CH-6501 Bellinzona. ☎ 91-825-7056, fax 91-825-3614.

■ Landmarks & Historical Sites

The Three Castles of Bellinzona. Admission is 8Sfr for all three castles.

Castelgrande (often called Castle Uri) was built in the sixth century and then rebuilt at various times throughout the ages. It features two massive asymetrical towers, complemented by additions from the 11th and 14th centuries that give it a maze-like feel. You can walk here via a very scenic path starting at Piazza Collegiata or take an elevator from Piazza del Sole. Open daily from 10 am-6 pm, the Castelgrande was completely restored to its original state in 1991 and is now home to museums and restaurants. ☎ 91-825-8145.

Open daily, 10 am-6 pm from February-December, **Castello di Montebello** (Castle Schwyz), left, dates back to the 13th century, and today is home to both a civic and archeological museum. This is the finest medieval castle in Bellinzona. ☎ 91-825-1342.

Castello di Sasso Corbaro (Unterwald Castle) is a block-like structure that was built in 1479 for the Duke of Milan, and it is used for temporary art exhibitions today. This castle (the smallest of the three) is just uphill from Castello di Montebello, and is open from April-November, from 10 am-6 pm daily. ☎ 91-825-5906.

■ Where to Stay

Hotel Unione is one of Bellinzona's finest hotels, in the heart of the city, and offering all modern amenities. Breakfast included in rates. ($$). Via Generale Guisan 1, CH-6500 Bellinzona. ☎ 91-825-5577, fax 91-825-9460, www.hotel-unione.ch.

Hotel Internazionale has clean and comfortable accommodations in the heart of Bellinzona, and includes a nice in-house restaurant with Italian, Swiss and International fare at reasonable rates. ($$). Viale Stazione 35, CH-6500 Bellinzona. ☎ 91-825-4333, fax 91-826-1359.

Hotel Gamper is near the train station in a quiet setting, except for the occasional train that passes nearby. It has very charming rooms, as well as a pizzeria and Italian restaurant that serves local dishes and regional wines. There is also a little sidewalk café that serves light snacks and coffees. ($-$$). Viale Stazione 29, CH-6500 Bellinzona. ☎ 91-825-3792, fax 91-826-4689.

Hotel Minotel Unione is at the foot of the castles in the town center, close to the rail station and two miles (3,2 km) from the highway. Very stylish, with all amenities. ($$). Via G. Guisan 1, CH-6500 Bellinzona.

Hotel San Giovanni features rustic and simple rooms in the old part of Bellinzona. ($-$$). Via San Giovanni 7, CH-6500 Bellinzona. ☎/fax 91-825-1919.

Tsui-Fok offers cheap rooms in a beautiful old building in the old town. ($). Clean and simple, with an in-house café, close to hiking trails. Via Nocca 20, CH-6500 Bellinzona. ☎/fax 91-825-1332.

Youth Hostel Montebello has 70 sleeping beds in a huge old mansion, and is suitable for handicapped persons. Just minutes from the train station. ($). Via Nocca 4, CH-6500 Bellinzona. ☎ 91-825-1522, fax 91-825-4285, www.youthhostel.ch/bellinzona.

■ Where to Eat

Grotto Paudese is in the wee hamlet of Paudo, just a 12-minute drive southeast of Bellinzona on a small, local road. This is a great little spot (sitting on the edge of the road with terrific views of the Alps), which also offers four rooms for an overnight stay. Very pretty and unpretentious; the staff is friendly and the restaurant and rooms are spotless. All the meals are homemade and regional. You won't find a better spot for local ambiance and real Bellinzona cuisine. ($). CH-6582 Paudo. ☎/fax 91-857-1468.

For fine regional dining, you'll want to try **Castlegrande**, in the 13th-century castle of the same name. This restaurant is sophisticated, with a serious wine list, and a formal waitstaff. ($$-$$$$). Closed Monday. Monte San Michele. ☎ 91-826-2353.

Locarno

J ust 14 miles (22 km) west of Bellinzona, Locarno is known as Ticino's sunniest town and is home to some 20,000 inhabitants. Sitting on the northern shores of Lake Maggiore, and encircled by mountains, it is a haven for all types of tropical and subtropical plants and trees, and is known for producing some of Europe's best figs and olives. Locarno is also famous for its annual International Film Festival, which takes place every August. The city is actually a trio of communities: **Locarno**, **Muralto** and **Minusio**. These three villages have a few auto-free streets, lots of tiny shops and cafés, and many fun places to sit and people-watch. The 40-mile-long Lake Maggiore, connecting Switzerland and Italy, provides many opportunities for excursions and water sports.

■ Information Sources

The Locarno **Tourist Office** is part of the Lago Maggiore Tourism Bureau (Ente Turistico Lugano Maggiore). Open March-October, Monday-Friday, 8:30 am-7 pm, Saturday, 10 am-4 pm; November-February, Monday-Friday. 9 am-12:30 pm, 2-6 pm. ☎ 91-791-0091 or 91-751-0333, fax 91-785-1941. This office offers guided walking tours of the city every Tuesday from March-October at 9:45 am for 5-10Sfr. Via Bernardino Luini 3, CH-6600 Locarno.

■ Adventures

Isole di Brissago (**The Brissago Islands**) are in the middle of Lake Maggiore, and reachable via ship from Locarno, Ascona or Porto Ronco. They offer a mixture of subtropical plants and trees and, since their opening in April of 1950, have hosted over four million visitors. The main island, St. Pancrace or the Big

Island, features a rich collection of exotic plants, while the Small Island, or St. Apollinaris, is home to natural vegetation left untouched. The mild climate of this region makes it possible for subtropical plant species to grow and thrive in an outdoor setting. Plant species are found here that are native to China, South Africa, Central and South American, Australia and the Oceania Islands. Roman artifacts have been found on these small islands dating back to 125 AD. It wasn't until 1949 that Ticino purchased this land, making it an official cantonal Botanical Park. There are over 1,500 species of plants, with markers designating the name of each plant. The park also features a fine restaurant, dining terrace, a convention center and a scientific research laboratory. The park is open from April-October from 9 am-6 pm. Admission is 7Sfr for adults and 3Sfr for children six-16. For more information, contact the Amministrazione, Isole di Brissago, Parco Botanico del Canton Ticino, CH-6614 Isole di Brissago. ☎ 91-791-4361, fax 91-791-0763, www.isolebrissago.ch.

Another fun adventure is to spend half a day or even a whole day exploring the **Gambarogno Riviera** found alongside Lake Maggiore's south shore as it nears the Italian border. Here you'll find 125 miles (200 km) of superb trails and hiking paths. The Locarno Tourist Office can provide you with maps of the area.

■ Landmarks & Historic Sites

The main section of Locarno is highlighted by a broad square known as the **Piazza Grande**. You'll find lots of shopping opportunities on the north side of this piazza, while on the south are the Public Gardens. From here you'll find the narrow Via Francesco Rusca, which then divides into four smaller walkways that all lead you to the Old Town. To the east of the train station is the Muralto district, while on the northeast side is the Minusio region of Locarno.

The **Santuario della Madonna dell Sasso** is considered to be one of the most important sights of Locarno. It sits high in the hamlet of Orselina at 1,165 feet (355 m). You can either hike to the top or take the funicular that leaves every quarter hour from 7 am-11 pm daily. A round-trip costs only 5.6Sfr for adults or 4Sfr for children. This church was founded in 1480 by a friar and contains religious artwork and a small museum next to it. Open daily from March-October, 7 am-10 pm (closes at 9 pm in the off-season). ☎ 91-743-6265.

■ Where to Stay

Hotel Romitaggio sits in the middle of the vineyards and features a large sun terrace that overlooks the Mogadino plains. Clean and modest with a friendly staff. ($$-$$$). CH-6597 Agarone-Locarno. ☎ 91-859-1577, fax 91-859-1600.

Hotel Garni Gottardo is an ultra-modern, beautifully decorated hotel only a few feet from the lake and train station. Most rooms have a balcony facing the lake, but be sure to request one anyway. Breakfast is included. ($$). Very clean and tidy. Via S. Gottardo 18, CH-6600 Muralto-Locarno. ☎ 91-743-3183, fax 91-743-4454.

Hotel Carmine is a large, modern five-story hotel that includes Internet connections in every room. ($$). CH-6602 Muralto-Locarno. ☎ 91-735-3060, fax 91-735-3061.

Garni Stazione is a cute little inn with a family atmosphere. Close to the train station, town center and the bus stop. Breakfast included. ($-$$). Piazza Stazione, CH-6600 Locarno. ☎ 91-743-0222, fax 91-743-5406.

The Locarno **Youth Hostel Palagiovani** is open year-round on the west side of Lugano's city center (just west of the Piazza San Francesco), and offers 188 beds starting at 32Sfr. ($-$$). Open in the summer from 8-10 am, 3-11:30 pm; winter from 8-10 am, 4-10:30 pm. Via Varenna 18, CH-6600 Locarno. ☎ 91-756-1500, fax 91-756-1501, www.youthhostel.ch/locarno.

■ Where to Eat

Restaurant Cittadella is in the heart of the Old Town of Locarno, and has a fine dining area upstairs, with a more informal "grotto" on the main level. Here, you'll find regional and seasonal specialties such as fresh fish, duck, goose and shrimp. ($-$$$$). Reservations required. The upstairs restaurant has a fixed-price menu at times. Open daily from noon-1:30 pm, 7-10 pm (closed on Monday in June and July). Via Cittadella 18, CH-6600 Locarno. ☎ 91-751-5885, fax 91-751-7759.

Ristorante Zurigo features a chestnut-lined terrace on the lakefront. The Italian food is some of the best in the region and the portions are hearty. ($-$$). Reservations are recommended. Open daily from 11 am-11 pm. Viale Verbano 9, CH-6900 Locarno. ☎ 91-743-1617, fax 91-743-4315.

Ascona

This is the quieter sister town of Locarno, and has a lovely town square that is simply referred to as *La Piazza*. For centuries this village has been home to fishermen, craftsmen and farmers – who for years led their cows through the streets at night from nearby pastures to their home barns. During the summer months the huge Piazza is filled to capacity with hundreds of locals and visitors enjoying all kinds of concerts – from classical to jazz to hip-hop.

Ascona is also well known for its sophistication and elegance, and is filled with art galleries and high-end boutiques. Often referred to as the "Queen of Lago Maggiore," it has been home to some of the world's most notable artists, writers and philosophers, including Karl Jung and Hermann Hesse, among others. With just 5,000 citizens, it offers over 3,000 hotel beds and some of the finest overnight accommodations within Ticino. It is also home to an annual New Orleans Jazz Festival.

The **Tourist Office Lago Maggiore** of Ascona is in Casa Serodine, Piazza San Pietro, CH-6612 Ascona. ☎ 91-791-0091, fax 91-785-1941. There is no train station here, so if you don't have a car, your best bet is to get off the train in Locarno and hop a bus or taxi for the quick ride (five minutes) to Ascona. Bikes can be rented for 20Sfr daily at **Facci Claudio** on Via Ascone 12, CH-6612 Ascona. ☎ 91-791-1341.

■ Landmarks & Historic Sites

Casa Serodine is a three-storied early-Baroque house with a fanciful façade and ornate stucco work, dating back to 1620. There is a nice **museum of modern art** (Museo Comunale d'Arte Moderna) on Via Borgo 34, CH-6612 Ascona. Open March-December, Tuesday-Sunday, 10 am-noon, 3-5 pm. ☎ 91-756-3185. The **Collegio Pontifico Papio** features a lovely Renaissance courtyard and its church, the **Chiesa Santa Maria dell Misericordia** has Gothic frescos dating from the 14th century.

■ Where to Stay

Hotel Ascona is a four-star hotel only five minutes from La Piazza, set in the midst of a tropical garden with spectacular views of the lake and surrounding mountains. It includes all modern amenities, with an outdoor heated pool,

HOTEL PRICE CHART	
$	30-75Sfr ($20-$49)
$$	76-205Sfr ($50-$109)
$$$	206-299Sfr ($110-$200)
$$$$	300Sfr+ ($200+)

sauna, whirlpool, solarium and dining terrace. ($$$-$$$$+). Via Collina, CH-6612 Ascona. ☎ 91-785-1515, fax 91-785-1530.

Hotel Castello is a 13th-century castle that has been restored and renovated to feature modern rooms in a beautiful setting at the end of Ascona's lakeside promenade. This hotel has stone stairways, thick stone walls and retains much of its original fortress works. The in-house restaurant, Locanda de' Ghiriglioni is one of the best in the area, with fine dining in a cozy setting. There is also a lakeside garden/terrace and a wine bar as well. ($$$-$$$$+). Open March-November. Lakeside Promenade, CH-6612 Ascona. ☎ 91-791-0161, fax 91-791-1804.

Casa Berno Ascona sits high above Lake Maggiore, surrounded by a subtropical garden. This hotel offers golfing and hiking excursions led by the knowledgeable hotel staff. There are two in-house restaurants that serve up rich buffets as well as regional specialties on a nightly basis, along with a very fine wine selection. Sauna, fitness room and massages are also available. ($$$-$$$$). CH-6612 Ascona. ☎ 91-791-3232, fax 91-792-1114.

Casa Wülfingen sits on the southwest slope of Monte Verita in a quiet location and features a fine view of Ascona – only 10 minutes away on foot. This charming, rustic inn is a good spot for hikes and walks, and also features a private beach. ($$$-$$$$). Via Rondonico 101, CH-6612 Ascona. ☎ 91-785-1820, fax 91-785-1821.

Hotel Mulino is close to the lake and old town, and all rooms have a balcony or sun terrace. Features a heated swimming pool. ($$-$$$). Via della Scuole 17, CH-6612 Ascone. ☎ 91-791-3692, fax 91-791-0671.

Hotel Sole is perfect for families or solo travelers and includes a windsurfing school and swimming pool. A good spot for walks and views of the lake. All rooms have balconies, and the in-house restaurant serves up tasty Italian fare. ($$). Via Leoncavallo 76, CH-6614 Brissago-Ascona. ☎ 91-793-1148, fax 91-793-1211.

■ Where to Eat

Al Pontile serves a great combination of French, Italian and local dishes, but what makes us keep coming back here is the ambiance. The interior is dark and romantic, with lanterns and an overall warm ambiance that is unique. The desserts are delicious. ($-$$$$). Open daily from 11:30 am-2:30 pm, 6-9 pm. Reservations recommended. Closed Mondays from January to March. Via Longalago G. Motta 31, CH-6612 Ascona. ☎ 91-791-0101.

DINING PRICE CHART	
Prices based on a typical entrée, per person, and do not include beverage.	
$	15-25Sfr ($10-$16)
$$	26-45Sfr ($17-$29)
$$$	46-70Sfr ($30-$47)
$$$$	71Sfr+ ($47+)

Trattoria della Ruga is in the heart of the city and features Italian and Ticinesi specialties, including a fine homemade ravioli or a succulent rabbit dish. The wine list includes over 140 varieties. ($-$$$). Open daily from 9:30 am-2:30 pm, 5 pm-1 am. Closed Monday. Via Village 28, CH-6612 Ascona. ☎ 91-791-2743, fax 91-791-2877.

Restaurant Da Ivo is a pleasant and homey restaurant run by hosts Alfredo and Luisa Cormano, who dish up regional and Mediterranean fare. Lobster, swordfish and grilled calf are complemented by fine Ticinesi, Italian and French wines. ($-$$$). Open 11:45 am-2:30 pm, 5:45-11 pm. Closed Monday. Via College 7, CH-6612 Ascona. ☎ 91-791-6093, fax 91-791-3393.

Osteria Nostrana is a hopping place on the wharf of the promenade. Good pizzas and pastas, but most folks come here to people-watch. ($-$$). Via Longalago G. Motta, CH-6612 Ascona. ☎ 91-791-5158.

Ristorante della Posta is a unique little find in the tiny village of Ronco, which sits high above Ascona overlooking Lake Maggiore and the Brissago Islands. It offers international, Italian and Mediterranean dishes at very reasonable prices. ($-$$). Open 11:30 am-2 pm, 6-9:30 pm daily. Closed mid-November to early February. It also features a few small rooms for a cheap overnight stay. A former post office, it is one of the few buildings in this village, and very easy to find. ☎ 91-791-8470, fax 91-791-4533.

Suggested Reading

Killing Dragons, The Conquest of the Alps
Ferbus Fleming
Atlantic Monthly Press, New York, 2000

The White Spider: The Classic Account of the Ascent of the Eiger
Heinrich Harper
Putnam Books, 1959, 1960, 1976, 1998

Scrambles Amongst The Alps, in the years 1860-1869
Edward Whymper
National Geographic Society, 1871, 2002

The Prisoner of Chillon
Lord Byron
Woodstock Books, 1993

Heidi
Johanna Spyri
Morrow & Co., Inc. 1996

Daisy Miller
Henry James
Harper & Brothers, 1892, 1912, 1996

The Bernese Alps
Kev Reynolds
Cicerone Press, 1992, 1997

Swiss Kitchen
(Die Echte Schweizer Küche)
Eva Maria Borer
The Windmill Press
1965, 1985

Index